EBD 3/25/89

The Literature of
AMERICAN MUSIC

in Books and Folk Music Collections:

a fully annotated bibliography

SUPPLEMENT I

by
DAVID HORN
with
RICHARD JACKSON

The Scarecrow Press, Inc.
Metuchen, N.J., & London 1988

Library of Congress Cataloging-in-Publication Data

Horn, David, 1942–
  The literature of American music in books and
folk music collections.

  Includes index.
  1. Music--United States--History and criticism--
Bibliography. I. Jackson, Richard, 1936–   . II. Title.
ML120.U5H7 Suppl. 1   016.781773   87-9630
ISBN 0-8108-1997-X

To my mother and to the memory of my father

--David Horn

To the memory of my mother

--Richard Jackson

CONTENTS

PREFACE

This book is the first supplement to The Literature of American Music in Books and Folk Music Collections: a fully annotated bibliography, published by Scarecrow Press in 1977. In its main sections it contains annotations for books published from mid-1975 to the end of 1980, and, in addition, for a number of books which were either overlooked in the compilation of the original book or were included without annotation in the Appendix. The total number of annotated entries is 996; a further 323 unannotated pre-1981 items brings the overall total to 1,319.

When the first book was published it was never intended that eleven years should elapse before the appearance of Supplement I. While the reasons for the delay will be of little concern to users of this book, its consequences are. Chief among these is the gap that exists between the date of the book's publication and the terminal publication date for annotated entries. It became apparent, during the book's compilation, that putting back this terminal date would probably result in even greater delay; consequently, the decision was made to leave it at 1980. Though this was done with some regret, it was based on the belief that this bibliography's concern with an in-depth approach is its primary characteristic, and one which makes the struggle to be up-to-date of less significance in the long term. At the same time, however, it was also apparent that a first step could be taken towards filling in the gap, in the shape of an unannotated listing. Such a list, covering 1981-85 imprints, is included here as Appendix A.

Like most supplements, this book is in one sense an offspring whose umbilical connection to its parent it is best not to cut. Although it has little capacity for independent existence, it does have some room to begin to develop a different character, as readers will perhaps observe. One result of this is that the two books should preferably be seen as having a reciprocal relationship.

On a wider front, it is hoped that a similar relationship will exist between this project and others recently published. See, for example, the books in the 1981-85 Appendix by De Lerma (S/A.287), Skowronski (S/A.291), Hefele (S/A.364), Booth (S/A.505), Hoffmann (S/A.647), and Taylor (S/A.648); mention should also be made of the 1986 books, The Literature of Rock, II: 1979-1983, by Frank

Hoffmann and B. Lee Cooper (Scarecrow Press), and Popular Music: a reference guide, by Roman Iwaschkin (Garland). Precise bibliographical duplication is in any case an unlikely event, but what is more interesting and important than overlap per se (or, indeed, than competition) is seeing the ways in which different means of constructing a subject area, different bibliographical approaches, and different styles complement and interact with one another. In this way the study of a subject is not only recorded and reflected on, it is moved forward.

In terms of material covered, the same basic attempt has been made in this supplement as was made in the first book: to include all English-language material known to the compilers and judged to be of interest; in addition, to provide a representative sample of books in languages other than English. Books from the main period in question which we have failed to see, or which are of more minor interest, are itemized in the unannotated listings that conclude each of the book's main sections. As before, the following types of material are excluded: periodical articles,[1] dissertations, serial publications, fiction,[2] popular song collections (except for a few with substantial linking narrative), "art" music scores, and general reference works. Cultural background is also excluded, with the exception of a small number of books giving more than just a passing mention to music.

In the base volume one musical area, jazz, was treated more selectively than others (see "Preface," p. vii). This time a similar approach has been used for rock, rock & roll, and pop. Critics of the first book rightly pointed out that the section on rock was thin. A considerable effort has been made to remedy this, but even so some selectivity was judged to be necessary. Although the rate at which the literature of rock has expanded has exceeded that of any other area of American music, there was a risk, as with jazz before, that the section would overshadow the others. An additional factor influencing this decision was the appearance of the bibliographies by Taylor, Hoffmann, and Iwaschkin referred to above.

The expansion in writing on rock has led to the one major organizational change in Supplement I. Instead of being included as a final item in Section I, "Popular Currents," "Rock, Rock & Roll, Pop" now has its own section, Section J. Some other, more minor changes have also been introduced in response to shifting patterns in the literature, or to offer an improved arrangement of material. The various changes which should be noted are as follows:

- A.1.a, originally "Bibliographies of Music" (General Works), has been expanded to include general discographies, while bibliographies of 18th-century music have been moved to B.1.

- A.7.d, "Musical Instruments," is now divided by instrument.

- F.4, originally "Spanish-American Folk Song," has been expanded to cover other particular ethnic groups.

- F.11, "Country Music," has been more fully sub-divided.

- G.1, originally "Guides to the Social and Cultural Background," has been dropped, and a new sub-division for "Reference Works" added to the following heading, "Black Music in Works on Black Culture and Society."

- G.5, originally "The African Heritage," has been dropped, as it no longer seemed appropriate to have a separate listing for African music (books linking Africa and Afro-America appear elsewhere according to their emphasis).

- Section G has been renumbered to take account of these alterations.

- I.2, originally "Social and Cultural Studies of Popular Music," has been renamed "The Popular Music Life," and sub-divided.

- I.4-I.7: the original headings have been regrouped, with additions, under the one head, "Words and Music," and the entire section renumbered.

- I.11.e, "Broadway Musical Comedy," now becomes I.8.e, and has been divided into five sub-sections.

- I.13, "Rock and Roll, and Rock," has become a separate part, Section J, with the title "Rock, Rock & Roll, Pop."

- Appendix: the original Appendix of unannotated items has been replaced by lists at the end of the principal sections of the bibliography.

Among other features of the supplement, the presence of an appendix (Appendix A), listing titles newly published in 1981-85, has already been noted. One category excluded from this list is that of revised editions of books included in the original bibliography. Consideration was given to including these in the main text of this volume, with revised annotations, but although in one particular case (see item 1369) that would have provided a welcome opportunity to improve on the original note, it seemed on balance to be preferable to reserve the main text for books making their first "full" appearance. (In one or two instances, however, an abridged, retitled publication is included in the main text, chiefly for clarification of its history.)

Because a number of revised editions have been important ones, some provision for them seemed essential, and so a selective list of them is provided as Appendix B.

Finally, the original all-in-one index has been divided into two, for names and subjects, and a third, a title index, has been added.

References to entries in the 1977 bibliography are indicated throughout Supplement I by the abbreviation LOAM (Literature of American Music), followed by the item number. An item number followed by "A" indicates the entry appeared in the LOAM Appendix.

One last feature of this supplement remains to be noted, and it is among the most important. At one point during work on the book, when progress was particularly slow, I was very fortunate in being able to enlist the help of Richard Jackson (New York Public Library). I owe Richard a considerable debt of gratitude, for without his contribution the book would have taken yet longer to complete (as it was, he was the first, by several months, to finish his share). He has been remarkably patient, not only with his colleague's tardiness, but with his questions, his changes of mind, and his incorrigible tendency to redraft.

Richard maintains that one of us is kinder to books than the other. I doubt if this is so (at least not now), but in any event the precise contribution of each compiler is not indicated in the text, not to disguise who holds which views, but for the more practical reason that a not inconsiderable number of annotations are, in their final form, joint efforts.

As was the case with the original book, the work necessary to compile this one would not have been possible without financial help. I would like to record my gratitude to the University of Exeter, the Sir Ernest Cassel Educational Trust, the British Academy, and the British Association for American Studies for their generous support of this project.

Once again I have been fortunate with the advice, encouragement, practical help and hospitality which I have received. I would like to thank in particular Simon Frith, Mick Gidley, Dave Laing, Richard Middleton, Ilse and Eric Moon, Pat Rom and Bill Eshelman. I am also most grateful to the Librarian of the University of Exeter, John Stirling, and to Heather Eva and her staff in the Inter-Library Loan Dept.; to many staff in the Library & Museum of the Performing Arts, Lincoln Center, New York, and at Rutgers Institute of Jazz Studies; a special word of thanks to Cecil Lytle (University of California, San Diego) for his role in arranging an exchange for me at the University in 1983, to Garrett Bowles and his family for participating in that exchange, and to Linda Barnhart and Wendell Hall at the University Library for their valued friendship during our stay.

My debt to my wife, Gill, is if anything even larger this time than last. She has carried out the same burdensome tasks--typing, indexing, filing--with the difference that, by now, my writing is harder to decipher, my files more prone to grow chaotic, my state of

mind more frequently in need of love and encouragement. I am
deeply grateful. Our children, Kate and Robert, having lived
through one bibliography, have now endured a supplement with
that same good grace as before. I have probably never told them
how good it is, on emerging from the unreal world of bibliography,
to find them there, just being themselves. It's a pleasure to do
so now, with love and thanks.

David Horn

Exeter,
December 1986

NOTES

1. The latest American music reference book, the very impressive
   New Grove Dictionary of American Music (Macmillan, 1986), for
   some reason lowers its standards of accuracy when describing
   The Literature of American Music, which it notes as including
   articles (Vol. 1, p. 211). Two further errors occur: 1) the
   1977 work is cited as a revision of a booklet published in
   Exeter in 1972, whereas, as the Preface to the 1977 book insists,
   "it is basically a wholly different book" (p. v); 2) in the text
   of the "Bibliography" article, LOAM is described as including
   "no indication of scope of coverage" (Vol. 1, p. 208).

2. Rock and pop fiction is listed in Paul Taylor's Popular Music
   Since 1955 (S/A.648).

A. GENERAL WORKS

1. Bibliography and Reference

a. Bibliographies of Music and Discographies

See also nos. S.21, S.25, S.57, S.135, S.136, S.137, S.811

S.1.   AMERICAN MUSIC Before 1865 in Print and on Records: a
       biblio-discography; preface by H. Wiley Hitchcock.   Brook-
       lyn: Institute for Studies in American Music, 1976.
       (I.S.A.M. Monographs, No. 6). 113p.
           Produced by a team of researchers at I.S.A.M. under the
       guidance of H. Wiley Hitchcock and Rita A. Mead, this work offers
       a clear picture of the availability, in the Bicentennial year, of early
       American music; it is also a valuable reference tool for a wide variety
       of users--teachers, performers, librarians, concert promoters. The
       first section is a bibliography of 199 items in three sections: music
       in performance editions (single publications, editions in series, an-
       thologies), music in facsimile reprints, and music in books (complete
       compositions only). All items are music "of which the written and/or
       published sources are securely documentable as antedating 1865 (or
       thereabouts)" (p. vi). Thus all folk music, except publications "ex-
       plicitly based on pre-1865 sources," is omitted. The second section
       is a discography, listing 543 recordings in alphabetical composer
       (anonymous title) sequence, with record label numbers. (This was
       based on work done in the late 1950s by Irving Lowens, and by H.
       Wiley Hitchcock in the mid-'60s.) The index lists composers, com-
       pilers and titles, and brings together information dispersed by the
       decision to use a classified arrangement. (A supplement, "American
       Music Before 1865 in Print and on Records: a biblio-discography:
       Supplement to Music on Records," by James R. Heintze," in Notes,
       34 (1978), pp. 571-580, adds to the discography the large number
       of recordings issued in 1976 itself, as well as listing some overlooked
       items released earlier.)

S.2.   INDEX of the Recorded Anthology of American Music (New
       World Records). Brooklyn: Institute for Studies in Amer-
       ican Music, (197-?). (I.S.A.M. Special Publications, No.
       2). 10p.
           The 100-LP series of records, the Recorded Anthology of

<u>American Music</u>, which appeared during the three years 1975-1978, funded by the Rockefeller Foundation, will long remain both a landmark in the establishment of American music as a field of study, and a wonderfully revealing and useful set of records for teaching or just listening. This stapled index, providing access to the collection by composer, selective title and selective subject, served as a stopgap measure until a more permanent index appeared. This happened in 1981, with the publication of <u>Index to the New World Recorded Anthology of American Music</u>, prepared by Elizabeth A. Davis (New York: Norton); this much fuller index lists all the contents, and provides indexes for names, titles, genres, as well as a subject index to the liner notes. (The series itself has continued to appear; these additional records do not appear in either list.)

S.3.   JACKSON, Richard. <u>U.S. Bicentennial Music 1</u>. Brooklyn: Institute for Studies in American Music, 1977. (I.S.A.M. Special Publications, No. 1). 20p.

This is "a selective list of musical Americana published at the time of the Bicentennial" (p. 3). It lists in ten sections (choral, band, organ and piano, chamber, orchestra, songs, stage works, popular music collections and sheet music, reprints and facsimiles, plus a section for Charles Ives) music "that specifically celebrated (or exploited) the Bicentennial ... and reprints and new editions of older American music published between 1970 and 1976." Representative samples of educational and choral folk music arrangements are also included, but unpublished operas and concert music commissioned for the celebrations, and recordings are left for a subsequent booklet. Details of publisher, date, pagination and price are given wherever ascertainable, and a list of publishers' addresses is supplied.

S.4.   KRUMMEL, D. W., ed. <u>Bibliographical Inventory to the Early Music in Newberry Library, Chicago, Illinois</u>. Boston: G. K. Hall, 1977. 587p.

The Newberry Library's music collection ("one of the most important music collections in the United States--Introduction) is well endowed in the area of Americana up to the early 20th century. It is not entirely alone in this, of course, but the particular bibliographical classification scheme used in this inventory allows the extent of the early American material to be readily ascertained, and fruitful browsing to take place, in addition to the traditional practices of verification of bibliographical details, etc. The basic principle of organization of printed material is geographical, supported by chronological ordering of individual items. American printed materials for 1701-1860 appear in Section 9. There are 1,530 items in all, subdivided into six sections: books & treatises, libretti & other dramatic texts, songsters & other word books, tutors & instruction books, anthologies & selected "art music," tune books & other religious collections. (The sheet music collection of some 80,000 items is not included; such material always has to wait, it seems, but a catalog--and one of the Harding Collection at the Bodleian Library in Oxford--would be an invaluable contribution to American music bibliography.) Details are provided in the form of photomechanically reproduced catalog cards. The library's more modest manuscript collection, listed in Section 1, where it is geographically sub-divided, includes 29 American items, among them several arrangements by Theodore Thomas of European compositions. The indispensable indexes cater to approaches by composer and editor, by printer, engraver, artist, copyist and publisher.

b. Bibliographies of Music Literature

See also nos. S.4, S.21, S.24

S.5.   COOPER, David Edwin. International Bibliography of Discographies: classical music and jazz of blues, 1962-1972; a reference book for record collectors, dealers, and libraries; with a preface by Guy A. Marco. Littleton, Colo.: Libraries Unlimited, 1975. (Keys to Music Bibliography, No. 2). 272p.

Though surpassed in thoroughness of coverage by the first two volumes of the Bibliography of Discographies (Classical Music, by Gray and Gibson, no. S.6, and Jazz, by Daniel Allen, no. S/A. 363), Cooper's work remains a valuable one-volume guide, particularly for the non-specialist. One of its merits may not be an intentional feature: although he aimed to be comprehensive, Cooper failed to identify some of the more obscure sources of discographical information, especially in jazz, and hence his listings tend to concentrate on material more likely to be found in libraries.

The book is organized in three parts. Part 1, Classical Music, has subsections for general guides, buyers' guides and subject discographies (e.g., electronic, film), for historical recordings and label discographies, and for composers and performers. American music is represented in all sections, and musical comedy is included in the designation "classical." Part 2, Jazz & Blues, lists general guides, buyers' guides and subject discographies, label discographies, and discographies of individual performers (mostly American); there are also short sections for chronological discographies. Part 3 is a summary of national discographies, catalogs, and major review sources. The total number of items is slightly under 2,000; coverage includes books, whole books, discographies within books, and articles. A detailed, 37-page index concludes the work. (Formerly LOAM A3).

S.6.   GRAY, Michael H., and GIBSON, Gerald D. Bibliography of Discographies. Vol. 1. Classical Music, 1925-1975. New York: Bowker, 1977. 164p.

An auspicious beginning to what is proving to be a significant series, this bibliography gives details of 3,307 discographies published between the given dates. Composers, performers, instruments, forms and genres are included in one alphabetical subject sequence; general works, label discographies and buyers' guides--all listed by Cooper (no. S.5)--are held over to a later volume in the series (comparison of their main classical sequences suggests that Gray and Gibson have the edge over Cooper in thoroughness). Coverage includes books, parts of books, and articles. The compilers examined each discography themselves whenever possible; items not seen are enclosed in square brackets. An index provides access by names of authors and editors, by series titles, and by distinctive volume titles. The representation of American music is not especially impressive; a later edition would presumably mark an improvement, following the increase in the recording of American composers begun during (if not fully maintained after) the Bicentennial. (The other published volumes in the series are listed as S/A.363, S/A.507.)

S.7. MARCO, Guy A. Information on Music: a handbook of reference sources in European languages. Vol. 1. Basic and Universal Sources. Littleton, Colo.: Libraries Unlimited, 1975. 164p.
_____. _____. Vol. 2. The Americas, by Guy A. Marco, Ann M. Garfield, Sharon Paugh Ferris. Littleton, Colo.: Libraries Unlimited, 1977. 296p.
        This annotated bibliography of sources of musical information is broadly conceived and therefore inevitably selective in many areas, but it provides a useful starting point from which to begin searching. The main coverage of the USA is found in Vol. 2, pp. 22-93. Here 232 items are listed in five major categories, with subdivisions: "direct information sources" (writing about folk and popular music, opera, church and religious music, musical life in regions and localities, instruments, black American music); biographical sources; guides to other sources (bibliographies); lists of music, discographies. Coverage includes books, dissertations, articles, unpublished papers, and whole journals. A number of general reference works appear alongside the more specialized ones. "Reference sources" are interpreted as including histories, and the definition is occasionally stretched to admit critical studies (e.g., Charles Keil's Urban Blues, LOAM 860). Annotations are succinctly informative. Items relevant to the USA appear also in more general sections, especially in Vol. 2, pp. 22-23, "North America," and in Vol. 1, chapter 6, "General Discographies." Vol. 1 has its own indices, but those in Vol. 2, which cover both volumes, are to be preferred. (A third volume, Europe (Littleton, Colo., 1984) contains an "update" of Vol. 2: a further 23 items, of which fifteen are particularly relevant to the USA.)

S.8 MEGGETT, Joan M. Music Periodical Literature: an annotated bibliography of indexes and bibliographies. Metuchen, N.J.: Scarecrow Press, 1978. 116p.
        A modest but useful compilation that includes a number of items relating to American music studies; these occur in particular in Part 2, which has sixteen entries, some bibliographical and some historical, concerned with the history of music periodicals in the USA, and in Part 5, which is devoted to indexes and bibliographies solely interested in music. This section contains no subdivisions (e.g., by

period, country, etc.) but there is a subject index, and this usefully includes references from individual names to particular item numbers, even though the annotations to these items do not mention the
names in question. Although some popular music reference items
are omitted (e.g., Steenson (LOAM 810), Moon (LOAM 919) and
Cooper (no. S.5), it is the paucity of ongoing specialist periodical
indexes in this particular field that is most striking (making regrettable the cessation of Tudor and Tudor's Popular Music Periodicals
Index (LOAM 1162) in 1976, despite the limits on its coverage). A
new edition of Meggett's book would no doubt include Norbert
Ruecker's Jazz Index (Frankfurt, 1977+).

c. Biographical Dictionaries

   See also nos. S.23, S.38, S.61, S.62

S.9.   NULMAN, Macy. Concise Encyclopedia of Jewish Music.
        New York: McGraw-Hill, 1975. 276p. illus.
        "The 500-odd entries listed alphabetically include definitions
of Jewish musical terms and vocabulary, the origin and structure of
Biblical and post-Biblical instruments, histories and descriptions of
Jewish musical organization and movements, biographies of representative composers and musicians, descriptive musical works, and
principal published collections" (page ix). A grand undertaking,
and the book has many felicitous aspects (footnotes with many entries, cross-references, many photos), but the author's high purpose is continually thwarted by omissions (where are Aaron Copland,
Leonard Bernstein, Fanny Brice, to name only three?), sloppy
scholarship (no exact birth or death dates and few locations of these
events are given for individuals), etc. The emphasis on what the
author considers international highlights of Jewish music renders the
work of limited value to those interested in the many aspects of
Jewish music in America.

2.   Histories

S.10.   DAVIS, Ronald L. A History of Music in American Life.
        Malabar, Fla.: Robert Krieger, 1980-1982, 3v. illus.,
        bibliogs.
        Whatever their faults, most previous histories of American
music, from Ritter to Hitchcock (and on), have character. Davis'
large work, the result, according to his acknowledgments, of a
"fourteen-year writing project" (no mention of time spent thinking,
or listening to music) is a very detailed but bland, plodding, ultimately unexpressive history of the surfaces of American musical
creativity and activity. The accusation made by Robert Stevenson
against John Tasker Howard and others (see LOAM 20, 24, 43), of
failing to consult original sources and relying instead on the second-

hand, applies here all over again, with an addition--of having nothing
to say. (The work sometimes seems intended to be an introduction--
but in three volumes?)

The volumes have separate titles: "The Formative Years,
1620-1865," "The Gilded Years, 1865-1920," and "The Modern Era,
1920-Present." There is evidence of concern to consider the whole
range of music across these years, including folk and popular idioms
(but not Indians...); thus there are chapters on minstrelsy in Vol.
1; on the musical stage, Tin Pan Alley, blues and ragtime, and early
jazz in Vol. 2; on popular song, country music, rock and soul, plus
further accounts of the musical and of jazz in Vol. 3. In general,
Davis is more confident in the areas of concert music and opera, but
whatever the subject, evidence of close listening to the music itself
is hard to find (there are no examples); on the other hand, and
despite the title and occasional chapters such as "Early Concert Life"
in Vol. 1, neither is there any well-developed sense of the interconnections between music and "life."

There are no footnotes, but each volume has a substantial
bibliographical essay, in chapters, and each volume also has its own
index.

S.11.　KINGMAN, Daniel. American Music: a panorama. New
York: Schirmer; London: Collier Macmillan, 1979. 577p.
bibliogs., discogs.

Aimed firstly at teachers and students, but useful to a wider
audience, this well-presented survey of the entire corpus of American music has a particular characteristic which it uses to good advantage: instead of the conventional, single chronological sequence,
Kingman favors an approach involving "separate treatment of distinct but interrelated streams" (p. xxvi). This permits great
flexibility (one can begin virtually anywhere), and avoids the hier-
archies of importance which often beset single sequence histories.
Kingman identifies six "intermingling and mutually influential
streams" (p. xxv): folk (Anglo-American, Afro-American, American
Indian, Spanish, French, and modern); sacred music "in the possession of the folk"; offspring of the rural South (country, blues,
rock); Broadway; jazz; art music. The text is admirably clear,
informative (about historical, cultural, and musical aspects), and
unprejudiced. Each chapter contains music examples, and is followed by recommended reading and listening, and by suggestions
for projects. Index.

S.12.　ZUCK, Barbara A. A History of Musical Americanism. Ann
Arbor: UMI Research Press, 1980. (Studies in Musicology, No. 19) 383p. bibliog.

The particular "Americanism" in question is that found in
US art music from the late 19th century up to 1945. Two fundamental types are isolated at the outset: "compositional" Americanism--
the incorporation of native idioms--and "conceptual" Americanism--
not peculiar to composers alone, though concerned with the difficulties they face vis-à-vis performance and recognition. The three-part

history which follows describes and discusses trends and events as
they involve and intertwine both types. Part 1 is concerned with
the roots and early history of the phenomenon to 1920, from Fry,
Heinrich, and Bristow in the first part of the 19th century, by way
of the Civil War era, the foundation of the Music Teachers National
Association (1876), to the late 19th/early 20th century composers
such as MacDowell, Farwell, Cadman, Mason, and Gilbert (Ives, "a
special case," is also briefly discussed in this context). Part 2,
in many ways the core of the book, covers changes wrought by the
Depression and the war years (the "definitive decade," according to
Virgil Thomson [quoted on p. ix]). Here attention focuses on the
interweaving of social, political, and artistic aims, as seen in the
adaptation of Gebrauchsmusik, the relationship between the composer
and the political left, the emergence of folksong as a source, the
work of the WPA and composers' involvement therein, and the responses of composers to World War 2. Particularly crucial throughout this section are the ideas of Charles Seeger (the book's dedicatee). Part 3 narrows the focus to look, with examples, at three
individual composers: Blitzstein, Harris, and Copland. 70 pages of
notes, a large, useful bibliography, and a general index complete
the work.
     As a history of trends, opinions, and activities, this revised
doctoral dissertation (University of Michigan, 1978), is both knowledgeable and informative. But although the author is sensitive to
the arguments involved, what is perhaps missing is an awareness
of the fundamental nature of the conflicts, at cultural, social, and
artistic levels, and of the fact that not infrequently it is the variety
of conflicts generated by the idea and processes of "Americanism"
(between high and low, imported and native, etc.), rather than the
degree to which assimilation has taken place, that is perceived today
as giving the music its character.

3. Miscellaneous Studies and Historiography

See also no. S.139

S.13. CLARKE, Garry E. Essays on American Music. Westport,
        Conn.: Greenwood Press, 1977. 259p. bibliog.
     These eight essays range widely, if with little obvious co-
hesion, over the American cultivated tradition, from Billings to
Rochberg. Basic biographical information is combined with cultural
history and, especially, with some close scrutiny of the music itself (a generous number of music examples is included) to provide
informative portraits of the various subjects covered: "Yankee
tunesmiths" (in particular Swan, Belcher, and Billings); Gottschalk;
the "American-Europeans" (Parker, Paine, MacDowell); Griffes, Ives;
Quincy Porter; Thomson, and the "New Eclecticism" (a chapter beginning with Cage, and going on to discuss the ideas and work of
George Crumb, James Drew, Robert Morris, and George Rochberg).
The lack of a linking theme is disconcerting, however. It may not

be as hazardous to send unlinked essays into the world as it is to climb unroped up a steep rockface, but it requires great strength of character to avoid the drop into the void. Even if your subjects have that strength, your essays are better roped. Support is provided, at any rate, in the shape of extensive notes, a twelve-page bibliography, and an index.

S.14.   GRAUE, Jerald C., ed. Essays on Music for Charles Warren
          Fox; introduction by Edward G. Evans; foreword by Rob-
          ert S. Freeman. Rochester, N.Y.: Eastman School of
          Music, 1979. 253p. illus., bibliog. refs.
          Includes an essay by Robert Stevenson, "American Awareness
of the Other Americas to 1900," which chronicles some of the ways
in which events in Latin America were reflected and commented on
by sheet music composers and in more extensive compositions such as
Frederic Grant Gleason's Montezuma. Music examples.

S.15.   GRUBBS, John W., ed. Current Thought in Musicology;
          with the assistance of Rebecca A. Baltzer, Gilbert L.
          Blount, and Leeman Perkins. Austin: University of
          Texas Press, 1976. 313p. bibliog. refs.
          Based on lectures given at seminars held at the University
of Texas in 1968, 1969 and 1971, this volume includes two essays of
particular relevance to American music. In "The Ecstatic and the
Didactic: a Pattern in American Music" by Charles Hamm, the pattern referred to is a recurring one in which the impulse to "improve"
what is seen as a poor state of musical health by turning to the past
and drawing up rules for guidance in technique, taste and morality,
exists side by side with the "ecstatic" approach which holds that
the personal, sensual experience of music cannot be bad and should
have no formal restraints placed upon it. Hamm illustrates this pattern by discussing two pairs of composers, Andrew Law and William
Billings, Daniel Gregory Mason and Charles Ives. Elliott Carter's
essay, "Music and the Time Screen," describes how, "out of a consideration for the special temporality of music," he "attempted to
derive a way of composition that deals with its very nature" (p. 63).
Developments in his approach to the dimension of time are discussed,
with particular attention to the Cello Sonata, the Second String
Quarter, the Double Concerto, and the Concerto for Orchestra.
There are several music examples in the text.

S.16.   LOWENS, Irving. Music in America and American Music: two
          views of the scene; with a bibliography of the published
          writings of Irving Lowens. Brooklyn: Institute for Studies
          in American Music, 1978. (I.S.A.M. Monographs, No. 8).
          61p.
          These are two lectures delivered while the author was Sen-
ior Research Fellow of the Institute for Studies in American Music
during 1975-76. Drawing examples mainly from the 18th and 19th
centuries, he first points out differences between music in America,
which "includes everything musical that takes place here, regardless

of its race, creed or national origin," and American music, which
"includes only that aspect of the art that was created by Americans"
(pp. 8-9), and suggests that the former is in greater need of
scholars' attention, "at least until we find out what took place
here." In his second lecture, Lowens goes further into what con-
stitutes "American music," submitting that while the concept may
now be an anachronism, there is a tradition of musical composition,
"sprung from national roots," and it is this tradition that is most
able to communicate with contemporary America.

The 43-page selective bibliography, by Elizabeth Aubrey
and Margery Morgan Lowens, is in five sections: books; papers;
abstracts and articles; reviews, editions and compilations; recordings. It is a testimony, both to the size and quality of Lowens'
contribution to music criticism in America, and to his own willing-
ness to be as concerned with music in America as with American
music.

S.17.   McCUE, George, ed. Music in American Society, 1776-1976:
        from Puritan hymn to synthesizer. New Brunswick, N.J.:
        Transaction Books, 1977. 201p. bibliog. refs.
        To help mark the Bicentennial in St. Louis a series of work-
shops was held, exploring the diverse manifestations of the American
character in American music. This volume represents the permanent
record--twelve papers, based on the workshop themes but prepared
specially for this publication; each is by a participant in the workshops, and an authority in his/her field. The contributors are:
William Schuman on a composer's view of Americanism in music;
Edward Jablonski on areas that are particularly American; Austin
B. Caswell on the hymn; Roy V. Magers on Ives's optimism, as illustrated in the Fourth Symphony; Kenneth B. Billups on "the other
side of black music" (i.e., not jazz and blues); Charlotte J. Frisbie
on the music of the American Indians; Joseph Hickerson on folk song
collecting; K. Peter Etzkorn on sociological features of popular music; Dan Morgenstern on jazz as music "born in and nurtured by
urban civilization" (p. 143); John Easton on developments in compositional techniques since 1950; Mary Elaine Wallace on the musical
theater; and Frank Peters on musical corporations. The problem
many of the contributors face is that their (apparent) brief to write
at an introductory level and assume no prior knowledge, combined
with the breadth of their subjects, leaves them perilously thinly
clad; what seemed a good idea for a workshop can soon assume the
sartorial overconfidence of Hans Christian Andersen's fairy tale king
when obliged to display itself on the printed page. Indexes of
names and titles.

S.18.   SHEPHERD, John, et al. Whose Music? a sociology of mu-
        sical languages, by John Shepherd, Phil Virden, Graham
        Vulliamy, Trevor Wishart; foreword by Howard S. Becker.
        London: Latimer, 1977; New Brunswick, N.J., Transac-
        tion Books, 1980. 300p. bibliog.
        This ground-breaking book by four British critics proposes

that "any particular kind of music can only be understood in terms of the criteria of the group or society which makes and appreciates that music" (p. 1). Other writers have suggested a similar thesis, but none of them have developed it quite so rigorously nor shown so persuasively that, in Becker's words, "analyses of social class systems speak in translatable ways to analyses of musical forms" (p. xiii). (In doing so, the authors take issue with the established assumption that it is possible to isolate objective musical "facts.") The argument is pursued from a variety of perspectives through the book's eight chapters; all are important reading for anyone interested in understanding how music expresses meaning. Their relevance to the study of American music is twofold: the first connection, more theoretical, is that the case made by John Shepherd in the first three chapters, that "meanings of society are encoded and creatively articulated by music" (p. 60), can both be applied to and tested by music of the USA in a particularly acute way, because of the encounter in the USA between the western culture of which Shepherd speaks here and non-western musical traditions. (Shepherd himself has indicated how this might be done in "Sociomusicological Analysis of Popular Musics," Popular Music, 2, [1982], pp. 145-177.)

The second connection lies in the specific examples used in three of the chapters. Phil Virden and Trevor Wishart, in "Some Observations on the Social Stratification of Twentieth-Century Music (Chapter 5), include an illuminating analysis of the blues as an example of how and why the music of dispossessed groups expresses the characteristics of immediacy, implicitness, "intensionality," and circularity. In Chapter 6 Graham Vulliamy re-examines the views of the mass culture critics and illustrates their failure both to differentiate between varieties of popular music and to discern the alternative criteria of the Afro-American tradition with a short study of the different ways in which the rock "community" perceives its music. Chapter 8, "On Radical Culture," by Trevor Wishart, sets out to demonstrate that all cultural criticism, even that considered "radical," is beset by notions of the universality of what are in effect culture-specific phenomena; in the course of proposing a new approach, Wishart makes the (probably unprecedented) juxtaposition of Percy Bysshe Shelley and John Cage as examples of the difficulties experienced in turning radical ideas into practical ones (Cage's particular dilemma is shown as being that between a dislike of the "control" exercised by the composer on the one hand, and the need for political/social interference on the other).

S.19.   SMALL, Christopher. Music, Society, Education: a radical examination of the prophetic function of music in Western, Eastern, and African cultures with its impact on society and its use in education. London: Calder; New York: Schirmer, 1977. 234p. bibliog. refs.
_____. _____. 2nd rev. ed. London: Calder, 1980; New York: Riverrun Press, 1982. 234p. bibliog. refs.
A highly stimulating, often polemical and/or visionary study,

by a New Zealander teaching in London, of what he sees as the im-
passe at which the West finds itself vis-à-vis its art--turned from a
process in which people participate into a knowable object to be ad-
mired--and of the potential of other attitudes to music to lead the
way out. Under consistent, well-argued attack is the dominance
(not necessarily the existence) of the "scientific world view," that
the world can be "mastered" and reduced to objective knowledge,
denying "the reality of experience, a reality in fact of greater significance in our lives than the structure of atoms or of the galaxies"
(p. 97). Staunchly defended is the view that art, which "enables
us to live in the world" (p. 4), by structuring our feeling and perception, holds the key to the future. Much of the Western classical
tradition is perceived as reflecting the scientific view; that different
aesthetics, hence world views, are possible is seen in certain developments within the classical tradition (late Beethoven, the Ro-
mantics) but more especially in post-classical 20th-century music
(Debussy and on), in the music of other cultures, and--the reason
for the book's inclusion here--in the music of the United States, a
culture that "has long contained within it the vision of a potential
society which is perhaps stronger and more radical than anything in
European culture" (p. 3). This is explored in Chapter 6, "A Different Drummer," where the independent strand running from New
England psalmody (before regular singing) and Billings, through to
Ives, Cage, and especially Partch, together with the blues, is seen
as offering alternative paths both in sound itself and in the social
concept of music making. Rock & roll and rock are briefly discussed
in the following chapter, "Plus Ça Change," as having promised, but
substantially failed to break the mold. Index.

4. Women in Music

See also S.502 and Section J.7(b)

S.20.   AMMER, Christine. Unsung: a history of women in Ameri-
         can music. Westport, Conn.: Greenwood Press, 1980.
         317p. bibliog.
         A pioneering study "of the role played by women in Ameri-
can music, as performers, composers, and teachers, during the past
two hundred years" (p. ix). The author concedes that her work is
not exhaustive: singers are omitted, many women "active in American music" have been left on one side, and she is aware that she
may not be backing all the winners in contemporary music. Nevertheless, it is an impressive, scholarly study. Of the eleven chapters, nine are historical and are devoted to distinctive areas of
music-making, beginning with organist Sophia Hewitt (Handel &
Haydn Society, 1820), and continuing with violinists (Camilla Urso,
Maud Powell, etc.); pianists (Teresa Carreño, Julia Rivé-King, Amy
Fay, Olga Samaroff); New England composers (Amy Beach, Margaret
Lang, Mabel Wheeler Daniels); all-women orchestras, mainly in Boston; composers "in European idioms" (Mary Carlisle Howe, Marion

Bauer, Ruth Crawford Seeger, etc.); composers "in American idioms" (Julia Smith, Florence Price, Margaret Bonds, Julia Perry, Alice Parker, Gena Branscombe); opera composers and conductors (Sarah Caldwell, Judith Somogi, etc.); and teachers. There are two chapters on post-1950 developments in composition and performance. The ten-page bibliography includes books, dissertations, and articles. Index.

S.21.   BLOCK, Adrienne Fried, and NEULS-BATES, Carol. Women in American Music: a bibliography of music and literature. Westport, Conn.: Greenwood Press, 1979. 302p. illus.

A substantial contribution to research on the roles played by women in American music and musical life, and to performances of compositions by American women, this bibliography consists of 5,024 items, including literature about women in the form of books, articles, dissertations and reviews, and scores by women composers both separately published and in anthologies and articles. All the women included were either native-born or have spent ten years or more in the United States. Each item listed is accompanied by an abstract; those for secondary literature are detailed annotations, ranging in length from 50-250 words, while those for scores consist mainly of symbols denoting duration, instrumentation, author of text, existence of recording, etc. In layout, style and organization the bibliography closely resembles RILM Abstracts, to whose computers the editors and their team of assistants had access.

There are eight main sections. The first three are devoted to general material, and the remainder cover five consecutive historical periods: Colonial times to 1820, 1820-1870, 1870-1920, 1920-1950, 1950-1978. Especially through author-subject and composer-author indexes follow. For each period section there are subsections for women in art music, listing general literature, literature on women as composers, patrons, educators and performers, and published scores. Up to 1920 there is also limited coverage of women in vernacular music. This is the least successful part of the enterprise (for example, Bessie Smith is included in the pre-1920 section, somewhat surprisingly, and then allocated the derisory total of one book, one chapter in a book, and two articles). The editors fail to make clear the reasons for their policy in excluding vernacular music after 1920; one assumes they--or the computer--balked at the huge quantity of material, but in the absence of any stated reason there is a suggestion of an unwarranted evaluative distinction.

S.22.   LEPAGE, Jane Weiner. Women Composers, Conductors, and Musicians of the Twentieth Century: selected biographies. Metuchen, N.J.: Scarecrow Press, 1980-1983. 2v. illus.

Of the 34 women featured in these two volumes, 26 are American--a bias which necessitates the book's inclusion here, but which neither justifies the global implication of the title nor accurately reflects the world position; even within its US coverage the work is unbalanced, as all the women are white. Thus the author's welcome intention to redress an imbalance creates inequalities of its own. The biographies themselves are useful, if a trifle laudatory, summaries, often incorporating interview material and press reviews; they also provide selective discographies and, for the composers, partial lists of compositions. There are no bibliographies. The Americans included in the first volume are: Victoria Bond, Antonia Brico, Radie Britain, Ruth Crawford Seeger, Emma Lou Diemer, Margaret Hillis, Jean Eichelberger Ivey, Barbara Anne Kolb, Pauline Oliveros, Eve Queler, Marga Richter, Louise Talma, Rosalyn Tureck, and Nancy Van de Vate. In Vol. 2 we find Beth Anderson, Sarah Caldwell, Vivian Fine, Kay Gardner, Miriam Gideon, Doris Hays, Daria Semegen, Susan Smeltzer, Julia Smith, Elinor Remick Warren, Judith Lang Zaimont, and Ellen Taaffe Zwilick. Both volumes have an index.

S.23.   NOTABLE AMERICAN WOMEN, 1607-1950: a biographical
        dictionary; Edward T. James, editor; Janet Wilson James,
        associate editor; Paul S. Boyer, assistant editor. Cam-
        bridge, Mass.: Belknap Press, 1971. 3v.
        NOTABLE AMERICAN WOMEN: the modern period; a bio-
        graphical dictionary; edited by Barbara Sicherman, Carol
        Hurd Green, with Ilene Kantrov, Harriette Walker. Cam-
        bridge, Mass.: Belknap Press, 1980. 773p.
        This substantial reference work contains full biographies of
numerous women musicians. Both the original set and the later
volume conclude with a classified listing by occupation. In the
former, there are three relevant headings: Composers (two names
only, Amy Beach and Carrie Jacobs-Bond), Music Educators and
Patrons (seven names), and Performing Musicians (42 names); in the
1980 volume all relevant names are collected under the one heading,
Music, and 26 names are listed, among them Frances Densmore, Billie Holiday, Jeanette MacDonald, and Helen Traubel. Though both
"serious" and "popular" musicians are included, there is a tendency,
numerically, to favor the former group, especially in the 1971
volumes; this despite the fact that, if the criterion is genuinely
"notability," the popular styles have produced far more candidates.

S.24.   SKOWRONSKI, JoAnn. Women in American Music: a bib-
        liography. Metuchen, N.J.: Scarecrow Press, 1978.
        183p.
        An annotated listing of biographical and critical material
contained in 1,305 books and articles; the references are arranged
in four historical sections (1776-1834, 1835-1868, 1869-1938, 1939-
1976), with an additional chapter for general history, and another
for bibliographies, dictionaries and indexes. Within each section entries are arranged alphabetically by author. Easily the largest section is the fourth (1939-1976), which contains items 329-1176. The
coverage of musical areas and styles is wide (it includes art music,
opera, jazz, blues, popular singers) but the results are far from
comprehensive. Concert music and opera are well covered, but much

periodical literature from the popular and folk areas has gone un-
noticed (a result of over-reliance on two periodical indexes: Music
Index and Readers' Guide); this leads to surprising omissions from
the name index (e.g., Aunt Molly Jackson, Barbra Streisand) and
under-representation (e.g., Sara and Maybelle Carter). There is
no provision, either in the separate sections or in the index, for an
approach by subject (e.g., women in jazz).

5. Vocal Music

a. Song

S.25.   CARMAN, Judith, et al. Art-Song in the United States,
          1801-1976: an annotated bibliography, by Judith Carman,
          William K. Gaeddert and Rita M. Resch; with a special
          section, Art-song in the United States, 1759-1810, by
          Gordon Myers. New York: National Association of
          Teachers of Singing, 1976. 308p. bibliog.
        Conceived as a "practical tool for the studio teacher of
voice and the mature singer" (Preface), this is a selective, but still
extensive, list of art songs by American composers, chosen according to their usefulness in developing vocal technique and for programming purposes, their quality, and their historical value. 1,366
songs are listed in the main sequence, and almost 350 composers are
represented (some with one song, some--notably Ives and Rorem--
with over 50). All the songs exist in published form, either individually or in collections, but no effort was made to ascertain
their current availability. Very detailed notes accompany each entry,
giving in most cases information on poet, publication date, composition date if known, dedication (if to a singer), key or tonality,
range, tessitura, meter, tempo, length, difficulty level, suitable
voice type, mood and subject, character of vocal line, character of
piano score, special difficulties, uses and evaluation. The section
on art-song from 1759-1810 lists a further 38 songs by early American composers with the same details, and Appendix A contains entries
for a further 35 songs not included, for various reasons, in the main
list. Other appendices provide a list of publishers and sample recital programs. There are indexes by subject and poet, by composer, and by title.

S.26.   EVANS, Mary Garrettson. Music and Edgar Allan Poe: a
          bibliographical study. Baltimore: Johns Hopkins Press,
          1939. (Repr. New York: Greenwood Press, 1968.) 97p.
        The principal section of this book, a bibliography of musical
settings of Poe texts, lists the settings alphabetically by composer.
Whenever possible the author appends brief biographical information
on the composer (and from these one may ascertain just how many
are American). The biographical data were obtained from the composers themselves in a great many instances.

6. Church Music

a. General Works

S.27.   HOOPER, William Lloyd. *Church Music in Transition.* Nashville, Tenn.: Broadman Press, 1963. 208p. bibliog.
A generally good, if lightweight history of church music told in ten chapters followed by notes, a bibliography, a general index, and a useful index to hymnals mentioned in the text. The prose is littered with biblical quotations, and is written in the simplified terms that church leaders sometime use to address their flock. The book was probably intended for Baptists; certainly, the publisher is attached to that denomination.

b. Hymnody

S.28.   BUTTERWORTH, Hezekiah. *The Story of the Hymns; or, Hymns That Have a History: an account of the origins of personal religious experience.* New York: American Tract Society, 1875. 256p. illus.
_____. *The Story of the Tunes: for home reading, praise meeting, and lectures on sacred music.* New York: American Tract Society, 1890. 257p. illus.
BROWN, Theron, and BUTTERWORTH, Hezekiah. *The Story of the Hymns and Tunes.* New York: American Tract Society, 1906; New York: George H. Doran, 1923. (Repr. Grosse Pointe, Mich.: Scholarly Press, 1968.) 564p. illus.
The Brown-Butterworth book is a revised version of Butterworth's two earlier compilations. It establishes fourteen categories of hymns, and, selecting examples in each, provides information on hymn writers, tunes, and composers. Many of the texts are of British origin, but a substantial number of the settings are American. Indexes of names and hymns.

S.29.   GOODENOUGH, Caroline Leonard. *High Lights on Hymnals and Their Hymns.* Rochester, Mass.: the author, 1931. (Repr. New York: AMS Press, 1974.) 505p.
As in Charles Seymour Robinson's *Annotations Upon Popular Hymns* (no. S.36) and other reference works in the subject, this collection deals with the literary form, not with hymn tunes; hence, it is about authors, not composers. The authors discussed are grouped into chapters ("British Hymnists--Women"), the ninth and tenth being devoted to Americans. Laboriously compiled, the book is, unfortunately, based largely on secondary sources which were to hand at the time. As a result it includes little not available elsewhere, and old errors are repeated.

S.30.   HAEUSSLER, Armin. *The Story of Our Hymns: the handbook to the hymnal of the Evangelical and Reformed*

Church. St. Louis: Eden Publishing House, 1952. 1088p.
bibliog.

It took six years (1945-51) to compile this estimable work.
Not only does it contain articles on the historical background of the
561 selections in The Hymnal of the Evangelical and Reformed Church
(1941); it also has four articles, biographies of authors, translators,
composers, arrangers, eight indexes, a foreword and a preface, and
a nine-page bibliography. The article "The Hymnody of the Evangelical and Reformed Church" contains a twenty-page "list of titles
[with extensive notes] of various psalters, hymnals, and tune-books
used by the congregations of the Reformed Church in the United
States" (p. 22).

S.31. HIGGINSON, J. Vincent. Handbook for American Catholic
Hymnals. New York: Hymn Society of America, 1976.
334p. bibliog.

This is a fine, exhaustive, well-organized research tool. To
anyone used to handbooks to the hymnals of single denominations
(e.g., The Hymnal 1940 Companion (Episcopal), Polack's The Handbook to the Lutheran Hymnal [1942], etc.), the format used here
may appear a little confusing. The book is divided into four parts:
I) a discussion of texts; II) a discussion of tunes; III) "Tunes-
Sources"; IV) biographies of composers and authors. The texts
and tunes discussed are grouped according to the Ecclesiastical
Year, as are the hymns in Catholic hymnals. The author's thoughtful "Helpful Suggestions" (after the Contents) should be consulted
first.

S.32. HIGGINSON, J. Vincent. Hymnody in the American Indian
Missions. New York: Hymn Society of America, 1954.
(The Papers of the Hymn Society, No. 18). 40p.

This "general survey" (p. 4) of Roman Catholic missions is
limited to two aspects of the subject: "first, schemes used to bring
the hymns to the Indians ... second, a general survey of the hymn
books with a more detailed report on certain examples" (p. 4). The
author, a Roman Catholic musician and writer, is careful: his report is fine and scholarly, with many bibliographical footnotes.
While some will cherish the mission work described, others will find
in the booklet confirmation of the processes of cultural defamation.

S.33. HUGHES, Charles W. American Hymns Old and New: notes
on the hymns and biographies of the authors and composers. New York: Columbia University Press, 1980.
621p. bibliog.

A scholarly companion to the hymnal American Hymns Old
and New, but a useful layman's book also. Arranged by hymn title,
the book provides details of authors, composers, publication date,
tune title, meter, number of stanzas, and includes brief comments on
texts and tunes. Biographical sketches of around 500 authors and
composers are also given, some quite detailed. The excellent bibliography includes books and articles.

S.34.   McCUTCHAN, Robert Guy. Our Hymnody: a manual of the
        Methodist Hymnal. New York: Methodist Book Concern,
        1937. 619p. bibliog.
        Methodist hymnals have always displayed transatlantic links:
John Wesley's first collection, a now very rare volume entitled Collection of Psalms and Hymns, was published in Charleston, South
Carolina in 1737, and while English authors have tended to dominate
not only British but American editions, the increasing American contribution in texts and music (from John Greenleaf Whittier to Fanny
Crosby, from Thomas Hastings to "Amazing Grace") has become a
characteristic feature. McCutchan's manual to the American hymnal
offers information hymn-by-hymn on authors and composers. There
are also indexes of first lines, tunes, and names. (The same author
compiled a guide, Hymn Tune Names: their sources and significance
[New York: Abingdon Press, 1957], which includes information on
numerous American tunes.)

S.35.   PORTER, Ellen Jane. Two Early American Tunes: fraternal
        twins? (a study of a hymn family). New York: Hymn
        Society of America, 1975. (The Papers of the Hymn So-
        ciety, No. 30). 19p. bibliog.
        An excellent, non-technical booklet about the tunes, "Won-
drous Love," and "Captain Kidd," the latter apparently American in
origin though it is said to have originated shortly after Kidd was
hanged in London in 1701 (see Downes and Siegmeister, A Treasury
of American Song, 1940). Both tunes have been used with hymn
texts, and it is on this aspect that the author dwells. Other than
the bibliography of secondary sources, there are six tables. No index.

S.36.   ROBINSON, Charles Seymour. Annotations Upon Popular
        Hymns. New York: Hunt & Eaton; Cincinnati: Cranston
        & Curtis, 1893. 581p. illus.
        A line in the preface reads: "... the hymns [here] have
been chosen mostly from Laudes Domini, issued in 1884, and New
Laudes Domini, issued in 1892...." The caption title on p. (5)
reads: "Annotations Upon the Hymns of Laudes Domini." Both
books mentioned were compiled by Robinson; they were collections
of Protestant hymns and sacred songs. The entries, concerning the
background of hymn texts--nothing here about hymn tunes--are
numbered 1 to 1,215. As in other hymn-book companions, the numbers match the numbers of a hymn book, in this case both editions
of Laude Domini (1, for example, being the hymn "Praise to Christ").
The annotations typically give morsels of biography, source of the
hymn, and a spiritual interpretation of the hymn (rather like a mini-
sermon). A drawing of the author, himself a hymn-writer, and details of his biography may be found on p. 297. Author index and
first-line index, but no title index.

S.37.   WELLS, Amos R. A Treasure of Hymns: brief biographies
        of the hundred and twenty leading hymn-writers with

their best hymns. Boston: United Society of Christian
Endeavor, 1914. 392p.

_____. _____; with preface by H. Augustine Smith.
Boston: W. A. Wilde, 1945. (Repr. Freeport: Books
for Libraries Press, 1971). 392p.

Thirty-six of the hymnwriters featured are American; they
receive short, sympathetic biographies, with the text of the chosen
hymn. Index of names.

c. Gospel Hymn

S.38.   ANDERSON, Robert, and NORTH, Gail. Gospel Music En-
         cyclopedia; introduction by Don Butler. New York:
         Sterling Publishing Co.; London: Oak Tree Press, 1979.
         320p. illus., discog.

Essentially a biographical reference work on contemporary
gospel performers (individuals and groups). There are 172 entries
in the main part of the book, all but twenty or so devoted to white
musicians. (There is very little overlap with the gospel performers
included in Gentry, LOAM 605). Generosity with pious and/or con-
gratulatory phrases is characteristic of most entries, which seem to
prefer at the same time to divulge as little precise factual information
as possible. Finding illuminating remarks on the music would be
tantamount to discovering that "famous stone that turneth all to
gold." Entries for groups list personnel, and there are over 150
publicity-style photographs--an impressive display of blow-dried
piety. In addition to the main sequence of biographical sketches
there are sections for Dove Award winners (1969-78), members of
the Gospel Music Hall of Fame (motto: Blessed are the meek?
What would Fanny Crosby have said?) with 25 short biographies, a
listing of gospel radio and television stations, fifteen representative
hymns, and a "major recording" discography. Index.

S.39.   BLACKWELL, Lois S. The Wings of the Dove: the story of
         gospel music in America; introduction by Brock Speer.
         Norfolk, Va.: Donning, 1978. 173p. illus., bibliog.

A rather superficial history of the subject, though one written with respect and sincerity. The author, who can write passages
of real warmth and flair, should perhaps have attempted something
a little less grand than the history of a whole genre of music. Certain groups, such as the Speer family and the LeFevre family, are
very well covered. All of black gospel music, however, receives only
one chapter out of a total of nineteen. The bibliography is disap-
pointing.

S.40.   HEMPHILL, La Breeska Rogers. La Breeska: an auto-
         biography. Nashville: Hemphill Music Co., 1976. 220p.
         illus.

A sincere, if ordinary, autobiography by the gospel singer
and wife of the country-singing Protestant minister, Joel Hemphill,

who began The Hemphills in Louisiana in the 1960s. No surprises here. Statements such as "The chances of a woman achieving full maturity depend largely upon her husband" will not endear the author to many female readers.

S.41. HOLM, Dallas. This Is My Story; with Robert Paul Lamb, foreword by David Wilkerson. Nashville: Impact Books, 1980. 139p.

In the manner of Chico Holiday and Tennessee Ernie Ford (nos. S.400, S.403), Holm celebrates his life of evangelism through song. But unlike these other performers, he was apparently never mired in rock or country music stardom: with the exception of a short stint in a local rock band, Holm has more-or-less spent his professional life in pop religious music. At the time of writing this book, he was singer with the crusades of David Wilkerson, a revivalist.

S.42. SIZER, Sandra S. Gospel Hymns and Social Religion: the rhetoric of nineteenth-century revivalism. Philadelphia: Temple University Press, 1978. 222p. bibliog. refs.

It is perhaps unlikely that students of the expressive resources of popular music would look to a study of Moody and Sankey's (and others') hymns for a lead, but this is an important book which has much to offer both in the field of American religious history and in that of popular culture. The popular hymnody of 19th-century revivalism, especially its language, is analyzed on the basis of perspectives drawn from cultural anthropology, which views texts as embodiments of complex cultural structures (Clifford Geertz, Claude Lévi-Strauss); the principal analytical approach is centered on Kenneth Burke's concepts of rhetorical "strategy" and "identification," in particular on the interpretative "strategy" whereby gospel hymns, through the language they use, "articulate a structure of the world and simultaneously create a community with its own specific identity" (pp. 18-19). In the analysis itself, "passivity and passion," centered on a community of feeling, are proposed as the main "strategic foci" of gospel hymns (p. 34); these are set in a linguistic and social context. In her final chapter, the author discusses how, superficial appearances to the contrary, this community was "deeply implicated in social and political identities" (p. 137). An appendix gives guidance on the methods used for analyzing the hymns. Index of names and subjects.

d. Moravians and German Pietists

S.43. CUMNOCK, Frances, ed. Catalog of the Salem Congregation Music. Chapel Hill: University of North Carolina Press, 1980. 682p. illus.

A particularly fine thematic catalog of the music manuscripts belonging to the Archives of the Moravian Church in America, housed at the Moravian Music Foundation, Inc., in Winston-Salem. A long

(44-page), helpful introduction outlines the historical background in Europe and America, and describes the nature of the Moravian community and the role and organization of its music. Particular attention is given to detailing the contribution of successive music directors, from Paul Tiersch and Johann Friedrick Peter to Christian Friedrick Schaaf, and to discussing the content, form and significance of Johannes Reuz's catalogs of 1808. The present catalog is in three main sections, one for each documented collection (those of the Salem Congregation, and Salem Sisters), and one for a group of liturgies. In each, arrangement is in folio number order, and each entry follows the same format: folio call number, composer's name (with dates), title, music incipit, title page information (with quotes from the 1908 catalogs), information derived from the music itself (tempo, key, number of measures), inventory of parts, and miscellany. There are indexes of composers and of text incipits.

S.44. GOMBOSI, Marilyn. A Day of Solemn Thanksgiving: Moravian music for the Fourth of July, 1783, in Salem, North Carolina. Chapel Hill: University of North Carolina Press, 1977. 215p. illus.
 Applying to music the restoration techniques practiced on buildings at Winston-Salem, North Carolina, the editor provides a fine modern edition of music for voices and instruments, "based on manuscript parts contained in the Salem Congregation music and preserved in the archives of the Moravian Music Foundation...." (p. 35). It is cited here for its scholarly introductory chapters on the Moravian church and its music, on music in Salem prior to July 4th, 1783, and on the "Day of Solemn Thanksgiving" itself. There are also substantial editorial comments and notes, accompanied by a bibliography of sources and documents, and an index.

7. Musical Life

a. General Works

Note: For general works on the musical life of particular periods, see S.140, S.146-S.149, S.205-S.225

S.45. FENNELL, Frederick. Time and the Winds: a short history of the use of wind instruments in the orchestra, band and the wind ensemble. Kenosha, Wis.: G. Leblanc, 1954. 59p.
 This little book is included here, not so much for the interest of its general historical overview (beginning with Monteverdi), or for the eminence of its bandsman-conductor author, as for its information of the foundation of the Eastman School wind ensemble in 1952, and for notes on conductors such as Theodore Thomas.

S.46. HART, Philip. Orpheus in the New World: the symphony orchestra as an American cultural institution. New York:

Norton, 1973. 562p. illus., bibliog.
Strongly underpinned by financial and other statistics, this
is a wide-ranging survey of the past, present, and future of the
symphony orchestra in the USA. The historical-critical survey
covers a period beginning before Theodore Thomas up to the American Symphony Orchestra League and Helen M. Thompson, with sections on Henry Lee Higginson (patron), Arthur Judson (manager),
and James Caesar Petrillo (American Federation of Musicians). This
is followed by a detailed study of six orchestras: Philadelphia,
Utah, Louisville, Buffalo, Albuquerque, and Cincinnati. Subsequent
sections are devoted to economic problems, the audience and the
repertory, and the future. Appendices include lists of major orchestras, information on attendances, details of work stoppages,
1954-72, and a financial summary of 82 orchestras in 1970-71. There
is a four-page bibliography and an index.

S.47.　MUELLER, Kate Hevner. Twenty-Seven Major American Sym-
　　　　phony Orchestras: a history and analysis of their reper-
　　　　toires, seasons 1842-43 through 1969-70. Bloomington:
　　　　Indiana University Press, 1973. 398p.
　　　　The major section of this remarkable contribution to repertoire studies consists of a catalog of works performed in a 130-year
period. Arranged alphabetically by composer (with each composer's
dates and nationality), for each title it provides details of timing,
of the orchestra(s) who performed it, and of the year(s) in which it
was performed. The catalog is preceded by a substantial amount of
prefatory material, the chief purpose of which is to begin to analyze
and measure the rise and fall in popularity of individual composers,
thereby suggesting the kinds of use to which the data could be put.
Numerous lists and graphs illustrate the discussion, among them
three lists of American composers, one a "popularity pyramid," the
other two giving (in musical and alphabetical sequences) the number
of orchestras in which each composer's works have been played
(Copland and Gershwin come top, Barber and Creston second). No
analysis is attempted of individual orchestras.

b.　Regional Studies (excluding opera)

　　Note: this section includes regional studies covering particular
　　periods

New England

S.48.　DICKSON, Harry Ellis. Gentlemen, More Dolce Please! ; an
　　　　irreverent memoir of thirty years in the Boston Symphony
　　　　Orchestra. Boston: Beacon Press, 1969. 162p. illus.
　　　　A delightful, light-hearted memoir by a BSO violinist of
forty years standing, who has also served as assistant conductor of
the Boston Pops Orchestra. Dickson slights himself (one cannot even
find here the date he joined the orchestra) but fills his charming

(some would say a bit old-fashioned) tale of devotion with many
stories of Serge Koussevitsky, Pierre Monteux, Charles Munch,
Leopold Stokowski, Leonard Bernstein, and others. There are also
details on various orchestra players, Boston's Symphony Hall,
touring, festivals, and many other subjects. (The title is from a
remark by Koussevitsky.) No index.

S.49. LAMBERT, Barbara, ed. Music in Colonial Massachusetts
       1630-1820: a conference held by The Colonial Society of
       Massachusetts, May 17 and 18, 1973. Vol. 1. Music in
       Public Places. Boston: Colonial Society of Massachusetts,
       1980. (Publications of the Colonial Society of Massachu-
       setts, Vol. 53). 404p. illus., bibliogs.

A stated aim of this volume is to "demonstrate that music
played a much larger part in the lives of the inhabitants of colonial
Massachusetts than had been previously supposed" (p. vii), a goal
which the authors of the four substantial contributions to the book
incontestably achieve through the sheer volume of their accumulated
evidence, all of it from primary sources. The first, "Selected
American Country Dances and Their English Sources," by Joy Van
Cleef and Kate Van Winkle Keller, was not given at the conference
itself (it takes the place of a paper deemed inappropriate to the
theme). It documents in detail the different individual dances and
their music, and shows just how common dancing was in the New
England colonies. Raoul François Camus then discusses "Military
Music of Colonial Boston," followed by Arthur F. Schrader, whose
"Songs to Cultivate the Sensations of Freedom" provides words,
music and full scholarly documentation for a sample of fourteen American Revolutionary War songs. In the longest contribution, Carleton
Sprague Smith's "Broadsides and Their Music in Colonial America,"
the author examines various categories of broadside ballad (ballads
concerning the settlement, the frontier, dissatisfaction with the
Crown, crime, etc.), matching up verses with their contemporary
tunes wherever possible and providing both text and music. The
extent of the material shows it to have been a rich cultural resource, and one from which much could be learnt. A commentary on
the 71 music examples in the book is provided by Israel J. Katz.
All the papers are copiously illustrated, with many facsimiles. An
index of the sources of the illustraitons is followed by a general index. (For publication details of volume 2, see no. S/A.38.)

S.50. WILSON, Ruth Mack. Connecticut's Music in the Revolution-
       ary Era; with the assistance of Kate Van Winkle Keller.
       Hartford: American Revolution Bicentennial Commission
       of Connecticut, 1980. (Connecticut Bicentennial Series,
       No. 31). 142p. illus., bibliog. refs.

A most valuable regional history of late 18th-century musical
life. The narrowing of the focus onto a particular era, while occasionally restricting, offers a good opportunity for in-depth study,
which the authors seize enthusiastically. Returning to primary
sources, they demonstrate in detail the variety of Connecticut musical

life, both sacred and, increasingly, secular at this period, with accounts of singing teachers, regular singing, the growth of dance, ballad opera, military music, and, towards the end, theater music. Index.

TANGLEWOOD

S.51   HOLLAND, James R. Tanglewood; foreword by Michael
        Tilson Thomas. Barre, Mass.: Barre Publishers, 1973.
        96p. illus.
        A picture book of the festival, in its contemporary form,
with a brief historical introduction. A complete listing of the staff
and members of the festival's resident orchestra, the Boston Symphony, as it existed in 1972, appears on p. 96.

S.52   HOWE, M. A. De Wolfe. The Tale of Tanglewood: scene of
        the Berkshire Music Festivals; with an introduction by
        Serge Koussevitsky. New York: Vanguard Press, 1946.
        99p. illus.
        A brief but thorough and attractively-written history of the
early years of the famous festival, from its inception in 1934 to the
beginning of the post-war era. (The book was finished soon after
a period of time, 1942-1944, during which the war caused the suspension or curtailment of Festival activities.) Howe (1864-1960), a
prolific biographer, is particularly good on tales of the history of
the locale; his account includes prominent references to Hawthorne
and Melville, both of whom at one point lived nearby, within a few
miles of each other. The final section of the book gives complete
programs of festival concerts, 1934-1946.

S.53.   KUPFERBERG, Herbert. Tanglewood. New York: McGraw-
        Hill, 1976. 280p. illus., bibliog.
        An affectionate history of the Tanglewood festival from the
days of Henry Hadley and Gertrude Robinson Smith through the
eras of Koussevitzky and the Boston Symphony Orchestra, Munch,
and Leinsdorf to the "troika" of the 1970s (Bernstein, Ozawa, and
Schuller). The stylish text, detailed without being over-demanding,
is complemented by an impressive array of photographs, many from
the early days of the festival. There is also a brief chronology
and an index.

S.54.   MAHANNA, John G. W. Music Under the Moon: a history
        of the Berkshire Symphonic Festival, Inc. Pittsfield,
        Mass.: Printed by Eagle Printing and Binding Co.,
        1955. 123p. illus.
        This is a first-rate documentary study of the Festival by
the then County Editor of the Berkshire Evening Eagle newspaper.
The facsimile of Gertrude Robinson Smith's first organizing letter of
1934 and the many inside photographs are fascinating. A note on
the title page acknowledges that the narrative is "gleaned from the
Official Minutes of the Corporation."

Pennsylvania, Ohio, Kentucky

S.55.   ARIAN, Edward. Bach, Beethoven, and Bureaucracy: the
         case of the Philadelphia Orchestra. University, Ala.:
         University of Alabama Press, 1971. 158p. bibliog.
    This is a compact, well-documented study of the Philadelphia
Orchestra's history and operating procedures as of the early 1970s.
It was written by a twenty-year veteran player in the orchestra who
switched to political science. The author believes that the economy
measures adopted by the orchestra have led to stagnation of repertory, alienation of orchestra members, and disservice to the community. Though he begins his preface by saying that "America today is
experiencing a widespread questioning of authority and values" (p.
ix), he claims a little later that he did not approach the book "in
the spirit of an exposé, but with a concern for both the future of
such organizations and the effective use of public subsidy" (p. x).
(His suggestions are scarcely radical: federal subsidy, a new board
of directors, an arts administrator....)

S.56.   CARDEN, Joy. Music in Lexington Before 1840. Lexington:
         Lexington-Fayette County Historic Commission, 1980.
         148p.
    An evident richness of musical life in the Kentucky town is
unveiled by the author's researches into local documentary sources.
Rather than link the results into one chronological narrative, she
organizes it into accounts of particular groups and activities; music
"enthusiasts," concerts and dances, education, business, church.
Index.

S.57.   FELLERS, Frederick P. and MEYERS, Betty. Discographies
         of Commercial Recordings of the Cleveland Orchestra
         (1924-1977) and the Cincinnati Orchestra (1917-1977).
         Westport, Conn.: Greenwood Press, 1978. 271p. bib-
         liogs.
    The two orchestras whose recordings are listed here are
given a section each (the first devoted to the recordings of the
Cleveland Orchestra, is the longer). Each section has its own introduction, composer and performing artist indexes, and bibliography. The discographies are arranged chronologically by date of
recording session. Each entry contains the session number, the
date, the composer and title of composition, the matrix number, label
number, and the original recording speed.

S.58.   GROSSMAN, F. Karl. A History of Music in Cleveland.
         Cleveland: Case Western Reserve University, 1972.
         201p. illus.
    An attractive, straightforward, though almost totally un-
documented narrative of music in the Ohio city. There are scarcely
any notes to speak of and no bibliography. The book is long on
repertory (names of pieces played by various clubs, schools, orchestras, etc.) but short on biographical information. There is a

little on the musical life of the various organizations but nothing about the composition of audiences. Names such as Johann Beck, Arthur Shepherd, Edwin Kraft, Arthur Loesser, Herbert Elwell, and James H. Rogers appear with some frequency. The author (1886-1969)--his picture appears with those of others between pp. 52 and 53)--died before the book was published; his work is lauded in the foreword by Edward G. Evans, Jr.

S.59. MADEIRA, Louis C. Annals of Music in Philadelphia and History of the Musical Fund Society from Its Organization in 1820 to the Year 1858; edited by Philip H. Goepp. Philadelphia: Lippincott, 1896. (Repr. New York: Da Capo, 1973). 202p. illus.

Goepp (1864-1936) compiled this chronicle of Philadelphia's music from material left by Madeira (who died shortly after the book was begun). He sees the city's musical history as dividing into four parts: a period when music was viewed as a "Bohemian, semi-respectable dissipation," the result in part of Quaker influence; a stage during which, under the impact of growing intellectual freedom, music was actively encouraged; an era of the transmission of impetus from the European classical tradition; and an age of great virtuosi, during which permanent musical institutions were established. Much of the book is devoted to an account of the Musical Fund Society.

S.60. WETZEL, Richard D. Frontier Musicians on the Connoquenessing, Wabash, and Ohio: a history of the music and musicians of George Rapp's Harmony Society (1805-1906). Athens, Ohio: Ohio University Press, 1976. 294p. illus., bibliog.

A fascinating study of the music and musical life of the religious-separatist communities of the Harmony Society which existed in the states of Pennsylvania, Indiana, and Pennsylvania again between 1805 and 1906. The Community was founded by the German millenialist Johann Georg Rapp (later, simply George Rapp, 1757-1847) and his followers, who came from Germany for the purpose and who numbered in hundreds. The book is scholarly, well-written, and has four appendices: the first three contain "examples of music composed and used by the Harmonists" and the last one "is a catalog of the musical items found in the Economy Archives." (One of the Society's settlements in Pennsylvania was named Economy Village.) A small 33-1/3 r.p.m. recording of excerpts from the Harmonists' music is included with the book. Index.

Arkansas, Louisiana, Missouri

S.61. PANZERI, Louis. Louisiana Composers. New Orleans: Dinstuhl Printing and Publishing, 1972. 102p. illus., bibliogs., discog.

This little book contains brief biographies of composers who have lived in Louisiana as well as those who were born there.

Therefore, along with such natives as Louis Moreau Gottschalk
(whose biography is somewhat mutilated), we are given entries for
composers such as H. Owen Reed, who attended Louisiana State
University between 1933 and 1937. Facts and other data are, unfortunately, frequently garbled (such as the use of a picture of the
Brazilian pianist Egydio de Castro e Silva in the entry for Costa
Rican-born composer Castro Carazo). There are many good photos,
however, and the twelve appendices of ("ASCAP Members Born in
Louisiana," "Early Louisiana Composers," etc.) are useful.

S.62. PEBWORTH, James R. A Directory of 132 Arkansas Com-
          posers. Fayetteville: University of Arkansas Library,
          1979. 89p. bibliog.
      Bio-bibliographical directory of composers born or long-
term resident in Arkansas, including writers of country music (e.g.,
Johnny Cash) and western swing (e.g., Leon McAuliffe) as well as
concert music (e.g., William Grant Still). Entries give full name,
dates, short biography, representative list of compositions, and
a list of citations in general reference works (about 100 of these
are listed in the bibliography at the back). An appendix contains
a list of publishers with their addresses.

S.63. WELLS, Katherine Gladney. Symphony and Song: the
          Saint Louis Symphony Orchestra; the first hundred years,
          1880-1980. (Woodstock, Vt.): Countryman Press, 1980.
          227p. illus., discog.
      A handsome work--generous dimensions, beautiful type, wide
margins, sharply reproduced illustrations--by a diligent author, who
states in her foreword that she pursued "the course of attempting
to record the progress, the growth, the 'life and times' ... of the
Saint Louis Symphony Orchestra through its conductors and its principal thrust ... the subscription concerts." This is an excellent
history, accompanied by twelve appendices (one a discography arranged by conductor) and two indexes (one for proper names, the
other general).

                    The West and South-West

S.64. CALMAN, Charles Jeffrey. The Mormon Tabernacle Choir;
          color photography by William I. Kaufman. New York:
          Harper & Row, 1979. 203p. illus.
      This history was sparked by the 50th anniversary of the
radio program featuring the all-volunteer Salt Lake City-based
chorus. (The group itself began in 1847.) It is a large, well illustrated book, written in a popular style, and published on slick
paper. There is a section of fourteen Mormon hymns and anthems
associated with the choir. An appendix lists all past and present
members.

S.65. MacMINN, George R. The Theater of the Golden Era in

California. Caldwell, Idaho: Caxton Printers, 1941.
529p. illus., bibliog.

Along with the "gold seekers, adventurers, settlers, solid
citizens, and parasites of every variety [who] swarmed to the California frontier from virtually every part of the world," came also
"stage artists of every kind and quality" (preface). This instructive and diverting study of theater on that frontier, 1848-1860--
especially in San Francisco--is described by the author as "an attempt at a chapter in social history" (ibid.). It contains three
chapters of relevance to music history, each one an indication of
the variety of available entertainment and edification. Chapter 4,
"Stars and Favorites," is dominated by the intriguing figure of
Dr. D. G. Robinson, celebrated for his comic songs and farces, all
of them locally topical. Several song texts are quoted. Chapter 8,
"The World of Music," recounts tales of the numerous foreign-born
and native musicians who came to give concerts, among them Henri
Herz (who, when a house collapsed on his piano, remarked, "Never
mind, I have two"--(p. 267), Stephen C. Massett, Elisa Biscaccianti
("The American Thrush"), Catherine Hayes ("The Swan of Erin"),
and Anna Bishop. Chapter 9 turns to minstrelsy, and to the varied
talents of Bill Birch, Charley Backus, Eph Horn, and Sam Wells.
All the author's many, mostly contemporary, sources are given in
footnotes and listed in the bibliography. The numerous illustrations
are fascinating, and there is an index.

S.66. JONES, Isabel Morse. Hollywood Bowl; foreword by Merle
       Armitage. New York: Schirmer, 1936. 203p. illus.
The detailed, intricate, "inside" story of the outdoor Cali-
fornia concert facility written by the then music reviewer of The
Los Angeles Times. People as widely varied as Carrie Jacobs Bond,
Arthur Farwell, Percy Grainger, and Otto Klemperer had parts in
that story, as well as architect Lloyd Wright (the son of Frank
Lloyd Wright) who built concert shells there in 1927 and 1928, both
destroyed. Fascinating photos, but no index.

S.67. KOOPAL, Grace G. Miracle of Music: the history of the
       Hollywood Bowl. (Los Angeles: W. Ritchie), 1972.
       373p. illus.
Charles Edward Toberman, the "Father of the Hollywood
Bowl," and the dedicatee and copyright owner of this good-looking
book, provides an introduction, which begins: "Many books and
countless articles have been written about the Hollywood Bowl, but
none has given the complete chronological history, both 'On Stage'
and 'Behind the Scenes'...." He continues "[Koopal] has had
access to the original records and minutes of ... various groups ...
to the archives of the Bowl itself, the actual programs ... and the
personal recollections of those still living...." Koopal's bias, however, may be noted on p. 158, in her discussion of Nicolas Slonimsky's introduction of "ultra-modern" music to Bowl concerts in 1933:
"The nadir was reached however with the presentation of Edgar
Varesese's [sic] 'Ionization' ... horrendous even in the Bowl where

some of the noise was dissipated by the vast expanse, but imagine
what it must have been like within the walls of living rooms of millions of [NBC Network] radio listeners!" A valuable feature is provided by the lists contained in Book II, "The History Makers,"
(e.g., "Cavalcade of Conductors and Soloists in Hollywood Bowl
1921-1972"). No index.

c. Operatic Life

    (i) General Works

S.68.   BISHOP, Cardell. The San Carlo Opera Company, 1919-
           1955: grand opera for profit. Cudahy, Calif.: the
           author, 1978. 259p. illus., bibliog.
    Those who can overlook its errors in spelling, grammar,
and syntax can find a fascinating wealth of detail in this vanity
publication. (The process of reproduction used here appears to be
some sort of xerography.) The San Carlo, apparently out of New
York (the book does not contain any information as to its home
base), was mainly a touring organization; it was the brain child of
one man, Fortune Gallo, who maintained until his death in New
York on March 8, 1970 that his only income was from tickets sold
to San Carlo performances. Somehow he had the secret of how to
make European opera pay in the United States. Appendices here
list San Carlo's repertory and singers (but not the conductors, orchestra members, chorus members, or dancers). The so-called bibliography is actually the notes section. (At least one factual error
should be noted: the Hugh Thompson encountered on p. 176 is not
the son of "composer and critic Virgil Thomson." Thomson never
married and never had children.)

S.69.   KELLOGG, Clare Louise. Memoirs of an American Prima
           Donna. New York: Putnam, 1913. 382p. illus.
    A fascinating, outspoken, and opinionated memoir by the
American soprano (1842-1916) who created the role of Marguérite in
Gounod's Faust when it was given its US premiere in 1863. She
sang from 1861 until 1887, shortly after marrying her manager, Carl
Strakosch, the nephew of the impresarios Maurice and Max Strakosch.
Particularly interesting here are first-hand comments about Gotts-
chalk, Thalberg, Longfellow, Max Maretzek, Christene Nilsson, and
Kellogg's friend, Adelina Patti. Kellogg was reportedly a difficult
person, but she left an absorbing book.

S.70.   LYON, Hugh Lee. Leontyne Price: highlights of a prima
           donna. New York: Vantage Press, 1973. 218p. illus.,
           discog.
    An earnest, well-researched, but superficially told biography
of the operatic soprano. Fingerprints of the author's magazine experience are in evidence. We are told Leontyne's favorite colors,
that she likes red roses, and that her 1959 separation from singer

William Warfield, whom she married in 1952, was due to the fact that
"they just did not come together enough and really be able to live
together." (p. 136). Some useful data are included, albeit in the
language of fan worship. In appendices are listed the (slightly
garbled) principal events of Price's life ("1961--Girl of the Golden
West. Mimi. Metropolitan Opera ... 1961--debut Metropolitan Opera,
January 27, 1961"), opera debuts ("1962--Ernani. Donna Elvira.
Metropolitan Opera"), a Price discography (rudimentary), and her
honors and memberships. No index.

S.71. MAPLESON, James Henry. The Mapleson Memoirs, 1848-
      1888. London: Remington; New York: Clarke, 1888.
      2v. illus.
      _____. The Mapleson Memoirs: the career of an operatic
      impresario 1858-1888; edited and annotated by Harold
      Rosenthal. New York: Appleton-Century, 1966. 246p.
      illus.
      The English impresario, known as "The Colonel," brought
his company to the USA for successive seasons between 1878 and
1886; during this period, based at the New York Academy of Music
but also touring extensively, he widely influenced the shaping of
operatic taste and performance. His entertaining memoirs are not,
his modern editor tells us, entirely reliable, but with Rosenthal's
watchful pen to correct many slips of memory, they provide a useful
source for the study of operatic performance and of the operatic life
at this time. Mapleson's final tour, during the winter of 1885-86,
finds him in financial straits in San Francisco, and making a "re-
treat across America," via Cheyenne, Louisville, Cincinnati, etc.,
each successive venue delighting in publicizing (and exaggerating)
the company's accumulative mishaps. The 1966 edition includes a
selective biographical index, with brief facts about many of the
personalities encountered in the book, and a general index. (Formerly LOAM A55).

S.72. NORTHOUSE, Cameron. Twentieth Century Opera in Eng-
      land and the United States. Boston: G. K. Hall; Lon-
      don: George Prior, 1976. 400p.
      The main part of this reference work consists of a chron-
ological list, in one single sequence, of first performances of 20th-
century English and American operas, 1900-1974. The format of
each entry is identical: composer's name, opera title, city of first
performance, date, and librettist's name; where applicable, the
educational institution at which the first performance was given is
added. No further information (theaters, performers, directors,
etc.) is given. Appendices provide information on additional operas
for which complete information was not obtained, on operas based on
literary works, and on published scores (full and vocal) and libretti.
The index provides access via name and title.

S.73. TRAUBEL, Helen. St. Louis Woman; with Richard G. Hubler;
      with an introduction by Vincent Sheean. New York:

Duell, Sloan and Pearce, 1959. 296p. illus.
Vivacious autobiography of the operatic soprano (1899-1972)
who starred at the Met in the 1940s, and whose defection to take up
a night club career was a cause célèbre in 1953. The final fifty or
so pages describe her first appearance outside of a high culture
context--on a TV show with Jimmy Durante ("I was being appreciated
for almost the first time"--p. 246)--her subsequent night club
career (she introduced her performance of "St. Louis Blues" with
the line, "Now I will sing you a folk ballad made famous by the
peasants of my native village"--p. 248), her handling by the "serious" critics, and a less than successful Hollywood experience making
a movie musical based on Steinbeck's Sweet Thursday, with music by
Rodgers and Hammerstein (Pipe Dream 1955). She apparently never
regretted her change of direction--"all culture has is hard seats"
(p. 253). An appendix lists her appearances, at the Met and elsewhere, 1937-1958.

(ii) New York

S.74. ROBINSON, Francis. Celebration: the Metropolitan Opera;
      picture editor, Gerald Fitzgerald. Garden City, N.Y.:
      Doubleday, 1979. 287p. illus.
      A lavish, slick picture book with loving commentary by a
long-time Met worker. For those who like pictures of singers, conductors, and production stills, this book is endlessly fascinating.
For those with a taste for the unpleasant and scandalous (things not
unknown in Met history) there is little to savor. For "celebration"
read "self-congratulation." Each of the book's thirteen sections is
devoted to a different aspect of the company. Most of the illustrations are from the Lincoln Center, not the "old" house.

S.75. RUBIN, Stephen E. The New Met in Profile; photographs
      by Alix Jeffry. New York: Macmillan, 1974. 202p.
      illus.
      "This book doesn't pretend to be a study of the Metropolitan
Opera company as much as a collection of profiles of its members"
(preface). As such it is a good, if lightweight, production. There
are interviews (with, for instance, singers Leontyne Price, Birgit
Nilsson, et al., conductor James Levine, stage director Nathaniel
Merrill), a chapter on fans (which includes excerpts from several
interviews), an introductory essay, and a name index. The "new
Met" is never defined; does the author mean the Met after Rudolf
Bing retired as General Manager? Or the Met when the house was
opened in Lincoln Center? The pictures are good, however, and the
book, though created for an immediate, contemporary market, already
seems to fill a historical purpose.

(iii) Chicago

S.76. CASSIDY, Claudia. Lyric Opera of Chicago; foreword by

Saul Bellow; recollections by Carol Fox; graphic design
by R. D. Scudellari. Chicago: Lyric Opera of Chicago,
1979. 233p. illus.
    Basically a big, lavish collection of pictures (many of them
in color), this book also contains a generous historical-critical text,
written with devotion and enthusiasm by one-time Chicago newspaper
music critic Claudia Cassidy, widely known for the roughness and
venom of her pen. Here she is all charm and grace, full of civic
pride and a fondness for poetic images. The best features are the
generous annals that encompass from the Lyric's first performance
(Feb. 1954) to 1979, and Bellow's fine, moving foreword.

S.77.   DAVIS, Ronald L. Opera in Chicago. New York: Appleton-
        Century, 1966. 383p. illus.
    The standard modern coverage of the subject, this is a full-
blown history beginning with a performance of Bellini's La Sonnambu-
la on July 29, 1850 featuring four visiting singers and ending with
the 1965 season of the Lyric Theatre of Chicago. During the 165-
year interim, companies and singers come and go and there are many
high points and low points. The following names are frequently encountered: Cleofante Campanini, Samuel Insull, Harold McCormick,
Nellie Melba, Amelita Galli-Curci, Mary Garden, Fausto Cleva, Maria
Callas, and Carol Fox. A wide range of sources was used: Chicago
newspapers, music journals, memoirs, biographies, scrapbooks, programs, various books about Chicago and about opera, and interviews. The annals, from the 1910-11 season to that of 1965, are indispensable.

S.78.   MOORE, Edward C. Forty Years of Opera in Chicago. New
        York: Liveright, 1930. (Repr. New York: Arno Press,
        1977). 430p. illus.
    This dry and witty account begins with the opening in 1889
of Chicago's first home of opera, the so-called Auditorium, designed
by Louis H. Sullivan and his associate Dankmar Adler (the Chicago
Grand Opera Company was not formed until 1910), and ends with
the opening of the house at Twenty Wacker Drive in 1929. An appendix provides annals of the Chicago Grand Opera Co., the Chicago
Opera Assn., and the Chicago Civic Opera Co. for 1910 through
1929. No index.

(iv) San Francisco

S.79.   BLOOMFIELD, Arthur J. The San Francisco Opera: 1923-
        1961. New York: Appleton-Century-Crofts, 1961. 251p.
        illus.

        _____. The San Francisco Opera: 1922-1978. Sausalito,
        Calif.: Comstock Editions, 1978. 532p. illus.
    The first book is a solid, if somewhat plodding, history of
the opera company, made hard to use by the absence of an index.
Four appendices provide a kind of annals: complete cast lists (last

names only), officers and directors (mostly lacking attributions of office held), etc. The second book, called "1st edition," is in effect a second edition, though one which has undergone considerable rewriting. The tone is lighter, the illustrations are different, there is coverage of a further eighteen years, and--best of all!--an index.

d. Musical Instruments

   (i) Organ

S.80.   ARMSTRONG, William H. Organs for America: the life and work of David Tannenberg. Philadelphia: University of Pennsylvania Press, 1967. 154p. illus., bibliog.
      A fine, well-written, carefully-documented study of the 18th-century emigrant (1728-1804) who built organs at Lititz, Pennsylvania. Tannenberg was not the first organ builder in America but he was an early one. "He built or helped to build almost fifty pipe organs for churches and individuals in six states [and] ... The quality of [his] work was such that he is recognized today as one of the master organ builders, to be ranked alongside the Silbermanns and Arp Schnitger in Europe." (p. xii). "Tannenberg thought of himself ... first of all [as] a member of the religious community properly called the Unitas Fratrum (Unity of the Brethren) but more commonly, Moravians." (p. 3). (The foreword, by E. Power Biggs, is used mainly as a platform for Biggs' touting of the so-called "tracker" organ-key action, which was used by Tannenberg as it was by all organ builders of the time.) Excellent bibliography and index.

S.81.   BARNES, William Harrison. The Contemporary American Organ: its evolution, design and construction. New York: J. Fischer, 1930. 341p. illus.
      _____. 8th ed. Glen Rock, N.J.: J. Fischer, 1964. 389p. illus., bibliog.
      The author, who was Associate Editor of the magazine The American Organist and a practicing organist, states in his Introduction that "the chief purpose of this work is to acquaint the reader with the details of present day organ building, as practiced by the leading builders of America, particularly with regard to the mechanisms employed." This he does in 21 chapters, concluding remarks, and a supplement on electronic instruments, using non-technical language. The drawings and photographs are excellent but the book as a whole is, of course, somewhat dated, especially the section on electronic instruments, though this was altered in the later editions. Later editions also have indexes; earlier ones do not.

S.82.   BARNES, William Harrison, and GAMMONS, Edward B. Two Centuries of American Organ Building: "from tracker to tracker." Glen Rock, N.J.: J. Fischer, 1970. 142p. illus.

A sketchy history (if, indeed, it can be called a history) of the organ in America and the organ builder, covering roughly 1750 to 1950. The method seems to be to mention a few facts about well-known organ makers and give a typical stop list. Only five organ companies are discussed as the "Later Nineteenth Century Builders" in a short chapter that covers pp. 34-49. There are some biographical sketches of organists in the latter sections. There are also chapters titled "The Theatre Organ" and "The Organ 'Revival' or 'Reform' Movement." Almost as an afterthought, we are provided with a "History of the Organ Action" in an appendix. The plates are excellent, but the slim content does not live up to the grand title. (A picture of Barnes may be found on p. 118 and one of Gammons on p. 123). No index.

S.83. THE BICENTENNIAL TRACKER: in commemoration of the Bicentennial of the United States of America 1776-1976 and the twentieth anniversary of The Organ Historical Society, Inc., 1956-1976; Albert F. Robinson, editor. Washington, Ohio: Organ Historical Society, 1976. 192p. illus.

A special Bicentennial issue of the society's regular periodical The Tracker, this is an impressive collection of 25 articles, some quite lengthy, and many illustrations about aspects of organs and organ history in the USA. Four pieces are about the Society itself. The collection is in eight sections: (1) The Organ Historical Society, Inc.; (2) The Contributions of Honorary Members (including E. Power Biggs and William H. Barnes); (3) The Development and Design of American Organs; (4) The Organ Builders; (5) The Organs; (6) The Secular Pipe Organ; (7) The Organ Case; and (8) The Composers and Organists. An excellent index concludes the work.

S.84. OGASAPIAN, John. Organ Building in New York City: 1700-1900. Braintree, Mass.: Organ Literature Foundation, 1977. 269p. illus., bibliog.

"This study represents an effort to remedy, at least in part, the lack of secondary material on individual (New York City organ) builders' careers, production, and stylistic traits" (p. vi). "It originated as the author's Doctoral dissertation, submitted to Boston University's Graduate School in January of 1977." (p. vii). To the eleven chapters the preface adds a fine brief resumé of the bibliography (as of 1977) of the history of American organ building. The author candidly acknowledges much help in his researches; the publishers could probably have done with some assistance themselves, as the production is poor. Index.

S.85. OWEN, Barbara. The Organ in New England: an account of its use and manufacture to the end of the nineteenth century. Raleigh, N.C.: Sunbury Press, 1979. 629p. illus., bibliog., discog.

Almost half of this huge work is taken up by four appendixes (one devoted to biographical sketches of New England organ builders,

the other three being "Stoplists of some representative organs referred to in the text," "On the use of the stops of the organ," and
"Inventory of the estate of Wm. M. Goodrich, dec'd"), a stupendous
bibliography and discography, dozens of illustrations, and a detailed
index. The body of the "account," Chapters 1-15, is a chronological
examination of the subject. A first-rate scholarly study.

S.86.   ROWELL, Lois. American Organ Music on Records. Brain-
        tree, Mass.: Organ Literature Foundation, 1976. 105p.
        bibliog. refs.
        An alphabetical composer discography containing 415 entries,
including some non-commercial recordings. The details given include
performer, organ played, its builder and location, date of recording
or date of issue. There are indexes of performers, organ builder,
instrument location, album titles, and record label.

        (ii) Piano

S.87.   BRADLEY, Van Allen. Music for the Millions: the Kimball
        piano and organ story. Chicago: Regnery, 1957. 334p.
        illus.
        The Kimball company was founded in 1857 and was still going
strong (though dramatically less strong than in its 19th-century
days) when this centennial history was produced. The company
manufactured and sold reed organs, pipe organs, and pianos, but
the last-mentioned instruments were its sole interest after the 1920s.
The story told here is straightforward, affectionate, uncritical, and
bright--the classic "official" biography. The truth of the matter--
far removed from the concerns of this book--is the kind of complex,
troublesome, contradictory theme that is shared by the biographies
of other American 19th-century captains of industry such as Marshall
Field and Isaac Singer (those on a less grand scale than the Carne-
gies and Mellons): put simply, the populace is benefited by the
manufacturer's comparatively cheap, excellent goods, but the manufacturer gains a saintly reputation and gets financially richer and
richer in the process. This is fine, except ... William Wallace Kimball (1828-1904), the shrewd, aggressive, beloved founder of the
Kimball company, died a multi-millionaire in his ornate Chicago man-
sion on Prairie Street.

S.88.   EHRLICH, Cyril. The Piano: a history. London: Dent,
        1976. 254p. illus., bibliog.
        Told largely from the viewpoint of economic history, this
very readable study includes a fifteen-page chapter (Chapter 7) on
the growth of piano making and selling in the USA. There are
several tables, one of which gives details of annual production, 1880-
1930, of representative manufacturers. Also relevant is the account
of the Steinway family in Chapter 3, including the marketing techniques of brother William. An appendix lists the names of piano
makers since 1851, with dates. Index.

(iii) Guitar

S.89.   ACHARD, Ken. The Fender Guitar. London: Musical New
          Services, Ltd., 1977. 68p. illus.
      "This book intends to tell the story of [Leo Fender, who
was born in California] and his guitars" (introduction). While only
the least demanding could say that the author's first intention is
realized (Achard does not even provide the date of Fender's birth),
the second one certainly is. There are photos of all the Fender
instruments plus serial numbers, dimensions, extracts from various
Fender patents, and a chart of the features of Fender models. No
index.

S.90.   ACHARD, Ken. The History and Development of the Ameri-
          can Guitar. London: Musical New Services, 1979.
          200p. illus.
      A detailed, liberally illustrated history of the various makes
of guitar, from the foundation of the C. F. Martin's company to the
1970s. The author's aim is "to relate the evolution of the well-known
makes each to the other, and to demonstrate the interesting developments which occurred at each stage of the history" (p. iii). The
emphasis is technical, rather than musical or social; performers
(such as Les Paul, Barney Kessels) are mentioned in connection with
models, not with their performance styles. In addition to Martin,
other prominent manufacturers include Fender, Gibson, Gretsch,
Guild, and Rickenbacker.

S.91.   BISHOP, Ian Courtney. The Gibson Guitar from 1950. Lon-
          don: Musical New Services, 1977-79. 2v.
      These two well-illustrated volumes provide players and col-
lectors with historical and technical information on all the various
Gibson models produced since 1950. Vol. 2 includes corrections and
additions to Vol. 1, and an index to both volumes. (For the early
history of the company, the author refers the reader to a pamphlet,
The Gibson Story, by Julius Bellson [Kalamazoo, Mich., 1973].)

S.92.   BROSNAC, Donald. The Electric Guitar: its history and
          construction. Los Angeles: Panjandrum Press, 1975.
          95p. illus., bibliog.
      A short history of the electric guitar precedes an illustrated
catalog of "historically significant" models, with commentary. There
follows a sequence of short chapters divulging a variety of technical
and practical information (on, for example, pick-ups, wiring circuits,
making a solid-body guitar) for guitar players and craftsmen.

S.93.   BROSNAC, Donald. The Steel String Guitar: its construc-
          tion, origin and design. Los Angeles: Panjandrum Press,
          1973. 93p. illus.
      _____. _____. 2nd ed. Los Angeles: Panjandrum
          Press, 1975. 112p. illus.
      Organized along similar lines to no. S.92, this handbook first

briefly surveys the instrument's history, especially in the USA, then provides an illustrated catalog of selected "guitars of special merit," 1836-1973. The remainder of the book consists of practical information on construction.

S.94. EVANS, Tom, and EVANS, Mary Anne. Guitars: from the Renaisance to rock; music, history, construction, players. New York: Paddington Press, 1977. 479p. illus., bibliog.

This large, reliable compendium of reference information, practical details, and historical outline includes large sections on the steel-string acoustic guitar (pp. 218-335) and the electric guitar (pp. 336-435), both of which focus attention mainly on developments in the USA. Each section has the same format: an introduction; an illustrated descriptive catalog of instruments (called a "gallery"); practical information on construction, again with illustrations; and a historical outline of the music and its players. In the first of two sections, this historical part covers blues, country music, the urban folk revival, and singer-songwriters; in the second it outlines the use of the electric instrument in jazz, blues, popular entertainment (especially Les Ford), and rock. There is a glossary and an index.

S.95. THE GUITAR PLAYER BOOK, by editors of Guitar Player Magazine. Saratoga: Guitar Player Books, 1978. 403p. illus.
_____. Rev. and updated ed. Cupertino, Calif.: Guitar Player Books, 1979. 403p. illus.
_____. Rev. and updated 3rd ed. Cupertino, Calif.: Guitar Player Books; New York: Grove Press, 1983. 403p. illus.

This anthology of pieces from Guitar Player (founded in 1967) amply reflects that journal's range of interests--biographies of guitarists, insights into their styles, practical information on guitar purchase and construction, historical and technical details on the development of the instrument and its makers. The pieces on individual musicians occupy the bulk of the book; generally based on interviews, they cover rock, jazz, blues and classical performers, and concentrate on down-to-earth practicalities. Sixty-nine musicians are featured in the 3rd ed., which contains pieces that originally appeared between 1971 and 1983. Index.

S.96. LONGWORTH, Mike. Martin Guitars: a history. Cedar Knolls, N.J.: Colonial Press, 1975. 219p. illus.
_____. _____. London: Omnibus Press, 1975. 118p. illus.

The celebrated firm of C. F. Martin & Co. has a history of guitar production in the USA dating back to 1833. Longworth's meticulous book is essentially a catalog of the many different styles of instrument--guitars, mandolins, ukuleles--produced over the years, with full descriptions, production details, and illustrations. The catalog is preceded by a brief history of the firm (all but six

years of its life have been spent in Nazareth, Pa.), biographical
sketches of the members of the Martin family, and general information on guitars. Tables giving full specifications of all models from
1898, and charting the history of instrument prices, conclude the
book.

(iv) Other Instruments

S.97.   ELIASON, Robert E. Early American Brass Makers. Nash-
         ville: Brass Press, 1979. (Brass Research Series, No.
         10). 56p. illus.
A beautifully written and researched account of four distinguished American manufacturers of brass instruments: Thomas D.
Paine, J. Lathrop Allen, Elbridge G. Wright, and Isaac Fiske. Each
maker receives a section of the book; an appendix lists the surviving
instruments of three of them. There are numerous pictures of instruments and a generous smattering of facsimiles of letters, prints, music, and labels. The book is in the tradition of, and in a sense, a
kind of companion piece to the author's earlier Keyed Bugles in the
United States (no. S.98).

S.98.   ELIASON, Robert E. Keyed Bugles in the United States.
         Washington, D.C.: Smithsonian Institution Press, 1972.
         (Smithsonian Studies in History and Technology, No. 19).
         44p. illus.
An informative general history of the brass instruments,
which flourished in the USA from 1810 into the 1950s and '60s. Pictures of some of the instruments accompany the text.

S.99.   HOOVER, Cynthia A. Music Machines--American Style: a
         catalog of the exhibition; with introductory notes by Erik
         Barnouw and Irving Kolodin. Washington, D.C.: Smith-
         sonian Institution Press for the National Museum of
         History and Technology, 1971. 139p. illus., bibliog.
         (_____.) The History of Music Machines. New York:
         Drake, 1975. 139p. illus., bibliog.
An excellent Smithsonian exhibition catalog of mechanical
instruments, well illustrated, and with nine sections for different
groups, each with information on the instruments, and each with the
names of pieces, performers, composers, and record numbers of the
illustrated music accompanying the exhibits. It is also more than
"just a catalog," however--hence its subsequent re-publication without
any mention of the exhibition (though the reasons for anonymity are
less clear). Besides the informative commentary, the book also contains thoughtful essays on broadcasting (by Erik Barnouw) and recording (by Irving Kolodin); there is also a foreword by Daniel J.
Boorstin.

S.100.   KRIVINE, John. Juke Box Saturday Night. Secaucus,
         N.J.: Chartwell Books, 1977. 159p. illus.

This large-format picture book by a British collector relates the history of the machines, beginning well before their "golden age" is considered to have begun in 1935 and continuing into the 1950s, when they declined in popularity. The accompanying historical commentary provides a well-informed survey of the development of juke boxes, of their design, their economic and commercial aspects, and the records they played. The text and choice of pictures display the cardinal virtues for this kind of study: vast but unobtrusive knowledge and a light touch. The majority of the illustrations are in color and are well produced; some of the smaller number of black-and-white photographs are of poorer quality. Index.

e. Publishing

S.101. WOLFE, Richard J. Early American Music Engraving and Printing: a history of music publishing in America from 1787 to 1825 with commentary on earlier and later practices. Urbana: University of Illinois Press, 1980. 321p. illus., bibliog.

Covering the same period as the bibliographies of Sonneck-Upton (LOAM 2) and Wolfe himself (LOAM 4), this is a meticulously researched companion volume which "attempts to answer such questions regarding the engraving, printing, publishing, and selling of music in America during the colonial and federal periods as a collector, librarian, musicologist, historian, bibliographer, researcher, or other interested person would be likely to ask" (p. xiv-xv). There are chapters on the Anglo-European background, on music publishing in the American colonies, on the establishment of a music publishing industry in Philadelphia, New York, Boston, Baltimore, and Charleston, on the early American firm of music publishing, and on the day-to-day customs and conditions of the trade. Much information is also given on ink and paper, on engraving and punching tools, and other practical details. Index.

f. Education

S.102. TELLSTROM, A. Music in American Education: past and present. New York: Holt, Rinehart and Winston, 1971. 358p. illus., bibliog.

This is a fine, tightly-packed history of the subject, no doubt intended as a text book. The author, credited on the title page as Chief of the Bureau of Music of New York State, writes in his preface: "The general plan of this book has been to assign the first chapter of each section to the evolution and establishment of a major educational movement. The following chapter or chapters demonstrate how the principles involved were transposed into action in the area of music education." There are fourteen chapters. The 27-page bibliography, which is given in chapter arrangement, is outstanding.

S.103.   ULRICH, Homer. <u>A Centennial History of the Music Teach-</u>
<u>ers National Association.</u>   Cincinnati: Music Teachers
National Association, 1976.   306p.
Histories of organizations can be terribly dull, but not so
this one.   The first four chapters make for interesting and entertaining reading, and MTNA doings are regularly related to events
of the day.   It is true, though, that the remaining four chapters
are valuable more for the reference material they contain; the titles
of these chapters are "The Divisions of MTNA," "The State Associations," "The Boards and Special Programs," and "Student Auditions and Student Support."   Best of the four excellent appendices
is a list of authors and titles of "Convention Papers and Journal
Articles" arranged by subject category.   (The other appendices are
devoted to a list of chapter members, a "tabular view of MTNA conventions," and the MTNA constitution.)   The big disappointment
about the book is the lack of an index.

g.   <u>Phonograph</u>

S.104.   CLARK, Ronald W.   <u>Edison: the man who made the future.</u>
New York: Putnam, 1977.   256p.   illus., bibliog.
A good overview of Thomas Alva Edison's life (1847-1931)
and his place in the society of the time, written by a British biographer.   The book is included here for the information it contains
on Edison's invention of the phonograph in 1877, his perfection of
it in the 1880s, and his recording and selling of cylinders and flat
discs.   (His low opinion of Claude Debussy, stated by John Philip
Sousa, is quoted on p. 168.)

S.105.   HITCHCOCK, H. Wiley, ed.   <u>The Phonograph and Our</u>
<u>Musical Life: proceedings of a centennial conference,</u>
<u>7-10 December 1977.</u>   Brooklyn: Institute for Studies
in American Music, 1980.   (I.S.A.M. Monographs, No.
14).   91p.   bibliog. refs.
This lively conference, commemorating the centenary of
Edison's invention of the phonograph, "sought to explore the immense and pervasive influence that the phonograph, phonorecords,
tape recordings, and related electronic developments have had on
every segment of the musical community" (editor's foreword).
These same segments of the musical community--audience, performers, scholars and critics, and other media--provide the structural
divisions of the proceedings, which consist of sixteen short papers
(average length five or six pages) and discussion.   The whole is
preceded by a panel's views on a specially commissioned work by
John Cage ("Address").   The contributors of papers are: (on the
audience) William Ivey, Jane Jarvis (Muzak), and James Goodfriend;
(on the composer) William Bolcom, Roger Reynolds, and Eric Salzman;
(on the performer) Martin Williams, David Baker, and Charlie Gillett; (on the scholar and critic) Richard Crawford, John Rockwell,
Charles Hamm, and David Hamilton; (on other media) Claire Brook,
Cynthia Adams Hoover, and Allan Miller.

S.106.   SCHICKE, C. A. Revolution in Sound: a biography of the
         recording industry. Boston: Little, Brown, 1975.
         246p. illus.
         This introductory survey falls into two parts. The first is
a historical account of the development of the recording industry to
the end of the 1960s, with particular attention to technological
changes and some interest also in commercial and social aspects. The
second, shorter section is an overview of modern record production
processes. Here and there (especially in the chapter "Booze, Broads
and Payola") the author tangles unsuccessfully with questions relating to music. The lively style occasionally edges close to the naive.
Index.

Additional Items

General and Historical

S.107.   SCHOEN-RENE, Anna Eugenie. America's Musical Inherit-
         ance: memories and reminiscences. New York: Putnam,
         1941. 244p.

Church Music

S.108.   MORAVIAN MUSIC FOUNDATION. Moravian Music For the
         Bicentennial. Winston-Salem, N.C.: Moravian Music
         Foundation, 1975.

S.109.   NININGER, Ruth. Church Music Comes of Age. New York:
         Fischer, 1957. 157p.

S.110.   OYER, Mary. Exploring the Mennonite Hymnal: essays.
         Newton, Kansas: Faith and Life Press, 1980. 140p.

S.111.   PETERSON, John W. The Miracle Goes On; with Richard
         Engquist. Grand Rapids, Mich.: Zondervan, 1976.
         220p.

S.112.   SALLEE, James. A History of Evangelistic Hymnody. Grand
         Rapids, Mich.: Baker Book House, 1978. 103p.

S.113.   TERRELL, Bob. J. D. Sumner. Gospel Is My Life. Nash-
         ville: Impact Books, 1971. 208p.

S.114.   VAN ALSTYNE, Frances. Fanny Crosby's Life Story. New
         York: Every Where Publishing, 1903. 160p.

S.115.   _____. Memories of Eighty Years: the story of her life,
         told by herself, ancestry, childhood, womanhood, friend-
         ships, incidents and history of her songs and hymns.

Boston: Earle, 1906. 253p.

S.116. _____. Fanny Crosby's Story of Ninety-Four Years;
retold by S. Trevenna Jackson. New York: Revell,
1915. 192p.

Musical Life

S.117. ALVERSON, Margaret Blake. Sixty Years of California
Song. Oakland: the author, 1913. 275p.

S.118. BERGMANN, Leola Nelson. Music Master of the Middle West:
the story of F. Melius Christiansen and the St. Olaf
Choir. Minneapolis: University of Minnesota Press,
1944. 230p.

S.119. CARTER, Morris. Isabella Stewart Gardner and Fenway
Court. Boston: Houghton Mifflin, 1925. 254p.

S.120. COOPER, Dennis R. The Florida West Coast Symphony
Orchestra: a silver anniversary history. Sarasota:
Florida West Coast Symphony Orchestra, 1974. 61p.

S.121. NEW YORK SINGING TEACHERS' ASSOCIATION. 20 Years
of the New York Singing Teachers' Association: a
record of agreement on essentials. Philadelphia: Pres-
ser, 1928. 193p.

S.122. NUTTER, Charles Read. The Harvard Musical Association.
Boston: The Association, 1937. 65p.

S.123. SHERMAN, John K. Music and Theater in Minnesota History. Minneapolis: University of Minnesota Press,
1958. 63p.

S.124. SCHLESINGER, Janet. Challenge to the Urban Orchestra:
the case of the Pittsburgh Symphony. Pittsburgh: the
author, 1971. 163p.

S.125. SIMKINS, F. B., ed. Art and Music in the South. Farm-
ville, Va.: Longwood College, 1961. 132p.

S.126 THARP, Louise. Mrs. Jack: a biography of Isabella
Stewart Gardner. Boston: Little, Brown, 1965. 365p.

Operatic Life

S.127. ALDA, Frances. Men, Women, and Tenors. Boston:
Houghton Mifflin, 1937. 307p. (Account of New York

operatic life by New Zealand-born soprano, who married impresario Gatti-Casazza.)

S.128.   ARONSON, Rudolph. Theatrical and Musical Memoirs. New York: McBride, Nast, 1913. 283p.

S.129.   HACKETT, Karleton. The Beginning of Grand Opera in Chicago (1850-1859). Chicago: The Laurentian Publishers, 1913. 60p.

Instruments

S.130.   FERGUSON, John Allen. Walter Holtkamp, American Organ Builder. Kent, Ohio: Kent State University Press, 1979. 142p.

S.131.   OGASAPIAN, John. Henry Erben: portrait of a nineteenth-century American Organ Builder. Braintree, Mass.: Organ Literature Foundation, 1980. 42p.

Phonograph

S.132.   GAISBERG, Fred. The Music Goes Round. New York: Macmillan, 1942. 273p.

S.133.   PALEY, William S. As It Happened: a memoir. Garden City, N.Y.: Doubleday, 1979. 418p. (Founder of CBS.)

B. THE MUSICAL TRADITION TO 1800

(See also S.49, S.80, S.860, S.871)

1. Reference Works

S.134. FULD, James J., and DAVIDSON, Mary Wallace. 18th-
Century American Secular Music Manuscripts: an inventory. Philadelphia: Music Library Association, 1980.
(MLA Index and Bibliography Series, 20). 225p. bibliog.
   A bibliography detailing "about half the presently located
secular manuscripts as examples of musical and social history"
(p. viii). Geographically arranged (by state, then library), the 85
mss. vary from single pieces to collections of over 400, and include
keyboard sonatas, marches, bugle calls, theater music, and ballads.
Each manuscript is described and its contents listed. The compilers
calculate that 75% of the titles are not found in printed form in the
Sonneck/Upton (LOAM 2) or Wolfe (LOAM 4) bibliographies; they
also avoid covering the songsters listed in Lowens (no. S.137).
(The position regarding overlap with another MLA publication,
Popular Secular Music in America Through 1800: a preliminary checklist of manuscripts in North American collections, by Kate Van Winkle
Keller (Philadelphia: MLA, 1981), is more confusing. Carolyn Rab-
son--review in American Music, 1, No. 3, [Fall 1983], pp. 94-96--
suggests that all of the mss. in Fuld-Davidson may be in Keller.)
Index of titles and types.

S.135. HEARD, Priscilla S. American Music 1698-1800: an annotated bibliography. Waco, Tex.: Markham Press Fund,
Baylor University Press, 1975. 246p. bibliog.
   Like Hixon (LOAM 1), this meticulous bibliography is designed to help those interested in American music before 1800 to
find their way around in Evans' American Bibliography. The first
section in Heard's book, "Entries Which Include Musical Notation,"
covers the same ground as Hixon, but is arranged in Evans (i.e.,
chronological) order, with the items subsequently added by the
American Antiquarian Society inserted into their appropriate places.
This arrangement permits the gradual development of music in the
colonies and the new Republic to be seen more easily than does the
alphabetical one. In addition, the author provides library locations,
and many brief, factual annotations. The second section, "Entries

Pertaining to Music," covers a type of material not indexed in Hixon (some 500 items in all, many of them hymns or song texts). A third section is devoted (as is Hixon's "Part Two") to entries not in the microprint edition of Evans; here again, Heard includes material pertaining to music, while Hixon does not. The index combines authors, composers and titles in one sequence; the absence of any provision for individual titles under composers' names in the index means Hixon's alphabetical arrangement is to be preferred in the first instance by those approaching the field via a particular name. Hixon's useful biographical sketches have no counterpart in Heard's volume. These two factors suggest the volumes should be viewed as in a certain degree complementary.

S.136.   KELLER, Kate Van Winkle, and RABSON, Carolyn, eds.
The National Tune Index: 18th-century secular music.
New York: University Music Editions, 1980. 80 micro-
fiches.
_____. _____. User's guide. New York: Univer-
sity Music Editions, 1980. 94p.
This huge, scholarly work is a computer-generated inventory with details of almost 40,000 secular items--melodies, songs, dances--collected from 452 printed sources and 68 mss. in libraries in North America and Britain. The work divides into five parts, "designed to help identify the tunes and song texts, to suggest their relationship to one another, and to lead the researcher directly to the original sources with speed and accuracy" (preface). Obtaining that "speed and accuracy" is likely to require patience and discipline, and frequent recourse to the User's Guide (which is included on two microfiche as well as being available in printed form). The five lists are: title, first lines, tune name and refrain; incipits in scale degrees; incipits in interval sequences; incipits in stressed-note sequences; bibliographical information and contents of all sources.

S.137.   LOWENS, Irving. A Bibliography of Songsters Printed in
America Before 1821. Worcester, Mass.: American Anti-
quarian Society, 1976. 229p. bibliog.
Lowens defines "songster" for his purposes as "a collection of three or more secular poems intended to be sung" (p. ix), a definition broad enough to permit the inclusion of numerous almanacs, guide-books, etc., the songs in which make up only a small fraction of the total contents. In most cases a songster contains no music (though there are frequent references to suitable tunes), but ones with musical notation are included, "if the texts and not the tunes are central" (p. xi). The impressively thorough, accurate bibliography lists 649 items, chronologically arranged from 1734 to 1820. Entries are by title, with a full transcription of each title page (or reconstruction, based mainly on advertisements, in the case of the considerable number of unlocated items), together with citations of entries in other bibliographies, locations in American libraries, contents notes, and references to other, related songsters. The indexes include a geographical directory of printers, publishers, booksellers

and engravers, an alphabetical index of compilers, authors, pro-
prietors and editors, and a title index. In his introduction Lowens
draws attention to some features of the songster type: the prevalence of epithets such as "patriotic," "sentimental" and "comic" on
the title-pages, the absence of salaciousness in the subject matter,
and the large number of Masonic items.

S.138.   SPECHT, R. John. Early American Vocal Music in Modern
         Editions. Albany, N.Y.: New York State American
         Revolution Bicentennial Commission, 1974. 16p.
    The compiler (choral director at Queensborough Community
College in New York City) introduces his useful little pamphlet by
saying, "Interest in the celebration of the American Bicentennial encouraged publishers to issue modern performing editions of many
early-American vocal works.... Undoubtedly some publications have
been overlooked; but the list is as complete as the writer's diligence
and active involvement in choral music can make it" (p. 2). Publishers' addresses are included.

                    2. General Studies

S.139.   CRAWFORD, Richard. A Historian's Introduction to Early
         American Music. Worcester, Mass.: American Anti-
         quarian Society, 1979. pp. 261-298. bibliog. refs.
    Crawford's stated aim in this fine essay is to invite his-
torians, especially historians of colonial America, who customarily
neglect music and musical life, to make fuller use of musical re-
sources--"to learn about early American life through their ears as
well as their eyes" (p. 262). Offering first a series of "landmarks"
in early American music, 1640-1800, he proceeds by way of example
to demonstrate some of the processes which can be detected beneath
the surface (and should therefore interest historians) in the sacred
and secular musical life of both rural and urban colonial America.
His main conclusions from this survey are: (i) music making was
carried on at a distance from the chief sources of cultural power and
wealth; (ii) Protestant psalmody was a written tradition practiced as
an oral one, and was intended to be accessible to both; (iii) the
disjunction between urban and rural musical life can be seen in the
different relationships that existed between creator, performer, and
audience; and (iv) psalmody is unusual in being notated music practiced most creatively in rural, not urban communities. In conclusion,
Crawford demonstrates that a lack of technical knowledge need be no
impediment to a historian's study of music by analyzing a Billings
anthem and a dance piece (recordings of which are provided on an
accompanying soundsheet), in terms of the contrasting ways in which
music can express time.
    The case Crawford makes is the more convincing for its
implied insistence on the historian's approaching music as itself culturally expressive (not merely as something useful for illustrating

history), and for its stress on the mutual benefits for music and history in the kind of rapprochement he describes. What could perhaps be said more clearly is that such rapprochement is only part of the interdisciplinary web the proper study of American music requires. (The text is reprinted from The Proceedings of the American Antiquarian Society, 89, No. 2 [1979].)

S.140.   SILVERMAN, Kenneth.   A Cultural History of the American
         Revolution: painting, music, literature, and the theatre
         in the colonies and the United States from the Treaty of
         Paris to the Inauguration of George Washington, 1763-
         1789. New York: Crowell, 1976. 699p. illus., bibliog.
The quarter-century from 1763 to 1789 has long been recognized as one of immense significance for its political developments; Silverman's achievement in this mighty work is to show that the same period was one of "startling innovations" (p. xv) in cultural life, of no less significance for the country's development. It is, as its author says, an intricate book: the interrelations of biography, sociology, politics and aesthetics make it so. It is also clearly and effectively organized. There are three historical parts (1763-1770, 1770-1783, 1783-1789), and within each the first section broadly surveys the individual arts, while the second ("broadly narrative") "treats all the arts together as a related response to a succession of critical events" (p. xvi). Chronology is outlined at the start of each part by a calendar. Musical life in this scheme has a particular slot in each of the separate surveys. It is also well integrated into the main narrative, and many contemporary musical figures appear there (Andrew Adgate, James Lyon, Alexander Reinagle) along with subjects such as concerts, instruments, singing schools, and "Yankee Doodle." Most prominent among the individual names are those of Francis Hopkinson, Andrew Law, Daniel Read, and--above all-- William Billings. The text is supported by extensive documentation, notes, and an index.

3.   Individuals

S.141.   NATHAN, Hans.   William Billings: data and documents.
         Detroit: Information Coordinators for the College Music
         Society, 1976. (Bibliographies in American Music, No.
         2). 69p. illus., bibliog.
Our knowledge of Billings the man (1746-1800) will probably always be fragmentary, and we shall continue to know him best through his magnificent music--"leaping upon the mountains, skipping upon the hills." But the picture we have of his life is much fuller now, following the researches of McKay and Crawford (LOAM 202), and of Hans Nathan. The latter's book, more modest in aims and scope, is concerned to construct a brief but lucid and accurate biographical narrative out of the information contained in the various documents, some newly discovered, which relate to the composer. The method is unusual, and effective: Nathan's own text proceeds

chronologically, referring to, and frequently quoting from these contemporary sources; alongside the narrative the texts of the more important documents are printed in modern type. This "complementary anthology" (preface) serves the scholar, who needs the full texts; it also serves to invite all readers to live in two eras at once--to reflect on Billings from a modern vantage point, and to be present in the Boston of his day. Various facsimiles and illustrations make their contribution to conveying the period flavor, and at the same time to producing a very handsome sourcebook.

The biography is followed by two bibliographies: the first a detailed, annotated catalog of the editions of Billings' music, of his manuscripts, and of his literary contributions; the second a listing of literature of Billings, divided into twelve early and 54 modern items.

C. THE CULTIVATED TRADITION IN THE 19TH CENTURY

1. Arbiters of Taste

S.142.   CURTIS, George William. Early Letters to John S. Dwight:
          Brook Farm and Concord; edited by George Willis Cooke.
          New York: Harper, 1898. 293p.
          Curtis (1823-92), editor of Harper's Weekly, noted abolition-
ist and early campaigner for women's rights, studied music with
Dwight and remained on personal terms with him. (The editor's
introduction is informative on Dwight's Journal.) These letters,
which extend up to 1847, contain some accounts of musical life in
New York and the North East (e.g., visits of European such as Ole
Bull in 1843), but are chiefly of interest for their views of European
and American culture. To Curtis, the United States was still, musically, a nation "content with foreign fragrance" (p. 177) (cf.
Dwight's own views, LOAM 100). For other, often more detailed, insights into Curtis' views on music, see his article in Putnam's
Monthly Magazine (March 1853), Dwight's Journal of Music (April
10, May 1 & 22, 1852), and The Harbinger (Dec. 7, 1845, Feb. 7
& March 21, 1846).

2. History and Reference

S.143.   JOHNSON, H. Earle. First Performances in America to
          1900: works with orchestra. Detroit: Information Co-
          ordinators for the College Music Society, 1979. (Bib-
          liographies in American Music, No. 4). 446p. illus.,
          bibliog.
          The fruit of extensive research--following the footsteps of
Sonneck--in newspapers, periodicals, concert programs and scrapbooks, this reference work lists the first American performances,
beginning in the late 18th century, of 1,140 orchestral works (including a number of choral works with orchestra, plus some chamber
music) by over 300 composers. Arrangement is by composer, and
the entry for each work begins with the place and date of the first
performance, and the name of the performing body and/or individual
artists; this is followed in many instances by the details of first performances in other cities. The text is enlivened by numerous excerpts from contemporary reviews (not, we are assured, included in
order to ridicule the "amazingly wrong-headed forthrightness of early

critics"--p. xv). Appendices provide lists of leading musical journalists before 1900, of major auditoriums, theaters and concert halls,
and of the musical works grouped by form, with references to their
entry number in the main body of the work. Somewhat surprisingly, there is no attempt to provide a chronology of the first performances listed.

3. Individual Composers

S.144.   CIPOLLA, Wilma Reid. A Catalog of the Works of Arthur
         Foote, 1853-1937. Detroit: Information Coordinators for
         the College Music Society, 1980. (Bibliographies in
         American Music, No. 6). 193p. illus., bibliog., dis-
         cog.
         A thorough, well-presented catalog of published and unpub-
lished material. Foote's original musical works (a total of 336) are
listed in eight categories--vocal, choral, piano, organ, chamber, orchestral, unpublished, miscellaneous songs and hymns. Entries
typically provide information, where appropriate, on date and place
of composition, location of ms., publisher, author of text, dedication, first performance, and reviews. Foote's own arrangements
(often under pseudonyms) of 156 pieces are also listed, followed by
details of arrangements of his music by other composers. The remaining sections are devoted to discography (nineteen discs and ten
piano rolls), Foote's literary works, critical literature on him, and
a list of sources. There are six detailed indexes.

S.145.   SCHMIDT, John C. The Life and Works of John Knowles
         Paine. Ann Arbor: UMI Research Press, 1980.
         (Studies in Musicology, No. 34). 756p. illus., bibliog.
         Paine (1839-1906) may have been "the dean of American
composers" of the latter years of the 19th century (according to John
Tasker Howard, quoted on p. 11), but he had been poorly treated
by scholars before the appearance of this hugh biographical and
critical study. Schmidt's detailed work (this despite the destruction
of many personal papers after Paine's death) more than adequately
atones for this neglect; whether one could go on to say that Paine
is hereby reinstated in his rightful place is another matter. That
would take a work of more flair and appeal; a ton weight is not a
perfect implement with which to signal a rebirth.
         But for scholars and students the scrupulous amassing of
information and its logical organization is invaluable. Nine biographical chapters trace Paine's life from his Maine background via
his early Harvard years (1862-1866), his time in Berlin, to his
Harvard professorship (he taught there from 1871 till 1905, and his
work for music education must rank alongside that as a composer),
to his maturity as a composer, and his declining years. There follow a further eight chapters in which each of Paine's extant compositions is scrutinized, genre by genre, in a descriptive analysis.
No fewer than 437 music examples illustrate these chapters, many

from works no longer in print. Appendices provide a list of works, a list of music courses taught at Harvard, with enrollment figures, and a selective roster of his students. Notes to the text occupy almost 70 pages. There is also an index.

4. Musical Life in the 19th Century

(For regional studies, see A.7.b.
See also nos. S.42, S.60, S.65)

S.146. DUNHAM, Henry M. The Life of a Musician. New York: Printed by Richmond Borough Publishing and Printing Co., 1931. 235p. illus.
A somewhat inconsequential memoir by an organist-composer who was a teacher on the faculty of the New England Conservatory from the last decades of the 19th century to the early ones of the 20th. It is sprinkled with names such as B. J. Lang, John Knowles Paine, and George W. Chadwick, but Dunham did not know these men well and we find out nothing substantial about them. What we do learn about is the author's own fairly routine life and thoughts. His widow tells us in the Dedication that "these recollections were Mr. Dunham's chief diversion and greatest joy during the last years of his life."

S.147. GIPSON, Richard McCandless. The Life of Emma Thursby, 1845-1931. New York: New-York Historical Society, 1940. (Repr. New York: Da Capo, 1980.) 470p. illus.
This is a detailed and valuable, if completely laudatory and traditional biography of the American soprano. Drawn upon and quoted from liberally by the author was an archive preserved by Ina Love Thursby, the singer's younger sister, which was subsequently given to the New York Historical Society in New York City. The archive consists of more than four thousand press notices, programs, letters, diaries, photographs, and miscellaneous memorabilia "numbering many thousands of items" (p. x). There are no notes and no bibliography though there is a chronology of Thursby's concert appearances (she never sang in opera).

S.148. JOHNS, Clayton. Reminiscences of a Musician. Cambridge, Mass.: Washburn & Thomas, 1929. 132p. illus.
Though the author (1857-1932), who was a composer mainly of songs, writes that these reminiscences "cover, for the most part, a period of forty-six years--from 1882 to 1928" (p. vii), they are neither broad nor deep. Nor are they very informative. Though he studied with John Knowles Paine, knew Paderewski, and met Liszt and Brahms, he writes mostly about his travels and social events in Europe. Paine receives one mention. (Johns taught for years at the New England Conservatory in Boston, though one would never know it from this book.) No index.

S.149.   RYAN, Thomas. Recollections of an Old Musician. New
York: Dalton, 1899. (Repr. New York: Da Capo,
1979.) 274p. illus.
A delightful memoir of 19th-century musical life in Boston
by the clarinetist of the Mendelssohn Quintette Club, which gave its
first concert in 1849. Here are recollections and brief word pictures of performers, composers, and patrons such as Charles C.
Perkins, B. J. Lang, Ole Bull, August and Wulf Fries, John
Bigelow, Jenny Lind, and Patrick S. Gilmore. One wishes for more
books like this one. No index.

Additional Items

S.150.   ADAMS, Juliette Graves. Chapters from a Musical Life; a
short autobiographical narrative. Chicago: Crosby
Adams, 1903. 135p.

S.151.   AMERICAN MUSICAL DIRECTORY 1861. New York: Thomas
Hutchinson, 1861. (Repr. New York: Da Capo, 1980.)
260p.

S.152.   KONKLE, B. A. Joseph Hopkinson, 1770-1842, Jurist-
Scholar-Inspirer: author of 'Hail Columbia'. Philadelphia: University of Pennsylvania, 1931. 361p.

S.153.   WARE, W. Porter. P. T. Barnum Presents Jenny Lind:
the American tour of the Swedish nightingale. Baton
Rouge: Louisiana State University Press, 1980. 284p.

D. THE CULTIVATED TRADITION IN THE 20TH CENTURY

1. 20th-Century Music in General
(with particular reference to the USA)

S.154.   APPLETON, Jon H., and PERERA, Ronald C., eds. The
Development and Practice of Electronic Music. Englewood
Cliffs, N.J.: Prentice-Hall, 1975. 384p. illus., bibliog., discog.
Four central, technical chapters on various aspects of electronic music by A. Wayne Slawson, Gustav Ciamaga, Joel Chadabe,
and John E. Rogers, are framed by two historical overviews: the
first, by Otto Luening, is concerned with the origins of electronic
music in Europe and the United States and its development up to the
1970s; the second, by Gordon Mumma, outlines the course of live
performance with electronic media and investigates the influence of
new technology on rock and jazz. The eight-page bibliography includes books and articles, while the useful international discography
lists recordings, mainly on US labels, of the music of over 200 individuals and groups. Index. (Formerly LOAM A74.)

S.155.   BRINDLE, Reginald Smith. The New Music: the avant-
garde since 1945. London: Oxford University Press,
1975. 206p.
The author's "concise picture of the more adventurous evo-
lutions of music since 1945" (p. vii) deliberately avoids many major
figures of the period, preferring to concentrate on those whose work
shows unmistakable signs of avant-gardism. Though full of admittedly personal views, the text is also analytical in nature, with a
rich supply of musical examples. Chapter 12, "Cage and Other
Americans," marks the chief appearance of American composers (besides Cage, Morton Feldman and Earle Brown are closely inspected),
but Cage in particular appears passim.

S.156.   BRINKMANN, Reinhold, ed. Avantgarde, Jazz, Pop:
Tendenzen zwischen Tonalität und Atonalität; neun
Vortragstexte. Mainz:Schott, 1978. (Veröffentlichungen
des Instituts für Neue Musik und Musikerziehung, Darm-
stadt, Band 18). 119p. bibliog. refs.
Contemporary trends in American music are the chief focus
of these German-language conference papers from Darmstadt, 1977.
Dieter Schnebel summarizes the achievement of the avant-garde (Cage,

etc.). Reich, Glass and Riley's "periodic" music form the subject of Ernstalbert Stiebler's contribution, while Clytus Gottwald concentrates on Reich, and Johannes Fritsch explains the tonality system of Harry Partch. Diverging trends in 1970s jazz are pointed out by Ekkehard Jost. Niels Frédéric Hoffmann, in the longest paper, traces the antecedents of some of pop music's harmonic characteristics (with music examples). Two papers on rock conclude the volume: Hans-Christian Schmidt asks how progressive is the rock music aesthetics of the '70s, and Sieghart Döhring explores the counterculture world of Frank Zappa.

S.157. EWEN, David. Composers of Tomorrow's Music: non-technical introduction to the musical avant-garde movement. New York: Dodd, Mead, 1971. 176p. illus.
These are rather brief, unscholarly essays on ten big-name twentieth-century composers, among whom we find Charles Ives, Milton Babbitt, John Cage, Harry Partch and Edgard Varèse. Each chapter is about twenty small pages in length. Sources of quotations are not cited exactly (some sources are not cited at all), and no lists of works, bibliography, or notes are provided. (Many might argue, too, over Ewen's choice of composers of "tomorrow's music," since five of the ten are now dead.) Index.

S.158. HAMM, Charles, et al. Contemporary Music and Music Cultures, by Charles Hamm, Bruno Nettl, and Ronald Byrnside. Englewood Cliffs, N.J.: Prentice-Hall, 1975. 270p. bibliogs., discogs.
The nine original essays in this volume focus on the way music "interacts with those social, political and cultural processes that distinguish the twentieth century" (preface). Six essays are directly concerned with aspects of American music. Hamm writes (Chapter 2) on the relationship between changes in music and changes in society in post-1945 America, with particular attention to Piston, Babbitt and Cage, and (Chapter 5) on the processes of acculturation, as illustrated by the interaction that began in the USA in the 1950s between a homogeneous body of popular music and other types such as country and folk. Nettl (Chapter 4) discusses the impact of the spread of Western musical styles on African music and on the musical culture of the North American Indian, and also (Chapter 7) investigates the setting of words to music in English-language folk song in the USA. Byrnside contributes (Chapter 6) an examination of factors involved in the formation of a musical style, more especially early rock, and (Chapter 8) a discussion of basic features of jazz improvisation, relating them to improvisation in other bodies of music. Chapters 7 and 8 contain numerous music examples and translations. Most chapters have a brief bibliography and discography, but there is no index.

S.159. MARTIN, William R. and DROSSIN, Julius. Music of the Twentieth Century. Englewood Cliffs, N.J.: Prentice-Hall, 1980. 400p. illus., bibliog.

Parts IV and V of this introductory volume are devoted to American composers (three of whom are Latin American). Part IV is entitled "Principal American Composers" and includes sections on Ives, Varèse, Carter, Copland, Piston, Schuman, Barber, Villa-Lobos, Chávez, and Ginastera. Part V is entitled "Other American Composers" and includes Thomson, Harris, and Still (in a chapter entitled "Nationalists"); Cowell, Ruggles, Sessions, and Foss ("Experimentalists and Progressives"); and Moore, Blitzstein, and Menotti ("Dramatists"). A discussion of John Cage and a few other Americans is featured in the section "Chance Music, Multimedia and Instrumental Exploration." Some music examples are included.

S.160. ROSSI, Nick, and CHOATE, Robert A. Music of Our Time: an anthology of works of selected contemporary composers of the 20th century. Boston: Crescendo, 1969. 406p. illus., bibliog.

The subtitle may be misleading: this is not a selection of scores, but a series of introductory chapters on forty 20th-century composers, whose careers are briefly surveyed, and one of whose works is scrutinized. Part 2 is entirely given over to American music: twenty composers (preceded by an outline of jazz) are considered chronologically (from Ives to Wuorinen) by date of birth. The chapters vary in length from six to fourteen pages (Antheil gets the longest) and almost all contain numerous music examples from the chosen works. In many instances, biographical information was obtained from the composers themselves; some were also the sources of the numerous photographs. The bibliography lists books and articles on each composer, but rations most of them to two or three items each. Index. (Formerly A83.)

S.161. VINTON, John. Essays After a Dictionary: music and culture at the close of Western civilization. Lewisburg, Pa.: Bucknell University Press; London: Associated University Presses, 1977. 170p.

The "dictionary" in question is the Dictionary of Contemporary Music (LOAM 259), which Vinton edited. These seven essays, dating from 1972 to 1975, are only distantly related to that project. Four of them center on American music and musical life, the most interesting being a selection of Virgil Thomson's reviews for the New York Tribune, 1940-1943, together with the outspoken memos these reviews provoked from the paper's chief editorial writer, the man responsible for hiring Thomson, Geoffrey Parsons. The other relevant essays are concerned with the Contemporary Music Project (CMP), an overview of American musical history (written for a Swedish reference book), and a brief look at 20th-century American orchestral music. Examples drawn from American music occur frequently in another essay, called "A Change of Mind," a piece which, as the only one relevant to the book's weighty subtitle, calls to mind Bishop John Earle's "grave divine"--"one who knows the burden of his calling and hath struggled to make his shoulders sufficient" (Microcosmographie, London, 1628). No index.

S.162.   WHITTALL, Arnold. Music Since the First World War.
London: Dent, 1977; New York: St. Martin's Press,
1977.   277p.   bibliog.
A major study, aimed at advanced students, and employing
a primarily technical, analytical approach.   While principally concerned with Europe, Whittall turns on numerous occasions to consider American composers also: in Part 1, "The Survival of
Tonality," a second chapter on symphonic music briefly reviews
Copland; in Part 2, "Twelve-Note Music," Sessions and Babbitt are
prominent (Chapter 9); in Part 3, "From Past to Future," Cage,
Varèse, and Carter are given close attention.

2.   20th-Century American Art Music

a.   Reference and Collected Biography

S.163.   AMERICAN MUSIC CENTER. Catalog of the American Music
Center Library. (Vol. 1).   Choral and Vocal Works;
compiled by Judith Greenberg Finell.   New York:
American Music Center, 1975.   198p.
_____.   _____. Vol. 2.   Chamber Music; compiled by
Karen McNerney Famera.   New York: American Music
Center, 1978.   164p.
Founded in 1940 by a group of American composers who
felt the need for a central information center "to foster and encourage the composition of contemporary music and to promote its production, publication, distribution and performance" (p. iii), the
Center has made available the information it holds in various forms.
These excellent catalogs are particularly valuable sources because
they include both printed music and manuscripts.   The first volume,
arranged in one alphabetical composer sequence, provides information
on title, voicing and accompaniment, and publisher (or indication of
manuscript).   Dates appear somewhat irregularly.   Vol. 2 is a
classified listing in three main sections: instrumental music (sub-
divided by number of players), voice(s) with chamber ensemble
(sub-divided by voice), and miscellaneous (including multi-media).
Each entry contains details of instrumentation, publisher (unless
manuscript), date, physical description, and duration.   The total
number of items listed is 3,226.   There is an index of composers
with index references for each individual work.

S.164.   ANDERSON, E. Ruth, comp. Contemporary American Composers: a biographical dictionary.   Boston: G. K. Hall,
1976.   513p.
_____.   _____. 2nd ed.   Boston: G. K. Hall, 1982.
578p.
The sheer number of entries (4,000 or so in the first edition, a further 500 in the second) prompts the unworthy thought:
will all the composers listed continue to compose when they find out,
via this book, just how extensive the competition is?   A more

positive approach doubtless inspired the compiler when she began a
five-year piece of detective work, turning up in all some 6,000
names. The criteria for eventual inclusion were: the individual
must have been born no earlier than 1870, be an American citizen
or have resided in the USA for an extended period, and have had
at least one original composition published, commercially recorded,
performed in an urban area, or selected for an award in composition.
Much information was collected by questionnaire, supplemented by
other sources such as concert announcements, publishers' lists. A
typical entry contains brief biographical details--the barest of bare
professional bones--a list of works, and an address. In general,
composers who wrote or write in jazz, popular or rock idioms only
are excluded, though there are exceptions (e.g., Duke Ellington,
whose entry eschews all mention of the word "jazz"). A list of all
the women composers in the book is appended (457 in the first edition).

S.165.   GLEASON, Harold and BECKER, Warren. 20th-Century
         American Composers. 2nd ed. Bloomington, Ind.:
         Frangipani Press, 1980. (Music Literature Outlines,
         Series 4). 232p. bibliog.
     To anyone beginning to study the works of one of the
seventeen composers represented here, this is an essential reference
tool in an exemplary series (the preface modestly calls it an "efficient resource"). Each composer section includes: (1) biography
(in outline form); (2) list of compositions by form (with dates of
composition or publication, publisher, and, for vocal works, name of
author); (3) style summary (with specific works--occasionally
measures--mentioned); (4) a quotation by the composer; (5) bibliographies (which are in sections and are usually quite extensive).
The last eleven pages are devoted to a general bibliography. The
seventeen composers are: Barber, Carpenter, Carter, Copland,
Hanson, Harris, Ives, Moore, Piston, Riegger, Bernard Rogers,
Ruggles, William Schuman, Sessions, Randall Thompson, and Virgil
Thomson. (The 1st ed., by Gleason, took the form of a privately
printed series, beginning in 1969, distributed by Levis Music
Stores, Rochester.)

S.166.   SHIRLEY, Wayne D. Modern Music, Published By the
         League of Composers, 1924-1946: an analytic index;
         edited by William & Carolyn Lichtenwanger. New York:
         AMS Press, 1976. 246p.
     Following its demise in 1946, Modern Music received many
accolades, pointing to its pioneering role in fighting for recognition
of twentieth-century music; one among them, which the magazine's
sole editor, Minna Lederman, confessed had deeply moved her, was
from Virgil Thomson, who declared, "no other magazine and no book
has told the musical story of its time so completely, so authoritatively, so straight from the field of battle and from the creative labora-
tory" (quoted by Minna Lederman in The Life and Death of a Small
Magazine [Brooklyn: ISAM, 1983], p. 198). Although devoted to all

contemporary music, it was in its coverage of the American scene
(predominantly the serious composers, but including also film music
and jazz) that Modern Music was especially effective, and Minna
Lederman's particular achievement was to persuade composers to become critics as well.

All this is reflected in this fine index, which is in a sense
a further accolade, for the great care and detail taken in its construction are a tribute to the store set upon each page of the
magazine. There are entries, in one sequence, for authors, titles,
and subjects (names and topics), with plentiful sub-divisions as
necessary. The part played by composer-critics is apparent in the
substantial author entries for, among others, Marc Blitzstein, Paul
Bowles, Elliott Carter, Theodore Chanler, Aaron Copland, Henry
Cowell, Lou Harrison, Frederick Jacobi, Roger Sessions, and Virgil
Thomson. (Modern Music itself was reprinted by AMS Press in
1967.)

S.167.   WENK, Arthur. Analyses of Twentieth-Century Music
         1940-1970. Ann Arbor, Mich.: Music Library Associa-
         tion, 1975. (MLA Index and Bibliography Series, No.
         13.) 94p.
         _____. _____. Supplement: 1970-1975. Ann Arbor,
         Mich.: Music Library Association, 1976. (MLA Index
         and Bibliography Series, No. 14.) 57p.
         _____. _____. Supplement. 2nd ed. Boston: Mu-
         sic Library Association, 1984. (MLA Index and Bib-
         liography Series, No. 14.) 132p.
The main volume contains a bibliographic checklist of articles on some 150 composers in 39 periodicals (23 of which are in
English) and in a selection of biographies, book-length studies, doctoral dissertations and Festschriften. Over 40 American composers
are listed, eleven of whom have three or more entries under their
names; these are Babbitt, Barber, Carter, Copland, Harris, Ives,
Piston, Ruggles, Sessions, Thomson, and Varèse.

The 1984 ed. of the Supplement updates the 1975 ed. (to
1982?) and also adds coverage of 41 periodicals and 41 Festschriften
not indexed in the main checklist. A further seven American composers have three or more entries: Cage, Cowell, Crumb, Finney,
Foss, Hovhaness, Persichetti. Author indexes.

S.168.   WILLIAMS, Michael D. Source: Music of the Avant Garde;
         annotated list of contents and cumulative indices. Ann
         Arbor, Mich.: Music Library Association, 1978. (MLA
         Index and Bibliography Series, No. 19.) 52p.
The eleven issues of Source: Music of the Avant Garde
produced in California (first at Davis, then at Sacramento) between
1967 and 1973 were remarkable documents of the West Coast's desire
for compositional innovation. Unusual in a number of aspects, the
journal's most distinguishing feature was the high proportion of its
contents given over to compositions, which ran the whole gamut of
notational styles, from conventional notes and staves to pieces of fur.

The first part of this index is an annotated list of these compositions, around 180 in all, arranged alphabetically by composer. The majority are American, though, as the compiler indicates: "the scope of Source ... broadens from the American West Coast avant garde in the early issues to a European emphasis in some of the later issues" (p. 7). A shorter index of articles and essays, arranged by author, is followed by lists of the contents of the six recordings issued with the journal, and by name and title indexes. (The editors of Source were Larry Austin (1-8), Stanley Lunetta (6-11), and Arthur Woodbury (6-10). John Cage (8), Alvin Lucier (10), and Stan Friedman (11) acted as guest editors.)

b. Critical Works

See also S.12

S.169.   GARLAND, Peter, ed. Soundings: Ives, Ruggles, Varèse. (Berkeley): Soundings Press, 1974. (201p.) illus.
All the issues of Garland's remarkable, if irregular, journal of contemporary American music, Soundings, are wont to be highly individualistic, arresting both to the eye and the brain, and happy to defy easy categorization. This particular, separately published volume, an escapee for some undisclosed reason from the fold of an already erratic family, is like its cousins in these characteristics. Typically consisting of a text partly typed, partly handwritten, partly in score, partly in pictures, it comprises thirteen contributions on, around, or in honor of the three composers of the title. Lou Harrison's two pieces, "Ruggles, Ives, Varèse" and "About Carl Ruggles," both originally appeared elsewhere (for the latter, see LOAM 344), as did Philip Corner's "Thoreau and Ives With Specifics for This Time," a kind of prose composition using quotations from Thoreau and Ives--and Corner--in a collage effect. Corner is the major contributor, having three other, equally unusual pieces, a short one on Ruggles, an analysis of Varèse's Density 21.5, and a lengthy discussion of Ives, in which chunks of analysis, couched in colloquial language, rub shoulders, Ives-like, with sections ruminating on wider human themes of concern to Ives and his music. Other contributions include two by James Tenney, on Ives and Varèse, a score by Malcolm Goldstein, "Majority--1964," reproductions in black and white of some Carl Ruggles paintings, photos of Varèse, and Garland's own "Americas," a "journal" of musings on American culture, dedicated to Varèse. (Soundings itself is currently published by Garland from 948 Canyon Road, Santa Fe, N.M. 87501.)

S.170.   GOLDMAN, Richard Franko. Selected Essays and Reviews, 1948-1968; edited by Dorothy Klotzman. Brooklyn: Institute for Studies in American Music, 1980. (I.S.A.M. Monograph, No. 13.) 262p. illus.
Goldman (1910-1980) was an outstandingly versatile figure

on the American music scene, as teacher, composer, conductor, and writer. This generous selection of his criticism is drawn from five journals, among them The Juilliard Review (which he founded) and The Musical Quarterly (for which he reported on music in New York for twenty years); most of it concerns contemporary American music and musical life. The most substantial pieces are two on Wallingford Riegger, one on Elliott Carter (who provides a foreword to the book), and one on John Philip Sousa; other subjects include Copland concerts at Juilliard in 1960-61, a memoir of Henry Cowell, and a scathing attack on the culture industry as embodied in a 1965 report, The Performing Arts: Problems and Prospects. In addition there is a broad cross-section of his "Current Chronicle" and his record reviews, both for The Musical Quarterly. A witty and questioning writer, his approach ranges with equal success from the more-or-less expository narrative (Sousa), to the personal appreciation (Cowell), to the perceptively interpretative. Index.

S.171.   KEELE UNIVERSITY, England. First American Music Conference, Friday, April 18-21, 1975. (Keele, Staffs.: Keele University Music Department, 1978.) 201p. bibliog., discog., refs.
As part of its pioneering efforts to establish American music studies in British academic institutions Keele University assembled a distinguished group of scholars to address its first conference, which was angled (although no underlying theme was stated) almost entirely towards 20th-century American art music by white composers. The proceedings, issued three years later by the Music Dept., consist of ten papers, and the discussion on the Americanness of American music (a favorite conference theme; cf. McCue, no. S.17) that concluded the weekend. To these have been added an introduction by Professor Peter Dickinson, the guiding light behind Keele's venture, and an interview between Dickinson and Aaron Copland, conducted at Keele in October 1976. The papers are devoted to: quotations and collage, with special attention to Rochberg (Karl Aage Rasmussen), chance and choice in Foss (Jane Waugh), Ives and the national character (David Wooldridge), spatial form in Ives (Robert P. Morgan), Elliott Carter (Arnold Whittall), stylistic evolution in Varèse (David Harold Cox), art and science in Varèse (Paul Griffiths), areas of common ground between rock and art music (Tim Souster), experimental music and the vernacular tradition, as seen especially in Heinrich (Michael Nyman), and the political music of Christian Wolff (Keith Potter). No index.

S.172.   MERTENS, Wim. Amerikaanse repetitive muziek: in het perspectief van de Westeuropese muziekevolutie. Bierbeck, Belgium: W. Vergaelen, 1980. 163p. illus., bibliog.
_____. American Minimal Music: La Monte Young, Terry Riley, Steve Reich, Philip Glass; translated by J. Hautekiet; preface by Michael Nyman. London: Kahn & Averill; New York: Broude, 1983. 128p. illus., bibliog.

Though its practitioners vary in their interpretation of minimalism, its basic characteristics as outlined by Mertens are reduction of musical means, repetition as a structural principle, and a non-narrative orientation. In concise chapters on each of the four composers under discussion, Mertens provides instructive introductory accounts of their music, with examples, and proceeds on the basis of this to compare their underlying concepts and idealogy with those of Western classical music. He then traces the development of these concepts, in particular that of the musical work as process not object, through the music of Schoenberg, Webern, Stockhausen, and Cage. Finally, he returns to ideology, to examine the minimalist philosophy in the light of the European thinking of T. W. Adorno, Jean-François Lyotard, and Gilles Deleuze. By this time the four composers themselves are no longer being mentioned.

c. Individual Composers

ERNST BACON

S.173.   HORGAN, Paul. Ernst Bacon: a contemporary tribute.
         (Orinda, Calif., 1974?) 23 leaves. illus.
         This is a mimeographed, unbound, undated group of
sheets, possibly issued by Bacon himself. Horgan's tribute requires only the first two leaves; the balance is devoted to an excellent catagorized catalog of Bacon's compositions, with the last four leaves (there are two numbered "22") devoted to excerpts from reviews of his musicals and literary works. (Besides Notes on the Piano [LOAM 357], Bacon also wrote Our Musical Idioms [Chicago: Open Court, 1917], and Words on Music [Syracuse: Syracuse University Press, 1960].)

LEONARD BERNSTEIN

S.174.   BERNSTEIN, Leonard. The Unanswered Question: six
         talks at Harvard. Cambridge, Mass.: Harvard University Press, 1976. (The Charles Eliot Norton Lectures
         1973.) 428p. illus.
         Bernstein's much publicized attempt, in the wake of
Chomsky's linguistic theories, to seek validation for a "notion of a worldwide, inborn musical grammar" (p. 7) has received extremes of praise and scorn; it did, undeniably, give considerable impetus to the application to music of linguistic theory and methodology. In themselves, the lectures were a multi-media tour de force, which the printed page only palely reflects; nevertheless they contain "a rich mélange of brilliant and wild theoretical speculations, illuminating descriptions of a variety of musical phenomena, and just plain personality" (Ray Jackendoff, reviewing the book in Language, 53, No. 4 [1977], pp. 883-4).
         The book is included here for two reasons: for that force

of Bernstein's personality which is so cogently expressed on each
page, and tells much about the man; and for the centrally important,
though brief, reference to Ives in the book's title, and in Chapter
5, "The Twentieth Century Crisis." The question posed by Ives in
his piece is interpreted by Bernstein as meaning "Whither music?"
The piece itself "spells out the dilemma of the new century" (p. 269)
between tonality and atonality, and Bernstein goes on to assert that
tonal music appeals to an innate quality, whereas atonal music does
not.

S.175. GOTTLIEB, Jack, ed. Leonard Bernstein: a complete catalogue of his works; celebrating his 60th birthday August
25, 1978. (New York): Amberson, 1978. 68p. illus.,
discog.
    Though not nearly as highly developed as other catalogs of
20th-century composers (e.g., Holst, Shostakovich), this is a useful
reference work. It offers a classified list of works, a chronological
list of works, an alphabetical title index, and various other compilations: a calendar of his life, a discography of Bernstein as composer,
lists of honors, of films and videos, of original television scripts, of
his writings, of writings about him, and of his publishers' addresses.
An appreciation by Lukas Foss precedes the catalog.

S.176. WEBER, J. F. Leonard Bernstein. Utica, N.Y.: the
author, 1975. (Discography Series, XIII.) 16p.
    A discography of commercially issued recordings of Bern-
stein's music. Works are listed chronologically, from Sonata for
Clarinet and Piano (1941-2) to Dybbuk (1974), and the recordings
of each work are also given in chronological order. Information
covering performers, recording date, timings, US and foreign release numbers and dates of release and deletion is given when known.
Alongside English label numbers there are references to reviews in
The Gramophone. (A more up-to-date listing, in Carol J. Oja's
American Music Recordings: a discography of 20th-century U.S.
composers [Brooklyn: Institute for Studies in American Music,
1982], contains substantially the same information as Weber's discography, arranged differently and without timings and bibliographical
references.) The address given on Weber's booklets is 1, Jewett
Place, Utica, N.Y. 13501.

JOHN CAGE

S.177. CAGE, John. Empty Words: writings '73-'78. Middletown,
Conn.: Wesleyan University Press, 1979. 187p.
    This further installment of Cage's writings (cf. LOAM 305-
308) is divided unevenly between a small number of more-or-less
conventional prose pieces and various examples of Cage's fascination
with nonsyntactical language, especially his "mesostics" (see LOAM
305). The essays are: a preface to his Lecture on the Weather, a
note on "how the piano came to be prepared," and a lecture on the
future of music. The longest of the other contributions is the title

piece, which makes, Cage says, "a transition from a language without sentences ... to a 'language' having only letters and silence (music)" (p. 133). The influence of Thoreau is again acknowledged, but whether he would approve of the treatment once more meted out to his ghost--by I Ching et al.--is another matter. Mesostics are devoted to James Joyce, Norman O. Brown, Morris Graves, and others.

S.178.   CAGE, John. Pour les oiseaux: entretiens avec Daniel Charles. Paris: Belfond, 1976. 254p. bibliog.
_____ . For the Birds: John Cage in conversation with Daniel Charles. Boston: Marion Boyars, 1981. 239p. bibliog. refs.
A book with a peculiarly Cagean history: it began life in 1968 as a series of interviews for the French periodical La Revue d' esthétique; the original taped interviews, which were translated into French for that series and the 1976 edition, went missing before they could be used for an English edition; the 1981 version (by Richard Gardner) was achieved by translating the French translation. Despite--or because of--this, the book is arguably one of the most informative in existence about John Cage (b.1912). The ten interviews are full of straightforward details of his background, thoughts and ideas. Cage gives open, easily phrased answers to the (sometimes rather formal) questions of his interviewer (in an "Afterword" Cage remarks on his difficulty in handling a French academician's questions, and on changes in the nature of their dialogue when he admitted this). One section, entitled in the English version, "Sixty Answers to Thirty-three Questions," and placed before the interviews, is in the curious multi-dimensional, multi-typeface style familiar from other Cage books, but the majority of the prose here is "normal."

S.179.   CHARLES, Daniel. Gloses sur John Cage. Paris: Union Générale d'Editions, 1978. 292p. bibliog. refs.
A collection of astute interpretative essays all previously published elsewhere, and grouped here in three parts. Part 1, "Approaches," discusses various central features of Cage's aesthetics: silence, indeterminism, chance and the interpreter, anarchy. Part 2, "Presentations," is devoted to particular works by Cage--the Sonatas and Interludes, the Piano Concerto, Rozart Mix, Song Books, Musicircus, Etcetera, and the five works for soloists, 1954-1956, each of whose titles includes an indication of the piece's length. Part 3, "Perspection," is more miscellaneous, and includes pieces on utopianism, chance, and on mushrooms and Japanese gardens.

S.180.   METZGER, Heinz-Klaus, and RIEHN, Rainer, eds. John Cage. Munich: Text & Kritik, 1978. (Musik-Konzepte, Sonderband) 174p. illus., bibliog., discog.
A collection of original and reprinted criticism in German by Heinz-Klaus Metzger, Hans G. Helms (including the English text of a 1972 interview with Cage), Daniel Charles, Dieter Schnebel, Christian Wolff (a letter to Metzger), Rainer Riehn, Hans Rudolf

Zeller, and Clytus Gottwald. Also included is the translation of an impromptu address given by Cage to the members of the Residentie-Orkest, The Hague, during rehearsals of "Atlas Eclipticalis" in 1976; this has detailed notes by Michael Nyman. The accompanying documentation includes chronologies of Cage's life and work, an excellent six-page bibliography, and a two-page discography.

S.181.   TOMKINS, Calvin. The Bride and the Bachelors: the heretical courtship in modern art. New York: Viking Press, London: Weidenfeld & Nicolson, 1965.   246p. illus.

_____. The Bride and the Bachelors: five masters of the avant garde. New York: Viking Press, 1968; Harmondsworth: Penguin, 1976.   306p.   illus.

Based on pieces written for the New Yorker in the early 1960s, this frequently reprinted work on the avant garde takes an in-depth look at the careers, attitudes, and achievements of Marcel Duchamp, John Cage, Jean Tinguely, Robert Rauschsenberg, and (in the new edition) Merce Cunningham--all of whom Tomkins sees as united in asking, in various ways, the basic heretical question: "why worry about art when life is what matters?" (p. 4).   The chapter on Cage is a lengthy (75-page), illuminating biographical and critical study which sets out Cage's underlying ideas: his intention to overthrow the notion of the purpose of art as being to "organize life into meaningful patterns" (p. 73), his attempt to remove his own tastes, ideas, and imagination, his adoption of chance procedures, and traces their development through his career.   The account concludes with the Philharmonic Hall concert of Feb. 1964--a debacle which, above all, brought no credit to the New York Philharmonic, or its subscribers.

ELLIOTT CARTER

S.182.   CARTER, Elliott. The Writings of Elliott Carter: an American composer looks at modern music; compiled, edited, and annotated by Else Stone and Kurt Stone. Bloomington: Indiana University Press, 1977.   390p.   illus.

One of the rare breed of "composers whose spectrum of interests is broader and more urgent than could be satisfied with 'mere' composing" (editors' introduction, p. xiii), Carter (b.1908) is represented in this chronologically-arranged collection by around 70 pieces, written between 1937 and 1976--reviews, articles, eulogies, program and liner notes--which provide a valuable commentary on his own music, and a percipient, often arresting view of the changing American musical scene.   Almost one half of the pieces were written for Modern Music between 1937 and 1946, and here the reader finds Carter at his most outspoken; a mellower, more detached approach emerges with the passage of the years.   Among the other composers featured are Piston, Riegger, Gilbert, Sessions, and--by far the most prominent, and clearly a significant influence--Ives.   Many others are mentioned in the numerous reports on New

York musical life. Other subjects include film music, "the rhythmic basis of American music," the role of the American composers,
and the influence of Expressionism. A superlative index permits
ready access by name and subject.

S.183.   WEBER, J. F. Carter and Schuman. Utica, N.Y.: the
         author, 1978. (Discography Series, XIX.) 20p.
     In the same series as Weber's Bernstein and Varèse dis-
cographies (nos. S.176 and S.202), this slim reference work lists
commercial recordings of Elliott Carter and William Schuman.
Originally compiled as bicentennial contributions to the Journal of
the Association for Recorded Sound Collections, the listings employ
the same basic structure and methods as the earlier volumes. Like
them, they are dated in terms of recent releases, but still useful.

HENRY COWELL

S.184.   SAYLOR, Bruce. The Writings of Henry Cowell: a des-
         criptive bibliography. Brooklyn: Institute for Studies
         in American Music, 1977. (I.S.A.M. Monographs, No.
         7.) 42p.
     Cowell was not only a prolific composer, he also produced
a considerable body of writing, varying "from hard-core theoretical
treatises and in-depth studies of other composers' work to pieces
of musical propaganda for popular magazines" (foreword). This
bibliography lists 237 items, including books, articles and reviews
(the largest section, containing 197 entries), and prefaces to scores
and notes to recordings of his music. The book and article sections are both in chronological order, providing an opportunity for
study of changes and developments in Cowell's attitudes. The composer's liner notes to Ethnic Folkways recordings, and his unpublished manuscripts, are excluded. Concise annotations accompany
each entry. There is no attempt, either in the notes or in the
prefatory material, to assess the value of Cowell's writings (a pity,
since, in all honesty, few people are likely to have the opportunity--
or the inclination?--to examine all these pieces again).

CHARLES T. GRIFFES

S.185.   ANDERSON, Donna K. Charles T. Griffes: an annotated
         bibliography-discography. Detroit: Information Coor-
         dinators for The College Music Society, 1977. (Bib-
         liographies in American Music, No. 3.) 255p. illus.
     The bibliography, occupying 140 pages, is a substantial-
looking listing of 525 annotated items about Griffes, and represents
a thorough search for information and opinion in the form of books,
parts of books, articles, dissertations, reviews, program notes,
newspaper correspondence, album liner notes, etc. (material in all
but a few histories is excluded--hence Wilfrid Mellers' chapter [in
LOAM 27] is missing). Many of the annotations include a brief
extract from the item in question. A great many of the items listed

are of small significance in assisting us to evaluate Griffes himself, but they would, no doubt, illuminate the study of his critical reception. A pity, therefore, that the chosen arrangement--alphabetical by author (title for unsigned material) in one sequence--should be so unexpressive, allowing no distinctions to be easily made between kinds of items, and refusing the items themselves any scope to relate to one another. Some kind of categorization of the material, with a chronological sub-arrangement, would have displayed the painstakingly gathered collection in a rather better light.

Several useful listings follow: a chronology of published works; a discography, arranged by label (with full details and with references to reviews in the bibliography) and by composition; a list of first performances, arranged by work and by date (but no references to reviews); and an index of performers. Surprisingly, there is no general index of references to Griffes' works, so that, for example, one must peck around like the white peacock on the cover to find all the reference in the bibliography to the piece named after it. (For a sister volume, a masterly catalog by the same author, see The Works of Charles Tomlinson Griffes: a descriptive catalogue [Ann Arbor: UMI Research Press, 1983].)

ROY HARRIS

S.186.   STRASSBURG, Robert. Roy Harris: a catalog of his works.
         Los Angeles: California State University, 1973. 48p.
         illus., discog.

The John F. Kennedy Memorial Library at California State University received a bequest of his autographs from Harris (1898-1979) in 1973. The catalog is a classified one, dividing the works into ten groups with chronological arrangement within each group, and with information on the duration of each piece and publication details. There is also a short biographical portrait, a list of honors and commissions, and a discography of 78s and LPs.

SIDNEY HOMER

S.187.   HOMER, Sidney. My Wife and I: the story of Louise and
         Sidney Homer. New York: Macmillan, 1939. (Repr.
         New York: Da Capo, 1978). 269p. illus.

For those looking for chatty inside information on the composer Sidney Homer (1864-1933) or his great singer wife Louise (1871-1947), this is the perfect source, though all but the most tolerant readers may be irked by the author's fondness for philosophizing, for the "poetic" turn of phrase, and for abundant use of "upright" epithets such as "blessed," "dear," and "precious." Homer was a pupil of Rheinberger and Chadwick (he adored both of them), a counterpoint and theory teacher himself, and a not altogether serious composer of a smattering of chamber and piano pieces and many songs. His wife was a Metropolitan Opera mezzo for almost 30 years beginning at the turn of the century. They were the parents of six children, she the aunt of composer Samuel Barber (who bore a certain resemblance to her). A major flaw of the book is the lack of an index. (Barber and Menotti are mentioned on pp. 265 and 266. Louise Homer was also the subject of Louise Homer and the Golden Age of Opera, by Anne Homer [New York: Morrow, 1974].)

CHARLES IVES

S.188.   CLINKSCALE, Edward H., and BROOK, Claire, eds. A Musical Offering: essays in honor of Martin Bernstein. New York: Pendragon Press, 1977. 301p. illus., bibliog. refs.

This Festschrift contains a nine-page essay by H. Wiley Hitchcock on "Charles Ives's Book of 114 Songs" (pp. 127-135), in which some of the remarks made by Ives in his "Postface" are illuminated by references to 19th-century American attitudes and to the composer's own utterances on music and life. Hitchcock also shows the variety of the collection by picking out songs with different features--radical harmonies, sentiment and nostalgia in the "household song" idiom, texts of poetic elegance, and vernacular elements.

S.189.   HITCHCOCK, H. Wiley. Ives. London: Oxford University Press, 1977. (Oxford Studies of Composers, 14.) 95p. bibliog.

The aim of the series in which this little book appears is "to provide short, scholarly, critical surveys of composers about whom no major work is already available, or whose music is in need of re-assessment" (back cover). Ives, of course, is far from being the easiest composer to handle briefly and with precision, but Hitchcock's brave attempt, while inevitably having to call a halt to many discussions of the music just as they are warming up, is a valuable, often insightful overview. There is little biographical data, other than what is offered by the short foreword; the book concentrates on musical description and analytical comment, dividing Ives' music into five groups: songs, choral music, keyboard music, chamber music, orchestral music. Many music examples are provided. Hitchcock is well aware of the implications of Ives' remark, "the fabric of existence weaves itself whole" (quoted in the foreword), and attempts whenever possible to integrate comment on Ives' views of culture and philosophy.

S.190.   HITCHCOCK, H. Wiley and PERLIS, Vivian, eds. An Ives Celebration: papers and panels of the Charles Ives Centennial Festival-Conference. Urbana: University of Illinois Press, 1977. 282p. illus., bibliog. refs.

The New York/New Haven Ives Conference (October 1974) was "the first international congress ever to be dedicated to an American composer" (preface). These excellent published proceedings (not only papers and panel discussions, but also selected contributions from the floor) are thus the first of their kind, also, to be devoted to a single American composer, and they mark that particular crossroads clearly and proudly, signposts thrusting out arms in every conceivable direction (except down). There are four main sections: (i) Ives and American culture (papers by Robert M. Crunden, Frank Rossiter and Neely Bruce); (ii) on editing Ives (the experience of John Kirkpatrick, James Sinclair and Lou Harrison); (iii) on performing Ives (conductors John Manceri, Gunther Schuller, Nicholas Slonimsky, Lehman Engel and Arthur Weisberg; and performers Nancy and Alan Mandel, Eugene Gratovich and Regis Benoit, Daniel Stepner and John Kirkpatrick); (iv) Ives and present-day musical thought (Robert P. Morgan on spatial form, Allen Forte on atonality, the views of composers Roger Reynolds, Charles Dodge, Lou Harrison, Salvatore Martirano and Gordon Mumma, and a fascinating attempt by William Brooks to see Ives in terms of Structuralist thought). There is also a panel at which various European views of Ives are put forward. Fifteen foreign participants were also asked to contribute "statements concerning their experience and views of Ives's music, or those of their compatriots," and these are reproduced in an appendix. A full list of participants and an index are also included.

S.191.   THE OPEN UNIVERSITY. Ives and Varèse; prepared for
          the course team by Ian Bonighton and Richard Middleton.
          Milton Keynes: Open University Press, 1979. 107p.
          illus., bibliog.
     The Open University (or OU) offers adults in Britain who, for whatever reason, did not attend university as students, the chance to complete a degree course from home. Units in the various courses are taught by a combination of broadcasting and the use of printed and recorded materials. The well-prepared texts (which are available commercially) are frequently valuable in themselves, and this one, part of a course on the rise of modernism in music, is no exception; not only is the text stimulating and perceptive, the integrated exercises and the accompanying book of scores provide extra incentive to careful listening and reading.
     The section on Ives begins with a lucid outline of his life and of the central thrust of his thinking; this is followed by consideration of technical features of his music (polytonality, etc.). Three works are then examined closely, with examples: the Concord Sonata, "General William Booth Enters Into Heaven," and the Fourth Symphony. Ives' place in 20th-century music is discussed in conclusion, and there is a list of his works. For Varèse, a biographical outline is followed by discussion of his ideas and attitudes, and by inspection of two works: Octandre and Density 21.5; a list of works is given here also. As a bonus, the appendix provides the text of an essay by Robert P. Morgan, "Rewriting Music History--Second Thoughts on Ives and Varèse," reprinted from Musical Newsletter, 1973.

S.192.   SIVE, Helen R. Music's Connecticut Yankee: an introduc-
          tion to the life and music of Charles Ives. New York:

Atheneum, 1977. 141p. illus., bibliog., discog.
Aimed probably at a teenage audience, this is a somewhat
uninspiring biographical-critical study, with press-release overtones.
Ives is described as a revolutionary, but it is clear from the tone
and style of the book that it is a fairly cosy revolution, no head-
less bodies to be seen. If the many paradoxes of Ives and his music are hard to bring out fully in this type of literature, then at
least the subject of his fascination with sound could be more fully
explored, rather than impressionistically described. There seems
little justification, either, for omitting most sources of quotation,
and all mention of the Ives' adoption of their daughter, Edith. The
bibliography is minuscule, the discography (a selective list of compositions with suggested recordings) only slightly less so. Index.

PHILIP JAMES

S.193.   JAMES, Helga. A Catalog of the Musical Works of Philip
          James (1890-1975). Southampton, N.Y.: the author,
          1980. 62p. illus.
          Philip James belonged "loosely to a group of urbane and
industrious New York-based composers ... most of whom were born
within a decade or so before the turn of the century" (p. xiii).
The catalog, compiled by his widow (with unspecified editorial assistance from Judith Finell Music Services, Inc.), lists his output
in 28 categories, with details of date of composition, instrumentation,
duration, dedication, first performance, publication, etc., as appropriate. A short biographical sketch and shorter "stylistic description" precede the catalog proper. There is a title index.

OTTO LUENING

S.194.   LUENING, Otto. The Odyssey of an American Composer:
          the autobiography of Otto Luening. New York: Scrib-
          ner's, 1980. 605p. illus., bibliog., discog.
          With a wit and a worldliness not commonly found in com-
posers' memoirs, Luening (b.1900) tells of his variegated life as
composer, conductor, performer, and teacher in Europe (where he
knew inter alia, Joyce, Busoni, Richard Strauss) and the USA
(where he was born and grew up--Wisconsin; where he earned a
precarious living in Chicago in the 1920s, and where he went on to
teach at Eastman, Bennington, Columbia (etc.) and to be associated
in one way or another with very many of the country's leading musical figures, among them Cowell, Partch, Ruggles, and Thomson).
Truly diversified--or just dappled? The question does pose itself,
but a composer who can write on gambling at Reno on one page and
electronic music on the next has to make us catch our breath. Besides sharing his experiences, Luening is generous too with his
thoughts on composing, on teaching, and on musical life in America.
Added bonuses come in the form of a selected list of compositions
(chronological, 1917-1980, with publishers), a discography arranged
by record label, and a select list of writings for books and journals.
There is also an index.

GIAN CARLO MENOTTI

S.195. GRUEN, John. Menotti: a biography. New York: Macmillan; London: Collier Macmillan, 1978. 242p. illus.
Gruen appears to have enjoyed the full cooperation of Menotti (b.1911) for this biography, and as a result is able not only to pass on Menotti's personal recollections and opinions but to communicate the animation with which he seems able to respond to each and every situation. A lively book, therefore, dominated by Menotti's personality, as the story moves from his Italian boyhood, his arrival in the USA to study at the Curtis Institute in Philadelphia (at Toscanini's suggestion), on through the first achievements of his career and his significant successes (The Medium, The Consul, Amahl) to his later, slightly waning star, and decision to live in Scotland. Two features stand out: the succession of musical works, mostly for the stage, and each described (though not analyzed) in its chronological place; and the profound friendships Menotti has formed throughout his life (with Samuel Barber, Robert "Kinch" Horan, Thomas Schippers, and others). Menotti's own memories are given verbatim as often as possible, as are those of many of his friends and associates. This gives weight and authenticity to the portrait; at the same time, it often seems divorced from its time and context. Index.

LEO ORNSTEIN

S.196. MARTENS, Frederick H. Leo Ornstein: the man, his ideas, his work. New York: Breitkopf & Hartel, 1918. (Repr. New York: Arno, 1975). 89p. illus.
A brief study of the pianist-composer (b.1892), whose radical approach to composition was the cause of much heated discussion in the 1910s. A 22-page biography sketches Ornstein's early life (he was not 30 when the book appeared) his childhood in Russia, the family's flight to the USA in 1907, his training as a pianist, his early concert career and first major compositions. There follow an outline of his musical philosophy, and some consideration of his pianistic technique and of individual compositions, with examples. (Ornstein subsequently devoted himself solely to teaching and composition, founding the Ornstein School of Music in Philadelphia.)

NED ROREM

S.197. ROREM, Ned. An Absolute Gift: a new diary. New York: Simon and Schuster, 1978. 286p.
This is the seventh in Rorem's series of diaries (see LOAM 343), though it is not strictly a diary: it contains reviews, articles, and a speech. There are excerpts from Rorem's diary, but most of the other pieces here were published elsewhere first. Rorem states in his foreword that the collection is "the latest in a series about so-called creative concerns. The series was begun partly as an antidote to a random diary (itself a distraction from the composer's

full-time job), partly as a result of periodical invitations." Rorem's
ideas are always interesting and his command of the language exceptional (if too "literary" for some tastes). (The book's title is
from the W. H. Auden poem, "The Composer.") Index.

WILLIAM SCHUMAN

See also no. 183

S.198.   ROUSE, Christopher. William Schuman Documentary: bio-
          graphical essay, catalogue of works, discography, and
          bibliography; with introductory note by Leonard Bern-
          stein. (Bryn Mawr, Pa.): Theodore Presser, 1980.
          54p. illus., bibliog., discog.
    The concise biographical essay occupies 26 pages, and in-
cludes some general assessment of individual musical works; though
factually informative, it tends to steer clear of any hint of criticism.
The list of works is arranged by category (orchestral, choral, etc.),
and chronologically within each category. It includes dates of com-
pletion and first performance, instrumentation, timing, and publisher. The discography, in one alphabetical sequence, provides information on performers and record issue numbers; no dates are
given. The bibliography is divided into sections of writings on and
by Schuman, and includes books, chapters in books, and articles.
The compiler stresses that the section on Schuman is selective, containing only the most important material; nevertheless it is surprising
to see that Schuman has been the subject of so few critics' concen-
trated attention.

ARTHUR SHEPHERD

S.199.   LOUCKS, Richard. Arthur Shepherd, American Composer.
          Provo, Utah: Brigham Young University Press, 1980.
          256p. illus., bibliog.
    The "professional craftsmanship" of Arthur Shepherd
(1880-1958) was a salient characteristic, according to William S. Newman's preface. To help us judge for ourselves (few works being
published), pages 67-225 are given over to facsimiles of the autographs of 32 works. Loucks provides a biography, from Shepherd's
early years in Idaho, his studies in Boston, his work for the Salt
Lake Theater, his relationship to the Wa-Wan movement and Arthur
Farwell, to his long period of teaching and composition in Cleveland.
He also briefly analyzes Shepherd's stylistic development, and provides a detailed catalogue of works, a bibliography of books, articles, and typescripts, and an index.

EDGARD VARÈSE

S.200.   METZGER, Heinz-Klaus, and RIEHN, Rainer, eds. Edgard
          Varèse: Rückblick auf die Zukunft. Munich: Text &
          Kritik, 1978. (Musik-Konzepte, 6). 118p. bibliog.,

discog.

Most of the material in this anthology of Varèse criticism consists of German translations of pieces previously published in English: Varèse's own essay, "The Liberation of Sound" (from Contemporary Composers on Contemporary Music, LOAM 263), Henry Miller's "With Edgard Varèse in the Gobi Desert" (from his The Air-Conditioned Nightmare), Gunther Schuller's "Conversations with Varèse" (from Perspectives of New Music, 3, No. 2 [1965]), Chou Wen-Chung's analysis of Ionisation (a shortened version; the full English text appears in no. S.201), and Arnold Whittall's "Varèse and Organic Athematism" (from Music Review, 27, No. 4 [1967]). There are original German contributions from Dieter Schnebel, Hans Rudolf Zeller and Heinz-Klaus Metzger, with chronologies of Varèse's life and works by Rainer Riehn. There is also a good eleven-page international bibliography of books and articles, and a two-page discography of LPs.

S.201.   VAN SOLKEMA, Sherman, ed. The New Worlds of Edgard
          Varèse: a symposium, with papers by Elliott Carter,
          Chou Wen-chung, Robert P. Morgan. Brooklyn: In-
          stitute for Studies in American Music, 1979. (I.S.A.M.
          Monographs, No. 11.) 90p. illus.
     The symposium on which this volume is based took place at the City University of New York in April 1977. Carter's paper (the briefest) is an overall assessment, Morgan discusses rhythm in Varèse, and, in the longest contribution, Chou Wen-chung analyzes Ionisation in depth, concentrating on the function of timbre in its formal and temporal organization. Both Morgan's and Chou's papers include numerous music examples. The book concludes with a digest of the discussion that closed the symposium.

S.202.   WEBER, J. F. Edgard Varèse. Utica, N.Y.: the author,
          1975. (Discography Series, XII.) 13p.
     Like the others in this series (see nos. S.176 and S.183), this is a discography of commercially issued recordings arranged chronologically by work. Beginning with Amériques (1918-22) and ending with Nocturnal (1960-61), the compiler lists 58 different recorded performances. Recordings are listed chronologically under each title, with details of performers, timings, and US and European releases (with dates of release and deletion). There are also refer-ences to reviews in The Gramophone.

S.203.   WEHMEYER, Grete. Edgard Varèse; mit gezeichneten Auf-
          nahmen von seiner Musik von L. Alcopley. Regensburg:
          Bosse, 1977. 251p. illus., bibliog.
     Varèse himself cautioned against the attempt to analyse his works; the process at work in the music was to be grasped by listening. As the author embarks on a series of essays on each of Varèse's works, she attempts to overcome this problem by incorporat-ing the abstract line drawings—or, as they are called, "drawn re-cordings"—of Varèse's friend, the artist L. Alcopley. Arranged

down the margins of the pages of descriptive text like stills from a
cartoon film, the drawings offer a visual impression of listening to
Varèse's music. Wehmeyer describes her own text as deliberately
provocative and personal; it is also informative on Varèse's works
and provides many insights. Her general conclusions oppose the
conventional wisdom and see Varèse as continuing the tradition of
neo-romanticism. In addition to the descriptive/analytical text there
are more general essays and numerous reference aids: a chronology
of Varèse's life, a catalog of his works, 64 pages of music illustrations in full score, and a good bibliography. An index is inserted
as an unpaged addition.

JOSEPH WAGNER

S.204. BOWLING, Lance, ed. Joseph Wagner: a retrospective of
        a composer-conductor. Lomita, Calif.: Charade Record
        Co., 1976. 34p. illus.
    A modest but helpful compilation of information about the man
whom Nicolas Slonimsky, in his contribution, refers to as "the most
undiscovered among American composers." Wagner (1900-1974), born
in Massachusetts, lived and worked in various parts of the USA, as
well as in Europe and Latin America, ending his days in Hollywood
(he was composer-in-residence at Pepperdine University). The composer of orchestral, band, chamber, vocal, and instrumental music,
he was also employed as a guest conductor from Finland to Chile,
was the founder of the Boston Civic Symphony, and wrote two text-
books on orchestration. A catalog of his works is included here,
together with Slonimsky's assessment (dating from 1954 and 1976),
which describes Wagner's style as "pragmatic modernism." There are
also (mostly glowing) excerpts from reviews of Wagner as conductor
(the reviewers are uncredited), and brief opinions of him from a
variety of musical figures.

d. 20th-Century Musical Life

For regional studies, see A.7.b

S.205   BINDER, Abraham W. The Jewish Music Movement in Ameri-
         ca: an informal lecture. New York: National Jewish
         Music Council, 1963. 17p. bibliog. refs.
         _____. _____. New ed., with additional resource in-
         formation. New York: Jewish Music Council of the
         National Jewish Welfare Board, 1975. 36p. bibliog.,
         discog.
    A lecture delivered in Jerusalem in 1952, briefly outlining
the renaissance in Jewish music that followed the formation of the
Society for Jewish Folk Music in Petrograd in 1908, and in particular
the various forms this renaissance took in the USA: choral societies,
publishing firms, recordings of the music of the synagogues, music
education, musicology, the establishment of academic institutions.

Irene Heskes' "resource addenda" to the new edition includes a
discography of compositions, a list of publishers, and suggested
choral works for performance.

S.206. BROWN, Malcolm H., ed. Papers of the Yugoslav-American
        Seminar on Music. Bloomington: Indiana University
        School of Music, 1970. 208p. bibliog. refs.
        These 25 papers were presented at a seminar held in Sveti
Stefan on July 6-14, 1968. Each participant discusses one aspect of
musical life and practice in Yugoslavia or the USA, and all but one
of the papers are paired together, providing opportunity for comparison. The American contributors and their topics are: Nancy
Hanks--Support for music; Charles Wuorinen--Schooling of young
composers; Wilfred C. Bain--Scope of music studies in America music institutions; Lukas Foss--American music in the 1960s; Howard
Taubman--Music and the mass audience; Milos Velimirovic--Musicolo-
gical studies; Edward N. Waters--Problems of music bibliography;
Vladimir Ussachevsky--Application of modern technology to music;
Barbara Krader--Philosophy of folk and traditional music study;
Bruno Nettl--Ethnomusicology in American music education; Juan
Orrego-Salas--Folk and popular music as sources in national schools
of composition; H. Wiley Hitchcock--Nationalism and anti-nationalism
in American music histories.

S.207. BROWNE, Ray B., et al., eds. Challenges in American
        Culture; edited by Ray B. Browne, Larry N. Landrum,
        William K. Bottorff. Bowling Green, Ohio: Bowling
        Green University Popular Press, 1970. 278p. illus.,
        bibliog. refs.
        A miscellany of studies, drawn from papers presented at
a meeting of the American Studies Association in Toledo, Ohio, in
1969. Two are on musical subjects: Neal Canon, in "Art for Whose
Sake: the Federal Music Project of the WPA," examines the tensions
inherent in the linking of music with concern for social change in
the 1930s; Neil Leonard explores Theodore Dreiser's interest in music and its appearances in his work.

S.208. CHAPIN, Schuyler. Musical Chairs: a life in music. New
        York: Putnam, 1977. 448p. illus.
        Autobiography of the impresario (b.1923), describing his
career as concert agent (he managed Jascha Heifetz's US tour for
several years), his work for Columbia Records (1959-63), for the
Lincoln Center (as Vice-President for programming, 1964-68), and
as Assistant Manager, then Manager of the Metropolitan Opera,
1972-75. Leonard Bernstein features prominently in the narrative,
as composer and conductor.

S.209. EISLER, Hanns. A Rebel in Music: selected writings;
        edited with an introduction by Manfred Grabs; Margorie
        Meyer, translator. Berlin: Seven Seas Books; New
        York: International Publishers, 1978. 223p. bibliog.

refs.
The main result in book form of Eisler's period of emigration in the USA (1934-48) was the work jointly written with Theodor W. Adorno, Composing for Films (LOAM 1306). This present work collects many of his shorter pieces, including some from this period and from his earlier visits, in 1935-36. Among them are a letter describing his first impressions of the US in 1935; the text of a broadcast given in Strasbourg in 1935, entitled "A Musical Journey Through America"; a short piece on his first reaction to Hollywood; an article on film music, "From My Practical Work"; a 1938 speech (to the choir of the International Ladies' Garment Workers Union) on "Labor, Labor Movement and Music," which includes observations on popular music and jazz ("Duke Ellington ... [is] really talented, but [he] makes his fortune in night clubs and his development as an artist is therefore handicapped" [p. 141]); the text of his statement prepared for the House Committee on Un-American Activities, when he was summoned before it in 1947; and a lecture given in Prague in 1948 on "Basic Social Questions of Modern Music," which begins with his views on music as a consumer commodity in American society.

S.210. FINELL, Judith Greenberg, ed. The Contemporary Music
Performance Directory: a listing of American performing
ensembles, sponsoring organizations, performing facilities,
concert series, and festivals of 20th century music. New
York: American Music Center, 1975. 238p. bibliog.
Another of American Music Center's useful publications (see also nos. S.163, S.226, S.227). The work is organized in the sections indicated in the subtitle, with each section sub-arranged state by state. Information varies for each section: that for performing ensembles offers directors' names, complete addresses and telephone numbers, with a brief statement about the group, while that for concert series, in addition to the above type of detail, includes notes on kinds of music performed and total number of concerts. The bibliography and index are excellent.

S.211. HITCHCOCK, H. Wiley. After 100 (!) Years: the editorial
side of Sonneck; in memoriam Oscar George Theodore
Sonneck, 1873-1928; a lecture, with Oscar George Theo-
dore Sonneck, his writings and musical compositions; a
bibliography by Irving Lowens. Washington, D.C.:
Library of Congress, 1975. (Louis Charles Elson
Memorial Lecture.) 39p. bibliog. refs.
Sonneck is generally thought of as a rather dour, intensely serious scholar, obsessively pursuing his impersonal activities; but, following a few hints in others' descriptions of the great man, Hitchcock shows us he had a lighter side, and that this lighter side was closer to his true nature than excessive aloofness and sobriety. Sonneck's three kinds of editorial activity--his editorship of Musical Quarterly, his scholarly handling of primary sources (in particular his many uses of (!), varying from "sic" to "ugh!"), and his

anonymous or pseudonymous writings, taking advantage of the "editorial we"--are all shown to be rich in indications that, while he might not have been vaudeville material, Sonneck had a playful sense of fun, one that clearly helped to keep him sane. When one thinks of the amount of unpromising material he must have read, his remark, "We need a little more fun in music," could be seen as a cri de coeur. Lowens' bibliography lists 149 books and articles by Sonneck in chronological order, various musical compositions (mainly songs), eight portraits, and numerous articles about him, including obituaries.

S.212.   LOURIE, Arthur. Sergei Koussevitzky and His Epoch: a
         biographical chronicle. New York: Knopf, 1931. 253p.
         illus.
         This is a flowery, adoring biography of the Russian-born conductor-bass player (1874-1951) who has been more praised for his passion for music than for his conducting technique. It was published when Koussevitsky (to use the correct spelling) was 56. He came to the Boston Symphony as its conductor in 1924 and remained so for 25 years. The author, a Russian composer (1892-1966) who came to the USA in 1941 and became a citizen, tells us: "In writing this biography I have not been content merely to discuss the facts of Koussevitzky's life and the materials referring to his activities which I had at my disposal, but have attempted at the same time a general outline of the musical art of the first quarter of this century..." (p. 217). This serves little purpose. (A previous reader of the copy of the book this annotator saw, had written in the margin next to one of the sections concerning early 20th-century music: "What has this got to do with Koussevitsky?") (See also no. S.220.)

S.213.   MANNES, David. Music Is My Faith: an autobiography.
         New York: Norton, 1938. (Repr. New York: Da Capo,
         1978.) 270p. illus.
         Mannes (1866-1959) was a violinist-teacher-humanitarian who with his wife, Clara Damrosch Mannes (Walter Damrosch's daughter), founded the Mannes School of Music on New York City's upper East Side in 1916. But Mannes' school is only part of the story, of course, which begins in New York, when he was born. From 1891 to 1912 he was a violinist in Damrosch's New York Symphony Orchestra, and its concert master for fourteen of these years. He was active almost until his death. His daughter, Marva, ends her preface by saying, "As the reader will notice, I have spurred my father's memory by interjecting questions and comments at certain intervals of his narrative--which ... was originally written by us children" (p. 20). There are particularly good cameos of Ignace Paderewski, James Reese Europe, Walter Damrosch, Ernest Bloch, and many others. No index.

S.214.   MUSSULMAN, Joseph A. Dear People ... Robert Shaw:
         a biography. Bloomington: Indiana University Press,

1979. 267p. illus., discog.

An admiring biography of the career of conductor Robert Shaw (b.1916), from his association with Fred Waring's Glee Club in 1938, up to his move to Atlanta in the late 1960s and subsequent work there with the Atlanta Symphony Orchestra. The central one of the book's three sections, "The White-Hot Years," traces in particular the history of the Robert Shaw Chorale from its foundation in 1948, through its many tours, both at home and overseas. At all stages of his career Shaw is seen to have been involved with significant episodes in America's musical life--live music on radio, choral renaissance, changes in the record industry, in concert management, in patronage, encouragement of native composers, etc.; it is this awareness of the different factors affecting musical life that makes Mussulman's portrait more than merely a recitation of biographical fact. The discography is a selected list of recordings, 1944-1977, with record numbers, and there is an index.

S.215.   PERLIS, Vivian. Two Men for Modern Music: E. Robert
        Schmitz and Herman Langinger. Brooklyn: Institute
        for Studies in American Music, 1978.   (I.S.A.M. Mono-
        graphs, No. 9.)   35p.   illus., bibliog. refs.
    Based on two lectures the author gave as I.S.A.M. Re-
search Fellow for 1976-77, and drawing on material from two recently
discovered archival collections, this is an account of the careers of
two men actively involved (but in different areas) in the dissemination of modern music in America between the world wars: Schmitz
(1889-1949), French-born conductor and pianist, founder of the
Pro-Musica Society, and Langinger (b.1900), Austrian-born engraver
for Henry Cowell's New Music Society.

S.216.   PORTER, Andrew. A Musical Season: a critic from abroad
        in America. New York: Viking Press, 1974.   313p.
    Englishman Andrew Porter's first tenure of the post of New
Yorker music critic covered one year, 1972-73. This is his music
criticism from that period--informed, enjoyable writing which (as he
describes in Music of Three Seasons, no. S.217) deliberately shows
greater concern for the work than the performance, and is particularly directed towards contemporary music. Among American works
reviewed here are pieces by Babbitt, Carter, Crumb, Ruth Crawford
Seeger, Sessions, and Thomson. Index.

S.217.   PORTER, Andrew. Music of Three Seasons: 1974-1977.
        New York: Farrar, Straus, Giroux, 1978.   667p.
    Porter's second term on the New Yorker began in 1974;
this hefty selection from his next three years' criticism is devoted
substantially, but not exclusively to New York. The list of American
works discussed is long and includes stage works by Barber, Floyd,
Glass, Alva Henderson, Kirchner, Menotti, Moore, Sessions, and
Thomson, as well as other pieces by Bolcom, Carter, Crumb, Del
Tredici, and Wuorinen. Very full index.

S.218.   RABIN, Carol Price. A Guide to Music Festivals. Stock-
         bridge, Mass.: Berkshire Traveller Press, 1979. 199p.
         illus., bibliog.
   Thorough handbook to all styles of American music festivals,
from fiddlers' conventions to grand opera. For each festival listed
there is a short historical summary, including a list of prominent
performers, and a description of the areas, together with information
on addresses and dates.

S.219.   SELTZER, George, ed. The Professional Symphony Or-
         chestra in the United States. Metuchen, N.J.:
         Scarecrow Press, 1975. 486p. bibliog.
   Well-organized, wide-ranging anthology of some 90 previously published pieces by American (predominantly) and European
writers, varying from two to twenty pages in length, and aiming
to provide a composite view of the "whole animal" of the symphony
orchestra from a wide variety of disciplines. There are seven sections: on history (European origins and US development; writers
include John H. Mueller, Joseph Wechsberg, and Oscar Levant);
on the conductor (general pieces by Schuller, Steinberg, Ormandy,
and others, with appreciations of Bernstein, Solti, and Toscanini);
on the orchestra musicians (mostly short pieces; the longest is by
Donal Henahan on the New York Philharmonic players); on the
audience (including socio-economic analysis by William J. Baumol
and William G. Bowen, and Thomas H. Hill and Helen M. Thompson
on youth concerts); on the music (the shortest section); on
business aspects (the longest, with pieces on management, unions,
subsidies, the problems facing black musicians, etc.); and on the
future (Harold C. Schonberg, Bernstein, et al.). The editor adds
a brief preface to each section, and there is an index.

S.220.   SMITH, Moses. Koussevitzky. New York: Allen, Towne
         & Heath, 1947. 400p. illus., discog.
   This is a full-scale biography of the conductor by a one-
time Boston music critic. He says in his foreword that the book is
"in no sense an 'authorized' biography" and, while he acknowledges
the help of the Lourié biography (no. S.212), he states that its value
"was unfortunately lessened greatly by its numerous errors, by the
author's excessively worshipful attitude toward his subject, and by
the book's inadequate factual content particularly as to omissions of
important matter about Koussevitsky's origins and early life." The
author attempts here and there to reproduce in prose Koussevitsky's
heavily accented pronunciation of English (a questionable exercise)
and he details the Boston Symphony Orchestra's Union problems
(Koussevitsky himself was apparently anti-Union). The appendices,
which list the American works in his repertory, the world premieres
he conducted, and the commissions of the Koussevitsky Foundation
(founded 1942), are most handy. Index.

S.221.   TAUBMAN, Joseph. In Tune with the Music Business;
         introduction by Edward M. Cramer. New York: Law-

Arts Publishers, 1980. 279p.
Edward M. Cramer, author of this book's introduction and
current president of the performing rights organization, Broadcast
Music, Inc., states on p. xvi: "[Taubman's] book is not for bedtime
reading. It is a text and is compactly written. It requires effort by
the reader because it must be studied, but once mastered should
serve as a continuing useful reference." This technical work is
mainly about copyright and entertainment law in the USA. The
author states in his foreword (p. xiii) that the book "is an outgrowth
of my lectures in the course, 'The Business of Music,' in [New
York's] New School for Social Research, for the past several years."

S.222.   UNIVERSITY OF ROCHESTER. Institute of American Music.
American Composers' Concerts, and Festivals of American Music, 1925-1971: cumulative repertoire. Rochester:
The Institute, 1972. 76p.
The creation of Howard Hanson, the annual American Composers' Concerts at the Eastman School of Music provided many composers with the opportunity to hear their music performed, and at
same time cultivated an audience for their music; fittingly, this
catalog is dedicated to Hanson by its unstated compiler, Ruth
Watanabe, in her foreword. The main section is a list, arranged alphabetically by composer, of the music performed, with dates. Other
information includes lists of recordings by the Eastman-Rochester
Symphony Orchestra (conducted by Hanson), the Eastman Wind Ensemble (conducted by Frederick Fennell and Donald Hunsberger),
and the Eastman-Rochester Pops Orchestra (Fennell). Eastman
School publications and prize-winners are also listed.

S.223.   WALLACE, Robert K. A Century of Music-Making: the
lives of Josef & Rosina Lhevinne. Bloomington: Indiana University Press, 1976. 350p. illus., bibliog.,
discog.
A long, restrained, reverential--though necessary--dual
biography of the Russian-born pianists and teachers Josef (1874-
1944) and Rosina (1880-1976) Lhevinne (spelled Levin by Josef's
father in Russia; Josef adopted the new spelling when he came to
the USA in 1919). They lived in New York, playing solo and duo
recitals and giving private lessons. They also toured extensively
and, beginning with its founding in October 1924, were associated
with the Juilliard School of Music. Rosina Lhevinne remained there
almost until her death at the age of 96, perhaps the most famous
piano students of her later years being Van Cliburn and John
Browning. The youthful author of this, the Lhevinnes' only biography to date, was Rosina Lhevinne's secretary, beginning when he
was 24 and she was 88. "A year after that," he states in his preface, "I began work on part of this biography--as my dissertation in
the 'Cultural History' niche of the English department at Columbia
University...." The book "was written with the approval and cooperation of Rosina Lhevinne, and she is principal among its primary
sources." So it is "approved"--a mixed blessing. Personal recollec-

tions are valuable, but the memory of an octogenarian is not always to be relied on. Further, people and events are presented as she wished them presented. The author says he checked her memory where possible, otherwise "we must rely on her veracity...."

e. Outstanding Critics

S.224.   POTTER, Hugh M. False Dawn: Paul Rosenfeld and art in America, 1916-1946. Ann Arbor, Mich.: University Microfilms International for the University of New Hampshire, 1980. 255p. bibliog. refs.

Though best known for his music criticism, Rosenfeld "chafed constantly under what he regarded as this limited view of his critical talent" (p. 3). Not the least merit of this study is that Potter recognizes Rosenfeld's versatility, and, guiding the reader through the range of the critic's thought as it was applied to music, painting, photography, and literature, stresses the interconnections. The most fundamental critical impulse he detects in Rosenfeld's words: "To know what is going on in the life of a civilization, to measure its force and direction, you have but to examine its art" (quoted on p. 188); this was the basis of Rosenfeld's attempt to isolate and trace the growth of "Americanism" in the arts. When studying the music criticism Potter uses not only Rosenfeld's published books (LOAM 276, 277, 377) but his many articles for The Dial, The New Republic, and Modern Music. While the 1920s criticism is seen as dominated by Varèse, the later work is characterized by "expanding horizons"; the last years even brought a revision in Rosenfeld's previously hostile attitude to folk song and jazz. Bibliographical references are to be found in the endnotes; no index.

S.225.   POUND, Ezra. Ezra Pound and Music: the complete criticism; edited with commentary by R. Murray Schafer. New York: New Directions, 1977. London: Faber, 1978. 530p. illus.

Pound (1885-1972) came to music criticism largely because of his interest, unusual at the time, in troubadour melodies, and his consequent concern with performance methods. The criticism, superbly marshalled and edited here by R. Murray Schafer, is mainly of interest for what it tells us of his theories and of the ideas he was to try to incorporate into his own music. Such is the extent of Schafer's contribution, however, that much direct information about Pound may also be obtained. Of the three sections, London 1908-21, France and Italy 1921-27, and Rapollo 1928-41, the first is the longest, containing all Pound's New Age criticism (cf. LOAM 301). The second section is the most relevant to this bibliography, as it contains Schafer's accounts of the Pound-Antheil friendship, of performances of Pound's music, and of the gradual process by which that music became known in the 1920s. The text of Antheil and the Treatise on Harmony is given, with commentary (for instance, on Antheil's own contribution to the ideas). Some account is also given of Pound's Villon opera, Le Testament.

Additional Items

S.226.   AMERICAN MUSIC CENTER. Compositions, Libretti, and
         Translations, Supported by the National Endowment for
         the Arts Composer/Librettist Program. New York:
         American Music Center, 1978. 35p.

S.227.   _____. The National Endowment for the Arts Composer/
         Librettist Program Collection at the American Music
         Center. New York: American Music Center, 1979.
         304p.

S.228.   CELENTANO, John, and REYNOLDS, C. A Catalogue of
         Contemporary American Chamber Music. Lawrenceville:
         American String Teachers' Association, 1975.

S.229.   CHASINS, Abram. Leopold Stokowski: a profile. New
         York: Hawthorn Books, 1979. 313p.

S.230.   McLENDON, James W. Biography as Theology: how life
         stories can remake today's theology. Nashville: Abing-
         don Press, 1974. (Includes a chapter on Ives.)

S.231.   THE MUSICAL Blue Book of America. New York: Musical
         Blue Book Corp., 1915-1922. (Biennial publication, ed.
         Emma L. Trapper, then H. Greene.)

S.232.   ROBINSON, Paul. Stokowski. New York: Vanguard
         Press, 1977. 154p.

S.233.   VERMORCKEN, Elizabeth Moorhead. These Two Were Here:
         Louise Homer and Willa Cather. Pittsburgh: University
         of Pittsburgh Press, 1950. (Repr. Norwood, Pa.:
         Norwood Editions, 1977; Philadelphia: West, 1978.)
         62p.

S.234.   ZIMMERMANN, Walter. Desert Plants: conversations with
         23 American Musicians. Vancouver: the author, 1976.
         373p.

E.   THE MUSIC OF THE AMERICAN INDIAN

1.   Reference Works

S.235.   LEE, Dorothy Sara.   Native North American Music and
Oral Data: a catalogue of sound recordings 1893-1976;
foreword by Willard Rhodes.   Bloomington: Indiana
University Press, 1979.   463p.
Computer-produced catalog of the recordings of North
American Indian music held at the Archives of Traditional Music,
Indiana University.   The 500 separate accessions include field, commercial, and broadcast recordings.   Information given includes collector, performer, depositor, editor, accession number, culture
group, year recorded; there are added entries in the catalog for
many of these, plus indexes of culture groups and of the subject
descriptive terms also used in the entries.

2.   General Studies

(See also S.284)

S.236.   BIERHORST, John.   A Cry from the Earth: music of the
North American Indians.   New York: Four Winds Press,
1979.   112p.   illus., bibliog. refs.
Accompanied by an LP (Folkways FC 7777), this is an attractively produced, basically introductory volume for schools, sur-
veying the different uses of music, its role in daily life and at times
of great emotion or danger.   Spanning a period from the late 18th
to the mid-20th century, it draws on the work of many important
collectors and introduces examples from a wide range of tribes and
regions.   Numerous music illustrations are included, many transcribed from field recordings.

S.237.   FICHTER, George S.   American Indian Music and Musical
Instruments; with instructions for making the instruments;
drawings and diagrams by Marie and Nils Ostberg.   New
York: McKay, 1978.   115p.   illus., bibliog.
An attractive book for younger readers.   The first half is
devoted to clear commentary on the music and some examples of the
music itself (the latter "based on the Bulletins of the Bureau of
American Ethnology," according to the copyright page).   The second

half is devoted to instructions and diagrams for constructing some
Indian instruments (for those with ready access to rawhide).

S.238.   FRISBIE, Charlotte J. Music and Dance Research of South-
         western United States Indians: past trends, present
         activities, and suggestions for future research. Detroit:
         Information Coordinators, 1977. (Detroit Studies in Mu-
         sic Bibliography, No. 36.) 109p. illus., bibliog.
         The retrospective part of this critical review sets out to
describe the orientations, methodologies and concerns of research
carried out between 1880 and 1976. This is followed by one chapter
which attempts to identify present research approaches, and by another in which possible future directions are indicated. Music and
dance are treated separately throughout. An appendix contains information on archives gathered in response to a questionnaire sent
out in 1975. The extensive bibliography (which could have benefited
from a subject index) covers 42 pages and includes books and articles.

S.239.   HERNDON, Marcia. Native American Music. Darby, Pa.:
         Norwood Editions, 1980. 233p. bibliog.
         A Native American herself, the author combines the ad-
vantages of that perspective with those of a trained ethnomusicologist
to produce a thoughtful, undogmatic, anthropologically-based survey
"from a topical, theoretical, and historical point of view" (preface).
The centrally important chapter is the third, in which she examines
and contrasts the respective world views of Euro-American and Native Americans. This enables her to draw some conclusions about
Native American art: it is "intuitive-experimental," an "art of
utility," and "art of participation and efficacy through action" (pp.
85-88). Turning more specifically to music, she defines and describes (following Bruno Nettl--see LOAM 399 and no. S.244--with
reservations) six music areas, explores ways in which music is used
for its power, discusses the role of music in nativistic movements,
such as the Ghost Dance, in the Native American church, and in
ceremonials of the Kwakiutl and the Eskimo, and describes its close
association with the life cycle. Finally, this topical material is tied
in with Nettl's music areas and the characteristics of each area are
enumerated, with music examples. The 24-page bibliography is excellent, and there is an index.

S.240.   HIGHWATER, Jamake. Ritual of the Wind: North American
         Indian ceremonies, music, and dances. New York:
         Viking Press, 1977. 192p. illus., bibliog., discog.
         Finely illustrated with (mostly historical) photographs, this
is a powerful but all-too-often generalized and emotive account of
"the way in which (Indian) ceremonies and dances perfectly reflect
the otherwise obscure principles of Indian sensibility" (p. 11).
Wind is identified as a vital conceptual metaphor in Indian religious
life, and its association with dance (the "breath-of-life made visible"--p. 16) is of central importance. Music features mainly in a

chapter entitled "The Initiation," describing songs sung at various ceremonies. The main focus of the book is on ritual action as the "most tenacious aspect of Indian life" (p. 170). (Charges amounting to plagiarism are leveled at the author by Charlotte J. Frisbie in Ethnomusicology, 24, No. 3 [Sept. 1980], p. 589.)

S.241.   HOFMANN, Charles. War Hoops and Medicine Songs. Boston: Boston Music Co., 1952. 34p. illus., bibliog., discog.

A small but good collection of songs intended primarily for a younger audience, and aimed at encouraging performance. Most of the melodies were transcribed by Catherine Ficcio.

S.242.   McALLESTER, David P., ed. Readings in Ethnomusicology. New York: Johnson Reprint Corporation, 1971. 370p. illus., bibliogs.

American Indian music is the subject of three of the articles in this classic collection of ethnomusicological scholarship. George Herzog's "Plains Ghost Dance and Great Basin Music" (1935) is the earliest. Willard Rhodes, in "A Study of Music Diffusion Based on the Wandering of the Opening Peyote Song" (1958), examines several versions of the one song, sacred and secular. David P. McAllester's "Indian Music in the Southwest" (see LOAM 414) briefly discusses the music of the Pueblos, Apaches and Navahos.

The volume also contains "Prolegomena to a Study of the Principal Melodic Families of British-American Folksong," by Samuel P. Bayard (1950), a 45-page "prelude to studies ... [in] melodic identification" (p. 65).

S.243.   MAY, Elizabeth, ed. Music of Many Cultures: an introduction; foreword by Mantle Hood. Berkeley: University of California Press, 1980. 431p. illus., bibliogs., discogs.

A series of introductory ethnomusicological essays, including one by David P. McAllester on "North American Native Music." Illustrated with photographs of instruments, a map, and music examples, it outlines the various characteristics of Indian music by regions and tribe.

S.244.   REESE, Gustave, and SNOW, Robert J., eds. Essays in Musicology in Honor of Dragan Plamenac on His 70th Birthday. Pittsburgh: University of Pittsburgh Press, 1969. 391p. illus., bibliog.

Includes "Musical Areas Reconsidered: a Critique of North American Indian Research," by Bruno Nettl, in which the author suggests modifications to the scheme of musical areas he began earlier (North American Indian Musical Styles, LOAM 399), and comments on the concept of musical areas in general.

84 / Literature of American Music

3. Music of Particular Tribes

S.245.   BAHR, Donald M., et al. Piman Shamanism and Staging
          Sickness, by Donald M. Bahr, Juan Gregorio, David I.
          Lopez; Alberto Alvarez, editor. Tucson: University of
          Arizona Press, 1974. 332 illus., bibliog.
   "Singing is the ultimate resort of shamans attempting to
divine an unknowable sickness" (p. 234); both in diagnosing and
curing an illness, the shaman's use of songs represents a request
for assistance. This ethnological study of the Piman shamans of
Arizona, drawing on material supplied by Juan Gregorio, a Papago
Shaman from South Roca, does not examine the songs as such,
but includes a substantial number of texts as well as information on
the role of the song.

S.246.   CLARK, Laverne Harrell. They Sang for Horses: the im-
          pact of the horse on Navajo and Apache folklore. Tuc-
          son: University of Arizona Press, 1966. 225p. illus.,
          bibliog.
   This study of the symbolic significance of the horse in
myths, tales, and legendary lore includes consideration of how that
significance has been defined and clarified in song. Texts of a
number of songs are given, in English translations.

S.247.   DENSMORE, Frances. Music of the Maidu Indians of Cali-
          fornia. Los Angeles: Southwest Museum, 1958. (Pub-
          lications of the Frederick Webb Hodge Anniversary Pub-
          lication Fund, 7.) 67p. illus., bibliog.
   "The life and history of the Indians of California has been
a sad one," remarks Carl S. Dentzel in his preface to this study-
collection, "and precious little about them has been preserved.
Among the significant remains has been some of the music of their
ceremonies." The songs collected here were all obtained at Chico
in the Sacramento Valley in 1937; Miss Densmore recorded them from
the singing of Amanda Wilson and Pablo Sylvers, the only two members of the Maidu in Chico to remember the old songs. The 53 songs
are grouped into nine categories, the largest of which are songs of
ceremonial dances, and songs of social dances. The music of each
song is provided, and some translations are given; there are also
notes and commentary on musical structure, and melodic analyses.

S.248.   FRISBIE, Charlotte J., ed. Southwestern Indian Ritual
          Drama. Albuquerque: University of New Mexico Press,
          1980. 372p. illus., bibliog.
   Among these ten papers presented at an Advanced Seminar
sponsored by the School of American Research in Albuquerque in
April 1978 are two specifically on song. Barbara Tedlock's study of
song of the Zuni Kachina society shows that there is a native song
classification system involving full command of the process of composition, and that composition is an individual activity, modified by the

group in performance. Leanne Hinton examines vocables in Havasu-
pai song, suggesting that sung syllables are preferred to language
when "social solidarity is being expressed, and where people are
seeking a sensation of spirituality" (p. 299). Other papers touching
on music are "Singing for Life: the Mescalero Apache Girls' Puberty
Ceremony," by Claire R. Farrer, "Ritual Drama in the Navajo House
Blessing Ceremony," by Charlotte J. Frisbie, and "Shootingway, an
Epic Drama of the Navajos," by David P. McAllester. Index.

S.249.   GOODMAN, Linda. Music and Dance in Northwest Coast
          Indian Life. Tsaile, Arizona: Navajo Community College
          Press, 1977. (Occasional Papers, Vol. 3, No. 3.) 38p.
          illus., bibliog., discog.
          Like the booklets by Haefer (no. S.250) and Rhodes (no.
S.255), this introductory text is part of a curriculum development
project. Attractively designed and produced, it focuses on the music
of the Nootka and Kwakiutl, describing the links between music and
environment, the various categories of song, the instruments, the
song texts, and summarizing the general characteristics of Northwest
coast music.

S.250.   HAEFER, J. Richard. Papago Music and Dance. Tsaile,
          Arizona: Navajo Community College Press, 1977. (Oc-
          casional Papers, Vol. 3, No. 4.) 37p. illus., bibliog.,
          discog.
          Neatly produced introductory booklet covering the cultural
background, features of music and dance, instruments, the place of
music in culture, and song types. There is equal attention to historical and contemporary musical categories.

S.251.   LUCKERT, Karl W. Coyoteway: a Navajo Holyway healing
          ceremonial; Johnny C. Cooke, Navajo interpreter. Tuc-
          son: University of Arizona Press, 1979. 243p. illus.,
          bibliog.
          Coyoteway is a nine-night healing ceremonial, during which
songs are chanted. Many texts are included in the descriptions
here, given in free English translation and accompanied by some music notation. All the songs were recorded by Man With Palomino
Horse, one of two surviving Coyoteway singers. Index.

S.252.   McINTOSH, David S. Folk Songs and Singing Games of the
          Illinois Ozarks; edited by Dale Whiteside; illustrations by
          Greg Trafidlo. Carbondale: Southern Illinois University
          Press; London: Feffer & Simons, 1974. 119p. illus.,
          bibliog.
          Song collection with words and melodies, notes on sources,
and general commentary. Included are numerous items of local significance.

S.253.   MITCHELL, Frank. Navajo Blessingway Singer: the auto-
          biography of Frank Mitchell, 1881-1967; edited by

Charlotte J. Frisbie and David P. McAllester. Tucson: University of Arizona Press, 1978. 446p. illus., bibliog.

Blessingway is a centrally significant Navajo song ceremonial; performed to ensure good health, it is "preventative in purpose, prophylactic rather than curative" (p. 1). The materials for this autobiography were gathered over a period of eighteen years, Frisbie joining McAllester in 1963, at which point Mitchell became convinced of the importance of passing on his knowledge, and the recording of his life story began. The parts of the narrative which make most reference to song and singing are Chapter 6 ("In the Beginning," a myth of Indian origins which includes examples of Earth's Surface songs, Placing of the Mountain songs, and others); Chapter 7, in which Mitchell describes how he became interested in learning to be a Blessingway singer; and Chapter 8, where the role of a Blessingway singer is described. But the entire narrative is concerned, at bottom, with cultural processes, roles, and relationships, and the place of song ritual in these is constantly to the fore.

S.254. ORTIZ, Simon. Song, Poetry and Language: expression and perception. Tsaile, Arizona: Navajo Community College Press, (1977?). (Occasional Papers, Vol. 3, No. 5.) 12p.

Navajo poet Ortiz battles without total success to articulate a profoundly felt idea: how song (for his father, for himself, and by extension for his people) conjoins the process of perception of the world outside oneself with that of expression of one's feelings towards it. This conjunction emphasizes that the meaning of song lies in the point of relationship between the outer and the inner worlds.

S.255. RHODES, Robert. Hopi Music and Dance. Tsaile, Arizona: Navajo Community College Press, 1977. (Occasional Papers, Vol. 3, No. 2.) 30p. illus., bibliog., discog.

More general than the other booklets in this series, in order to "avoid the specifics which would or could offend Hopi's or which they feel should not be broadly disseminated" (p. 2), the text includes brief descriptions of ceremonies, dances, and of how songs are composed. (Rhodes is the author of Selected Hopi Secular Music: Analysis and Transcription, unpublished Ed.D. thesis, Arizona State University, 1973.)

S.256. SPINDEN, Herbert Joseph. Songs of the Tewa; translated by Herbert Joseph Spinden, preceded by an essay on American Indian poetry.... New York: published under the auspices of the Exposition of Indian Tribal Arts, 1933. (Repr. New York: AMS Press; Santa Fe, N.M.: Sunstone Press, 1976.) 125p. illus., bibliog. refs.

A collection of some 70 song texts in English ("home songs," sacred chants, ceremonial songs, magic songs, and prayers) is preceded by a 65-page essay in which the author, while centering his

attention on the Tewa of New Mexico, widens his field of vision to
consider the place of poetry in Indian arts, the various song types
(reincarnation lullabies, guardian spirit songs, vocational songs,
etc.) and techniques of translating Indian poetry.

S.257.   UNDERHILL, Ruth Murray. Singing for Power: the song
         magic of the Papago Indians of Southern Arizona.
         Berkeley: University of California Press, 1938 (repr.
         1968). 158p. illus.
A beautifully written study, compassionate and understanding, with evocative, unsentimental descriptions of Papago song
ritual in its role as "a magic which called upon the powers of Nature
and constrained them to man's will" (introduction). The songs on
which the study is based (and which are given in translation) were
"culled from fourteen months of patient communion with the old men"
(p. 8). In the sequence of ceremonies described, these songs are
used as a means to cause events to happen; thus in the ritual of
drinking liquor from giant cactus when the rainy season is near,
the songs are the magic which will "pull down the clouds." Such
song for the Papago is not composed but is itself a magic given to
the worthy (who combine the qualities essential for a poet--heroism
and practicality) on behalf of all.

S.258.   WOODS, W. Raymond, and LIBERTY, Margot, eds. An-
         thropology on the Great Plains. Lincoln: University of
         Nebraska Press, 1980. 306p. bibliogs.
         Includes "Plains Indians Music and Dance," by William K.
Powers, which summarizes "the anthropological status of Plains music
and dance and suggests some theoretical and methodological considerations for further study" (p. 214). Excellent bibliography.

Additional Items

S.259.   CUMMINS, Marjorie W. The Tache-Yokuts: Indians of the
         San Joaquin Valley, their lives, songs and stories.
         Fresno, Calif.: Pioneer Publishing Co., 1979. 174p.

S.260.   DIAMOND, Stanley, ed. Theory and Practice: essays
         presented to Gene Weltfish. The Hague: Mouton, 1980.
         362p. (Includes "The First Snake Song," by David P.
         McAllester.)

S.261.   GLASS, Paul, ed. Songs and Stories of the American In-
         dians; with rhythm indications for drum accompaniment.
         New York: Grosset & Dunlap, 1968. 61p.

S.262.   HUENEMANN, Lynn. Songs and Dances of Native America:
         a resource text for teachers and students. Tsaile,
         Arizona: Education House, 1978. 254p.

S.263.   KATZ, Jane B., ed. This Song Remembers: self-portraits
          of Native Americans in the arts. Boston: Houghton
          Mifflin, 1980. 207p. ("Performing Arts," pp. 125-154.)

S.264.   LAUBIN, Reginald, and LAUBIN, Gladys. Indian Dances of
          North America: their importance to Indian life; foreword
          by Louis R. Bruce. Norman: University of Oklahoma
          Press, 1979. 538p.

S.265.   McALLESTER, David P., ed. Hogans: Navajo Houses and
          House Songs; house poems from Navajo ritual translated
          and arranged. Middletown, Conn.: Wesleyan University
          Press, 1980. 113p.

S.266.   PIETROFORTE, Alfred. Songs of the Yokuts and Paiutes;
          edited by Vinson Brown. Healdsburg, Calif.: Nature-
          graph Publishers, 1965. 64p.

F. FOLK MUSIC

Note: this section is primarily, though not exclusively, concerned with the folk music of white Americans. Works specifically devoted to black folk music will be found in Section G.

1. General Works on Folk Music

S.267.   BOULTON, Laura. The Music Hunter: the autobiography
        of a career. Garden City, N.Y.: Doubleday, 1969.
        513p. illus.
   Laura Bolton's career as a collector represented "thirty-five years of determined and dedicated effort to secure the tapes and records of the music of peoples on all five continents..." (introduction, by Andrew W. Cordier). The densely packed record of that odyssey is singularly short on specific scholarly information, on the author, her associates, or her 28 expeditions (which included the North Western and South Western USA); a genteel travel diary, it belongs with that school of collecting which sees music as readily transcending barriers (of race, culture, politics), rather than expressing cultural dynamics. The index is somewhat unsystematic.

S.268.   MERRIAM, Alan P. The Anthropology of Music. (Evans-
        ton): Northwestern University Press, 1964. 358p.
        bibliog.
   "There is an anthropology of music, and it is within the grasp of both musicologist and anthropologist" (p. viii): with this assertion Merriam moved to close the gap between the two disciplines, and "to provide a theoretical framework for the study of music as human behavior" (ibid.). Besides its importance as a pioneering study, the book is cited here for the numerous occasions on which examples are referred to of music behavior from the USA: Flathead Indians appear frequently and in various contexts (physical and verbal behavior, composition, interrelationships between the arts, etc.); jazz musicians are discussed under the rubric of the social behavior of musicians, and jazz in the context of "music as symbolic behavior" and of "music and cultural dynamics." In all instances the particular interest is in comparative study with music and musical practice from other parts of the world (especially Africa). The bibliography is a long list of references cited, and there is a thorough index.

2. Folk Music in the United States

a. Reference Works

S.269. AMERICAN FOLKLORE Films and Videotapes: an index.
        Memphis: Center for Southern Folklore, 1976. 338p.
        illus.
Formed in 1972 "to document folk traditions of the South,
through films, photographs, and taped recordings," the Center
(directors: Bill Ferris and Judy Peiser) began in 1974 to collect
information for a catalog of existing films and videotapes. The
completed index lists over 1,800 titles, and supplements are planned.
A subject index lists the titles of films on musical topics, of which
there is a substantial number, either under one of the nineteen major subdivisions of "Folk Music" (among them Afro-American, Bluegrass, Cajun, Indian) or under personal names. For full information
on each film the user then turns to the main section, where films
are listed alphabetically by title, with details of length, format,
date, producer, distributor, and a descriptive annotation. An additional section gives details of special collections not available for
rental or purchase. Jazz and blues documentaries are also covered
by Meeker (LOAM 921); each index includes films not listed in the
other, but Meeker's coverage of this particular area is generally
more thorough, and his annotations more penetrating.

S.270. BAGGELAAR, Kristin, and MILTON, Donald. Folk Music:
        more than a song. New York: Crowell, 1976. 419p.
        illus.
        _____. The Folk Music Encyclopaedia. London: Omni-
        bus Press, 1977. 419p. illus.
The U.S. title conceals the fact that this is a (mainly biographical) reference work (the UK title is an unnecessary inflation).
The compilers' approach is extremely selective, including only individuals "who have made or are still making the most conspicuous
impact on the folk song and its development" (p. vii). In addition
to individuals (who include in their number notable collectors), there
are entries (even more selective) for genres, instruments, festivals,
journals, and organizations (bluegrass, fiddle, Newport, Sing Out,
and National Folk Festival Association). "Folk" is not defined, but
is interpreted to include early country music, the folk song revival,
bluegrass, blues, and folk rock. The compilers evidently wrote to
many of the individuals for information; not all replied (they are
generally quoted when they did), but were included anyway. The
resulting unevenness is not compensated by any particular sharpness
of insight; a generous space allocation for each entry tends to result in a diffuse, non-critical style.

S.271. BRIEGLEB, Ann, ed. Directory of Ethnomusicological Sound
        Recording Collections in the U.S. and Canada. Ann Ar-
        bor, Mich.: Society for Ethnomusicology, (1971).
        (Special Series, No. 2.) 46p. bibliog.

Organized state-by-state, then alphabetically by city, this directory provides three categories of information for each of the 124 archives and private collections listed: name, address, phone number, curator, hours of opening, and indication of public or private status; playback facilities available; description of the content of the collection. There is an index to the geographical content of collections, in which North America's representation is strong. For long a much-used handbook, Briegleb's work has become outdated in some respects (e.g., curators' names and phone numbers) and has been largely superseded, as far as American traditional music is concerned, by the large and estimable new directory, Resources of American Music History, by D. W. Krummel, et al. (Urbana: University of Illinois Press, 1981), yet retains its usefulness in certain areas. Its descriptive notes are sometimes more detailed than the newer book, with its duty to summarize whole collections of American music, not just the ethnic parts, can manage (though, it should be noted, the opposite is also true); and its concern with worldwide traditional musics means that not infrequently a collection of Americana is seen to belong in or alongside a wider or more diversified collection--thus providing some view of context.

S.272.   FLANAGAN, Cathleen C., and FLANAGAN, John T.
         American Folklore: a bibliography, 1950-1974. Metuchen,
         N.J.: Scarecrow Press, 1977. 406p.
         The period covered by this bibliography follows on where Haywood (LOAM 429) stopped (though the compilers do not mention this, and are not very generous in their remarks on their predecessor). Of the sixteen sections, containing in all over 3,500 items (books, articles, and chapters in symposia and collections), the sixth, "Ballads and Songs," is most relevant to American music. In this some 670 items are listed in three parts: Collections; Criticism; History and Theory. Besides the mainstream of Anglo-American ballad and folk song there is coverage also of non-English folk material, country music, and black folk music. None of these is as thoroughly covered as the main tradition, and for some subjects (e.g., blues) the coverage is so slender as to be misleading. There are frequent short annotations. Other relevant material appears in sections 5 ("General Folklore"), 11 ("Folk Heroes"), and 16 ("Obituaries"). There is an author index, but the lack of an index to topics and to persons as subjects is a drawback to full use of the book (e.g., there is no easy way to locate all books and articles on Woody Guthrie or Aunt Molly Jackson).

S.273.   INDIANA UNIVERSITY. Archives of Traditional Music.
         A Catalog of Phonorecordings of Music and Oral Data
         Held by the Archives of Traditional Music. Boston:
         G. K. Hall, 1975. 531p.
         This substantial collection, numbering a quarter of a million individual items, includes a large quantity of American music in recorded form. (Its particular overall strengths are the music of Africa, Afro-America, Latin America, North American Indians,

and Indiana.) Arrangement is by accession order, with indexes of geographical areas, culture groups and subjects, collectors, performers, recording companies. HRAF (Human Relations Area Files) symbols are included in the reproduced catalog entries, which also provide details of country of origin, title, performer, date and record issue number. Wire recordings, cylinders, discs and tapes are represented; some unissued field recordings are also included, but the catalog concentrates on commercially issued material.

S.274.   LUMPKIN, Ben Gray. Folksongs on Records; with Norman
         L. ("Brownie") McNeil. Issue Three: cumulative, in-
         cluding essential material in Issue One and Two. Boul-
         der, Colo.: Folksongs on Records; Denver: Alan
         Swallow, 1950. 98p. illus., bibliog.
         Now principally of value to the collector of 78s, this was a
brief but pioneering attempt in its day to come to terms with the
discography of folk song. Over 4,000 records are listed by the two
main compilers (assisted, apparently, by over 40 contributors).
The United States is strongly represented. The four categories of
the main listing are "Folksongs, Ballads, Spirituals, Work Songs,"
"Indian (American) Songs and Dances," "Folk Dance Records and
Albums," and "Library of Congress Pressings." Arrangement is by
performer, except in the American Indian section, or by title in the
case of anthologies. The index provides for access by type (Child
ballads, Irish songs, etc.), but not by song title. (Such a list
was intended, "if demand is sufficient," according to Lumpkin's
"Plans for Future Issues," but neither the list nor the further issues
were published. (Issues One and Two were published in the late
1940s.)

S.275.   SANDBERG, Larry, and WEISSMAN, Dick. The Folk Music
         Sourcebook. New York: Knopf, 1976. 260p. illus.,
         bibliogs., discogs.
         This excellent reference guide to source materials on North
American "folk and folk-based music," produced under the aegis of
the Denver Folklore Center, is a larger, more comprehensive version
of a catalogue compiled by Harry Tuft, proprieter of the Center, and
Phyllis Wagner in 1966. It combines in an attractive presentation
thorough bibliographical and discographical listings with detailed information on performance, and thus proves useful to scholars, performers, and casual listeners. There are four sections. (i) Listening (mainly by Sandberg) is an annotated listing ("as comprehensive
as the availability of information allows"--p. 3) of recordings, with
some biographical and critical comments on individual artists. The
main divisions are: Black American music (including blues, ragtime
and gospel), North American Indian music (by David McAllester),
Chicano music (by Philip Sonnichsen), Canadian folk music, Cajun
music, Anglo-American music (divided into regions, instrumental albums, and sea songs), Western swing, and Contemporary music and
the folk song revival (with a contribution by Ralph Rinzler); (ii)
Learning (by Weissman) is an extensive annotated bibliography of

songbooks, reference works, and instrumental books; (iii) Playing contains information on the manufacture, purchase, and care of primary folk instruments (banjo, dulcimer, guitar, mandolin, etc.), with a section by David Ferretta on the five-string banjo, and some basic instruction on performance; (iv) Hanging Out lists organizations, festivals, centers, periodicals, films, videotapes and archives. Glossary and index.

S.276.   TUDOR, Dean, and TUDOR, Nancy. Grass Roots Music. Littleton, Colo.: Libraries Unlimited, 1979. 367p. bibliog.
        A "pre-selected evaluative guide to the best and most enduring recorded grass roots music ... available on long-playing discs and tapes" (p. 11), aimed both at the librarian and the individual collector. Approximately 1,700 records are included, represented in some 850 annotated entries (for those with personal or institutional budgets of less than $7,500 (1978), 220 key albums are identified). The cut-off date is 1974. "Grass roots music" centers on white folk and folk-derived music, including the main folk tradition, folk revivals, old time music, bluegrass, southwestern (Western swing, cowboy songs), country (the largest section), sacred music (very short), and troubadours (singer-songwriters). A preliminary section entitled "Ethnic Offerings" is disappointingly small. Each section has a knowledgeable introduction, "synthesizing" existing knowledge in an uncontroversial way. Annotations are generous, informative, only occasionally diffuse. Bibliographical guidance is provided in a list of 100 books and 21 periodical citations, and there is a label directory and an artists' index. (For the other volumes in this series, "American Popular Music on Elpee," see nos. S.540, S.661, S.817. For a cumulative edition of all four volumes, see S/A 517.)

b. General Studies

S.277.   BECK, Horace P., ed. Folklore in Action: essays for discussion in honor of MacEdward Leach. Philadelphia: American Folklore Society, 1962. 210p. bibliog. refs.
        Samuel P. Bayard's piece, "Decline and 'Revival' of Anglo-American Folk Music" takes a pessimistic view of the situation facing folk music ("there seems to be no function the inherited folk music can perform in our society"--(p. 20), one which he was to change later ("I had yet to learn that the condition was only temporary"--Guntharp, no. S.326, p. 11). The volume also includes "The Folk Ballad and the Literary Ballad: an essay in classification," by Tristram P. Coffin, and "Anglo-Irish Balladry in North America," by G. Malcolm Laws.

S.278.   BRUNVAND, Jan Harold. The Study of American Folklore: an introduction. New York: Norton, 1968. 383p. bibliog. refs.
        _____.   _____. 2nd ed. New York: Norton, 1978.

460p. bibliog. refs.
A basic, reliable guide to folklore types, with definitions
of genres, outlines of their major characteristics, summaries of the
contributions of important scholars, and detailed bibliographic guidance. For the second edition the material is reorganized to come
together in chapters 10-12, which contain clear accounts of folksongs,
ballads and folk music (definitions, characteristic features, types),
and outline the first principles of folk music analysis.

S.279.   CARD, Caroline, et al., eds. Discourse in Ethnomusicology:
essays in honor of George List; editors Caroline Card,
John Hasse, Robert L. Singer, Ruth M. Stone. Bloom-
ington: Ethnomusicology Publications Group, Indiana
University, 1978. 298p. illus., bibliog.
Of the set of seven essays forming the section "Studies:
the Americas," three are directly relevant to music in the USA:
Frank J. Gillis investigates the metamorphosis of the Old World
Derbyshire ballad "The Derby Ram" into the New World jazz tune
"Oh, Didn't He Ramble"; John Hasse's piece, "The Study of Ragtime: a Review and a Preview," is a very useful examination of
ragtime literature, including dissertations; and Paula Tadlock discusses black and white shape-note singing in Mississippi. Two of
the other pieces should be noted also: Barbara Seitz's discussion
of the Mexican corrido, and Abraham Cáceres' preliminary comments
on the marimba in the Americas. A bibliography of George List's
writings is included.

S.280.   JACKSON, Bruce, ed. Folklore & Society: essays in
honor of Benj. A. Botkin. Hatboro, Pa.: Folklore As-
sociates, 1966. 192p. bibliog. refs.
This Festschrift for a famous song scholar includes seven
items of musical interest: Willard Rhodes, "Folk Music, Old an New";
Kenneth S. Goldstein, "The Ballad Scholar and the Long-Playing
Record"; Charles Haywood, "Negro Minstrelsy and Shakespearean
Burlesque"; MacEdward Leach, "John Henry"; Judith McCulloh,
"Some Child Ballads on Hillbilly Records" (repr. Los Angeles: John
Edwards Memorial Foundation, 1967--see LOAM 616); Ruth Rubin,
"Slavic Influences in Yiddish Folksong"; and Ellen Stekert, "Cents
and Nonsense in the Urban Folksong Movement: 1930-1966."

S.281.   NEVELL, Richard. A Time to Dance: American country
dancing from hornpipes to hot hash; with drawings and
wood engravings by Randy Miller. New York: St.
Martin's Press, 1977. 272p. illus., bibliog.
An attractive book providing a history of American country
dancing, profiles of country dancing in various locations around the
country, instructions on how to do some of the dances, actual tunes,
and anecdotes about and quotes from miscellaneous dancers, musicians,
and callers. While this is a book primarily about dance, the author
duly acknowledges the role of music: "The music is undoubtedly the
mainstay of the dancers" (p. 128). That mainstay is usually per-

formed by a lone fiddler or a fiddler and pianist or a group of instrumentalists. It is usually traditional and performed with or without written out parts. Musicians will probably be most interested in the section marked "Collections of Fiddle Tunes" that begins on p. 261.

3. Anglo-American Folk Song Studies and Collections

(See also S.341)

S.282. BRONSON, Bertrand Harris. The Ballad As Song. Berkeley: University of California Press, 1969. 324p. bibliog. refs.

These are eighteen essays by a noted scholar, all but two originally published in various American and European journals between 1940 and 1968; they chart Bronson's persistence in bringing together the traditional British and American ballads and the music to which they were sung. This is especially prominent in three pieces: "Folk Song and the Modes," "On the Union of Words and Music in the 'Child' Ballads," and "Toward the Comparative Analysis of British-American Folk-Tunes." Other pieces discuss the morphology of ballad tunes, and the interdependence of tune and text (both of these with particular reference to the British Isles). Items of specifically American interest include reviews of books by George Pullen Jackson and Frank C. Brown, an overview of developments in folk song in the USA, 1910-1960, and a consideration of the effects of recording on folk song. Index.

S.283. BRONSON, Bertrand Harris, ed. The Singing Tradition of Child's Popular Ballads. Princeton, N.J.: Princeton University Press, 1976. 526p. bibliog.

Despite the title, this is not a new book, but a one-volume abridgement of the same compiler's massive work of scholarship, The Traditional Tunes of the Child Ballads (LOAM 464).

S.284. BROWNE, Ray B., et al., eds. New Voices in American Studies; edited by Ray B. Browne, Donald M. Winkelman and Allen Hayman. West Lafayette, Ind.: Purdue University Studies, 1966. 165p. bibliog. refs.

Included in these papers from the Mid-America Conference on Literature, History, Popular Culture and Folklore, held at Purdue University in 1965, are three of musical interest. Bruno Nettl outlines some influences of Western civilization on North American Indian music, C. E. Nelson undertakes a survey of the versions of the ballad "Thomas Rhymer" (five of which are recorded by Child), and Donald M. Winkelman, in "Some Rhythmic Aspects of the Child Ballad," makes a case for the importance of rhythmic symmetry in understanding ballad structure and the folk process.

S.285. BURT, Olive Woolley. American Murder Ballads and Their

Stories. New York: Oxford University Press, 1958.
272p. illus.

Teacher-turned-journalist Mrs. Burt's book has one of the
more bizarre beginnings in American music literature: "I suppose
my interest in murder ballads was first awakened in my infancy and
on my mother's knee" (foreword). Good preparation for a Utah
childhood, perhaps; but it also gave her an obsessive interest
which, on the evidence of the book, she pursued with flair and not
a little relish. The fruit of her nationwide collecting is a body of
a hundred or so ballad texts ("each song tells of an actual murder
committed in this country"--p. xii-xiii) which she organizes into
eight broad subject groups (e.g., "friends and relations," "the
profit motive," "a matter of pigment"). In each case the texts are
linked by a narrative which mixes personal experiences and anecdotes with a retelling of each episode--an unscholarly method, possibly, but also an informative and often absorbing one. Each chapter is prefaced by a list of the songs it features, with an indication
of those for which unaccompanied melodies are also given (about one
quarter). These titles are omitted from the index proper, which
contains entries for names, and for regions.

S.286.   CHASE, Richard, ed. American Folk Tales and Songs and
Other Examples of English-American Tradition as Pre-
served in the Appalachian Mountains and Elsewhere in
the United States; music edited with the assistance of
Raymond Kane McLain, Annabel Morris Buchanan, and
John Powell. New York: New American Library, 1956.
(Repr. New York: Dover Publications, 1971). 239p.
illus., bibliog.

Chase (b.1904), "one of the more audacious of the folk-
revival entrepreneurs of the 1930s" (David Whisnant, All That Is
Native and Fine (Chapel Hill: University of North Carolina Press,
1983], p. 202), was closely involved with the White Top Folk Festival
in Virginia, where he worked with McLain, Buchanan, and Powell.
(Charles Seeger described White Top in 1936 as "reactionary to the
core" [Whisnant, p. 207].) His collection is evenly divided between
tales and songs. Sections 2-5, pp. 107-223 present a selection of:
ballads, songs, and hymns; games and country dances; fiddle tunes;
and "odds and ends." Tunes are mostly given in shape-notes, with
guitar chords. There is a title index. (Chase also compiled an earlier, more modest volume, Old Songs and Singing Games [Chapel Hill:
University of North Carolina Press, 1938], while he was a director
at White Top.)

S.287.   COHEN, Anne B. Poor Pearl, Poor Girl! the murdered-
girl stereotype in ballad and newspaper. Austin: University of Texas Press, 1973. (Publications of the
American Folklore Society, Memoir Series, 58.) 131p.
illus., bibliog.

The murder of Pearl Bryan in Kentucky in 1896 not only
resulted in a celebrated court case, but inspired a number of ballads

(135 texts are known to the author, belonging to six basic types) over a 70-year time span. This comparative study of newspaper accounts and ballads draws out and analyzes the various formulae (words, scenes, characters, actions) employed, showing the same ones at work in each medium. Particularly revealing is the discussion of stereotypes, which demonstrates how distinguishing features of the original story are gradually blurred in successive versions and stereotyped elements take over. A number of texts are given (some deriving from a 1927 recording by Vernon Dalhart).

S. 288. THOMPSON, Harold W., ed. A Pioneer Songster: texts from the Stevens-Douglass manuscript of Western New York 1841-1856; assisted by Edith E. Cutting. Ithaca, N.Y.: Cornell University Press, 1958. 203p. bibliog.
The songs included here were written down by family members largely from the singing of one Artemas Stevens; many years after its compilation that manuscript passed into the hands of Stevens' great-grandson, Harry S. Douglass, of Wyoming County, western New York state. The texts are 89 in number and are divided into three sections: "Songs and Ballads from the British Isles," "American Songs and Ballads," and "Minor Groups--English and American." Each section has background notes, as does each text. There is a song-title, first-line index. The introduction by Thompson is both informative and entertaining.

S. 289. WARNER, Frank M. Folk Songs and Ballads of the Eastern Seaboard: from a collector's notebook. Macon, Ga.: Southern Press, 1963. 51p.
A popular and well-traveled performer, Warner (b.1903) was always profoundly sympathetic to the songs he sang; in the words of Carl Sandburg, "in voice and style he can be dynamic and gustatory or soft and shadowy, according to the song and the people it came from" (quoted on the sleeve of Our Singing Heritage, Elektra 153). His long career as a collector (he was introduced to the fascination of folk song by Frank C. Brown at Duke University in the 1920s and began collecting not long afterwards) provided the wide experience on which this understanding was based. With his wife Anne he combed the eastern seaboard for material, one of their most notable discoveries being Frank Proffitt, from whom they learned "Tom Dula" (see no. S.314). This volume of four lectures given at Wesleyan College, Macon, Georgia, on April 22-23, 1963, is informed by the same spirit of enthusiasm, understanding, and experience. They are entitled, "From a Collector's Notebook," "Let's Sing," "Folk Songs and Our American Heritage," and "The Function of Folk Songs." Texts of many songs are included, but there is no index. (For the fruits of the Warners' collecting in printed form, see Anne Warner, ed., Traditional American Folk Songs From the Anne & Frank Warner Collection [Syracuse: Syracuse University Press, 1984].)

4. Other Ethnic Groups

a. General

S.290. GRAME, Theodore C. America's Ethnic Music. Tarpon
        Springs, Florida: Cultural Maintenance Associates,
        1976. 232p. bibliog.
        This important, but virtually unknown book puts a pas-
sionately argued case for placing America's musical history in a
proper multicultural perspective. Conceding the enormity of the
task, Grame embarks on a process of opening the field with a series
of studies on specific aspects of American ethnic music, concentrating his attention on the least known traditions. Before this, in a
deeply-felt and hard-hitting first chapter, "Music and the Melting
Pot," he denounces a lack of awareness of the importance of ethnicity in America's musical history, and is critical first of those
composers and scholars who "exploited" Indian materials from a Euro-
centered, melting pot perspective, and, second, of widespread attitudes towards the music of European immigrants ("a melting-pot
ideology required that a melting-pot music be created"--pp. 14-15).
The subsequent studies center on: a short study of multi-ethnic
music in Pittsburgh; the Scottish songs of Elizabeth McLennan who
emigrated in 1925, and whose songs "lie almost totally dormant" (p.
44); immigration songs illustrative of how and why immigrants came
to the USA; songs of derision and conflict (song in situations of
inter-ethnic tension); religious song (Greek Orthodox, Byzantine
Catholic, Snake-handling Protestants, Black Baptist, Jewish); rites;
festivals; secular vocal music; the ethnic musician; ethnic recordings and radio.

b. Spanish-American

S.291.   CAMPA, Arthur L. Hispanic Folklore Studies of Arthur L.
         Campa. New York: Arno Press, 1976. (79p.) bibliogs.
         This reprint volume of books and articles by a pioneer
scholar in Hispanic-American studies contains two items of particular
musical interest. Spanish Folk-Poetry in New Mexico (Albuquerque:
University of New Mexico Press, 1946) is a book-length study and
collection (224p.) of folk songs, which Campa groups in four sec-
tions--romance, corrido, décima, and canción. There is also an introductory section, with geographical and historical background and
a general discussion of folksinging in New Mexico. The songs (texts
only) each have a preliminary note, and informants' names are provided. The Spanish Folksong in the Southwest (originally issued in
University of New Mexico Bulletin, Modern Language Series, Vol. 4
No. 1, 1933) is an earlier, shorter (67p.) study and collection,
divided into sections for the ballad, the décima, and the canción
popular.

S.292. DICKEY, Dan William. The Kennedy Corridos: a study of

the ballads of an American hero. Austin: Center for
Mexican American Studies, University of Texas, 1978.
127p. illus., bibliog.
President Kennedy's death in November 1963 was strongly
felt among Mexican Americans, and corridos on the subject began to
be heard very soon after the event. In Texas twenty 45 rpm recordings were available within weeks, and these are the focal point of
this scholarly study, which differs from Paredes' work (no. S.293)
in its emphasis on commercial recordings and on the continuing corrido tradition. Formal analysis of the Kennedy corridos is preceded
by more general discussion of the development of the corrido and
the history of its recorded form. Appendices give the Spanish texts
of a number of the corridos with English translations.

S.293. PAREDES, Américo. A Texas-Mexican Cancionero: folk-
        songs of the Lower Border. Urbana: University of Il-
        linois Press, 1976. 194p. illus., bibliog., discog.
        refs.
A fascinating collection of 66 songs from the Lower Rio
Grande, Texas-Mexican border. As a native of the region, and a
performer of its music, Paredes has a personal investment in the
songs, which gives a piquancy to his text; all the songs come from
his own body of knowledge. They are arranged in five groups:
Old Songs from Colonial Days (6), Songs of Border Conflict (34),
Songs for Special Occasions (8), Romantic and Comic Songs (11),
The Pocho (i.e., Americanized Mexican) Appears (7). For each
song the author provides melody and guitar chords, Spanish verses,
and English prose translation. He is at pains to point out that
his versions "are not the minutely faithful transcriptions of specific
performances required for scholarly analysis and should not be
taken as such" (p. xiv). Paredes' own text is particularly informative: a general introduction discusses the social situation in which
the songs were performed, and in addition each group has its own
introduction, presenting the historical background. There are seventeen photographic illustrations (of singers, and of historical events).
Subject index.

S.294. ROBB, John Donald. Hispanic Folk Songs of New Mexico;
        with selected songs collected, transcribed, and arranged
        for voice and piano. Albuquerque: University of New
        Mexico Press, 1954. (University of New Mexico Publica-
        tions in the Fine Arts, No. 1). 83p.
        _____. Hispanic Folk Music of New Mexico and the
        Southwest: a self-portrait of a people. Norman: Uni-
        versity of Oklahoma Press, 1980. 891p. illus., bibliog.
        John D. Robb's own massive collection of Southwestern folk
music, begun in 1942 and now the J. D. Robb Collection at the Fine
Arts Library, University of New Mexico, forms the basis of these
two volumes, which vividly illustrate "the ramifications of Spanish
influence throughout the Western hemisphere during Spain's golden
age, an influence that is still felt strongly in the American Southwest

four hundred years later" (p. 16). The original work, which the later volume substantially expands, contains the music of fifteen songs, and commentary. The second work contains the melodies and texts of around 400 secular and religious songs, and the melodies of some 175 instrumental pieces. Part 1, secular song, the largest of the three parts, is divided into fourteen sections by genre (romance, corrido, canción, etc.) and subject (occupation, patriotism, courtship and marriage, etc.). Part 2, religious song, includes six song types (alabado, alabanza, etc.), while Part 3, instrumental melodies, includes 108 matachines and related dances, plus a variety of social dance melodies (cuadrilla, polka, etc.). Both types of vocal music have detailed documentation, including name and age of informant, place and date of recording, and notes. The texts are given in Spanish and English translation, and are followed by the unaccompanied melodies, transcribed by Robb himself. Piano-vocal arrangements of selected songs are given in an appendix. Three indexes (titles, first lines, and general) complete a most impressive volume.

S.295.   ROBINSON, Barbara J., and ROBINSON, J. Cordell. The
         Mexican American: a critical guide to research aids;
         foreword by Carlos E. Cortes. Greenwich, Conn.:
         Jai Press, 1980. 287p.
         An annotated bibliography of bibliographies, directories,
dictionaries, and other reference sources. There is no section for
music as such, but the subject index entries under "music" and
"folk music and songs" refer the reader to some 30 works which include music in their coverage.

S.296.   TEXAS-MEXICAN BORDER MUSIC. Vol. 1. An Introduction,
         1930-1960; edited by Chris Strachwitz. Berkeley, Calif.:
         Arhoolie Records, 1974. 16p. illus., discog.
         _____. Vols. 2 & 3. Corridos Parts 1 & 2, by Philip
         Sonnichsen. Berkeley, Calif.: Arhoolie Records, 1975.
         32p. illus., bibliog. refs., discog.
         These booklets accompany the first issues of the invaluable
five-record set of musica nortena (Folklyric 9003-7). In the first,
Strachwitz provides a brief introduction, biographical notes on the
performers, and a chronology of border history, as well as lyrics of
the songs on the record (in Spanish and English). Sonnichsen's
text, more substantial, has very detailed information on the various
corridos (Gregorio Cortez, Joaquín Murieta, etc.), with source
notes, and a short essay on the "golden age" of the recorded corrido; once again, there are textual transcriptions in Spanish and
English.

c.   Other Groups

S.297.   BOYER, Walter E., et al., eds. Songs Along the Mahan-
         tongo: Pennsylvania Dutch folksongs; edited by Walter
         E. Boyer, Albert F. Buffington, and Don Yoder. Lan-

caster, Pa.: Pennsylvania Dutch Folklore Center, 1951.
(Repr. Hatboro, Pa.: Folklore Associates, 1964). 231p.
illus., bibliog.
An evocative collection of 62 sacred and secular items, arranged in social groups: childhood, courtship and marriage, the farm, the "snitzing" party, apple butter making, the tavern, "American life," a New Year's blessing, the camp ground. Each song is given in Pennsylvania Dutch and English, and the text and melody are preceded by informative commentary. There is a pronunciation key and a song index.

S.298. GRONOW, Pekka, comp. The Columbia 33000-F Irish
Series; a numerical listing; with an artist index compiled by Bill Healy and a title index compiled by Paul F. Wells. Los Angeles: John Edwards Memorial Foundation, 1979. (JEMF Special Series, No. 10.) 77p. illus., bibliog.
An important contribution to our understanding of how and to what extent record companies catered for minority groups, this discography provides details of the 563 78rpm Irish-American records issued by Columbia between 1925 and 1937, plus the small postwar series (1947-51) of 33 records, featuring such performers as the Flanagan Brothers, Shaun O'Nolan, and Frank Quinn. Arranged in catalog number order, entries give details of performer, matrix and take numbers, titles, date where known, and reissue numbers; no locations are given. There is a table of release dates, and the volume is enhanced, not only by excellent indexes, but by the reproduction of contemporary advertisements, often including portraits.

S.299. GRONOW, Pekka. Studies in Scandinavian-American Discography. Helsinki: Finnish Institute of Recorded Sound, 1977. 2v.
Between them, these two volumes of discography list all known Finnish-American records up to the 1940s, whether made in Finland or the USA, and most of the other Scandinavian-American recordings of the same period. Vol. 1 covers Victor, Odeon/Okeh, Brunswick and Vocalion, while Vol. 2 covers Columbia (and is a revision of the author's American Columbia Scandinavian "E" and "F" series [Helsinki, 1974]). The introductions to the listings are a mine of detailed historical information on the recording companies concerned and in particular their ethnic series policy. No artist or title indexes are provided to the discographies, which are in catalog number order, with performer names, description of performance (taken from label), matrix, title, credits, date of recording, and, not infrequently, release dates.

S.300. NETTL, Bruno, ed. Eight Urban Musical Cultures; tradition and change. Urbana: University of Illinois Press, 1978. 320p. bibliog. refs.
This "group of ethnomusicological studies devoted to the fate of traditional musics in modern cities" contains one piece on the

United States: Ronald Riddle's fascinating investigation of "Music Clubs and Ensembles in San Francisco's Chinese Community." (A full account of Chinese music in San Francisco appeared in Riddle's later work, Flying Dragons, Flowing Streams [Westport: Greenwood Press, 1983].)

S.301.   PAWLOWSKA, Harriet M., ed. Merrily We Sing: 105 Polish folksongs; with an analysis of the music by Grace L. Engel; foreword by Emelyn Elizabeth Gardner. Detroit: Wayne State University Press, 1961. 263p. bibliog.

Like the other books in this section, this collection of Polish-American songs reminds us of the importance of the music of ethnic groups in the United States. Offered "as a symbol of the gifts to the United States from the people of Polish heritage" (preface), it is also a sign of cultural identity and tenacity. The songs are arranged in six groups and are given as beautifully designed and printed single-line melodies, with Polish and English texts. The six groups are idiosyncratically titled: (i) "People Sing Because a Mood Moves Them to Do So"; (ii) "When People Are Filled with Laughter, They Sing"; (iii) "Singers and Weavers of Ballads, Tales of Infinite Variety and Enduring Sameness"; (iv) "There Is No Theme Which a Singer Cannot Feel and, Feeling It, Does Not Fashion Into Song"; (v) "The Singer Etches Portraits of Travelers Who Have Been Here and Gone..."; (vi) "Sometimes People Sing for the Joy of Singing, Caring Not Where They Begin or Stop or What They Sing." Engel's "analysis of the music" is a five-page discussion of the general characteristics of Polish folk song. Notes on each song are included at the back of the book.

S.302.   WRIGHT, Robert L. Swedish Emigrant Ballads. Lincoln: University of Nebraska Press, 1965. 209p. bibliog. refs.

"As leaflets or street-prints hawked about Sweden for a few öre apiece, usually anonymous, [these ballads] tell of the wonders of the great land in the West.... [and] provide insight into the human experience of the more than a million Swedes who were to become Swedish-Americans" (pp. 18-19). The text of these original songs of the emigration (1850-1900) are given in Swedish and English, and include "Songs of Justification," "Songs of Disillusionment," "Songs of Nostalgia," "Songs of Disaster." Nineteen melodies are given in the appendix.

5.   Regional Studies and Collections

a.   The South

See also S.837

S.303.   JAMESON, Gladys V., ed. Wake and Sing: a miniature anthology of the music of Appalachian America. New

York: Broadcast Music, Inc., 1955. 47p.
A volume of "hymns, ballads, folk songs, fiddle tunes and songs for children." The music is described as being suitable for choirs, schools, special programs and group singing. The book was published for the centennial of Berea College, Berea, Kentucky. Twelve of the songs are single melody lines, the balance (ca. 28) are in three or four parts. Brief notes are provided for each song.

ALABAMA

S.304.   BROWNE, Ray B., ed. The Alabama Folk Lyric: a study
in origins and media of dissemination; collected and edited with an introduction and notes by Ray B. Browne. Bowling Green, Ohio: Bowling Green University Popular Press, 1979. 480p. bibliog. refs.
Based on the author's 1956 UCLA dissertation, this is a substantial, scholarly collection of the melodies and texts of 192 songs. There are nine broad categories: love songs, sentimental songs, pseudo-Negro songs, social commentary songs, parodies of songs, satiric songs, funny songs, animal songs, and literary songs. The songs themselves are given in the versions collected by Browne in the early 1950s, with headnotes (including the name of the singer, place and date) and notes on other versions. The introduction wrestles with the problem of defining folk song, explains the selection criteria for the volume (which includes a desire to present as large as possible a number of songs hitherto unpublished in other collections), and draws attention to the importance of the popular songbook or "songster" in the transference of songs from the popular to the folk tradition. Index of titles, first lines, refrains and choruses.

S.305.   CARMER, Carl. Stars Fell on Alabama; illustrated by Cyrus
LeRoy Baldridge. New York: The Literary Guild, 1934. 294p. illus.
Carmer spent six years in Alabama in the late 1920s and early '30s (he taught in Tuscaloosa), visited most parts of the state and became quite deeply familiar with its people and its ways; if he had an overriding impression it was probably of an awe-inspiring mixture of enchantment and malevolence. His very evocative personal portrait contains a number of interesting first-hand accounts of music-making among both the white and black population; though they read a little as if fictionalized, this seems to have been in the interests of readability rather than the exercise of fancy. Part 2, "In the Red Hills," contains vivid descriptions of local fiddlers, of an all-day Sacred Harp "singing," and of folk singing. The extent to which music and folklore permeated black life is abundantly clear; particularly interesting are the ring shout in Part 1, Chapter 3, the baptism in the same chapter, the various folk songs (including "John Henry") and spirituals in Parts 3 ("Black Belt") and 4 ("Conjure Country"). A list of fiddle tunes is included at the back of the book.

GEORGIA

S.306.   COLLINGS, Henrietta, ed. Georgia's Heritage of Song.
         Athens, Ga.: University of Georgia Press, 1955. 81p.
         illus.
Modest collection of songs with piano accompaniment, intended mainly for teachers, to "enrich the study of a unit on Georgia
history" (p. 3). In addition to folk songs, Indian songs, and Negro
songs, there are songs about Georgia, musical settings of poems by
Georgia poets, hymns, and songs of the 1860s.

S.307.   FOXFIRE 3; edited with an introduction by Eliot Wigginton.
         Garden City, N.Y.: Anchor Press, 1975. 511p. illus.
         FOXFIRE 4;   ; afterword by Richard M. Dorson.
         Garden City, N.Y.: Anchor Press, 1977. 496p. illus.,
         bibliog.
         FOXFIRE 6;   . Garden City, N.Y.: Anchor Press,
         1980. 507p. illus., bibliogs.
Foxfire magazine, an unusual enterprise run by high school
students in Georgia, has become justly renowned for its investigations into living Georgia traditions. Each of these books is a collection of articles that originally appeared in the magazine, and each
contains material on Appalachian musical instruments. Foxfire 3 includes portraits of seven banjo and dulcimer makers, representing
different styles, documents their technique in detail, and provides
background in the shape of transcribed interviews (pp. 120-213).
Foxfire 4 adopts a similar approach to fiddle makers (pp. 186-225)
and adds a bibliography by Dorson, and a list of periodicals and
resources on Appalachia. Foxfire 6 illustrates and documents the
gourd banjo as made by Leonard Webb, and also includes a bibliography on the subject (pp. 54-83).

S.308.   KILLION, Ronald G., and WALLER, Charles T. A Treasury
         of Georgia Folklore. Atlanta: Cherokee Publishing Co.,
         1972. 267p.
Based on material collected by the WPA Federal Writers
Project in the late 1930s. Chapter 10 (pp. 229-262) provides the
texts of numerous folk songs, among them work songs, play songs,
spirituals, and English and Scottish ballads.

KENTUCKY

S.309.   FUSON, Harvey H., ed. Ballads of the Kentucky High-
         lands. London: Mitre Press, 1931. 219p.
A collection of around 100 texts (no music) in seven sections: "Old Ballads and Songs," "Other Ballads and Songs," "Short
Sayings in Rhyme-Jigs," "Play Songs," "Nursery Rhymes," "War
Songs," and "Old Religious Songs." The singer (source) of each
text is identified (some are from Fuson's own memory), and there is
an alphabetical index at the front (instead of a contents list). The
lengthy poetic introduction (pp. 5-39)--Fuson was also a poet--draws

liberally on the compiler's knowledge of his native region to discuss
the background and importance of the people's particular skill with
oral literature. Straying beyond the state line, he goes on to discuss the relationship between the ballad tradition and the work of
Poe, Foster, John Howard Payne, and Joel Chandler Harris.

S. 310.   RITCHIE, Jean. Singing Family of the Cumberlands.
          New York: Oxford University Press, 1955. 282p.
          illus.
          _____. _____. New York: Oak Publications, 1963.
          258p. illus.

Well-loved folksinger's story of her childhood in Kentucky--
a fond, folksy, evocative portrait of a large Appalachian family and
(especially) of their music-making. Many songs are quoted, with
melodies. The arrival of radio and the spread of hillbilly music are
seen as leading to a decline in the amount of home-made music.

S. 311.   ROBERTS, Leonard, ed. In the Pines: selected Kentucky
          folksongs; music transcriptions by C. Buell Agey; con-
          sultants, Jan Philip Schinan. Pikeville, Ky.: Pikeville
          College Press, 1978. 319p. illus., bibliog.

The second of two fine collections by Roberts, this volume
contains 143 songs, "drawn from an archive of material accumulated
over a period of twelve years, from 1947 to 1955" (p. xvi). Some
of the collecting was done by students of Roberts, and they are
duly given credit. The book is divided into two sections: (i) Ballads; (ii) Folksongs. Each song is transcribed by Agey as a single-
line melody with chord names. There are abundant notes, and both
title and first line indexes.

S. 312.   ROBERTS, Leonard, ed. Sang Branch Settlers: folksongs
          and tales of a Kentucky mountain family; music trans-
          cribed by C. Buell Agey. Austin: University of Texas
          Press for the American Folklore Society, 1974. (Memoir
          Series, Vol. 61). 401p. bibliog.

Roberts writes in the foreword to this rich and fascinating
collection: "The folktales and folksongs in this volume were collected
from 1951 through 1955 from one family living in Harlan and Leslie
counties, Kentucky. This family, the Couches, had lived in the
small area of the Kentucky mountains for one hundred years.... I
felt an in-depth study of the family was the obligation of the serious
folklorist. The quest was long and, after four years of interviewing
and taping, I left the lore of the family still unexhausted." The
book is divided into four sections: (i) Introduction (in which the
interviews with various members of the family are transcribed word-
for-word); (ii) Folksongs and Hymns (100 in all with melodies); (iii)
Folktales and Riddles; and (iv) Appendix, which contains notes, the
type numbers of the folktales, a genealogy of the Couch family, a
ten-page bibliography, and an index of titles and first lines of the
songs. (Originally published in 1959 in a slightly different arrangement in two parts by the University of Kentucky Press: the folk-

ways, legends, and experiences as a book entitled Up Cutshin and Down Greasy, and the songs and tales in a microcard volume entitled Tales and Songs of the Couch Family.)

MARYLAND

S.313.   CAREY, George G., ed. Maryland Folk Legends and Folk
         Songs. Cambridge, Md.: Tidewater Publishers, 1971.
         120p. illus.
   A modest but attractive collection of several folk stories and thirty-two folk-song texts. The texts have brief annotations and citations to other folk-song collections. A substantial amount of the material apparently came from repertoire of Alice Ridgeway Tucker, who died in 1944; the balance of the texts were selected by the editor from the Maryland Folklore Archive at the University of Maryland in College Park.

NORTH CAROLINA

S.314.   WEST, John Foster. The Ballad of Tom Dula: the docu-
         mented story behind the murder of Laura Foster and the
         trials and execution of Tom Dula. Durham, N.C.:
         Moore Publishing Co., (1970?). 212p. illus., bibliog.
   The North Carolina ballad became famous in the 1958 version by the Kingston Trio; this was based on the adaptation by Alan Lomax and Frank Warner from the singing of North Carolina traditional musician Frank Proffitt, who first sang it for Warner in 1938. Proffitt himself recalled it "as the first song he ever heard his father pick on the banjo" (Sandy Paton, in the booklet accompanying Frank Proffitt, Folk-Legacy Records, FSA1, p. 9). The actual events behind the ballad, which are the concern of this book, took place in Wilkes Co., N.C., in 1866-1868.

S.315.   WETMORE, Susannah, and BARTHOLOMEW, Marshall, eds.
         Mountain Songs of North Carolina. New York: Schirmer,
         1926. 43p.
   A collection of fourteen songs arranged with piano accompaniment by Marshall Bartholomew, preceded by a dated one-page introduction and followed by a succinct one page of notes. Though the accompaniments to the songs are sparse, the collection emanates from the "folk-song-as-art-song" approach. Mercifully, this has more or less passed from us. The genre itself, however, is perfectly respectable; these are charming pieces which no doubt have little to do with the original folk songs.

SOUTH CAROLINA

S.316.   SMITH, Reed, ed. South Carolina Ballads; with a study of
         the traditional ballad today. Cambridge, Mass.: Har-
         vard University Press, 1928. (Repr. Freeport: Books
         for Libraries Press, 1972.) 174p. bibliog.

This "small sheaf of surviving South Carolina ballads"
(preface) is a collection of fourteen ballads and two traditional
songs, with 43 variants and twelve tunes. Headnotes provide comment on each ballad, and on versions found elsewhere in the country. The collection is preceded by a lengthy theoretical essay on
more general questions relating to the ballad, starting "with the
popular ballad as we have it exhibited in Child's great collection,
and [working] forward in time to modern instances and contemporary analogies" (ibid.). (The same author also wrote "The Traditional Ballad and Its South Carolina Survivals," Bulletin of the
University of South Carolina, No. 162, 1925.)

TENNESSEE

S.317. BURTON, Thomas G., and MANNING, Ambrose N., eds.
        The East Tennessee State University Collection of Folk-
        lore: folksongs; musical notations and analysis by
        Annette Wolford. Johnson City, Tenn.: East Tennessee
        State University, Institute of Regional Studies, 1967.
        (Monograph No. 4.) 114p.
_____. The East Tennessee State University Collection
        of Folklore: folksongs II; Annette Wolford, assistant
        editor. Johnson City, Tenn.: Research Council of East
        Tennessee State University, 1969. 119p.
A line in the introduction of the second volume reads:
"The first five reels of magnetic tape of the East Tennessee State
University Collection of Folklore are published in Monograph No. 4
... the folksongs recorded in Beech Mountain, North Carolina, are
presented in this volume." These are beautifully, thoughtfully
edited little books, especially the second one. In both books the
songs are given in keyless single-line melodies with complete texts,
and information on the singer and the date each song was taped is
also provided. Both books also have abundant annotations, identify
the mode of each song, give Child numbers where appropriate, and
include title-first line indexes. The second one has biographical
sketches and a bibliography of the books cited in the annotations.
Models of their kinds.

WEST VIRGINIA

S.318. BOETTE, Marie, ed. Singa Hipsy Doodle and Other Folk
        Songs of West Virginia; music notes drawn by John
        Laflin: illustrated by Marcia Ogilvie. Parsons, W. Va.:
        McClain Printing Co., 1971. 177p. illus.
Anthology of over 100 songs (texts, melodies, and chords
for autoharp): Child ballads; colonial, early American and soldier
songs; Appalachian songs; spiritual and religious songs; children's
and play-party songs; parlor songs; and songs from the manuscript
collection of Dr. Patrick W. Gainer, a West Virginian ballad scholar.
Each song has an introductory comment, and there are indexes of
titles and first lines.

S.319.   BUSH, Michael E., ed.   <u>Folk Songs of Central West Virginia</u>.
Ravenswood, W. Va.; the editor, 1969-1970.   2v.
These paperbound books were reproduced entirely--both
text and music--from handwritten originals.   Each contains over 40
songs.   There are no introductions and no credits except those given
above (with the exception of identification of persons pictured on the
covers).   The tunes, in shape notes, are given in single-line form
(most with guitar chords indicated).   Those tunes in the major mode
are all transcribed in C major; those in minor are in A minor.   Some
are modal.   Almost all of the songs are sourced and many have background notes.   (The last page of each volume includes the directive:
"For information write: Song Book, P.O. Box 127, Glenville, W. Va.
26351.")

S.320.   COX, John Harrington, ed.   <u>Folk-Songs Mainly from West</u>
<u>Virginia</u>; introductory essay and supplementary refer-
ences by Herbert Halpert.   New York: National Service
Bureau, 1939.   88p.   bibliog.
_____.   <u>Traditional Ballads from West Virginia</u>; intro-
ductory essay and supplementary references by Herbert
Halpert.   New York: National Service Bureau, 1939.
109p.   bibliog.
_____.   <u>Traditional Ballads and Folk-Songs Mainly from</u>
<u>West Virginia</u>; editors George Herzog and Herbert Hal-
pert, 1939; George W. Boswell, 1964.   (Philadelphia):
American Folklore Society, 1964.   (Publications, Bibliographical & Special Series, Vol. 15.)   218p.   bibliog.
The first two mimeographed booklets had a very limited cir-
culation.   Boswell was asked (by Tristram P. Coffin) to prepare a
one-volume edition, and this is the 1964 version.   A fine collection
of texts and unaccompanied tunes not included in Cox's earlier
<u>Folk-Songs of the South</u> (LOAM 507).   Each item has its full share
of information, but the original notes are reduced somewhat in the
later edition, and a new bibliography has been substituted for the
original (which appeared in identical form in both 1939 publications).
(Formerly LOAM A100 and A101.)

b.   The West

See also F.8.a

TEXAS

S.321.   PUBLICATIONS OF THE TEXAS FOLK-LORE SOCIETY.
This famous series contains many essays on musical subjects
relating to Texas and the Southwest.   All the relevant volumes are
listed here, in the numerical order of the series, with details of the
authors and titles of the essays on music they contain.   (The presence of music examples is indicated by the letter M.   For explanation
of the asterisk (*) see no. 26 in the series.)

Publications of the Texas Folk-Lore Society, 1; edited by Stith
Thompson. Austin: Texas Folk-Lore Society, 1916.
(Repr. as Round the Levee. [Austin, 1935].) 111p.
R. E. Dudley and L. W. Payne, "Texas Play-Party Songs
and Games"; B. D. Wood, "A Mexican Border Ballad"

_____, 2; edited by J. Frank Dobie. Austin: Texas Folk-Lore
Society, 1923. (Repr. as Coffee in the Gourd. [Austin,
1935; Dallas: Southern Methodist University Press, 1969].)
110p. bibliog. refs.
*John R. Craddock, "The Cowboy Dance" (including
examples of the calls); Dorothy Scarborough, "The 'Blues'
as Folk Songs'; W. P. Webb, "Miscellany of Texas Folklore" (including texts of the songs of or by hobos, railroads, slums, cowboys and Negroes).

_____, 4; edited by J. Frank Dobie. Austin: Texas Folk-Lore
Society, 1925. (Repr. as Happy Hunting Ground [Hatboro,
Pa.: Folklore Associates, 1964].)
F. S. Curtis, "Spanish Songs of New Mexico" (with music)"
M; J. Frank Dobie, "Verses of the Texas Vaqueros (with
music)" M.

_____, 5; edited by J. Frank Dobie. Austin: Texas Folk-Lore
Society, 1926. (Repr. as Rainbow in the Morning [Hatboro,
Pa.: Folklore Associates, 1965].) 190p. bibliog. refs.
*L. W. Payne, "Some Texas Versions of the 'Frog's Court-
ing'"; Mattie Austin Hatcher, "A Texas Border Ballad";
Natalie Taylor Carlisle, "Old Time Darky Plantation Melo-
dies"; R. C. Harrison, "The Negro as Interpreter of His
Own Folk Songs"; *Gates Thomas, "South Texas Negro
Work-Songs". (Included in the reprint is an unnumbered
Society publication of 1912, "Some Current Folk-Songs of
the Negro and Their Economic Interpretation," by Will H.
Thomas.)

Texas and Southwestern Lore; edited by J. Frank Dobie.
Austin: Texas Folk-Lore Society, 1927. (Repr. Dallas:
Southern Methodist University Press, 1967.) (Publications
..., 6). 259p. bibliog. refs.
J. Frank Dobie, "Ballads and Songs of the Frontier Folk"
M; *John R. Craddock, "Songs the Cowboys Sing"; Ina
Sires, "Songs of the Open Range"; Arbie Moore, "'The
Texas Cowboy'"; J. Evetts Haley, "Cowboy Songs Again";
Julia Beazley, "The Ballad of Davy Crockett" M; *George
E. Hastings, "'Annie Brean From Old Kaintuck'" M; L. W.
Payne, "Songs and Ballads--Grave and Gay" M.

Follow de Drinkin' Gou'd; edited by J. Frank Dobie. Austin: Texas
Folk-Lore Society, 1928. (Repr. Dallas: Southern Methodist
University Press, 1965.) (Publications ..., 7). 201p.
bibliog. refs.
B. A. Botkin, "The Play-Party in Oklahoma"; *H. B. Parks,
"Follow the Drinking Gourd" M; *Mary Virginia Bales, "Some

Negro Folk-Songs of Texas" M; Nicolas J. H. Smith, "Six
Negro Folk-Songs" M; Newton Gaines, "Some Characteristics of Cowboy Songs" M; J. Frank Dobie, "More Ballads
and Songs of the Frontier Folk" M.

Man, Bird, and Beast; edited by J. Frank Dobie. Austin: Texas
Folk-Lore Society, 1930. (Repr. Dallas: Southern Metho-
dist University Press, 1965.) Publications..., 8). 185p.
bibliog. refs.
Jovita González, "Tales and Songs of the Texas-Mexicans"
M; L. W. Payne, "Recent Research in Balladry and Folk
Songs."

Southwestern Lore; edited by J. Frank Dobie. Austin: Texas
Folk-Lore Society, 1931. (Repr. Dallas: Southern Metho-
dist University Press; Hatboro, Pa.: Folklore Associates,
1965.) (Publications..., 9). 198p. bibliog. refs.
Joaquin Mora, "Songs the Vaqueros Sing" M; George E.
Hastings, "'Hell in Texas'" M; Ernest E. Leisy, "'Oh, Bury
Me Not'"; Edward Ford Piper, "'A Love-of-God Share'" M.

Tone the Bell Easy; edited by J. Frank Dobie. Austin: Texas
Folk-Lore Society, 1932. (Repr. Dallas: Southern Metho-
dist University Press, 1965.) (Publications..., 10). 199p.
bibliog. refs.
J. Frank Dobie, "Mustang Gray: Fact, Tradition, and
Song" M; Mabel Major, "British Ballads in Texas" M;
Samuel E. Asbury and Henry G. Meyer, "Old-Time White
Camp-Meeting Spirituals" M.

Puro Mexicano; edited by J. Frank Dobie. Austin: Texas Folk-Lore
Society, 1935. (Repr. Dallas: Southern Methodist University Press, 1969.) (Publications..., 12). 261p. bibliog.
refs.
*Paul S. Taylor, "Songs of the Mexican Migration" M.

Straight Texas; edited by J. Frank Dobie and Mody C. Boatright.
Austin: Texas Folk-Lore Society, 1937. (Repr. Hatboro,
Pa.: Folklore Associates, 1966). (Publications..., 13).
348p. bibliog. refs.
Frances Densmore, "The Alabama Indians and Their Music"
M; Helen Ashworth Moore, "The Play Party in Victoria
County" M.

Coyote Wisdom; edited by J. Frank Dobie, Mody C. Boatright, and
Harry H. Ransome. Austin: Texas Folk-Lore Society,
1938. (Repr. Dallas: Southern Methodist University Press,
1965.) (Publications..., 14). 300p. illus., bibliog. refs.
Lillian Elizabeth Barday, "The Coyote: Animal and Folk
Character"; J. W. Hendren, "An English Source of 'The
Trail to Mexico'" M; Samuel E. Asbury, "'There Were Three
(Two) Crows'" M.

Texian Stomping Grounds; edited by J. Frank Dobie, Mody C. Boat-
right, and Harry H. Ransome. Austin: Texas Folk-Lore
Society, 1941. (Publications..., 17). 162p. bibliog.
refs.
    J. Olcutt Sanders, "Honor the Fiddler!"; Helen Gates,
"'Toodala'" M; Laura Atkins, "Some Play Party Games of
South Texas" M.

Backwoods to Border; edited by Mody C. Boatright and Donald Day.
    Austin: Texas Folk-Lore Society, 1943. (Repr. Dallas:
    Southern Methodist University Press, 1967.) (Publica-
    tions..., 18). 235p. bibliog. refs.
    J. Frank Dobie, "A Buffalo Hunter and His Song" (i.e. "The
Buffalo Skinners") M; Catharine Marshall Vineyard, "'The
Arkansas Traveler'"; Vanita Parrett, "Cowboy Dance Calls";
*Violet West Sone, "Rope-Jumping Rhymes."

From Hell to Breakfast; edited by Mody C. Boatright and Donald
    Day. Austin: Texas Folk-Lore Society, 1944. (Repr.
    Dallas: Southern Methodist University Press, 1967.) (Pub-
    lications..., 19). 215p. bibliog. refs.
    Ruby Terrill Lomax, "Negro Baptizings";
*John A. Lomax, "Adventures of a Ballad Hunter"; Mody
C. Boatright, "More About 'Hell in Texas'"; Ernest Speck,
"The Song of Little Llano."

Gib Morgan, Minstrel of the Oil Fields, by Mody C. Boatright. Aus-
    tin: Texas Folk-Lore Society, 1945. (Repr. Dallas:
    Southern Methodist University Press, 1965.) (Publications
    ..., 20). 104p. illus.

Mexican Border Ballads and Other Lore; edited by Mody C. Boat-
    right. Austin: Texas Folk-Lore Society, 1946. (Repr.
    Dallas: Southern Methodist University Press, 1967.)
    (Publications..., 21). 135p. bibliog. refs.
    *Brownie McNeil, "Corridos of the Mexican Border" M.

Texas Folk Songs; edited by William A. Owens; musical arrangements
    by Willa Mae Kelly Kochs. Austin: Texas Folk-Lore So-
    ciety, 1950. (Publications..., 23). 302p. bibliog. (An-
    thology; see LOAM 515)

Folk Travelers: Ballads, Tales, and Talk; edited by Mody C. Boat-
    right, Wilson M. Hudson, Allen Maxwell. Austin: Texas
    Folk-Lore Society, 1953. (Publications..., 25). 261p.
    bibliog. refs.
    Joseph W. Henderson, "Bonny Barbara Allen" M; Robert
C. Stephenson, "The Western Ballad and the Russian Bal-
lada"; idem., "Signature in Ballad and Story"; Américo
Parades, "The Love Tragedy in Texas-Mexican Balladry";
Elizabeth Harley, "Come Boy, Come Buy" M (on singing
salesmen).

Texas Folk and Folklore; edited by Mody C. Boatright, Wilson M.
        Hudson, Allen Maxwell. Dallas: Southern Methodist Uni-
        versity Press, 1954. (Publications..., 26). 356p.
        A reprint anthology, including all or part of those pieces
        marked with an asterisk * in the above lists.

Mesquite and Willow; edited by Mody C. Boatright, Wilson M. Hud-
        son, Allen Maxwell. Dallas: Southern Methodist Univer-
        sity Press, 1957. (Publications..., 27). 203p. bibliog.
        refs.
        Brownie McNeil, "The Child Ballad in the Middle West and
        Lower Mississippi Valley"; R. C. Stephenson, "Dialogue in
        Folktale and Song."

Madstones and Twisters; edited by Mody C. Boatright, Wilson M.
        Hudson, Allen Maxwell. Dallas: Southern Methodist Uni-
        versity Press, 1958. (Publications..., 28). 169p. bib-
        liog. refs.
        Américo Parades, "The Mexican Corrido: Its Rise and
        Fall."

And Horns on the Toads; edited by Mody C. Boatright, Wilson M.
        Hudson, Allen Maxwell. Dallas: Southern Methodist Uni-
        versity Press, 1959. (Publications..., 29). 237p. bibliog.
        refs.
        Américo Parades, "The Bury-Me-Not Theme in the South-
        west"; Walter Starkie, "Cante Jondo and Flamenco in An-
        dalusia and Hispano-America"; Everett A. Gillis, "Texas
        Singing Schools."

Singers and Storytellers; edited by Mody C. Boatright, Wilson M.
        Hudson, Allen Maxwell. Dallas: Southern Methodist Uni-
        versity Press, 1961. (Publications..., 30). 298p. bib-
        liog. refs.
        MacEdward Leach, "The Singer or the Song" (a plea for a
        study of the aesthetics of the ballad and folksong);
        Vincente T. Mendoza, "Some Forms of the Mexican Canción";
        James Ward Lee, "Arkansas Variants of Some Texas Folk-
        songs."

A Good Tale and a Bonnie Tune; edited by Mody C. Boatright,
        Wilson M. Hudson, Allen Maxwell. Dallas: Southern
        Methodist University Press, 1964. (Publications..., 32).
        274p. (see LOAM 420.)

The Sunny Slopes of Long Ago; edited by Wilson M. Hudson and
        Allen Maxwell. Dallas: Southern Methodist University
        Press, 1966. (Publications..., 33). 204p. illus., bib-
        liog. refs.
        Everett A. Gillis, "Laureates of the Western Range"; James
        Ward Lee, "The Penny Dreadful as a Folksong"; Jack

Solomon, "The Ballad of Bob Williams."

Hunters and Healers; folklore types and topics; edited by Wilson M.
    Hudson. Austin: Encino Press, 1971. (Publications...,
    35).
    Norman L. ('Brownie') McNeil, "Origins of 'Sir Patrick
    Spens'"; John Q. Anderson, "'The Gatesville Murder':
    the Origin and Evolution of a Ballad"; Hermes Nye, "Bar-
    bara Ellen and the Lincoln Continental: or, The Commercial
    Folk Festival"; Henry Schmidt, "The Huapango: a Dithyram-
    bic Festival."

Diamond Bessie and the Shepherds; edited by Wilson M. Hudson.
    Austin: Encino Press, 1972. (Publications..., 36). 158p.
    illus.
    Ann Miller Carpenter, "The Railroad in American Folk Song,
    1855-1920."

Observations and Reflections on Texas Folklore; edited by Francis
    Edward Abernethy. Austin: Encino Press, 1972. (Publi-
    cations..., 37). 151p. illus.
    Patrick B. Muller, "Folk Songs and Family Traditions";
    Bill C. Malone, "From Folk to Hillbilly to Country: the
    Coming of Age of America's Rural Music"; Francis Edward
    Abernethy, "Singing All Day and Dinner on the Grounds."

The Folklore of Texan Cultures; edited by Francis Edward Aber-
    nethy; music director, Dan Beaty. Austin: Encino Press,
    1974. (Publications..., 38). 366p. illus., bibliog. refs.
    Edwin W. Gaston, "Early Texas Indian Songs and Tales";
    Dan Beaty, "Lebanese Song Style" M.

Some Still Do: Essays on Texas Customs; edited by Francis Edward
    Abernethy. Austin: Encino Press, 1975. (Publications...,
    39). illus.
    Joe Angle, "Fiddlers and Festivals: a Texas Tradition."

What's Going On? (in Modern Texas Folklore); edited by Francis Ed-
    ward Abernethy. Austin: Encino Press, 1976. (Publica-
    tions..., 40). 309p. illus.
    Charles Clay Doyle, "'As the Hearse Goes By': the Modern
    Child's Memento Mori"; Francis Edward Abernethy,
    "Give the World a Smile Each Day" (on modern gospel
    music); Joseph F. Lomax, "Zydeco-Must Live Oh!";
    Guy Logsdon, "Western Swing"; Bill C. Malone, "Grow-
    ing Up with Texas Country Music"; Jan Reid, "Post-
    script: The Improbable Rise of Redneck Rock."
Paisanos: a folklore miscellany; edited by Francis Edward Abernethy.
    Austin: Encino Press, 1978. (Publication..., 41). 180p.
    illus., bibliog. refs.
    Peter M. Stephan, "Minstrelsy at the Market Place; or, What

the Traveling Texan Found for Entertainment in Ante-Bellum
New Orleans"; Lawrence Clayton, "Facts and Fiction in
Three Lomax Outlaw Songs."

6. Instrumental Folk Music

S.322.   AHRENS, Pat J.   Union Grove: the first fifty years.   Columbia, S.C.:   the author, (1974).   243p.   illus., bibliog., discog.

This is a loving pictorial tribute to and commentary on the
50th anniversary (1974) of the old-time fiddlers' convention held an-
nually at Union Grove, South Carolina.   The author, who is knowledgeable and enthusiastic (if occasionally sentimental), calls it "the
nation's oldest, continuous" fiddling convention.   There are nine ful-
some historical chapters and a tenth devoted to biographies of some
of the leading musicians.   The beautifully reproduced pictures, old
and new, are fascinating, and the bibliography and discography are
probably definitive.

S.323.   BURMAN-HALL, Linda C.   Southern American Folk Fiddle
Styles.   Los Angeles: John Edwards Memorial Founda-
tion, (1976?).   (Reprinted from Ethnomusicology, 19,
No. 1 [1975].)   (Reprint No. 32.)   pp. 47-65.   bibliog.

A revised portion of the author's Ph.D. dissertation
("Southern American Folk Fiddling: Context and Style," Princeton
University, 1973), this article describes the conventions of perform-
ance, examines the musical characteristics of the fiddle tune, and
distinguishes the various regional substyles (Blue Ridge, Southern
Appalachians, Ozark, and Western).

S.324.   CHRISTESON, R. P., ed.   The Old-Time Fiddler's Repertory.   Columbia: University of Missouri Press, 1973-
1984.   2v.   bibliogs.

These two finely produced volumes contain 459 fiddle tunes
collected by the compiler, mainly but not exclusively in Missouri,
from the late 1940s.   Christeson (b. 1911) came from an area--
Pulaski County, Missouri--where "old-time fiddling and square dancing flourished and were integral components of the mores of the
people" (Vol. 1, p. viii).   His compilations, while serving scholars,
are dedicated to the maintenance of a much-loved tradition.   Each
volume is organized into four sections: breakdowns, quadrilles, miscellaneous pieces, and waltzes.   Some tunes have piano accompaniments (more so in Vol. 1); no bar marks are provided ("they aren't
necessary and they would violate tradition"--Vol. 2, p. viii).   Each
volume has background notes on the fiddlers, and headnotes to
each tune; the latter, often brief, give the informants' names, and
sometimes dates and places.   There are also tune indexes.   (Vol. 1
formerly LOAM A98.)

Folk Music / 115

S.325. EPSTEIN, Dena J. The Folk Banjo: a documentary his-
        tory. Los Angeles: John Edwards Memorial Foundation,
        (1976?). (Reprinted from Ethnomusicology, 19, No. 3
        [1975].) (Reprint No. 33.) pp. 347-371. illus., bib-
        liog.
        Testing out effectively the method she employs in her Sin-
ful Tunes and Spirituals (no. S.521, where some of this information
also appears), Epstein dispels a number of long-established legends
concerning the provenance of the banjo by offering a chronological
"assembly of contemporary documents" (p. 350) which demonstrates
the African origin of the instrument, its construction methods, and
its presence on the plantations. She also provides a table of
references summarizing this literature.

S.326. GUNTHARP, Matthew G. Learning the Fiddler's Ways;
        foreword by Samuel P. Bayard; introduction by Robert
        C. Doyle. University Park: Pennsylvania State Uni-
        versity Press, 1980. 159p. illus.
        In Buffalo Valley, Central Pennsylvania, Guntharp and
Doyle encountered a vivacious fiddle tradition and set out to document it. Setting their account against the physical background of
Buffalo Valley, they give detailed descriptions of fiddling style,
transcriptions of fiddle tunes, and interviews with non-performing
fiddlers. Two common styles are singled out for a closer look:
square dance (with particular attention to an old-time fiddler Harry
Daddario) and bluegrass (concentrating on bluegrass fiddler Marvin
Kretzer). A glossary and numerous photos are included, but no
index.

S.327. MITSUI, Toru. Eikei Amerika Minzoku-Ongaku no Gakki.
        (The Instruments of Anglo-American Traditional Music.)
        Toyo Rashi: Traditional-Song Society, 1970. 141p.
        An account of the structure, playing techniques, history,
and performers of the fiddle, Appalachian dulcimer, and five-string
banjo, with shorter sections on other instruments. (In Japanese.)

S.328. RITCHIE, Jean. Jean Ritchie's Dulcimer People. New York:
        Oak, 1975. 128p. illus., bibliog., discog.
        Short portraits of dulcimer makers and players, with prac-
tical information on construction and tuning, and with numerous musical illustrations. Includes a detailed bibliography and discography.
(For an in-depth portrait of dulcimer making, see Dulcimer Maker:
the craft of Homer Ledford, by R. Gerald Alvey [Louisville: University Press of Kentucky, 1984].)

7. The Religious Folk Song Tradition of White Americans

S.329. BRUCE, Dickson D. And They All Sang Hallelujah: plain-
        folk camp-meeting religion, 1800-1845. Knoxville:

University of Tennessee Press, 1974. 155p. illus.
Drawing on anthropological and sociological perspectives,
Bruce offers a discerning interpretation of the role of religion in
Southern frontier life in the first half of the 19th century, and in
particular of the nature and function of the camp meeting. The book
is scattered with references to camp meeting spiritual songs (an index of first lines is included), but one chapter, Chapter 5, has particular relevance to music. Entitled "And We'll All Sing Hallelujah:
the Religion of the Spiritual Choruses," it is an attempt to analyze
the content of camp meeting spirituals--especially hymns with
chorus refrains--and to relate the themes to frontier life and attitudes. Biographical mention is made of tunebook compilers such as
William "Singing Billy" Walker, Ananias Davisson, and B. F. White.

S.320. COBB, Buell E. The Sacred Harp: a tradition and its
        music. Athens, Ga.: University of Georgia Press,
        1978. 245p. illus., bibliog.
    Acknowledging the extent of his debt to the labors of
George Pullen Jackson, Cobb offers a work that attempts not to
open up new ground as much as "to pay tribute to the tradition
and the people of the Sacred Harp [and] to set down, in a more
complete form than has been done before, the inner workings, the
local variations, and the style of that tradition for those who know
it only at a distance" (preface). Thus this is a valuable synthesis
of research into this unique body of religious folk song, which
takes its name from the 1844 songbook of B. F. White and E. J.
King (LOAM 528). Beginning in general terms, Cobb describes a
typical "singing"--what happens, the attitudes and values embodied,
and the essential texts. He then outlines the characteristic features
of the music as printed (pentatonicism, crossing of voices, etc.)
and of singing style. These he now places in historical context,
with an overview of the background of the tradition in New England
singing schools, and the role of the singing master and of the camp
meeting in its taking root and flourishing in the South. The next
chapters, on the successive revisions of the original book, and on
the various singing conventions as they developed, mark Cobb's own
more original contribution, concentrating on variation within the
overall tradition. A final chapter considers the future. Appendices
are devoted to dates and locations of singings, and to a selection of
music. The bibliography lists books and articles, and there is an
index.

S.331. KARSON, Burton, ed. Festival Essays for Pauline Alder-
        man: a musicological tribute; associate editors Joan
        Meggett, Eleanor Russell, and Halsey Stevens. Salt
        Lake City, Utah: Brigham Young University Press,
        1976. 279p. illus., bibliog. refs.
    This Festschrift contains three essays of interest to stu-
dents of American music. Glenn C. Wilcox writes on a little-known
Georgian advocate of musical reform in the field of notation, Edwin
T. Pound (1833-1919), who published numerous shape-note tunebooks

in the last quarter of the 19th century. Pound's Songs for All with Supplement (first edition 1882) uses four separate notational systems, combined with his own staff and letter system, copyrighted in 1884. All these systems are illustrated in the text.

Johannes Riedel's discussion of the songs of Henry Russell re-examines, with examples, the extent to which American public sentiment and social climate influenced him and his ability to portray that sensibility. Thirty-three melodic motifs are also listed, with brief comment.

In the third essay, Henry Leland Clarke briefly considers, with examples, the musical elements of the blues, and identifies as their most distinguishing features what he calls "homing melody," in which "every phrase comes to rest on the same note, and not always from the same direction." This Clarke calls "one of the rarest phenomena in musics of the world" (p. 238).

S.332. LORENZ, Ellen Jane. Glory, Hallelujah! the story of the campmeeting spiritual. Nashville, Tenn.: Abingdon Press, 1980. 144p. bibliog.

The usefulness of this volume--its concise history of the growth of camp meetings, its clear account of the characteristics of the spiritual, the importance attached to the publishing history of the hymnals and songsters--is considerably lessened by the uncertain tone, which at times anticipates an audience of children, and at other times hints at considerable scholarship. Thus fictionalized attempts to re-enter the camp meeting world sit uneasily alongside the authentic contemporary accounts collected by E. S. Lorenz (author of Practical Church Music [New York; Revell, 1909]), on which the author draws. The text includes a collection of 48 spirituals, reproduced from various original sources, with annotations.

S.333. PATTERSON, Daniel W. The Shaker Spiritual. Princeton, N.J.: Princeton University Press, 1979. 562p. illus., bibliog.

An outstanding work of scholarship and devotion, this collection of Shaker song offers what Patterson considers to be the best of some 8,000 to 10,000 songs contained in Shaker manuscript song books. These manuscripts are seen as providing "a chance to study the complete life history of a well-documented folk-song repertory created by one distinctly bounded group." Patterson confesses," "I do not know of another branch of American folk song for which this would be possible" (p. xiv). Three initial chapters provide a detailed introduction: on early forms of religious folk song, on the institutional background of Shaker song, and on the relation of the Shaker spiritual to traditional song. A note on Shaker notation and the transcription methods used in the book precedes the collection itself, which is in thirteen parts (divided into categories such as "Solemn Songs," "Early Laboring Songs," "Ballads," "Anthems"). Each section has an introduction, and each song an often quite substantial discursive note. The songs themselves, mostly from 1825-1870, but some recorded by Patterson himself, are given as single melody lines, with texts, and sources. There are numerous illustrations (both lithographs and photographs) and diagrams, notes on variants, checklists of Shaker song manuscripts and additional manuscripts cited, and indexes of persons, subjects, first lines, titles, and non-Shaker songs.

S.334.   RICHMOND, Mary L. Shaker Literature: a bibliography. Hancock, Mass.: Shaker Community, 1977. 2v.
This thorough, painstaking annotated bibliography is in two parts: Vol. 1 contains material by the Shakers themselves, and Vol. 2 contains writing about them. Volume 1, which comprises books, pamphlets, broadsides, and periodical articles, has a section for music leaflets. Here 26 items are listed, most of them published by the Canterbury, N.H. Shakers during the 1870s; all are printed in conventional notation, the changeover from the Shakers' own system to what they termed "hide and seek" notes having taken place, reluctantly, in the early part of that decade. Library locations are given for these items. Volume 2 provides one alphabetical sequence (by author, or title for anonymous works) of around 1,250 books, parts of books, and pamphlets about Shakers, followed by a second sequence of some 850 periodical articles. All the items are annotated, but there is no breakdown by subject and no subject index to facilitate access to the material on Shaker music these lists contain. Instead, the user must rely on a cross-reference system from one entry to other related ones. There is a list of addenda, a supplement covering 1973-74, and a title and joint author index.

S.335.   STANISLAW, Richard J. A Checklist of Four-Shape Shape-Note Tunebooks. Brooklyn: Institute for Studies in American Music, 1978. (I.S.A.M. Monographs, No. 10.) 61p. bibliog.
The 305 entries provide a useful bibliography of the various editions of approximately 100 shape-note tunebooks published between 1798 and 1860, plus those which, although published after this date, are closely connected with earlier volumes. Arrangement is alphabetical by author/compiler, with a title index. Entries give details of title, imprint, pagination and/or dimensions, library locations, and a note as to whether the tunebook is "urban" ("contains music that is European in style") or "rural" ("contains music of folk-hymn and indigenous styles"). There are some annotations. The bibliography lists 57 secondary sources. There is also a chronological summary covering 1798-1859, and a list of additions and amendments supplied by Paul C. Echols.

S.336.   THOMASON, Jean. Shaker Manuscript Hymnals from South Union, Kentucky; with comment on the musical notation by Fann R. Herndon; introduction by Julia Neal. Bowling Green, Ky.: Kentucky Folklore Society, 1967. 56p.
Fifteen manuscript hymnals from 1830-1881 in the Kentucky Library at Western Kentucky University are each individually described. The authors are identified, musical features and subject matter

briefly discussed, and sample verses quoted. Some facsimile pages are included. The appendix gives fuller details of each of the books that has named authors and tunes.

8. Occupational Folk Song

a. Cowboys

See also I.8.f

S.337.   FELTON, Harold W., ed. Cowboy Jamboree: western songs
& lore; musical arrangements by Edward S. Breck; illustrations by Aldren A. Watson; foreword by Carl Carmer.
New York: Knopf, 1951. 107p. illus.
Apparently based substantially on Margaret Larkin's Singing
Cowboy (LOAM 560), this is a collection of twenty songs, with simplified piano accompaniments intended particularly for children. Each
song is preceded by a brief commentary on the subject of the song
(but not the song itself).

S.338.   HARRIS, Charles W., and RAINEY, Buck, eds. The Cowboy: six-shooters, songs, and sex. Norman: University of Oklahoma Press, 1976. 167p. illus.
Includes a chapter by Guy Logsdon on "The Cowboy's Baw-
dy Music" which briefly surveys the history of cowboy song collecting, the fostering of the romantic image and the expurgation of
texts, and the perpetuation of cowboy culture via films and recordings.

S.339.   LEE, Katie. Ten Thousand Goddam Cattle: a history of
the American cowboy in song, story and verse. Flag-
staff, Ariz.: Northland Press, 1976. 254p. illus.,
bibliog., discog. refs.
Singer, filmmaker, radio and television personality Katie
Lee's book deserves to be better known. The subtitle and the preface ("I am attempting here more than just a book of songs.... The
cowboy and his songs are nothing without some knowledge of what
goes on around him.... I have, therefore, taken us deeper into
the land that was, and is, his home"--p. ix) together lead us to
expect a focus on the cowboy from both diachronic and synchronic
viewpoints. But the book's virtues are less ambitious and more
specific. The framework is a highly personalized narrative of Katie
Lee's travels and performances, during the course of which she encounters a number of cowboy songwriters and pieces together the
history of numerous songs. We not only receive the results of this
"research done over a lifetime" (p. x), we actually witness the research in progress. Her "attempt to restore writer to lyric and
composer to music" reaches its climax in the long search for the
author of her favorite song, "Old Dolores." She duly visits the
town itself, and the song's author, newspaperman-lawyer James

Grafton Rogers (no cowboy, he) becomes the central character, along with other favorite writers Gail Gardner and Billy Simon. Katie Lee's prose is not to everyone's taste. Self-consciously "Western" and often verbose ("I packed half a house in the trunk of Mr. Ford's first T-bird, crawled into a plush seat under a chrome wheel, turned the key, took a slug of hot coffee, pushed the throttle and said 'Let's go, Thunder'"--p. 4), she is nevertheless capable of evocative descriptions of the West. A useful feature is the appendix, a "compendium of songs" which are the scholarly fruits of her labors: texts and melodies of 54 songs, with comments, and bibliographical and discographical information. There is also a glossary, an extensive bibliography of collections, folios, and background, but no index.

S.340.   WHITE, John I. Git Along, Little Dogies: songs and song-
         makers of the American West; with a foreword by Austin
         E. Fife. Urbana: University of Illinois Press, 1975.
         221p. illus., bibliog., discog.

A collection of authoritative essays, some previously published, on particular cowboy songs and songwriters. The author, celebrated in the 1930s for his recordings and radio appearances as "The Lonesome Cowboy," draws on personal contact and a substantial collection of data, biographical, musical, bibliographical and discographical. Following an autobiographical chapter accounts are given of "Git Along, Little Dogies"; Owen Wister's venture into songwriting; Joseph Mills Hanson's "The Railroad Corral;" cowboy singing; Harry Stephens; Will Barnes; D. J. O'Malley; Romaine Lowdermilk; Gail Gardner; Badger Clark; Curley Fletcher ("The Strawberry Roan"); "Zebra Dun"; "Home on the Range"; "The Little Old Sod Shanty On the Claim"; Lowell Otus Reese's "Great Grandad"; White's own "Great Grandma"; singer Carl T. Sprague; and collectors N. Howard Thorp and John A. Lomax. Throughout the book the author's main concern is to put on record as many facts as possible concerning the precise origin of a song, often--as Fife says in his foreword--"determining its authorship and establishing its role in the evolution of the popular song tradition of Anglo-America" (p. xiii). In addition to the selective bibliography and discography there is a listing of White's own recordings, and an index.

b.   Lumberjacks

S.341.   CAZDEN, Norman, ed. The Abelard Folk Song Book: more
         than 101 ballads to sing. New York: Abelard Schuman,
         1958. 127p. illus., bibliog.

A great many of the songs in this "practical, singable assortment of folk songs and ballads" (p. 1) come from the repertoire of George Edwards, of the Catskills. The breadth of his repertoire--and hence of the book--suggests "that the tradition discovered here is not so much peculiar to one region as it is a product of that highly mobile worker, the lumberman" (ibid.). The songs are divided into two sections, "Songs For Every Day" and "Songs for Saturday Night," and are harmonized for piano accompaniment, with guitar chords provided also. A volume for popular use, it has a complementary scholarly side also: each song is headed by a descriptive note and, at the end of each section, there is information on origins, other versions, noteworthy features, and bibliographic references.

S.342. GRAY, Roland Palmer, ed. Songs and Ballads of the Maine Lumberjacks; with other songs from Maine. Cambridge, Mass.: Harvard University Press, 1924. (Repr. Detroit: Singing Tree Press, 1969.) 191p.

This is a collection of some 50 texts (no music), each preceded by background notes. In his introduction, the compiler informs us, "the sheaf of songs and ballads comprising this volume I gathered in Maine during a long residence there while professor in the State University." Several texts are quite contemporary: one, for instance, is called "President Wilson" and is dedicated to him (but there are none about Paul Bunyan, though he was a creation of the Maine lumberjacks). (Formerly LOAM A111.)

S.343. RICKABY, Franz, ed. Ballads and Songs of the Shanty-Boys. Cambridge, Mass.: Harvard University Press, 1926. 244p. illus.

A fascinating volume which would merit reprinting, this is a collection of the songs and ballads of the shanty-boys (lumbermen) of the Michigan, Minnesota, and Wisconsin forests. The songs are from the "Golden Age of American Lumbering," identified by the editor as 1870-1900. There are 51 pieces (texts only), with variants; tunes are furnished for some, but for others are only indicated (some have neither tune nor indication, but are included in the belief that "half a loaf is better than none" (p. viii). The brief preface and lengthy introduction are rich in information and sentiment. There is a section of notes on the songs, a title index, and a first-line index. The photos are excellent.

c. Sailors

S.344. NEESER, Robert W., ed. American Naval Songs & Ballads. New Haven, Conn.: Yale University Press, 1938. 372p. illus., bibliog.

"It has been the aim of the editor ... to gather in one collection the best of the songs, ballads, and short poems relating to the Navy and naval life and achievements, whether produced within the service itself or on the outside...." The collection is limited to texts only; no music is included, and for the great majority of songs and ballads no tunes are indicated. All the vocal texts are taken from broadsides or old collections, and twenty of the broadsides are printed as handsome facsimile illustrations. The texts and poems are given in chronological groups form the Revolution to the Civil War.

No 20th-century material is included. No title index, but the good bibliography offers library sources for each book listed.

9. Protest and Social Song Movements

(See also F.10)

a. General Studies

See also S.1151

S.345. MYRUS, Donald. Ballads, Blues, and the Big Beat. New
York: MacMillan: London: Collier-MacMillan, 1966.
136p. illus., discog.
An introduction to topical folk song for teenagers. There
are short, lively chapters on 1960s protest singers and troubadours
(Dylan, Paxton, Ochs, Sainte-Marie), on the "founders" of the tradition, black and white (Seeger, Guthrie, Leadbelly, etc.), on
selected women performers (Baez, Mahalia Jackson, Elizabeth Cotten,
Odetta), on folk-rock and blues, on early country music, and on
folk song scholarship.

S.346. RODNITSKY, Jerome L. Minstrels of the Dawn: the folk-
protest singer as a cultural hero. Chicago: Nelson-Hall,
1976. 192p. illus., bibliog., discog.
Rodnitsky's thought-provoking, well-argued and documented
study sets out to examine "the history of American folk-protest with
particular stress on the evolution of the protest song, the protest
singer, and the social forces that shaped the protest tradition during
the twentieth century in general and the 1960s in particular" (preface). He outlines three particular goals: "to analyze the extent to
which popular protest music has been a radical, politico-cultural influence since 1945; to describe how folk-protest was absorbed by
popular music in the late 1960s; and finally to provide social and cultural portraits of four key writer-performers who became cultural
heroes during the 1960s" (ibid.). The first two goals are achieved
in the first part, the last in the second, entitled "Folk Heroes--Links
in the Chain." Here sections are devoted to detailed biographical
and critical portraits of Woody Guthrie, Phil Ochs, Joan Baez, and
Bob Dylan. A last section, "Coda: the End of an Era," considers
the decline of the genre since the late 1960s. (For two contrasting
assessments of Rodnitsky's view of the protest singer, see the reviews by Hughson Mooney, Journal of American History, 64, December 1977, pp. 851-53, and R. Serge Denisoff, Contemporary Sociology, 6, March 1977, pp. 269-70.)

b. Woody Guthrie

S.347. GUTHRIE, Woody. Seeds of Man: an experience lived and

dreamed. New York: Dutton, 1976. 401p.
_____. _____. New York: Pocket Books, 1977.
434p.

One of the numerous cuts made in the manuscript of Woody's
Bound For Glory (LOAM 597) by his editor, Joy Doerflinger, was the
account of a trip made by Woody, his father, and two uncles to the
Chisos Mountains in Texas in 1931, in search of a silver mine family
lore recorded as having been discovered by Woody's grandfather.
In 1947, not long after the tragic death of his daughter Cathy in a
domestic fire, Woody took up the story again, changing silver to
gold, replacing an uncle with a friend, adding and inventing all
manner of colorful characters, delighting in their language, and
generally allowing his imagination space to breathe. "The story bil-
lowed as he wrote," according to Joe Klein (no. S.348, p. 343).
"His descriptive passages were, at once, glorious and dizzying ...
[but] the cumulative weight of all the words was, ultimately, numb-
ing" (ibid., p. 344). Edited after Woody's death in 1967 by William
Doerflinger, editor at Dutton's, the narrative as we have it is a
testimony to Woody's distinctive ability to draw equally on the experience of ear and eye, and to imbue all he wrote with a profound
humanity.

S.348. KLEIN, Joe. Woody Guthrie: a life. New York: Knopf,
        1980. London: Faber and Faber, 1981. 475p. illus.
        An outstanding biography, which performs the rare feat of
creating a fascinating narrative out of the peripatetic life of an
American vernacular musician. True, Guthrie's story by itself is an
absorbing one--possibly the outstanding example in American music
of the interweaving of music and politics--and his character and
achievements would color the palest narrative style; but the traditional image of the man as a folk-hero reincarnate that is necessary
to most accounts of Guthrie would not survive the kind of close, detailed scrutiny meted out in this book. The immense amount of detail
made available to the author by the access provided to Guthrie's unpublished papers by his second wife Marjorie, as well as by his own
interviews, is handled with skill and sensitivity; Klein avoids judging
the subject, yet the picture which emerges has an at least partially
demythologizing effect. Klein has no particular thesis, and is not
drawn to making Guthrie a symbolic figure (note the subtitle--a life),
but offers the material on which he can be re-assessed ("it seems,"
wrote Dave Laing, "that the actual Woody Guthrie was far closer to
the bohemian logophile than to the proletarian folk-song hero"--Popu-
lar Music, 2 [1982], p. 308). Detailed source notes are provided,
and there is an index.

S.349. ROBBIN, Edward. Woody Guthrie and Me: an intimate
        reminiscence. Berkeley, Calif.: Lancaster-Miller, 1979.
        160p. illus., bibliog.
        Robbin's acquaintance with Guthrie began in 1938, when he
was Los Angeles editor of the People's World, and a broadcaster--as
Woody was--over KFVD radio. This "potpourri of memories" was

written, Robbin says, in an unavailing attempt to "exorcise Woody's ghost from my spirit" (p. 156). It mostly concerns their friendship in the late 1930s and early '40s, and is an affectionate, if sketchy, portrait. The most substantial item is the transcript of a 1976 interview with singer Will Geer. There are also accounts of conversations around the same period (reconstructed from memory) with Guthrie's first and second wives, Mary and Marjorie. No index.

10. Folk Song Revival and Folk Rock

(See also S.346)

a. General Studies

S.350.   LAING, Dave, et al. The Electric Muse: the story of folk
         into rock, by Dave Laing, Karl Dallas, Robin Denselow
         and Robert Shelton. London: Eyre Methuen, 1975.
         182p. illus., bibliog. refs., discogs.
         One American and three British critics attempt to trace "the
myriad forms taken by what has been loosely called the 'folk revival'," and to examine "its effects on the dominant popular music of
the period, rock" (introduction). Each author has one section of
the book, the first two (Shelton and Laing) being more exclusively
concerned with America, and the second two with Britain. Shelton
describes the various ingredient styles of the American Folk revival
--Anglo-American ballads, blues, gospel, etc.--and introduces the
pioneers and outlines the early split between purists and those of
a more commercial orientation. Laing chronicles developments in rock
in the 1960s and early '70s under the impact of the folk revival,
which revitalized an idiom grown limp after the dissipation of the
power of early rock & roll. Briefly mentioning key musicians such
as the Byrds, Dylan, Lovin' Spoonful, Crosby, Stills, Nash and
Young, Joni Mitchell, James Taylor and Joan Baez, he demonstrates
the crucial role of folk elements, not only in the economic success of
the music, but in its cultural influence. Dallas explores the roots of
folk tradition with particular reference to Britain, and attempts to
show the kinship between these and the developments of "electric
folk." Much of his material is relevant to the USA also. Denselow
is concerned with British songwriters "who have attempted to as-
similate something of the feel of English traditional music within a
rock context" (p. 139). Index.

S.351.   VASSAL, Jacques. Folksong: une histoire de la musique
         populaire aux Etats-Unis. Paris: Albin Michel, 1971.
         348p. illus., bibliog.
         _____. Electric Children: roots and branches of modern
         folkrock; translated and adapted by Paul Barnett. New
         York: Taplinger, 1976. 270p. illus., bibliog., discog.
         Written originally to introduce French audiences to--and
interest them in--American and British folk rock, its antecedents,

and its practitioners, Vassal's book is useful for the range of its coverage, and for its occasional forays into territory not well covered elsewhere (e.g., the records of Tom Paxton), but in essence contains little not found in other sources in greater depth. It is in three parts. Part 1, "Roots," briefly outlines the history of black and white folk music, with an emphasis on songs of social comment. (There is an odd chapter on Indian music, called "Reds," which turns out to be chiefly about two folk rock performers of native American extraction, Buffy Sainte-Marie and Peter La Farge.) Part 2, "Branches," might have been better called "Trunks," since these are the pillars of Vassal's argument. Here are quite close examinations of Woody Guthrie, the urban folk revival (Seeger et al.), Dylan, and the "new generation" (in this case, Paxton, Phil Ochs, Joan Baez, Judy Collins). Discussion of individuals tends often to be constructed as a series of reviews of their LPs. Part 3, "Electric Children," is an overview of more recent developments in the USA and Britain (updated by the translator). The discography lists album titles but no label names or numbers; the bibliography includes books, articles, and songbooks. Index.

S.352. VON SCHMIDT, Eric, and ROONEY, Jim. Baby, Let Me Follow You Down: the illustrated story of the Cambridge folk years. Garden City, N.Y.: Anchor Books, 1979. 314p. illus.

What appears at first to be an elaborate picture book (it is indeed liberally illustrated) turns out to be also a vivid account of the late 1950s genesis and '60s flowering of the Cambridge (Massachusetts) folk scene, the seminal festival out of which came Joan Baez, Bob Dylan, Bonny Raitt, and many less well known. The narrative incorporates verbatim excerpts from interviews with over 60 participants. Beyond that, the authors were themselves participants, and have a strong sense of the "musical community ... whose common bond was a rediscovery of the many basic forms of American folk music" (foreword). No index.

S.353. WHISNANT, David E. Folk Festival Issues: report from a seminar, March 2-3, 1978, sponsored by The National Council for the Traditional Arts. Los Angeles: John Edwards Memorial Foundation, 1979. (Special series, No. 12.) 28p. illus., bibliog.

A summary record of a seminar held in Washington, D.C. to consider some of the issues (philosophical, social, cultural, etc.) "deriving from and related to folklife festival production." Discussion ranged over the concepts embodied in past festivals, the current situation, the probable impact of new social factors, and the need for new presentational mechanisms.

b. Individual Performers

JOAN BAEZ

S.354.   BROWNE, Ray B. et al., eds. Heroes of Popular Culture;
          edited by Ray B. Browne, Marshall Fishwick, Michael
          T. Marsden. Bowling Green, Ohio: Bowling Green
          University Popular Press, 1972. 190p. bibliog. refs.
     Two musical "heroes" of popular culture are the subjects
of essays in this volume. The first is Joan Baez, called "a pacifist
St. Joan" by Jerome Rodnitzky in his piece. The second is Burt
Bacharach, whose elevation to hero status may surprise some, but
who for Bruce Lehof is a "newstyle man in a newstyle world" (newstyle heroes do not "stand for something," they "move for something" [sic.]--p. 165).

S.355.   SWAN, Peter. Joan Baez: a bio- disco- bibliography;
          being a selected guide to material in print, on record,
          on cassette and on film, with a biographical introduction.
          Brighton: John L. Noyce, 1977. 23p.
     The 94-item bibliography of American and British material
includes 51 articles by and about Joan Baez, fifteen books, chapters
and pamphlets, 22 background books, and six songbooks. Each entry is briefly annotated. The discography, also annotated, lists 29
Joan Baez LPs with a further six to which she contributed. Five
films are given in the filmography. Index of names.

S.356.   SWANEKAMP, Joan. Diamonds & Rust: a bibliography and
          discography on Joan Baez. Ann Arbor, Mich.: Pierian
          Press, 1980. 75p. illus.
     More thorough than Swan (no. S.355), this is an annotated
bibliography of 184 items, chronologically arranged, with indexes of
article titles, subjects, and periodical titles (33 sources are given);
these are followed by an alphabetical album discography, with label
numbers, dates, and lists of contents, an album chronology, a listing of songs released as singles, with composers and label numbers,
and indexes of composers and song titles.

JUDY COLLINS

S.357.   CLAIRE, Vivian. Judy Collins. New York: Flash Books,
          1977. 77p. illus., discog.
     Constructed much as the same author's book on Linda Ron-
stadt (no. S.1240), this contains a biographical section derived from
unsourced secondary sources and a "music" section devoted to a
critical investigation of the singer's records. The writing is generally
laudatory; the critical section is lightweight. The discography is a
chronological list of Collins' albums; provided for each is the record
number, the release date, and the titles and composers of the songs
included. No index.

11. Country Music

a. General Reference Works and Discography

See also nos. S.275, S.276

S.358.   DELLAR, Fred, and THOMPSON, Roy. The Illustrated Encyclopedia of Country Music; with Douglas B. Green.
New York: Harmony Books; London: Salamander Books,
1977. 256p. illus., discogs.

Basically a biographical dictionary, though with some entries
for instruments and styles, this is an efficient, attractive production,
a useful starting point for essential career information, if not for
anything more telling than that. It features some 450 entries--a very
respectable total, and one which includes the less well-known as well
as the illustrious, the early as well as the modern. Entries are frequently constructed around the sequence of an artist's records; many
have selective album discographies. The numerous illustrations consist of portraits and reproduced album covers, the majority in color.
(Reviewing the book in Old Time Music, No. 27 [Winter 1977/78], p.
31, Tony Russell hazarded the guess that many of the old-time and
bluegrass entries are the work of Douglas B. Green.)

S.359.   FABER, Charles F. The Country Music Almanac. Lexington, Ky.: the author, 1978-1979. 2v.

A miscellany of ranking lists, in typed and stapled form;
several are idiosyncratic, but most are useful within the limitations
of the genre. The two volumes are divided by period: the first
covers 1922-43, the second 1944-78. Each volume contains essentially
the same type of material: "The Five Hundred Greatest Country Music Performers," "The Country Music Charts" (in Vol. 1 this is
based on inspired guesswork, the precise date being unavailable),
"The Top Twenty Records Each Year," "The Top Twenty Songwriters." The first section in each case contains a selective
"Chronology of Country Music Recordings" (for "recordings" read
"events"). (Available from the author at 3569, Cornwall Drive,
Lexington, Ky. 40503.)

S.360.   GENNETT RECORDS of Old Time Tunes: a catalog reprint.
Los Angeles: John Edwards Memorial Foundation, 1975.
(JEMF Special Series, No. 6.) 20p. illus.

The illustrated catalog reprinted here is one released by
Gennett (the label of the Starr Piano Company of Richmond, Indiana)
in January 1928, and lists all the hillbilly records issued during the
previous year on the Electrobeam Gennett label. A brief introduction
by John K. MacKenzie describes the significance of the catalog.

S.361.   OSBORNE, Jerry. 55 Years of Recorded Country/Western
Music; edited by Bruce Hamilton. Phoenix, Ariz.:
O'Sullivan Woodside, 1976. 164p. illus.

Though chiefly intended as a collector's pricing guide, this is also a useful discography (especially given the continued absence of standard country discographies). There are three main sections: (i) an "alphabetical-chronological" 78 rpm listing, in which arrangement is by performer (Roy Acuff to York Brothers), with recordings listed in record label number order; (ii) an alphabetical listing of 45s, which is not chronological but which includes label names and numbers (whereas (i) includes both sides of each record, (ii) lists only the "A" side); (iii) an alphabetical listing of "future gold records"--records often ignored by collectors but which may have value "someday." Arrangement is once again by artist, with record label and number given after each title. A substantial, 30-page dealers' and collectors' directory is included at the back of the book.

S.362.   SAKOL, Jeannie.   The Wonderful World of Country Music.
         New York: Grosset & Dunlap, 1979.   240p.   illus.
         An illustrated reference book containing, in one alphabetical sequence, entries for a wide variety of country music phenomena: individuals, festivals, events, publications, television and radio programs, etc. The coverage is selective, the style personal, and several features have no value (e.g., illustrations of the homes of country music stars), but some of the information, especially on individuals, is useful; there are also some unusual items for an encyclopedia, such as a transcript of a television interview (December, 1977) with Dolly Parton by Barbara Walters. An index provides access to names and topics that have no entry of their own.

b.   Miscellaneous Guides and Surveys

S.363.   CORNFELD, Robert.   Just Country: country people,
         stories, music; with Marshall Fallwell.   New York:
         McGraw-Hill, 1976.   176p.   illus., bibliog.
         Fallwell's full-page black-and-white portraits (of George Jones, Maybelle Carter, Eddy Arnold, and others), sparingly used for greater effect, are the most striking thing about this illustrated introduction. The numerous other illustrations, some historical, some commercial, and some more of Fallwell's, are also effective, if overshadowed. Cornfeld's text (for which Fallwell also contributed two chapters) is far from overshadowed, although the designer seems to suggest we should think it elementary. It is a capable, affectionate narrative, in broadly historical sequence, of the styles and the stars. Cornfeld also reveals, intermittently, a sharp ear for what makes a musical identity. The book concludes with a series of short portraits (by Fallwell) of some Nashville performers thought to be the future stars.

S.364.   LAZARUS, Lois.   Country Is My Music!   New York: Mess-
         ner, 1980.   192p.   illus., bibliog.
         Possibly intended for a younger audience, this is an overview of the modern country music scene in Nashville and elsewhere.

There is some comment on music as such, and one chapter, "Black Blues and Country," discusses black-white interaction.

S.365.   RUBENSTEIN, Raeanne. Honkytonk Heroes: a photo album of country music, photographs by Raeanne Rubenstein; text by Peter McCabe. New York: Harper & Row, 1975. 154p. illus.
    While this is essentially a picture book--and the pictures, in black and white, are exceptional--the abundant text is equally arresting. Knowing, witty, kind, and truthful, it seems to have been written (and perhaps was) by a loving but sophisticated fan. The introduction is one of the best capsule history-essays on country music. The book has its faults, however: many performers are omitted altogether (there are five pictures of Dolly Parton but none of Minnie Pearl) and there is no index.

c.   Country Music Lyrics

    See also S. 376

S.366.   HORSTMANN, Dorothy. Sing Your Heart Out, Country Boy. New York: Dutton, 1975. 393p. bibliog., discog.
    This outstanding book is a collection of the lyrics of some 310 country music songs; what makes it unusual and valuable is that each lyric is preceded by information from its author (or his or her heir) on its background. The songs are grouped into fifteen subject categories, such as "Songs of Home," "Honky-Tonk Songs," etc. Horstmann provides historical commentary for each category. The time period covered by the lyrics is a little vague: the compiler writes in her preface that the book contains lyrics of the "finest ... and best-loved songs written over the past fifty years plus some a good deal older than that" (p. xi). A brief foreword is provided by Bill Anderson (the Southern Editor of Billboard), and there is an index of song titles.

d.   History and Criticism

    (i) General

S.367.   CARR, Patrick, ed. The Illustrated History of Country Music, by the editors of Country Music magazine. Garden City, N.Y.: Doubleday, 1979. 359p. illus.
    "Illustrated histories" are perhaps expected to place illustration before historical text, but this particular work defies that expectation. It is a careful, scholarly, full-blown account in twelve historical chapters, from the pre-history of the music to the modern scene. The principal (and outstanding) contributors are Charles Wolfe (on the background, the 1920s, and the contemporary trends), and Douglas B. Green (on the 1930s, the 1940s, and the revival of

the "mountain sound" after Hank Williams). Green collaborated with
Bob Pinson on the chapter on Texas, and with William Ivey on chap-
ters on Nashville and "the death of rock and the rise of country."
The other writers are J. R. Young (on singing cowboys), Roger
Williams (on Hank Williams), and Nick Tosches (on rockabilly).
There is, regrettably, no bibliographical or discographical informa-
tion, but there is a large index.

S.368.　GREEN, Douglas B. Country Roots: the origins of country
　　　　　music; foreword by Merle Travis. New York: Hawthorn
　　　　　Books, 1976. 235p. illus., bibliog., discog.
　　　　　　Green disclaims all idea that his book might be thought "a
scholarly history," preferring to propose it as "an interpretative look
at the history of country music, one that will impart both knowledge
and, it is hoped, a little insight to the expert and devoted fan and
give a sense of perspective to the neophyte" (p. 3). It is probably
the second audience that will profit most from a clearly organized,
reliable and enjoyable text, but Green is a very knowledgeable writer, perhaps especially on western themes, and worth reading by anyone. The eleven chapters each take one subject: European folk
traditions; Appalachian old time music; blues; country; singing cowboys; Cajuns; bluegrass; western swing; gospel music; rockabilly;
country-folk; country-rock; honky-tonk, country pop and the Nashville sound. They are all liberally illustrated with black-and-white
photographs, all of which have descriptive captions which often add
details on individuals which would seem out of place in the main text.
There is also a chronology, 1877-1975, a lengthy discography and a
bibliography of books, both organized according to the book's chapter headings, and an index.

S.369.　MITSUI, Toru. Kantori Ongaku no Rekishi. (A History of
　　　　　Country Music.) Tokyo: Ongaku-no-Tomo Sha, 1971.
　　　　　336p. illus., bibliog., discog.
　　　　　　A professor of English and a prolific critic, Mitsui has been
very influential in introducing Japanese audiences to the history and
background of much American music. Here, with a debt acknowledged
to Bill C. Malone's Country Music U.S.A. (LOAM 606), he provides a
thorough history of country music, from its folk roots to its modern
sound, in ten chapters. (The book was reprinted in 1974 and 1976.)
General index, and index of names. (In Japanese.)

S.370.　RUBIN, D., ed. The American South: portrait of a cul-
　　　　　ture. Baton Rouge: Louisiana State University Press,
　　　　　1980. 379p.
　　　　　　Includes an essay, "Southern Country Music: a Brief
Eulogy," by Katie Letcher Lyle, which discusses the most common
themes in country music and their persistence.

S.371.　TOSCHES, Nick. Country: the biggest music in America.
　　　　　New York: Stein and Day, 1977. 258p. illus.
　　　　　_____. Country: living legends and dying metaphors

in America's biggest music. New York: Scribner's, 1985. 260p. illus.

For all its (in some respects) well-earned reputation as a disrespectful, ribald tilt at some country music shrines, the first thing about Tosches' book is that it is learned. Whether on arcane British ballads, obscure 1920s singers, or minutiae of the record industry, Tosches' restless exploration of "the darker areas of country music history, not its current popularity" (rev. ed., p. ix), is replete with information and erudition. As the sources of this knowledge are rarely acknowledged the originality of his ideas is not easy to test. What chiefly distinguishes them--and maybe serves to disguise part of their heritage--is the colorful language to which they are wedded: some of Tosches' stuff may be second-hand, but he struts it with flair.

Though there are thirteen chapters, the essentials of the book are contained in five essays on aspects of country music history, separated by short, picturesque--and a mite self-indulgent--interludes. The five pieces are all constructed in what appears to be a diffuse, rambling way, but this seems deliberately designed to bring out connections. Basic themes are apparent in each: the ballad inheritance; the growth of rockabilly (with particular attention to Jerry Lee Lewis); sexual images; black-white interaction (especially with reference to fiddle and guitar); the record industry. One of the shorter pieces is concerned with "yodeling cowboys," and two with "forgotten" musician Emmett Miller. The revised edition recasts some prose, corrects some facts and adds some new ones, but changes little of substance. Index.

(ii) Bluegrass

S.372.   HILL, Fred. Grass Roots: illustrated history of bluegrass and mountain music. Rutland, Vt.: Academy Books, 1980. 121p. illus., bibliog.

Pleasant if unexceptional introductory history with a particular emphasis on bluegrass. A brisk and affectionate survey of old-time music up to and including Roy Acuff precedes three chapters on bluegrass--the first on Bill Monroe and the rise of the genre; the second on the ups and downs of bluegrass bands of the 1950s; the third on the subsequent revival. Indexes of names and titles.

S.373.   MITSUI, Toru. Bluegrass Ongaku. (Bluegrass Music.) Toyohashi: Traditional-Song Society, 1967. 159p. illus.

_____. _____. 2nd rev. ed. Tokyo: Bronze-sha, 1975. 222p. illus.

To this illustrated study in Japanese belongs the distinction of being the first book on bluegrass (see John Edwards Memorial Foundation Quarterly [JEMFQ], 12, No. 41 [1976]). A series of introductory chapters lays out the hillbilly background. Following this Mitsui sets out to define bluegrass, to describe the role of each

instrument and the characteristics of singing style and of bluegrass
melodies, and to discuss texts and repertoires. The last chapters
turn to the musicians themselves (Monroe, Scruggs, Flatt, Reno, the
Stanley Brothers), and to the performance of the music.

(iii) Modern

See also no. S.383

S.374. BANE, Michael. The Outlaws: revolution in country music.
(New York?): Country Music Magazine Press, 1978.
154p. illus.
The term "outlaw," in country music circles, was borrowed
from a 1972 song by Lee Clayton ("Ladies Love Outlaws") and applied
to the group of anti-Nashville establishment musicians that included
Waylon Jennings and Willie Nelson. Bane's colloquial account insists,
to begin with, that we are aware who the first outlaw was: Hank
Williams. He then provides portraits of the main protagonist outlaws
(they had thought of calling themselves "cowboys," but "'outlaw'
sounded meaner than 'cowboy'; after all, Roy Rogers was a cowboy"
--(p. 11): Tompall Glaser, Waylon Jennings, Jack Clement, Willie
Nelson, and David Allan Coe. Basically biographical, with considerable interview material, these energetic accounts are most informative
when discussing the musicians' various experiences with the system.
The overall impression may not be the intended one: it is of the
parochialism that even "revolution" does not diminish.

S.375. CORBIN, Everett. Storm Over Nashville: a case against
modern country music. Nashville, Tenn.: Ashlar Press,
1980. 202p. illus.
The charge against modern country music is that it has
conspired to murder traditional country music, and has falsely described itself as country music when it has degenerated into pop-rock.
Accused are record companies, the music press, radio and television
stations, individual performers, and some organizations. The plaint-
iff, militant traditionalism, seeks not only to prove the charges, but
to demonstrate that traditional country music, with its virtues of
simplicity, purity (...), both deserves to live and is the true country music. In the event, despite the undoubted correctness of much
of his argument, Corbin's case is badly presented and repetitive, and
often fails to hit its targets squarely.
Similar battles have been fought in other musical areas;
what makes Corbin's book interesting despite its flaws is the immediacy of its details. As a Nashville-based journalist he provides many
examples of day-to-day events and humdrum details characteristic of
Nashville life in particular, which are shown to be symptomatic of
greater issues. In his account of the music he admires and for
which he is fighting, Corbin's rambling style again undermines his
success, but several people stand out as representative: Roy Acuff
(who is interviewed), Vernon Dalhart, Vernon Oxford, Ernest Tubb

(while among the targets of his hostility are Eddy Arnold and Dolly Parton). The odd saga of the Jimmie Rodgers stamp, meanwhile, is a modest, concluding tribute to the value of perseverance.

S.376.   GAILLARD, Frye. Watermelon Wine: the spirit of country music. New York: St. Martin's Press, 1978. 236p. illus.

The central theme of Gaillard's stimulating book is the tension between tradition and commercialism in country music. He explores the roots of this tension--the "estrangement of country and folk" (p. 34)--but his attention is directed mainly at the post-Williams generation of country music rebels. These writers and performers have adopted outspoken postures against the establishment, but their achievement Gaillard sees as being one of the reunification, not the further polarization, of traditional country music concern and compassion with the demands of entertainment. Besides Cash and Williams, Gaillard focuses on Waylon Jennings, Tompall Glaser, Kris Kristofferson, Joan Baez, Willie Nelson, Doug Sahm, and Vince Matthews. One chapter is concerned with Loretta Lynn and the changing image of women, and another on black country music stars. The "diverse and evolving sensibilities of country music" are illustrated in a selection of 55 lyrics.

S.377.   GRISSIM, John. Country Music: white man's blues. New York: Paperback Library, 1970. 299p. illus.

Touring the late-1960s country scene in Nashville and California, watching, interviewing, with a keen journalistic eye and ear, Grissim gives us one of the most informative and enjoyable books on country music. The central pillars of the book are astutely described encounters with a variety of individuals: record producers Jerry Kennedy, Shelby Singleton, Billy Sherill, and Scott Turner, and performers Waylon Jennings, Johnny Cash, Merle Haggard, and Jerry Lee Lewis. (All but Cash are based on interviews.) Supporting these are shorter portraits of Buck Owens, Glenn Campbell, Commander Cody (and His Lost Planet Airmen), Loretta Lynn, Jeanie C. Riley, and others. Other chapters are devoted to the Nashville studio scene, the Grand Ole Opry (before its move), and various aspects of the country music life and mores. No index.

e.   Regions and Places

See also nos. S.375, S.377

TENNESSEE

S.378.   HURST, Jack. Nashville's Grand Ole Opry; text by Jack Hurst; introduction by Roy Acuff. New York: Abrams, 1975. 404p. illus., discog.

Glossily illustrated history-cum-photograph album of the country music radio and television program, from its inception to the move to Opryland in 1974. The text plays a secondary role but does contain a substantial amount of original material. The illustrations, the book's raison d'être, move beyond a purely documentary function into one more of celebration, even adulation, but do so with that same combination of formality and informality that often characterizes the music itself. Among the more general chapters are ones devoted specifically to Uncle Dave Macon, Hank Williams, women artists, and Bill Monroe. The discography is a four-page listing of LPs, and there is an index to texts and illustrations.

S.379.   PETERSON, Richard A. Single-Industry Firm to Con-
         glomerate Synergistics: alternative strategies for sell-
         ing insurance and country music. Los Angeles: John
         Edwards Memorial Foundation, 1975. (Reprint No. 34.)
         pp. 341-357. bibliog. refs.

(Reprinted from Growing Metropolis: Aspects of Development in Nashville, ed. James Blumstein & Benjamin Walter [Vanderbilt University Press, 1975].) Peterson explores the changes in the business management strategy of the National Life and Accident Insurance Company towards its celebrated radio station, WSM Nashville, and in particular, the Grand Ole Opry, seeing the decision to develop Opryland as a departure from the "one product" philosophy that marked the earlier years of the relationship.

S.380.   TASSIN, Myron, and HENDERSON, Jerry. Fifty Years At
         the Grand Ole Opry, foreword by Minnie Pearl; introduc-
         tion by Mother Maybelle Carter. Gretna, La.: Pelican,
         1975. 112p. illus.

A commemorative picture book with many historical and contemporary photographs. The accompanying text is an affectionate tribute to Nashville past and present by two authors with a long experience of the Opry.

S.381.   WOLFE, Charles K. Tennessee Strings: the story of
         country music in Tennessee. Knoxville: University of
         Tennessee Press, in cooperation with the Tennessee
         Historical Commission, 1977. 118p. illus., bibliog.

An enlightening, if all too brief, historical survey, from the folk background to modern Nashville, by way of the mountain musicians, the rise of radio (Grand Ole Opry), and the post-war developments, honky-tonk and bluegrass. The singular importance of Tennessee--"constantly in the forefront of the music's development" (preface)--is amply demonstrated in a narrative that includes the legendary (Uncle Dave Macon, George D. Hay, Roy Acuff, Chet Atkins) and the less well-known. But although the rationale for a regional history is admirably expressed--"one cannot pretend to understand the music without understanding the social context that produced and maintained it" (ibid.)--this does not result, unfortunately, in any very penetrating attempt to locate the significance of the music "in the commonly agreed meanings of the group or society in which the ... music is located" (John Shepherd, et al., Whose Music?, no. S.18, p. 7). Index.

TEXAS

S.382. CLAYPOOL, Bob. Saturday Night at Gilley's; principal
        photographer Tony Bullard. New York: Grove Press,
        1980. 176p. illus.
        Colorful history and description of the raw and raunchy
Pasadena honky-tonk, opened in 1971, and of the partnership between country-rock performer (and cousin of Jerry Lee Lewis)
Mickey Gilley and the formidable Sherwood Cryer, who conceived
and runs this huge (and hugely profitable) enterprise. The second
part of the book, concerned with the use of Gilley's to make the
movie Urban Cowboy (starring John Travolta) is less interesting,
except for the description of the threat to the very identity of the
establishment which resulted from the "Hollywood invasion."

S.383. REID, Jan. The Improbable Rise of Redneck Rock;
        photographs by Melinda Wickman. Austin, Tex.:
        Heidelberg Publishers, 1974. 342p. illus.
        A close-quarters account of the growth of country rock in
Austin, and of its main protagonists. The author is a journalist
who, though a Texan by birth (his own ambivalent attachment and
sense of involvement are important ingredients in his story), came
to Austin in 1970. The research for the book occupied a year in
1973-74, and involved considerable interviewing. Reid begins, in
Part 1, not with the performers but with those who laid the foundation for the development of the Austin scene--club owners,
managers, etc., especially Kenneth Threadgill, the founders and
staff of the Armadillo (in particular Eddie Wilson, Stan Alexander,
and Mike Tolleson), and Larry Watkins. Part 2 presents a series
of portraits of musicians: Jerry Jeff Walker, Steve Fromholz, B.
W. Stevenson, Willis Alan Ramsey, Bobby Bridger, Rusty Wier,
Kinky Friedman, Michael Murphey, and Willie Nelson. The book concludes with a rather tetchy, disillusioned account of a Willie Nelson
"picnic" festival at Dripping Springs. No index.

f. Musicians

    (i) Collected Profiles

S.384. CHALKER, Bryan. Country Music. London: Phoebus,
        1976. 95p. illus.
        A slick picture book of country music stars for the UK fan
audience. Color pictures are included when at all possible. The
commentary provides a basic outline and biographical snippets, in
the style assumed to be necessary for popular appeal.

S.385. DAVID, Andrew. Country Music Stars: people at the top
        of the charts. New York: Domas Books, 1980. 96p.
        illus.
        An attractively designed and illustrated fan book, featuring

double-page displays (full-page photo on the right, biography on the left) of 39 country music recording artists. Each potted biography is accompanied by a "scorecard": number of gold records, Grammy and other awards, top albums, "memorable" singles, current recording label. No discographical information is provided. Index.

S.386. DAVIS, Paul. New Life in Country Music; foreword by Cliff Richard; introduction by George Hamilton IV. Worthing, Sussex: Henry Walter, 1976. 111p. illus.

This little British paperback gives thirteen short biographical sketches of country music performers, with emphasis on their religious attachments. Cliff Richard states in his brief foreword: "The artists ... featured in this book are well known ... exponents of country and western music. And their ... Gospel music stems from their personal Christian commitment...."

S.387. DEW, Joan. Singers & Sweethearts: the women of country music. Garden City, N.Y.: Doubleday, 1977. 148p. illus.

A thoughtful collection of in-depth personal profiles, all well illustrated, and all derived largely from interview material. The author sets out her aim in the introduction as being "to present information and observations that in my opinion most clearly define [these performers] mentally, emotionally, and musically, but I am not presumptuous enough to think that all the layers of complexity have been stripped away. The private inner core remains intact and untouched" (p. 6). The five in question are Loretta Lynn, Tammy Wynette, June Carter, Dolly Parton, and Tanya Tucker.

S.388. GRAY, Andy. Great Country Music Stars. London: Hamlyn, 1975. 176p. illus., bibliog.

This contains a history of sorts by a writer for London's New Musical Express. It is, however, mainly an excuse for photographs--"20 in colour and approx. 200 in black and white," to quote the dust jacket, of (chiefly contemporary) "stars" (a photo of the author appears on p. 67). Many were taken in Europe--and European country music performers are included at the end. The book abounds in handsome toothy smiles and bouffant hair-dos. The bibliography abounds in eight titles.

S.389. GURALNICK, Peter. Lost Highway: journeys and arrivals of American musicians. Boston: Godine, 1979. (Repr. New York: Vintage Books, 1982). 362p. illus., bibliog., discog.

A companion volume to Guralnick's Feel Like Going Home (LOAM 830), this second set of profiles is as elegantly--and passionately--written as the first, but has a wider coverage of music styles (in particular a strong representation of country music), and a deeper understanding of popular culture. Although the portraits first appeared independently in a variety of journals (Rolling Stone, Boston Phoenix, etc.), they are linked by the author's preoccupation with the way blues, country music, and rockabilly fed off each other in the 1950s and '60s. Also binding the pieces together is Guralnick's sense, described in his introduction, that his various subjects are united by a common experience, which he expresses in the image of the road. The road is a metaphor for "all the psychic dislocations that a career in show business necessarily entails" (p. 3), and for the seeming inevitability with which commercial success leads to a severing of a performer's roots. (Guralnick may be unaware of another famous use of the road metaphor--by Sidney Bechet, for whom "the road goes away ... and the road comes back" [Treat It Gentle, no. S.737, p. 4].) The portraits (mostly based on interviews) are divided into four sections: influential figures (Ernest Tubb, Hank Snow, DeFord Bailey, Rufus Thomas, Bobby Bland), rockabilly (Scott Moore, Charlie Feathers, Elvis Presley, Charlie Rich, Sleepy LaBeef, Mickey Gilley, Jack Clement), country music outlaws (Waylon Jennings, Hank Williams, Jr., Merle Haggard, James Talley, and Stoney Edwards), and blues (Howlin' Wolf, Otis Spann, Big Joe Turner). There is also a conversation with Sam Phillips. Index.

S.390.   MALONE, Bill C. and McCULLOH, Judith, eds. Stars of Country Music: Uncle Dave Macon to Johnny Rodriguez. Urbana: University of Illinois Press, 1975. 476p. illus., bibliog., discogs.

The 21 original essays in this fine collection come from American and British contributors, who in general set out to summarize existing knowledge on particular individuals in a scholarly but approachable way. Apart from the first (Norm Cohen on early pioneers) and last (Bill C. Malone on the "shower of stars" since 1945), each essay is on an individual or group. The musicians covered are: Uncle Dave Macon, Vernon Dalhart, Bradley Kincaid, Carter Family, Jimmie Rodgers, Gene Autry, Bob Wills, Roy Acuff, Bill Monroe, Ernest Tubbs, Hank Williams, Lester Flatt and Earl Scruggs, Chet Atkins, Johnny Cash, Loretta Lynn, Merle Haggard, Charley Pride, Tom T. Hall, and Johnny Rodriguez.

The essays average 20 pages in length, and all have bibliographies and discographies. There is a combined index of names and titles.

(ii) Individual Musicians

ROY ACUFF

S.391.   SCHLAPPI, Elizabeth. Roy Acuff: the Smokey Mountain Boy. Gretna, La.: Pelican, 1978. 299p. illus., bibliog., discog.

A thoroughly-researched, devoted biography by a writer who is not ashamed to admit that she intended, initially, only to be a collector of Acuff memorabilia; her collecting was so assiduous, the results so plentiful that she began, gradually, to consider herself a

biographer. Acuff himself (b.1903) provided much help and information, and many other colleagues and acqaintances were interviewed (a
list appears in the biography, with dates). The essentials of Acuff's
life and career are told in two chapters, "The Early Years" (Tennessee boyhood, medicine show experience in the late 1920s, the
Opry in the late '30s), and "The Big Time" (to the 1970s). Most of
the other chapters are devoted to particular aspects of his music or
his life outside music: there are sections on the Smokey Mountain
Gang, on the "Acuff sound," on his publishing ventures with Fred
Rose, on his movies, on his involvement in politics (with an analysis
of his running for governor of Tennessee in 1948), and on his
character. Appendices offer a chronology of his oversea tours,
1949-1971, with descriptions, and a file discography. The thorough
bibliography includes articles, record album notes, newspaper articles and songbooks, as well as the author's personal sources, and
there is a full index. (The same author contributed the chapter on
Acuff to Stars of Country Music, no. S.390.)

CHET ATKINS

S.392.   ATKINS, Chet. Country Gentleman; with Bill Neely. Chi-
          cago: Regnery, 1974. 226p. illus.
          Born near Luttrell, Tennessee (about twenty miles north of
Knoxville) in 1924, Atkins ranks as one of the country's outstanding
and most influential guitarists, though one would hardly guess it
from this book. A chatty, small-scale autobiography, it relates in
highly modest terms most of the "downs" of Atkins' career, and a
few of the "ups," as he moves from small-time live performer to
radio, to recordings, to concert and symphony orchestra appearances. There is little of substance on his music, or on the Nashville
scene of which he has long been an integral part. The book's foreword, by William Ivey, provides a brief but excellent overview of
country music history.

GENE AUTRY

S.393.   AUTRY, Gene. Back in the Saddle Again; with Mickey
          Herskowitz. Garden City, N.Y.: Doubleday, 1978.
          252p. illus., discog.
          When the best-selling record of the most popular of Holly-
wood's "singing cowboys" is a ditty about a reindeer, some horseplay
is likely on the part of critics and historians. Autry (b.1907) takes
such things in good part; he has, in any case, a saddlebag full of
anecdotes, about his early days in Texas and Oklahoma, his first
recordings, his Hollywood career, etc., and what they show is a
generous, "self-confessed square," with no great illusions about the
quality of his achievements, and who never quite understood why
his limited talent garnered so much popular esteem. He regards his
music as pre-eminent in his life: "Music has been the better part of
my career. Movies are wonderful fun and they give you a famous
face. But ... songs are forever" (p. 18-19). As to his contribution

to country music, "I sure won't claim that I improved the quality of it ... [but] I believe I helped make it a little more respectable" (p. 133). The discography, 1929–1964, lists song titles, year by year, with composer credits but no other discographical details. There is also a filmography, 1934–1953, with fuller details, and an index.

JOHNNY BOND

S.394. BOND, Johnny. Reflections: the autobiography of Johnny Bond. Los Angeles: John Edwards Memorial Foundation, 1976. (Special Series, No. 8.) 79p. illus., discog.
Bond's somewhat scant recollections of his time on radio in Oklahoma in the '30s, his lengthy career as lead guitarist for Gene Autry, and his contribution as a songwriter, barely do justice to any of the areas of his life. Rather more space is occupied by the filmography of singing westerns (38 in all) and by a detailed discography, 1941–1957. There are also excerpts from Bond's scrapbooks, a list of his songs recorded by other artists, a chronology (b.1915), and the sheet music for six songs.

CARTER FAMILY

S.395. ORGILL, Michael. Anchored in Love: the Carter Family story. Old Tappan, N.J.: Fleming H. Revell, 1975. 192p. illus.
A well-meaning but inadequate, over-sentimental biography. In a family history marked by separation, divorce, and alcoholism-- among other things--for an author to present everything as quite so pristine and exemplary risks distortion at the very least.

JOHNNY CASH

S.396. CASH, Johnny. Man in Black. Grand Rapids, Mich.: Zondervan, 1975. 244p. illus.
_____. _____. London: Hodder & Stoughton, 1976. 224p. illus.
Cash's confessional autobiography--he accepts the phrase "spiritual odyssey" as appropriate--testifies to three things: to the destructive power of amphetamines and barbiturates (Cash was an addict for many years); to the love of June Carter Cash, which played a large part in curing him; and to the sincerity of his religious conversion. The latter acts as a framework for the book, as well as being its constantly recurring theme. The drug story takes up the central portion, where it is told with troubled candor. Before that, Cash describes something of his Arkansas childhood (the cotton-picking, the radio-listening), his first recordings for Sam Phillips, and his initial steps to national prominence. Nowhere is his singing or songwriting given much scrutiny, though a number of song lyrics are reproduced. Numerous other musicians appear, most notably long-term friend Carl Perkins. No index. (Formerly LOAM A126.)

JUNE CARTER CASH

S.397.   CASH, June Carter. Among My Klediments. Grand Rapids,
         Mich.: Zondervan, 1979. 152p. illus.
         (A "klediment," curious term, is defined by the author in
her introduction as a thing one holds close or dear.) An autobiography, liberally strewn with poems and Bible verses, of the singer/
guitarist/autoharp player, daughter of Maybelle Carter and wife of
Johnny Cash. The book is in five sections: "The Early Years"
(names of people and places but few opinions); "Ambition," "Johnny
Cash" (in which we read how Cash was "rescued" from drugs),
"Home and Children," and "Special Moments and People." The
presence of music in the author's life is mentioned, but she rarely
writes about music as such. There are many photos of family and
friends.

JIMMIE DAVIS

S.398.   WEILL, Gus. You Are My Sunshine: the Jimmie Davis
         story. Waco, Tex.: Word Books, 1977. 187p. illus.
         Davis (b.1902, Louisiana) has been rated one of the "most
intriguing country singers of the pre-war era" (Nick Tosches,
Country, no. S.371, p. 121). His career began with his 1929-33
series of Victor recordings, which marked him as an "urbane, eclec-
tic performer who was influenced by black music as well as by the
rural white traditions" (ibid., p. 123); by the late 1930s his repertoire had become more middle-of-the-road, preceding his entry into
politics and his election as Louisiana Governor in 1944 (he was
elected again in 1960). In the 1950s he turned almost exclusively to
gospel. For all this diversity and popularity, Davis has been the
object of very little close study. This book in no way changes that.
The publisher, more accustomed to inspirational religious texts, is
hardly likely to be keen on scrutiny of Davis' risqué, blues-influenced
lyrics of the early '30s; it also appears the author is averse to
bothering readers with too many dates and similar hard facts ("during this period Jimmie and his band leader Charlie Mitchell wrote a
tune called 'You Are My Sunshine,' which remains today one of the
three most popular songs ever written"--p. 60). It turns out the
real subject is something more holy even than Davis' gospel offerings:
the American Dream, no less--"that's what Jimmie Davis' story is all
about" (introduction).

ALTON DELMORE

S.399.   DELMORE, Alton. Truth Is Stranger Than Publicity;
         edited, with an introduction, commentary, and discog-
         raphy, by Charles K. Wolfe. Nashville, Tenn.: Country
         Music Foundation Press, 1977. 188p. illus., discog.
         Autobiographies of early country musicians are rare and
valuable documents (see also Harkreader, no. S.402); Wolfe calls this
one "perhaps our fullest and most detailed picture of early country

music by one who was there" (p. v). The elder of the brothers
who formed the Delmore Brothers, premier exponents of close-harmony
vocals with attractive guitar accompaniment, Alton (1908-1964) began
this unghosted autobiography in the late 1950s, a few years after
the death of Rabon (1916-1952) had effectively ended his musical
career. The last portions as we have them were written in 1963;
they take the story up to the mid-1940s. The manuscript remained
in the family till Wolfe heard about it in 1974. He considers it possible that more exists, but none has been found.

It is a vivid, deeply-felt account, told in a homespun idiom
which occasionally aspires to become "literary." Particularly memorable are the descriptions of Alton's rural Alabama childhood (the
family were sharecroppers), of the brothers' first steps in their
careers (winning a local contest, gaining an audition and recording
for Columbia in Atlanta), of their time on the Grand Ole Opry (no
punches pulled here, when required), and of the numerous fellow
musicians of their acquaintance (especially Uncle Dave Macon).
Alton's story is occasionally bitter, but more often tinged with resig-
nation: "you live and learn, but sometimes it is too late when you
learn"--p. 62). Wolfe adds a final chapter bringing the story up to
1964, and appends a fine discography, 1931-1961, of the Columbia,
Bluebird, and King recordings. An index would have been a most
useful addition.

TENNESSEE ERNIE FORD

S.400.   FORD, Tennessee Ernie. This Is My Story, This Is My
         Song; line drawings by Lorin Thompson. Englewood
         Cliffs, N.J.: Prentice-Hall, 1963. 179p. illus.
         A miscellany of autobiographical and moralistic tales, about
Ford's childhood (he was born in Bristol, Tennessee on February
13th, 1919), his family, and his church (denomination not named but
Protestant). There is much talk about religion and leading the clean
life. A photograph of Ford carrying a rifle and accompanied by his
small son "on one of our deer hunts" faces p. 85.

TOM T. HALL

S.401.   HALL, Tom T. The Storyteller's Nashville. Garden City,
         N.Y.: Doubleday, 1979. 221p.
         Not a full autobiography (some portions of his early life
are told in a form of flashback) but rather a wry portrait of the
twists and turns of Hall's fortunes in Nashville, post-1964, as songwriter, singer, and sometime songplugger. Interesting for its (not
very objective) accounts of the various ingredients that form the
city's country music scene (recording, publishing, etc.), and not
least for its comments on his own approach to songwriting and on
some particular songs (e.g., "Harper Valley PTA"), it has little to
offer concerning other individuals (the copyright page proclaims:
"The stories in this book are true; however, to protect the privacy
of certain individuals involved, certain names, dates, places, and

likenesses have been altered). Though he admits to some faults, and
that "my life was not of my own making" (p. 215), Hall is proud of
having become a winner in a town and a business where losers take
nothing. No index. (Hall also wrote, How I Write Songs, Why You
Can. [New York: Chappell Music, 1976].)

SIDNEY J. HARKREADER

S.402. HARKREADER, Sidney J. Fiddlin' Sid's Memoirs: the autobiography of Sidney J. Harkreader; edited by Walter D.
Haden. Los Angeles: John Edwards Memorial Foundation, 1976. (Special Series, No. 9.) 37p. illus., bibliog., discog.

All-too-brief recollections of the Grand Ole Opry fiddler
(b.1898), "rediscovered" in the 1970s. He describes the early days
of the Opry and numerous memorable occasions in its history, and
follows that with an account of his Tennessee boyhood (his first
mail order fiddle cost $3.95 in 1913), and of his travels with Uncle
Dave Macon in the 1920s. The text of an interview with Harkreader
by the editor is also included. The discography lists all known recordings, from the 1924 New York session with Uncle Dave to 1929.

CHICO HOLIDAY

S.403. HOLIDAY, Chico and OWEN, Bob. Holiday In Hell. Ana-
heim, Calif.: Melodyland Productions, 1974; Springsdale,
Pa.: Whitaker House, 1976. 177p. illus.

"This is Chico's first book," reads a passage on the back
cover of this paperback, "and Bob's eighth." It can begin turning
your life right-side up." (If you are already in that happy state,
you are presumably spared from reading it.) The title refers to the
period of big commercial success of this country-turned-gospel
singer (or as he repeatedly referred to here: "the skinny Italian
singer."--e.g., p. 115), before his wife, Sally, helped bring him to
religion. There are brief forewords by Johnny Cash and Pat Boone.

WAYLON JENNINGS

S.404. ALLEN, Bob. Waylon and Willie: the full story in words
and pictures of Waylon Jennings & Willie Nelson. New
York: Quick Fox, 1979. 127p. illus., discog.

A respected country music journalist, and editor of Nashville! magazine, Allen seems to be caught here between the publisher's eye on the market for rapidly produced, plentifully illustrated
fan biographies, and his own capability of providing something much
more satisfying. This is not the "full" story, and it is heavily reliant on published sources. But there are perceptive moments, and
Allen's comments on the music of the two artists are valuable. The
discographies, one for each, contain chronological lists of LPs, with
lists of track titles. (As if to refute the charge that he himself did
no interviewing, Allen published an interview with Nelson in Journal
of Country Music, 8, No. 2 [1980], pp. 3-28.)

BRADLEY KINCAID

S.405. JONES, Loyal. Radio's "Kentucky Mountain Boy," Bradley Kincaid; music transcribed by John M. Forbes; introduction by Archie Green. Berea, Ky.: Appalachian Center, Berea College, 1980. 189p. illus., bibliogs., discog.

Interest in Kincaid (b.1895, Garrard County, Kentucky) centers not only on his recordings (for Gennett and Brunswick in the 1920s, Victor and Decca in the '30s, on various LPs in his later years) but on his activities as a broadcaster (from Chicago, Cincinnati and elsewhere, where he was "the first artist to become a radio star using almost entirely authentic folk music"--p. 28) and song collector. Jones' short, affectionate biography, drawing on Kincaid's own recollections, is followed by 50 song transcriptions (texts, melodies, and guitar chords), a listing of Kincaid's repertory, with many of his own comments on individual songs, a bibliography of his thirteen published songbooks, 1928-1945, a discography, and a bibliography of sources (books, articles, correspondence, and interviews). No index.

KRIS KRISTOFFERSON

S.406. KALET, Beth. Kris Kristofferson. New York: Quick Fox, 1979. 96p. illus., discog.

A pulp biography--strictly for the non-discriminating. The discography is a chronological list of the singer-movie actor's LP albums with title contents indicated.

LORETTA LYNN

S.407. LYNN, Loretta. Coal Miner's Daughter; with George Vecsey. Chicago: Regnery, 1976. 204p. illus.
_____. _____. New York: Warner Books, 1977. 269p. illus., discog.

Of all the outstanding women country singers of the 1960s and '70s, Loretta Lynn remained closest to her country roots, and (with Dolly Parton) drew most heavily on her experience in her music. Just what these roots and this experience were--the intense poverty of her childhood in Butcher Hollow, Kentucky, in the Depression and after, marriage at thirteen (and a mother of four by eighteen)--is made abundantly clear in her colloquially told autobiography. All parts of her subsequent life story--her early married life in Washington State, her first records (for Zero in 1960) and her rise to success--are narrated with the same disarmingly matter-of-fact approach. A fascinating story; small wonder it made a successful motion picture (Universal Pictures, 1980, starring Sissy Spacek).

S.408. ZWISOHN, Laurence J. Loretta Lynn's World of Music; including an annotated discography and complete list of songs she composed. Los Angeles: John Edwards Memorial Foundation, 1980. (Special Series, No. 13.) 115p. illus., discog.

The annotated discography, 1960-1979, occupies the major part of the book. Discographical detail includes date, master and release numbers, title and composer credits; the linking commentary is of a critical rather than biographical nature. The extent of Loretta Lynn's songwriting is demonstrated in the chronological list of her songs, 119 in all. Other items include a list of albums, 1963-1980, an interview with Don Grashey (manager of Zero records, for whom she made her first recordings), and musicians Speedy West and Harold Hensley, who played on her first sessions, and a transcript of a conversation with Teddy Wilburn, one of the Wilburn Brothers who assisted her career in Nashville. There is also an index of song titles.

JIM AND JESSE McREYNOLDS

S.409.   SEARS, Nelson. Jim and Jesse: Appalachia to the Grand Ole Opry. Pennsylvania: Nelson Sears, James McReynolds and Jesse McReynolds, 1976. 164p. illus., discog.

Laudatory, self-consciously homespun biography of the country music duo from Southwest Virginia, Jim and Jesse McReynolds, whom it celebrates as bastions of all those virtues still found in Appalachia but which the rest of us carelessly forgot. It contains only a little about their actual music. The appendices include a chronological list of Jesse's songs, some song texts, and a discography, 1951-73.

MOLLY O'DAY

S.410.   TRIBE, Ivan M., and MORRIS, John W. Molly O'Day, Lynn Davis, and the Cumberland Mountain Folks: a bio-discography. Los Angeles: John Edwards Memorial Foundation, 1975. (Special Series, No. 7.) 35p. illus., bibliog., discog.

An eleven-page biography of Molly O'Day (born La Verne Williamson in Kentucky in 1923), highly talented country singer of the 1940s, and of her husband and partner Lynn Davis (b.1914), is followed by short sketches of other musicians associated with them, a listing of song titles from their songbooks, a discography, and a note on electrical transcriptions. The extent of Molly O'Day's influence is demonstrated by a list of her songs recorded by others, with discographical details.

DOLLY PARTON

S.411.   JAMES, Otis. Dolly Parton: a personal portrait. New York: Quick Fox, 1978. 95p. illus., discog.

Within the strict limitations of these fan publications (see also Kalet, no. S.406), this is a relatively high-class production; occasional sources are cited and surface "reality" is questioned here and there. Plenty of photos of the star attraction herself, of course, and a few of her with other people (often not identified). The discography is skimpy but generally better than most in books of this kind (record numbers are consistently given and a producer is occasionally mentioned).

S.412.   NASH, Alanna. Dolly. Los Angeles: Reed Books, 1978.
295p. illus., discog.
_____.   _____. New York: Berkley, 1979. 372p.
illus., discog.
_____.   _____. St. Albans: Panther, 1979. 397p.
illus., discog.
The author interviewed Dolly Parton at some length for this biographical study, and frequent quotations from the interviews enliven the text, as does material furnished by numerous other friends and associates. Further sources were the author's own observation of Parton in performance, and published accounts (especially Joan Dew's interview--see no. S.387--which remains a more perceptive piece). A long, elaborate book, it traces the Parton story from the birth into a lower-income family in East Tennessee in 1946, through her move to Nashville in 1964 to become both songwriter and singer (she accomplished both aims), her tours (1967-1974) with Porter Waggoner, and subsequent career. Parton credits Nashville's Fred Foster with helping to shape her image and point her towards pop (as opposed to pure country) music; Chet Atkins she claims as another major influence. The discography is sketchy, and there is no index.

MINNIE PEARL

S.413.   PEARL, Minnie, and DEW, Joan. Minnie Pearl: an autobiography. New York: Simon and Schuster, 1980.
256p. illus.
Not the least fascinating aspect of the comic country girl act which Minnie Pearl brought to much perfection was that it was, indeed, an act. The story she tells is of a small town, middle-class Tennessee childhood and education. Sarah Ophelia Colley was born in Centerville, studied drama and dancing in Nashville, and taught dancing on tour in the 1930s, before, partly by chance, the Minnie Pearl character was born. Her enjoyable, natural-sounding narrative contains much about the Grand Ole Opry, which she joined in 1940, and about other country stars such as Eddy Arnold and Tennessee Ernie Ford. No index.

RILEY PUCKETT

S.414.   LARSEN, John, et al. Riley Puckett (1894-1946): discography; compiled in cooperation with Tony Russell, Richard Weize; biographical essay by Charles K. Wolfe.

Bremen: Archiv für Populäre Musik, 1977. (Schriften des Archivs für Populäre Musik: Bibliographien und Discographien, Band 8.) 45p.

The eleven-page essay by Wolfe offers critical as well as biographical information on Puckett and on the Skillet Lickers. The detailed discography which follows covers all Puckett's recordings under his name or by groups headed by him; it does not include the Skillet Lickers' recordings, or those by "McMichen's Melody Men." Information includes personnel, instruments, place, date, matrix and release numbers, titles and composer credits. Indexes of titles and of composers and authors.

TEX RITTER

S.415.   BOND, Johnny.   The Tex Ritter Story. New York: Chappell Music Co., 1976. 397p. illus., bibliog. refs. discog.

Informal biography of "America's Most Beloved Cowboy," Woodward "Tex" Ritter (1905-1974), who made no fewer than 60 singing "B" Westerns between 1936 and 1945, but whose voice on the soundtrack of the High Noon theme song is probably his best remembered performance. Singer-songwriter Bond, who knew Ritter for over 30 years and performed with him often, tells the story of Ritter's years as a Broadway actor, a western star, and a (ceaselessly touring) country recording artist, with the help of many stories and anecdotes from Ritter's family and friends. The large appendix provides a chronology, a list of the Broadway shows in which Ritter performed, a detailed discography (1932-1973), a filmography (1936-1972), and the lyrics of nineteen songs which he made famous.

JIMMIE RODGERS

S.416.   BOND, Johnny. Jimmie Rodgers: an annotated discography. Los Angeles: John Edwards Memorial Foundation, 1978. 70p. illus., bibliog.

"Largely a synthesis of recording data previously available" (Porterfield, no. S.418, p. 387), this is a thorough discography of Rodgers' recording career, 1927-1933. The 63 sessions are listed chronologically, with full details of venue, date, time of day, master numbers, song titles, timings, composer/autor credits, personnel (small groups), release numbers and dates, and US LP reissue numbers. The generous annotations offer lively, if a trifle disorganized comment on different aspects of the recordings, and draw on the opinions of other Rodgers experts. An appendix provides a complete list of releases for each title--US and foreign 78, 45 rpm and LP issues--and there is a title index. Norm Cohen adds a concise introduction, where he discusses some features of Rodgers' repertoire, influence, and impact on country music.

S.417.   PARIS, Mike, and COMBER, Chris. Jimmie the Kid: the life of Jimmie Rodgers. London: Eddison Press, 1977.

211p. illus., bibliog., discog.

This British contribution to Jimmie Rodgers literature was the first full-length study since 1935 (Carrie Rodgers' My Husband, Jimmie Rodgers, LOAM 640). Though overshadowed by Porterfield's biography (no. S.418), it remains valuable as a concise, objective work. Several aspects and events of Rodgers' life receive little or no attention (e.g., his first marriage), and in other areas Paris and Comber are frequently driven to speculation; but in most essentials the story remains the same. Extensively illustrated, the book also contains a final chapter tracing Rodgers' influence, exploring the reason for his popularity, and summarizing the essence of his music, in particular his treatment of the blues. The bibliography lists books and articles, and there is an index.

S.418. PORTERFIELD, Nolan. Jimmie Rodgers: the life and times of America's Blue Yodeler. Urbana: University of Illinois Press, 1979. 460p. illus., bibliog. refs., discog.

Born out of what its author confesses is a "lifelong, bumbling, inexplicable love for Jimmie Rodgers and his music" (p. 364), this is an immensely readable, skillful biography which uses the tools of the scholar and the fruits of the tireless investigator of sources, to put its author's enthusiasm to fine, telling use. Not least of the book's merits is a profound understanding, part inherited, part acquired, of Rodgers' place in the society and culture of his time, and of Rodgers' own sense of the world he lived in. This, and all the detail of Rodgers' life and career, is effortlessly told--as befits the subject matter--the flow of narrative disguising the hard graft of research. At the same time the author's sympathetic approach to his cast of characters ensures that, while one man may be the focus of attention, the people in his life are no mere ciphers. Scholarship is evident not merely in the use of varied source material (interviews, newspapers, etc.), but in the integration and interpretation of historically vital information (such as the significance of Ralph Peer's copyright procedure). Porterfield avoids slowing down the narrative with analysis of the songs themselves, but is content to place each in its context and comment on it in general terms. The excellent discography includes names of composers and copyright holders, and release dates. Index.

HANK WILLIAMS

S.419. CARESS, Jay. Hank Williams: country music's tragic king. New York: Stein and Day, 1979. 253p. illus., bibliog., discog.

This is a colloquially told but nonetheless deeply felt popular account of the singer's life. It draws liberally on previous biographies (especially those of Jerry Rivers (LOAM 644) and Roger Williams (LOAM 645) and reference sources (e.g., Melvin Shestack's Country Music Encyclopedia, LOAM 609), but also boasts a number of original interviews with Williams' family and associates. There are passages of eloquence and several shrewd observations; there are

also some faintly embarrassing moments (such as the passage contemplating Hank and Eternity), and the tone is sometimes defensive,
often excessively laudatory. But though other accounts may avoid
these traps and be more scholarly and detailed, this one, by a sensitive fan, should not be overlooked. The discography is long, but
poorly displayed on the page and lacking some basic information
(e.g., dates). Index.

HANK WILLIAMS, JR.

S.420. WILLIAMS, Hank, Jr. Living Proof: an autobiography;
        with Michael Bane. New York: Putnam, 1979. 222p.
        illus.
        The author was a small child when his famous father died,
aged 29, in 1953. The legacy proved hard for the growing boy to
live with, and his candid, eye-opening story describes some of the
results. But besides the two failed marriages, the drink, the drugs,
and the near-fatal mountain climbing accident in the Rockies--and
his subsequent efforts to rebuild his life--there is a lot of perceptive writing on his songs.

BOB WILLS

S.421. STRICKLIN, Al. My Years With Bob Wills; with Jon McConal.
        San Antonio, Tex.: Naylor, 1976. 153p. illus.
        Stricklin was the pianist with Bob Wills and His Texas Play-
boys from 1935 to 1942; he first met Wills (who referred to him, according to Bill C. Malone, as "the old piano pounder," Country Music U.S.A. [rev. ed., University of Texas Press, 1985], p. 172, in
1931 when working for radio station KFJZ in Fort Worth. His affectionate memoir has little to say about Wills' music, though he occasionally mentions pieces which the band performed. He is at his
best in the vivid glimpses he provides of Wills in action--at recording
sessions, on tour, playing for dances (and, strangely enough, for
funerals). The book is dedicated to Wills' wife Betty, who is quoted
on the dust jacket as saying it "left me with the feeling of love and
respect Al had for his 'boss' during those years and his 'friend'
through all the years."

S.422. TOWNSEND, Charles R. San Antonio Rose: the life and
        music of Bob Wills; with a discography and filmusicog-
        raphy by Bob Pinson. Urbana: University of Illinois
        Press, 1976. 395p. illus., bibliog., discog.
        A long, magnificently detailed biography of the Texas mu-
sician who pioneered western swing. Besides the help offered by
Wills himself (1905-1975) before his death, the author's sources included a vast number of interviews, conducted over an approximately
ten-year period; this material is so central that Townsend is led to
describe his book as "basically oral history" (p. xii). Wills' life and
career are very fully chronicled; Townsend's central focus is on
Wills as a popular entertainer ("I have been economical in trying to

point out deep social meanings, hidden or overt, in his music"--
p. xiii). Musical commentary, while not prominent, is scattered
throughout the book; Townsend is definite in his attribution of
strong black influence, especially blues, and in his description of
Wills' music as a type of jazz--a new type, combining elements from
folk and country music, but fundamentally jazz (see, for example,
pp. 57-59, 101-106). Each chapter is followed by copious notes and
references, and there is an essay on sources, which lists all the
interviews in alphabetical order of interviewee, as well as the radio
and television air shots and transcriptions, manuscripts, newspapers,
magazines and books used in the mammoth project. Pinson's discography is exemplary, covering all Wills' recording sessions, 1929-
1973. The "filmusicography" is described as "preliminary"; it lists
film titles, dated, principal stars, songs, participating band members, and lead vocals for Wills' fifteen films, made 1940-1946.
There is also a full index.

TAMMY WYNETTE

S.423.   WYNETTE, Tammy.   Stand By Your Man: an autobiography;
         with Joan Dew. New York: Simon & Schuster, 1979.
         349p. illus.
         _____. _____. New York: Pocket Books, 1980.
         360p. illus.
         _____. Stand By Your Man. London: Hutchinson,
         1980. London: Arrow Books, 1981. 349p. illus.
         When Tammy Wynette demurred at writing her autobiography
while not yet 35, it was pointed out to her that these eventful years
had provided her with a chance to do "more than many people do in
a lifetime." Coming at the end of her ghosted autobiography, this
statement leaves the reader, who has by now shared the stormy experience of four broken marriages, with little alternative but to agree,
even if the failure of much of the text to acknowledge a world outside the narrow one the book describes is perhaps equally remarkable. The most interesting part is the one which exists outside
country music but has a relationship to it--the account of the singer's
Mississippi childhood and youth (she was born in Itawamba County,
Mississippi, in 1942, and picked cotton on her grandfather's farm from
a child); in her daily life two worlds touched--the grinding reality,
and the fantasy of becoming a country music star. The main part
of the story, from her first recordings on, provides some insight into
the country music world by means of an unplanned cumulation of
snippets; but there is little about music itself save some scattered
comments (e.g., on the role of church music, on some of her songs).
The main attention is centered on the ups and downs of the singer's
personal life, in which the figure of George Jones is particularly
prominent. Somewhat surprisingly, there is a detailed index.

12. Cajun Music

S.424.   CONRAD, Glenn R., ed. The Cajuns: essays on their
history and culture. Lafayette: Center for Louisiana
Studies, University of Southwestern Louisiana, 1978.
432p. illus., bibliog. refs.
_____. _____. 2nd ed. 1978. 262p. bibliog.
refs.
Includes "Acadian Folk Songs as Reflected in 'La Délaissée',"
by Elizabeth Brandon, which examines variations of one well-known
song brought to Louisiana from France.

S.425.   RUSHTON, William Faulkner. The Cajuns: from Acadia to
Louisiana. New York: Farrar, Straus, Giroux, 1979.
342p. illus., bibliog.
This attractive portrait of the customs and history of the
Cajuns includes a sixteen-page chapter entitled "French Accordian
Folk Music," which centers on Ambrose Thibodeaux and his live
broadcasts from Fred's Lounge in Mamou, Louisiana.

Additional Items

General

S.426.   BERGER, Melvin. The Story of Folk Music. New York:
S. G. Phillips, 1976. 127p. (For younger readers.)

S.427.   JAMESON, Gladys. Sweet Rivers of Song: authentic ballads, hymns, folksongs from the Appalachian region.
Berea, Ky.: Berea College, 1967. 81p.

S.428.   LUNSFORD, Bascom Lamar, and STRINGFIELD, Lamar, eds.
30 and 1 Folksongs (From the Southern Mountains). New
York: Fischer, 1929. 56p. (In arrangements for piano
accompaniment.)

S.429.   MUNN, Robert F. The Southern Appalachians: a bibliography and guide to studies. Morgantown: West Virginia
University Library, 1961. 106p.

S.430.   RAINE, James Watt, ed. Mountain Ballads for Social Singing;
music collected by Cecil J. Sharp. Berea, Ky.: Berea
College Press, 1923. 27p.

Ethnic Groups

(a) Spanish-American

S.431.   BLOCH, Peter. Le-Le-Lo-Lai: Puerto Rican music and its performers. New York: Plus Ultra, 1973. 197p.

S.432. CAMPA, Arthur Leon, ed. Spanish-American Folksongs
From the Collection of Leonora Curtin. (Albuquerque?):
Independent Music, 1946. 66p.

S.433. DURAN, Gustavo, ed. 14 Traditional Spanish Songs From
Texas; transcribed from recordings made in Texas,
1934-1939, by John A., Ruby T. and Alan Lomax.
Washington, D.C.: Pan American Union, 1942. 20p.

S.434. HEISLEY, Michael. An Annotated Bibliography of Chicano
Folklore from the Southwestern United States. Los
Angeles: Center for the Study of Comparative Folklore
and Mythology, University of California, Los Angeles,
1977. 188p.

S.435. RAEL, Juan B. The New Mexican Alabado; with transcription of music by Eleanor Hague. Stanford, Calif.:
Stanford University Press, 1951. 154p.

S.436. STARK, Richard B., ed. Music of the Bailes in New Mexico; with Anita Gonzales Thomas and Reed Cooper. Santa
Fe,, N.M.: International Folk Art Foundation, 1978.
118p. (Fiddle tunes)

S.437. STARK, Richard B., ed. Music of the Spanish Folk Plays
of New Mexico; assisted by T. M. Pearce, Ruben Cobos.
Santa Fe: Museum of New Mexico Press, 1969. 359p.

S.438. TINKER, Edward L., ed. Corridos and Calaveras; with
notes and translations by Américo Paredes. Austin:
University of Texas Press, 1961. 58p.

S.439. TULLY, Marjorie, and RAEL, Juan. Annotated Bibliog-
raphy of Spanish Folklore in New Mexico and Southern
Colorado. Albuquerque: University of New Mexico
Press, 1950. 124p.

S.440. VAN STONE, Mary R., ed. Spanish Folksongs of New
Mexico; with a foreword by Alice Corbin. Chicago:
R. F. Seymour, 1928. 44p.
_____. _____. New ed. Fresno, Calif.: Academy
Guild Press, 1964. 44p.

S.441. WORKS PROGRESS ADMINISTRATION. New Mexico. The
Spanish-American Song and Game Book. New York:
Barnes, 1942. 87p.

(b) Other Groups

S.442.　BALYS, Jonas, ed. Lietuviu dainos Amerikoje (Lithuanian Folksongs in America). Boston: Lietiviu Enciklopedijos Leidykla, 1958. (Treasury of Lithuanian Folklore, 5.) 326p.

　　　　　_____.　_____. Silver Spring, Md.: Lietuviu Tautosakos Leidykla, 1977. (Treasury of Lithuanian Folklore, 6.) 342p.

S.443.　BERGMAN, Marian. Russian-American Song and Dance Book. New York: Barnes, 1947. 95p.

S.444.　BLEGEN, Theodore C., and RUUD, Martin B., eds. Norwegian Emigrant Songs and Ballads; songs harmonized by Gunnar J. Malmin. London: Oxford University Press; Minneapolis: University of Minnesota Press, 1936. (Repr. New York: Arno, 1979.) 350p.

S.445.　DOYLE, David Noel, and EDWARDS, Owen Dudley, eds. America and Ireland, 1776-1976: the American identity and the Irish question. Westport, Conn.: Greenwood Press, 1980. 348p. ("Irish Traditional Music in the United States," by W. H. A. Williams, pp. 279-283.)

S.446.　GRAME, Theodore C. Ethnic Broadcasting in the United States. Washington, D.C.: American Folklife Center, Library of Congress, 1980. 171p.

S.447.　KANAHELE, George S., ed. Hawaiian Music and Musicians: an illustrated history. Honolulu: University of Hawaii Press, 1979. 543p.

S.448.　KOLAR, Walter W. A History of the Tambura. Vol. 2. The Tambura in America. Pittsburgh: Duquesne University Tamburitzans, Institute of Folk Arts, 1975.

S.449.　MEEK, Bill, ed. Songs of the Irish in America. Skerries Co. Dublin: Gilbert Dalton, 1978. 64p.

S.450.　REAVY, Joseph M. The Music of Corktown: the Reavy collection of Irish-American traditional tunes. Melrose Park, Pa.: the author, 1979.

S.451.　RUBIN, Ruth. Voices of a People: Yiddish folk song. New York: Yoseloff, 1963. 496p.

　　　　　_____.　_____. 2nd ed. New York: McGraw-Hill, 1973. 558p.

Regions

S.452.   CARNEY, George O., ed. Oklahoma's Folk Music Tradi-
         tions: a resource guide. Stillwater: Oklahoma State
         University, 1979. 104p.

S.453.   COCHRAN, Robert, and LUSTER, Michael. For Love and
         For Money: the writings of Vance Randolph; an anno-
         tated bibliography. Batesville, Ark.: Arkansas College
         Folklore Archive Publications, 1979. 115p.

S.454.   MASSEY, Ellen Gray, ed. Bittersweet Country. Garden
         City, N.Y.: Doubleday, 1978. 434p. (On Ozark folk-
         lore and customs.)

S.455.   SHEARIN, Hubert G., and COMBS, Josiah H. A Syllabus
         of Kentucky Folk-Songs. Lexington, Ky.: Transylvania
         Printing Co., 1911. 43p.

Instrumental

S.456.   CLINE, Dallas. Cornstalk Fiddle and Other Homemade In-
         struments. New York: Oak, 1976. 63p.

S.457.   COOPER, Reed. Folk Fiddle Music from New Mexico. Ber-
         keley, Calif.: Manzano Press, 1978. 18p.

S.458.   IRWIN, John. Instruments of the Southern Appalachian
         Mountains. Norris, Tenn.: Museum of Appalachia Press,
         1979. 95p.

S.459.   JARMAN, Harry E., ed. Old-Time Dance Tunes; edited by
         Bill Hansen. New York: Broadcast Music, 1951. 80p.

S.460.   REINER, David, ed. Anthology of Fiddle Styles. Pacific,
         Mo.: Mel Bay, 1979.

Occupational

S.461.   FOWKE, Edith, ed. Lumbering Songs from the Northern
         Woods; tunes transcribed by Norman Cazden. Austin:
         University of Texas Press for the American Folklore So-
         ciety, 1970. (Publications of the American Folklore So-
         ciety, Memoir Series, Vol. 55.) 232p.

S.462.   TIERNEY, Judith, ed. A Description of the George Korson
         Folklore Archive in the D. Leonard Corgan Library of
         Kings College, Wilkes Barre. Wilkes Barre, Pa.: Kings
         College Press, 1973. 46p.

Protest, Folk Song Revival, Folk Rock

S.463. ATKINSON, Bob, ed. Songs of the Open Road: the poetry
of folk rock and the journey of the hero; foreword by
Oscar Brand; commentary by Joseph Campbell and Walt
Whitman; epilogue by C. G. Jung; illustrations by E.
Friedman. New York: New American Library, 1974.
144p.

S.464. GLAZER, Tom, ed. Songs of Peace, Freedom, and Protest.
New York: David McKay, 1970. 357p.

Country Music

S.465. AMERICAN SOCIETY OF COMPOSERS, AUTHORS AND PUB-
LISHERS. Country and Western Music: ASCAP music
on records. New York: ASCAP, 196-? 122p.

S.466. ARNOLD, Eddy. It's a Long Way From Chester County.
Old Tappan, N.J.: Hewitt House, 1969. 154p.

S.467. BERMAN, Connie. The Official Dolly Parton Scrapbook;
foreword by Dolly Parton. New York: Grosset & Dunlap,
1978. 95p.

S.468. CONN, Charles. The New Johnny Cash. Old Tappan, N.J.:
Revell, 1973. 94p.

S.469. FOWLER, Lana Nelson. Willie Nelson Family Album. Amaril-
lo, Tex.: Poirot, 1980. 160p.

S.470. FUCHS, Walter. Die Geschichte der Country-Music:
Zentren, Stile, Lebenslaufe. Bergisch Gladbach; Lubbe,
1980. 544p.

S.471. HEMPHILL, Paul. The Good Old Boys. New York: Simon
& Schuster, 1974. 255p.

S.472. HICKS, Daryl. God Comes to Nashville: spotlights on Music City personalities. Harrison, Ark.: New Leaf Press,
1979. 160p.

S.473. HOLLARAN, Carolyn. Meet the Stars of Country Music.
Nashville, Tenn.: Aurora, 1977-1978. 2v.

S.474. HOLLARAN, Carolyn. Your Favorite Country Music Stars.
New York: Popular Library, 1975. 283p.

S.475. KOSSER, Michael. Those Bold and Beautiful Country Girls:
an illustrated tribute to the women of country music.

Leicester, Eng.: Winward; New York: Mayflower, 1979. 127p.

S.476. LEDFORD, Lily May. Coon Creek Girl. Berea, Ky.: Appalachian Center, Berea College, 1980. 31p.

S.477. LINEDECKER, Cliff. Country Music Stars and the Supernatural. New York: Dell, 1979. 317p.

S.478. OFFEN, Carol, ed. Country Music: the poetry. New York: Ballantine, 1977. 120p. (Anthology of texts.)

S.479. SMITH, L. Mayne. An Introduction to Bluegrass. Los Angeles: John Edwards Memorial Foundation, (1966?). (Reprint No. 6.) (Reprinted from Journal of American Folklore, 78 [1965], pp. 245–256.)

S.480. STROBEL, Jerry, ed. Grand Ole Opry: WSM picture-history book. Nashville, Tenn.: WSM, 1979. 156p.

S.481. VAN RYZIN, Lani. Cutting a Record in Nashville. New York: Watts, 1980. 85p.

S.482. WALTHALL, Daddy Bob. The History of Country Music. Vol. 1. Houston: Walthall Publishing Company, 1978. 210p.

S.483. WERNICK, Peter, ed. Bluegrass Songbook. New York: Oak, 1976. 128p.

S.484. WORTH, Fred L. The Country and Western Book. New York: Drake, 1977. 94p. (Quiz book.)

G. BLACK MUSIC

1. Black Music in Works on Black Culture and Society

a. Reference

S.485.   PEAVY, Charles D. Afro-American Literature and Culture
         Since World War II: a guide to information sources.
         Detroit: Gale Research, 1979. (American Studies In-
         formation Guide Series, Vol. 6.) 302p.
    Despite the suggestion in the subtitle, this annotated bib-
liography is not concerned with reference books, but with critical
and biographical writing. It is in two parts: subjects, and individual authors. The first part includes a section for music containing 46 items (books and articles). The choice, unfortunately,
is wholly unbalanced (e.g., five out of the 46 entries are for parts
of Ralph Ellison's Shadow and Act (LOAM 1016), but absent are
basic works by Haralambos (LOAM 892), Heilbut (LOAM 897), Oliver
(LOAM 818), Spellman (LOAM 1058), to name but a few). Subject
and author idnexes.

S.486.   SPRADLING, Mary Mace, ed. In Black and White; Afro-
         Americans in Print; a guide to Afro-Americans who have
         made contributions to the United States of America from
         1619 to 1969. Kalamazoo, Mich.: Kalamazoo Library,
         1971. 127p.
         _____.   _____. 2nd ed., 1976. 505p.
         _____.   In Black and White: a guide to magazine ar-
         ticles, newspaper articles, and books concerning more
         than 15,000 black individuals and groups. 3rd ed.
         Detroit: Gale, 1980. 2v.
    A useful, though very selective, bio-bibliographical dic-
tionary, the 3rd ed. contains a good representation of black musicians
and of those categories of performers who are relevant to black music
but are normally excluded from specialist music reference works.
Entries typically contain a short biography, followed by a list of
references (71 in the case of Duke Ellington) in reference works,
books, periodicals, and newspapers. The most valuable of these are
the references to the post-1950 black press: Ebony, Jet, Negro Digest, etc.; unfortunately--and disappointingly--the pre-1950 period
is less well covered, with the result that earlier figures are provided
with references which concentrate on later, second-hand sources

rather than on contemporary reports. (Eileen Southern's Biographical Dictionary of Afro-American and African Musicians [Westport:
Greenwood Press, 1981] partially redresses the balance, but would
it not be possible for someone to do a really thorough job on The
Chicago Defender, etc.?)

S.487.   SZWED, John F., and ABRAHAMS, Roger D.   Afro-American
          Folk Culture: an annotated bibliography of materials
          from North, Central and South America and the West
          Indies. Philadelphia: Institute for the Study of Human
          Issues, 1978. (Publications of the American Folklore So-
          ciety, Bibliographical and Special Series, Vol. 31.)   2v.
          An important bibliography, whose unequivocally stated pur-
pose goes beyond the (narrow) limits normally accepted for bibliographic influence: the compilers' aim is to provide the means for
shattering long-accepted myths about the deculturation of people of
African descent in the New World. It is possible for a bibliography
to achieve this because the lack of such a reference tool has contributed hitherto to the reinforcement of the processes by which (in
Eugene Genovese's terms) Afro-Americans of each succeeding generation are forced to re-invent their past by reason of lack of access to
the insights and research of preceding generations. Cross-cultural
comparison is a vital means of changing attitudes, hence the rationale
for a book covering the entire Americas.
          Coverage is restricted to published materials—books, parts
of books, pamphlets, articles, and record liner notes—and extends
to the end of 1973. Folklore is widely defined ("what we are most
interested in here are the expressive and symbolic aspects of the
lives of ordinary people"—p. xiii). Organization is by country,
with preliminary sections for bibliographies and general works. The
North American section occupies most of Vol. 1, where it amounts
to 3,331 entries, all in one alphabetical sequence. A large number
have one- to three-line annotations, provided by a team of helpers.
The size of this single listing renders it difficult to use, making the
subject index indispensable. From this it is possible to tell that a
wide range of vocal and instrumental music is covered: sacred and
secular song, specific types of work song, minstrelsy and vaudeville,
blues, ragtime, jazz, drumming bands, etc. The presence of material on related areas (from dance, verbal duels, and tale telling to
dress, medicine, and religion) is clearly advantageous. (Unfortunately, no index of people as subjects is provided.)

b.   Histories, Studies, and Collections

     See also S.520

S.488.   BENSTON, Kimberly W.   Baraka: the renegade and the
          mask.   New Haven, Conn.: Yale University Press,
          1976.   290p.   bibliog.
          To an extent unrivalled by any other black writer, Amiri

Baraka (LeRoi Jones) has continued to explore, both in literary
works and cultural criticism, the central importance of music in the
black experience. Benston's perceptive study reveals how fundamental Baraka's concern with music is to all his work. One chapter
in particular is devoted to an investigation of the essential elements
in his attitude to music, as demonstrated in Blues People (LOAM
689) and, to a lesser extent, Black Music (Loam 1052). Placing
Baraka's music criticism first in the context of that of other black
writers, Benston elucidates his belief in an African-derived aesthetic
and in the crystallization of African essence into archetypal Afro-
American forms such as the blues. The controversy aroused by his
emphasis on African culture is also discussed, with an exposition of
the Hegelian elements in Baraka's thoughts. (For another view of
Baraka's writings on music, see Paul Burgett, Aesthetics of the Music of Afro-Americans, unpublished Ph.D. thesis, Eastman School of
Music, 1976, pp. 91-181. Burgett also gives detailed consideration
to Alain Locke.)

S.489.   BLASSINGAME, John W.   Black New Orleans, 1860-1880.
          Chicago: University of Chicago Press, 1973. 301p.
          illus., bibliog.
          Although the extent to which it discusses music specifically
is not extensive, this fine study of the "economic and social life of
the Negro in New Orleans during Reconstruction" (preface) is included here because, alternative theories notwithstanding, New Orleans remains uniquely important in the history of black music in the
USA, and Blassingame's book demonstrates how, in all its diverse
patterns and structures, "the city's Negro community was sui gene-
ris" (p. xvi). The chapters on family life in particular are essential
reading for the understanding of the community at the period when
so much of the music that was later to flourish was in its formative
stages.

S.490.   HENDERSON, Stephen.   Understanding the New Black
          Poetry: black speech and black music as poetic refer-
          ences. New York: Morrow, 1973. 394p.
          An anthology of black poetry, including a selection of
spirituals, blues, and folk rhymes. One of the main themes of the
lengthy introduction is the ways in which music "lies at the basis
of much of Black poetry, either consciously or covertly" (p. 47).
Various types of musical influence--adaptation of song forms, use
of tonal memory, language from the jazz life--are distinguished.

S.491.   LEVINE, Lawrence W.   Black Culture and Black Conscious-
          ness: Afro-American folk thought from slavery to free-
          dom. New York: Oxford University Press, 1977. 522p.
          bibliog. & discog. refs.
          This crucially important study sets out to illuminate the
consciousness and value systems of Afro-Americans by an examination
of their thought as embodied in folk expression from the antebellum
era to the 1940s. Drawing deep and wide on both song and narrative,

Levine traces the profoundly creative responses of black America to
its evolving situation of "racial, social, and economic exploitation"
(preface), taking the reader as he does so to the heart of the culture's symbolic universe. His choice of subject--a people articulate in their lifetime, who "have been rendered historically inarticu-
late by scholars" (ibid.)--his use of the rich reservoir of sources
(song and narrative texts, contemporary accounts, autobiographies,
etc.) as historical documents, and his clear assertion of the need to
understand an expressive form in cultural terms, make what is undoubtedly a major contribution to historiography also highly significant in music literature.

Although Levine is at pains to stress the wholeness of the
world he describes, it is pertinent here to point to those parts of
the book where music is most prominent. Chapter 1, "The Sacred
World of the Black Slaves," analyzes the means by which, though
physically enslaved, the slaves, by assimilation and transformation,
prevented spiritual slavery by their creation of a world apart. The
slave spiritual in particular provides evidence of the vitality and independence of slave culture, and through that, of slave cosmology.
The creative process in the slave's sacred song centers on a system
of spontaneous communal creation to which the individual makes important contributions. What was at work in the songs, Levine argues,
was a means of ensuring that slavery could never destroy central
communality, nor wholly isolate the individual. The texts, at the
same time, provided the slaves with a way to find the worth and
harmony denied them in their physical lives, by extending "the
boundaries of their restrictive universe backward until it fused with
the world of the Old Testament, and upward until it became one with
the world beyond" (p. 32-33). The slaves found value by "literally
willing themselves reborn" (ibid.).

Chapter 3, "Freedom, Culture, and Religion," discusses
gospel music in the context of changed religious consciousness, seeing the paradox of a message indicating the dissolution of the old
sacred world couched in a style revitalized by reference to musical tradition, as a model of black acculturation to 20th-century sensibility. Chapter 4, "The Rise of Secular Song," examines how black
thought, as expressed in song, changed after slavery. Transformation, assimilation, re-creation are once again key terms, but ones at
work now within a shift from a collective to an individual ethos, as
work song (discussed on pp. 202-216) gives way to blues--"the first
almost completely personalized music that Afro-Americans devleoped"
(p. 221), but one in which individuality and communality still interact, albeit in a more complex relationship. The nature of this relationship is explored both in songs (mainly texts) and performance
(aspects of religious ritual), and dissemination via recordings (creating a larger, more unified audience). The extent to which secular
song may be seen as a repository of responses to the black social situation is explored in a section "Secular Song and Protest," while the
theme black culture vis-à-vis larger society is further examined in
"Secular Song and Cultural Values--Black and White." The endnotes,
pp. 447-505, represent a vast bibliographical (and to a lesser extent
discographical) resource, and there is an index.

S.492. SAXON, Lyle, ed. Gumbo Ya-Ya: a Collection of Louisiana
    Folk Tales. Boston: Houghton Mifflin, 1945. 581p.
    illus.
    The material for this evocative anthology was gathered by
workers on the WPA Louisiana Writers' Project; the editorial work was
carried out by Saxon and Edward Dreyer, with Robert Tallant acting
as special writer. Dealing chiefly, though far from exclusively, with
New Orleans, its 24 chapters include several on music: (1) "Kings,
Baby Dolls, Zulus, and Queens" is a picturesque account of the
Mardi Gras Indians and their music; using material gathered by
blacks, principally by Robert McKinney, it attempts to capture the
flavor of the occasion rather than dispassionately describe it; (2)
street cries of New Orleans, including examples; (4) "Axeman's Jazz,"
an account of a murderer who terrorized New Orleans in the late
1910s and expressed (in a letter to the Times-Picayune) a passion for
jazz; (19) "Riverfront Lore," with illustrations of song texts; (21) a
collection of song texts with linking commentary illustrating Creole
songs (with English translations), white folk ballads, work songs,
blues, "Junkermen" blues, and spirituals. In addition, Chapters (8)
and (9) on Creoles and Cajuns provide useful background, if little
on music. Index.

S.493. SMITHERMAN, Geneva. Talkin and Testifyin; the language
    of black America. Boston: Houghton Mifflin, 1977.
    291p. bibliog.
    An interesting and useful survey of black English, with
consideration of its history and structure, its modes of discourse,
and its implied world view. Music itself receives little attention,
though much of the general discussion is relevant and could form a
valuable background to the hitherto little explored but potentially
rewarding subject of the creative influence of language in a musical
context (i.e., the extent to which the grammatical structures, etc.,
of black English played and play a crucial formative role in musical
form and rhythm).

S.494. TALLANT, Robert. Mardi Gras. Garden City, N.Y.:
    Doubleday, 1948. (Repr. Gretna, La.: Pelican, 1976.)
    263p. bibliog.
    A colorful history and description of the celebrated New
Orleans carnival, particularly informative on the clubs, the balls, the
various social groups, and the parade itself. Though Tallant has no
special interest in music, his account refers often to areas of musical
activity--marching bands, jazz, songs, and the Mardi Gras Indians'
own particular music--and is essential reading for anyone wanting a
sense of the uniqueness of New Orleans society. (For closer attention to the music of the Indians, see David Elliott Draper, The Mardi
Gras Indians: the ethnomusicology of black associations in New Orleans. [Ph.D., Tulane University, 1973].)

c.   Anthologies of Criticism

S.495.   HARPER, Michael S., and STEPTO, Robert B., eds.
         Chant of Saints: a gathering of Afro-American literature,
         art, and scholarship. Urbana: University of Illinois
         Press, 1979. 486p. illus.
         Originally published in two issues of the Massachusetts Re-
view (fall and winter, 1977), this seminal anthology takes its title
from a poem by Sterling Brown, to whom the volume is dedicated.
For Stepto, all the essays "share an abiding interest in ... a culture's effort ... to translate data and prosaic fact into metaphor"
(p. xv). In keeping with the title, several contributions have a
musical subject. Frederick Turner provides a moving tribute to the
New Orleans trombonist Jim Robinson (1892-1976). Sherley A.
Williams, building on the works of Stephen Henderson (see no.
S.490), examines the blues roots of contemporary Afro-American
poetry. Mary F. Berry and John W. Blassingame discuss the African
and slavery roots of contemporary black culture, and include slave
songs and blues in their argument. The post-1962 recordings of
John Coltrane are the subject of a poetic interpretation by Kimberly
W. Benston. Duke Ellington's autobiography, Music Is My Mistress
(LOAM 1105), is viewed by Albert Murray in the context of black
autobiography. Jazz, and especially Coltrane, figure prominently in
three of the seven poems by Michael Harper, among them the remarkable "Narrative of the Life and Times of John Coltrane: Played
By Himself."

                2.   Black Music - General Works

a.   Reference

     See also nos. S.273, S.884, S.885

S.496.   DETROIT PUBLIC LIBRARY. Catalog of the E. Azalia Hack-
         ley Memorial Collection of Negro Music, Dance, and
         Drama. Boston: G. K. Hall, 1979. 510p.
         The collection listed in this catalog (reproduced from the Li-
brary's catalog cards) was founded in 1943 in memory of an educator
and performer who devoted much of her life (1867-1922) to promoting
black music. It contains, according to the introduction, approximately
12,000 cards; these represent books on black music and music by
composers; sheet music (including songs on black themes by non-
blacks, and ranging from concert to popular music idioms); broadsides and posters; and photographs of black performers. (For a
biography of Hackley, see Azalia: the life of Madame E. Azalia
Hackley, by M. Marguerite Davenport [Boston: Chapman & Grimes,
1947].)

S.497.   MEADOWS, Eddie S. Theses and Dissertations on Black

American Music. Beverly Hills, Calif.: Theodore Front, 1980. 18p.

A bibliography of around 250 theses and dissertations, divided into thirteen historical and generic categories (e.g., "Origin and Acculturation," "Spirituals-Folksongs," "Modern Jazz"). Entries include author, title, degree awarded, institution, and date. Some are also provided with annotations. (For further comment and additions, see James R. Heintze's review, American Music 1, No. 2 [Summer 1983], pp. 91-92.

b. Critical Studies

S.498. DENNISON, Tim. The American Negro and His Amazing Music. New York: Vantage Press, 1963. 76p.

An oddity in the literature on black music. Dennison founded the "Association for the Preservation and Development of the American Negro Spiritual" circa 1957. This booklet is his "guided missile," launched in the cause of the purification of the spiritual, to encourage "a reformation and a renaissance in American Negro music and halt this everlasting rolling around in the fleshpots of jazz" (p. 44). Specifically, Dennison calls for a national all-Negro symphony orchestra, and an effort to "find that Negro Beethoven.... We have too many budding Louis Armstrongs already" (p. 59). Gershwin also falls victim to these intrepid ballistics; Porgy and Bess is "earthy, sexy, corrupt, violent, comical, irreligious, blasphemous, hypocritical, desecrating to the spirituals, immoral, and altogether derogatory to the American Negro" (p. 47) .... Well, it ain't necessarily so.

S.499. HANDY, D. Antoinette. Black Music: opinions and reviews; introduction by Edgar A. Toppin. Ettrick, Va. (P.O. Box 103): BM & M, 1974. 86p. illus., bibliog. refs.

Thirty-three brief articles, originally written for the Richmond Afro-American in 1972-73, and mainly concerned with local events (not all star-billings) involving black musicians from jazz, gospel and orchestral music. Some pieces also ponder significant contemporary issues (e.g., black musicians in symphony orchestras). Generally arresting and challenging in style, the book is perhaps most valuable as an insight into black critical preoccupations in changing times. No index.

c. Collected Biography

S.500. ABDUL, Raoul. Famous Black Entertainers of Today. New York: Dodd, Mead, 1974. 159p. illus.

In a series of biographical works aimed at young people, this book includes interviews with, or portraits of, ten black musical

personalities: choreographer-musical director Alvin Ailey, soprano
Martina Arroyo, gospel singer-composer Alex Bradford, conductor
James DePriest, singer Aretha Franklin, composer-lyricist Micki
Grant, critic and composer Carman Moore, singer Diana Ross (no
interview), actor-singer Ben Vereen, and pianist André Watts.
Index.

S.501.   BERRY, Lemuel. Biographical Dictionary of Black Musicians
         and Music Educators. Vol. 1. Guthrie, Okla.: Educa-
         tional Book Publishers, 1978. 389p. bibliog.
     An ambitious but unfortunately flawed undertaking, this
dictionary provides biographical data of greatly varying thoroughness
and reliability for some 2,000 individuals, including composers, art
music performers, jazz, blues and soul musicians, popular vocalists,
teachers, and musicologists. Around one-third of the entries appear
in an appendix, with virtually the same amount of detail, thus creating two sequences of names. Coverage of most fields is extensive,
but that of the blues has many omissions, and some surprising ab-
sences can be noted also in contemporary jazz (e.g., Anthony Braxton, Herbie Hancock). The major problem is that the entries tell
the user virtually nothing--and do so with great inaccuracy. The
most detailed entries are usually those for teachers and composers;
all too often, however, they are like that for Wayne Shorter: "he
has been on the jazz scene for a short period of time. However, he
has had the opportunity to perform with both Horace Silver, May-
nard Ferguson and Art Blakey" (p. 171; Leroi Jones/Amiri Baraka
recognized Shorter's ability in the late 1950s). Page 222 tells us
Howlin' Wolf "has a number of records to his credit." Dates of birth
are not consistently provided, and comparison with other reference
works suggests there are many errors. Several lamented musicians
apparently still lived and breathed in 1978 (e.g., Eric Dolphy, d.
1964; Bud Powell, d.1966). Other eccentricities include the presence
of white musicians (Tommy Dorsey, Scott La Faro, Virgil Thomson),
mis-spellings causing names to be misfiled ("Coletrane, John"), and
malapropisms such as the memorable description of Charlie Parker
as a "bonified jazz saxophonist" (p. 151).

S.502.   BOGLE, Donald. Brown Sugar: eighty years of America's
         black female superstars; designed by Joan Peckolick.
         New York: Harmony Books, 1980. 208p. illus., bib-
         liog.
     A lucid, articulate history of black women in 20th-century
show business, told as a series of biographical portraits of outstanding performers, organized by decade. Bogle's basic thesis is that
"no matter what the period, the divas were able to pick up on the
temper of the time, to answer the specific needs of their age, and
to use their style to make personal statements to us all" (p. 16).
His portraits briefly discuss career, character, and artistry, with
a sharp eye for the effects the performers had on their particular
era. The extremely fine black-and-white illustrations contribute to
the exploration of image. Among the many music stars featured,

the greatest attention is paid to these: Ma Rainey, Bessie Smith, Florence Mills, Josephine Baker, Ethel Waters, Ivie Anderson, Billie Holiday, Lena Horne, Dorothy Dandridge, Katherine Dunham, Hazel Scott, Marian Anderson, Pearl Bailey, Eartha Kitt, Diahann Carol, Leontyne Price, Aretha Franklin, Diana Ross, and Donna Summer. Index.

S.503.   MAPP, Edward. Directory of Blacks in the Performing Arts. Metuchen, N.J.: Scarecrow Press, 1978. 428p.
The compiler describes his book as a "compendium of biographical and career facts on over 850 black individuals, living and deceased, who have earned a degree of recognition for their work in the performing arts" (preface). Music is well represented; the classified index reveals that there are entries for 44 composers, 14 concert singers, 25 conductors, three disc jockeys, 20 "entertainers," nine folk singers, seven gospel singers, 91 jazz musicians, 42 "musicians," 15 opera singers, 30 pianists, and 170 singers. (There is considerable overlap in these categories, with many people appearing more than once.) The information given is divided into categories: date(s), education, special interests, address, honors, career data, and various types of professional credit (clubs, radio, records, theater, etc.) with dates. Mapp's approach is somewhat inconsistent: "career data" varies from the detailed (e.g., Sisseretta Jones) to the perfunctory (e.g., Wilson Pickett); compositions are credited to Ella Fitzgerald, but not to Miles Davis. The book's value lies in bringing together performers normally scattered among several reference sources; these more specialized sources, however, generally offer more detail.

3.   Black Composers and Concert Performers

(See also S.70)

S.504.   ABDUL, Raoul. Blacks In Classical Music: a personal history. New York: Dodd, Mead, 1977. 253p. illus.
This handy collection of pieces, derived from Abdul's newspaper reviews, would probably fulfill the research needs of many high-school students, but for other users most of the pieces, on black performers, operas by black composers, etc., are rather brief and superficial. Almost all subjects here are dealt with more substantially in other sources. The ideas are not particularly striking and the writing not particularly graceful. The illustrations are sixteen impressive portrait photographs of various black performers and composers.

S.505.   BAKER, David, et al., eds. The Black Composer Speaks; a project of the Afro-American Arts Institute, Indiana University, edited by David N. Baker, Lida M. Belt and Herman C. Hudson. Metuchen, N.J.: Scarecrow Press, 1978. 506p. illus., bibliogs.

Interviews with fifteen black American art music and jazz composers (one born in Nigeria): T. J. Anderson, David Baker (also one of the book's editors), Noel Da Costa, Taleb Rasul Hakim (b. Stephen A. Chambers), Herbie Hancock, Ulysses Kay, Undine Smith-Moore, Oliver Nelson (probably the last interview before his death in 1975), Coleridge-Taylor Perkinson, George Russell, Archie Shepp, Hale Smith, Howard Swanson, George Walker and Olly Wilson. Each answers the same basic questions, which fall into two parts: general (e.g., influences, black artists in society) and music (e.g., method of composition, works in progress). Most replies are quite detailed, the briefest being those given by Anderson and Russell. Each interview is followed by a list of compositions with dates, and with publication and recording details where applicable, and by a bibliography of works by and about each composer. Combined author and title index.

S.506.   DE LERMA, Dominique-René.   Black Concert and Recital
         Music: a provisional repertoire list.   Bloomington, Ind.:
         Afro-American Music Opportunities Association, 1975.
         40p. bibliog.
         This first volume in a projected series "lists 245 works by
40 composers" (preface).   The works are both published and in
manuscript and the composers range alphabetically from Francis
Harris Abbot to Arthur Cunningham.   The arrangement is by composer, with details given on some of each composer's work.   Medium
index.

S.507.   LaBREW, Arthur R.   The Black Swan: Elizabeth T. Green-
         field, songstess.   Detroit: (the author), 1969.   86p.
         illus.
         Elizabeth Taylor Greenfield (1824-1876) occupies a particu-
larly important place in the history of black American concert singers
as being one of the earliest to establish a reputation both at home
and abroad (she performed in England for Queen Victoria).   LaBrew
offers background information on her, but the most valuable aspect
of his book is the collection of excerpts from newspaper reviews of
the tours she undertook in 1851-1853, following her concert debut
at Buffalo.   The first of LaBrew's books (see also nos. S.517 and
S.594), this is not without its clumsiness, but demonstrates the
value of black music research based on contemporary sources.   (La-
Brew also edited a volume of music by Francis Johnson [1792-1844],
Selected Works of Francis Johnson [Detroit: LaBrew, 1976?].)

S.508.   McBRIER, Vivian Flagg.   R. Nathaniel Dett: his life and
         works (1882-1943).   Washington, D.C.: Associated
         Publishers, 1977.   152p. illus., bibliog. refs.
         A biographical study of the composer, pianist and teacher,
laying stress not only on his significance from creative and peda-
gogical points of view, but also on his role as "a serious social
thinker, aggressively active even then in the cause of Black liberation" (preface).   In tracing Dett's early life in Ontario and New York

State, his education and his career up to his final years at Bennett
College in Greensboro, North Carolina, the author naturally focuses
much attention on his period at Hampton Institute (1913-32), where
his untiring work on behalf of music in general and black music in
particular produced such rich fruits, but which ended, shabbily,
with his summary dismissal. Some musical works are examined, with
examples, in their chronological context. Though admiring, the
author's tone is not over-adulatory. Included in the appendices are
a list of published and unpublished works, a selection of Hampton
concert programs, and further music examples illustrating, without
comment, aspects of Dett's technique and style. No index.

S.509.   TURNER, Patricia. Afro-American Singers: an index and
          preliminary discography of long-playing recordings of
          opera, choral music, and song. Minneapolis: Challenge
          Productions, 1977. 255p. bibliog.
          While black jazz and blues musicians have been well served
discographically, another side of black music, the considerable contribution to the art of singing in the concert and operatic traditions
made by black performers on record, has been less well documented.
This reference book goes some way towards correcting this. Its
aim is "to identify and list those Afro-American singers whose musical
careers have consisted primarily of performance on the concert stage
and in opera; to provide a brief biographical statement for each
singer, to quote from a record review or reviews; and to cite all
long-playing recordings of each singer" (preface). About 120 singers
have been identified altogether (they are listed on pp. 227-28), but
only those who have recorded on LP (about two-thirds) appear in
the main section of the book. This is an alphabetical listing with
date and place of birth when known, excerpts of reviews, list of
records (with record label and number, and date of issue), and
reference to source of biographical information in books or journals.
A second, much smaller performer section lists the recordings of
several choral groups. The various works performed on the recordings listed are grouped and indexed in nine categories: composers,
arias, spirituals, Lieder, art songs, folk and traditional, songs
from musicals and other popular songs, religious songs, and Christmas songs. In each of these sections the name of the singer and
the record number is given. The bibliography lists books and articles, relevant journal titles, and a number of record catalogs.
An index lists singers and composers in separate sequences.

BLIND TOM

S.510.   GIANNONE, Richard. Music in Willa Cather's Fiction. Lin-
          coln: University of Nebraska Press, 1968. 254p. illus.,
          bibliog.
          Pervasive though the presence of music is in Willa Cather's
novels, on relatively few occasions is the music recognizably American. One of the most celebrated appearances of an identifiable
American musician, Blind Tom Bethune, in the guise of Blind

d'Arnault in My Antonia, is examined in Giannone's chapter on this
work, Chapter 6.

S.511.   SOUTHALL, Geneva H.   Blind Tom: the post-Civil War
         enslavement of a black musical genius.   Minneapolis:
         Challenge Productions, 1979. 108p. bibliog. refs.
         The first part of a projected trilogy devoted to the life of
Blind Tom Bethune (1849-1909), the prodigy whose pianistic skills
and musical memory astounded 19th-century audiences, but who was
destined to live out his life regarded by most who saw him as a
freak or an imbecile. This volume covers the period from Tom's
birth (as Thomas Greene Wiggins in Harris County, Georgia) to the
"legal guardianship" trial (a form of re-enslavement) of 1865. The
author's exhaustive search through the records provides a rich
historical and political background, especially of the presecessionist
South, in whose political life General Bethune, Tom's second master,
was very active as an editor and journalist. Tom himself remains
indistinct (though his relentless exploitation is vividly clear--and
passionately denounced); far more sharply in focus are the typical
audiences--whether those fed on circus tricks or on more conventional notions of genius--with their inability to see beyond caricature
("a wonderful chattel," "a freak of idiotism"). Willa Cather, who saw
Tom perform, offers a contrast (and, perhaps, a more imaginative
description than occurs in the biography) in My Antonia, Book 2,
where she speaks of Tom ("Blind d'Arnault") as "vitalized by a sense
of rhythm that was stronger than his other physical senses--that not
only filled his dark mind, but worried his body incessantly" (see
no. S.510) (A second book in the trilogy, The Continuing Enslavement of Blind Tom, was published in 1983.)

PAUL ROBESON

S.512.   DENT, Roberta Yancy, ed.   Paul Robeson Tributes and
         Selected Writings; assisted by Marilyn Robeson and Paul
         Robeson, Jr.   New York: The Paul Robeson Archives,
         1976. 112p. illus.
         Among the selection of Robeson's own writings included
here are "Some Aspects of Afro-American Music" (written for The
Afro-American, Dec., 1956), and "What I Want From Life," which is
in part a discussion of the bonds between Africa and Afro-Americans.

S.513.   FREEDOMWAYS.   Paul Robeson, the Great Forerunner, by
         the editors of Freedomways.   New York: Dodd, Mead,
         1978. 383p. illus., bibliog.
         To the English critic Benny Green, Robeson was "one of
the archetypal artists of the 20th century.... When he sings I hear
the unsullied expression of the human spirit" (quoted on p. 5); but
his contribution to black music has continued to be sadly neglected.
Only recently has his overall contribution to American--indeed,
world--culture begun to be re-examined (this often in protest at the
political attempt to reduce him to insignificance), and then with com-

paratively little attention to the role of music in his life. This collection of essays, while concentrating on Robeson's social and political ideas and activities, does include a seven-page piece by Anatol I. Schlosser, "Paul Robeson's Mission in Music." Included also are tributes to Robeson from Lena Horne and Pete Seeger, and Robeson's own "The Culture of the Negro." The bibliography, by Ernest Kaiser, is extensive. (A more substantial one is Lenwood G. Davis's A Paul Robeson Research Guide [Westport: Greenwood Press, 1982].)

S.514.　　GILLIAM, Dorothy Butler. Paul Robeson, All-American. Washington, D.C.: New Republic Book Company, 1976. 216p. illus., bibliog.

An "unauthorized" biography (Robeson's son declined to help or hinder), but written with access to the Paul Robeson Archives in New York as well as to sections of FBI files, and aided by interview material. The story of "the man who rose from a poor preacher's son to millionaire theatrical, screen, and concert star, and whose political beliefs caused him to be scorned and humiliated in later years" (p. ix) is effectively and movingly told. The author seeks to illuminate the way Robeson became a focus for "complicated social, political and theatrical forces," but the narrative impetus of so varied a life tends to prevent this. As often happens in books on Robeson, music--his singing, his approach to and use of song, his role in awakening ears to black music--is little discussed outside of purely biographical contexts.

S.515.　　HAMILTON, Virginia. Paul Robeson: the life and times of a free black man. New York: Harper & Row, 1974. 217p. illus., bibliog.

Covering much the same ground as Gilliam (no. S.514), this biography is equally successful in clarifying how, in Sterling Stuckey's words, "Robeson's fate illustrates the extent to which guardians of the culture are willing, when frightened, to attempt to blot from history a man's meaning, his very existence" (New York Times, October 21, 1973, quoted on p. 194).

S.516.　　NAZEL, Joseph. Paul Robeson: biography of a proud man. Los Angeles: Holloway House, 1980. 216p. bibliog.

Nazel's book is not a biography, despite the subtitle, but a lucid, hard-hitting study of Robeson's profound commitment, in all his various roles, to the cause of black society and culture. There are relatively few direct references to Robeson the musician (Chapter 4, centering on his views of black culture, contains the majority), but Nazel views the different aspects of his subject as basically indivisible ("he was singer/actor/activist--an inseparable trilogy, bound together as the soul is to the body, giving life and meaning, one to the other"--p. 13), and an appreciation of Robeson the musician is considerably deepened by the understanding Nazel brings. Many of Robeson's writings, speeches, and interviews are quoted, and the text of his appearance before the House Un-American Activities Committee in 1956, is reproduced.   No index.

4.   Black Musical Life in the Slave Era

(See also no. S.521)

S.517.   LaBREW, Arthur R.   Black Musicians of the Colonial Period: a preliminary index of names compiled from various sources.   Detroit: LaBrew, 1977.   182p.   illus., bibliog.
_____.   _____.   (New ed.)   Detroit: LaBrew, 1981. 209p.   illus., bibliog.
Over 50 newspapers were the main source for this impressive, pioneering work, which offers far more than the notion of "index" might imply.   The entries for the musicians, drawn from advertisements (particularly for recapture of escaped slaves) and news items, are arranged chronologically by the year the name appears in the source.   They include biographical information and notes on which musical skill each practiced; detail taken from advertisements often includes an evaluation also.   (LaBrew notes that the ability to sing was rarely mentioned, and suggests that this was because voice alone was an insufficient means of identification.)   The chronological arrangement permits a number of interesting facts to emerge, such as the earliest mention of the banjo: in the middle and upper colonies in 1749.   Preceding the index is a long introduction, including a chronological account of musical activity among blacks, based on the results of the research.   There is also an alphabetical index, and the text includes reproductions of a number of advertisements. LaBrew laments his inability to find a publisher for his work—and one can fully sympathize.   Such valuable research deserves wider dissemination.

5.   Folk Song

a.   Collections

See also S.492

S.518.   BREWER, J. Mason.   American Negro Folklore; illustrated by Richard Lowe.   Chicago: Quadrangle Books, 1968. 386p.   illus.
Anthology of folklore materials (tales, proverbs, rhythms, etc.).   Part 3 is devoted to songs and contains words and melodies of seventeen spirituals, six folk blues, ten slave "seculars" and work songs, eight ballads, and six miscellaneous items.   Most are reprinted from earlier sources.   Index.

S.519.   PORTER, Grace Cleveland, ed.   Negro Folk Singing Games

and Folk Games of the Habitants; traditional melodies
and text transcribed by Grace Cleveland Porter; accompaniments by Harvey Worthington Loomis. London:
Curwen, 1914. (Repr. Folcroft, Pa.: Folcroft Library
Editions, 1978.) 35p.

The thirteen items, partly collected by the editor, and
partly by Louise Clarke-Prynelle for Henry Krehbiel, are given with
piano accompaniment, and each is preceded by a description of the
game. The editor's source was Mammy Mary, whose own story of a
Georgia plantation is given in her own words (or, at least, in the
stylized form that passed for black talk).

b. Studies

S.520. DUNDES, Alan, ed. Mother Wit From the Laughing Barrel:
readings in the interpretation of Afro-American folklore.
Englewood Cliffs, N.J.: Prentice-Hall, 1973.
_____. _____; a new printing, with addendum. New
York: Garland, 1981. 674p. bibliog.

An important collection of previously published material
(64 items in all), providing a variety of interpretations of different
aspects of black folklore--origins, speech, beliefs, humor, etc.
Though virtually all the pieces can be read with interest from the
musical standpoint, there are a number with specifically musical subjects (the original dates of publication are given in parentheses):
D. K. Wilgus, "The Negro-White Spiritual" (1959); Richard Alan
Waterman," African Influence on the music of the Americas"
(1952); Janheinz Jahn, "Residual African Elements in the Blues"
(1961); Gertrude P. Kurath & Nadia Chilkovsky, "Jazz Choreology"
(1956); Guy B. Johnson, "Double Meaning in the Popular Negro
Blues" (1927); Mimi Clar Melnick, "I Can Peep Through Muddy
Waters and Spy Dry Land: Boasts in the Blues" (1967); Willis
Laurence James, "The Romance of the Negro Folk Cry in America"
(1958); Robert Winslow Gordon, "Negro 'Shouts' from Georgia"
(1927); John Lovell, "The Social Implications of the Negro Spiritual"
(1939); H. B. Parks, "Follow the Drinking Gourd" (1928); Alan
Lomax, "I Got the Blues" (1948); Russell Ames, "Protest and Irony
in Negro Folklore" (1950); Chadwick Hansen, "Social Influences on
Jazz Style: Chicago, 1920-30" (1960); Samuel C. Adams, "The Acculturation of the Delta Negro" (1947); Richard M. Dorson, "The
Career of 'John Henry'" (1965); Marshall and Jean Stearns, "Fron-
tiers of Humor: American Vernacular Dance" (1966) (on man-and-
wife vaudeville acts).

The editor provides introductory paragraphs to each piece
but no index.

S.521. EPSTEIN, Dena J. Sinful Tunes and Spirituals: black
folk music to the Civil War. Urbana: University of
Illinois Press, 1977. 433p. illus., bibliog.

This truly remarkable book achieved what had been thought

impossible: a history of early black folk music and musical life that
is not largely speculative but documented in immense detail. Years
of tireless, painstaking research were spent systematically investigat-
ing early historical materials (travel accounts, memoirs, letters,
etc., etc.) for any references to black music; a mass of primary
sources was uncovered, and these are gathered and organized here
into a chronological account from the earliest days of the slave trade
to 1867. Part 1, "Development of Black Folk Music to 1800," presents evidence from the earliest reports of African music in the
colonies, on instruments, on dancing and singing, on the role of music in daily life, concluding with the first stages of acculturation and
the question of conversion to Christianity. (A distinguishing feature here is the prominence of source material specifically concerning
the West Indies; this is justified by the author, to compensate for
a relative paucity of mainland material for the early years, because
of the substantial common factors between the islands and the mainland in the first stages of their colonial history.) Part 2, "Secular
and Sacred Black Folk Music, 1800-1967," concentrates on mainland
America and is concerned in turn with black music in New Orleans,
acculturated dancing and associated instruments, worksongs, characteristics of secular folk music, and the background and nature of
religious folk music. Part 3, "The Emergence of Black Folk Music
During the Civil War," is substantially devoted to the collecting of
songs on the Sea Islands off S. Carolina and Georgia, culminating
in the first collection of slave music, Slave Songs of the United
States (LOAM 768). The genesis and publication history of the
book are described in detail, together with information on the compilers, William Francis Allen, Charles Pickard Ware, and Lucy
McKim Garrison.

Interpretation and analysis of the data is not the author's
primary objective--indeed, the documents generally speak very elo-
quently for themselves--but she is confident, in her conclusion
that, although not all controversies have now been resolved (even
after twenty years' work), the documents "establish certain facts
beyond any question" (p. 343). These "facts" relate to the trans-
plant of African music, instruments, and musical practices in the
New World and their persistence, albeit in changed forms; to the
process of acculturation (rather than the disappearance of black culture); to the omnipresence of secular black folk music in the antebellum South; and to the distinctiveness of black spirituals.

Appendices include excerpts from Allen's diaries, a chronological table for sources of the banjo, and several facsimiles. The
massive, 42-page bibliography includes annotations; the index is
similarly thorough.

S.522.   LOMAX, Alan.   The Rainbow Sign: a southern documentary.
          New York: Duell, Sloan and Pearce, 1959. 209p.
          These are valuable "tape-recorded documentaries" (p. 20)
of black life in the South, with particular reference to music; represented are two people--Nora, a folk singer, and Reverend Renfrew,
a 70-year-old minister--and a revival church service (prayer,

responses and sermon), the latter from North Mississippi in 1942. These are preceded by an essay on black life in the USA and a religious srevice in Haiti. Lomax states (p. 4): "Strip America of [the Southern Negro folk singer's] creations and we would appear unexpressed in the world's eyes, for jazz clothes our vast technology and our puritan democracy in humanity." (Emphasis added.) (The title of the book is from the spiritual sometimes called "Home In That Rock"--"God gave Noah the rainbow sign/ No more water but the fire next time.")

6. Spirituals and Religious Music

(except Gospel--see G.11.c)

a. Collections

S.523.   COHEN, Lily Young. Lost Spirituals; with thirty-six illustrations by Kenneth K. Pointer, and forty-one plates of musical compositions as composed by Negroes and set down in music by the author. New York: Walter Neale, 1928. (Repr. Freeport: Books for Libraries Press, 1972.) 143p. illus.
   The 41 melodies and texts from South Carolina (usually one verse and refrain only) are incorporated in anglicized form into the author's narrative of her personal reminiscences, archly told in the third person; "a child of prosperity who had the good fortune to be born and brought up in the South during the '70s and '80s and who enjoyed the love of the faithful colored servants of that time" (p. xvii), she describes the songs as growing "like wild flowers in their sweet crudeness, with only the warmth of the Negro heart to foster them" (p. xviii). Included in the text is a description of an Emancipation Day parade by a black military company with fife and drum corps. The songs themselves include lullabies, spirituals, play and dance songs, and songs of the watermelon vendor; all were originally in Gullah dialect.

S.524.   JACKSON, Judge, ed. The Colored Sacred Harp. Ozark, Ala.: J. Jackson, 1934. 96p.
   _____.   _____. Rev. ed. Montgomery, Ala.: Paragon Press, 1973. 96p. illus.
   Seventy-seven songs are given in four-part harmony, using four shape notes. Jackson, born in Montgomery County in 1883, learned sacred harp singing around Ozark, and was active in the Dale Co. Colored Musical Institute, from where the idea came for the original compilation. Besides editing and arranging the collection, Jackson contributed a number of original compositions (27 contributed in all). He died in 1958. (See also Joe Dan Boyd, "Judge Jackson: Black Giant of White Spirituals," Journal of American Folklore 83, No. 330 [Oct.-Dec. 1970], pp. 446-451.)

S.525. JOLAS, Eugène, ed. Le nègre qui chante; chansons tra-
duites et introduction per Eugène Jolas. Paris: Editions
des Cahiers Libres, 1928. 85p.
The collection of French verse translations of 38 songs
(mainly spirituals, with some folk songs and blues) is preceded by
a twenty-page introduction.

S.526. LOGAN, William A., ed. Road to Heaven: Twenty-eight
negro spirituals; collected by William A. Logan; edited
by Allen M. Garrett. University, Ala.: University of
Alabama Press, 1955. 37p.
The dust jacket of this collection states "Dr. Garrett ...
contributed the sympathetic and understanding introduction," but
"condescending" might describe it more accurately. Other than that
(Garrett's "suggested bibliography," which follows this introduction,
contains four titles), there is a brief, unsigned preface, a section
of notes about the songs, and a first-line index. The songs are
given in single lines, copied in large, not-very-sophisticated autog-
raphy. The selection is of interest, however. The black collector
was born in 1871, and he made it a practice to set down the spirituals sung by the oldest members of various church congregations.
"In this fashion," states the preface, "he was able to add to his collection many spirituals which date from the period of the War Between
the States." The order of the songs is geographical by state of
origin. No title index.

S.527. SCHWARZER GESANG I: Spirituals, englisch-deutsch; aus-
gewählt, übersetzt und mit einem Schallplattenverzeichnis
versehen von Paridam von dem Knesebeck. Munich:
Nymphenburg, 1961. 71p. discog.
_____. II: Blues, englisch-deutsch; herausgegeben, mit
Nachwort und Schallplatten-Überblick von Joachim Ernst
Berendt. Munich: Nymphenburg, 1962. discog.
Bilingual anthologies (original English and German translation) of the texts of 62 spirituals, eight hollers and worksongs, sixteen blues about the country and the city, 25 classic blues, six
prison blues, and twelve blues from Kansas City and the swing tra-
dition.

b. Jubilee Singers

S.528. JOHNSON, J. Rosamond, ed. Utica Jubilee Singers Spirituals, As Sung by the Utica Normal and Industrial Institute
of Mississippi; taken down by J. Rosamond Johnson; with
introduction by C. W. Hyne. Boston: Ditson; Chicago:
Lyon & Henly; London: Winthrop Rogers, 1930. 149p.
illus.
The Utica Jubilee Singers first sang outside Utica in the
early 1900s, and made their first broadcast in 1926. It was through

radio that they became widely known, their weekly audience in the late 1920s being estimated at over three million (p. xv). At the time of publication of this collection they had also made twenty records. The 38 spirituals are presented by Johnson in harmonies "exactly as sung" by the singers. Hyne's introduction discusses the definition of the spiritual, its origins, and its method of creation (drawing on J. R. and James Weldon Johnson, Harry T. Burleigh and others); he also provides a classification of Negro music, religious and secular.

c. Studies and Reference Works

See also nos. S.520, S.582

S.529. DJEDJE, Jacqueline Cogdell. American Black Spiritual and Gospel Songs from Southeast Georgia: a comparative study. Los Angeles: Center for Afro-American Studies, University of California, 1978. (Monograph Series, No. 7.) 105p. bibliog.
    A comparative ethnomusicological analysis of a representative sampling of spirituals and gospel songs, based on field research in S.E. Georgia and N.E. Florida. Close attention is given to individual musical elements (form, scale, tonality, melodic contour, intervals, etc.) and to methods of ornamentation and embellishment. A table of similarities and differences summarizes the findings. The text includes many music examples, and sample transcriptions of performances of gospel and spiritual songs, with analysis of their tuning systems, are included in the appendices.

S.530. WILLIAMS, Ethel L., and BROWN, Clifton L. Afro-American Religious Studies: a comprehensive bibliography with locations in American libraries. Metuchen, N.J.: Scarecrow Press, 1972. 454p.
    Pages 160-166, "Spirituals, Gospel Songs, Music, Poetry," provide a useful, if far from complete 93-item bibliography of books, articles, dissertations, and collections. The remainder of the bibliography offers the student of black music a valuable listing of background material. Appendix 2 lists manuscript collections. Name index.

7. Ragtime

(See also no. S.279)

S.531. BERLIN, Edward A. Ragtime: a musical and cultural history. Berkeley: University of California Press, 1980. 248p. illus., bibliog.
    Some hamburgers are all bun and no middle; this one is most generous with the meat, but serves it in sliced bread. Part 2 of the

book, the "musical history" of the subtitle, is a very fine 109-page study of piano ragtime, with many music examples. Following discussion of the characteristics and musical sources of early piano rags, Berlin analyzes the features of what he terms a "cohesive style" (approximately the first decade of the century) and its subsequent "erosion" in the 1910s. Preceding this central section--and mainly responsible for the "cultural" epithet in the subtitle--is an investigation of how ragtime was perceived by contemporaries; i.e., what critics (mainly) and performers (to a lesser extent) understood to be its origins, its distinguishing features and its aesthetic value. This section sits uneasily beside the more analytic one: its emphasis on vocal ragtime makes a useful historical point, but the expectation that this "cultural" history will shed light on what follows is not fulfilled; authentic "cultural" history (of the black vernacular world out of which it arose, of the relation of this society to the dominated one, of the growing popular culture industry in late 19th century America) would indeed have done that.

The final section, on changing critical attitudes to ragtime, continues the theme of Part I, but is in effect a postscript. Scholarly documentation abounds throughout, and includes a good bibliography and a location index for piano rags in selected anthologies. There is also a general index.

S.532. JASEN, David A., and TICHENOR, Trebor Jay. Rags and Ragtime: a musical history. New York: Seabury Press, 1978. 310p. illus.

Not so much a history, more a critical catalog on historical principles, this book is the "culmination of more than twenty-five years of constant study, research, collecting and performing" by both authors. Following an introduction on "ragtime as a form and a fad," the book proceeds chronologically from 1897-1978 (Tom Turpin to William Bolcom), dividing the authors' selection from the repertoire into eight chapters, some of which deal with several composers, one of which is devoted to a single individual (Jelly Roll Morton). Around 50 composers are featured, prominent among them Scott Joplin, James Scott, Joseph Lamb, Zez Confrey, and James P. Johnson. In each chapter an introduction is followed by the catalog; this takes the form of a short biography of each composer, and a list of selected rags, for each of which the authors provide details of publishing date, publisher, discographical information where relevant (roll or record number, with occasional dates, and names of performers other than the composer), a note on structure, and a critical commentary (with some music examples). Towards the end of the book, especially in the final section on the revival, comment on individual pieces becomes sparse. An appendix gives the dates of other important ragtime composers, and there is an index.

S.533. WALDO, Terry. This is Ragtime; with a foreword by Eubie Blake. New York: Hawthorn Books, 1976. 244p. illus., bibliog., discog.

An excellent historical account of the growth and development

of ragtime, and of its changing fortunes through successive revivals.
Waldo combines historical accuracy, succinct social and cultural discussion and basic musical commentary, and writes in an informal,
accessible style. Ten chapters take the story from the roots of ragtime through its classic period (with particular attention to Joplin,
but also to Lamb and Scott), its exploitation by the music business
at the turn of the century, the achievements in New York of Will
Marion Cook, Williams & Walker, James Reese Europe, Eubie Blake,
and James P. Johnson, continued ragtime activity in St. Louis (influence of the blues) and elsewhere, to the series of revivals from
the 1940s to date. Accepting the revivals as an important, integral
part of the story, Waldo sets them in the context of the revival of
New Orleans jazz, giving accounts of Lu Watters (with interviews)
and Turk Murphy, and going on to describe the commercial aspects
of 1950s interest in the music, alongside the pioneering book by
Blesh and Janis (They All Played Ragtime, LOAM 799), a work
which awakened interest in "authentic" ragtime and led to the performances of Max Morath. He concludes with the reinstatement of
Joplin in the 1970s, the influence of Marvin Hamlish's music for
The Sting (of which he disapproves), and the revivals of Treemon-
isha in Atlanta and Houston. An interview with Gunther Schuller
is featured. A fifteen-page LP discography, a bibliography of books,
articles, music collections, and liner notes, and an index complete
the volume.

EUBIE BLAKE

S.534.   CARTER, Lawrence T. Eubie Blake: keys to memory.
          Detroit: Balamp Publishing, 1979. 116p.
          The 31 brief chapters here provide a composite, anecdotal
portrait of Blake, but one of little depth; the chief merit of the book
is the large number of verbatim quotations from Blake as an elderly
man.

S.535.   ROSE, Al. Eubie Blake. New York: Schirmer, 1979.
          214p. illus., discog.
          An affectionate biographical portrait, based on a series of
taped conversations with Eubie Blake (1883-1983), then well into his
nineties but with a power of recollection--like most of his faculties
--as yet undimmed. Rose's decision to transfer substantial amounts
of Blake's own speech directly into the text assures the pianist's
own vivid presence, but also edges the book uncertainly towards
autobiography. Blake's early years in Baltimore, his partnership
with Noble Sissle, and his career up to Shuffle Along (1921) are told
with an awareness of the importance of context (as, for instance, in
the accounts of Bert Williams' contribution to opening up avenues for
black performers in show business); the account of the later career
is much less detailed. When it comes to the renewal of public interest, beginning in the 1960s, the narrative grows somewhat breathless
and unreflective, but here, as elsewhere, Blake's sunny personality

is pre-eminent. There is a selected list of his compositions, with
details of collaborators and year of composition, a discography of 78s
and LPs, a filmography, and piano rollography by Michael Montgomery, a filmography, and an index.

SCOTT JOPLIN

S.536.   HASKINS, James. Scott Joplin; with Kathleen Benson.
          Garden City, N.Y.; Doubleday, 1978. 248p. illus.,
          bibliog.
          The motivation for this widely researched biography lay in
the author's perception that, while Joplin's music was suddenly all
the rage in the early 1970s, there was a marked lack of interest in
the man himself. Haskins' ambitious aims--given the paucity of
previously known documentation--are amply fulfilled: not only is
the portrait more detailed than any previous attempt, particularly
on Joplin's early years, it is also informative on the cultural and
social background. All the author's many sources (including interviews) are acknowledged in extensive notes. Some hoped-for material eluded his researches, however: "Despite intensive efforts,
there are still facts I cannot document.... What I have done, therefore, is to take the facts I have documented together with the interview material I have gathered and the undocumented legends about
Joplin, and made what I consider educated conjectures about what is
not known" (p. xii). Index.

8.   Blues

a.   Reference

S.537.   ARNAUDON, Jean-Claude. Dictionnaire du blues. Paris:
          Filipacchi, 1977. 291p. illus., bibliog.
          A biographical dictionary of over 400 entries, combining
concise, detailed career data with brief critical evaluation. Coverage
is restricted to exponents of rural and urban blues, and excludes
many who, in the compiler's eyes, are more closely identified with
jazz, rock & roll, and soul. Among those excluded by the strict application of this judgment are Bessie Smith, Jimmy Rushing and
Fats Domino. Both Bogaert (LOAM 805) and Harris (no. S.538)
have more entries and a broader coverage, but against that Arnaudon's book has a greater unity and has best solved the problem of
being factually informative and readable.

S.538.   HARRIS, Sheldon. Blues Who's Who: a biographical dic-
          dionary of blues singers. New Rochelle, N.Y.: Arling-
          ton House, 1979. 775p. illus., bibliog.
          Elephantine both in size and memory, this remarkable refer-
ence book sets down in impressive detail the lives and careers
("condensed to the bare facts without embellishment"--p. 9) of 571
blues singers. Drawing on his own research by interview and

correspondence, and on a myriad of published sources, Harris presents his information in a compact, telegraphic style, following a set pattern that normally includes dates of birth and death, background, career, personal details (of husband or wife and children), songs, awards, influences (by and on), and bibliographic references. (Many entries also provide a few sample "quotes," short, laudatory, generally imprecise remarks drawn from published sources and all out of context; an unnecessary embellishment, which does not work as a substitute for critical summary by the compiler.) Coverage deliberately excludes instrumentalists such as Pete Johnson, but includes a substantial number of white performers (Ramblin' Jack Elliott, Janis Joplin). Additional material includes a bibliography of books and magazine titles, useful indexes of films, radio and television programs, theatrical shows and song titles. The final 76-page index is of names, places and other subjects. The photographic illustrations, many from the author's own collection, are excellent.

S.539.   HERZHAFT, Gérard. Encyclopédie du blues: étude bio-
         discographique d'une musique populaire négro-américaine.
         Lyon: Fédérop, 1979. 346p. illus., bibliog.
    The need for subject dictionaries in a great many areas of American music is a pressing one, and in none more than blues. Herzhaft's half-hearted attempt to balance his book between topical and biographical entries fails, not dishonorably, because biographical data is the dominating element--so much so that the subject entries for regions, cities, styles and instruments in most cases are themselves constructed around short biographies (mainly of performers who do not otherwise achieve the status of a separate entry). Herzhaft's coverage is less precisely defined than Arnaudon's (no. S.537), less extensive than Harris's (no. S.538). It excludes white performers, but includes a number of (mostly celebrated) musicians whose music is more readily associated with other styles (e.g., Little Richard, Tina Turner). Entries have a tendency to be discursive and often lack precise information. The addition to many entries of guidance on available LPs is a welcome bonus. Index.

S.540.   TUDOR, Dean, and TUDOR, Nancy. Black Music. Littleton,
         Colo.: Libraries Unlimited, 1979. 262p. bibliog.
    Very useful discographical guide to LPs, covering blues, gospel, rhythm and blues, soul, and--more modestly--reggae. The authors present a selection of around 650 entries, representing some 1,300 discs; their generous annotations handle questions of the style and significance of individual performers with confidence (except possibly in the gospel section, which, in addition contains the poorest ratio of entries to issued recordings) and accuracy. Each section has a brief historical and stylistic introduction, and there is bibliographical guidance also, the literature (113 books and 21 periodical citations) being listed in an annotated bibliography at the back. There is also a label directory and an index. (For other volumes in the series, "American Popular Music on Elpee," see no.s S.276, S.661, S.817. For a cumulative edition of all four books, see S/A 517.)

b. Mainly Historical

S.541. BAS-RABÉRIN, Philippe. Le blues moderne, 1945-1973.
Paris: Albin Michel, 1973. 266p. illus., bibliog.,
discog.

_____. _____; nouvelle édition revue et augmentée.
Paris: Albin Michel, 1979. 254p. illus., bibliog.,
discog.

This study of post-war blues explores in turn three main
themes: the adaptation of bluesmen and their music to the conditions of post-war America; the decline in popularity of the blues in
the black community, and the rise of rhythm and blues and soul;
and the discovery and assimilation of the blues by white rock musicians and audiences. At least half the book is devoted to aspects
of the last of these, which the author handles with greater confidence than he does the earlier material. The bibliography has a
number of inaccuracies, and the discographical information is, like
the legendary box of string, too short to be used. Index.

S.542. OAKLEY, Giles. The Devil's Music: a history of the blues.
London: British Broadcasting Corporation, 1976; New
York: Taplinger, 1977. 287p. illus., bibliog., discog.
_____. _____. Rev. ed. London: Ariel Books/BBC,
1983. 287p. illus., bibliog., discog.

Written to accompany a BBC television series, this is a
straightforward, reliable history of the blues from slavery to the
post-war era; clear in outline, factually sound, and well-illustrated,
it ranks as a successful assimilation of existing knowledge and documentation. Oakley is strong on the social history and cultural significance of the music, less prepared to get involved in the music
itself. Although the canvas is broad, he pays close attention to detail in the form of particular musicians, particular songs (many lyrics
are quoted). The only original material comes from interviews conducted for the series (e.g., with Little Brother Montgomery, Bukka
White). In addition to bibliographic references in the notes, there
is a short, annotated book bibliography, and a very selective list
of recommended recordings. General and title indexes.

c. Regional Studies

S.543. BEYER, Jimmy. Baton Rouge Blues: a guide to the Baton
Rouge bluesmen and their music. Baton Rouge, La.:
Arts and Humanities Council of Greater Baton Rouge,
1980. 48p. illus., discogs.

Short biographies of nineteen blues musicians associated with
Baton Rouge, prefaced by a brief account of the development of the
blues in the city, of the work of Harry Oster, and of the recordings
made by J. D. Miller. Those musicians with the more detailed biographies are: Robert Pete Williams, Slim Harpo, Lonesome Sundown,
Lightnin' Slim, Silas Hogan, Lazy Lester, Moses Smith, Arthur Kelly,

Henry Gray, and Tabby Thomas. Each entry has a short discography.

S.544.   FERRIS, William. Blues From the Delta. Garden City,
         N.Y.: Anchor Press, 1979. 226p. illus., bibliog.,
         discog.
         Though partly re-written and partly re-organized, this is
substantially the same study as LOAM 821. In truth, the relationship is not made sufficiently clear; a note on the verso says "Parts
of this book have appeared, in slightly different form, in ..." etc.,
but the author himself offers no guidance as to what he has changed
and why. The strength of this documentary portrait of the creative
processes in the Delta blues remains its use of material obtained
from local contemporary sources, in particular the detailed transcript of a Clarkdale house party. The bibliography and discography
are considerably enlarged, and an index has been added.

d.   Collected Portraits

     See also S.389, S.559, S.1136

S.545.   CHARTERS, Samuel. Sweet as the Showers of Rain: the
         Bluesmen, volume II. New York: Oak Publications,
         1977. 179p. illus.
         Charters' second and final volume of regional studies of
pre-war blues styles, a partner to The Bluesmen (LOAM 827), concentrates on singers from Tennessee, Georgia and the Carolinas.
Following the same method as he used in the earlier book, he describes the distinguishing features of each regional background
clearly and evocatively, provides salient biographical information,
then centers his attention on recordings with equal weight given to
music and lyrics, and with numerous examples. Chief among the
musicians whose work is described are the Memphis Jug Band, Gus
Cannon, Furry Lewis, Frank Stokes, Sleepy John Estes, Memphis
Minnie, Peg Leg Howell, Barbecue Bob, Blind Willie McTell, Blind
Blake, Buddy Moss, Blind Boy Fuller and Gary Davis. There is a
discographical note on available recordings, and an index of names
and titles.

S.546.   NEFF, Robert, and CONNOR, Anthony. Blues. London:
         Latimer, 1976. 141p. illus.
         A soundscape of the voices of blues musicians, describing
"their music, their pasts and their futures, hopes and fears, failures and ideas" (introduction). Based on conversations with musicians in the early 1970s, and presented without comment in one
single sequence, the text effectively moves from casual recollection
to telling anecdote, from strong opinion to more meditative reflection.
Fifty-six musicians are featured, among the most prominent being
James Cotton, Willie Dixon, Honeyboy Edwards, John Lee Hooker,
Brownie McGhee, Esther Phillips, Hound Dog Taylor, and Muddy

Waters. There are over 80 black and white photographs, some full page, and very brief biographical details of each musician are given in note form at the end.

S.547.   WILSON, Burton.   Burton's Book of the Blues.   Austin,
    Tex.:   Spelco Press; the author, 1971.   77p.   illus.
    _____.   _____: a decade of American music, 1967-
    1976.   Rev. ed.   Austin, Tex.:   Edentata Press, 1977.
    77p.   illus.
    Black-and-white photographs, by Wilson, of blues per-
formers, with a smattering also of rock and country stars.

e.   Individual Artists

JOHN LEE HOOKER

S.548.   FANCOURT, Leslie.   John Lee Hooker: a discography.
    Faversham, Kent: the author, (197-?).   19p.
    The original research into Hooker discography was done by
Dave Sax, whose work was published in Leadbitter and Slaven (LOAM 808).   This chronological listing (of American issues only, like the original) revises that work and extends it from 1966 to 1974.

B. B. KING

S.549.   SAWYER, Charles.   The Arrival of B. B. King.   Garden
    City, N.Y.:   Doubleday, 1980.   274p.   illus., discog.
    _____.   B. B. King: the authorized biography.   Poole,
    Dorset: Blandford Press, 1981; London: Quartet
    Books, 1982.   274p.   illus., discog.
    A sympathetic, admiring biography of King (b.1925), whose confidence the author clearly enjoyed.   Sawyer's chief concern is the "social significance of (King's) life story" (p. vii)--his rise from sharecropping to be the "preeminent artist of a neglected genre," who finally achieves recognition as "the reigning master of his craft" (p. 106)--and this significance lies in its power to sym- bolize the "death of Jim Crow" (p. vii).   The story of King's early years in the Mississippi Delta is particularly well told.   This and the more sketchy Memphis period, when King took his first steps on the road to fame, are presented in a conventional biographical man- ner; thereafter, with his subject committed to a life of incessant touring, first on the "chitlin circuit," then in the more lucrative "prestige entertainment rooms of Middle America" (p. 105), Sawyer abandons detailed chronology in favor of overall portraits of the lifestyle and developments characteristic of successive periods of King's career, pointing out high and low spots, and--especially-- attempting to analyze both his subject and the circumstances affect- ing him.   The absence of a shapeless narrative of one-night stands is no great loss, but does produce other, unsolved problems (e.g., the Horatio Alger-ism which obsesses the author would be more

convincing if seen against a more telling portrait of the relentless grind of life on the road). A chapter on King's musical style ("The Music Alone") comes last, and looks lost. There are 50 pages of appendices, an odd collection of other lost material ranging from details of plantation organization and lynchings to an analysis of a King solo. The discography lacks personnel and precise dates. Index.

BESSIE SMITH

S.550. ALBERTSON, Chris, ed. Bessie Smith, Empress of the Blues; compilation and biography by Chris Albertson; notes on Bessie Smith's singing style by Gunther Schuller; musical arrangements by George N. Terry; edited by Clifford Richter. New York: Walter Kane, 1975. 143p. illus., discog.

This collection of 30 songs recorded by Bessie Smith (nineteen of them composed by her), in arrangements for voice and piano, has prefatory material, the highlight of which is the superbly produced selection of photographic portraits by Carl Van Vechten et al.

f. Interpretation

See also S.331

S.551. BIGSBY, C. W. E., ed. Approaches to Popular Culture. London: Arnold, 1976. 280p. illus., bibliog. refs.

Among the essays in this volume, which range over such topics as the relationship between popular culture and Structuralism, Marxism and linguistics, there is a short piece by Paul Oliver, entitled "Blue-eyed Blues: the Impact of the Blues on European Popular Culture." This is a twelve-page summary of the development of interest in the blues in Europe, and of the growth of blues-inspired music, from skittle to acid rock. Oliver sees the blues as having been "sucked dry" of all it can offer popular music; well before this point was reached, he notes, black audiences "quit the blues like it had never been" (p. 239). The editor's introductory essay, "The Politics of Popular Culture," although it does not discuss music, touches on themes that could be further explored in a popular music context, e.g., the presence or absence of a "transcendent dimension"--the ability to hint at other worlds and times beyond the present time and place--in popular culture, and the role of alienation, which Bigsby calls "the condition of maximum receptivity to a mass art ... which no longer links man to his own past, but which provides a temporary connection across class in the present" (p. 9).

S.552. GARON, Paul. Blues and the Poetic Spirit; with a preface by Franklin Rosemont. London: Eddison Press, 1975. 178p. illus., bibliog.

A highly original, often belligerent study, bringing sur-
realism and psychology to bear on blues lyrics, in order to illuminate "the blues and the mind, the blues as thought," in particular
the "psychological determinants of blues songs and their poetic implications" (pp. 17-18). The central chapter (Chapter 5, "Imagination, Instincts and Reality") looks at the blues' handling of the con-
ventionally repressed emotions involved in sexuality and aggression,
and explores the poetic treatment of specific themes (travel, male
supremacy, work, magic, etc.). Where most critics decline to see
more than occasional elements of revolt in the blues, Garon perceives the idiom as offering a "sustained poetic attack on the super-
structure of an exploitative society" (p. 65). A shorter chapter on
symbols, images, and the dream provides a challenging conclusion.
      If the potential of this approach is not fully realized, it is
partly because, in the earlier chapters, Garon circles round the
subject for too long, and partly because his very high level of intolerance of other systems and points of view effectively closes as
many doors as it opens. This subject, however, is one Pandora's
box that has a great many keys.

S.553.   MURRAY, Albert. Stomping the Blues; produced and art
         directed by Harris Lewine. New York: McGraw-Hill,
         1976. 264p. illus.
      The central thesis of this important, challenging book has
four main strands: (i) while "the blues" may be associated with
baleful spirits, blues music may not; it is rather a "fundamental
ritual of purification, affirmation, and celebration" (p. 83), and
Murray demonstrates this in the music, and in its social roles and
contexts; (ii) blues lyrics are less important than the music; (iii)
the music is not created as a personal release from suffering so much
as in response to the demands of a particular craft ("it is a far
greater matter of convention, and hence tradition, than of impulse"
--p. 126); mastery of this craft requires sophisticated knowledge,
hence it is not so much in rural blues (important as these are) as in
the idiom of the "consecrated professionals" such as Armstrong,
Ellington, Parker, Young, that is found the combination of earthiness
and refinement necessary to "reflect the subtleties and complexities
of contemporary experience" (p. 213)--i.e., to dispel the blues.
      This last argument produces the emphasis throughout the
book on blues-playing jazz musicians ("jazz" is a word Murray himself
does not use, however) which makes it unique among "blues" books.
Another unique feature is the relationship between the text and the
illustrations and captions. Instead of merely harmonizing with the
arguments, the many excellent photographs and their texts perform
the role of a subtle counterpoint, pointing to people, places, times,
objects, fashions, where the main text is centered more on generalities.

S.554.   TITON, Jeff Todd. Early Downhome Blues: a musical and
         cultural analysis. Urbana: University of Illinois Press,
         1977. 296p. illus., bibliog.

This impressive scholarly study takes as its pivotal point a "representative sample" of 48 "downhome" blues from 1926 to 1930 (Titon prefers "downhome" to "country," as it evokes not just a place but a feeling associated with that place, and locates that feeling "in the mental landscape of black America"--(p. xiv); but far from being an exercise in reification the book is fundamentally about processes--the social, cultural and mental processes of creation, and the processes of dissemination into the larger culture. Part 1 describes the social and cultural background of down home blues in southern agrarian life in the late 19th and early 20th centuries; this leads to a discussion of how the singers who come from this background see their music. Part 2, the central section, presents the song sample (texts, melodic transcriptions, discographical detail and general commentary). Titon follows this with a pioneering piece of musical analysis in which he dissects aspects of form, tone, rhythm, melody; he then demonstrates that this is a far from sterile exercise by using the information gained to create a "model that produces new blues melodies" (p. 169). (The influence of Chomsky is acknowledged.) This still leaves the question of how singers generate texts, and this Titon discusses in a chapter on formulaic structure (he also investigates themes in what is perhaps the weakest part of the study). Part 3 turns its attention to the movement of the blues onto a wider stage, in particular to the attitudes of the white-dominated record industry. An outline of the history of early blues recordings leads to a telling discussion of the techniques of record advertising--the use of stereotypes, etc.--suggesting urban white America's growing unease. The bibliography lists interviews, books, and articles, and there is a general index.

g. Collections of Music and Texts

See also S.527

S.555. NICHOLAS, A. X., ed. Woke Up This Morning: poetry
        of the blues. New York: Bantam Books, 1973. 122p.
        discog.
        Transcriptions of the texts of 48 blues by sixteen blues singers, beginning with Leadbelly and Ma Rainey, and ending with John Lee Hooker and B. B. King. About two-thirds come from the pre-1942 era. The editor's introduction, the brevity of which presents no obstacle to his polemics, includes a somewhat myopic onslaught on critic Paul Oliver.

9. Rhythm and Blues, Soul, Gospel

a. Rhythm and Blues

See also S.540, S.1098, S.1130, S.1161

S.556. FERLINGERE, Robert D. A Discography of Rhythm & Blues and Rock 'n' Roll Vocal Groups, 1945 to 1965. Pittsburg, Calif.: the author, 1976. 700p.

A hard-to-find book (despite its size), this is a looseleaf compilation listing some 15-20,000 recordings. Arrangement is by group name; most, but not all, of the groups are black.

S.557. GONZALEZ, Fernando L. Disco-File: the discographical catalog of American rock & roll and rhythm & blues vocal harmony groups, 1902-1976; race, rhythm & blues, rock & roll, soul. 2nd ed. Flushing, N.Y.: the author, 1977. 449p.

A monumental discographical achievement, listing over 31,000 titles by vocal groups on 78s and 45s. While the volume as a whole covers a 75-year period, from the Dinwiddie Quartet (actually a religious group) to Manhattan Transfer, the bulk of the listings fall into the period from the late 1930s (Golden Gate Quartet, etc.) to the late 1960s. The (computer-produced?) list is alphabetical by group name, with cross-references to changes of name. Under each name titles are listed "alpha-numerically," i.e., alphabetically by record label, numerically within each label sequence (the order is not strictly chronological, therefore, although the end result is sometimes the same). Details are provided of titles, master numbers, and of recording and release dates where known (depending usually on the generosity or otherwise of record companies), but not of personnel or recording location. Subsequent re-releases as single are also noted. Positions 1-3 on Billboard charts are indicated, as are a cappella and instrumental recordings. There are appendices of bootlegs and unissued items. Coverage as a whole extends beyond r & b and rock & roll to include some gospel and jazz performances (criteria here are clearly difficult to establish), and soul (Supremes, Four Tops, etc.). (Publication address: P.O. Box 1812, Flushing, N.Y. 11352.)

S.558. LEICHTER, Albert. A Discography of Rhythm & Blues and Rock & Roll, Circa 1946-1964; a reference manual. Staunton, Va.: the author, 1975. 189p.

A looseleaf listing of 78s and 45s by title. Details are provided of performer or group name (no personnel as such), release date when known (usually year only), record label and number. Around 1,000 records are included. The usefulness of the book is limited by its arrangement and its smallish coverage, but it can at least serve as a partial complement (title index) to Gonzalez' vocal groups discography (no. S.557). (Publication address: 580 Hilltop Drive, Staunton, Va. 24401.)

S.559. LYDON, Michael. Boogie Lightning: how music became electric; photographs by Ellen Mandel. New York: Dial Press, 1974. 229p. illus.

_____. _____. New foreword by B. B. King. New York: Da Capo Press, 1980. 229p. illus.

A collection of essays, profiles, and interviews centering

on the theme of how the electrification of instruments, especially the guitar, enabled black music to "steer musical values back to their primeval source in sensual-mystical delight" (p. 12). With a mixture of thoughtful prose and journalese, Lydon investigates the contributions of several key figures in rhythm and blues: John Lee Hooker, Bo Diddley, producer Ralph Bass, the Chiffons, Aretha Franklin, Ray Charles. These "star" profiles, mixing interview material, biographical data, and critical assessment, are balanced by contemplative pieces on the implications of recorded sound for one's concept of music (this becomes a paean to Chuck Berry), and on the electric guitar itself. (Formerly LOAM A182)

S.560.   OTIS, Johnny. Listen to the Lambs. New York: Norton, 1968. 256p.

When Arnold Shaw interviewed Otis for his book Honkers and Shouters, (no. S.561) he found him "a rapid, well-structured talker," but was still "unprepared for the flow of words" (p. 166). Otis' own book opens with a searing account of the causes of the 1965 Watts riots, and goes on to produce a forceful onslaught on racism and social injustice. Himself an extremely significant figure in rhythm and blues history, as songwriter, drummer, bandleader, record producer, Otis (b. 1921) tells some stories of his life in the music business for their own sake, but chooses many of them to illustrate his central theme. He has a unique perspective on it: for he writes not from a clearcut black or white position, but from that of a white man (he was the son of Greek immigrants) who decided in his youth that "if our society decided that one had to be either black or white, I would be black" (p. 12). As an American ethnic drawn to black life and enabled by black music to "pass" for black, Otis is not of course, alone (cf. Mezz Mezzrow), but his outspoken sentiments, in the music context, make him different.

S.561.   SHAW, Arnold. Honkers and Shouters: the golden years of rhythm and blues. New York: Collier Books, 1978. 555p. illus., bibliog., discog.

For sheer detail on a particular slice of black music history Shaw's book is hard to beat, and the relative paucity of studies in rhythm and blues makes it doubly valuable. Drawing in particular on an inside knowledge of the record business in the 1940s and '50s, and on extensive interviews with performers and significant figures in the recording industry, he constructs a basically historical account from the 1930s roots to the "end of an era." The first two sections, "Roots" and "Components," proceed chronologically from bluesmen like Leroy Carr and Big Bill Broonzy to pioneer rhythm and blues performers such as Louis Jordan, Cecil Gant, T-Bone Walker, etc. Each chapter is constructed by linking together biographical accounts of these and other individuals, to form a narrative. Using the same technique, the following sections proceed chronologically within geographical areas: California, the Midwest, the East Coast, the South. The text includes 25 separate interviews ("grooves") with major figures. The weight of biographical detail

in particular prevents true historical perspective from emerging:
some of these can be gained from Charlie Gillett's The Sound of the
City (LOAM 1350), but a history of rhythm and blues, with due attention to its social and cultural setting, is still needed. Index.

S.562.   TOPPING, Ray. New Orleans Rhythm & Blues Record Label
         Listings; foreword by John Broven. Bexhill-on-Sea:
         Flyright Records, 1978. 68p.
     A discography listing the rhythm and blues records issued
between the early 1950s and the mid-1970s on over 100 record labels
produced by companies based in and around New Orleans. The order in which the labels are given is apparently random, but under
each label heading the issues are listed numerically by record number, with artist, title and matrix number. There is an index to the
labels, and some guidance on the dating of a number of the recordings (dates are not given in the listing itself) is provided at the
back of the booklet, mainly in the form of references to trade journal announcements. No artist or title index.

S.563.   WATSON, Deek. The Story of the "Ink Spots"; with Lee
         Stephenson. New York: Vantage Press, 1967. 72p.
     Lightweight, anecdotal account by the founder of the vocal
group. Beginning in Indianapolis in the 1920s with a group called
"The Percolating Puppies" (they performed for coffee-drinkers),
Watson tells briefly of street-corner singing, early breaks, foreign
tours, work with Glenn Miller and in Hollywood (where, such was
the prevailing fashion, their version of "The Last Round-Up" was
very popular).

b. Soul and Motown

See also S.540

S.564.   AMISTAD 2; edited by John A. Williams and Charles F.
         Harris. New York: Random House, 1971. 338p.
     This important collection of black American writing includes
a seminal essay by Mel Watkins, "The Lyrics of James Brown" (pp.
21-43), which tellingly explores the ways aspects of black life are
expressed in Brown's songs.

S.565.   BENJAMINSON, Peter. The Story of Motown. New York:
         Grove Press, 1979. 180p. illus., discog.
     This "story of how Motown grew and changed, and why"
(p. xi) is particularly informative on the commercial side of the company's history--or, rather, on that electrically charged area where
business and music meet. Berry Gordy dominates the book; his
biography provides its framework, his accomplishments its narrative,
and his character (his hard-headed business sense, his musical per-
specacity) its principal human interest. Whatever is under discus-
sion--the features of the Motown sound, the hard-won professionalism

of its performers, the machine-like qualities that were to develop, the expansion of the business, the social questions raised--proceeds from Gordy out; few performers get close scrutiny (unlike in Morse, LOAM 893)--all are to a considerable degree subservient. Though clearly hugely impressed, Benjaminson is as quick to point to failings as to successes. But one point emerges above all others: by changing the general outlook for black performers and by achieving huge financial success, Motown opened the way for black music to move into the mainstream. Profusely illustrated, and with a discography of top twenty hits, 1961-1971, and an index.

S.566.   CUMMINGS, Tony.   The Sound of Philadelphia.   London:
          Methuen, 1975.   157p.   illus.
          English critic Cummings' main interest, in this finely de-
tailed regional history, written in a readily accessible style (a very rare breed), is in the early 1970s Philadelphia soul sound and scene. "Why is it," he asks, "that America's fourth largest city ... has been the place where soul music has again emerged with all the power, energy and dollar capacity of Detroit in the sixties?" (p. 8). His own preference is not for a sociological explanation, but for "a startling web of coincidences" (ibid.). That may sound like a copout, but should not detract from the usefulness of a very informative book, which, before reaching '70s soul, maps out in five historical chapters the development of black music and rock & roll in Philadelphia from the late '40s (successive chapters are devoted to gospel, doowop quartets, jazz, rock & roll, and the so-called "beat concert style"), and seeks in particular to portray the interconnections between the performers, the producers, the arrangers, the labels, and the media. Cummings conducted many interviews, and quotes extensively from them in the text. Many individual performers make brief appearances, and in both the historical and the contemporary accounts there are just as many little known as famous names. Some of the most interesting information concerns arrangers and producers such as Thom Bell, Kenny Gamble, Leon Huff, Weldon McDougal, and media involvement (in particular Dick Clark's American Bandstand program, nationally networked from WFIL-TV in Philadelphia). The book is liberally illustrated and has a name index, but no discographical information.

S.567.   HOARE, Ian, ed.   The Soul Book.   London: Eyre Methuen,
          1975.   206p.   bibliog. refs.
          A thoughtful and sometimes outstanding survey of significant
areas of soul by four British critics. The task of laying out the historical background, especially in gospel music, and of describing the first great soul pioneers (Ray Charles, Sam Cooke, James Brown, Clyde McPhatter, etc.) falls to Tony Cummings. Simon Frith outlines the Motown story succinctly, with many enlightening comments on the company's aims and achievements, and on its relationship to black society, adding a stout defense against the venom of some parts of the music press (in the USA and Britain). Clive Anderson describes the genesis of Memphis soul, with separate sections on Stax artists,

William Bell, Otis Redding, the Staple Singers, and others; moving
further south, he also includes some account of soul as recorded in
Muscle Shoals and of the largely independent activity in New Orleans. The best piece is by Ian Hoare, on black lyrics and soul's
interaction with white culture. Hoare maintains that "The use of
words in soul music is as much a part of its strength as the vitality
of its rhythms and the expressive power of its vocal and instrumental
styles" (p. 120), and demonstrates this with a sharp analysis of
thematic content. His discussion of the borrowing of black styles
by white rock music draws on Britain for most of its illustrations,
while his final theme--the influence of white rock lyrics on soul--is
exemplified in particular in the songs of Smokey Robinson, Sly
Stone, and Curtis Mayfield. Anderson's linear approach returns to
conclude the book with an outline of soul in the 1970s. Index.

S.568.   LARKIN, Rochelle. Soul Music! New York: Lancer Books,
         1970. 169p. illus., discog.
         This paperback contains thirteen chapters dealing with in-
dividual performers Aretha Franklin, James Brown, Dionne Warwick,
and Ray Charles; with record companies; and collectively, with groups
such as the Duells, the 5th Dimension, and Sly and the Family Stone.
The discography (albums only?) gives no record numbers, but the
photos used throughout are beautiful and often haunting. The
author's enthusiasm sometimes betrays defensiveness, and there is
a tendency to be undiscriminating. No index.

S.569.   PETRIE, Gavin, ed. Black Music. London: Hamlyn, 1974.
         128p. illus.
         Selected from the British magazine, Black Music, these are
short, interview-based portraits of a range of contemporary black
performers, among them James Brown, Ray Charles, the Staple
Singers, the O'Jays, the Three Degrees, the Chi Lites, Thom Bell,
Bill Withers, The Pointer Sisters, Barry White, the Isley Brothers,
Harold Melvin, Smokey Robinson, the Stylistics, Al Green, Bobby
Bland, and Billy Preston. The photographic illustrations (some in
color) are impressive; the journalists are unacknowledged.

RAY CHARLES

S.570.   CHARLES, Ray, and RITZ, David. Brother Ray: Ray
         Charles' own story. New York: Dial Press, 1978;
         London: Macdonald & Jane's 1979. 340p. illus., dis-
         cog.
         Colloquially told, disarmingly candid autobiography, based
on many hours of interview material which Ritz fashioned into a
coherent, chronological narrative (his contribution was clearly considerable: he speaks of convincing Charles in 1976 "to let me write
the story of his life"--p. 312). Staunch independence of view and
action is the greatest hallmark of Charles' character as expressed
in the book; lack of sentimentality another. But there is poignancy
too, particularly in the early chapters, describing his boyhood in

Greensville, Georgia (when blindness developed he was the only blind person in town), and at blind school in St. Augustine, Florida. The book traces his musical apprenticeship in Florida, Seattle, Los Angeles, New York, and his slow, steady progress to the top. The combined influences of blues, gospel and jazz--not forgetting country music--and the adoration in particular of Nat King Cole-- emerge as centrally important (Charles views his music as having "roots which I've dug up from my own childhood, musical roots buried in the darkest soil"--p. 174), although their treatment tends to be episodic, fragmentary. For Ritz, the manner and tone of Charles' speech and his efforts to recapture it--and through it to express something of his music--are the controlling factors. The discography has a commentary, but is a bit short on discographical detail. No index.

SAM COOKE

S.571.   McEWEN, Joe. Sam Cooke: a biography in words and pic-
         tures; edited by Greg Shaw. New York: Sire Books/
         Chappell, 1977. 48p. illus., discog.
         A short fan biography of the gospel singer who helped lay
the foundations for soul. Cooke's life (1935-1964), from his Chicago
childhood to his murder in Los Angeles, is told in a calm, straightforward style. McEwen draws on recognized sources such as Heilbut's The Gospel Sound (LOAM 897); he also conducted some interviews of his own. The numerous illustrations are of varying quality
(and one appears twice); the discography is fine. No index.

DIANA ROSS

S.572.   HASKINS, James. I'm Gonna Make You Love Me: the story
         of Diana Ross. New York: Dial Press, 1980. 154p.
         illus., discog.
         _____. _____. New York: Dell, 1982.
         As with some of Haskins' numerous other biographies for
younger readers, this is a generally conscientious, if somewhat superficial and overly "professional" study, with a tendency to idolize.
The discography is composed of the "singles and albums that made
the Billboard and Cash Box Top 100 lists," and contains no record
numbers. No index.

STEVIE WONDER

S.573.   DRAGONWAGON, Crescent. Stevie Wonder. New York:
         Flash Books, 1977. 94p. illus., discog.
         Informed, fan-oriented biography that makes considerable
use of press stories and includes an account of traveling with Wonder
in 1974. Each album, up to Songs in the Key of Life, is quite closely
inspected, especially from the point of view of the lyrics. The role
of Motown and the steady growth of Wonder's spirituality are also
central.

S.574.   ELSNER, Constanze. Stevie Wonder. London: Everest
         Books, 1977. 360p. illus., discog.
         A long, adoring biography by a German journalist. Its
greatest value is in the large quantity of interview material it contains, with Stevie Wonder himself, with close friends and associates,
and with many Motown figures. Most frequently quoted and/or referred to are producers Hank Cosby, Berry Gordy, and Clarence
Paul, publicist Ira Tucker, Jr., musician Malcolm Cecil, singers Marvin Gaye and Madelaine "Gypsie" Jones, and singer-songwriter Lee
Garrett. The amount of detail is impressive, though its more discerning use, together with a more critical eye (especially towards
the endless adulation of Wonder's acquaintances), and a knowledge
of black music history would have done the subject greater justice.
(The author's comments on the lyrics of Wonder's songs are rather
vacuous, having few points of reference; music as such rarely
features at all.) The discography, more thorough than most of its
kind, covers singles and albums, and includes recording dates and
release numbers. There is also a listing of UK and US chart positions. Index.

S.575.   FOX-CUMMING, Ray. Stevie Wonder. London: Manda-
         brook Books, 1977. 123p. discog.
         Unpretentious pocket-size popular biography, aimed at a
British market (the cover includes the logo, "Daily Mirror Pop
Club"), with generous quotations from the British music press. A
chronology of "Stevie Wonder's Career Highlights," 1950-1977, and
a brief discography of UK singles and albums are included.

S.576.   HASKINS, James. The Story of Stevie Wonder. New York:
         Lothrop, Lee & Shepard, 1976. 104p. illus., discog.
         Principally intended for younger readers, this is an inform-
ative biography, often more so than Dragonwagon's study (no. S.
573), though both use much of the same interview material. Haskins gives detailed consideration to Wonder's blindness, to the
growth of his musical talent, and his early success. There is less
attention to the songs themselves than in Dragonwagon, but a fuller
character portrayal. Index. (Haskins is also the compiler, with
Kathleen Benson, of an illustrated tribute, The Stevie Wonder Scrapbook [New York: Grosset & Dunlap; London: Cassel, 1978].)

c.   Gospel Music

     See also nos. S.529, S.530, S.540

S.577.   GOREAU, Laurraine. Just Mahalia, Baby. Waco, Tex.:
         Word Books, 1975. 611p. illus.
         _____. Mahalia. Berkamsted, Harts: Lion, 1976.
         592p. illus.
         The much-loved singer (1911-1972) first suggested to Laur-
raine Goreau in 1967, "on a wave of dissatisfaction with so much in

print which was erroneous," that her fellow New-Orleanian should
write "the 'real' book of her" (preface). (This, therefore, was
after Mahalia's own autobiography [LOAM 899] was published.) From
then until Mahalia's death, Goreau interviewed her extensively,
traveled with her, studied her memorabilia. After 1972 she embarked
on a course of "total research" (ibid.), carrying out a huge program
of interviewing with family, friends, musicians, associates, correspondence, and on-the-spot research in New Orleans, Chicago, and
elsewhere. The result is a massively detailed, close-quarters account,
one of the most meticulous of any popular music figure. Unfortunately, there are some problems, Goreau's chosen style, intended pre-
sumbaly to recapture the intensity of Mahalia's personality and lifestyle, is a restless, staccato prose, full of incomplete sentences
("Summer revival, familiar now. The one-day Chicago circuit, then
gather up the caravan car and move on out. Hallelujah. Thank You,
Jesus"--p. 113, UK ed.), which when combined with a sense that at
least some detail could have been used more discriminatingly, is likely to become tedious. For research purposes, the book offers further difficulties: there is no index, no documentation, and a dis-
inclination to pinpoint events with dates, all of which impedes the
use of what is undoubtedly very valuable material.

S.578.   JACKSON, Irene V., ed.   Afro-American Religious Music:
         a bibliography and a catalogue of gospel music.   West-
         port, Conn.: Greenwood Press, 1979. 210p. illus.
    The bibliography is an unannotated listing of 873 items
(books, articles, dissertations) in six sections: general Afro-
America; ethnomusicology, dance, and folklore; African and Afro-
American folksongs; religious folksongs; black church/black religious;
Caribbean. The catalogue is a list of the Library of Congress's
holdings of black gospel songs copyrighted between 1938 and 1965.
Arranged by composer, it provides information whenever possible
on arranger, publisher and copyright year. It is preceded by some
practical hints on how to identify black gospels. There is a subject
index to the bibliography and a name index only (why no title index?) to the catalogue.

S.579.   RICKS, George Robinson.   Some Aspects of the Religious
         Music of the United States Negro: an ethnomusicological
         study with special emphasis on the gospel tradition.
         New York: Arno Press, 1977. 419p. bibliog.
    An unaltered reprint of the author's Ph.D. dissertation
(Northwestern University, 1960), this study combines statistics and
ethnomusicology (under the guidance of Melville J. Herskovitz and
Alan P. Merriam) in a pioneering exploration of the continuity of
black religious music, and of the correlation between musical practice, church affiliation, and social class in the black community. The
book begins with an account of the conditions of development and the
stylistic characteristics of the music of three periods: pre- and
post-Civil War, and the 20th century; the third period receives the
greatest attention. Ricks then proceeds to an analysis of the musical

style of spirituals, jubilees, and gospels in order to "obtain a quantitative description of the existing forms," and to "determine their relationships by musicological comparison" (p. 14). Selecting ten samples of each type (but omitting to say where they come from), and providing full transcriptions, he analyzes each group with reference to tonal range, melodic intervals, formal structures, etc.

(Much of the literature on gospel music in particular is in dissertation form. For a selective list, see nos. S.623-S.628. For comment on Ricks' findings, see William H. Tallmadge's notes to the album, Jubilee to Gospel [JEMF-108].)

S.580.   RODEHEAVER, Homer. Singing Black: twenty thousand
         miles with a music missionary. Chicago: Rodeheaver
         Co., 1936. (Repr. New York: AMS Press, 1975.) 96p.
         illus.
         Bishop Arthur J. Moore, of the Methodist Episcopal Church
South, writes in the introduction: "The world knows Homer Rodeheaver as one of the greatest evangelistic song leaders of all time, but it was my privilege to have him as travelling companion and faithful friend through all the experiences of desert and jungle here described." The desert and jungle in question are African, and the time is the mid-1930s. There is more about religion than music in this travelogue, as Moore delivers sermons and Rodeheaver (1880-1955) leads (occasionally identified) hymns, plays the trombone, and performs magic tricks; though Rodeheaver does write in the original preface that he made the trip "to find out the source of the negro spirituals," and offers occasional, somewhat basic comments on the subject.

S.581.   ROSENBERG, Bruce A. The Art of the American Folk
         Preacher. New York: Oxford University Press, 1970.
         265p. bibliog. refs.
         Continuing and developing the pioneering work on oral
formulas of Milman Parry and Albert B. Lord, this is a fascinating study of the techniques of oral composition used by (mainly black) folk preachers in the creation of chanted sermons. The sample for the study was drawn from sermons recorded for the project in the late 1960s in several geographical areas: Southern California, Virginia and Georgia, Kentucky and Tennessee, and Oklahoma. The preachers most closely scrutinized are Rev. Ruben Lacy (a former blues singer), Rev. Elihue H. Brown, and Rev. D. J. McDowell. Particular use is also made of a sermon recorded for a commercial company by Rev. C. L. Franklin of Detroit (Aretha Franklin's father). Following an opening historical account, Rosenberg considers a succession of aspects of the sermon: content and structure, chanting, formulaic qualities, theme, process of composition; the subject of audience response is also introduced in various contexts. Specifically musical considerations arise in the discussion of chanting, but the pre-eminent roles of rhythm and meter are important throughout. In his conclusions, the author proposes a theory of spontaneous creation based, not on memorizing formulaic systems, but on the

preacher's "ability to compose spontaneously the vocabulary at his command to fit his metrical pattern" (p. 102). A substantial part of the text (pp. 125-249) is given over to transcriptions of seventeen sermons, with introductory notes. In several instances, the transcriptions offer two versions on the same theme.

S.582. WALKER, Wyatt Tee. Somebody's Calling My Name: black sacred music and social change. Valley Forge, Pa.: Judson Press, 1979. 208p.

A doctoral thesis (Colgate University, 1975) revised for more popular consumption, Walker's book veers away from the scholarly towards the subjective. Its central theme, that black religious music is a barometer of the black social situation, is persuasively argued (Walker is a minister in Harlem and knows how it's done), the force of the argument deriving much from the author's own experiences (e.g., with Martin Luther King). Not that the subject matter is all contemporary; Walker provides a historical overview of spirituals, "Dr. Watts" hymns, and gospel music, and illustrates his discussion with both music and text examples. Problems arise when strength of feeling takes precedence over documented evidence and over-simplification passes unchallenged (e.g., the book's opening sentence: "The music of the black religious experience is the primary root of all music born in the United States"--p. 15). The book concludes with suggestions for maintaining and improving modern black church music practice. Index.

S.583. WARRICK, Mancel, et al. The Progress of Gospel Music: from spirituals to contemporary gospel, by Mancel Warrick, Joan R. Hillsman, Anthony Manno. New York: Vantage Press, 1977. 99p. bibliog., discog.

Intended principally, though not exclusively, for use in education, this is a slim and, sadly, sketchy account of the roots and characteristics of black gospel music. The text is partly redeemed by a generous number of musical examples, and a suggested classroom curriculum. Name and song title indexes are included.

S.584. ZARETSKY, Irving I., and LEONE, Mark P., eds. Religious Movements in Contemporary America. Princeton, N.J.: Princeton University Press, 1974. 837p. bibliog.

An important, and--to music scholars at least--insufficiently well known article by anthropologist Morton Marks, entitled "Uncovering Ritual Structures in Afro-American Music," occupies pp. 60-134. Marks explores three distinct types of music--Brazilian carnival, Afro-Cuban santería, and North American black gospel music-- as examples of culture contact between African and European culture, in his search for explanations of how certain rituals generate meaning. Particular attention is paid to the relationship between linguistic and musical structures, and especially to the notion of "style-switching" between codes within a repertoire. The discussion of santería and its music includes an examination of the migration of the religion to New York and its impact there, in the early 1960s. Section 5, on gospel music, explores "channel cues"--changes in intonation pattern, rhythm, etc.--and their role in creating a ritual setting, which Marks describes as a "trance-event." A comparison of a gospel song and a New York Puerto Rican song, both on the theme of "going home," leads to a conclusion in which the "enormous role that African culture forms have played in the New World in the shaping of national popular cultures" (p. 115) is stressed. Musical transcriptions are included in an appendix to the essay.

Additional Items

General

S.585.   ABRAHAMS, Roger D. and SZWED, John F., eds. Discovering Afro-America. Leiden: Brill, 1975. 94p. (Includes "Reflections on the State of Black Music and the Black Musician," by Leonard Goines.)

S.586.   ABRAHAMS, Roger D. Talking Black. Rowley, Mass.: Newbury House, 1976. 101p.

S.587.   LAYNE, Maude Wanzer. The Negro's Contribution to Music. Charleston, W. Va.: Mathews, 1942. 88p.

S.588.   STROTHOFF, Wolfgang. Verzeichnis deutschsprächiger musikpädagogischer Schriften zur afro-amerikanischen Musik. Bremen: Archiv für Populäre Musik, 1977. 28p.

S.589.   VAN VECHTEN, Carl. Keep Inchin' Along: selected writings about black art and letters; edited by Bruce Kellner. Westport, Conn.: Greenwood Press, 1979. 300p.

S.590.   VLACH, John M. The Afro-American Tradition in the Decorative Arts. Cleveland: Cleveland Museum of Art, 1978. 175p. (Exhibition catalog; Chapter 2, "Musical Instruments," pp. 20-26.)

Concert Performers

S.591.   GORDON, E. Harrison. Black Classical Musicians of the 20th Century. Vol. 1. Edison, N.J.: MSS Information Corp., 1977.

S.592.   SCHUYLER, Philippa Duke. Adventures in Black and White; with a foreword by Deems Taylor. New York: Speller, 1960. 302p. (The 1950s tours of the concert pianist [1932-1967].)

Black Musical Life in the Slave Era

S.593.   ARMSTRONG, Orland Kay. Old Massa's People: the old
slaves tell their story. Indianapolis: Bobbs Merrill,
1931. 357p.

S.594.   LaBREW, Arthur R. Studies in 19th-Century Afro-American
Music. Detroit: the author, 1976.

S.595.   TAYLOR, Jo Gray. Negro Slavery in Louisiana. Baton
Rouge: Louisiana Historical Association, 1963.

Folk Songs and Spirituals

S.596.   BREWER, J. Mason. American Negro Folklore. Chicago:
Quadrangle, 1968. 386p.

S.597.   BREWER, J. Mason. The Word on the Brazos: Negro
preacher tales from the Brazos bottoms of Texas. Austin:
University of Texas Press, 1953. 109p.

S.598.   COURLANDER, Harold, ed. A Treasury of Afro-American
Folklore: the oral literature, traditions, recollections,
legends, tales, songs, religious beliefs, customs, sayings, and humor of peoples of African descent in the
Americas. New York: Crown, 1976. 618p.

S.599.   CRITE, Allan Rohan. Three Spirituals from Heaven to
Earth. Cambridge, Mass.: Harvard University Press,
1948. 165p.

S.600.   _____. Where You There When They Crucified My Lord?
a Negro spiritual in illustrations. Cambridge, Mass.:
Harvard University, 1944. 93p.

S.601.   DITON, Carl, ed. Thirty-six South Carolina Spirituals;
for church and general use. New York: Schirmer,
1930. 54p.

S.602.   FISHER, William Arms, ed. Seventy Negro Spirituals. Boston: Ditson, 1926. 212p.

S.603.   FREY, Hugo, ed. A Collection of 25 Selected Famous Negro
Spirituals. New York: Robbins-Engel, 1924. 47p.

S.604.   HATFIELD, Edwin Francis, ed. Freedom's Lyre; or, Psalms,
Hymns and Sacred Songs for the Slave and His Friends.
New York: S. W. Benedict, 1840. (Repr. Miami:
Mnemosyne, 1969.) 265p.

S.605.   JESSYE, Eva A. My Spirituals; edited by Gordon Whyte
          and Hugo Frey. New York: Robbins-Engel, 1927.
          81p.

S.606.   JOHNSON, Hall, ed. The Green Pastures Spirituals; ar-
          ranged for voice and piano. New York: Fischer, 1930.
          40p.

S.607.   _____. Thirty Negro Spirituals; arranged for voice and
          piano. New York: Schirmer, 1949. 82p.

S.608.   JUBILEE AND PLANTATION SONGS: characteristic favor-
          ites as sung by the Hampton Students, Jubilee Singers,
          Fisk University Students, and other concert companies.
          Boston: Ditson, 1887. 80p.

S.609.   LILJE, Hanns, et al. Das Buch der Spirituals und Gospel
          Songs. Hamburg: Furche, 1961. 231p.

S.610.   MAGRIEL, Paul D., ed. Chronicles of the American Dance.
          New York: Holt, 1948. 268p. (Includes a section on
          William Henry Lane ["Juba"] by M. A. Winter.)

S.611.   TAYLOR, Marshall W., ed. A Collection of Revival Hymns
          and Plantation Melodies; musical compilation by Josephine
          Robinson. Cincinnati: M. W. Taylor & W. C. Echols,
          1883. 272p.

S.612.   THARPE, Sister Rosetta. Eighteen Original Negro Spirituals.
          New York: Mills Music, 1938. 32p. (Published to fol-
          low up on Sister Tharpe's Cotton Club success in 1938.)

S.613.   TRENT-JOHNS, Altona, ed. Play Songs of the Deep South.
          Washington, D.C.: Associated Publishers, 1944. 33p.

S.614.   WHITE, Clarence Cameron, ed. Forty Negro Spirituals.
          Philadelphia: Presser, 1927. 129p.

Ragtime and Blues

S.615.   BLUMENFELD, Aaron. The Art of Blues and Barrelhouse
          Improvisation. Berkeley, Calif.: the author, 1979.
          218p.

S.616.   COLLECTORS CLASSICS. Bexhill-on-Sea: Blues Unlimited,
          1964-1966. (A series of 15-page pamphlets, by various
          authors: 1 - Muddy Waters; 2 - John Lee Hooker; 3 -
          Chuck Berry & Bo Diddley; 4 - Howlin' Wolf; 5 - Survey
          of Pre-War Blues Artists Reissued on EP and LP (1951-
          1964); 6 - Charley Patton; 7 - Elmore and Homesick

> James; 8 - Chicago Blues; 9 - Texas Blues; 10 - Blues
> Boy King; 11 - Touch Me, Lord Jesus; 12 - Cajun Music;
> 13 - Memphis; 14 - Son House.)

S.617. EVANS, Mark. Scott Joplin and the Ragtime Years. New
        York: Dodd, Mead, 1976. 120p. (For younger read-
        ers.)

S.618. KIRBY, Edward "Prince Gabe." Memories of Beale Street.
        Memphis, Tenn.: Penny Pincher Sales, 1979. 73p.

S.619. RASMUSSON, Ludvig. Blues. Stockholm: Almqvist &
        Wiksell, 1979. 140p.

Soul

S.620. BERMAN, Connie. Diana Ross, Supreme Lady. New York:
        Popular Library, 1978. 174p.

S.621. LAMAISON, Jean-Louis. Soul Music. Paris: Albin Michel,
        1977. 183p.

S.622. PASCALL, Jeremy, and BURT, Rob. The Stars and Super-
        stars of Black Music. London: Phoebus; Secaucus:
        Chartwell, 1977. 128p.

*   *   *

Dissertations on Black Religious Music

(see no. S.579)

S.623. BAKER, Barbara. "Black Gospel Music Styles, 1942-1975."
        University of Maryland, 1978.

S.624. BOYER, Horace C. "An Analysis of Black Church Music,
        With Examples Drawn from Services in Rochester, New
        York." Eastman School of Music, 1973.

S.625. BURNIM, Mellonee V. "The Black Gospel Music Tradition:
        symbol of ethnicity." Indiana University, 1980.

S.626. JACKSON, Irene V. "Afro-American Gospel Music and Its
        Social Setting, with Special Attention to Roberta Martin."
        Wesleyan University, 1974.

S.627. MAULTSBY, Portia K. "Afro-American Religious Music,
        1610-1861." University of Wisconsin, 1974.

S.628. RAICHELSON, Richard M. "Black Religious Folksong: a study in generic and social change." University of Pennsylvania, 1975.

1. Reference Works

S.629.   CASE, Brian, and BRITT, Stan.   The Illustrated Encyclo-
         pedia of Jazz.   New York: Harmony Books; London:
         Salamander Books, 1978.   223p.   illus., discogs.
A handsomely produced volume, well illustrated with color
reproductions of record sleeves and with photographs (by Valerie
Wilmer), but more accurately described as a biographical/critical
guide to leading jazz musicians than an encyclopedia.   There are
entries, alphabetically arranged, for over 400 individuals from all
periods of jazz, with some bias towards the post-war period both in
names included and length of entries, and with a fairly modest representation of blues artists.   The entries themselves, which vary in
length from a short paragraph to two whole pages, are assessments
in a biographical framework, rather than impersonal, factual career
accounts.   All are well informed, and make interesting reading, despite a certain tendency to hyperbole.   All have selected lists of LPs
at the end, with American and European labels given, and most entries refer to individual recordings in the text, in a manner remi-
niscent of Jazz On Record (LOAM 958).   There are no entries for
movements, cities, clubs, terms, etc.   Name index.

S.630.   FEATHER, Leonard, and GITLER, Ira.   The Encyclopedia
         of Jazz in the Seventies; introduction by Quincy Jones.
         New York: Horizon Press, 1976; London: Quartet
         Books, 1978.   393p.   illus., bibliog., discog.
The third volume in Feather's series of encyclopedias, this
one covers the ten-year period since The Encyclopedia of Jazz in
the Sixties (1966; see LOAM 904).   Like its predecessors it is principally a biographical dictionary, an indispensable compilation of
data on around 1,300 musicians, singers, composers, and arrangers
active in this period.   For those (a considerable proportion) who
were also featured in previous volumes, the entry focuses on their
activities in this particular decade, but includes a brief recapitula-
tion of the essential information on their earlier careers.   A typical
entry gives instrument, date of birth, career details, a brief assessment, and a selective list of LPs.   In addition to the biographies
there are selections from the celebrated blindfold texts from Down
Beat (including a long one with Miles Davis), popularity polls, a

piece on jazz education by Down Beat publisher Charles Suber, a guide to films by Leonard Maltin, a list of recommended records, and a (partial) bibliography of (English language) books.

S.631.　HIPPENMEYER, Jean-Roland. Jazz sur films; ou, 55 années de rapports jazz-cinéma vus à travers plus de 800 films tournés entre 1917 et 1972; filmographie critique.　Yverdon:　Editions de la Thièle, 1973.　125p.　illus.

Despite the excellence of Meeker (LOAM 921), this is a useful compilation, as it lists films chronologically.　Around 600 films are included in the main sequence, both feature films and ones devoted to a specific jazz subject.　(Feature films with jazz scores but no jazz performance element in the films themselves are listed separately.) Approximately half the entries are annotated, and the annotations vary considerably in length, some amounting to lengthy commentaries that include references to reviews.　Title and name indexes are included.

S.632.　LEE, Bill. Jazz Dictionary; with foreword by Stan Kenton. (New York):　Shattinger International Music Corp., 1979.　64p.　illus.

Many of the terms defined here are technical ones encountered in the performance, recording, and study of jazz (recording jargon is especially strongly represented).　The colloquial language of jazz musicians is also represented, though not so thoroughly.　Outnumbering each of these categories is technical musical terminology not intended, originally at least, to describe features of jazz.　The preeminence of such terms is surely not an accurate reflection of "jazz language"; it may be the compiler's wish that jazz musicians and students should talk of "agogic accents" and "torsional vibration"--but that's another question entirely.　Useful as a technical directory with a jazz slant; for the language of jazz, prefer Gold (LOAM 905).

S.633.　RECLAMS JAZZFÜHRER, by Carlo Bohländer and Karl Heinz Holler.　Stuttgart:　Reclam, 1970.　991p.　illus., bibliog.

_____.　2nd ed., by Carlo Bohländer and Kurt Oehl. Stuttgart:　Reclam, 1977.　998p.　illus., bibliog.

All students of German literature know the value of the Reclam volumes, but scarcely any non-German students of jazz know the immense potential usefulness of this jazz reference book.　It includes a biographical dictionary of impressive proportions (approximately 2,500 names in the 2nd ed.), with biographical outlines, concise stylistic commentaries and selective discographies.　There are also sections for instruments, with a brief history of each instrument's use in jazz and information on its main exponents; for subjects (including jazz terminology); and for compositions (a thematic catalogue of around 500 jazz standards, with title, composer, copyright year, publisher, musical incipit, and commentary).　The whole volume is helpfully supplied with a network of cross-references and with a multitude of references to source materials.

S.634.   SUMMERFIELD, Maurice J.   The Jazz Guitar: its evolution
         and its players.   Gateshead, England: Ashley Mark,
         1978.   238p.   illus., bibliogs., discogs.
         Basically a biographical dictionary, containing details of
the lives of 115 jazz guitarists (from John Abercrombie to Hungarian-
born Attila Zoller).   Each entry is illustrated, and provides details
of place and date of birth (and death, where appropriate), and
career outline; most entries are supplemented by a short selected
discography and bibliography.   While the shorter pieces (100-250
words) are usually strictly factual, the longer ones (300-500 words)
contain some general evaluation.   In addition, the book includes a
short, summary history of the guitar in jazz, and a brief account of
the various instruments.

S.635.   VOIGT, John.   Jazz Music in Print, by John Voigt and
         Randall Kane.   Winthrop, Mass.:   Flat Nine Music, 1975.
         unpaged.
         _____.   Jazz Music in Print.   2nd ed.   Boston: Horn-
         pipe Music, 1978.   unpaged.   bibliog.
         _____.   _____.   1979 supplement.   Boston: Hornpipe
         Music, 1979.   unpaged.
         An attempt to index "all published works of the most sig-
nificant jazz composers and players" (introduction).   The compiler
admits that it is doubtful whether "the music presented to the buying
public [can] be called jazz," but proceeds anyway, on the basis of
an emphasis on performers rather than composers, editors or publishers.   Publishers' addresses are included.

S.636.   WÖLFER, Jürgen.   Handbuch des Jazz.   Munich: Heyne,
         1979.   271p.   illus., bibliogs., discogs.
         This concise reference work provides German readers with
a layperson's subject dictionary, covering terms, places, styles, instruments, record companies and similar topics.   In the manner of
a "Sachwörterbuch," no entries for individuals are provided, although
there is a name index.   Many of the 400 or so entries are for words
that the reader would encounter in average jazz literature; explanations are simple, unpretentious, and a cross-reference system alerts
the user to the relationships which are always there to be explored
(and which subject dictionaries can perhaps suggest better than
other forms of reference work).   Entries are often accompanied by
brief bibliographical and discographical notes.   (For further comments
on the subject reference work, and for an example in rock literature,
see Kneif, no. S.1100.)

                         2.   Discographies

         Note: for a full bibliographical listing of jazz discog-
         raphies, the reader is recommended to consult Daniel
         Allen, Jazz (see no. S/A. 363).

a. General

S.637. McCOY, Meredith, and PARKER, Barbara, eds. Catalog
of the John D. Reid Collection of Early American Jazz.
Little Rock: Arkansas Arts Center, 1975. 112p.
illus.
John D. Reid (1907-1974) was a Victor recording engineer
with a particular love for New Orleans and other early jazz. The
importance of his collection, in the Arkansas Arts Center since 1964,
is that it not only contains a large body of commercial jazz recordings (mainly 78s), but also a small corpus of original recordings
made by Reid himself, and a quantity of documents--memorabilia,
photographs, and correspondence. Much of the latter was not cata-
loged when the book was produced (and still is not, apparently),
but some non-recorded materials are included. Most of the book is
devoted to entries for sound recordings. These are grouped in
five sections: (i) "original" recordings--these were made between
1939 and 1949 with various musicians; most prominent is Sidney
Bechet, for whom Reid had a special liking (they were longtime
friends; one particular session, recorded by Reid in Boston in 1945,
with Bunk Johnson, was released commercially in 1983 on Fat Cat's
Jazz FCJ 1002); (ii) blues; (iii) bands; (iv) piano and organ solos;
(v) gospel and spirituals. Most of the collection dates from 1935
to 1945; it totals 4,000 records (though one possible interpretation
of an ambiguous sentence in the introduction would indicate there
are 10,000 in all).

b. Special

See also S.816

S.638. RUPPLI, Michel. Atlantic Records: a discography. Westport, Conn.: Greenwood Press, 1979. 4v.
From its small beginnings in New York in 1947, as an independent black music label (see Gillett, LOAM 13), up to October
1978 Atlantic recorded master numbers of approximately 36,000 titles,
ranging from jazz, blues, rhythm and blues through soul into the
white pop and rock market. This mammoth listing presents them all,
arranged according to Atlantic's master number sequence, which in
most cases equates with chronological order. Information was obtained mainly from Atlantic studio files. Personnel listings, generally
complete for jazz sessions, are less so in other areas. Besides
giving place and date of each session, with titles and US release
numbers, the discography also provides timings whenever known.
Vol. 1 covers 1947-66, Vol. 2 1966-70, Vol. 3 1970-74, Vol. 4 1974-
78. Vols. 1-3 each have their own index of session leaders, and
Vol. 4 has a cumulative index to session leaders in all four volumes.

S.639. RUPPLI, Michel. The Savoy Label: a discography. Westport, Conn.: Greenwood Press, 1980. 442p.

The Newark-based company, whose founder-owner Herman Lubinsky "had parlayed a hole-in-the-wall race record store into an independent label" (Ross Russell, Bird Lives, LOAM 1136, p. 169), is most celebrated for its pioneer 1940s bebop recordings of Charlie Parker, et al. But its roster extended across the black music field and included performers from rhythm and blues (Big Maybelle, Big Jay McNelly) and gospel (James Cleveland, Alex Bradford). All are listed here in a chronological discography for 1939-1965. Details for the post-1965 era are more sketchy, as the company's files are missing for this period. Where different matrix series were in use simultaneously, listings are given place by place.

c. Discographies of Individuals and Bands

Note: many discographies of individual musicians and of bands are issued as small booklets. What follows is a listing of the more substantial publications. For further information, see Allen (no. S/A 363).

(i) Collective Works

S.640.   EVENSMO, Jan. Jazz Solography Series. Hosle, Norway: Evensmo, 1975-83. 14v.
This ongoing series of critical discographies (replacing the one begun in 1969--see LOAM 934) combines a high standard of discographical information with informative linking commentary; an unusual feature is the provision of figures for length of solos (in numbers of bars). The individual volume titles are as follows:
Vol. 1.   The Tenor Taxophone of Leon Chu Berry.
Vol. 2.   The Tenor Saxophones of Henry Bridges, Robert Carroll, Herschal [sic] Evans, Johnny Russell.
Vol. 3.   The Tenor Saxophone of Coleman Hawkins, 1929-1942.
Vol. 4.   The Guitars of Charlie Christian, Robert Norman, Oscar Aleman (in Europe).
Vol. 5.   The Tenor Saxophone and Clarinet of Lester Young, 1936-1942.
Vol. 6.   The Tenor Saxophone of Ben Webster, 1931-1943.
Vol. 7.   The Tenor Saxophones of Budd Johnson, Cecil Scott, Elmer Williams, Dick Wilson, 1927-1942.
Vol. 8.   The Trumpet and Vocal of Henry Red Allen, 1927-1942.
Vol. 9.   The Trumpets of Bill Coleman, 1929-1945, Frankie Newton.
Vol. 10.   The Trumpet of Roy Eldridge, 1929-1944.
Vol. 11.   The Alto Saxophone, Trumpet and Clarinet of Benny Carter, 1927-1946.
Vol. 12.   The Trumpets of Dizzy Gillespie, 1937-1943, Irving Randolph, Joe Thomas.
Vol. 13.   The Tenor Saxophone and Clarinet of Lester Young, 1936-1949. Rev. ed.

Vol. 14. The Flute of Wayman Carver, the Trombone of Dickie
Wells, 1937-1942, the Tenor Saxophone of Illinois
Jacquet.

S.641. LANGE, Horst H. The Fabulous Fives. Lübbecke: Uhle
and Kleimann, 1959. 32p.
_____. _____; revised by Ron Kewson, Derek
Hamilton-Smith and Ray Webb. Chigwell: Storyville Publications, 1978. 150p. illus., bibliog.
The revised edition is a finely produced discography (as
one expects from this specialist publisher), comprising separate listings for eight early white jazz bands: The Original Dixieland Jazz
Band, Earl Fuller's Famous Jazz Band, Louisiana Five, New Orleans
Jazz Band, Original Georgia Five, Original Indiana Five, Original
Memphis Five (a.k.a. Ladd's Black Aces, Lanin's Southern Serenad-
ers, etc., etc.), and Southern Five. Each discography is chronologically arranged, and provides information on personnel, date,
matrix numbers (all takes), titles (with composer credits where
given on the original records), record labels and numbers (including, for unissued takes, the company's file instructions to 'hold'
or 'destroy'). The ODJB listing also includes details of film appearances, broadcasts, and La Rocca's private recordings. The
numerous illustrations include contemporary advertisements, record
labels, and photographs. There are indexes of personnel, titles,
artist credits, catalogue numbers, and label illustrations. The members of the publishing team involved take the precaution of disso-
ciating themselves from Lange's claims in his preface for the primary
role of white musicians in the creation of early jazz.

(ii) Individuals

BIX BEIDERBECKE

S.642. CASTELLI, Vittorio, et al. The Bix Bands: a Bix Beiderbecke discobiography, by Vittorio Castelli, Evert (Ted)
Kaleveld, Liborio Pusateri. Milan: Raretone, 1972.
223p. illus.
An impressive discography, 1924-30, with linking biographical narrative. Arrangement is chronological, and full discographical
details are provided (band, place, date, personnel, matrix and take
numbers, titles, release numbers, LP reissue numbers). An unusual
and most welcome feature is the "solo-play" which follows: for each
title on the session the form of composition (AABA-32, etc.) is given,
together with a breakdown of the choruses including the number of
bars played by soloists and band. There are various indexes:
titles (with composer/author credits), musicians and orchestras,
78rpm release numbers, and the contents of microgroove reissues.
(Formerly LOAM A196.)

206 / Literature of American Music

BUNNY BERIGAN

S.643.   DANCA, Vince. Bunny: a bio-discography of jazz trum-
          peter Bunny Berigan. Rockford, Ill.: Vince Danca,
          1978. 64p. illus.
          The prolific Bunny Berigan (1908-1942) made some 600 re-
cordings. This booklet provides discographical details for only the
"most popular, many in the jazz idiom" (p. 31); some 220 items are
listed, with personnel, place, date, matrix and release numbers.
Preceding the discography is an affectionate memoir of the trumpeter. (Available from 2418 Barrington Pl., Rockford, Ill. 61107.)

ORNETTE COLEMAN

S.644.   WILD, David, and CUSCUNA, Michael. Ornette Coleman
          1958-1979: a discography. Ann Arbor, Mich.: Wild-
          music, 1980. 76p. illus., bibliog. refs.
          A discography listing a substantial number of private
readings as well as commercial releases. Chronologically arranged,
the listing provides details of group name, personnel, place and
date, matrix and take numbers, titles, composer credits, length of
take, instrument on which Coleman performs, record label and number (or indication of private recording). In addition there is a
stylistic appreciation by Cuscuna, and a biography by Wild. There
are several indexes, including ones for titles, performers and album titles. Additional information appears in disc'ribe (Wildmusic,
1980-), an occasional journal devoted to supplementary material for
Wildmusic publications.

JOHN COLTRANE

S.645.   DAVIS, Brian. John Coltrane Discography. Hockley, Es-
          sex: Brian Davis and Ray Smith, 1977. 42p. + supple-
          ment.
          Beginning with Coltrane's first recording session with Dizzy
Gillespie in November 1949, this discography lists, with the usual
discographical details, all disc recordings by Coltrane with his own
and other groups up to his final session in New York on March 17th,
1967. A particular effort is made to list as many reissues as possible, including those on Japanese labels. The seven-page supplement lists private recordings, and draws on research by Nils Winther
Rasmussen and Jan Lohmann. (For points of comparison with Wild's
discography see Wild, no. S.646.)

S.646.   WILD, David. The Recordings of John Coltrane: a discog-
          raphy. Ann Arbor, Mich.: Wildmusic, 1977. 72p. + 2
          supplements.
          Like Davis (no. S.645) this is a chronological listing of
Coltrane's recordings from November 1949 to March 1967, with full
discographical details, including reissues. Wild adds two features
not present in Davis: composer credits after each title, and dura-

tions. He also includes private tapes as an integral part of his listing (Davis gives a less complete discography of these in a supplement). Neither discography provides details of the order of soloists (in the manner of Evensmo), though Wild apparently has the information, but chooses to reserve it for subsequent, fuller publication as part of a larger book on Coltrane. Wild's two supplements provide corrections and additions plus an index of musicians (but none of titles).

DUKE ELLINGTON

S.647.   AASLAND, Benny.   The "Wax Works" of Duke Ellington: the 6th March 1940-30th July 1942 RCA Victor Period. Järfälla, Sweden: Dems, 1978. unpaged, illus.
_____.   _____: 31st July 1942-11th Nov. 1944, the recording ban period.   ...1979. unpaged, illus.
These are specialized discographies ("for advanced collectors," but not without a fascination for backward ones also), providing details (a) of the 106 recording sessions, stage performances, and broadcasts in the 28-month period up to the Petrillo ban, and (b) of the 222 sessions (mainly, but not exclusively, broadcasts) in the period of the ban itself. Title sections give dates and initials of soloists; chronological sections give venue, date, personnel, titles, and record numbers (original and reissues), or indication of the existence of an acetate. Credits are not included. Microgroove listings proceed label by label, and are followed by reproductions of the liner notes to the relevant volumes in the RCA "Works of Duke" Series. Other volumes are planned.

S.648.   TIMNER, W. E.   The Recorded Music of Duke Ellington and His Sidemen: a collector's manual. Montreal: the author, 1976. unpaged.
_____.   _____. Rev. and updated ed. Montreal: the author, 1979. unpaged.
A "handy reference source for any fellow collectors" (introduction) in five sections: (i) a list of orchestras--i.e., band names and pseudonyms under which Ellington records have been issued, bands other than his own with whom Ellington recorded, etc.; (ii) a key to personnel; (iii) a chronological list of recordings, including studio sessions, movie soundtracks, concerts, radio and television broadcasts, private recordings, by Ellington orchestras and by his foremost sidemen with other bands (this listing is not a complete discography, as it lacks issue numbers, but place, date, personnel, titles and label names are all given); (iv) a title index, with chronological sub-arrangement (no fewer than 117 versions of "Mood Indigo"!); (v) an "attendance list" of Ellingtonians in chart form.

STAN GETZ

S.649.   ASTRUP, Arne.   The Stan Getz Discography. Texarkana, Tex.: Jerry L. Atkins; Hellerup, Denmark: Arne

Astrup, 1978. 101p. illus.
Covers 1943-1978, and includes studio recordings, live sessions and broadcasts--the standard range of discographical information, clearly presented, with a listing of album titles, arranged by
record company, as an appendix. No artist or track title indexes,
unfortunately.

BILLIE HOLIDAY

S.650.   MILLER, Jack. Born to Sing: a discography of Billie
         Holiday. Copenhagen: Jazzmedia, 1979. 147p. illus.
Miller's work extends and improves on Jepsen's 1969 Holiday
discography (LOAM 944) in a number of ways: it furnishes details
of numerous radio broadcasts, television shows and other live performances not in Jepsen; it gives extensive lists of LP reissues; it
provides full lists of items for those sessions when Billie sang on
some, but not all, of the numbers recorded; it supplies occasional
explanatory notes and comments; it includes an artist name index.

JELLY ROLL MORTON

S.651.   WRIGHT, Laurie. Mr. Jelly Lord; with special contributions
         by John H. Cowley, John R. T. Davies, Mike Montgomery,
         Roger Richards, Horace Spear. Chigwell, Essex: Story-
         ville Publications, 1980. 243p. illus., bibliog.
A superlative discography--or, perhaps chrono-discography?
--detailing all Morton's recordings (piano rolls, 78s, Library of Congress sessions, broadcasts, microgroove reissues), and integrating
into the text a substantial amount of biographical and other information. The main discography provides details of personnel and instruments, recording locations and dates, matrix and take numbers, title
and composer credits, and issue numbers. As in this volume's
predecessor (Morton's Music, LOAM 941), John R. T. Davies provides
short pieces of musical notation to identify alternative takes. Footnotes offer further details, such as issue dates, reverse matrices,
and these are frequently followed by "inter-session notes"--nuggets
of information on Morton's movements and on the precise identities
of the musicians on each session (often the subject of intense research and speculation), drawn from printed sources and interviews.
The listing of Library of Congress recordings uses new information,
provided by John H. Cowley, including some of Alan Lomax's notes
on the contents of each acetate. The microgroove reissues section
consists of chronological charts, with code letters for each LP label.
A final section, "Miscellaneous Mortonia," includes the lyrics of unissued LC recordings, a list of copyright holders of Morton's compositions, and a photo scrapbook. Indexes of names, places, and titles
complete a model volume.

HARRY RESER

S.652.   TRIGGS, W. W. The Great Harry Reser. London: Henry

G. Waker, 1980. 200p. illus.

Discography of the popular 1920s dance band leader and banjoist. Reser (1896-1965) made the historian's task more complex by his frequent use of pseudonyms; this is a painstaking, devoted piece of research. A biographical outline and an assessment of Reser's musicianship precede the discography itself, which proceeds label by label (Reser seems to have gone from one to the next like a winetaster), with information on matrix numbers, date and place of recording, titles, release numbers. No personnel are given: it is intended to produce a second volume with this information. The text contains many notes and comments and is illustrated with contemporary photographs and black-and-white reproductions of sheet music covers.

ZOOT SIMS

S.653.   ASTRUP, Arne. The John Haley Sims (Zoot Sims) Discography. Lyngby (Klintevej 25, DK-2800 Lyngby): Danish Discographical Publishing Co., 1980. 103p. illus.

Chronologically arranged discography, covering 1943-1979, with details of personnel, place, date, matrix numbers, titles, and release numbers. Broadcast performances are included. A thorough work, which unfortunately lacks a name index; the only title index provided is a partial one for album titles.

CLARK TERRY

S.654.   RADZITZKY, Carlos de. A 1960-1967 Clark Terry Discography, With Biographical Notes. (Antwerp): United Hot Club of Europe, 1968. 48p. illus.

Designed to complement the discography of Terry's 1947-60 recordings by Malcolm Walker, published in Jazz Monthly, December 1961-April 1962 (five parts), this work includes a short, three-page biography, and full discographical information (though the compiler cautions he is "not a professional discographer"). Terry's recordings with Duke Ellington are excluded, and there are no indexes. (Additions and corrections appeared in Jazz Journal, 21 [Oct. 1968] and 22 [Jan. 1969].)

CLARENCE WILLIAMS

S.655.   BAKKER, Dick M. Clarence Williams on Microgroove. Alphen aan den Rijn: Micrography, 1976. 44p.

Thorough microgroove discography, compiled to expand on the incomplete (and, apparently, sometimes inaccurate) information in this area given by Lord (no. S.656).

S.656.   LORD, Tom. Clarence Williams. Chigwell, Essex: Storyville Publications, 1976. 625p. illus., bibliog.

Phenomenally detailed bio-discography of Williams' life (1893?-1964) and recordings. The meticulously presented discograph-

ical information for each item includes: performer credits (as on
record label), instrumentation and personnel, location and date, matrix and take details, record label and catalog number, composer
credits, copyright composer, copyright holder and date. Following
the listing for each session there is a series of schematic diagrams
for each item recorded in the session (breakdown into choruses,
with indication of who plays when), with key and timing. This is
a wonderful adjunct to a discography. The linking biographical
paragraphs are strictly factual and incorporate material from newspapers, contemporary accounts and more recent critical comment.
The material that follows the main bio-discography is equally rich in
information and includes: a short appreciation, transcriptions of
some typical Williams piano phrases, a discography of sessions once
(but no longer) thought to be his, a list of compositions owned by
his publishing company and recorded by other artists, a title list of
his own compositions (almost 500 in all), a roster of musicians associated with him, with dates (of records <u>and</u> live engagements), an
index of record catalog numbers (for comment on the microgroove
list, see Bakker, no. S.655) and indexes of titles, names, etc.

d. The Science of Discography

S.657. RUST, Brian. Brian Rust's Guide to Discography. Westport, Conn.: Greenwood Press, 1980. 133p. bibliog.
Discography may not have originated in the United States,
but the recordings of American musical idioms, especially jazz, and
the doings of American record companies, have been more thoroughly documented by discographers than have those of any other
country or region. So it is appropriate to include a general volume
on the subject here. Rust's book is not, despite the implications of
the title, a practical guide to would-be discographers (the creation
of a discography is broadly treated in just one short chapter), so
much as a concise summary of the generalities: overviews of the
purpose and history of the "science," and consideration of the major
types of discography, and a brief survey of record labels. Bibliographic information is provided in the form of a listing of journals
known to review discographies, an annotated bibliography of book-
length discographies, and a list of discographical magazines.

S.658. WYLER, Michael. A Glimpse At the Past: an illustrated
history of some early record companies that made jazz
history. West Moors, Dorset: Jazz Publications, 1957.
32p. illus.
Based on articles originally published in The Melody Maker
in 1954-1955, this limited edition publication provided collectors of
the time with much helpful information on the background to fourteen
jazz record labels, among them "Black Swan," "Famous," "Black
Patti" and "Herwin." Though for the most part superseded by
Rust's The American Record Label Book (no. S.815), some of Wyler's
entries are more detailed. All the labels are illustrated.

e. Annotated Record Guides

S.659.   JONES, Morley. Jazz. New York: Simon & Schuster;
          Poole, Dorset: Blandford Press, 1980.   (Listener's
          Guide Series.)   133p.   illus.
          An introductory, no-frills guide to jazz on LP for the non-
specialist.   Unlike similar guides, this one opts to give general biographical and (to a lesser extent) critical information on individual
artists, and to follow this with a brief list of recommended records
(rather than to work from particular records out).   Too much space
is devoted to biography, and too little to conveying an understanding of the music and its styles.   The basic arrangement is chronological in ten chapters (from "New Orleans" to "Fusion and Beyond").
Around 300 LPs are listed, with label names only--no further discographical details are supplied.   (The dust-jacket, of the UK edition
at least, credits authorship to the series editor, Alan Rich.)

S.660.   LYONS, Len.   The 101 Best Jazz Albums: a history of
          jazz on records.   New York: Morrow, 1980.   476p.   il-
          lus., bibliog., discogs.
          Authors of record guides, in whatever subject area, usual-
ly find they have to become to some extent purveyors of historical
knowledge, if they want the help they are offering to be both com-
prehensible and respectable.   This is the only guide to give equal
weight to both history and guidance, and so aim at nothing less
than the "history of jazz on records" of the subtitle.   To do so
within an imposed limit of 101 records is partly self-defeating, but
this restriction in numbers at least permits an expansion in the space
available for consideration of each record, so that the lively, informed discussions of individual musicians become like short essays,
providing biographical and background data, stylistic comment, as
well as references to other recordings.   In general the canonized
members of the jazz fraternity grab most of the attention ("I believe
it is far better to immerse oneself deeply in the masters than to
cover the ground more superficially"--preface), but a wider view of
jazz developments is provided in the introductions to each of the
book's seven historical chapters, so that the scene is well set before
each band of saints comes marching in.   Each chapter has a general
discography, listing other recommended records.   All records listed
were available in 1979.   There is an index of names, subjects, and
titles.

S.661.   TUDOR, Dean, and TUDOR, Nancy. Jazz. Littleton,
          Colo.: Libraries Unlimited, 1979.   (American Popular
          Music on Elpee.)   302p.   bibliog.
          From the rich but variable crop of jazz LPs, the Tudors
have picked and packaged some 1,300 of the "best and most enduring" recordings in this useful discographical guide.   They present
their guidance in around 650 generously annotated entries, aimed to
assist both librarians and individual collectors.   There are six

sections: general anthologies; ragtime; geographic origins and stylings (New Orleans, Chicago, New York, the territories); mainstream swing and big bands; bop, cool, modern; diverse themes (instructions, vocals, pop jazz). Each section has its introduction, and both here and in annotations the authors aim for a "summation and synthesis of existing thought" (p. 6), rather than original insight. One hundred thirty books and eighteen periodicals are briefly annotated in the bibliography, and there is a label directory and an artists' index. (For the other volumes in this series, see nos. S.276, S.540, S.817. For a cumulative edition of all four books, see no. S/A 517.)

3. General Books on Jazz

a. General Guides and Handbooks

S.662. COKER, Jerry. The Jazz Idiom. Englewood Cliffs, N.J.:
         Prentice-Hall, 1975. 84p.
         Useful outline guide for students on how to study jazz,
aimed particularly at performers. Included are: a brief guided tour
through jazz histories to date; guidance on how to transcribe and
to study transcriptions and on the development of aural faculties;
hints for studying jazz keyboard; practical help with improvisation
and arrangement.

S.663. COKER, Jerry. Listening to Jazz. Englewood Cliffs, N.J.:
         Prentice-Hall, 1978. 148p. discogs.
         Written with admirable clarity, this is a succinct, nontech-
nical introduction to the basic features of jazz, stressing the qualities and importance of improvisation. From an outline of the formal
structures (the "vehicle," the chorus, chord progressions), and a
description of the role of the instruments in the rhythm section,
Coker moves on to focus on the improvising soloist, first in general
terms according to types of vehicle (be-bop tune, modal tune, etc.);
he then selects six outstanding improvisers (Armstrong, Hawkins,
Young, Parker, Davis, Coltrane), isolates the essentials of their
style, and examines at close quarters one individual recording of
each. Suggestions for further listening are included, as well as a
chronology, an overview of jazz history, and a glossary.

S.664. GRIDLEY, Mark C. Jazz Styles. Englewood Cliffs, N.J.:
         Prentice-Hall, 1978. 409p. illus., bibliog., discog.
         _____. Jazz Styles: history and analysis. 2nd ed.
         Englewood Cliffs, N.J.: Prentice-Hall, 1985. 445p.
         illus., bibliog., discog.
         _____. _____. Instructor's Manual and Discography.
         Englewood Cliffs, N.J.: Prentice-Hall, 1985. 107p.
         A student's and general reader's guide to understanding
the stylistic aspects of jazz--and the best of its kind. Sensibly combining a historical approach with one which cuts across chronology

in search of salient features, Gridley allows understanding to grow
via an interplay of the two approaches. The book is in four parts.
Part 1 outlines the basic ingredients of the music, tests definitions,
introduces techniques for listening and for understanding improvisation. Parts 2-4 are chronologically organized: "pre-modern"
(with sections on early jazz, swing, Ellington and Basie); modern
to the early 1960s (bop, 1950s, Davis); the early '60s and the early
1970s (Coleman, Evans et al., Mingus, Coltrane, etc.). The emphasis throughout is on an attempt to describe stylistic developments
in non-technical language, and to pick out the essential hallmarks
of the styles of individual musicians (biographical detail is minimal).
A concentration on post-1940 music is justified by the author because
"almost two-thirds of the jazz history which is available to us on
records has been made since 1940" (p. vii). Included in appendices
are a useful discussion of chord progressions, a guide to record
buying, a glossary, a discography of the many recordings cited in
the text, and a short guide to further recordings. Missing is any
attempt to understand jazz on a socio-cultural basis also--Gridley
classes this as an "external" factor to be "eliminated" (p. 336).
Index.

The second edition, though "eighty percent ... rewritten
for greater readability" (preface), is substantially the same in terms
of organization and content; the main differences are a greater
amount of space devoted to the roots of jazz and its early practitioners, more coverage of the 1970s, especially jazz-rock, and the
keying of the text to the Smithsonian Collection of Classic Jazz. The
discography is moved to the accompanying manual, which also contains advice for teachers and suggested exam topics.

S.665.   NANRY, Charles. The Jazz Text; with Edward Berger.
         New York: Van Nostrand, 1979. 276p. illus., bibliog.,
         discog.
         An introduction to jazz "aimed at students of the music and
its performers" (preface), and distinguished from other similar books
by a markedly sociological approach, which subordinates individual
jazz stars to the context that shaped them, to an extent unusual in
jazz literature. (It is noticeable that the author is more at home
with social movements, etc., than with critical appreciation of individuals: his sections on important figures, called "the personal
dimension," and made to bring up the rear in several chapters, are
[to prove the point?] rather flat potted biographies.) The book
falls into three parts: Part 1, an introduction, raises some major
themes, defines terms, and provides background. Part 2 is a concise historical survey in four chapters. Part 3 is an outline of basic
jazz research methodology, and an insight into the possibility of a
sociologically based approach.

S.666.   TANNER, Paul O. W., and GEROW, Maurice. A Study of
         Jazz. Dubuque, Iowa: Brown, 1964. 83p. bibliog.,
         discogs.
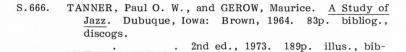   . 2nd ed., 1973. 189p. illus., bib-

liog., discog.

_____. _____. 3rd ed., 1977. 211p. illus., bibliog.,
discog.

_____. _____. 4th ed., 1981. 226p. illus., bibliog.,
discog.

Essentially a handbook for teachers at either secondary or
college level, this work has established a solid reputation as a reliable guide for teachers and students alike. Early chapters offer
clear, succinct advice on the basic elements of jazz, and on how to
listen to it. The bulk of the book is historically organized, from
"jazz heritages" to the contemporary era, and each has "suggested
classroom activities." An outstanding feature is the generous provision of music examples, and their integration into the text in a
readily understandable manner. Included at the back of the book
is a selection of "scores" (examples of successive styles, performed
on the accompanying disc), and a glossary. The main shortcoming of
the book is the absence of any sense of the importance of context.
Index. (Formerly LOAM A222.)

b. The Jazz Life

See also S.677

(i) General

S.667. BECKER, Howard S. Outsiders: studies in the sociology
of deviance. New York: Free Press of Glencoe; London:
Collier-Macmillan, 1963. 179p.

In the late 1940s Becker worked as a professional dance
band pianist in Chicago, using the opportunity to carry out research
by participant observation. In this famous study he draws on this
research, and on later experience in Champaign-Urbana and Kansas
City, to form the basis of two chapters, "The Culture in a Deviant
Group: the Dance Musician" and "Careers in a Deviant Occupational
Group: the Dance Musician." The community of musicians he describes "classify themselves according to the degree to which they
give in to [the standards of] outsiders; the continuum ranges from
the extreme 'jazz' musician to the 'commercial' musician" (p. 83). The
first chapter demonstrates how the musicians view themselves as set
apart from others, and how this feeling results in a conflict between
their own and their audience's standards (not just of music, but of
behavior, for the "setting apart" is used to justify different standards
in all branches of life); this in turn produces self-segregation. The
second chapter explores the consequences of choosing a career as a
dance musician, in particular the need to integrate into the music
business, the problems raised by freedom from outside control, and
the difficulties often encountered in family relationships.

S.668. DEXTER, Dave. Playback: a newsman/record producer's

hits and misses from the thirties to the seventies. New
York: Billboard Publications, 1976. 239p. illus.
An unashamedly "rambling, name-dropping, memory-pro-
voking tome" (p. 8), this is a diverting, anecdotal account of music
and musicians encountered during forty years as a jazz journalist
(Down Beat) and record producer (Capitol). Among the host of
musicians who appear in the loosely connected reminiscences are Mildred Bailey, Benny Carter, Julia Lee, Peggy Lee, Pete Johnson,
Frank Sinatra; Dexter's particular fondness for big bands is reflected in a high number of band leaders: Basie, Ellington, Goodman, Kenton, Miller, etc. A list of big band opening theme tunes
is included. Index.

S.669. HAMMOND, John. John Hammond on Record: an auto-
        biography; with Irving Townsend. New York: Ridge
        Press, 1977. 416p. illus., discog.
        _____. _____. Harmondsworth: Penguin Books,
        1981. 432p. illus., discog.
A significant figure in the discovery and promotion of jazz
musicians, especially in the 1930s, Hammond (b.1910) was born in
New York into Vanderbilt family affluence (on his mother's side).
From the same source he inherited a crusading zeal, and this,
coupled with his background, and with a socio-political outlook radical for one with that background, enabled him to pursue with conviction twin objectives: the dissemination of jazz (especially as
played by black musicians), and the lessening of racial discrimination ("to bring recognition to the Negro's supremacy in jazz was the
most effective and constructive form of social protest I could think
of"--p. 68). This pursuit occupies the heart of the book, which
describes his involvement with the recording of many musicians,
notably Billie Holiday, Fletcher Henderson, Bessie Smith, Count
Basie, Benny Goodman, Charlie Christian, Teddy Wilson--and, in
later years, rock stars Bob Dylan and Bruce Springsteen. Many
candid behind-the-scenes glimpses of the jazz life and of record
company mores make fascinating reading, as does Hammond's long
association with NAACP, which dated from the Scottsboro trials of
the 1930s. Name index.

S.670. MORRIS, Ronald L. Wait Until Dark: jazz and the under-
        world 1880-1940. Bowling Green, Ohio: Bowling Green
        University Popular Press, 1980. 231p. illus., bibliog.
A fascinating historical and sociological study of a little
investigated subject--the involvement of gangsters in the growth and
spread of jazz from turn-of-the-century New Orleans to the late
1930s. This involvement Morris terms "sponsorship" and his case
rests on replacing the stereotype of the mobster ("culturally atavis-
tic, materialistically mad, and terrifyingly destructive"--p. 7) with
one which sees him, as far as the patronage of music was concerned,
as "generous to a fault, seriously engaged in racial integration and
(exhibiting) remarkable restraint toward employees and customers
alike" (p. 9). Morris begins his account in the peak years of the

1920s, looking especially at Chicago and New York; he then turns
the clock further back to describe night club life before gangster
involvement revitalized it, the typical life of an early jazz musician,
and the New Orleans milieu (especially the Italian community) in
which the first links can be seen.   Chapters 6 and 7 take a close
look at the gangsters themselves, and at the nature of patronage.
Chapter 8 discusses the decline of the scene, and, as a postscript,
Chapter 9 ruefully considers the present.   Morris's greatest problems occur with the reluctance of many of those he attempted to
interview to furnish him with hardcore information, with the result
that much of his evidence is second-hand and he confesses to have
read a lot between the lines of jazz literature.   Added to this, he
is poorly served by his publishers--typos are frequent and stylistic quirks abound.   Nevertheless, the book remains an important
contribution to our understanding of the relationship between jazz
and social forces.   Included in the appendices are lists of Italian
jazz and jazz musicians clubs in New Orleans, circa 1905, and of
New York jazz clubs.   Index.

S.671.   OSTRANSKY, Leroy.   Jazz City: the impact of our cities
          on the development of jazz.   Englewood Cliffs, N.J.:
          Prentice-Hall, 1978.   274p.   bibliog., discog.
          The rise of jazz was partly dependent on, and fostered by,
social conditions in urban and urbanizing America.   Ostransky's tale
of four cities--New Orleans, Chicago, Kansas City, New York--re-
affirms and reinforces this with accounts of the way in which special
conditions in each place permitted jazz to flourish.   Mainly a synthesis of earlier research, his book offers greater than usual detail
on the early history of each city, attempting in particular to capture
their essential spirit.   This historical background is largely kept
separate in each case from the account of the growth of jazz that
follows it.   As a method this has some drawbacks, chief among which
are: (a) it implies a one-way influence from social conditions onto
jazz, and (b) it is too inflexible to allow for description of the complex of social and cultural and economic factors at work in both the
creation and the reception of jazz.   (For a more challenging and sophisticated account of Chicago in particular, see Berndt Ostendorf's
chapter "Social Mobility and Cultural Stigma: The Case of Chicago
Jazz," in his study Black Literature in White America [Totowa, N.J.:
Barnes & Noble, 1982], pp. 95-117.)   Index.

          (ii) Clubs and Festivals

S.672.   AGOSTINELLI, Anthony J.   The Newport Jazz Festival,
          Rhode Island, 1954-1971: a bibliography, discography
          and filmography.   Providence: the author, 1977.   64p.
          The bibliography lists books, articles in the jazz, music
and general press, and references in the Providence Journal-Bulletin
1954-75, and in the New York Times (1954-72).   The discography

lists recordings made at the festival in artist order, with dates, personnel, titles and record release numbers; there is a supplementary list of Voice of America radio broadcasts. The filmography lists feature and television films, with details of performers for a certain number of them.

S.673.   AGOSTINELLI, Anthony J. The Newport Jazz Festival, Rhode Island (1954-1971): a significant era in the development of jazz. Providence: the author, 1978. 63p.
A miscellany of accounts of the festival, quotes from press reports, etc., describing the beginnings of the festival, the opposition it encountered, its role in providing an opportunity for newcomers (and in revitalizing older hands), evidence of racial discrimination in the town, and the riots that ended its career. Some reflections by organizer George Wein are given in an appendix.

S.674.   GOLDBLATT, Burt. Newport Jazz Festival: the illustrated history. New York: Dial Press, 1977. 287p. illus., discog.
This handsome volume (around 300 photos) provides an authoritative history of the festival from its beginnings to its period in New York, 1972-76. To his own experience (Goldblatt attended each festival himself) the author added that of musicians, organizers, audience and townsfolk by conducting over 140 interviews. His account includes information on the many practical difficulties, discussion of the problems encountered over racial discrimination, and comment on the performers themselves. Many reviews are quoted. The climax, inevitably, comes in 1971 when violence brought the series in Newport itself to a close. (This episode is not illustrated.) Besides the full chronological discography there is a list of programs, 1954-76.

S.675.   GORDON, Max. Live at the Village Vanguard; introduction by Nat Hentoff. New York: St. Martin's Press, 1980. 146p. illus.
Snappy, entertaining recollections by the founder and owner of the celebrated New York nightclub, opened in 1934. Though most closely associated with jazz, a typical night of "Greenwich Village high jinks" in its early years was witnessed by a gathering of "poets, WPA writers, hustlers, insomniacs, college students ... tourists, broads on the make, musicians, moochers, all of them crowding the place every night to let off steam" (p. 31). In the early '40s a star attraction was Judy Holliday (with Betty Comden, Adolph Green, John Frank and Alvin Hammer, as "The Revuers"); their act was replaced by Josh White, Leadbelly, and Woody Guthrie (a long Guthrie letter to Gordon is given in full). Jazz portraits occupy the latter part of the book: Sonny Rollins, Miles Davis, Charles Mingus (a conversation between Gordon and Dannie Richmond), Rahsaan Roland Kirk, the Baroness Nica de Koenigswarter (friend of Parker, Hawkins, Monk and others), and a Russian tour with Thad Jones and Mel Lewis.

S.676.   GRIME, Kitty. Jazz at Ronnie Scott's; photography by
         Val Wilmer. London: Robert Hale, 1979. 188p. illus.
     England's most celebrated jazz club has had a regular place
for many years on the itinerary of US jazz musicians visiting Europe.
Here interviews held with them, and with some of their British
counterparts, are dismembered and the fragments reassembled to
form one series of "pathworks" describing certain subjects (the road,
the influences of Charlie Parker, learning the jazz trade, being a
jazz musician, etc.), and a second centered around instrumental
groups. Among the American jazz musicians most prominently featured in these gobbets are: Andrew Cyrille, Bud Freeman, Dizzy
Gillespie, Johnny Griffin, Woody Herman, Quentin Jackson, Thad
Jones, Jimmy Knepper, Charles Mingus, Roswell Rudd, and Archie
Shepp. Name and title index.

S.677.   HASKINS, Jim. The Cotton Club. New York: Random
         House, 1977. 169p. illus., bibliog. refs.
     For the whites who flocked to Harlem in the 1920s and '30s,
the Cotton Club epitomized what they were seeking in the way of
exotic entertainment. From the viewpoint of black music and dance
the club's considerable importance lay partly in the opportunities it
offered to make black artistry visible without recourse to the stereo-
typing of minstrelsy, and partly in the openings it gave to numerous
black performers who later became stars. Haskins' well-researched
synthesis of information on the history of the Club concentrates on
the succession of shows and performers, but does not lose sight of
the complex fabric of social and racial attitudes implied in the club's
existence and changing fortunes. He succeeds in placing the Club's
history clearly in its context, as just one--albeit the most famous--
of a group of similar establishments. His history takes us from the
development of the black community in Harlem through the foundation
of the Club in 1923 (by gangster Owney Madden) up to its transfer
to Broadway in 1936, and its four successful years there before
changing fashions forced its closure in 1940. Prominent among the
black musicians featured are Duke Ellington, Cab Calloway, Ethel
Waters, and Lena Horne. Among the important white musicians involved are songwriters Harold Arlen and Ted Koehler (whose "Stormy
Weather" was a resounding Cotton Club hit for Ethel Waters in
1933).

S.678.   LYONS, Jimmy. Dizzy, Duke, the Count and Me: the story
         of the Monterey Jazz Festival; with Ira Kamin; drawings
         by David Stone Martin; photographs by Peter Breinig....
         San Francisco: California Living Books, 1978. 184p.
         illus.
     Lyons was the founder of and driving force behind the
Monterey festival, and his colorful reminiscences about the festival
form the first part of the book--mostly anecdotal, randomly organized
snippets about musicians, the stuff of which footnotes are made in as
yet unwritten biographies. Kamin then contributes a detailed chronology of the festival, 1958-77, with information on each year's

program. "Gleanings" is the title of the final part, which contains
a miscellany of reviews and recollections by (among others) Ralph
J. Gleason, Leonard Feather and Richard Hadlock.   Index.

(iii) Photographic Studies

See also S.729

S.679.   BERENDT, Joachim-Ernst. Photo-Story des Jazz. Frank-
         furt: Kruger, 1978. 356p. illus., discog.
         _____. Jazz: a photo history; translated by William
         Odom. London: Deutsch; New York: Schirmer, 1979.
         355p. illus., discog.
         Of the 370 black and white photographs on display here,
relatively few are familiar from previous publications. Berendt's
stated aim was to include pictures "that communicate something
of both the personality and the music of the musicians"--an ambitious undertaking, but one at least partly realized in an always interesting, sometimes quite arresting, portrait gallery. Berendt
draws on his own large collection, and on that of Duncan P. Schiedt,
also using many contemporary photographs by William Caxton,
Giuseppe Pino, and others. The "history" component is insubstan-
tial--a basically chronological outline, and occasional dollops of necessary information. Most of the accompanying text is devoted, not to
history as such, but to brief biographies of the musicians; these
tend to be adulatory in nature and do not add greatly to the photographs. (For some reason, accompanying texts to musical photograph
albums tend to assume a low level of knowledge among their readers,
thereby severely limiting the expressiveness of the pictures; more
imaginative texts, or indeed a semiotic study of jazz photography,
would be a welcome development.) Index of names.

S.680.   BRASK, Ole. Jazz People; photographs by Ole Brask;
         text by Dan Morgenstern; introduction by James Jones.
         New York: Abrams, 1976. 300p. illus., bibliog.,
         discog.
         A photographic celebration, with excellent supporting text.
Following an excursion into jazz pre-history, for which a number of
archival illustrations are included, the book is constructed, in a
broadly chronological way, around the Danish photographer's evocative portraits, mainly from the 1960s and '70s. Text serves illustration, so gaps in the photographic record mean numerous major
musicians (Parker, Coltrane) receive little attention; but by the same
token, some benefit who do not regularly enjoy the spotlight in jazz
histories (e.g., Budd Johnson, Stuff Smith).

S.681.   DALE, Rodney. The World of Jazz. Oxford: Phaidon
         Press, 1980. 192p. illus.
         Coffee-table book, profusely illustrated with photographic
portraits of jazz musicians, selected from a variety of published and

unpublished sources, and chronologically organized. Dale's text
provides accompanying thumb-nail sketches of many of the musicians,
setting each of them briefly in place in jazz history, and offering a
basic introduction to the historical framework of the music. Index.

S.682.   PINO, Giuseppe. From Spirituals to Swing; photographs
         (by) Giuseppe Pino; text (by) Jean-Claude Arnaudon;
         English version (by) Fanni L. Jones (and) Willy Leiser.
         Montreux: International Booking Agency, 1979. un-
         paged, illus.
         Spiral-bound volume containing a modest but powerful col-
lection of photographs, arranged in sections: spirituals, blues,
swing. The spirit, rather than the reality, of the celebrated 1938
Carnegie Hall concert hovers behind the images, which mainly evoke
torchbearers of the music, photographed in the 1960s and 1970s.
Parallel French and English text, evoking the music in poetic terms.

S.683.   REDFERN, David. David Redfern's Jazz Album. London:
         Eel Pie, 1980. 159p. illus.
         British photographer David Redfern's work has been fea-
tured on many album covers and has illustrated many a journal article. This is an impressive sample of that work, in black-and-white
and color, covering the 1960s and '70s. The photographs were
taken in both the USA and Europe, at festivals and concerts, in
clubs, in the photographer's studio, on the road, backstage, and
cover a wide range of moods, poses and expressions, conscious and
unconscious. Index.

S.684.   WILMER, Valerie. The Face of Black Music: photographs
         by Valerie Wilmer; introduction by Archie Shepp. New
         York: Da Capo, 1976. unpaged, illus.
         Outstanding book of black and white photographs taken in
the USA and Europe between 1963 and 1975. Jazz and blues musicians, famous and not so famous, provide the subject matter, and
the camera catches them in performance, behind the scenes, at
home, on the road. But it is the "individual's inner core, rather
than the exterior" that the book sets out, ambitiously, to capture.
Most striking however is the emphasis on links: between the giants
and the unknown, between musicians and their roots, between the
various styles of black music. Accompanying the photographs are
selections from interviews with many of the musicians made by the
photographer herself.

c.   Practical Guides to Arranging, Composing, and Improvising/Jazz
     in Education

S.685.   BAKER, David N. Jazz Pedagogy. Chicago: Maher, 1979.
         195p. bibliogs., discogs.
         Challenging, polemical, but always practical, this wide-

ranging handbook on jazz education is the product of twenty years'
pioneering endeavor by one of the USA's leading jazz educators.
The "meat" of the book consists of detailed suggestions for course
construction, based on Baker's teaching at Indiana University;
these are followed by discussion of practical aspects of training a
college band and of running a smaller combo. He also considers
methods of teaching improvisation and problems in jazz education
that are familiar to the high schools.

S.686. KYNASTON, Trent P., and RICCI, Robert J. Jazz Im-
        provisation. Englewood Cliffs, N.J.: Prentice-Hall,
        1978. 218p.
        A clear practical guide for students who already possess a
mastery of technical facilities.

d. General Analytical and Critical Works

    See also S.553

S.687. ASRIEL, Andre. Jazz: Analysen und Aspekte. Berlin:
        Lied der Zeit, 1966. 288p. illus., bibliog.
        _____. _____. 2. Aufl. Berlin: Lied der Zeit,
        1977. 294p. illus., bibliog.
        Like another excellent German historical-cum-musicological
work, Alfons M. Dauer's Der Jazz: seine Ursprünge und Entwicklung (LOAM 988), this book is all but unknown in the anglocentric
world of jazz criticism. It is probably the major work on jazz to be
published in the German Democratic Republic. Its chief concern is
with the musical features of jazz, whether treated in terms of
chronological development, or synchronically (rhythm, form, arrangement, etc.), and it teems with music examples. There are lists of
outstanding practitioners in given areas of the music, and indexes
of names and subjects.

S.688. BRINKMANN, Reinhold, ed. Improvisation und neue Musik:
        acht Kongressreferate. Mainz: Schott, 1979. (Ver-
        öffentlichungen des Instituts fur Neue Musik und
        Musikerziehung, Darmstadt, Band 20.) 136p. bibliog.
        refs.
        These 1979 German conference papers include one by Ekke-
hard Jost on improvisation in jazz; also noteworthy is a more general
one, "What is improvisation?" by Carl Dahlhaus.

S.689. BRINKMANN, Reinhold, ed. Die neue Musik und die Tra-
        dition: sieben Kongressbeiträge und eine analytische
        Studie. Mainz: Schott, 1978. (Veröffentlichungen des
        Instituts für Neue Musik und Musikerziehung, Darm-
        stadt, Band 19.) 152p. bibliog. refs.
        Includes a paper in German by Ekkehard Jost on tradition
in free jazz and pop.

S.690. OSTRANSKY, Leroy. <u>Understanding Jazz</u>. Englewood
        Cliffs, N.J.: Prentice-Hall, 1977. 367p. bibliog.
        Although the author states that "What began ... as just a
revised edition of <u>The Anatomy of Jazz</u> turned out to be, in fact, a
new book" (p. x), it is probably best to think of this as a considerably revised and updated version of the earlier volume (LOAM
999). Several chapters, notably "The Musical Elements of Jazz,"
are substantially altered, mainly to make the new book less technical; others have only minor changes. Three new chapters, on
the 1960s and '70s, replace the previous concluding chapter, "Toward the Future." The bibliography is updated also. Index.

e. General Histories

S.691. BERENDT, Joachim-Ernst, ed. <u>Die Story des Jazz: vom</u>
        <u>New Orleans zum Rock Jazz</u>. Stuttgart: Deutsche Ver-
        lagsanstalt, 1975. 209p. illus., bibliog., discog.
        _____. _____. Reinbek: Rowohlt, 1978. 285p.
        illus., bibliog., discog.
        _____. <u>The Story of Jazz: from New Orleans to rock</u>
        <u>Jazz</u>. Englewood Cliffs, N.J.: Prentice-Hall; London:
        Barrie & Jenkins, 1978. 192p. illus., bibliog., discog.
        A collection of essays on successive historical periods of
jazz, each adequate as an introduction, but none substantial enough
to do more than scant justice to the subject. Reimer von Essen
writes on New Orleans, Manfred Miller on blues (and, later, on
blues today), Werner Burkhardt on Chicago, Dan Morgenstern on
the swing era, Leonard Feather on bebop, Ekkehard Jost on free
jazz, and Karl Lippegaus on rock jazz. Each commissioned author
brings out the salient points clearly and concisely--in some cases
making new ones--but each piece is overburdened by the recitation
of names. The editor's justification for the book--to ask experts "to
write on the styles and jazz forms that they have experienced, lived
through and researched" (p. 10)--is not reflected in markedly more
perceptive or authoritative criticism. There are, however, two unusual contributions: Leonard Feather describes the careers of Louis
Armstrong and Duke Ellington in parallel, with points of comparison
and contrast (a piece that would have been improved by removing
the need to construct it diachronically), and the editor's own musings
on a philosophy of jazz, which would stand more chance of achieving
the admirable aim of peeping "over the boundary wall with which the
followers of jazz have literally shut off their music from all surrounding phenomena" (p. 175), were they less beholden to Germanic ab-
straction. No index.

S.692. CHILTON, John. <u>Jazz</u>; foreword by George Melly. London:
        Hodder and Stoughton; New York: David McKay, 1979.
        (Teach Yourself Books.) 186p. illus., bibliog., discog.
        An excellent introductory history of jazz, which has much to

offer the knowledgeable listener also. Jazz historiography has many
pitfalls: the proliferation of musicians and recordings beckon the
historian into side alleys, the impassioned yet mundane (and often
exploited) jazz life tempts the writer to indulge in social and/or
moral judgments which are not always appropriate, while the claims
and counterclaims of both fans and musicians seem designed to un-
dermine objectivity. Chilton avoids all these, and shows at the same
time that one can still be sharp yet have no axe to grind; from the
music's ancestry to its free jazz and other modern developments,
his account is ready to take each period and style on its own merit.
An unusual, welcome feature is that, spaced evenly among the eleven
historical chapters are three non-technical, theoretical ones--on the
basis of jazz improvisation, the new harmonic and rhythmic concepts
of bop, and the fundamentals of modal and free jazz. Each chapter
has a list of recommended reading, and at the end of the book are
a fuller bibliography, suggestions for recordings, a glossary, and
an index.

S.693.   COLLIER, James Lincoln. The Making of Jazz: a compre-
          hensive history. Boston: Houghton Mifflin; London:
          Hart-Davis Macgibbon, 1978; New York: Dell, 1979;
          London: Macmillan, 1981. 543p. illus., bibliog., dis-
          cog.
          Aimed at "students and the lay public" (preface), this is
a sane, balanced history, written in a readily accessible style. Its
29 chapters are divided between the roots (4), the early years (7),
the swing age (8), and the modern era (from bebop on) (10).
While some chapters take a broad perspective, others are devoted to
single outstanding individuals (Morton, Armstrong, Ellington, Parker,
Coltrane). The writing mixes historical and biographical information
with passages of descriptive musical criticism; based on attentive
listening to recorded jazz, these lack the support of music examples,
but nevertheless frequently provide the reader with valuable points
of insight. (Collier has a happy way with metaphor--see, for instance, his description of Monk on p. 383.) The shortcomings of
the book stem from its relative lack of interest in the relationship
between music, culture and society, other than during the music's
formative years. The bibliography indicates an almost total reliance
on music, especially jazz, literature as source material. (Sources
are not cited in the text.) This leads to somewhat inadequate attempts to come to grips with the problems posed by complex individuals like Parker, where the author is obliged to fall back on amateur psychology and reveals hints of the "middle-class white critic"
syndrome usually absent elsewhere. The discography is a representative list of jazz on LP, and there is a reliable index.

S.694.   DAVIS, Nathan. Writings in Jazz. Dubuque, Iowa: Gor-
          such Scarisbrick, 1978. 172p. illus., bibliog., discog.
          Intended as a contribution to the study of jazz at high
school or junior college level, this is an introductory outline history
of the music, its social and cultural contexts, and its major

performers. Music examples are included, though the presentation of this aspect is much less thorough than in Tanner and Gerow (no. 666). Davis is not served especially well by his editors, but the text is generally clear and uncomplicated; it gains confidence as it enters the post-war period. Davis is a well-traveled jazz musician himself, who has played with many of the outstanding post-war figures; some of the fruits of these experiences have a habit of cropping up in the text, an initially disconcerting feature in an aspiring textbook, but one which, for the average reader at least, does give the book a more original air. Some original claims are made: e.g., on Kenny Clarke's drumming (p. 91) and Charlie Parker's birthdate (p. 93), adding an unusual spice to an otherwise unexceptional text.

S.695.   GODDARD, Chris. Jazz Away From Home. New York:
         Paddington Press, 1979.   319p.   illus., bibliog. refs.
         Although not a comprehensive history of the impact of jazz on Europe and its subsequent development there, this is a perceptive study of some parts of the story in France and England: of "how and when and in what form jazz reached Europe" (p. 7), its use in other musical contexts, and--perhaps the chief concern of the book-- the varied reactions of the musical establishment. Following an account of the background to the first bands to cross the Atlantic and of their arrival and reception--with particular attention to James Reese Europe, Will Marion Cook (and Sidney Bechet), the Original Dixieland Jazz Band and Paul Whiteman--Goddard examines the role of jazz in developments in the theatre and dance in the 1920s, the encounter with jazz of several European composers (Ravel, Milhaud, etc.), the development of jazz criticism (Goffin, Panassie, Lambert) and the use of jazz as fashionable background in the 1920s by European high society ("a sophisticated form of tokenism"--p. 219). An appendix contains transcripts of a number of interviews made in 1976-78 with American and European musicians. Index.

S.696.   TIRRO, Frank. Jazz: a history. New York: Norton,
         1977.   457p.   illus., bibliog., discog.
         A jazz musician borrows an idea and flies with it; the jazz historian can do the same, or, at the other extreme, he can load up too much baggage and fail to take off. Tirro tends toward the latter, though the problem is one of type of baggage as well as the amount: the stalwarts of jazz literature (Schuller, Stearns, Williams, etc.) are omnipresent, but although Tirro maintains his text is an attempt to introduce jazz history to the interested layman by incorporating research in sociology, cultural anthropology, history (as well as musicology), there is little evidence of wide reading in any of these areas.
         Aerodynamic difficulties do not end there: there is too much weight in the tail, and not enough up front. Jazz pre-history is an important subject; the question is whether, in a 350-page text, it should be allowed to occupy most of the first 150 pages--especially when that decision means ragtime and blues have as much room as

bebop and the 1950s! Further technical problems emerge when the
six main chronological chapters devoted to jazz, 1900-1960, are followed by a hodge-podge where Tirro finds a home, among others,
for Billie Holiday and the Modern Jazz Quartet, and which he apolo-
getically calls "Loose Ends and Peripheral Events"; what would we
say to the plane-builder who had a puzzling handful of parts left
when he'd finished?

    Still, the presence of numerous musical examples, including
structural schemes and transcriptions, holds out the promise of enlightening in-flight entertainment, should take-off occur (even if
text and illustration do not always fully complement each other).
Taken together with the generous bibliographies, the footnotes, and
the acknowledgment of sources, these transcriptions and schemes
suggest a work of scholarship--an engineering triumph; but they
are more usefully interpreted (since no device is used to its full potential) as contributions towards providing the reader with the means
to make the wings for himself.

S.697.   WALKER, Edward S. Don't Jazz--It's Music; or some notes
             on popular syncopated music in England during the 20th
             century. Walsall, Staffs.: the author, 1979. unpaged.
             illus.

    Though chiefly concerned with British musicians, this ac-
count of the growth of dance music and jazz in Britain contains mention of numerous influential appearances in Britain by American musicians, among them Noble Sissle and Paul Whiteman.

f.   Collected Criticism and Appreciation

    See also S.722

S.698.   BALLIETT, Whitney. Improvising: Sixteen jazz musicians
             and their art. New York: Oxford University Press,
             1977. 263p.

    Of the thirteen essays in this anthology, six appear here
in book form for the first time (having previously seen the light of
day, New Yorker style); they are pieces on King Oliver, Jess Stacy,
Sid Catlett, Stephane Grappelli, Jim Hall and Bob Wilber. Of the
remaining seven, four appeared in Such Sweet Thunder (LOAM 1012)
(those on Henry Red Allen, Earl Hines, Mary Lou Williams, Pee Wee
Russell), two in Ecstacy at the Onion (LOAM 1013) (essays on Red
Norvo and the MJQ), and the profile of Buddy Rich appeared in
Super-Drummer (LOAM 1137). Balliett brings these musicians together here because "their lives, in intertwining and overlapping,
form a scattershot history of the music ... as they themsleves have
lived it" (p.v.). Astute (as always) and illuminating portraits, all
except the Oliver and Catlett pieces containing interview material
with their subjects who offer musings on the mystery of improvisation. Index.

S.699.   BALLIETT, Whitney. New York Notes: a journal of jazz, 1972-1975. Boston: Houghton Mifflin, 1976; New York: Da Capo, 1977. 250p.

Following on from his Ecstasy at the Onion (LOAM 1013), this volume of Balliett's selective New York jazz chronicle, based on material first published in the New Yorker, maintains the previous standards of interest and readability without ever aspiring to great heights (a "workaday record" is how Balliett himself describes it). The regrettable decision to omit an index (all Balliett's other volumes have one) suggests someone, somewhere, does not rate very highly the book's lasting value for reference. The following musicians are featured in some of the longer pieces: Rollins, Hines, Christian, Mulligan, Ellis Larkins, Shaw, Krupa, Condon, Basie, Jimmy Rowles, Ellington, Parker, the MJQ, Mabel Mercer and Helen Humes. There are also reports on each of Newport-New York Festivals, 1972-1975.

S.700.   BERENDT, Joachim-Ernst. Ein Fenster aus Jazz: Essays, Portraits, Reflexionen. Frankfurt: Fischer, 1977. 428p. illus.

———.   ———. Rev. ed. Frankfurt: Fischer, 1978. 431p. illus.

A collection of essays on American and European music and musicians, in which pieces on individuals are balanced by discussions of broader subjects, relating jazz to other musics, and to social and political developments. Berendt makes clear in his introduction that he views jazz as a "political music," with a "message which goes beyond the purely musical." Included in the pieces on individuals are McCoy Tyner, Keith Jarrett, Tony Williams, Sun Ra, the Modern Jazz Quartet, Oscar Pettiford, and Charles Mingus ("and the shadow of Duke Ellington"). Other topics include jazz and religiosity (Coltrane, etc.), the art of the duet, the "new fascism" in rock and jazz, jazz in the 1980s. Index.

S.701.   COLLIER, James Lincoln. The Great Jazz Artists; monoprints by Robert Andrew Parker. New York: Four Winds Press, 1977. 185p. illus., bibliog. & discog. refs.

Sixteen essays, aimed at introducing the new reader (especially teenagers and college students) to jazz, range over the history of the music from its roots to Coleman and Coltrane. In general they are clear, intelligent summaries of existing thought and knowledge, with an awareness of the importance of context, which goes some way to redeeming the inevitable distortions in the "great individuals" approach. The main shortcoming is an absence of the sense of challenge to existing modes of thought which the study of jazz can bring. General index.

S.702.   FEATHER, Leonard. The Passion for Jazz. New York: Horizon Press, 1980. 208p. illus.

Like its predecessor, no. S.703, this is a pot-pourri of around 40 short, journalistic pieces originally published in the Los

Angeles Times and elsewhere. What caused Feather pleasure earlier in the decade evidently arouses passion in 1975-1980, but little
of that is communicated. The majority of the pieces are portraits
of musicians, often based on interview. No index.

S.703.   FEATHER, Leonard. The Pleasures of Jazz: leading per-
         formers on their lives, their music, their contemporaries;
         introduction by Benny Carter. New York: Horizon
         Press, 1976; New York: Dell, 1977. 200p. illus.
     A lightweight collection of more than 40 short pieces on con-
temporary jazz musicians, based on interviews. Written by Feather
for various journals and newspapers, chief among them the Los
Angeles Times, between 1966 and 1975, the pieces cover a wide
stylistic area, ranging from Eubie Blake to Chick Corea; they are
mostly very short, however, rarely exceeding three pages. The
longest is a ten-page interview with trumpeter Freddie Hubbard.
There are six sections in all: "Happenings," "Old Masters," "Big
Bandsmen," "Voices," "Combo Leaders," and "Other Pleasures." No
index.

S.704.   HARRISON, Max. A Jazz Retrospect. Newton Abbott:
         David & Charles; Boston: Crescendo, 1976. 223p.
         bibliog. & discog. refs.
     A collection of 27 pieces originally published in Jazz Monthly,
Jazz Journal, and Jazz Review between 1956 and 1973. Never as renowned a jazz essayist as his US counterparts Balliett, Feather, and
Williams, Englishman Harrison has consistently produced criticism of
a high order (the policy of Jazz Monthly in particular encouraged jazz
journalism to be serious and thoughtful in the context of an illustrated magazine). His earnest, intelligent writing offers many insights into the music of a wide range of musicians, grouped around
six themes: improvisation (Parker, Waller, Monk, Hampton), group
relations (e.g., Teddy Charles, Bunk Johnson, Hal McKusick, Jimmy Lunceford), extending the jazz language (James P. Johnson,
Dizzy Gillespie, David Mack, Ornette Coleman), formal variety (Tadd
Dameron, Duke Ellington, Jelly Roll Morton, Gil Evans), using expressive resources (e.g., Miff Mole, Serge Chaloff, Lennie Niehaus),
and cross-influences (e.g., Paul Whiteman). A pronounced feature
of his writing, which he shares with André Hodeir, is his fondness
for introducing notions drawn from European high culture, and a
corresponding lack of interest in American popular culture. Whatever its merits, when this approach has Nietzsche, Rilke, Roland,
and Ibsen appear in the first two pages, there are signs of over-
zealous Eurocentrism. Index.

S.705.   LARKIN, Philip. All What Jazz: a record diary, 1961-68.
         London: Faber & Faber; New York: St. Martin's Press,
         1970. 272p.
         _____. All What Jazz: a record diary, 1961-1971. Rev.
         ed. London: Faber & Faber, 1985. 312p.
     English poet Larkin (1922-1986) wrote these short record

reviews for the Daily Telegraph from 1961-1971 (the 1984 edition
adds the 1969-71 pieces "for the sake of completeness"--p. 29),
covering jazz and, to a lesser extent, blues releases. From a
stylistic point of view, rarely can the music have been spoken of
with such clarity, economy, and wit. The main difficulty is that
Larkin's taste in jazz extended very little into bebop and beyond.
To begin with, he is able to conceal this reasonably well, but his
efforts to be objective are severely taxed by jazz developments in
the 1960s. The central interest of the book begins to shift away
from the music itself as we mark the increasingly plainly (if often
humorously) stated hostility of the writer. Keenly aware of this
himself, on looking back over his articles, Larkin notes of the later
pieces, "they seem ... to carry a deepening sense of depression"
(p. 29), and regrets that the book as a whole "seemed to type me
as a disliker rather than a liker" (p. 30). Nevertheless his cry,
"I still insist I love jazz" (ibid.), can find too many echoes in the
text for anyone to challenge it. The best of the writing has that
invaluable gift of sending you to the records with renewed spirits
and fresh ears. A list of records reviewed serves as an index.
(Some further articles, not included here, can be found in Larkin's
other anthology, Required Writing: miscellaneous pieces 1955-1982
[London: Faber & Faber, 1983].)   (Formerly LOAM A 210.)

S.706.   SCHOUTEN, Martin. Billie en de President: verhalen uit
         de tijd van de jazz. Amsterdam: De Arbeiderspers,
         1977. 256p. bibliog. refs.
         Collection of essays by a Dutch journalist, including a
study of the Billie Holiday-Lester Young partnership (with music
examples), portraits of four pianists--Jimmy Yancey, Fats Waller,
Errol Garner, Thelonious Monk (also with some examples)--an account of modern jazz in the East Village from the late 1950s, and a
study of Bix Beiderbecke. Included also is a piece on composer
Philip Glass. Name index.

S.707.   TÉNOT, Frank, and CARLES, Philippe. Le Jazz. Paris:
         Larousse, 1977. 255p. bibliog.
         Collects together the articles on jazz written for the En-
cyclopédie Larousse, arranging them in three sections: (i) "les
phases de la musique noire," eight short chapters on blues, spirituals
and gospel, New Orleans, big bands, bebop, rock & roll, free jazz,
and "postfree"; (ii) seventeen portraits of major musicians; and (iii)
thirteen short chapters on instruments, their development in jazz,
and their major practitioners. The text is authoritative and well-
written; some of the portraits are extremely vivid (see, for example,
Lionel Hampton), without that descent into purple prose that often
characterizes the jazz writer straining for effect. Index of names,
and bibliography of books.

S.708.   TRAILL, Sinclair, ed. Concerning Jazz. London: Faber
         & Faber, 1957; London: Jazz Book Club, 1958. 180p.
         A collection of wide-ranging essays of varying quality,

specially written for the volume. Some may reveal more about late 1950s critics than about music, but all are substantial. Mezz Mezzrow's "In the Idiom" is a rambling, anecdotal piece, chiefly noteworthy for the speed with which Mezz can get off the subject. "Evolution and Appreciation: a Perspective," by Stanley Dance, is a capsule history of the relationship between music and audience, in general terms. Hugues Panassié's contribution, "A Soul and a Beat: the Essence of Jazz," searches for the basics, but won't find them in modern jazz at any price. Less frightened by post-war developments, Gerald Lascelles outlines, with solid judgement and discernment, the trends and influences in piano playing that have led towards the modern style. Mike Butcher pinpoints the main characteristics of the modern idiom in general in "Modern Jazz: the Bopsters and Beyond," a piece which eventually succumbs to name-listing. Breaking out of history, Douglas Hague provides a synchronic view of the range of US jazz activity in "The Jazz Scene: America." (Formerly LOAM A223.)

4. History and Criticism of Specific Periods

a. Origins to 1930

S.709.   CHILTON, John.   A Jazz Nursery: the story of the Jenkins' Orphanage Bands.   London: Bloomsbury Book Shop, 1980.   60p.   illus., bibliog. refs.
        A fascinating example of musical detective work. Chilton pieces together the history of Rev. Daniel Jenkins' band from Charleston, S.C., from its foundation in the late 19th century as a fund-raising enterprise for the orphanage. Its significance for historians of black music lies partly in the fact that a number of jazz musicians were schooled in the band (Gus Aitken, Cat Anderson, Peanuts Holland, Jabbo Smith) and partly in its influence outside Charleston, both in other parts of the USA and abroad. Chilton's account shows that many aspiring black musicians heard the band on tour in the 1910's and '20s, and that moreover the band's first visits to Europe antedated those made by James Reese Europe, Will Marion Cook, etc. The music they played, Chilton expects, was "a robust music that loosened up the formal ragtime arrangement and produced emphatic syncopations when playing marches and two-steps" (p. 30). The pinnacle of the band's fame was reached when it performed in the stage dramatization of DuBose Heywood's Porgy in New York and London in 1927-8.

S.710.   KAUFMAN, Fredrick, and GUCKIN, John P.   The African Roots of Jazz.   Sherman Oaks, Calif.: Alfred Publishing Co., 1979.   147p.   illus., bibliog., discog.
        Using methods drawn from ethnomusicology, informally presented, the authors aim to fill a gap as they see it in the available literature concerning the relationship between jazz and traditional African music. They begin by describing the conditions of

enslavement in West Africa and the provenance of the slaves, going
on to discuss aspects of West African music, and to provide an in-
depth portrait of music among the Egba people of Abeokuta, Nigeria.
Points of comparison with jazz are regularly noted (e.g., between
the unconventionality of griots and of bop musicians). Switching
their focus more directly onto jazz, the authors examine the music's
essential features, and relate them to African counterparts; this
study encourages them to declare "we found every musical element
within early jazz has been influenced by African traditional music"
--p. 78. Music examples are provided (of call-and-response, riffs,
etc.), and there is also discussion of instruments. The bibliography
and the references are noticeably anglocentric; in stressing the
uniqueness of their work the authors ignore the substantial contribution of Alfons M. Dauer (LOAM (988).

S.711.   LYTTELTON, Humphrey. The Best of Jazz: Basin Street
         to Harlem; Jazz masters and masterpieces 1917-30. Lon-
         don: Robson Books, 1978; New York: Taplinger, 1979.
         214p. illus., bibliog., discog.
         _____. _____. Harmondsworth: Penguin, 1980.
         238p. illus., bibliog., discog.
         English jazz trumpeter Lyttelton's BBC jazz program has
been the most widely heard jazz broadcast in the UK for many years
(not that the competition is fierce), and it is a measure of the
respect in which he is held that axe-wielding mandarins of the corporation, who know nothing and care less about the music, have
failed to remove him from their schedules. His volume of "jigsaw
fragments" (p. 11) takes the shape of a series of essays on outstanding musicians in early jazz, from the ODJB to Luis Russell.
There are chapters on James P. Johnson, King Oliver, Sidney
Bechet, Bessie Smith, Jelly Roll Morton, Fletcher Henderson, Louis
Armstrong, Bix Beiderbecke, Duke Ellington, McKenzie and Condon's
Chicagoans, Johnny Dodds and Jimmy Noone, and the Louis Arm-
strong-Earl Hines partnership on the immortal "Weather Bird."
Close examination of one or two particular recordings forms the basis of Lyttelton's method; this analysis is set against a biographical--
and occasionally social--background. More coherent as a unit than
most volumes of jazz essays, the book necessarily omits some influential figures, and is somewhat incomplete as jazz history. Its
great strengths are a perceptive musician's insight into the musical
heart of the pieces under examination, a lucid, witty style, and an
ability to distinguish between jazz myths that have real meaning and
those that are mere hyperbole. Index. (For the succeeding book,
see no. S/A 437.)

S.712.   OPEN UNIVERSITY. The Rise of Jazz; prepared by Richard
         Middleton for the course team. Milton Keynes: Open
         University Press, 1979. 76p. illus., bibliog.
         (For comment on Open University courses and their mate-
rial, see no. S.191; like that item, this manual deserves a place in
the bibliography of American music as an independent entity.) An

admirably clear introduction to early jazz, successfully combining historical outline, musical analysis, and awareness of the importance of socio-cultural issues. Beginning with definition, the text takes a celebrated recording (King Oliver's "Dippermouth Blues") and uses it as a basis for discussion of material and form, harmony and melody, rhythm, and instruments. A brief foray into the subject of modernism (like no. S.191, this unit is part of a course on modernism in music) is followed by a basically historical sequence of chapters: an account of the origins of jazz and of the importance of New Orleans, an examination of Chicago small band jazz, and, finally, an analysis of the growth of the big band in New York. Within this historical framework outstanding individuals are examined (Louis Armstrong, Bix Beiderbecke, James P. Johnson, Bessie Smith, Fletcher Henderson, Duke Ellington, Luis Russell), and particular stress is laid upon close scrutiny of representative recordings; musical examples appear in the text, and there is an invaluable set of transcriptions (in an accompanying volume, entitled Scores 8).

S.713.   WHITEMAN, Paul, and McBRIDE, Margaret. Jazz. New
          York: Sears, 1926. (Repr. New York: Arno Press,
          1974.) 298p. illus.
          Still a controversial figure, largely because he did not
spurn the accolade "King of Jazz" when the music his orchestra
played was demonstrably not jazz as it was being played by Armstrong, Oliver, etc., in Chicago, and because of the wealth the
title brought him while so many musicians struggled to make a living in the music, Paul Whiteman (1890-1967) has not yet been objectively assessed. Though it will settle few arguments, his book
has a part to play in any reassessment. It is only marginally autobiographical, being mainly concerned with the characteristics of
jazz as he sees them, with the social effect of the music, with the
instruments and their roles, with orchestration, recording, the requirements of a jazz musician (symphony-trained musicians are to be
preferred), and the future of the music--concerns he summarizes
as an effort to help "to give jazz a respectful hearing" (p. 11). In
spite of its period-piece air, the book is an early document in a
school of jazz appreciation that has steadfastly persisted, and which
believes jazz to be basically an idiom of composition and arrangement,
and which must seek "legitimacy" as such. Improvisation is not a
significant feature in Whiteman's version of jazz--his arrangements,
in Gunther Schuller's words were "not jazz--or perhaps only intermittently so--[but were] marvels of orchestral ingenuity" (LOAM
1038, p. 192). (Formerly LOAM A227.)

b. The Swing Era

S.714.   MILLER, Paul Eduard. Down Beat's Yearbook of Swing;
          introduction by Fletcher Henderson. Chicago: Down
          Beat, 1939. (Repr. Westport, Conn.: Greenwood

Press, 1978.) 183p. bibliog., discog.
_____. Miller's Yearbook of Popular Music. Chicago:
PEM Publications, 1943. 195p. bibliog., discog.

Much of this miscellany is now of very limited usefulness,
from the miniature history of jazz, the representative record library,
the valuation of collectors items, to the bibliography of circa 100
items (books and articles). Still valuable, however, are Chapter 3,
"Biographies of the Men of Swing," which gives details on 200 musicians, including minor figures, and Chapter 6, a vocabulary of
swing terms.

S.715. WALKER, Leo. The Big Band Almanac. Pasadena, Calif.:
Ward Ritchie Press, 1978. 466p. illus.

"Look in the almanac," said Bottom the Weaver, eager to
have natural lighting for the artisans' play, "find out moonshine."
How surprised he would have been to find potted biographies instead! For this almanac tells, not of celestial bodies, but of earthly
stars, twinkling in their show business courses: a biographical
dictionary, in effect, of bandleaders from the big band era. Each
entry begins with a note on the time and place of the leader's first
band, a list of sidemen and vocalists, and other information such as
theme song, sponsored radio shows, and recording affiliations. The
biographical sketch which follows is in a narrative style. There
are plentiful illustrations of bandleaders, bands, and vocalists, all
looking confident they know what day it is, even if a prophecy of
the big band's demise might surprise them. Name index.

c. Bebop and After

S.716. BUDDS, Michael J. Jazz in the Sixties: the expansion of
musical resources and techniques. Iowa City: University of Iowa Press, 1978. 124p. bibliog., discog.

Short, evaluative guide to stylistic innovation in 1960s
jazz. Following an introductory survey of jazz styles before 1960,
Budd presents a series of chapters focusing on specific musical
features--color and instrumentation, texture and volume, melody and
harmony, meter and rhythm, structural design. There is also consideration of the influences of bossa nova and rock. A number of
musical examples and chord sequences illustrate the text, which is
generally clearly written and contains several useful explanations,
though it plumbs no great depths. There is a discography of
records cited, a seventeen-page bibliography, and an index.

S.717. CARLES, Philippe, and COMOLLI, Jean-Louis. Free Jazz/
Black Power. Paris: Editions du Champ Libre, 1971.
327p. bibliog. refs., discog.
_____. Free Jazz, Black Power. Paris: Union
Générale d'Editions, 1972. 435p. bibliog. refs., discog.
_____. Free Jazz Black Power; aus dem französischen von

Federica und Hansjorg Pauli. Frankfurt: Fischer,
1974. 288p. bibliog. refs.
_____. _____. Hofheim: Raymund Dillmann, 1980.
253p. bibliog. refs.
Not for the first time a significant contribution to jazz
criticism has remained little known in English-speaking countries because of the lack of an English translation. Much of the criticism
we do have has been able to remain somehow innocent of considerations of social and political ideology. The basic thesis of this book
is that, with the growth of free jazz--and also, following the contribution of LeRoi Jones to the re-interpretation of black music--such
a posture of innocence is untenable; for not only free jazz, but the
whole of black music must, in the authors' view, be understood in
a way which brings social, political and economic conditions--and
specifically, the conflicting ideologies of the governing and the
governed--to the foreground.
    The book is in three parts. Part 1 sets out the politiciza-
tion at the heart of free jazz, and focuses on the role of economic
and cultural "colonization" of the music by dominant white interests,
a process in which much jazz criticism is seen as having a part.
Part 2, the longest section, is called "contributions to a history of
black jazz"; here the authors identify the social, economic and political processes at work earlier in black music--in the blues, work
songs, spirituals, etc.--and in different styles of jazz, demonstrating
how closely these idioms are linked to prevailing conditions. Part 3
returns to free jazz, to consider the "contradictions" implicit in its
various features (reflecting society's contradictions), and its radical
political implications. (The 1980 reissue lacks the biographical portraits of the earlier editions.)

S.718.   CORYELL, Julie, and FRIEDMAN, Laura. Jazz-Rock Fusion:
         the people, the music; preface by Ramsey Lewis. Lon-
         don: Marion Boyars; New York: Dell, 1978. 297p.
         illus., bibliog., discog.
    A series of interviews with 58 musicians involved in playing
"jazz-inspired improvisatory music" (p. xiii)--people "who had a
hand in shaping the course of music from the late sixties to the late
seventies" (preface). The interviews are grouped by instrument or
group of instruments (bass, brass, percussion, etc.), or by function (composer). Each interview includes a photograph, and is preceded by a biographical sketch. Most are short--barely two pages
long--but this is a useful sourcebook. The extensive discography
lists major albums and those on which the musicians appeared as
sidemen.

S.719.   FEATHER, Leonard. Inside Be-bop. New York: Robbins,
         1949. 103p. illus.
         _____. Inside Jazz; with a new introduction. New
         York: Da Capo, 1977. 103p. illus.
    Written at a time when, as Feather reminds us in his in-
troduction to the reprint edition, much of the jazz world was

implacably hostile to the new music (the original publisher changed the title to the more cautious Inside Jazz not long after the book was published), the book is, first and foremost, an interesting example of extended jazz criticism written in the midst of significant stylistic changes; it was also the first book to attempt to analyze in detail bop's musical characteristics. Of the book's three parts, "When," "How," and "Who," the first section is the longest, devoting considerable space to Parker and Gillespie within a concise summary of the history of bop from the late 1930s. Feather shows little social awareness, but a keen ear for stylistic changes, which subsequent critics have done little to improve on; his major failure was his denigration of Monk. "How" is an examination of bop harmony, phrasing, rhythm, etc., with music examples. "Who" is a collection of biographical sketches of around 90 musicians. No index.

S.720.   MORGAN, Alun, and HORRICKS, Raymond. Modern Jazz: a survey of developments since 1939; with a foreword by Don Rendell. London: Gollancz, 1956. (Repr. Westport, Conn.: Greenwood Press, 1977.) 240p. discog.
        Written at a time in Britain when post-war jazz developments were anathema to a great majority of jazz fans, but before some of the most significant recordings of the post-war era (Kind of Blue, etc.), this book now occupies a no-man's land of jazz criticism: not close enough to contemporary events to be valuable as a document of the period, but not even half complete as a map of the field. Nevertheless sections of the historically organized text can be read with profit: the low-key style (the authors are described in Peter Gammond's introduction as "gently persuasive as a pair of Savile Row tailors") tends to obscure the degree of perception, particularly on the roots of bebop and on the role not just of such seminal figures of Christian, Parker, Gillespie, but of the likes of Clyde Hart and Jimmy Blanton. Awareness of--and fascination with--the growing diversity between East Coast and West Coast schools is clearly reflected in the way many of the subsequent chapters are organized, while Horricks' interest in large ensembles may well be responsible for the presence of three chapters on orchestras--Kenton and Barnet, Ellington, and Basie. The closest inspection made is that of the Miles Davis 1948/9 group; here the habit of listing names yields to examination of specific tracks. Index. (Formerly LOAM A213.)

S.721.   RIVELLI, Pauline, and LEVIN, Robert. The Black Giants. New York: World, 1970. 126p. illus.
        _____. Giants of Black Music; new introduction by Nat Hentoff. New York: Da Capo, 1979. 126p. illus.
        Unlike much of the jazz press, Jazz & Pop magazine gave unequivocal support to the "New Jazz" in the 1960s. This collection presents some of the best articles and interviews, from the period 1965-69. Among the musicians featured are John Coltrane, Pharoah Sanders, Elvin Jones, Sunny Murray, Oliver Nelson, Horace Tapscott, Byard Lancaster, Leon Thomas, Archie Shepp, and Alice Coltrane.

The writers are Frank Kofsky, David C. Hunt, John Szwed, Will Smith, Nat Hentoff, and the editors. Hentoff's foreword to the reprint edition has no doubt that "the most recurrent theme in these interviews and essays is survival" (p. vi).

S.722. SINCLAIR, John, and LEVIN, Robert. Music and Politics. New York: World, 1971. 133p. illus.

A collection of "articles, reviews, interviews, polemics and manifestos--many of them controversial, none of them less than provocative," all originally published in Jazz and Pop magazine. Such volumes often have a disparate character, but these pieces, according to Pauline Rivelli's foreword, are connected "not only by their subject matter--the extramusical, political, and social aspects and significance of rock and the New Black Music--but by a bold and abiding revolutionary vision." Among the musicians Sinclair discusses are Chick Corea, Marion Brown, the Rationals, Maurice McIntyre, Sun Ra, Charlie Haden, the Jazz Composers' Orchestra Association, and Stanley Crouch. Levin's contributions include interviews with Sunny Murray, Jimmy Lyons, Willis Jackson, and Booker Little, with reviews of Eric Dolphy and Anthony Braxton, and a consideration of what he sees as rock's declining revolutionary thrust.

S.723. TAYLOR, Arthur. Notes and Tones: musician-to-musician interviews. Liege: the author, 1977. 301p. illus.
_____. _____. New York: Perigree Books, 1982. 296p. illus.

Arthur Taylor (b.1929) is a jazz drummer who left the US for Europe in the early 1960s; before that, he had known and played with many outstanding musicians. The 27 interviews in this excellent book were conducted between 1968 and 1972 in various European cities, as Taylor caught up with jazz musicians on tour. He was inspired, he says, "by the voices of musicians as they saw themselves and not as critics or journalists saw them. I wanted an insider's view" (foreword, 1982 ed.). Certain topics are deliberately repeated throughout the book: music, travel, critics, religion, drugs, racism, and the word "jazz"; Taylor also sought as much information as he could get about Charlie Parker and Bud Powell. The interviewees are (in alphabetical order): Art Blakey, Don Byas, Betty Carter, Ron Carter, Don Cherry, Kenny Clarke, Ornette Coleman, Eddie Lockjaw Davis, Miles Davis, Richard Davis, Kenny Dorham, Erroll Garner, Dizzy Gillespie, Johnny Griffin, Hampton Hawes, Freddie Hubbard, Elvin Jones, Philly Joe Jones, Carmen McRae, Max Roach, Sonny Rollins, Hazel Scott, Nina Simone, Leon Thomas, Charles Tolliver, Randy Weston, Tony Williams.

S.724. VUIJSJE, Bert. De nieuwe Jazz: met bijdragen van Simon Korteweg en Martin Schouten. Baarn: Bosch & Keuning, 1978. 224p.

Originally published in various Dutch journals, these are interviews with twenty musicians active in the 1970s. Seventeen are American: Sonny Rollins, Max Roach, Charles Mingus, Cecil Taylor,

Archie Shepp, Sun Ra, Milford Graves, Charlie Haden, Sunny Murray, Pharoah Sanders, McCoy Tyner, Jimmy Lyons, Sonny Sharrock,
Sam Rivers, Richard Abrams, Julius Hemphill, and David Murray.

S.725.   WILMER, Valerie. As Serious As Your Life: the story of
         the new jazz. London: Allison & Busby; London & New
         York: Quartet, 1977. 296p. illus., bibliog.
    Greater political awareness, a dislike of the "entertainer"
label, an ability to articulate what in earlier generations of jazz musicians were powerfully felt but generally unvoiced attitudes towards
the relationship of jazz to American society--these are some of the
hallmarks of the black jazz musicians of the late 1960s and the '70s
who are the subject of this important, illuminating, sometimes controversial study. The author's hope is that her book will make people
more familiar, not only with the names, views, and music of these
musicians, but also with what she holds to be a conspiracy against
them on the part of the media. As usual with this writer, there is
excellent interview material. The first chapters contain portraits
of great '60s innovators--Coltrane, Taylor, Coleman, Sun Ra, Ayler--
seen mainly through the eyes of their contemporaries. These are
followed by an account of the co-operative AACM (Muhal Richard
Abrams, et al.). Part 2 presents brief biographies of some '70 musicians, including Earl Cross, Art Lewis, Frank Lowe, and Leroy
Jenkins, and Part 3 salutes the central importance of the drummer
in modern jazz with portraits of Elvin Jones, Sunny Murray, Milford
Graves, and Ed Blackwell. The quasi-religious dedication of these
musicians to their "furnishing ideology" (p. 194) has its dangers for
personal relationships, as is shown in a section on women's role in
jazz, which also considers the obstacles to black women musicians.
The "conspiracy" theory, and the musicians' attempts to establish
their own outlets, are outlined in Part 5. Brief biographies of over
150 musicians appear at the end of the book, with a bibliography of
books, a list of journals, and a name index. The lack of a discography is unfortunate, and reinforces one's disappointment at the
book's reluctance seriously to consider the music itself.

                        5. Regions

                  (See also H.3.b.(ii))

S.726.   HESTER, Mary Lee. Going to Kansas City. Sherman, Tex.:
         Early Bird Press, 1980. 197p. illus.
    Based on interviews conducted in the 1970s, with musicians
closely identified with jazz in the "Heavenly City" in its heyday as a
preeminent jazz center, these are anecdotal portraits and self-
portraits that reveal the great degree of estimation in which most of
these musicians held and hold each other. Among those whose recollections are prominent are Jay McShann, Buster Smith, Eddie Durham,
Jo Jones, Stuff Smith, Joe Turner, Budd Johnson, Gene Ramey,
Buck Clayton, and Count Basie. Besides recalling and extolling

each other they also remember Lester Young, Charlie Parker, Herschell Evans, Walter Page, Hot Lips Page and Charlie Christian. The text would have benefitted from an editorial hand--it reads awkwardly at times--but the effect of the anecdotes is to reveal a jazz community with an almost familial intimacy and fellow-feeling. No index, but effective line drawings by the author's husband, Don Hester. (The Kaycee community is tellingly portrayed in the highly recommended documentary film, The Last of the Blue Devils.)

S.727. SCHAFER, William J. Brass Bands and New Orleans Jazz; with assistance from Richard B. Allen. Baton Rouge: Louisiana State University Press, 1977. 134p. illus., bibliog., discog.

A "gene pool" for jazz is how Schafer describes the New Orleans brass band (p. 8). His fine historical study makes clear how much of a contribution the band tradition made to jazz. But his aim is not to demonstrate linear influence; his target is to explore the "vortex where ... two rivers of American music meet"--the band tradition and the black heritage--"and thereby discover the unique art of the New Orleans Street bands" (p. 7). The book's main achievement is to reveal the rich tradition of the city's black brass bands--their early history, their characteristic playing styles, their repertoire, their musicians--and to show how the relationship between brass bands and jazz was a symbiotic one, "two musics coexisting and mingling, never quite merging" (p. 50) (a perennial chracteristic of New Orleans music, he might have added). The context of performance is particularly important, and Schafer focuses particularly on the funeral parade (Chapter 3, "Garlands of Flowers"). Here the combination of elements of ritual, music, theater and religion is seen as a rich expression of black culture. An appendix contains the facsimile reprint of the parts for a favorite brass band piece, "Fallen Heroes," by George Southwell, with brief musical comment. Additional material includes a roster of brass bands, a microgroove discography, a bibliography of books and articles, endnotes and index.

S.728. SCHIEDT, Duncan. The Jazz State of Indiana. Pittsboro, Ind.: the author, 1977. 256p. illus.

"Rather than jazz having issued solely from a Louisiana cornucopia, it in fact had innumerable wellsprings" (p. 150); Schiedt's valuable contribution to jazz historiography is a conscious attempt (following on from the work of Franklin Driggs and Ross Russell on Kansas City, and preceding Tom Stoddard's research on the West Coast) to draw attention to other, less fashionable centers than New Orleans in the rise of jazz, in particular to counterbalance the "regrettable neglect of this state [i.e., Indiana] in the jazz histories thus far written" (p. v). Indiana was important for its development of a distinctive style, which it achieved by interpreting music from elsewhere. The style in question is "Midwestern" and the time is the 1910s and '20s, before a Chicago style emerged. The significance of Schiedt's study is the evidence it provides for the contributions of a variety of ethnic groups in the fashioning and disseminating of the music.

Following an account of the "Hoosier heritage" (popular music in Indiana at the turn of the century) and of the "faint stirrings" in the 1910s, the author concentrates on aspects of jazz in the 1920s: profiles of Indiana musicians (Red Nichols, Jim Riley, Emil Seidel, Hoagy Carmichael, Speed Webb, etc.); a short discussion of the rise of the arranger; description of two prominent bands (The Royal Peacocks and the band led by Charlie Davis); the role of the campus bands; the continuing black tradition of the state in the late '20s with Leroy Carr, Slide Hampton and others. There is also a "scrapbook" of other places and people, and an index.

S.729. WEINBERG, Barbara. Jazz Space Detroit: photographs of black music, jazz and dance; text by Herb Boyd. Detroit: Jazz Research Institute, 1980. 64p. illus.

An impressive photo-record of the revitalized Detroit jazz scene of the 1970s; most of Barbara Weinberg's monochrome studies are of Detroit's "unheralded resident artists" ("for every skilled musician that left Detroit to make it elsewhere, there were dozens who stayed behind to keep the beat of jazz alive"--p. 20). The city's more illustrious jazz offspring are represented also, but without fanfare, for the book celebrates the continuing local jazz community. The accompanying text whets the appetite with just enough historical and contemporary information to make it clear that a full account--jazz space and jazz time Detroit--would be most illuminating.

6. Jazz Musicians

a. Collected Profiles

See also nos. S.698, S.699, S.702, S.703, S.721, S.723

S.730. CONVERSATIONS With Jazz Musicians. Detroit: Gale Research Co., 1977. (Conversations, 2.) 281p. illus.

Part of a series forming a wide-ranging oral history project, this volume devoted to jazz contains transcriptions of eleven interviews made by Zane Knauss, mostly in the summer of 1977. The interviewees are Louis Bellson, Leon Breeden, Dizzy Gillespie, Eric Kloss, Jimmy McPartland, Barry Miles, Sy Oliver, Charlie Spivak, Billy Taylor, Phil Woods and Sol Yaged.

S.731. GLEASON, Ralph J. Celebrating the Duke; and Louis, Bessie, Billie, Bird, Carmen, Miles, Dizzy and other heroes; preface by Studs Terkel. Boston: Little, Brown, 1975. 280p. illus., discog.

Many of the more perceptive jazz critics lack one basic gift: the ability to convey enthusiasm. Gleason's strength, developed over the years in the limited space allowed for liner notes, and for concert and record reviews, lies precisely here, not in any pretense at analysis. This collection of his pieces from 1952-1974 (he died in 1975) also displays his own close involvement with the music (he was personally acquainted with a large number of those he writes about) and his emotional investment in it. Following an essay on "Jazz: Black Art/American Art," there are portraits of Bessie Smith, Louis Armstrong, Jimmie Lunceford, Billie Holiday, Lester Young, Charlie Parker, Dizzy Gillespie, John Lewis and the MJQ, Carmen McRae, John Coltrane, Miles Davis, and Albert Ayler. Part 3 is a longer tribute to Duke Ellington, consisting mainly of a "ducal calendar," a chronologically arranged series of pieces follow- ing Ellington's progress from 1952 to 1974. Index. (Formerly LOAM A205.)

S.732. HENTOFF, Nat. Jazz Is. New York: Random House, 1976. 288p. illus., bibliog., discog.
     A series of personal portraits of major jazz musicians: Ellington, Holiday, Armstrong, Wilson, Mulligan, Davis, Mingus, Parker, Coltrane, Cecil Taylor, and Gato Barbieri. Hentoff's long involvement with jazz lends authority to the "inside" aspects of his profiles, as he seeks "to understand the intertwining of lives and sounds, of personal styles and musical styles, of societal dynamics and jazz dynamics" (p. 9). The hallmarks of Hentoff's approach are his sensitivity to political and social issues, coupled with his readiness to explore and often accept new developments in jazz which have stranded many other critics of his vintage. The potency of this mix is often undermined, however, by his journalistic style (see, for example, the other piece in the collection, on "the political econo- my of jazz"). Index.

S.733. HODES, Art, and HANSEN, Chadwick, eds. Selections from the Gutter: jazz portraits from "The Jazz Record". Berkeley: University of California Press, 1977. 233p. illus.
     Pianist Art Hodes and writer Dale Curran started The Jazz Record in New York in 1943. The only regular jazz magazine at the time, it continued until November, 1947 an amalgam of news, collec- tors' information, and pieces about musicians. The 78 short articles in this anthology represent, in Hansen's words, "an impressive com- posite portrait of the traditional jazz musician in the forties" (pref- ace). The magazine's great contribution was not so much its bio- graphical sketches, valuable though some of these are, as its cross- section of autobiographies of both black and white musicians, given orally to Curran and Hodes. Among the musicians whose recollec- tions are featured are Cow Cow Davenport, Big Bill Broonzy, Baby Dodds, George Lewis, and Jim Robinson; those of Mezz Mezzrow, Zutty Singleton, Kaiser Marshall, and George Wettling mainly concern other musicians. Hodes himself wrote several autobiographical pieces, and these are collected together as Part I, and form a vivid account of the jazz life in Chicago and New York from the 1920s. Part 2 is devoted to blues, boogie-woogie and ragtime, and includes pieces on Bessie Smith and Scott Joplin. Part 3 concerns New Orleans musicians

(Oliver, Armstrong, Morton, etc.). Part 4, "The Second Line," features the "next generation" (all white, and including Eddie Lang and Max Kaminsky), and Part 5 is a miscellany, with appearances by Hugues Panassié, Fats Waller, James P. Johnson, Lester Young and Bob Wilber. The usefulness of the book for reference is impaired by the lack of an index--an omission such a prestigious press should be ashamed of.

S.734.   JAZZ GUITARISTS: collected interviews from Guitar Player
          Magazine. Saratoga, N.Y.: Guitar Player Books, 1975.
          118p. illus.
          Interviews with 37 jazz guitarists, originally published in
Guitar Player Magazine between June 1969 and February 1975.
Leonard Feather provides an introduction. Index.

S.735.   ULLMAN, Michael. Jazz Lives: portrait in words and pic-
          tures. Washington, D.C.: New Republic Books, 1980.
          244p. illus., discog.
          The play on words in the title is significant: jazz lives
in the late 1970s because musicians such as those Ullman portrays,
representing a variety of styles, have lived their lives in many ways
as "innovative responses" (p. 7) to the peculiar conditions in which
jazz is produced and consumed. An interesting theme, but the format
of the book--23 portraits of individuals, some previously published--
does not allow its development, only its reiteration. Nineteen of the
portraits are of musicians: Joe Venuti, Doc Cheatham, Earl Hines
and Dizzy Gillespie (a joint chapter), Neal Hefti, Marian McPartland,
Sonny Rollins, Betty Carter, Horace Silver, Dexter Gordon, Tommy
Flanagan, Rahsaan Roland Kirk, Sam Rivers, Ken McIntyre, Karl
Berger, Ran Blake, Ray Mantilla, Anthony Braxton, and Charles
Mingus. The others are Maxwell Cohen (the New York lawyer who
fought the cabaret card system), artists' manager Maxine Gregg, and
producers John Snyder and Steve Backer.

b. Individuals

     Note: for discographies of individual musicians, see H.2,c

COUNT BASIE

S.736.   DANCE, Stanley. The World of Count Basie. New York:
          Scribner's; London: Sidgwick & Jackson, 1980. 399p.
          illus., bibliog., discog.
          The underlying premise of the biographer--that it is pos-
sible to single out one person from the crowd and make it seem, for
a while, as if the world revolves around him or her--is refreshingly
absent in Dance's "World of ..." series (see also LOAM 1040 & 1106,
and, to a lesser extent, no. S.753), which, taken together, begin to
point the way towards possible new directions for jazz historiography.
Basically a series of interviews with 34 musicians (Part 1 is centered

around Basie, Part 2 around the other mainstay of Kansas City jazz,
Jay McShann), this particular volume avoids one single chronology
and instead allows an intricate portrait to emerge of the complex interplay between musicians, on social and musical levels, characteristic
of the broad community formed by the bands (and, for that matter,
of the wider one of jazz as a whole). Basie and McShann are the
pivotal figures, to be sure, but, as the 25-page index demonstrates,
the real subject is the nature of the network of performers who make
up this "world." Included in the appendices are some Basie itiner-
aries, selected LP discographies of the Basie band and of 27 other
(including Jimmy Rushing, Lester Young, Buck Clayton, Buddy Tate,
and Jay McShann), and a four-page bibliography of books and articles.

SIDNEY BECHET

S.737. BECHET, Sidney. Treat It Gentle: an autobiography.
        London: Cassell; New York: Hill & Wang, 1960; London:
        Jazz Book Club, 1962; London: Transworld, 1964. 245p.
        illus., discog.
        _____. _____; with a new preface by Rudi Blesh.
        New York: Da Capo, 1978. 245p. illus., discog.
        Readers of jazz autobiographies tend to devour the jazz doc-
umentation they contain and to take the "story of self" with a large
pinch of salt. In the case of Bechet's remarkable book we need to
reverse the process. As an objective documentary source it is useful, particularly on New Orleans, but must be used with care; as an
account of a black musician's search within himself and his heritage
for what his music is expressive of and why, it is unrivaled. Here
jazz autobiography is no longer jazz history told in the first person,
but an attempt by a musician to explain himself by reference to his
culture; in Bechet's words, to understand "the part of me that was
there before I was. It was there waiting to be me. It was there
waiting to be the music" (p. 4).
        Bechet (1897?-1959) was persuaded to record his reminis-
cences in Paris in the early 1950s by Joan Reid; after the initial
work, editing passed to Desmond Flower and John Ciardi. In the
late '50s, at Flower's instigation, Bechet, though now ill, recorded
further material for the post-1936 period of his life; he wanted to
add to this, and was aware of its sketchy nature, but was unable
to do so. The editors appear to have been most careful to preserve
the style and spirit of Bechet's oral narrative. It is an approach
unique among jazz musicians for its gifts of metaphor and parable,
its poetry, and its mythic qualities, all of which are used to great
effect in the search for insights and explanations. Particularly
striking is the story of Omar, the murdered slave who was Bechet's
paternal grandfather. Omar becomes a symbol of the genesis of the
music in the folk memory ("It was Omar started the song ... the
good musicianers, they all heard it behind them. They all had an
Omar..."--p. 202). Bechet's account of his life moves from the New
Orleans of his birth through his first trip to Europe (with Will

Marion Cook's Southern Syncopated Orchestra), his career in the
1920s and '30s, to his return to France ("closer to Africa"), where
he settled permanently in 1950. Many musicians are mentioned, in
various lights, notably Louis Armstrong, Buddy Bolden, Bunk Johnson, Freddie Keppard, Tommy Ladnier, Manuel Perez, Noble Sissle,
and Clarence Williams. But Bechet's central concern remains the
search for meaning, not in factual linear chronicle, but, as in the
blues, in a consciousness in which past and present are one, and
in which the music mediates between man and the world. The discography is a full chronological listing, with record numbers but
without personnel. Index.

S.738.   HIPPENMEYER, Jean-Roland. Sidney Bechet, ou l'extraor-
          dinaire odyssée d'un musicien de jazz. Geneva: Tribune
          Editions, 1980. 237p. illus., bibliog., discog.
    Researched with the kind of devotion that Bechet continues
to inspire, this is not so much a biography as a detailed diary of
Bechet's life and career. The narrative, replete with dates, names,
places, titles, is written with an engagingly light touch and incorporates many revealing comments from Bechet's contemporaries at appropriate moments. Additional material includes a filmography, a
discography of available LP reissues, and a bibliography of sources.
No less interesting than the main text are the "témoignages et anecdotes" gathered together at the end of the book; these are further
comments, reflections, opinions on aspects of Bechet's life and career
by people who knew or encountered him. An unusual book; Hippen-
mayer clearly had the material for a full study but chose to present
it otherwise, and in so doing provided a rich fund of material for
future biographies. No index.

BUDDY BOLDEN

S.739.   MARQUIS, Donald M. Finding Buddy Bolden, First Man of
          Jazz: the journal of a search. Goshen, Ind.: Pinch-
          penny Press, Goshen College, 1978. 81p. illus.
    A revealing insight into the painstaking detective work re-
quired in the writing of jazz biography. This is the journal of an
eighteen-month period, from July 1970 through December 1971, in
Marquis' researches for his Bolden biography (no. S.740). It also
contains an account of finding a publisher, and of putting the book
together to go to press, plus some concluding reflections on the whole
project.

S.740.   MARQUIS, Donald M. In Search of Buddy Bolden, First Man
          of Jazz. Baton Rouge: Louisiana State University Press,
          1978. (Repr. New York: Da Capo, [1980?].) 176p.
          illus., bibliog.
    During research for this biography (possibly the least ex-
pected of all unlikely items in the jazz library) Marquis says, "numerous dead-ends ... led me to believe that other jazz historians were
smarter than I; they knew a book on Bolden was impossible" (no.

S.739, p. 6). But the final product is a vindication of his efforts: here is the plain, unadorned but now well-documented story of Bolden (1877-1931), his family history, early life and schooling, musical influences, life as a musician in New Orleans, demise, institutionalization in 1907 and death 24 years later. Numerous pieces of jazz lore are shown to be erroneous, but Bolden retains his importance as a jazz pioneer, and the context in which he performed (the dance-halls, his contemporaries) is clearly indicated. In his attempt to describe "how and what [Bolden] played" Marquis accepts the judgement that "his sound was unique and affected people deeply" (p. 99). If there is something lacking it is that complementary side to the historian's duty to demythologize, which is to understand why the legend existed in the first place, what need it was felt to satisfy. Factual accuracy is important, but is only one part of history. The bibliography includes all the primary sources consulted and interviews conducted. Index.

CAB CALLOWAY

S.741.   CALLOWAY, Cab, and ROLLINS, Bryant. Of Minnie the Moocher and Me; with illustrations selected and edited by John Shearer. New York: Crowell, 1976. 282p. illus.

Calloway's most famous hi-de-ho song is an appropriate title for his autobiography, for it epitomizes the unceasing desire to entertain which permeated his career. George T. Simon's description of him as "an extremely alert, appreciative and articulate man, full of wit and good humor" (LOAM 1045, p. 112) is ratified, but is only part of the picture. Calloway's account of his career from childhood (b.1907) and youth in Rochester and Baltimore, through apprenticeship in Chicago and New York, to his big break at the Cotton Club in 1930 and subsequent career as bandleader, vocalist, and musical theater actor, is bright, entertaining, honest oral history, critical and generous as the occasion demands; it is also a tribute to one ideal he holds above all others: professionalism.   Other views of Cab besides his own are incorporated in the form of recollections by musicians Milt Hinton and Benny Payne, and by members of his family.   His fame as a master of jive talk is commemorated in a reprint, included at the back of the book, of the text of the 1944 edition of The New Cab Calloway's Hepsters Dictionary, and of Prof. Cab Calloway's Swingformation Bureau, a tongue-in-cheek quiz published in 1939.   No index.

JOHN COLTRANE

S.742.   COLE, Bill. John Coltrane. New York: Schirmer; London: Collier Macmillan, 1976. 264p. illus., bibliog., discog.

Based (somewhat loosely, one imagines) on a doctoral dissertation (Wesleyan University, 1975), this is a musical biography, tracing the evolution of Coltrane's style and sound, and--most important--the religious philosophy they embody.   Though he

effectively analyzes many individual pieces (using music examples
drawn from the transcriptions of Andrew White), Cole is adamant
that such an endeavor by itself is an empty exercise ("to understand Trane ... it is necessary to recognize ... that behind his art
was his philosophy, and that this philosophy determined everything
he did and how he did it"--p. 10). The key to understanding is
in "the way of life of the traditional African, that is, the traditional
man" (p. 13). To interpret this, Cole draws heavily on the ideas
of Fela Sowande, particularly the latter's The Role of Music in African Society (Washington, D.C., 1969), important ideas which, however, are never wholly convincingly integrated and developed, but
tend to become decorative. There is also an overall patchiness
about the book, which is not helped by frequent personal digres-
sions. Index.

S.743.   SIMPKINS, Cuthbert Ormond. Coltrane: a biography.
         Perth Amboy, N.J.: Herndon House, 1975. 287p.
         illus., bibliog. refs.
         Few writers have appeared who can write dispassionately
about Coltrane (1926-1967). Simpkins is not one of them, but his
profound sympathy with his subject's music and with his emotional
and spiritual intensity enables him to portray both the gentle, private man and the fervent, obsessed musician convincingly as integral parts of the whole. Biographical information came from many
sources, oral (the acknowledgments list a hundred names, mostly
musicians) and printed, and is amplified by frequent quotations
from contemporary reviews, which permit the reader to glimpse
Coltrane's long hard road to any kind of acceptance. The story is
not dramatic--any drama ceases as Coltrane conquers drugs and
drink in the mid-1950s, but even before that the joint theme of musical and spiritual quest is emerging as the dominant one. Ambitiously, Simpkins attempts to capture both Coltrane's spiritual beliefs and something of the nature of his music in his prose (aided
by poetic interpolations); this makes it difficult for him to account
for either, though some theoretical comments on music are offered.
The appendices, however, contain some meatier analyses in the form
of reprinted articles by Zito Carno and others. Also included are
facsimiles of pages from Coltrane's workbook. No index. (Formerly
LOAM A220.)

MILES DAVIS

S.744.   KERSCHBAUMER, Franz. Miles Davis: stilkritische Unter-
         suchungen zur musikalischen Entwicklung seines Perso-
         nalstils. Graz: Akademische Druck u. Verlagsanstalt,
         1978. (Beiträge zur Jazzforschung, 5.) 238p. bibliog.,
         discog.
         A detailed musicological analysis of the development of
Miles Davis' style. The author divides the period 1945-1968 into
five chronological sections: bebop, cool jazz, mainstream (East
Coast), hard bop, and modal style, with a briefer overview of the

period 1968-1975 as a conclusion. Each of the main chapters follows the same pattern: general historical summary of the particular style; "musical" biography of Davis for this period; musical analysis (of repertoire, form, and themes; of instrumentation, arrangement, and sound; of the rhythm sections; of tonality; of the structure of im- provised solos, with comparisons between choruses); influence from and on other musicians of the period; summary. The longest of these sections--analysis of specific solos--are supported by 55 trans- criptions in the back of the book. There are also sonagraphic analyses, which mark a pioneering attempt to pin down rhythmic nuances characteristic of the different periods. The discography is a supplement to J. G. Jepsen's 1969 work (LOAM 944).

DUKE ELLINGTON

S.745.   ELLINGTON, Mercer. Duke Ellington in Person: an inti- mate memoir; with Stanley Dance. Boston: Houghton Mifflin; London: Hutchinson, 1978. 236p. illus.
     Though sometimes anecdotal, this is a highly interesting and illuminating portrait of Ellington by his son, who seems to get closer to the true man and musician than any other biographer. Many passages are full of insights, whether on aspects of the music, on the complexities of his character, on his relationships with mu- sicians, with women, with his family (those with Mercer were no- toriously fraught--the son admits to having felt hate as well as love) --insights of the kind only someone so close could have, but which people in similar situations seem rarely to express. Because of Mercer's virtually uninterrupted association with his father, the "in- timacy" of the title is fully justified; what makes the book unusual is that, because the association was in part a professional one, this intimacy extends to all areas of Ellington's ideas, life and career. It is a wide-ranging description of the man and his music, viewing him, as it were, from the inside out (public reception of Ellington and his music is present, but seen as Ellington himself would have seen it). One of the appendices lists the compositions omitted from the listing in Ellington's own Music Is My Mistress (LOAM 1105).

S.746.   JEWELL, Derek. Duke: a portrait of Duke Ellington. Lon- don: Elm Tree Books, 1977. 192p. illus., discog., bibliog.
     _____.   _____. Rev. ed. London: Sphere Books, 1978. 302p. illus., bibliog.
     Jewell, a British journalist who knew Ellington relatively well in the last decade or so of his life, declares his book "does not pretend" to be a definitive biography ("There will never be a definitive biography of Duke," he declares, categorically), but "simply his story written with affection and an attempt at under- standing" (p. 5). A readable, informative, if unchallenging por- trait, it lives up to this modest description; the most successful part is the account of the 1960s and '70s, to Duke's death in 1974 (the account of his early years is very thin--40 years covered in

under 40 pages). Critical comments on music are generally unmem-
orable, but the complexity of Ellington's character--or, at least, the
variety of veils with which he mystified all questioners--is clear.
The main drawback to the book is a weakness it shares with much
transatlantic jazz criticism: too much reliance on second-hand
sources (Jewell's failure to acknowledge his sources merely compounds
this), and an absence of any real sense of time, place or culture. The
discography is a selective list of albums; the "bibliography" merely
a list of six previous books on Ellington. Index.

HERB FLEMMING

S.747.   BIAGIONI, Egino. Herb Flemming: a jazz pioneer around
         the world. Alphen aan de Rijn: Micrography, 1977.
         90p. illus., discog.
         Biography of the trombomist and vocalist who was born in
Montana (ca. 1898) of Tunisian and Egyptian parents and whose recording career spanned 50 years, 1919-1969. Biagioni makes use of
unpublished autobiographical material left by Flemming on his death
in 1976. This tells of his travels with Sam Wooding, his experiences
in Europe, including Russia, his time in nightclub and theater pit
orchestras, his recordings with Fats Waller, Duke Ellington and
others. Flemming also comments frequently on the status of black
musicians.

BUD FREEMAN

S.748.   FREEMAN, Bud. You Don't Look Like a Musician. Detroit:
         Balamp Publishing, 1974. 125p.
         _____. If You Know of a Better Life! Please Tell Me.
         Dublin: Bashall Eaves, (1976?). 61p.
         Tenor saxophonist Bud Freeman (b.1906) "hadn't the moti-
vation to write a post-card" before he began the first of these
books, "although I have always been a story-teller" (preface to If
You Know of a Better Life!). His particular speciality as a racon-
teur is the short, funny anecdote (which would, it turns out, have
been well suited to the back of a post-card). For these two entertaining, if somewhat chaotic, collections he feeds us story after
story of fellow musicians (especially of his contemporaries from the
Chicago scene) and of his own experiences. The first book, much
more substantial, offers occasional time for reflection; it also has an
index.

DIZZY GILLESPIE

S.749.   GILLESPIE, Dizzy. To Be, Or Not ... To BOP: memoirs;
         with Al Fraser. Garden City, N.Y.: Doubleday, 1979.
         552p. illus., discog.
         _____. Dizzy: the autobiography of Dizzy Gillespie;
         with Al Fraser. London: W. H. Allen, 1980. 552p.
         illus., discog.
         This most ambitious of jazz autobiographies--product of a

five-year endeavor to create "the most complete, authentic, and authoritative autobiography of a jazz musician ever published" (preface)--is also the most diffuse, but in some ways the most singular. Gillespie's own narrative provides the central framework: a detailed, vivacious, only occasionally vainglorious account of his life and career, in which he frequently reveals a sharp, perceptive eye and keen memory, especially for changes in music and in its performance context. Cut into this lengthy chronological record at regular intervals are the recollections, obtained from interview, of a hundred or so acquaintances (150 were interviewed in all)--family members, friends, and, in particular, musicians, whose contributions range from the laconic to the loquacious. Though tighter editing would have much improved the result, this oral history technique offers a many-sided portrait of the book's subject, critical at times, laudatory at others, of a kind unusual in music autobiography. It also provides an excellent profile of an era and a way of life (be-bop), seen through the eyes of some of the main protagonists. Among the musicians who make contributions, the most frequently quoted are Milton Hinton, Budd Johnson, Max Roach, and arranger Walter Gilbert Fuller. A chronology of Gillespie's life, from his birth in South Carolina in 1917, up to his White House concert in 1978, precedes the text. The discography is a selected list of important recordings, intended to indicate Gillespie's development and innovations. There is also a filmography and an index.

BABS GONZALES

S.750. GONZALES, Babs. "Movin' On Down de Line". Newark, N.J.: Expubidence Pub. Corp., 1975. 143p. illus.
     Continuing in the same vein as I Paid My Dues (LOAM 1113), these are further vivid, if random, recollections of and outspoken comments on the music business, especially the drug scene, the shysters and other hangers-on. Many encounters with racism are a notable feature.

CONNIE HAINES

S.751. HAINES, Connie. For Once in My Life; as told to Robert B. Stone. New York: Warner Books, 1976. 223p. illus.
     Haines (b.1922) was a diminutive but dynamic singer with various big bands (Harry James, Tommy Dorsey, etc.); she was frequently heard on the radio in the mid-1940s, made more than one movie, had more than one sad marriage, and knew Frank Sinatra, Red Skelton, Lana Turner and others among the Hollywood famous. Later she turned to gospel songs, singing with Jane Russell and others, and, as this autobiography was written, was an ordained minister of the Unity Church. Her book scarcely lives up to her erstwhile talents; reams of recreated dialogue and an "inspirational" story line give it an air of upright soap opera.

HAMPTON HAWES

S.752.   HAWES, Hampton, and ASHER, Don.   Raise Up Off Me: a
         portrait of Hampton Hawes.   New York: Coward, McCann
         and Geoghegan, 1974.   179p.
         _____.   _____; new introduction by Gary Giddins.
         New York: Da Capo, 1979.   179p.
         Stunningly powerful autobiography by the Los Angeles-born
bebop pianist.   Hawes (1928-1977) provides us with probably the
most telling book on bebop--a disarmingly frank, unsentimental,
sometimes bitter story of the jazz life in an era ravaged by narcotics.
It is also, astonishingly, one of the funniest books on jazz.   With
skilled editing by Asher, Hawes tells his tale in a colorful colloquial
style that is remarkable for the vividness of its cameo portraits of
great musicians (Parker, Gray, Monk, and two short but exquisite
glimpses of Billie Holiday), and for the almost irrepressible powers
of observation, which only seem to decline as he tells how, pardoned
by President Kennedy and released from a jail sentence five years early, he struggled to make a comeback in the changed world of the 1960s.

EARL HINES

S.753.   DANCE, Stanley.   The World of Earl Hines.   New York:
         Scribner's, 1977.   324p.   illus., bibliog., discog.
         The taped recollections of Earl Hines (1905-1983) form the
largest single element in what is essentially a joint portrait, of
Hines himself and of the Chicago jazz scene in the 1920s and '30s.
Hines' autobiography runs to 120 pages.   A richly anecdotal, world-
ly account of his life from his childhood in Duquesne, Pennsylvania,
up to 1976, it dwells on the tapestry of life in Chicago jazz clubs,
especially the Sunset Cafe and the Grand Terrace.   A strict sense
of chronology is refreshingly absent (Dance provides an exact
chronology in an appendix) as innumerable fellow musicians cross
the stage and are almost invariably remembered with generosity.
The remainder of the book consists of more oral history, in the form
of the recollections of 21 musicians who worked with Hines and knew
the Chicago scene well.   The longest are those of Lois Deppe (whom
Hines knew from childhood), Charlie Carpenter and Budd Johnson.
Finely illustrated, the book also contains a short list of articles, a
representative LP discography, and an index.   (For general comments
on Dance's approach, see no. S.736.)

BUNK JOHNSON

S.754.   SONNIER, Austin M.   Willie Greary "Bunk" Johnson: the
         New Iberia years.   New York: Crescendo Publishing,
         1977.   81p.   illus., discog.
         The first part of this short but interesting volume contains
a brief biography of trumpeter Bunk Johnson (1880-1949), and a
discography of the recordings made in the 1940s, after his rediscovery.   Part 2 is devoted to the musicians of the New Iberia area
in the period 1900-1930 (Bunk lived and worked there from 1920,

and it remained his home after the "rebirth" of his career in 1942).
In addition to a list of sixteen bands, with their personnel, there
are biographical sketches of 47 musicians. The text is well illustrated with 49 photographs, those of the New Iberia musicians being
especially interesting. Transcriptions of two Bunk solos ("Milenberg
Joys," and "I Can't Escape From You") conclude the book.

J. J. JOHNSON

S.755.   BAKER, David. J. J. Johnson, Trombone. New York:
          Hansen House, 1979. (Jazz Monograph Series.)   68p.
          bibliog., discog.
          Aimed principally, but not exclusively, at the jazz perform-
er, this monograph series is designed as a "modus operandi for
studying, analyzing, imitating and assimilating" the styles of jazz
masters. Besides transcriptions there are samples of work sheets on
which the various facets of a player's style can be mapped out.
Brief biographical, critical, bibliographical and discographical information is also included.

STAN KENTON

S.756.   EASTON, Carol. Straight Ahead: the story of Stan Ken-
          ton. New York: Morrow, 1973. (Repr. New York: Da
          Capo, n.d.) 252p. illus.
          An admiring, but not overly reverential biography of the
bandleader, whose bands were notable (or notorious) for their full,
brassy sound, for the enormous, controlling contributions of their
arrangers, and their relative lack of swing and of distinctive solo
quality. Kenton's public life (twelve bands, 30 years on the road)
and its private, equally varied counterpoint (three wives, many
analysts) are described with a verve which prevents the portrait of
the complex, obsessional character becoming pretentious. Frequent
use of quoted material (from musicians, wives, children, etc.) contributes to a many-sided portrait; but the problematic question of
his reactionary social and racial views is unsatisfactorily handled
(being attributed to the innate contradictions of Waspishness). Perhaps the most striking thing to emerge from the book is that, in its
interminable cycle of band formation-touring-disbanding, the Kenton
outfit remained fundamentally uninterested in most of the rest of
jazz; it already had an all-consuming interest: itself.

S.757.   LEE, William F. Stan Kenton: artistry in rhythm; edited
          by Audree Coke. Los Angeles: Creative Press of Los
          Angeles, 1980. 727p. illus., bibliog., discog.
          Massive "official" biography of Kenton's career up to his
death in 1979, incorporating a huge amount of documentation in the
form of excerpts from the daily and music press at home and abroad,
and the recollections of friends, colleagues, members of the band,
fans, etc. The biographer himself assumes the role of coordinator,
offering linking narrative between these two basic types of information.

An unusual, worthwhile enterprise, made unfortunately hard to as-similate by the extremely one-sided, repetitious, undigested nature of much of the material; the book would have profited greatly from some negative opinions, and a much stronger editorial hand. There is also a dearth of purely musical information. The 150-old pages of appendices provide a list of band personnel, a filmography, a title listing, with dates, of Kenton's compositions and arrangements, a catalog of the recordings on Kenton's Creative World label, and a chronological discography of studio and live sessions, with details of location, date, titles, matrix and label numbers (but no person-nel). Index.

GEORGE LEWIS

S.758.   BETHELL, Tom.   George Lewis: a jazzman from New Or-
            leans.   Berkeley: University of California Press, 1977.
            387p.   illus., bibliog., discog.
         Painstakingly detailed, dispassionate biography of clarinet-tist George Lewis (1900-1968), based on original interviews conducted in 1966-76 (including six with Lewis), on the Tulane University ar-chival tapes, and on William Russell's unpublished New Orleans diaries and notebooks from 1942-49.   Besides Lewis himself, there are prominent appearances by numerous New Orleans musicians, es-pecially Bunk Johnson, Baby Dodds, Lawrence Marrero, Slow Drag Pavageau, and Jim Robinson.   The book's generally low-key approach is partly in deference to scholarship, no doubt, but is also due to Lewis' profound personal reserve ("it was always understood that the book would be about him, but not in any personal way"--p. 2). Lurking beneath the intricate but tidy surface, however, is a "re-visionist thesis" concerning the origins of jazz, according to which jazz is not an Afro-American form of music at all.   Denying all no-tions of cultural retention by black Americans, Bethell prefers a "simpler" solution: jazz was pioneered by blacks solely because it offered one of the few openings they were not obstructed from pur-suing.   These and similar at best contentious statements are not adequately explained, but their tenor is clear enough.   One is struck above all by the dismissive attitude towards the long, complex debate in the USA over the origins of black culture, and by the (British empirical?) intolerance of any idea that black artistic con-sciousness might be multi-layered and not at all susceptible to "simple" solutions.
         In reality, the book contains little evidence of this pre-liminary theorizing; one other claim, that New Orleans jazz continued to develop stylistically, is pursued, though perhaps not conclusively. But there is much of value in the biographical and historical detail, supported by accurate documentation and accessible via a good index.

GUY LOMBARDO

S.759.   LOMBARDO, Guy.   Auld Acquaintance; with Jack Altschul;
            introduction by Jules Stein.   Garden City, N.Y.:

Doubleday, 1975. 295p. illus.

"It is difficult to write with any objectivity on the Guy Lombardo band," wrote Albert McCarthy in 1971, "for it has become an institution and somehow criticism seems an irrelevance" (LOAM 1043, p. 64). The band's huge, and longlasting popularity has been a periodic affront to critics--especially jazz critics--many of whom did not feel as constrained as McCarthy; some tempered their wrath with humor, as did George T. Simon: "... [it is] a wonderful band to talk to. It never plays so loudly that you've got to say 'what?' ... If you catch it at dinner sessions you can even hear a mashed potato drop" (LOAM 1045, p. 321). Most galling of all to critics and jazz lovers has been Lombardo's loyal following among jazz musicians, most celebrated among whom was Louis Armstrong. According to James Lincoln Collier, the respect was mutual (Louis Armstrong [New York: Oxford University Press, 1983], p. 219). Lombardo's own, ghosted account has few troubles with objectivity, but is a dignified affair, telling of the band's Cleveland debut in 1924, the breakthrough in Chicago in 1927, and subsequent successful career. Above all, it is a family story: four brothers from Ontario--Guy (1912-1977), the eldest, Carmen, Lebert, and Victor--of whom Carmen (1903-1971) emerges as the most interesting and versatile--saxophonist, vocalist, and songwriter.

S.760.   CLINE, Beverly Fink. The Lombardo Story. Don Mills, Ontario: Musson, 1979. 158p. illus., discog.

A conscientious biography, with little speculation about motivations, and no unflattering details. The author clearly read much background material and conducted extensive interviews. The main text concludes with a transcript of an interview with Bill Lombardo, Guy's nephew, who conducted the band after his uncle died. There is no dialogue, thankfully, anywhere. The useful appendices contain lists of Carmen and Guy Lombardo's songs, assembled by Dave Kressley and Dick Scher, and a discography of Lombardo record albums available at the time of writing. (An earlier biography is The Sweetest Music This Side of Heaven, by Booton Herndon [New York: McGraw-Hill, 1964].)

McKINNEY'S COTTON PICKERS

S.761.   CHILTON, John. McKinney's Music: a bio-discography of McKinney's Cotton Pickers. London: Bloomsbury Book Shop, 1978. 68p. illus., bibliog. refs., discog.

Meticulously researched, as with all this author's work, this is a valuable factual record of an outstanding black band that has been rather overshadowed, in jazz criticism at least, by the bands of Ellington and Henderson, and yet was "the only black Territory band to achieve national fame during the 1920s" (p. 1). In his chronicle of the band's history, from its formation in 1921 through its heyday in the late 1920s under arranger Don Redman, to its decline in the 1930s and final break-up in 1938, the author draws extensively on the recollections of one of the longest-serving members of the band, guitarist and vocalist Dave Wilborn. (McKinney himself, one of the founders of the band and its manager for many years, died in 1969.) The discography includes, in addition to full details of personnel, matrix numbers, etc., the name of the arranger of each recorded item, and identification of all soloists. There is also a biographical directory of McKinney's musicians.

GLENN MILLER

S.762. SNOW, George, and GREEN, Jonathon. Glenn Miller & the
        Age of Swing. London: Dempsey & Squires, 1976.
        128p. illus., discog.
        A short but lively portrait, which sets out to provide, in roughly equal measure, both a basic biographical account of Miller's life and career, and a wider picture of the music and style of the big band era. In this Snow (who "conceived, designed and produced" the book) and Green (who wrote the text) are aided by an attractive collection of photographs. Their assessment is a balanced one, setting off Miller's many personal and professional shortcomings against his considerable arranging skill and his ability to reach and keep an audience.

JELLY ROLL MORTON

S.763. HILL, Michael, and BRYCE, Eric. Jelly Roll Morton: a
        microgroove discography and musical analysis. Salisbury
        East, South Australia: Salisbury College of Advanced
        Education, 1977. (Occasional papers, No. 16.) 37p.
        bibliog.
        The analysis (by Bryce) is of three Morton pieces: "Seattle Hunch" (piano solo), "Mr. Jelly Lord," and "Kansas City Stomps." It includes partial transcriptions and schematic diagrams. The discography (by Hill) is not a discography as such, but a two-part index (chronological and title) to Morton LP reissues. This is followed by a useful bibliography which includes a large number of articles.

DREW PAGE

S.764. PAGE, Drew. Drew's Blues: a sideman's life with the big
        bands. Baton Rouge: Louisiana State University Press,
        1980. 226p. illus.
        Though well-known and well-respected, first on the white territory band scene in the Southwest in the late 1920s and early '30s, then in the dance bands in Chicago and in the touring big bands, clarinetist Drew Page (b.1905) was never a star. This makes his autobiography unusual in jazz and dance band literature, and an interesting document for its portrait of the lifestyle (and semi-poverty) of the rank-and-file musicians of the era. His memory is crystal clear, and if the likable book rests on its accumulation of anecdotes, for once such a device seems highly appropriate. Page insists that,

for all the ups and downs, "I only regret that I didn't have all the fun there was to be had" (p. 217). Determined not to be nostalgic, he is disinclined to look for any significance in his own story, indeed finds himself "looking at these incidents quite abstractly, as though they'd happened to someone else" (ibid.). Most of the fellow musicians featured are sidemen too, though a substantial contribution comes from Harry James. Black musicians are encountered only rarely. Index.

CHARLIE PARKER

S.765.   BAKER, David. Charlie Parker, Alto Saxophone. New
          York: Hansen House, 1978. (Jazz Monograph Series.)
          71p.
          (For a description of this series, see Baker's J. J. Johnson,
Trombone--no. S.755.)

ART PEPPER

S.766.   PEPPER, Art, and PEPPER, Laurie. Straight Life: the
          story of Art Pepper; discography by Todd Selbert. New
          York: Schirmer; London: Collier Macmillan, 1979. 516p.
          illus., discog.
          A stunning performer on alto sax, Pepper (1925-1982) reveals an almost total lack of interest in thinking about music; his talent enabled him to perform "off the top"--"All I had to do was reach for it, just do it" (p. 475). Such insights as the book provides into his music comes from the interpolated contributions of other musicians which are cut--as are recollections of Pepper by friends and family, and several reviews--into the course of the narrative, and provide an effective change of angle to Pepper's own monochromatic vision. The story Pepper himself tells, as edited from tapes by his third wife, is a no-holds-barred but profoundly disquieting tale of drug addition, imprisonment (including San Quentin, 1961-66) and remorseless self-destruction. The irony of the title (a Pepper composition) as applied to Pepper's disoriented odyssey is not repeated in the text, which proceeds with an obsessive desire to set down each and every experience with as little comment or reflection as possible. Of the many questions the book makes no attempt to answer ("how could he...?" "why didn't he...?") the most perplexing is the one which asks: to what extent can the music be equated with the man? The discography is a comprehensive listing of Pepper's recordings (personnel, venues, dates, titles, release no.) from his first sessions with Stan Kenton in 1943 to his late 1970s comeback. Index.

BOB SCOBEY

S.767.   SCOBEY, Jan. He Rambled! 'Til Cancer Cut Him Down:
          Bob Scobey, Dixieland jazz musician and bandleader,
          1916-1963. Northridge, Calif.; Pal Publishing, 1976.

244p. illus., discog.

A handsome pictorial tribute to the traditional jazz trumpeter by his second wife. The book has a basic biographical structure (not always apparent), but its main focus is on the large number of interpolated quotations from Scobey's friends and fellow musicians (among them Clancy Hayes, Art Hodes, Lizzy Miles, and Bill Napier), and on the black-and-white illustrations. Quite a substantial portion of the text covers the trumpeter's last months following the diagnosis of cancer. The discography includes pictures of each LP album cover, and there is an index.

RALPH SUTTON

S.768.   SHACTER, James D. Piano Man: the story of Ralph Sutton.
Chicago: Jaynar Press, 1975. 244p. illus., discog.

Scholarly-looking but with a Waller-like sense of humor, Sutton (b.1922) commands equally varied piano styles (though he himself maintains "I'm a whorehouse piano player. Whorehouse piano swings"--p. 101). This biography is based on a series of interviews and correspondence with Sutton, his family and his associates; it tells of the early Waller influence, the first job with Teagarden, on through the pianist's time as resident pianist at Condon's 1948-56, up to his involvement with the World's Greatest Jazz Band (1969 on). Includes a varied account of a nightclub pianist's triumphs and travails. The discography contains details of commercial and private recordings, airchecks and transcriptions.

FATS WALLER

S.769.   VANCE, Joel. Fats Waller: his life and times. Chicago:
Contemporary Books, 1977. 179p. illus., bibliog.

Capturing the Waller personality in dull print is well nigh impossible (except with poetic licence, perhaps--see Eudora Welty's short story Powerhouse; even she concludes, "And who could ever remember any of the things he says? They are just inspired remarks that roll out of his mouth like smoke"); but Vance's short biographical study conveys a warm, evocative portrait, one which is also sharply aware of the various private and public contradictions. Fundamental to Vance's perception of Waller is the view that he failed to "resolve the emotional squeeze ... how to make the transition from childhood to adulthood" (p. 170) ("he was, for most of his career, a child-prodigy of teardrop-pure innocence, wrapped in a bulk of blistering and hilarious camaraderie and sensuality, but a child still"--p. 112, a passage that also serves to illustrate the author's style). Vance's interpretation, which includes comment on Waller's musical performances and his compositions, is generally astute, though it stops short of coming to terms with the basic tensions which a jazz musician of cross-over appeal like Waller best illustrates--between commodity and art, oral and literate, black and white, the possible and the perfect, own culture and catholicity, lowbrow and highbrow, corporeal and cerebral, etc., etc. Vance hints at some of these but develops no argument. Index.

S.770.   WALLER, Maurice, and CALABRESE, Anthony.   Fats Waller;
         foreword by Michael Lipskin.   New York: Schirmer,
         1977.   235p.   illus., discog.
         Waller's eldest son's knowledge of his father enables him to
create a vivid portrait of Fats in this biography.   Though demands
of "the road" constantly militated against a proper relationship, and
though awe was the young Waller's most common emotional response,
father clearly told son a lot about his life, his friendship, his attitudes, and neither the generally adoring tone of the book nor its
recreated conversations detract from its value as an accurate memoir.
         The essential story is here, told in some detail: the Vir-
ginia background of Fat's parents, his Harlem childhood, the influence and friendship of James P. Johnson and Willie "The Lion"
Smith, his relationship with Clarence Williams and Andy Razaf, his
rise from rent-shout pianist to Broadway composer, radio star, and
popular touring entertainer, his varying fortunes in the late '30s
and early '40s (e.g., his failure at Carnegie Hall in 1942), and his
death on a train in Kansas City in 1943.   Some themes stand out:
his prodigious appetites, his urge to make his music respectable,
his dislike of more low-brow musical idioms.   Like other Waller books,
however, this one fails to make clear the particular tragedy of a man
constantly pulled apart by the conflicting realities and aspirations:
can a black entertainer be an artist?   can a popular performer be
taken seriously?--characteristic of the society in which he found himself.   The excellent discography is supplemented with lists of Waller's published and unpublished compositions, and of his piano rolls.
Index.

PAUL WHITEMAN

See also no. S.713

S.771.   JOHNSON, Carl.   A Paul Whiteman Chronology (1890-1967).
         Williamstown, Mass.:   Williams College, 1977.   44p.
         illus., discog.
         _____.   Paul Whiteman: a chronology (1890-1967).
         (Rev. ed.)   Williamstown, Mass.:   Williams College,
         1979.   40p.   illus., discog.
         An outline chronology of the main events in Whiteman's life
in note form.   Set alongside the incidents relating specifically to
Whiteman (in heavy type) are notes of other contemporaneous events
in the popular music world (in lighter type)--a helpful device.   Unfortunately, despite the resources of the Whiteman Collection at Williams College, the compiler is unable to provide precise dates, all
occurrences being merely grouped by year.   Additional material includes a brief account of the Whiteman Collection, various lists (personnel, radio shows, motion pictures, etc.), concert programs, and
information on currently available Whiteman recordings.

LESTER YOUNG

S.772.   McDONOUGH, John.   Lester Young; notes on the music by

Richard M. Sudhalter. Alexandria, Va.: Time-Life
Records, 1980. 52p. illus.
For many years a book-length biographical and critical
study of Lester Young (1909-1959) was probably the most needed
item in the jazz library. This handsome booklet, written to accompany a boxed set of records in the "Giants of Jazz" series,
deserves a mention because it provides a thorough biographical outline and some illuminating comments on Young's tenor saxophone
style. (The contrast with Michael Brooks' sleeve notes for the
Columbia series, "The Lester Young Story" is very marked.) Since
the appearance of the Time-Life set Robert A. Luckey's Ph.D. thesis, A Study of Lester Young and His Influence Upon His Contemporaries (University of Pittsburgh, 1981) has become available; the
main event, however is the appearance of Lewis Porter's long-
promised study, Lester Young (Boston: Twayne, 1985), one
chapter of which appeared in The Black Perspective in Music, 9,
No. 1 (Spring 1981), pp. 5-24.

Additional Items

Discographies

S.773.   KOSTER, Piet, and BAKKER, Dick M. Charlie Parker.
          Vols. 3-4. Alphen aan den Rijn: Micrography, 1975-
          1976. (Completes work listed as LOAM 945.)

S.774.   MASSAGLI, Luciano, et al. Duke Ellington's Story on
          Records. (Vols. 10-16) Milan: Raretone, 1976-1983.
          (Completes work listed as LOAM 946. Volumes and
          dates are: 10 - 1956-57; 11 - 1958-59; 12 - 1960-62;
          13 - 1963-65; 14 - 1966-67; 15 - 1968-70; 16 - 1971-74.)

S.775.   STRATEMANN, Klaus. Buddy Rich and Gene Krupa: a
          filmo-discography. Lübbecke: Uhle & Kleimann, 1980.
          76p.

S.776.   WHITE, Bozy. The Eddie Condon "Town Hall Broadcasts,"
          1944-1945: a discography. Oakland: the author (?),
          1980. 108p.

Historical and Critical Works

S.777.   BACKUS, Rob. Fire Music: a political history of jazz.
          Chicago: Vanguard Books, 1976. 104p.

S.778.   CERCHIARI, Luca, et al. Il jazz degli anni settanta. Mi-
          lan: Gammalibri, 1980. 268p.

S.779.   FARK, Reinhard. Die missachtete Botschaft: publizistische

Aspekte des Jazz im kulturellen Wandel. Berlin: Volker Spiess, 1971. 302p.

S.780. FOSTER, Frank. In Defense of Be-Bop. Scarsdale, N.Y.: Foster Fan Club, 1980. 16p.

S.781. JACKSON, Arthur. The World of Big Bands: the sweet and swinging years; foreword by Edmund Anderson. Newton Abbot: David & Charles; New York: Arco, 1977. 130p.

S.782. LEFTON, Mark, et al., eds. Approaches to Deviance: theories, concepts, and research findings. New York: Appleton-Century-Crofts, 1968. 391p. (Includes "Sounds of Protest: jazz and the militant avant-garde," by Lloyd Miller and James K. Shipper.)

S.783. RENAUD, Henri, ed. Jazz classique et jazz moderne. Paris: Casterman, 1971. 2v.

S.784. RONCAGLIA, Gian Carlo. Una storia del jazz. Venice: Marsilio, 1979- .

S.785. SPITZER, David. Jazzshots: a photographic essay. Miami: Zerkim Press, 1979. 120p.

S.786. VIAN, Boris. Chroniques de jazz; texte établi et présenté par Lucien Malson. Paris: La Jeune Parque, 1967. 288p.
_____. _____. Paris: Union Générale d'Editions, 1971. 512p.

S.787. WHITE, Mark. The Observer's Book of Jazz. London: Warne, 1978. 192p.

S.788. WHITE, Mark. The Observer's Book of Big Bands. London: Warne, 1978. 192p.

Individual Musicians

S.789. BURKHARDT, Werner, and GERTH, Joachim. Lester Young: ein Porträt. Wetzlar: Pegasus, 1959. 48p.

S.790. FOX, Roy. Hollywood, Mayfair, and All That Jazz: the Roy Fox story. London: Frewin, 1975. 248p.

S.791. FRANCHINI, Vittorio. Lester Young. Milan: Ricordi, 1961. 96p.

S.792. GUTMAN, Bill. Duke: the musical life of Duke Ellington.

New York: Random House, 1977. 184p. (For younger readers.)

S.793.   HOSKINS, Robert. Louis Armstrong: biography of a musician. Los Angeles: Holloway House, 1979. 222p.

S.794.   KRAUT, Eberhard. George Lewis: Streifzug durch ein Musikerleben. Menden: Der Jazzfreund, 1980. 62p.

S.795.   MAURO, Walter. Louis Armstrong, il re del jazz. Milan: Rusconi, 1979. 216p.

S.796.   RIESCO, José Francisco. El jazz clasico y Johnny Dodds, su rey sin corona. Santiago, Chile: Imprenta Mueller, 1972. 351p.

I. POPULAR CURRENTS

1. General Reference Works

a. Song Indexes

S.797.   AMERICAN SOCIETY OF COMPOSERS, AUTHORS AND
         PUBLISHERS. ASCAP Hit Songs. New York: ASCAP,
         (1977?). 139p.
A year-by-year listing, 1914-1976, of ASCAP-licenced hit
songs, with a further list for 1892-1913 (before ASCAP was founded).
Precise criteria are not given, but the introduction states:
"ASCAP's performance records were carefully correlated with lists
and charts and surveys published in major music trade periodicals."
Composer/author credits, but no publishers are given, and there is
a title index. (Previous versions were published as 40 Years of Hit
Tunes in 1956, and ASCAP Hit Tunes in 1967 and 1971 [LOAM
A232].)

S.798.   AMERICAN SOCIETY OF COMPOSERS, AUTHORS AND
         PUBLISHERS. ASCAP Index of Performed Compositions.
         New York: ASCAP, 1952. 2v.
         _____. _____. New York: ASCAP, 1963. 3v.
         _____. _____. New York: ASCAP, 1978. 1423p.
These alphabetical title listings of "compositions in the
ASCAP repertory which have appeared in the Society's survey of
performances" are successive volumes (not new editions), each covering a particular period. Therefore the most recent publication
does not include all the songs listed in the previous books, as not
all were performed in the period covered. Huge compilations (the
1963 volumes contain over 200,000 titles), they provide information
on composer, author, and publisher only; no dates are given, and
no name indexes are provided. They are not definitive lists, being
confined to ASCAP members' compositions and to those that have
been performed, but they are useful identification tools for popular
songs.

S.799.   AMERICAN SOCIETY OF COMPOSERS, AUTHORS AND
         PUBLISHERS. 40 Years of Show Business Tunes: the
         big Broadway hits from 1917-1957. New York: ASCAP,
         (1958?). 149p.
Intended as a record guide for the media, this is a

259

selective, chronologically organized song list of musical theater items, with information on the show from which each song comes, composer's and author's name, publisher, and recordings. Title index.

S.800.   AMERICAN SOCIETY OF COMPOSERS, AUTHORS AND PUBLISHERS. 30 Years of Motion Picture Music: the big Hollywood hit tunes since 1928. New York: ASCAP, (1960?). 135p.

Like ASCAP's 40 Years of Show Business Tunes (no. S.799), this is primarily a record guide. Songs from the movies are arranged chronologically, 1928-1959, and alphabetically under each year. Details are given of movie title, recording artist, record number, composer/author credits, and publisher. Cover of some titles is very thorough: "I'm in the Mood for Love" is credited with 63 recorded performances, including jazz versions.

S.801.   BROADCAST MUSIC, INC. All Time Pin Up Tunes 1940-1962. New York: BMI, (1963?). 43p.

A year-by-year title list of songs which appeared under the "popular" heading in the monthly BMI "Pin Up Hits" sheets. Composer and author credits, and publishers' names, are included, but there are no indexes.

S.802.   BROADCAST MUSIC INC. BMI Performindex. New York: BMI, (194-?+).

Begun in the 1940s and issued at regular intervals (triennially?), this "practical catalog of music licensed by BMI and selected from its repertory" bases its selection "primarily upon reports of performances by the networks and more than 3,000 radio and television stations that logged performances" ("explanatory notes" Vol. 7, 1964). Each volume covers a particular period (Vol. 7 January 1960-April 1963). Unlike the ASCAP lists (no. S.798), the emphasis here is on a classified list (eight categories in Vol. 7: concert; country; film, theatre and TV; instrumental and jazz; Latin American; popular; religious; rhythm & blues). An alphabetical title list refers the user to the appropriate category in the classified list, where details are provided of composer's and author's name, publisher (in coded form), and, in most cases, recordings (also in coded form). Show or film titles are given in that section.

S.803.   CRAIG, Warren. Sweet and Lowdown: America's popular song writers; with a foreword by Milton Ager. Metuchen, N.J.: Scarecrow Press, 1978. 645p. bibliog.

The quest for the Holy Grail of the perfect popular song reference book, already red with the blood of many an industrious knight, claims another victim, this time one who, well down the arduous road, is seduced by a false idol--the Academy Award. Out of a mass of data collected, the actual legacy of this particular Lancelot is a work flawed by attachment to an ill-defined idea of success and popularity. From research on an original total of 274

composers and lyricists, entries appear for only 144, the remainder
being eliminated because they did not reach the author's required
total of hit songs for the period in which they worked. Their names
appear in an appendix. They include Jerry Bock, Cy Coleman,
Johnny Green, Frederick Loewe, Kurt Weill; no doubt such treatment
will encourage them all to try harder in the future. Those who make
the gra.e are not, however, rewarded with complete coverage. Each
entry for the survivors (most of whom worked in the period 1900-
1950, although there are three periods: to 1880, 1880-1920, 1920-
1969) includes a biographical sketch, followed by a chronological
listing of stage and screen productions on which the person worked,
and of "popular" songs; these are defined as "those [songs] which
sold sizable quantities of sheet music or individual [single] phonograph records," and/or are "listed in various histories as having
been popular" (p. 3). This means, for example, that only six of
the songs Rodgers & Hammerstein wrote for Oklahoma! are given.
Appendices provide "comparative rankings" for the 144, and a list
of "sources of data," all of which are existing reference books.
There are also indexes of titles and productions.

S.804.   HAVLICE, Patricia Pate. Popular Song Index. Metuchen,
           N.J.: Scarecrow Press, 1975. 933p. bibliog.
           _____. _____. First Supplement. Metuchen, N.J.:
           Scarecrow Press, 1978. 386p. bibliog.
           _____. _____. Second Supplement. Metuchen, N.J.:
           Scarecrow Press, 1984. 534p. bibliog.
     These volumes should not be confused with the song in-
dexes of Shapiro (Popular Music, LOAM 1161), Burton (The Blue
Book of Tin Pan Alley, LOAM 1147), and others whose main aim is
to identify authors, composers, dates, and titles. They belong
rather to the genre of index begun by Minnie Earl Sears (Song Index, 1926) and continued by Desiree De Charms and Paul F. Breed
(Songs in Collections, 1966); i.e., they are primarily locating devices to the words and music of songs that appeared in published
song collections. As such they can act as identification tools, but
only to a limited extent. The main volume is an index to the contents of 301 such song books published in 1940-1972 (among them
some reprints of earlier books), including "folk songs, pop tunes,
spirituals, hymns, children's songs, sea shanties and blues" (preface). Only song books containing both words and music are included. A bibliography of the song books is provided first; next
comes the index by title, first line of song and first line of chorus;
this is followed by a composer and lyricist index. The song title
entries in the second part contain the fullest entries for each song.
The first supplement indexes a further 72 song books published in
1970-1975, and the second 156 covering 1974-1981. Approximately
one-half of the song books included contain music by American
writers; a substantial number are associated with one person (composer or performer).

S.805.   LEIGH, Robert. Index to Song Books: a title index to

over 11,000 copies of almost 6,800 songs in 111 song
books published between 1933 and 1962. Stockton,
Calif.: the author, 1964. 273p.
Not primarily an index to popular song books, but approximately three-quarters of the song books indexed here appear also
in Havlice (S.804); the major difference between Leigh and Havlice
is the former's starting date (which Leigh chose because Sears' Song
Index supplement was published in 1934). Unlike Havlice, Leigh
does not provide information on composer and lyricist.

S.806.   LOWE, Leslie. Directory of Popular Music, 1900–1965; in
          seven sections. Droitwich, Worcestershire: Peterson,
          1975. 1034p.
Though basically a reference guide to popular music in
Great Britain, this massive work can be useful to those seeking information on US popular music, especially in the area of the reception and influence of American popular song abroad. The main section is a chronology of song titles, arranged by month of UK copyright deposit (this is not made sufficiently clear); following each
song title are details of writers, publishers, country of origin, the
show and/or film where the song was first featured, and recordings.
Section 2 is a directory of 600 stage shows, each with the date of
the opening performance either in London or New York (whichever
came first). This section contains cross-references to Section 1
for further details on each song. The other sections contain a
film directory (around 1500 films, with maker, date, and with cross-
references to Section 1), a title index, a list of UK music publishers, of Academy Award-winning songs, 1934-65, and of theme songs
and signature tunes of well-known artists.

S.807.   STECHESON, Anthony, and STECHESON, Anne. The
          Stecheson Classified Song Directory. Hollywood: Music
          Industry Press, 1961. 503p.
Intended primarily for the music trade, this directory lists
over 100,000 American popular song titles in approximately 400 subject categories. Besides yielding many general groupings ("animals,"
"railroad," "war") the approach can be quite specific ("alimony,"
"lawyer"). In addition, a type of keyword method is also used,
producing lists under terms such as "lazy" and "sorry." Publishers'
names follow each title, but writers' names are not always given.
Under "Songs Thru the Year" there is a chronology.

S.808.   WOLF, Edwin. American Song Sheets, Slip Ballads and
          Poetical Broadsides 1850-1870: a catalogue of the collec-
          tion of the Library Company of Philadelphia. Philadel-
          phia: Library Company of Philadelphia, 1963. (Repr.
          New York: Kraus, 197-?.) 205p. illus.
"In the 1850s," writes Wolf in his introduction, "songs of
topical interest began to appear with greater frequency.... It was
these jingles written for a moment in time which seem most fascinating
today" (p. iv). 2,722 items are listed (with 194 Confederate songs

in an appendix); entry is by title, and each typically gives first
line, number of verses, the air to which the song was sung, information on author and/or composer, and publisher, and a note on
ornaments and illustrations. 304 different designs are illustrated.

S. 809.   WOLL, Allen L. Songs From Hollywood Musical Comedies,
          1927 to the Present: a dictionary. New York: Gar-
          land, 1976. 251p.
     A quick-reference index to the more than 7,000 songs in
Hollywood musicals since 1927. An alphabetical song title listing
refers the user to a list of musical films in Section 2. Here the
films are given with year of release, names of major stars, director,
composer, and lyricist, and, for post-1950 musicals, song titles.
Information on currently available recordings is appended. The
1,187 musicals indexed are listed chronologically in Section 3, followed by a composer and lyricist index.

b. Discographies and Guides to Recordings

See also S.1115, S.1118

S. 810.   DOCKS, L. R. 1915-1965 American Premium Record Guide:
          identification and values, 78s, 45s and LPs. Florence,
          Ala.: Books Americana, 1980. 737p. illus., bibliog.
     "Intended to be a guide to scarce and sought-after
records," and not to more familiar items, Dock's work encompasses
a wide range of music: jazz, dance bands, big bands, personalities
(mainly 78s, 1915-20); blues (78s, 1920-early 1950s); country,
hillbilly, etc. (mainly 78s, early 1920s to early 1950s); rhythm and
blues, rock & roll, rockabilly (45s and selected LPs, 1940s to early
1960s). Useful for identification, but mainly serving the collector
who wishes to purchase; likely prices are given, almost all below
$100. Name index.

S. 811.   KOENIGSBERG, Allen. Edison Cylinder Records, 1889-
          1912; with an illustrated history of the phonograph.
          New York: Stellar Productions, 1969. 159p. illus.
     An artist and title listing, from the first commercially pro-
duced cylinders up to the introduction of the four-minute-long
"Blue Amberol" cylinder. No recording dates are given, but there
are references to dates of issue. (For a historical survey of Edison
cylinders and phonographs, see George L. Frow and Albert F.
Sefl, The Edison Cylinder Phonographs: a detailed account of the
entertainment models until 1929 [Sevenoaks, Kent: Frow, 1978].
Blue Amberols are listed in Sydney H. Carter's Blue Amberol Cylinders: a catalogue [Bournemouth, Hants.: Talking Machine Review,
n.d.].)

S. 812.   MURRELLS, Joseph, comp. The Book of Golden Discs.
          London: Barrie & Jenkins, 1974. 503p. illus.

_____.   _____.   New and completely revised ed.   Lon-
don: Barrie & Jenkins, 1978.   413p.   illus.
_____.   Million Selling Records, 1903-1983:   an illustrated
directory.   London: Batsford, 1984; New York: Arco,
1985.   528p.
        Veteran English popular music researcher Murrells' book
aims "to set out in chronological order the details and story of every
phonograph disc which has been certified or reliably reported to have
sold one million or more units globally" (preface).   Beginning in
1903, with Caruso's "Vesti la giubba," the book covers a longer
period than most books of hit records, thus serving an effective historical function; by not confining his interest to any one style or
group of styles, Murrells also produces a source of reference information that offers frequent interesting juxtapositions.   Within each
year discs are listed alphabetically by artist.   Details are provided
of record company (but no further discographical information), composer and author, and the background to the song.   There follows
a biographical sketch of the artist or group (in the case of performers with more than one million-seller, this usually occurs under
their first hit).   This last category often includes information hard
to trace elsewhere.   In addition to the artist and title indexes, the
back of the book contains a plentiful supply of statistics in table form
(records with most weeks at No. 1, artists with most No. 1 singles,
etc.).

S.813.   PITTS, Michael R.   Radio Soundtracks: a reference guide.
        Metuchen, N.J.:   Scarecrow Press, 1976.   161p.   illus.
        A guide to collecting old-time radio broadcasts on tape and
LP.   Only "basic entertainment programs" are included: radio big
band shows are not covered, but many other music shows are.   Arrangement is by title of show, with details of performers, length of
recording, etc.

S.814.   RANDLE, Bill.   The American Popular Music Discography:
        1920-1930.   Vol. 3.   The Columbia 1-D Series, 1923-
        1929:   a discography of popular music issued on Colum-
        bia Records numbers 1-D to 2061-D, with an appendix
        of 2062-D to 2600-D.   Bowling Green, Ohio: Bowling
        Green University Popular Press, 1974.   411p.
        An impressive beginning to a planned series of discographies
which apparently has not materialized, this volume has several features which recommend themselves to other discographers: the discographical details provided after each record label number include
composer credits, publisher's name, date of publication, date of
record's release, and original pressing order.   (Other information
covers artist's name, description of style, type of accompaniment,
master number, and title; no recording dates are given--these were
to be published later, with one volume covering the whole series.)
In addition, there is an outline of Columbia Records' history, a
roster of artists with references to issue numbers (these include
Vernon Dalhart, Ruth Etting, the Ipana Troubadours, Leo Reisman,

and Paul Whiteman), a title index, a publishers' index. (For another Columbia discography, see Dan Mahony's The Columbia 13/14000-D Series [LOAM 809], which is similarly detailed, suggesting the thoroughness of Columbia's files.)

S.815.   RUST, Brian. The American Record Label Book. New
         Rochelle, N.Y.: Arlington House, 1978. 336p. illus.
         Aimed principally at "the discriminating record collector of
all kinds of music," who wishes to know "exactly when his records
were made, what firm produced them ... what these labels look like,
and how common--or rare--are the items produced by this or that
company" (p. 9), these accounts of the history of some 250 record
labels are of interest to a variety of students of American popular
music, because of the close links between the music and the phonograph industry's fluctuating fortunes. The entries are arranged
alphabetically by label, and for each Rust draws deeply on his extensive knowledge of discography to provide precise historical and
descriptive information, coupled with general comment on the range
of music. Some labels all but defeat even him (see, for instance,
Famous Singers), while others have their matrices charted in detail.
The terminal date is 1942. Most labels are illustrated in black-and-
white.

S.816.   SEARS, Richard S. V-Discs: a history and discography.
         Westport, Conn.: Greenwood Press, 1980. 1,166p.
         illus.
         Recorded in 1943-49 and distributed exclusively to military
personnel, the V-Disc program, under the dynamic leadership of
Lieutenant Robert Vincent, amassed a vast quantity of excellent music, most of which, for copyright reasons, still remains unavailable.
The known quality of much of the music, and the number of musicians whose discography is incomplete without mention of their V-
Disc contributions, have created a need for a reference book. Sears
fills this gap in an admirably thorough way. The historical section
provides a 90-page review of the setting up of the V-Disc group,
and a survey of its operations. The annotated discography of Army
and Navy V-Discs, a massive compilation, is arranged alphabetically
by performer, and chronologically within each performer section.
Details are provided of place, issue number,s titles, playing time,
master and serial numbers, arrangers, vocalists, soloists; complete
personnel are not given for each session, but information is given
in notes, and there are cross-references elsewhere in the text from
the names of featured performers to the main entry. The majority
of the music falls into the categories of jazz band and popular
vocalist, though there are symphony orchestras and military bands
also. Supplementary information includes an appendix listing commercially issued EPs and LPs, and numerical/title indexes.

S.817.   TUDOR, Dean, and TUDOR, Nancy. Contemporary Popular
         Music. Littleton, Colo.: Libraries Unlimited, 1979.
         313p. bibliog.

Like the other three volumes in this series, "American Popular Music on Elpee" (nos. S.276, S.540, and S.661), this is a thoroughly prepared discographical guide. Its subject area is more diverse (from Josephine Baker to the Velvet Underground in one volume), and extends beyond the USA into British music (notably, but not exclusively, for rock). The book falls into two parts: mainstream popular music (vocal stylists, instrumental ensembles, novelty and humor, big bands, stage and film), and rock (rockabilly, rock and roll, acid rock, etc.), with no connection between them. About two-thirds of the 730 or so recordings listed for annotation occur in Part 1. As elsewhere in the series, the section introductions and the annotations aim, not at originality, but at being "a summation and synthesis of existing thought"; that is likely to suggest there are no widely diverging opinions among critics, but nevertheless the usefulness of the approach, especially to those seeking information outside of their sphere of knowledge, is apparent. The bibliography offers 141 book citations but only ten journals; there is a label directory and an index to both parts. (For a cumulative edition of all four books in the series, see S/A.517.)

S.818.   WHITBURN, Joel. Top Easy Listening Records 1961-1974.
         Menomonee Falls, Wisc.: Record Research, 1975. 152p.
         illus.
    As with other Whitburn compilations (LOAM 632, 890, 1340 and no. S.819), this listing is based on a particular Billboard hit chart: in this case, that amorphous category otherwise known as "adult middle-of-the-road," or MOR. Under each performer there are details of the records which reached the chart, date of entry, position reached, number of weeks in the chart, label name, and issue number. Annual supplements were issued 1976-1980.

S.819.   WHITBURN, Joel. Top LPs 1945-1972. Menomonee Falls,
         Wisc.: Record Research, 1973. 224p.
    Based on Billboard's "Top 100" album chart. Annual supplements have been issued, 1974-1980.

S.820.   WILE, Raymond R. Edison Disc Recordings. Philadelphia:
         Eastern National Park and Monument Association, 1978.
         427p.
    The famous Edison Diamond discs, one quarter-inch thick, vertically cut, and capable of containing five minutes of recorded sound on one side, were launched by Edison in October 1913; for many enthusiasts, they represent the peak of pre-electric recording. The entire output on these discs--literally hundreds of recordings--is charted here, from the end of 1912, when Edison first issued discs, through to the last issue (electrically recorded by then) in October 1929, and including the lateral-cut discs of the last few months. The listing is by series (the 50000 series being the biggest), and includes all the smaller ethnic series--Scandinavian, Polish, Yiddish, etc. Arrangement is by catalog number order, and

the information supplied covers coupling date, month of issue
(from 1915), "cut-out" (i.e., deletion) date, matrix number, artist
and title. Omitted are recording dates, take numbers, and personnel.

"The Edison repertoire over the thirty-odd years of its
existence," wrote Brian Rust, summing up both cylinders and discs,
"was rarely anything special" (no. S.815, p. 113). It was certainly broad, however, encompassing a variety of popular entertainers,
light classics, religious numbers, dance bands, novelty songs, jazz,
and some old-time items. Among the most frequent names are
B. A. Rolfe, Vaughn de Leath, Don Voorhees, Johnny Marvin, Vernon Dalhart, and Homer Rodeheaver. No name or title indexes are
provided.

c. Collected Biography

See also S.927

S.821. COLBERT, Warren E. Who Wrote That Song?, or Who In
        the Hell Is J. Fred Coots? an informal survey of Ameri-
        can popular songs and their composers. New York:
        Revisionist Press, 1975. 195p. illus.
        A highly selective, anecdotal reference book dedicated,
evidently, to providing information on the less well-known song
composers. (In discussing Nicholas Brodsky, Colbert writes:
"... this is a classic example of the very point I'm trying to make.
This is beautiful music ... this man should be known" (p. 21).)
There are sections entitled "Who Wrote That Song? and "Some Interesting Stories About Composers and Songs." Among those discussed
are Nacio Herb Brown, Ted Snyder, James F. Henley, Robert Allen,
Fred Fisher, Jimmy V. Monaco. A third section, "Alphabetical Listing of Most Popular Songs," includes dates with the song titles.
There is no index. (J. Fred Coots, in response to the existential
question in the title, provides a foreword.)

S.822. FISHER, John. Call Them Irreplaceable. London: Elm
        Tree Books; New York: Stein & Day, 1976. 224p.
        illus., bibliog.
        Stylish, generally laudatory portraits, for the general read-
er, of a select band of American and European entertainment legends,
including Al Jolson, Jimmy Durante, Fred Astaire, Bing Crosby,
Judy Garland, Danny Kaye, and Frank Sinatra. Fisher draws heavily on published sources for biographical and critical information, and
if his attempt "to distil the essence of their ephemeral art" produces
a brew less heady--and far more ephemeral--than these stars' performances, there are moments of perception into the qualities that
fashioned them.

S.823. SIMON, George T., et al.. The Best of the Music Makers:
        from Acuff to Ellington to Presley to Sinatra to Zappa

and 279 more of the most popular performers of the last fifty years, by George T. Simon and friends; foreword by Dinah Shore. Garden City, N.Y.: Doubleday, 1979. 635p. illus.

A wide-ranging, selective biographical dictionary of 284 performers who have displayed "staying power." Simon's method, he explains, was to set up a panel who selected the biographies; Simon himself then commissioned many of the pieces from writers he felt "were expecially qualified" (p. xv)--these are the "friends" of the title page, and include Carol Easton, Amy Lee, Dan Morgenstern, and John S. Wilson. Coverage extends to jazz, folk, country, and rock musicians. Entries typically cover one or two pages and include a quotation and a photo, as well as biographical data. No index.

S.824.   PERRY, Jeb H. Variety Obits: an index to obituaries in Variety, 1905-1978. Metuchen, N.J.: Scarecrow Press, 1980. 309p.

One of the greatest merits of Variety's obituaries is their relative lack of discrimination on the grounds of show business status; consequently, they amount in toto to a very large reference source of information on lesser known figures. This modest but useful index restricts itself to "those people who worked in the production-related areas of motion pictures, television, radio, the ligitimate stage, minstrelsy, and vaudeville" (p. vi). Those whose career was music, therefore, are included if they practiced their speciality in these areas. Many illustrious names appear (e.g. Garland, Gottschalk, Robeson); for these Variety becomes one more source of information--for the less famous, however, it could well be the only one. Each name is accompanied by the following details: age at death, date of death, professional speciality, location of obituary. The particular musical activities covered include compower/orchestrator/arranger, conductor, lyricist, minstrel, music director, musician, vaudevillian, and vocalist.

2.   The Popular Music Life

a.   The Popular Music Business

See also J. (Rock and Roll, Rock, and Pop)

S.825.   DACHS, David. Anything Goes: the world of popular music. Indianapolis: Bobbs-Merrill, 1964. 328p. illus.

A knowledgeable, if homiletic, account of the popular music business in the early 1960s, made or marred (according to one's taste) by a rigid belief in the ineffable superiority of earlier popular music styles (Gershwin, Rodgers, etc.). Dachs' title is two-edged: it aptly sums up his view of the prevailing "lunacy" of the contemporary music industry and the newer music, while casting a nostalgic glance at the master craftsmen such as Cole Porter. Whether or

not one shares Dachs' sense of revulsion at the prevalence of
"cheap music" and its exploitation by unscrupulous commerce (creating "a kind of crazy-mixed-up honky-tonk milieu that colors and
cheapens the quality of American life"--p. 321), his guided tour is
an informative one, taking the reader in detail through the neigh-
boring worlds of songwriters, publishers, A & R men, arrangers,
payola, disc jockeys, distributors, record industry economics, and
the different circumstances affecting specific, related styles (country
& western, folk, jazz, Broadway, Hollywood). Though not presented
as a scholarly offering, the book is replete with many statistics,
and with first-hand accounts (and opinions) from those involved in
the various areas. Index of names. (Formerly LOAM A235.)

S.826.   MEYER, Hazel. The Gold in Tin Pan Alley. Philadelphia:
         Lippincott, 1958. (Repr. Westport, Conn.: Greenwood
         Press, 1977.) 258p.
         An entertaining and informative history of the business
side of popular song; written before the arrival of rock & roll transformed the music business, and therefore dated in some respects, it
still offers interesting if sometimes tongue-in-cheek accounts of such
topics as song-plugging, the growth of performing rights societies,
the educational departments of popular song publishers, the rise of
the disc jockey and the A & R man (with special attention to Mitch
Miller), payola, the practicalities of popular songwriting, and the
making of a hit. (Formerly LOAM A241.)

b.   Media and Publishing

S.827.   DeLONG, Thomas A. The Mighty Music Box: the golden
         age of musical radio. Los Angeles: Amber Crest
         Books, 1980.   335p.   illus., bibliog.
         Informed and readable account of music on the radio in the
1920s-1940s, with more attention to changes and developments in
programming and techniques than to those in the music broadcast.
Much of the book divides into discussion of topics; the growth of
crooning, children's music, dance, Toscanini and the NBC Symphony
Orchestra, country and western, amateurs, superstars (Jessica
Dragonette, Fred Waring, Frank Munn). The bibliography lists
books and articles, and there are indexes of "selected subjects" and
names.

S.828.   DUNNING, John. Tune in Yesterday: the ultimate ency-
         clopedia of old-time radio, 1925-1976. Englewood Cliffs,
         N.J.: Prentice-Hall, 1976. 703p. illus.
         A "nostalgia reader" (p. x) as well as a historical reference
work, Dunning's book provides information--dates, networks, spon-
sors, personnel, etc.--on each show in narrative form. The emphasis is on drama, comedy and variety shows. Among those with a
strong musical content are shows featuring Abe Burrows, Andrews
Sisters, Bing Crosby, Eddie Cantor, Ethel Merman, Frank Sinatra,

Rudy Vallee. Also included are details of title shows such as the Chamber Music Society of Lower Basin Street (which featured, for example, the young Dinah Shore), the Grand Ole Opry, and Hollywood Barn Dance. Index of names and show titles.

S.829. FEIST, Leonard. An Introduction to Popular Music Publishing in America. New York: National Music Publishers' Association, 1980. 111p. illus., bibliog.
A short survey of the past and present of song publishing in America, by an author with a long involvement in the industry. In the sections on contemporary publishing, Feist's chief concern is with processes and functions. He names few names, and although "the recording of a song is what the songpublisher deals with" (p. 13), he puts very little detail into his sketch of the US recording industry. Figures for sales of printed music, 1958-78, and recordings, 1946-78, are, however, given in appendices.

S.830. PITTS, Michael R., and HARRISON, Louis H. Hollywood on Record: the film stars' discography. Metuchen, N.J.: Scarecrow Press, 1978. 411p. illus.
A discography of long-playing records of music and spoken word, made by motion picture performers since 1948. Arrangement is by performer, and the listing for each individual is subdivided (where appropriate) into the categories of LPs, original casts, soundtracks, and compilations. Some entries also include a representative sample of 45s. Discographical detail provided is limited to album title, label name and catalog number. No dates are given, and there is no listing of the individual tracks on each item, or of other performers. For those whose interest is primarily in the music, album titles alone are of limited usefulness, the more so given the high proportion of banal titles conjured up by record companies. Although designed in part as a complement to discographies such as Rust's Complete Entertainment Discography (LOAM 1159), which includes only 78s, this is not in the same discographical league. No indexes.

c. Clubs, etc.

S.831a. SYLVESTER, Robert. No Cover Charge: a backward look at the night clubs. New York: Dial Press, 1956. 301p.
A casual, generalized, but knowing memoir about the night club world (mostly in New York) of the past. While few hard musical facts are present--despite the importance of music in this world-- one does discover anecdotes about, and occasionally quotes from, the likes of Duke Ellington, Sonny Greer, Eddie Condon, Wingy Manone, Vincent Youmans, and Charlie Parker. No index.

S.831b. WEIL, Susanne, and SINGER, Barry. Steppin' Out: a guide to live music in Manhattan. Charlotte, N.C.:

East Woods Press, 1980. 155p. illus.
A line in the preface reads: "... rest assured that the 150 selections in this book are, for the most part, as stable as music rooms in Manhattan can be." For some time after it appeared, the book has remained amazingly reflective of the New York popular music scene. When it ceases to be useful at all as a guide book, it will probably be useful as a work of history. There are separate sections for each type of music: "Jazz," "Cabaret/Showcase," "Rock," etc. Each entry receives lively, often extensive, annotation. There are two indexes: one alphabetical, the other by neighborhood.

S.832. WOOTTON, Richard, and McKISSACK, Charlie. Honky Tonkin': a guide to music USA. London: the authors, 1977. 27p. illus.
WOOTTON, Richard. _____. 2nd ed., expanded, updated, and re-written. London: the author, 1978. 179p. illus., bibliog.
_____. Honky Tonkin': a travel guide to American music. 3rd ed. London: Travelaid Publishing; Charlotte, N.C.: East Woods Press, 1980. 180p. bibliog.
Originally intended for listeners to a Radio London program hosted by Charlie Gillett, this is an informal and informative gazetteer of clubs and other musical venues in the United States. Although only selective (it lists no venues in Kentucky or Mississippi, for instance) and aimed at a European audience, it could be a serviceable handbook for Americans also, footloose in Lubbock, Texas, or nonplussed in Akron, Ohio. Other information given includes record and book stores, radio stations, festivals, and an annotated list of magazine titles and addresses. The range of music covered is wide, "from blues, country, bluegrass, folk, modern rock through unusual genres like Cajun and Tex-Mex, as well as r & b and rock 'n' roll" (introduction to the second edition).

3. Historical and Critical Studies

See also S.1151

S.833. CARNEY, George O., ed. The Sounds of People and Places: readings in the geography of music. Washington, D.C.: University Press of America, 1979. 336p. illus., bibliogs.
Music is often plundered, in education, to make dull subjects more interesting; with more justification, it is also used as a filter enabling those chiefly interested in other subjects to see their subjects with different eyes; more rarely, it is linked with another subject in a genuinely interdisciplinary way, which acts reciprocally to the benefit of each. The (mostly reprinted) articles in this reader for students of cultural geography fall mainly into the second category, though some stray perilously close to the first,

and one or two hint at the possibility of the third. The musical subject matter is almost entirely American popular music. At its best, the encounter between music and geography suggests some fruitful lines of inquiry; these occur mainly when some of cultural geography's key terms are being applied--"spatial diffusion," "cultural hearth," "mental maps." That these connections are not fully explored is explained partly by the excessive space devoted to background outlines of relevant aspects of popular music history, and the generally introductory tone throughout. But another reason is the one-sidedness of most contributors' approaches; their study of music may illuminate their geography, but does their geography illuminate the music?

Nevertheless the book contains interesting evidence of a worthwhile effort to link the two subjects in some way. The text is in seven parts. Part 1 is devoted to a general piece on spatial aspects by Peter H. Nash, with references to popular and folk music. Part 2, on country music, contains broadly-based essays by Tamara and Larry K. Stephenson, Charles F. Gritzner, and Douglas K. Meyer, and three articles by the editor (one on bluegrass, two on country music radio). Part 3 contains a valuable contribution on white gospel quartets by A. D. Horsley. Part 4, on folk, is given over to a piece by James R. Curtis on Woody Guthrie and the Dust Bowl, and Part 5 contains approaches to rock & roll by Larry R. Ford and Ronald S. Murray. Two essays on the image of place make up Part 6, on popular music: a general piece by Ford and Floyd M. Henderson, and Henderson's individual contribution on the image of New York. The editor concludes the book, in Part 7, with a wide-ranging article on the roots of American music. Each piece is followed by study questions and, often, by bibliographies; there are many maps (mostly small) and the final sections list further readings and lists of teaching resources. No index.

S.834.   EWEN, David. All the Years of American Popular Music.
         Englewood Cliffs, N.J.: Prentice-Hall, 1977. 850p.
         Even to someone with Ewen's experience of the production line of popular music books for a middlebrow market, the task of an all-embracing volume covering "the entire world of [American] popular music in all its varied facets" (p. vii) must have been a daunting one. The result is certainly impressive in its range; not only is coverage claimed of "every style and field of popular music creativity" (ibid.), hundreds of individuals get a mention, and many distinctive popular music phenomena--the music business, the media, the role of certain specific places--are present also; historical and social changes are noted. A bias is apparent in the allocation of chapters: six to the period to 1865, five to 1865-1900, and the remaining 34 to 70-plus years of the 20th century.

Ewen's approach is to write consensus history for the curious, easily accessible in style and descriptive in manner, lacking analysis of any kind, and avoiding provocation. Not surprisingly the text, though detailed, is bland, well-versed in the surfaces of the subject, but unable to rise above a low level of discourse. He

clearly drew on a huge number of sources, but they are not even
selectively listed, and where references do appear in the text they
are incomplete. The index is the clearest guide to the book's in-
tentions: 74 pages crammed with names and titles, totalling over
11,000 entries in all.

S.835. HAMM, Charles. Yesterdays: popular song in America.
        New York: Norton, 1979. 533p. illus., bibliog.
        The sixteen chronological chapters of this fine scholarly
study represent the most extensive application so far of musicological techniques to the history of American popular song. Believing
that "popular song in America has a continuous, unbroken, and coherent history of some two hundred years," and that "any single
chapter of his history ... is best understood in the context of the
entire story" (introduction), Hamm presents a lucid, informative
historical chronicle that begins with the post-Revolutionary era and
ends with rock in the 1970s. The weight of attention goes to the
19th century, from James Hewitt's "The Wounded Hussar" via Irish
melodies, Italian opera, minstrelsy, the Hutchinson Family, German
songs, Stephen Foster, Civil War songs, to Charles K. Harris's
"After the Ball" and the birth of Tin Pan Alley. The book's distinguished feature is that the historical outline is filled in with a
splendid proliferation of musical examples and commentary, all integrated into the text. Other features include numerous illustrations (especially sheet music covers), seven appendices listing the
"most popular" songs from the late 18th century to 1958, a nine-
page bibliography of books and articles, and a general index.
        Underpinning Hamm's choice of subject matter is a defini-
tion of popular song which takes account of various characteristics:
musical, performance, context, economic (sold for profit), level of
ability (performers' and audience's), and physical form. Underpin-
ning his methodology is a bid to delimit the field by applying a different notion of popularity, one based on quantification: the songs
"listened to, bought, and performed by the largest number of
Americans" (p. xix). Despite the assured value and stature of the
text, these definitional questions raise a number of problems, particularly in the sphere of minority musical cultures, which are seen
as significant only when they influence, or aspire to become, the
"majority" taste. Though Hamm acknowledges song as expressing
social and cultural processes, this tenet is absent from his basic
methodology, and his approach leaves little room for consideration of
the dynamic relationship between majority and minority cultures, nor,
indeed, of the possibility of different esthetic systems. These factors create particular difficulties in the chapters on the 20th century, where the pre-eminence of Tin Pan Alley and rock produces a
somewhat distorted picture (blues and country music are ignored
save as influences), while the treatment of rock itself highlights
other problems--the lack of appropriate musicological methods both
to study popular performance techniques and to overcome the absence of printed musical sources. (For further comment on the
methodology, see Richard Middleton, "Popular Music, Class Conflict,

and the Music-Historical Field," in Popular Music Perspectives 2,
ed. D. Horn et al. [Gothenburg, Exeter, etc.: IASPM, 1985], pp.
24-46.)

S.836.   JEWELL, Derek.   The Popular Voice: a musical record of
          the 60s and 70s. London: Andre Deutsch, 1980. 256p.
          illus.
     A collection of Jewell's reviews, interviews, and profiles,
written mostly for the London Sunday Times between 1963 and 1978
(a "musical record" of London, therefore), ranging widely over
American and British jazz, rock, pop, and popular song (and British
musical theater, i.e., Lloyd Webber and Rice). Demonstrating the
diversity of the era ("breathtaking"--p. 11) is the main reason for
reprinting so many often unremarkable short pieces (average length
300-500 words) which no doubt made interesting wrapping for fish
and chips (in the quality fish and chip shops)--though even then
the contents may well have had more taste. Jewell's approach is a
catholic one, but he is clearly happiest when describing big bands
(Ellington, Herman), and popular singers (Fitzgerald, Crosby,
Sinatra).

S.837.   MALONE, Bill C.   Southern Music, American Music. Lex-
          ington: University Press of Kentucky, 1979. 203p.
          illus., bibliog.
     There have been few good regional studies of American pop-
ular music, and none before this one which attempted to cover all
genres, both separately and in their interactions. This worthy objective is somewhat undermined by the very richness of the subject
matter--the Southern folk-derived musical traditions and their transformation into national idioms is too vast a topic to be treated satis-
factorily in a book this short (155 pages of text) except at a fairly
introductory level. As such it succeeds well. Malone's writing is
lucid and his scholarship is shot through with a profound love of
the South's music. The structure is historical: from folk origins
(black and white) and the period of "national discovery" (Foster,
spirituals, folk song collections), through ragtime, blues and jazz,
hillbilly, Cajun and gospel, to "nationalization" (the South's music
becomes the nation's music), the rise of rock, modern gospel, and
soul, and the "resurgence" of country music in the 1970s. Malone's
conclusion is basically optimistic: although homogenization threatens
all popular music, it has led, in counteraction, to new, creative attempts to fuse tradition and modernity. The extensive bibliographic
essays, 26 pages long, is a very valuable addition. Index.

S.838.   MATLAW, Myron, ed.   American Popular Entertainment:
          papers and proceedings of the Conference on the History
          of American Popular Entertainment. Westport, Conn.:
          Greenwood Press, 1979. 338p. illus., bibliog.
     This 1977 Lincoln Center conference brought together per-
formers and scholars in recollection and discussion of many aspects
of popular entertainment: minstrel shows, vaudeville, and burlesque;

tent repertoire shows; circus, Wild West, and medicine shows; dance and "environmental entertainment" (i.e., amusement parks). Those papers most relevant to the role of music are Robert C. Toll's outline of the major stages in the evolution of blackface minstrelsy, Helen Armstead-Johnson's "Blacks in Vaudeville: Broadway and Beyond," and Max Morath's informal discussion of Bert Williams "and his associates." Don B. Wilmeth's bibliographical survey is a selective discussion and listing of some 250-300 items. Index.

S.839.   PALMER, Tony.   All You Need Is Love: the story of popular music; edited by Paul Medlicott. London: Weidenfeld & Nicolson and Chappell; New York: Grossman, 1976. 323p. illus.

In 1973-75 Palmer made a series of sixteen programs for British television on American (and some British) popular music, in the process of which he commissioned "essays relating to each episode, hoping these would focus my attention on what was considered important" (p. ix). When it came to a companion book, he abandoned the essays (by no less than Paul Oliver, Rudi Blesh, Leonard Feather, Stephen Sondheim, Charlie Gillett...) and wrote his own text ("not the text of the films, although it expresses the same point of view"--ibid.). Apart from an introductory one on origins, each chapter is devoted to a genre or part of a genre (from ragtime to rock, and including jazz, blues, vaudeville, musicals, country music, war and protest song), and each offers a skeletal outline of that genre, with copious illustrations. Except for quotations from his own interviews, Palmer acknowledges no sources (although he is clearly not above borrowing material--compare, for example, his p.105 with Ian Whitcomb's After the Ball [LOAM 1172] pp. 48-49.) Perceptive, but frequently opinionated, his text becomes hung up on questions of struggles to survive, exploitation, manipulation, commercialization; a '70s-style "moldy fig," he is convinced of the decline of the individual qualities that made each genre distinctive, and sees contemporary popular music as flowing down a "baubled sewer" (p. 300). Index.

S.840.   ROBERTS, John Storm.   The Latin Tinge: the impact of Latin American music on the United States. New York: Oxford University Press, 1979. 246p. illus., bibliog., discog.

An important, ground-breaking book which reveals for the first time the breadth and depth of the influence of Latin American music, particularly that of Cuba, Mexico, Argentina, and Brazil, on the popular music styles of the USA. Roberts first describes the "unity-in-diversity" of Latin American music, then proceeds historically to chart the influence from the 19th century to the present day. There are chapters on the first manifestations of influence (notably in the music of Gottschalk), and the "Latin strain" in New Orleans around the turn of the century; on the impact of the tango; on the "rumba era" of the 1930s; on the "watershed" of the 1940s, when "Latin elements began to move below the surface ... and establish themselves" (p. 126); on the "mambo time" of the 1950s, the retrenchment period of the 1960s, followed by a return to the mainstream in the 1970s with the advent of salsa. The text is rich in detail; among the profusion of names most frequent reference is made to Ray Barretto, Xavier Cugat, Dizzy Gillespie, Machito, Eddie Palmieri, Tito Puente, and Mongo Santamaria. The various processes by which the music becomes known--visiting musicians, immigration, sheet music, visits to Latin America by US musicians, etc.-- and the complex interactions between US and Latin American musical idioms, are outlined. If detail (sometimes admittedly trivial) can obscure argument from time to time, Roberts justifies his approach by maintaining that, as a first attempt to "put the record straight" much that is superficial has to be charted. One regret must, however, be the lack of music examples, especially of rhythmic patterns. The question of why the subject has been neglected is touched on only briefly, and somewhat acerbically, but would make another fascinating study in itself. The book contains no footnotes or references, but a glossary, a listing of relevant albums, a 58-item bibliography, and an index.

S.841.   ROBINETTE, Richard. Historical Perspectives on Popular
         Music. Dubuque, Iowa: Kendall/Hunt, 1980. 162p.
         illus., bibliog., discog.
         A skeleton outline of the history and basic characteristics
of popular music, devised "for use in an introductory music course
... at the college lower division or highschool level" (preface). So
bare are the bones that, rather than trouble its users with sentences, the book is designed "in an outline form"--as a series of
headings and subheadings, delineating major and less major features
and developments. These are grouped into seven historical units,
proceeding from "the pre-twentieth century base" through Afro-
American music, jazz, popular song, and the "basis of rock and
roll" (including rhythm and blues, and country music) up to the
various influences on music in the 1970s. The discography lists the
recordings recommended for each unit, and there is a glossary and
a set of worksheets. The overall picture is somewhat unbalanced;
there is, for example, no attention to the musical theater or to Tin
Pan Alley, and too much prominence given to white big band leaders.

S.842.   RUBLOWSKY, John. Popular Music. New York: Basic
         Books, 1967. 164p. illus.
         An introductory historical survey of some of the genres of
American popular music--musical theater, jazz, rock, etc., all
treated separately but briefly--with notes on outstanding individuals.
There is also discussion of the way the popular music industry is
organized. Index. (Formerly LOAM A244.)

4. Words and Music

a. Sheet Music

S.843. KLAMKIN, Marian. Old Sheet Music: a pictorial history;
    photographs by Charles Klamkin. New York: Hawthorn
    Books, 1975. 214p. illus.
        Handsome, instructive volume, angled towards the serious
collector, but containing much of interest to the materially unac-
quisitive student of popular music. The author's aim is to examine
"published American sheet music from its visual aspects ... with the
audio turned down" (p. 6); this visual aspect is important because
"there is no better way to get the information about musical history
in America than to study the covers of the published songs" (p.
191). A large number of covers are reproduced, some in color, and
with copious annotations. The bulk of the text is divided into brief
considerations of the covers of songs in a series of categories, among
them patriotic and political, transport, notable events, home and
family, social issues, minstrelsy, ragtime. There is also some discussion of early publishers and lithographers (Nathaniel Currier,
Gene Buck), and advice on collecting. Index.

S.844- LEVY, Lester S. Picture the Songs: lithographs from the
 54.   sheet music of nineteenth-century America. Baltimore:
    Johns Hopkins University Press, 1976. 213p. illus.,
    bibliog.
        Following his earlier attempts to trace America's social his-
tory through its songs, Levy here turns to illustrating "how a prime
and inexpensive form of art was delivered into the hands of the
public by the medium of sheet music for the piano" (introduction).
The lithographed sheet music cover was at one and the same time a
means of pictorially relaying items of news and "the art form most
readily and reasonably available to people of moderate means"
(ibid.). 100 covers, representing 50 lithographers, are included, in
chronological order. Opposite each lithograph Levy provides background information on the topic and the lithographer, with some consideration also of the composer of the music. Extensive background
bibliography and index.

S.855. PRIEST, Daniel B. American Sheet Music: a guide to col-
    lecting sheet music from 1775 to 1975, with prices. Des
    Moines, Iowa: Wallace-Homestead, 1978. 82p. illus.,
    bibliog.
        A list of some 1,500 song titles, with prices a collector
might expect to pay, and with composers' and lyricists' names. A
series of short chapters precedes the list; these give a brief history
of American popular music, describe the role of the songplugger,
provide a list of all-time best-selling songs, and discuss the business
side and the art of the cover design.

S.856. WESTIN, Helen. Introducing the Song Sheet: a collector's guide with current price list. Nashville, Tenn.: Nelson, 1976. 160p. illus., bibliog.

Informal layman's handbook, intended to familiarize would-be collectors with the categories of popular song sheets from 1880 to World War 2, and with their various features. The book includes practical remarks on condition, dating, and handling, as well as lists of representative works in the categories "Tin Pan Alley Titans," Negro composers, women composers, and instrumentals. There is also a miscellany of subject categories (tear-jerkers, alcohol, food, transport, etc.) and information on cover artists.

S.857.   WILK, Max. Memory Lane, 1890 to 1925: ragtime, jazz, foxtrot and other popular music and music covers. London: Studioart, 1973. 88,(36)p. illus.
_____. Memory Lane: the golden age of American popular music 1890-1925. New York: Ballantine Books, 1976. 88,(36)p. illus.

A "random assemblage" of 128 color reproductions of sheet music covers, with the music of twelve pieces (six by Joplin, already widely available), a mock-ironic introduction, and two pages of notes, tucked modestly away at the back of the book, giving dates for all the covers and brief notes on almost a quarter of them. The covers themselves are handsomely reproduced, and there is occasional evidence of planning in their arrangement, but the whole is rather shapeless, and the lack of decent commentary coy and irritating. Apparently intended as a nostalgic divertissement.

b.   General Guides and Studies

See also S.862

S.858.   SALZMAN, Eric, and SAHL, Michael. Making Changes: a practical guide to vernacular harmony. New York: McGraw-Hill Book Co., 1977. 22p.

"Students and musicians who want to learn something about harmony can find learned treatises and classical texts that, at their best, help prepare them for a gig in a provincial German town, circa 1760. Along with this useful knowledge comes a great deal of guilt, snobbery, and abuse" (introduction). Amen. Recognizing the lack of practical guidance to the harmony musicians--especially rock musicians--actually use, the authors provide, not a systematic course of instruction, so much as "a walk in the woods" (p. 14), during which they hope the reader will begin to develop an understanding of relationships. The harmony in question is that at the basis of popular music; its origins are various, but it is distinctively American in its compound nature. The many examples are either traditional (non-copyright) or were written by the authors for the book. They are often accompanied by a list of tunes which use the chord changes illustrated.

S.859.   SCHECHTER, Harold, and SEMEIKS, Jonna Gormely. <u>Pat-</u>
<u>terns in Popular Culture: a sourcebook for writers.</u>
New York: Harper & Row, 1980. 476p. illus.
This handbook for college teachers of written composition
courses includes some song lyrics (rock, folk, country, soul, "sentimental") in the popular culture items included. Chosen to help
illustrate an interesting theme--the ways in which popular culture
explores archetypes--the songs are to be used in a limited way: for
discussion of language and content, and for writing suggestions, and
not at all as music and performance (students evidently are not required to <u>listen</u> to the songs--only read them).

c.   Collections with Historical Narrative

See also S.867

S.860.   LAWRENCE, Vera Brodsky. <u>Music for Patriots, Politicians,</u>
<u>and Presidents: harmonies and discords of the first</u>
<u>hundred years.</u> New York: Macmillan, 1975. 480p.
illus., bibliog. refs.
While basically a large and excellent collection of reproductions of sheet music, lyrics, portraits, broadsides, title pages, and
a multitude of artifacts from the first hundred years of US history,
this book is also a well-researched, scholarly, amusing, and clearly-
written chronicle of the connections between historical and political
events, and political and patriotic music in the same period. Some
of the more "colorful" title pages of sheet music are reproduced in
full color; the majority of items are in black-and-white. Index.

S.861.   LEVY, Lester S. <u>Give Me Yesterday: American history in</u>
<u>song, 1890-1920.</u> Norman: University of Oklahoma Press,
1975. 420p. illus., bibliog.
At once entertaining and instructive, this third volume in
the author's series on popular song provides another convincing display of how popular music has mirrored many of the features, developments and events of an era. Nine of the ten chapters are each
devoted to one category of subject matter: entertainers, transpor-
tation, important public figures, women in the public eye, new territories, athletes and sportsmen, disasters and murders, leisure and
relaxation, progress; the final chapter covers a miscellany of topics.
Many song texts are quoted, and a number of songs are given with
words and melodies. Some 50 sheet music covers are reproduced,
mainly in black-and-white. The extensive bibliography includes
books and articles. Index.

S.862.   SCOTT, John Anthony. <u>The Ballad of America: the his-</u>
<u>tory of the United States in song and story.</u> New York:
Bantam Books, 1966. 404p. illus., bibliog., discog.
A product of the folk song revival era, this useful little
book is described by the compiler (with more accuracy than is shown

in the subtitle) as "an attempt to show how the story of the American people is revealed in their song." It is designed as a practical introduction to the national song heritage, with a particular relevance to use in education. The material is selected with three criteria in mind: clear expression of a given national mood or experience; fine examples of melodies and lyrics; effectiveness and popularity with contemporary audiences and performers. The songs are grouped in eight historical sections, from the colonial era to post-World War II. There are fourteen chapters in all (e.g., "The Westward Movement," "Farmers and Workers"). Most songs are in English, though one chapter, "Immigrants," is devoted to non-English songs and contains six items. Each chapter has a historical introduction, and each song is headed by generous background notes. The songs themselves are given as single-line melodies with guitar chords, and texts. There is a list of sources, an LP discography (both organized by the book's section titles), an index of titles and first lines, and a general index.

S.863.   SILBER, Irwin, ed. Songs of Independence. Harrisburg,
          Pa.: Stackpole Books, 1973. 249p. bibliog., discog.
          An illuminating anthology of the words and music of "songs associated with the development of American independence and political identity" (p. 11). Silber provides sufficient additional material to justify his claim that the book is a "study," and sufficient socio-political background to confirm that his approach is "at least as much sociological as it is musicological" (ibid.). The songs, from the Colonial and Revolutionary eras up to and including the War of 1812, are presented as single melody lines, with guitar chords (a small number are in four-part harmony). The arrangements are by Jerry Silverman (who is mentioned in the acknowledgments, but not on the title page). There are generous notes, and indexes of tunes, titles, persons, places, and events.

d. National and Regional Songs

S.864.   FEDOR, Ferenz. The Birth of Yankee Doodle. New York:
          Vantage Press, 1976. 204p. illus., bibliog.
          The title of this curious book is misleading, for it is not so much a history of the famous song as a hodgepodge of local history, etymology, genealogy, and lengthy quotations. For a study of the song itself, one still should use Oscar G. Sonneck's 1909 study (LOAM 1187) as at least a good starting point. Fedor's bibliography is poor, and his introduction a string of "inspirational" quotes from sources as diverse as Herbert Hoover, Abraham Lincoln, J. Edgar Hoover, and Adlai Stevenson.

S.865.   HALL, Ruth K. A Place of Her Own: the story of Eliza-
          beth Garrett. Sante Fe, N.M.: Sunstone Press, 1976.
          171p. illus., bibliog.

This is an apparently carefully researched biography ("intended primarily for young readers"--author's note) by a gifted amateur about the blind author of New Mexico's official state song, "O, Fair New Mexico," a tango. Ms. Garrett (1885?-1947), who composed many other secular and religious songs, was a daughter of Pat Garrett, the sheriff who shot Billy the Kid. She is described here as "half Chicano."

S.866.   TURNER, Martha Anne. The Yellow Rose of Texas: her
          saga and her song; with the Santa Anna legend. Austin,
          Tex.: Shoal Creek Publishers, 1976. 136p. illus.
     The story behind the well-loved song goes back to 1836, to the Battle of the San Jacinto, in which Texas forces overcame the Mexican troops under the command of General Antonio Lopez de Santa Anna; in this they were assisted, it appears, by a mulatto servant, Emily West, originally from New York, who was fully occupying the general's attentions (he had taken over a Texas plantation) when the Texans attacked. This, the emergence of the song, and its commercial history, are well told here in this carefully researched account. Like other scholars, however, the author is unable finally to solve the puzzle of the composer's identity--the mysterious "J.K." named as the composer on the first appearance of the song in 1858.

e. Popular Music in Times of Conflict

    (i) General

S.867.   AMERICAN WAR SONGS; published under supervision of
          National Committee for the Preservation of Existing
          Records of the National Society of the Colonial Dames
          of America. Philadelphia: privately printed, 1925.
          (Repr. Ann Arbor, Mich.: Gryphon Books, 1971).
          202p.
     An anthology of over 130 texts of songs from various campaigns (Revolutionary War, War of 1812, Mexican War, Civil War, Spanish-American War, World War I), with linking commentary, biographical information on authors and/or composers, and circumstances of composition. Much editorial work was apparently done by William Bond Wheelwright. Title, name and subject indexes.

    (ii) American Revolution

S.868.   ANDERSON, Gillian B. Freedom's Voice in Poetry and Song.
          Wilmington, Del.: Scholarly Resources, 1977. 888p.
     Focusing on the huge but little known body of Revolutionary political and patriotic song, this massive compilation has two main purposes: to "provide bibliographic control over song lyrics published in the colonial newspapers apart from their music" (p. x), and to provide a selection of music for the songs. The bibliographic control

is supplied by an inventory of 1,455 lyrics published between 1773 and 1783. Arranged geographically, then by newspaper, the inventory gives details wherever possible of first lines, titles, authors, tunes, and 18th-century source (in the case of a reprint). All these elements have their own index, the tune index being particularly thorough. The "educational" part of the book, the songbook, contains the music and texts of 92 songs and eight poems, chronologically arranged. Given the problems inherent in matching music to lyrics in the songs of this period (for the two were rarely published together), this songbook is an impressive and valuable achievement.

S.869. BRAND, Oscar. Songs of '76: a folksinger's history of
        the Revolution. New York: Evans, 1972. 178p. illus.
        A collection of 62 songs in single-melody lines with guitar
chords. In some cases, Brand writes, "the songs are 'jury' versions--verses and melodies selected and arranged (i.e., by Brand himself) from the many variants available" (p. 1). All are newly copyrighted by the compiler, who adds copious background and historical commentary, but does not indicate his sources.

S.870. CAMUS, Raoul F. Military Music of the American Revolu-
        tion. Chapel Hill: University of North Carolina Press,
        1976. 218p. illus., bibliog.
        A pioneering study, revealing not only the previously unsuspected extent of music in the revolutionary army, but also the importance of its role in the campaign. Camus begins by outlining the function and organization of military music in Europe, and the existing environment of military music in the colonies. He then proceeds historically, from the first shots of 1775, to 1783, producing an impressive amount of documentation (though not, surprisingly, about "Yankee Doodle"). Chapter 4 breaks the overall chronology to discuss, with examples, the various drum beats and signals, their military uses, and the traditions and ceremonies in which they were formalized. The appendices include lists of five tutors, drum manuals and collections of military music. Index.

S.871. RABSON, Carolyn, ed. Songbook of the American Revolu-
        tion; with illustrations by Nancy Hansen. Peaks Island,
        Maine: NEO Press, 1974. 112p. illus., bibliog.
        Celebrating the Bicentennial handsomely and a little in advance, this fine songbook presents texts and melodies in three sections: Ballads, Hymns, and National Songs. The hymns are given in four-part harmony with melodies in the tenor (as in the originals); most of the remainder appear as single melody lines, with added guitar chords. (For the latter, the original sources--contemporary ephemeral publications such as broadsides--often give the text only, and merely indicate possible tunes.) Historical information accompanies every song, and there is a general index (but not a song index, unfortunately, referring to specific pages where text and music may be found). Some concessions have been made to sensitivities of

persons unnamed: "Some verses have been omitted from several
songs, either because of space limitations or indelicacy of content"
(p. 4).

(iii) Civil War

S.872.   EMURIAN, Ernest K. Stories of Civil War Songs. Natick,
           Mass.: W. A. Wilde, 1960. 96p.
           This is one of some dozen little books by Rev. Emurian, a
southern Methodist minister, most of which tell the "stories" of hymns
and songs, and are aimed at a popular readership. Here twelve
Civil War songs are treated. The books by Emurian are breezy, unscholarly, and their "facts" must be taken with the proverbial grain
of salt. Legends are not always identified as such and--true or
false--are perpetuated; names and dates--the right ones or wrong
ones--are related with great confidence.

S.873.   EMURIAN, Ernest K. The Sweetheart of the Civil War:
           the true story of the song "Lorena." Natick, Mass.:
           W. A. Wilde Company, 1962. 72p. illus.
           This is perhaps the most consistently factual of Dr. Emu-
rian's books. Much authoritative assistance is indicated in his
"Acknowledgements" (pp. 71-72), and reproductions of authentic
old photographs can be seen throughout the book. The facts of
the "story" are important, of course, but they are stitched together
in Dr. Emurian's own sugary, at times unintentionally funny, prose.
To state what is perhaps a too well known fact: one must always
be vigilant to separate manner from matter. The charming song,
"Lorena" (1857), supposedly based on a true incident, was composed
by Joseph Filbrick Webster (1819-1875), the poem written by Rev.
Henry DeLafayette Webster (1824-1896) (the two men were not related). Though "Lorena" was very popular in mid-19th-century
America and still known in the 20th century, its composer is probably
best known for the hymn "The Sweet By and By" (composed 1867).

S.874.   SILBER, Irwin, ed. Soldier Songs and Home-Front Ballads
           of the Civil War. New York: Oak Publications, 1964.
           95p. illus.
           Though not so stated, this is an abridged version of
Silber's large, 1960 collection, Songs of the Civil War (LOAM 1191).
The 58 songs (as opposed to 129 in the original) are given as single-
line melodies with guitar chords. They are identical to the large
collection except for one unfortunate omission: Jerry Silverman's
piano accompaniments. (One cannot imagine performances of the
"home-front ballads" here--such as "Just Before the Battle, Mother,"
and "The Vacant Chair"--without piano.) The bulk of the interesting, if brief, introduction is taken from the original, as are
some of the headnotes and illustrations. Missing are the extensive
notes for each song that appear in the original. One unique feature,
however, is the presence of some evocative photographs. No song
title index.

5. Bands and Their Music

(See also S. 870)

S.875. BRIDGES, Glenn. Pioneers in Brass. Detroit: Sherwood
Publications, 1965. 113p. illus.

This is a valuable, if slightly crude, biographical dictionary
of over 50 mostly rather obscure 19th- and early 20th-century band
performers and conductors (many of whom were also composers, like
Herbert L. Clarke). Much information here can be found in no other
work. The articles, which must have been very difficult to compile,
seem carefully researched and written; each features at least one
photograph of the subject; each is concluded with a casual, selective
discography (all record and cylinder labels and numbers are omitted).

S.876. HALL, Harry H. A Johnny Reb Band from Salem: the
pride of Tarheelia. Raleigh, N.C.: North Carolina Confederate Centennial Commission, 1963. 118p.

A fine scholarly monograph, bulging with bibliographic and
other footnotes, and giving the history of the Salem, North Carolina
Regiment for three years (1862-65) during the Civil War. The band,
composed of Moravians, played concerts and served its regiment in
many ways. It was involved in the Battle of Gettysburg. The
band's members were prisoners of war for over three months in
1865. The author states that his study provided material for his
doctoral dissertation (foreword, p. vii) at Peabody College, Nashville,
and that "the major portion ... is based upon the Civil War diary of
Julius Augustus Leinbach (Lineback)" (p. 1), a member of the band.
Index.

6. 19th-Century Popular Music

S.877. AUSTIN, William W. "Susanna," "Jeanie," and "The Old
Folks at Home": the songs of Stephen C. Foster from
his time to ours. New York: Macmillan, 1975. 420p.
bibliog., refs.

Austin calls his fascinating, unusual study a "labyrinthine
exploration" (p. xiii), and indeed, as he pursues the many meander-
ing trails which lead out from Foster and his songs through a vast
complex of 19th- and--to a lesser extent--20th-century American
culture, there is a distinct danger of his readers losing the thread.
One's admiration for the writer's ability to make connections between
Foster and figures as diverse as Herman Melville, P. T. Barnum,
Philip Paul Bliss, W. E. B. DuBois, and Ray Charles is somewhat
tempered by a feeling that more rigorous control, and more pronounced theoretical base for the exploration, would have benefitted
the end result.

What distinguishes this book from most others on popular
music is its profound concern with meanings. Believing that Foster's

songs "elude mere musical description or analysis" (p. ix), Austin
sets out to investigate not one meaning but "a whole range of meanings in relation to each other" (p. xi) in their social and historical
contexts. The songs are divided into three broad groups: "Comic,
Ethiopian" ("Susanna" etc.), "Poetic," ("Jeanie with the Light Brown
Hair," etc.), and "Pathetic plantation" ("The Old Folks at Home,"
etc.); in addition to examining them in the context of Foster's life
and art, Austin looks at the variety of functions filled by each type
of song for distinct groups of people into whose lives they filtered--
how, for example, "Susanna" was used in mid-century California
gambling halls, how "Old Folks" and similar songs were influential
in the "people's songs" of Root and Work, and the gospel songs of
Bliss and Sankey. The concluding chapters highlight contrasting
20th-century clusters of meanings: for Charles Ives and other composers, for Ray Charles in his "Swanee River Rock," and for Pete
Seeger's "creative rearranging" of "Camptown Races" and others.
These and other interpretations, as Austin wisely remarks, "are important ... only to the extent that they reflect and affect our interactions with each other, in all kinds of music and in more than
music" (p. 356). (Formerly LOAM A233.)

S.878.   TAWA, Nicholas E.   Sweet Songs for Gentle Americans:
          the parlor song in America, 1790-1860.   Bowling Green,
          Ohio: Bowling Green University Popular Press, 1980.
          273p.   illus., bibliog.
          A meticulously thorough, scholarly re-examination of the
parlor song genre, "what it is; why, by whom, and for whom it
was written; its textual and musical commonplaces; and the characteristics of its lyrics and music" (preface). Tawa divides the time-
span covered into three periods: British domination (1790-1811),
the rise of American singers and composers (1811-1841), and American ascendancy (1841-1861). His method is to move, in a sense,
backwards along the line of communication, from the audience (social
levels, and changes therein) and the uses of the music (particularly
in education), back through the disseminators of the songs--the professional performers, the publishers, the retailers--eventually ar-
riving at the songs themselves, their subject matter and their musical characteristics. One intervening chapter breaks the sequence to
examine the relationship and the differences between the parlor song
and the minstrel song. Besides the vast array of documentation
there is a list of the 170 most popular songs in the extant collections, a bibliography of works consulted, a selection of music
examples, and a musical supplement of reprints of sixteen representative songs. Index.

7.   The Genteel Tradition

S.879.   BOND, Carrie Jacobs.   The Roads to Melody.   New York:
          Appleton, 1927.   (Repr. New York: Arno Press, 1980.)

223p. illus.

The composer (and, often, author) of a vast number of popular songs, some 170 of which were published--and most of which are now forgotten--Mrs. Bond (1862-1946) enjoyed a career which lasted 50 years (1894-1944), but the years 1900-1910 were the most fruitful. The songs she wrote at that time (among them "Just a Wearyin' for You" and "A Perfect Day," to name two survivors) place her firmly in the tradition of 19th-century sentimental parlor song composers. But she was in many ways a very forward-looking woman, and her story is both fascinating in its own right (even allowing for autobiographical licence) and significant in terms of the position of the woman composer. It was to songwriting that Mrs. Bond turned, in Chicago, following the untimely death of her husband, Frank Bond, in 1895, an event which left her in poverty. The struggle was hard, but through perseverance and the help of friends her songs became known. Characteristically resourceful, she set up her own music business at home, publishing her own songs, and even designing the sheet music covers. "A Perfect Day," composed in California, had a huge contemporary success; the words and music appear on pp. 175-78. (In an earlier article, "Music Composition as a Field for Women," Etude 38, No. 9 [1920], pp. 583-584, Mrs. Bond rehearsed some of the ideas which later found place in her book.) (The title of the book appears in the reprint as The Roads of Melody--the cover title of the original edition.)

8. Popular Music of the Stage and Screen

a. General Historical Works

S.880.   BLUMENTHAL, George. My 60 Years in Show Business: a chronicle of the American theater, 1874-1934; as told by George Blumenthal to Arthur H. Menkin. New York: Frederick C. Osberg, 1936. 336p. illus.

From program boy to impresario, and from burlesque to grand opera, Blumenthal's experience of the New York musical stage was nothing if not varied. His autobiography is very much about wheeling and dealing, but there are numerous insights into the nuts and bolts of the New York theater in the late 19th and early 20th centuries. Among those who make regular appearances are Oscar Hammerstein I, Victor Herbert (with more on the background to productions of his operas than on the man himself), and Emma Trentini; the cast of characters also includes Rudolf Friml, Mary Garden, Weber and Fields, and the booking agents Erlanger and Klaw.

S.881.   CHURCHILL, Allen. The Great White Way: a re-creation of Broadway's golden era of theatrical entertainment. New York: Dutton, 1962. 310p. illus., bibliog.

Churchill's enjoyable tale of Broadway from 1900 to the beginning of Prohibition in January 1920 is filled with legendary larger-

than-life-figures such as producers Erlanger and Frohman, actors
Belasco and Maude Adams, tales of financial wizardry (and hocus-
pocus), and much supporting theatrical lore. The only musical
figure to recur frequently in the narrative is George M. Cohan
(see especially pp. 133-40, 224-27, and, for his opposition to the
Equity strike of 1919, pp. 285-87). Chapter 9 is devoted to vaudeville, and chapter 11 to the period beginning about 1915, when
Broadway was invaded by the dance craze, and music began to
dominate theatres and restaurants alike. Here we also meet, all too
briefly, with the Jim Europe band, the partnership between Kern,
Wodehouse and Bolton that produced the musicals for the Princess
Theatre, and the dancing Castles. Though music is not treated
anywhere in great detail, its place and function as one ingredient
in the overall context of Broadway are apparent. Index.

S.882.   MARCOSSON, Isaac F., and FROHMAN, Daniel. Charles
          Frohman: manager and man; with an appreciation by
          James M. Barrie. New York: Harper, 1916. 439p.
          illus.
    Though he produced many plays with incidental music and
plays in which music stood out, such as Fluffy Ruffles (1909), The
Girl from Montmarte (1912), and The Doll Girl (1913), this otherwise
fascinating biography of Frohman (1860-1915), the outstanding
theater manager of the turn-of-the-century, who went down on the
Lusitania in 1915, contains little or nothing about songs or composers.

S.883.   TOLL, Robert C. On with the Show: the first century of
          show business in America. New York: Oxford Univer-
          sity Press, 1976. 361p. illus., bibliog.
    Proceeding from the belief that, as show business enter-
tained, "it reflected and spoke to its patrons' deepest concerns, de-
sires and needs" (introduction), Toll's historical account of the evolution in the 19th and early 20th centuries of the numerous species
of popular stage entertainment is part narrative, part explanation.
The central theme of the common people's shaping of show business
in their own image is explored through accounts of the beginnings
in the early 19th century, the Barnum phenomenon, the circus, the
minstrel show, popular dramas, vaudeville, etc. Musical performance,
though never analyzed, is never far away, and is a noteworthy element in the accounts of minstrelsy, of negroes in show business,
and of the evolution of the musical comedy; it is noted also in the
chapters on burlesque, vaudeville and the Ziegfeld Follies. The
many contemporary illustrations include sheet music covers, hand-
bills, cartoons, and photographs. The book concludes with a bibliographical essay, a chronological table in which events in society
and on stage are compared, and an index.

b. Blacks on Stage and Screen

S.884.   SAMPSON, Henry T. Blacks in Blackface: a source book

on early black musical shows. Metuchen, N.J.: Scarecrow Press, 1980. 552p. illus.

That the black contribution to the musical stage was significant has rarely been doubted, but it is obvious, following Sampson's revelation of the breadth and depth of black activity in this
book, that it has hitherto been grossly underestimated. Turning
for his information to contemporary black newspapers (which themselves both knew about and broadcast the highly creative nature of
the black musical stage), Sampson first provides an overview of the
development of black musical theater. Here, as elsewhere, his own
text is uncritical, but he includes numerous extracts from reviewers
in the black press, giving the flavor of their critical response. The
men behind the productions are portrayed in two successive chap-
ters--financial backers such as Sherman H. Dudley, and producers
such as Isham Jones, Bob Cole, and J. Rosamund Johnson--and
many of the black theaters themselves are briefly described. Two
chapters containing reference information form the heart of the book:
first, a series of synopses of around 150 shows, with details where
possible of producers, authors, composers, cast, musical numbers,
and plot; second, some 100 biographical sketches of major performers.
Appendices include a typical T.O.B.A. contract, and a partial list
of shows, 1900-1940. Index.

S.885. SAMPSON, Henry T. Blacks in Black and White: a source
book on black film. Metuchen, N.J.: Scarecrow Press,
1977. 333p. illus.

Some 300 independent, all-black-cast films were produced
up to 1950, and many of them were described as musical comedies,
or musical dramas, or featured music in some way. The music content of these films is not Sampson's primary concern, but much information of a reference kind about the music can be obtained from
the book. Synopses of over 100 of the films are provided, with
cast lists; among those appearing in these films are Bert Williams,
Josephine Baker, Lena Horne, Louis Jordan. There are also biographical sketches of over 70 performers, including Cab Calloway,
Dorothy Dandridge, and Bill "Bojangles" Robinson. A complete list
of the all-black films gives date, company, and cast (sometimes--but
not always--including musicians). Appendix C provides details of
film credits for featured players in these films, including a selection
of musicians (e.g., Eubie Blake, Ethel Waters). The index, unfortunately, is not comprehensive; for example, the presence of Sidney
Bechet in Moon Over Harlem (p. 157) is not indexed.

S.886. SCHIFFMAN, Jack. Uptown: the story of Harlem's Apollo
Theatre. New York: Cowles, 1971. 210p. illus.

For many years regarded as the hub of black show business,
the Apollo was founded by Schiffman's father, and managed by the
author himself from 1935. A vivid, anecdotal history, the book not
only chronicles all the memorable performances--from Bessie Smith via
the big bands and dancers like Bill Robinson to the postwar era of
Dinah Washington, Billie Holiday, Lionel Hampton, vocal groups such

as the Orioles, and soul star James Brown--it also takes care to describe the changing social context and the consequent modulations in both performers and audiences. Index.

c. Minstrelsy and Medicine Shows

S.887.   BROWNE, Ray B., ed. Rituals and Ceremonies in Popular
          Culture. Bowling Green, Ohio: Bowling Green Univer-
          sity Popular Press, 1980. 349p. illus.
    Included in this collection of 26 essays is a brief but inter-
esting contribution by David N. Lyon, "The Minstrel Show as Ritual:
Surrogate Black Culture," in which certain minstrel song texts are
analyzed, and reasons are suggested as to how and why minstrel
songs, created by whites, were accepted by the general public as
being of black origin.

S.888.   McNAMARA, Brooks. Step Right Up. Garden City, N.Y.:
          Doubleday, 1976. 233p. illus., bibliog.
    From the post-Civil War era well into the 20th century (into
the 1950s in some places), touring medicine shows gave work to black
and white musicians, whose job was to put the audience in the right
humor to buy the patent medicines. Although McNamara has relatively little to say about the music or the musicians, his book should
be noted as a fascinating illustrated history of this remarkable institution.   Special attention is paid to the Indian shows, in particular
those of the Kickapoo Indians and their imitators, where it was more
than likely you would see a "combination of burning wagon trains and
blackface minstrel routines" (p. 103).   Chapter 9 describes in brief
the various kinds of variety act that were part and parcel of the
shows.   (For information and comment on black musicians in the
medicine show, see Paul Oliver, Songsters and Saints: vocal traditions on race records [Cambridge: Cambridge University Press,
1984], and Bruce Bastin's notes to the recording, The Last Medicine
Show on Flyright 507/8.)

d. Burlesque, Vaudeville, Revue

S.889.   DiMEGLIO, John E. Vaudeville U.S.A. Bowling Green,
          Ohio: Bowling Green University Popular Press, 1973.
          259p. illus., bibliog.
    Vaudeville may have been the "vast intellectual wasteland
of its day" (p. 6), but it was also "the most popular form of entertainment in a period of American history where many significant
changes were taking place" (ibid.), and as such, DiMeglio convincingly asserts, needs closer examination.   His own study, based on
research into published and unpublished materials and on personal
interviews, is concerned less with performance aspects than with the

personal, professional, organizational, geographical, and, to a smaller extent, social background. Successive chapters examine the managers, the audiences, the typical vaudevillian and his/her lifestyle (the hardships and rewards of life on the road), the particular difficulties facing black vaudevillians, the importance of New York, and other centers in big cities and small towns. A final chapter summarizes vaudeville's role in the society of its day. Although the book pays no particular attention to music, several performers with strong musical credentials figure frequently, among them Fred Astaire, Eddie Cantor, Sammy Davis Jr., Al Jolson, and Ethel Waters. Index.

S.890. ISMAN, Felix. Weber and Fields: their tribulations, triumphs and their associates. New York: Boni and Liveright, 1924. 345p. illus.

Pioneers of a music hall tradition that drew its inspiration from the ethnic vernacular culture of the cities--especially New York's Lower East Side--and played a significant part in the development of popular culture in America, Joe Weber (1867-1942) and Lew Fields (1867-1941) lived out in show-biz saga from the penury of beer garden song-and-dance routines to wealth and celebrity (and retirement in Beverly Hills in 1930, after this book was written). Isman, who knew them well, is inclined to see their achievement, only partly tongue-in-cheek, in terms of a military campaign, in which the two "undersized, underfed and underloved" heroes (who were both nine years old when they made their first performances) outwit all opposition on their way to the top. This is an admiring, detailed biography, tracing the careers of "Weberfields" from that infant beginning, through their lengthy apprenticeship in dime museums, their success as ethnic comics, their gradual shift to the legitimate theater and the shows produced at 'Weber and Fields' Music Hall (1896-1904), to their personal feud, break up and later reconciliation. Isman recaptures something of their comic spirit, and also provides plenty of detail on business aspects, backstage schemings, and so forth. There is little on music or on the performance skills of Lillian Russell, Fay Templeton, and others who worked for and with them. The music of eight Weber and Fields songs is included at the back. No index.

S.891. KAHN, E. J. The Merry Partners: the age and stage of Harrigan and Hart. New York: Random House, 1955. 302p.

For fourteen years from 1872 Ned Harrigan (1844-1911) and Tony Hart (1855-1891) were a star attraction in New York's vaudeville with their sketches (which grew to full-length plays) on all manner of New York life, especially on the Irish, Italian and black communities. Song always featured predominantly in their performances ("make songs for the poor, and you plant roses among the weeds," Harrigan once remarked), and Harrigan himself wrote the lyrics of over 200 songs. Although Kahn treats his own research dismissively, speaking of "facts ... brashly filched from the labors

of older and, on the whole, wiser people" (p. xi), his biography is
a thorough one. Besides tracing their careers, Kahn describes
typical Harrigan and Hart performances, and demonstrates the inspiration Harrigan in particular found for songs, plays and performance in the ethnic groups of New York. Harrigan's partnership
with composer Dave Braham (1834-1905) is briefly described on
p. 151ff. The great strength of Kahn's book is its detailed portrait
of the popular stage in its historical and social context. No index.

S.892. MOODY, Richard. Ned Harrigan: from Corlear's Hook to
        Herald Square. Chicago: Nelson-Hall, 1980. 282p.
        illus., bibliog.
        Using a wealth of previously unavailable and/or untapped
source material--family documents and scrapbooks, programs, clip-
pings, manuscripts, interviews with descendants--Moody skillfully
recreates the life and times of this fascinating figure in American entertainment history--the senior partner in the Harrigan-Hart partnership, and the man who, in Sigmund Spaeth's words, created
"something as typically American as the minstrel show, or rag-time,
or jazz itself" (LOAM 1171, p. 195); that something was a mixture
of vaudeville, minstrelsy, and "some of the technique of musical
comedy and the modern revue" (ibid., p. 181). Moody's biography
enables us to see the evolution of this form, with frequent use of
Harrigan's unpublished mss. The story of the celebrated Mulligan
Guard is told in Chapter 6, and the music of the song is reproduced,
with six others, in the book. Harrigan's composer partner, Dave
Braham, is regularly featured in the book (Moody acknowledges a
debt to Harrigan's granddaughter for research on Braham's English
origins), and his way of working is outlined on pp. 154-55. But
the songs themselves--songs which "represent the beginning of urban popular song" (Charles Hamm, no. S.835, p. 281)--are not central to the interests of either Moody or Kahn (no. S.891). Much
more research could profitably be done on the Harrigan-Braham partnership. Index.

S.893. MORELL, Parker. Lillian Russell: the era of plush. New
        York: Random House, 1940. 319p. illus.
        One of the first--if not the first--of America's international-
ly-known superstars, Lillian Russell (aka Helen Leonard, 1861-1922)
built her career on a combination of sensual stage presence--in the
context of light opera!--and an appealing natural voice (which was
said to be able to hit high C eight times a night). Born in Chicago,
the daughter of an early feminist, she made her debut in 1880 at
Tony Pastor's variety theater in New York as a shy English maiden
("a vision of loveliness and a voice of gold," said Pastor). All this
and much more is thoroughly, readably related in this biography,
tracing her career from Gilbert and Sullivan to Weber and Fields,
Offenbach to melodrama, with all the intermittent hurly-burly of
failed marriages and a publicity machine and extravagant lifestyle
that only Hollywood could later rival. Use is made of Russell's autobiographical articles which appeared, "cautiously expurgated," in

Cosmopolitan magazine in 1922. Morell makes little attempt to assess Russell's role in the development of the female singing star in these crucial, formative years of American popular culture. (A study by John Burke, Duet in Diamonds [New York: Putnam, 1972] draws frequently on Morell in a portrait of Russell and her gargantuan one-time companion, Diamond Jim Brady.)

S.894.   SMITH, Bill. The Vaudevillians. New York: Macmillan,
         1976. 278p. illus.
         Various, generally less well-known vaudeville figures talk to Billboard magazine's Bill Smith, who reproduces their reminiscences in the first person. Among those featured are the singing comedian Billy Glason, the singing, dancing (and rope-twirling) husband and wife team of Will and Gladys Ahern, dancer-pianist John Bubbles, child vaudeville star turned accomplished singer Sylvia Froos, singer-comedian Jack Haley, and singers Rae Samuels and Arthur Tracy. Index.

S.895.   SOBEL, Bernard. A Pictorial History of Burlesque. New
         York: Bonanza Books, 1956. 194p. illus.
         Chapter 14, "Books and Music," considers some of the composers and lyricists who worked in burlesque; also included are an account of the first shows, beginning in 1869, a typical show format, information on burlesque in western honky-tonks, and a portrait of Minsky's. (Well on the decline in the 1920s, burlesque was eventually banned in 1939.) Index.

S.896.   SOBEL, Bernard. A Pictorial History of Vaudeville; fore-
         word by George Jessel. New York: Citadel Press,
         1961. 224p. illus.
         Sobel's descriptive historical account, though short, is knowledgeable and affectionate; it takes the reader from vaudeville's European origins, through its early American development, the minstrel show, to the peak of its history in the early 20th century, and its decline in the 1930s. On the way Sobel portrays "a vaude-villian's life and times" (the theaters, the touring life, the managers, etc.), the moguls (chief among them E. F. Albee, F. F. Proctor), and the Palace Theater on Broadway, vaudeville's principal attraction in the 1910s and '20s. This nicely illustrated history is followed by a large portrait gallery of vaudevillians, and a smaller one of eminent visitors from more "legitimate" areas of the theater. Index of pictures.

S.897.   ZEIDMAN, Irving. The American Burlesque Show. New
         York: Hawthorn Books, 1967. 271p. illus., bibliog.
         Bristling affectionately with the names of performers and producers, and with theatrical facts and figures, this history of what its author describes as "primarily a commercialized sex show" outlines the story of burlesque from its 19th-century predecessors, through the rise and fall of the "wheel show" in the 1910s-1930s, to the subsequent prevalence of strip. Though the text contains little

on individual musicians it provides an idea of the run-of-the-mill
exposure popular music received, and of the employment its practitioners earned, in the context of popular theatrical entertainment.
Index.

e. Broadway Musical Comedy

   (i) Reference Works

   See also S.799, S.884, S.906

S.898.   DRINKROW, John.   The Vintage Musical Comedy Book.
          Reading, England: Osprey, 1974. 146p. illus., discog.
          Concentrating on English shows, but with some information
on American productions, this is a modest reference book providing
highly selective credits, brief plot synopses and lists of principal
numbers for over 70 musicals (alphabetically arranged from Annie
Get Your Gun to the Vagabond King). One positive feature is the
inclusion of the owner of the performing rights for each show. Rudimentary discography (by Frank Rogers).

S.899.   DRONE, Jeanette Marie. Index to Opera, Operetta and Mu-
          sical Comedy Synopses in Collections and Periodicals.
          Metuchen, N.J.: Scarecrow Press, 1978. 171p. bibliog.
          The 74 reference sources and four periodicals indexed pro-
vide a fairly good coverage of plot synopses, but a substantial number of musicals are not represented in them; as a result Drone's
work, while it is as good as its sources allow, appears somewhat
patchy. Alphabetically arranged by work title, with a composer index and a bibliography of additional sources.

S.900.   GREEN, Stanley. Encyclopedia of the Musical Theatre.
          New York: Dodd, Mead, 1976. 488p. bibliog., discog.
          _____. Encyclopedia of the Musical. London: Cassell,
          1977. 488p. bibliog., discog.
          Green's objectives are clearly set out in his preface, where
he describes the work as "a ready-reference book containing succinct information regarding the most prominent people, productions,
and songs of the musical theatre, both in New York (incl. off-
Bway) and London." There are entries, therefore, for individuals
with a variety of functions: composers, librettists, lyricists, directors, producers, choreographers, actors, and actresses. A typical
entry provides biographical data followed by a chronological list of
stage shows with, in the case of performers, notes on the roles
played. Entries for the shows themselves provide information on
their authors, a note on any sources, a list of the best-known songs,
and selective production details (producer, director, designer, leading members of the cast). This is followed by a brief commentary on
the show itself and its fortunes, with, often, a note on the storyline.
Film versions are indicated also. Entries under selected songs give

the names of its creators, the show to which it belonged, and its drar tic context. Additional information at the back of the book includes lists of awards and prizes, and of long runs, a bibliography of published librettos and lyrics and of reference sources, and a discography of original and studio cast albums, and of selected recordings by performers, composers and lyricists. (Record label name only supplied.) A reliable, accurate work, which must, however, be used as it was intended--as a quick, handy guide to selective information.

S.901.   HODGINS, Gordon W.   The Broadway Musical: a complete
         LP discography. Metuchen, N.J.: Scarecrow Press,
         1980. 183p.
         Though less comprehensive than Hummel (no. S.902), this
discography can readily meet the needs of most users. Its coverage
is restricted to original cast albums, and to albums "released to
feature specific performers or groups of performers whether or not
that person or group ever actually appeared on stage in the musical
recorded" (p. iv). Only releases on major US labels are included.
Arrangement is alphabetical by show title, with details of record label
and number, year of release, cast, composer and author credits, and
song titles. There are six indexes: composer; lyricist and book
author; performer; song title (selective--complete for 94 shows,
partly complete for 112); composer-lyricist partnership; major record
company. An appendix lists records lacking adequate information.
The cut-off date appears to be 1978.

S.902.   HUMMEL, David.   The Collector's Guide to the American
         Musical Theatre. Grawn, Mich.: D. H. Enterprises,
         1977. unpaged.
         _____. _____. 2nd ed. Grawn, Mich.: D. H.
         Enterprises, 1978. 238p.
         _____. _____. Supplement 1. Grawn, Mich.:
         D. H. Enterprises. 1978. 79p.
         _____. _____. New ed. Metuchen, N.J.: Scarecrow
         Press, 1983. 2v. (940p).
         The earlier editions of this important discography and
reference book were closely tied to the compiler's own collection: a
basic chronological arrangement, beginning with The Beggars' Opera,
was organized within each year by the order in which Hummel acquired the recordings. The new edition, as well as massively increasing the coverage, opts for an alphabetical order of shows, all
versions being detailed under the one heading. Besides studio cast
albums, the book lists composers' home recordings, demos, backers'
auditions, and private live performances. The details provided for
each show include credits, production information, number of performances, and a list of songs. Name index.

S.903.   PARIS, Leonard A.   Men and Melodies. New York:
         Crowell, 1954. 197p.
         Sixteen American show composers and lyricists are featured

in this light-weight, highly-selective collection of biographies. The
earliest figures dealt with are Reginald DeKoven, Victor Herbert,
and Harry B. Smith, and the latest Kurt Weill, Richard Rodgers, and
Oscar Hammerstein II. The writing is noticeably short on fact and
long on anecdote. Index.

S.904.   RICHARDS, Stanley, ed. Ten Great Musicals of the Ameri-
          can Theatre. Radnor, Pa.:   Chilton, 1973.   594p.
          illus.
          _____. Great Musicals of the American Theatre, Vol. 2.
          Radnor, Pa.:   Chilton, 1976.   606p.   illus.
          These two volumes contain the complete book and lyrics for
20 musicals.   The editor provides brief introductory notes on each
show, its creators and its principal performers.   The shows included
are: (Vol. 1) Of Thee I Sing, Porgy and Bess, One Touch of Venus,
Brigadoon, Kiss Me Kate, West Side Story, Gypsy, Fiddler on the
Roof, 1976, Company; (Vol. 2) Leave It to Me, Lady in the Dark,
Lost in the Stars, Wonderful Town, Fiorello! Camelot, Man of La
Mancha, Cabaret, Applause, A Little Night Music.

S.905.   RICHARDS, Stanley, ed.   Great Rock Musicals.   New York:
          Stein and Day, 1979.   562p.   illus.
          Includes the complete book and lyrics for The Wiz, Two
Gentlemen of Verona, Grease, Your Own Thing, Hair, and Promenade.
(Jesus Christ Superstar and the lyrics to Tommy are also present.)
The editor contributes background commentary on the writers and
the productions.

          (ii) Histories and Studies

S.906.   BORDMAN, Gerald.   American Musical Theatre: a chronicle.
          New York: Oxford University Press, 1978.   749p.
          In the preface to his admirable book, Bordman speaks of
"the need for a thorough, accurate history," but the subtitle is a
more precise description of the book's form and purpose.   One turns
to a history of an art form for (among other things) an informed
awareness of the interplay between that art and the society and culture in which it is rooted, and for an ability to discern the significant among the insignificant hordes.   Neither of these is Bordman's concern (though he makes some attempt to relate the musical
to social and historical developments, falling as he does so for too
many historical clichés).   His aim is to provide a short, descriptive,
mildly critical account of every musical done on Broadway from 1866
to May 1978.   These accounts are chronologically arranged, season
by season, and contain basic factual information (opening dates,
theaters, authors and composers, plot summaries, leading performers)
and comment on book, lyrics, music, and the overall achievement (or
lack of it) of each show.   All this is woven into a paragraph or two
of readable narrative.   In order to impose some sense of history,

Bordman divides his text into five broad periods with "intermissions"; each period is introduced by a summary of historical and social trends. The succession of shows is interrupted in appropriate places by short biographies of leading figures.

A book to "dip into," as Bordman admits, rather than read from beginning to end, it is also an excellent reference book, having a higher level of accuracy than most reference works in this or the popular song field. Its reference capacities are enhanced by good indexes: shows, songs, and people.

S.907.   FEHL, Fred. On Broadway: performance photographs by
              Fred Fehl; text by William Stott with Jane Stott. Austin:
              University of Texas Press, 1978; London: Thames &
              Hudson, 1979. 419p. illus.

A collection of photographs of Broadway shows (including a number of musicals) from 1940 to 1968 by a pioneer of the art of theatre performance photography. The two or three photographs from each of the shows chosen are accompanied by the comments of actors, directors, critics, etc., mostly derived "from fugitive periodicals" (p. xxxv). Chosen from the Fehl archive at the University of Texas, the photographs are a vibrant record in which, as William Stott remarks in his introduction, "the people are alive, downstage, lustrous, ready to please."

S.908.   GOTTFRIED, Martin. Broadway Musicals. New York:
              Abrams, 1979. 352p. illus.

The sumptuous illustrations in this large, handsome volume might justifiably be regarded as an end in themselves (with a word of thanks to the designer, Nai Y. Chang); but Gottfried's text should not be overlooked. It aims "not to present an encyclopedic or historical account of musicals but to define, analyze, criticize, and celebrate them--to capture their spirit" (p. 6). While the illustrations effectively accomplish the last two functions, the text knowledgeably, if all too briefly, tackles the first three, with successive discussion of the "elements" of a musical (book, music, lyrics, design), of the art of directing (with special attention to George Abbott, Jerome Robbins, and Bob Fosse), of outstanding composers (Kern, Rodgers, Gershwin, Berlin) and of the modern era (in particular, Stephen Sondheim, and with a section on black musicals). Index.

S.909.   JACKSON, Arthur. The Book of Musicals: from Show
              Boat to A Chorus Line; foreword by Clive Barnes.
              London: Mitchell Beazley, 1977. 208p. illus., bibliog.,
              discog.
              _____. The Best Musicals ... (etc.). New York:
              Crown, 1977. 208p. illus., bibliog., discog.

An attempt to provide the general reader with an all-in-one book on the American musical (stage and, to a lesser extent, screen): eye-catching pictures, potted history, and reference information. The latter, which occupies half the book, consists of a

"who's who of show and film music," giving short biographies of
around 90 leading figures, a musical calendar, 1866-1977, a song
title index with references to show, plot summaries (very summary),
a list of long runs on and off Broadway, a filmography, an LP discography, and a book bibliography. Index.

S.910.   KISLAN, Richard. The Musical: a look at the American
            musical theater. Englewood Cliffs, N.J.: Prentice-
            Hall, 1980. 262p. illus.
      Kislan's "simple book, a book of fundamentals designed for
the beginner" (p. vii) cannot be unreservedly recommended as such.
Its first section, a series of short chapters on the various forms of
musical theater that preceded the "mature" musical itself (minstrelsy,
vaudeville, burlesque, revue, etc.), presents historical evolution in
a boiled-down, somewhat insipid form, ignoring all social developments. Part 2 solves the problem of simplifying the rich, complex
years of the mature musical by declaring that Jerome Kern, Rodgers
and Hammerstein, and Stephen Sondheim were/are the helmsmen who
"set the ship of tradition to sail in significant new directions"
(p. viii)--and by focusing on these figures' lives and works, to the
exclusion not merely of the likes of Gershwin and Porter, but of the
very idea of the theater as a living system of interrelationships.
Part 3 deals in turn with the elements of musical theater--book,
lyrics, score, dance, design--and is the most successful, drawing on
the author's practical experience. Index.

S.911.   MORDDEN, Ethan. Better Foot Forward: the history of
            American musical theatre. New York: Grossman Pub-
            lishers, 1976. 369p. illus., bibliog.
      Determined to avoid being thought dull, Mordden writes
history in a perky style that seems constantly to be on the verge of
telling a good joke. It turns out, however, that he doesn't know
any, and the resulting let-down focuses attention on the book's
rather hollow center. The 29 chronological chapters, from 19th-
century beginnings to the 1970s, and ending with praise for Sondheim's Follies and A Little Night Music, provide a detailed map of
the surfaces, particularly of the "hard realities of music, lyrics
and script" in preference to the "human side of musical comedy"
(p. x), and are useful for that. Mordden is at his best when there
is a whiff of an argument to be joined (as, for example, in his
views on most critics). Index.

      (iii) Practical Aspects

S.912.   BENNETT, Robert Russell. Instrumentally Speaking. Mel-
            ville, N.Y.: Belwin-Mills, 1975. 169p.
      Composer and master arranger (especially for Broadway),
Bennett (b.1894) would have a fascinating story to tell--but not
here. This is basically an instrumental book, in two parts: "The

Music Arranger in the Theater," and "The Game Is There for the
Hunting." Preface by Richard Franko Goldman.

S.91?. ENGEL, Lehman. The Critics. New York: Macmillan,
1976. 332p.
    A frequently devastating critique of the American news-
paper theater critics, with many references to their treatment of
musicals. Company, Cabaret, A Chorus Line, Sweet Charity, Hair,
and Candide are among the shows whose reviews are analyzed and
evaluated. Some critics receive scathing treatment (e.g., Martin
Gottfried--"Nobody knows everything. The question is whether
Gottfried knows anything"--p. 45), some a modicum of praise (e.g.,
Douglas Watt, Walter Kerr). A revealing insight into the power,
the responsibility (and lack of it), the foibles of theater critics--
and into the always explosive relationship between the critics and
the practitioners themselves. Index.

S.914. ENGEL, Lehman. The Making of a Musical. New York:
Macmillan; London: Collier Macmillan, 1977. 157p.
    Based on a curriculum developed by Engel at Music
Theatre Workshops under the aegis of BMI, this is a "step-by-step
analysis of the elements that comprise a musical show" (p. xvii).
In clear language the author sets out the essential features of the
music (song forms, musical elements), lyrics, and libretto (with an
interesting scene-by-scene comparison of Oklahoma! and West Side
Story with their "originals" Green Grow the Lilacs and Romeo and
Juliet). The discussion of the libretto also includes consideration
of the placement of songs, and some criticism of Pacific Overtures.
Index.

S.915. ENGEL, Lehman. Their Words Are Music: the great
theatre lyricists and their lyrics. New York: Crown,
1975. 275p. illus.
    With this critical anthology Engel aims "to trace the pro-
gress of lyric writing from some of our earliest musical theatre,
through a number of significant changes, to the present time" (p.
xii). The generous selection of lyrics opens with a section "Beginnings and Problems," covering the late 19th and early 20th
centuries; following this a chapter each is devoted to Cole Porter,
Lorenz Hart, Oscar Hammerstein II, Ira Gershwin, Howard Dietz,
E. Y. Harburg, Dorothy Fields, Marc Blitzstein, Harold Rome,
Frank Loesser, Betty Comden and Adolph Green, Alan Jay Lerner,
Sheldon Harnick, Tom Jones, and Stephen Sondheim. There are
also sections on Leonard Sillman's New Faces, and on Kurt Weill's
various collaborators (Maxwell Anderson, Langston Hughes, etc.).
Each of these chapters has a short introduction and a chronologically
presented selection of lyrics with linking commentary, which combines close examination of technical features with notes on dramatic
function, and to which Engel brings a vast theatrical experience.
(He forestalls criticism that his comments are too uniformly compli-
mentary by arguing that "it would seem pointless and arrogant to

select and comment on anything less than the best examples"--p.
xii.) These main chapters are followed by a "bouquet" of lyrics
from 47 successful shows, 1920-1974, and by samples of the work
of 35 (at the time) unproduced lyricists. There is also a note on
song form, and an index of show and song titles.

S.916.   ENGEL, Lehman. Words With Music. New York: Macmillan,
         1972. 358p. bibliog.
    From the vantage point of a lifetime in the musical theater,
Engel stands back from the details of performance runs, cast lists,
etc., to cogitate about what he sees as the essentials of the genre,
to perceive its standards, and to measure examples from the American musical stage against them. Fundamentally practical and em-
pirical in his approach, he begins by considering features such as
characters, subject matter, outer shape, going on to enumerate and
discuss six "needs of the musical" (feeling, subplot, romance,
"lyrics and particularization," music, comedy), finally ranging over
a miscellany of topics, among them audience response and adaptation
to libretto. He is not, he insists, "trying to say that any rigid
rules exist" (p. 8), but to see how, within their practical limitations,
shows apply the basic principles in their own particular ways. In
doing so, he widens the focus beyond the edges of the musical itself, and includes frequent comparisons with other forms of the
theater (Puccini is referred to more often than Kern; Pinter's Home-
coming rates more index entries than Porgy and Bess). Index.

S.917.   FRANKEL, Aaron. Writing the Broadway Musical. New
         York: Drama Book Specialists, 1977. 182p.
    One of the satisfactions of writing a musical, according to
Frankel (who both wrote and directed them) is "in conquering its
mountainous odds." Critics and historians (who are frequently dis-
satisfied) might benefit from the crampons, pitons and plain rope on
offer here; for this guide book proceeds by analyzing, with considerable insight, the basics of a musical. Taking two major shows,
My Fair Lady and Company, to provide the backbone of examples,
Frankel first dissects those essentials which, taken together, amount
to style; he then discusses in turn the elements and implements (the
founding and the building tools) of the book, the music, and the
lyrics. These discussions include topics as varied as writing for
the voice, categories of song, underscoring, and vocabularies suited
to context and/or character. Production aspects are also considered.
Index.

(iv) Miscellaneous Memoirs

S.918.   ANDERSON, John Murray. Out Without My Rubbers: the
         memoirs of John Murray Anderson; as told to and written
         by Hugh Abercrombie Anderson. New York: Library
         Publishers, 1954. 253p. illus.

"Ghosted" by his brother and completed shortly after his death, this is the brisk autobiography of the Broadway director, designer and lyricist whom Brooks Atkinson called "King of the revues." Anderson (1886-1954) came to prominence in 1919 with his designs for the Greenwich Village Follies; his staging was "artistically and technically in advance of all the other revues in New York" (Cecil Smith, LOAM 1228, p. 130). The center of the book is a busy, occasionally ironic, account of the 30-odd years after GVF: "as there has to be no particular denouement and nothing has to be resolved, the reader must look upon it as a sort of revue" (p. 60), and indeed a great many figures-performers, composers, directors, etc. are introduced, but none holds the stage for long. A chapter (or "scene") towards the end briefly refers to some of the galaxy of composers who played his old piano--i.e., with whom he collaborated. Index.

S.919.   ARMITAGE, Merle. Accent on Life; foreword by John
         Thomas. Ames: Iowa State University Press, 1965.
         386p. illus.
      Autobiography of the stage designer, writer and manager, including accounts of working with Mary Garden and as West Coast producer of Porgy and Bess.

S.920.   DE MILLE, Agnes. And Promenade Home. Boston: Little,
         Brown, 1956. 301p. illus.
      Autobiographical sequence to Dance to the Piper (no. S.921), witty, vivacious, with a gift for sparkling characterization (Kurt Weill "seemed to peer through decorum and lean against every idea as though he were pressing his mind to the windowpane of thought"--p. 78). Covering the busy early 1940s, the book includes Ms. De Mille's views on how a musical succeeds, the genesis of One Touch of Venus (Nash/Weill), and her involvement with Rodgers and Hammerstein's Carousel.

S.921.   DE MILLE, Agnes. Dance to the Piper. Boston: Little,
         Brown, 1951. 342p. illus.
      Entertaining, sometimes folksy autobiography of the choreographer who did so much to transform dancing on the American musical stage. Her "story ... of a spoiled, egocentric, wealthy girl" describes her early years, her first theatrical choreography in London, and her traumatic "brushes with Broadway" for Hooray for What (Arlen/Harburg) in 1937. The high point of the book is reached with her account of the genesis of Rodeo, with music by Aaron Copland, and of its performance in 1942 by the Ballet Russe. Shortly after this, and in a similar vein, she achieved a great success with her choreography of Oklahoma! (Ms. De Mille's childhood years are told in greater detail in her later book, Speak to Me, Dance With Me [Boston: Little, Brown, 1973].)

S.922.   FERBER, Edna. A Peculiar Treasure. New York: Double-
         day, Doran, 1939. 398p. illus.

Autobiography of the best-selling novelist (1887-1968) of
the 1920s and 1930s, whose Show Boat (1927) was turned into a musical by Jerome Kern and Oscar Hammerstein II. Ms. Ferber describes the genesis of the novel (pp. 288-91, 295-303), in particular
her visit to a show boat in North Carolina, and briefly comments on
the musical (pp. 304-06). Regular appearances are made (esp. pp.
283-84, 310-13) by George S. Kaufman, with whom Ms. Ferber collaborated in several plays.

(v) Individual Shows

S.923.   ALTMAN, Richard, and KAUFMAN, Mervyn. The Making of
          a Musical: Fiddler on the Roof. New York: Crown,
          1971. 214p. illus.
          Altman was Jerome Robbins' assistant on the original pro-
duction of Fiddler, and subsequently carried his staging ideas around
the world, recreating it for different productions. His account of
the genesis and production of Fiddler, 1960-1964, is unusual in the
literature of the musical theater for its detailed attention to just one
show. The well-established traditions of hard graft and high tension
are well caught without being overstressed. Following an introduction which centers on the 1964 tryouts, the book takes us back to
the early 1960s, drawing on the recollections of composer Jerry Bock
and lyricist Sheldon Harnick, to the beginnings of the show and the
emphasis on the concept of "tradition" which was present throughout.
A section on the problems and changes that arose with Joe Stein's
libretto clearly shows the workings of the "trial and error" approach.
The 1964 Washington, D.C. tryout, the reception of the show on
Broadway, the forceful nature of the leading star Zero Mostel (whose
eventual boredom threatened the show's success), and above all the
dominating personality of Jerome Robbins--aggressively determined,
inspired but difficult--are all vividly described. The narrative goes
on to detail other productions and the movie. There are cast lists
of the New York and Hollywood productions and there is an index.

S.924.   CHARNIN, Martin. Annie: a theatre memoir. New York:
          Dutton, 1977. unpaged. illus.
          The idea of a musical based on the comic strip, "Little
Orphan Annie," first occurred to Charnin in 1971. In addition to
that inspiration he was both lyricist and director of the show (book
by Thomas Meehan, music by Charles Strouse), and so was closer to
it than anyone else. His story of the show's history, up to the successful Broadway opening in April 1977, is informal, generous, and
understandably enthusiastic. Although his account is often sketchy
he gives inside details of writing, casting, financing, designing,
rehearsing, etc., and the book is fully illustrated with color and
black-and-white photographs.

S.925.   KREUGER, Miles. Show Boat: the story of a classic

American musical. New York: Oxford University Press, 1977. 346p. illus., discog.

Faced with an art form that has always laid emphasis on visual style and beauty, much musical theater appreciation descends into uncritical adulation ("dewy-eyed valentines" in Kreuger's phrase), offset by the occasional flourish--in the name of veracity-- from the pens of those who relish the destruction of myths and the debunking of heroes. In between the two, along the path of detailed historical scholarship that had hitherto been thought unsuitable for the musical theater (apparently), Kreuger pioneers an approach that pays tribute to the visual impact of the genre with a lavish presentation (the illustrations include set designs, cartoons, publicity shots, film stills and posters), and at the same time puts an individual show under the microscope of scholarship with a scrupulously careful, but still very readable, historical text. In doing so he demonstrates that as a genre the musical comedy benefits enormously from such attention. In succession he describes and analyzes the Ferber novel, the 1927 Ziegfeld production, the 1929 film, the 1932 Ziegfeld revival, the 1936 film (directed by James Whale), the post-war revival of 1946, the 1951 MGM film, and other major stage revivals of the last 25 years, paying considerable attention to production history, story changes, and critical reception. Kreuger's knowledge of stage and film history is impressive, and his judgments, which are inobtrusive and invariably telling, are based on this expertise. Seven appendices provide complete production listings for New York, London and America regional stagings, a graph showing which productions contained which songs, full details of castings for all film versions, a list of major radio productions, and a selected discography. There is also a full index. The one missing item is an overall assessment of the Kern-Hammerstein show and its significance; there are numerous insights, particularly into aspects of Hammerstein's contributions, but a coherent critical summary is absent.

f. Film Musicals

See also nos. S.800, S.809, S.885

S.926. CASPER, Joseph Andrew. Vincente Minnelli and the Film Musical. South Brunswick, N.J.: Barnes; London: Yoseloff, 1977. 192p. illus., bibliog.

Minnelli's thirteen film musicals, from Cabin in the Sky (1942) to On a Clear Day You Can See Forever (1970), rank among the highest achievements in the genre--indeed, for Casper, represent its pinnacle. Casper sees Minnelli as the first Hollywood director to have taken a serious attitude to the musical, and to have integrated its many component parts. In this process, drama was the "fundamental structuring element" (p. 34), and it is on dramatic aspects of his methodology that Casper's critique concentrates. This is so not just in the chapters on enactment, spectacle, and dance,

but also in the one on music, which deals, not with the music as
such but with "dramatic motivation and relations, technical position
and handling." Casper describes the motivation for song in the
Minnelli musical as having "something to do with the subliminal
life" (p. 119), and illustrates this in an "exegesis of selected musical numbers." This links with his view of the significance of the
Minnelli musical, which is as an expression of the importance of fantasy. The text is amply illustrated with stills from the movies, and
there is a filmography and an index.

S.927.　　CRAIG, Warren.　The Great Songwriters of Hollywood.
　　　　　San Diego:　Barnes; London:　Tantivy Press, 1980.
　　　　　287p.　illus.
　　　　　Imposing-looking but rather slight reference book devoted
to the Hollywood careers and song output of an elite group of
thirty-two composers and lyricists, each of whom "contributed substantially to motion pictures throughout their lifetimes," and each of
whom was honored in the Songwriters' Hall of Fame.　Craig provides
a short biographical sketch of each august personage, followed by
a chronological list of film songs, grouped under film title.　There
is also a photographic portrait, and numerous sheet music covers,
with some film stills.　Indexes of song titles, films, and people.

S.928.　　DRUXMAN, Michael B.　The Musical:　from Broadway to
　　　　　Hollywood.　South Brunswick, N.J.:　Barnes; London:
　　　　　Yoseloff, 1980.　202p.　illus.
　　　　　Concentrating on 25 film musicals, from On the Town
(1949) to A Little Night Music (1977), Druxman briefly outlines the
story of the adaptation process in each case from stage to screen.
One of his stated goals is to attempt to explore the reasons for the
frequent failure of successful stage musicals to translate to the
screen--an important theme, which, partly because he insists his
audience must be "the light reader of movie memorabilia," he fails
to do more than state in several different ways and contexts.
Plentifully illustrated.

S.929.　　HARMETZ, Aljean.　The Making of "The Wizard of Oz."
　　　　　New York:　Knopf, 1978.　329p.　bibliog.
　　　　　Absorbingly detailed account of the production history of
the celebrated 1939 film musical.　Successive chapters deal with the
MGM studio in 1938 (especially the roles of Arthur Freed and Mervyn
LeRoy), the (many) scripts and scriptwriters called in to adapt L.
Frank Baum's American fairy tale, the writing of the music (songs
by Harold Arlen and E. Y. Harburg, incidental music by Herbert
Stothart), the process of casting, the four directors, the actors
and actresses (Garland, Lahr, etc.), the Munchkins, the special
effects, and so on.　Most of the material came from interviews, and
from surviving papers relating to the film.　Published sources are
listed in the bibliography.　Index.

S.930.　　HURST, Richard Maurice.　Republic Studios:　between

poverty row and the majors. Metuchen, N.J.: Scarecrow Press, 1979. 262p. bibliog.
Republic Pictures, the major producer of B films from the
mid-1920s to the '50s, made no less than 386 B Westerns. Of these,
56 featured Gene Autry, and 81 Roy Rogers, the two leading "singing cowboys." "Not all fans or scholars of the Western film consider Autry's influence to be benevolent," says Hurst (p. 136) with
a degree of understatement (he presumably means influence on the
cinematic art, not middle-class morality)--and much the same might
be said of Rogers (though he could at least act). But this solid
history of the studio, in devoting its central chapter (Chapter 5)
to the phenomenal success of these westerns, and of Autry and
Rogers in particular, is determined to look on the positive side.
The presence of music in varying degrees is frequently noted, and
its role in popularizing the genre is discussed, but the music it-
self--its character, its function--is not analyzed. Long bibliography,
and index of subjects, names, and titles.

S.931.   PIKE, Bob, and MARTIN, Dave.   The Genius of Busby
         Berkeley.   Reseda, Calif.:   Creative Film Society, 1973.
         194p.   illus.
Most of the text is devoted to a substantial interview with
Berkeley, conducted by Martin in 1963. It is followed by a short
biography, and by a filmography, 1930-1962, with selected credits
(including song titles) and commentary. The text is in typescript,
but the many black-and-white illustrations are mostly well reproduced.

S.932.   ROTHEL, David.   The Singing Cowboys.   South Bruns-
         wick, N.J.:   Barnes; London: Yoseloff, 1978.   272p.
         illus., bibliog., discogs.
An enthusiast's book on the outstanding Hollywood singing
cowboys from 1935-1953. Most of the chapters are devoted to individual stars: Tex Ritter, Eddie Dean, Jimmy Wakeley, Monte Hale,
Rex Allen; the longest of these are on Gene Autry and Roy Rogers.
Biographically constructed, they concentrate on the stars' careers
and on the films themselves rather than on the music. A good deal
of interview material is included and there are annotated filmographies
and discographies of available LPs. No systematic listing of songs is
provided, though some filmographies have notes on some of the songs
sung. A chapter on "Unsung Singing Cowboys" offers a glimpse at
the career of those who toiled unrewarded in B Western factories.

S.933.   THOMAS, Lawrence.   The MGM years; with an introduction
         by Sidney Skolsky.   New York: Columbia House, 1972.
         138p.   illus., bibliog., discog.
Handsomely illustrated reference guide to 40 MGM musicals,
1939-71, from An American in Paris to Ziegfeld Follies. For each
show the details given includes cast list, credits, song titles, plot
summary and selection of critics' comments. Supplementary information is provided in the form of a song index, biographies of

of performers and directors, a chronology of MGM musicals, and an
index of movie titles. There is also a commentary on soundtrack
recording by Jesse Kaye.

S.934.   THOMAS, Tony, and TERRY, Jim. The Busby Berkeley
         Book; with Busby Berkeley; foreword by Ruby Keeler.
         Greenwich, Conn.: New York Graphic Society, 1973.
         184p. illus.
       Essentially a large (and impressive) picture book of stills
from all the Berkeley films--the majority of them musicals, the majority of them spectacular. It also contains a substantial biographical
section of Berkeley (titled "The Man Behind the Spectacle") and
coverage of his Broadway comeback as supervising producer of the
1971 revival of Vincent Youmans' No, No, Nanette. The literary tone
tends to be somewhat solemn, especially when discussing some of
Berkeley's most preposterous "numbers," like those in the 1952
movie, Million Dollar Mermaid.

g. Music for Films and Television

S.935.   BAZELON, Irwin. Knowing the Score: notes on film
         music. New York: Van Nostrand Reinhold, 1975.   352p.
         illus.
       High on his pedestal as King Kong on his skyscraper, com-
poser-teacher Bazelon first surveys the history of film music, and
finds much of it what others have called "gesunkenes Kulturgut"--
the gold of high culture stolen to be melted down in popular culture's bargain basement. But polemics aside, his subsequent chapters on the contemporary concert composer in film, on the technique
of film scoring, and on "what does film music actually do?" (the
longest section) are informative and stimulating, with frequent close
attention to specific examples of the use of music in film and a number of music illustrations. The book concludes with a set of interviews with film composers Elmer Bernstein, Leonard Rosenman, Jerry
Goldsmith, John Williams, Richard Rodney Bennett, Alex North, Lalo
Schifrin, Bernard Herrmann, David Raksin, Bernardo Segáll,
Laurence Rosenthal, Johnny Mandel, Paul Glass, John Barry, and
Gail Kubik. Index.

S.936.   BERG, Charles Merrell. An Investigation of the Motives
         for and Realization of Music to Accompany the American
         Silent Films 1896-1927. New York: Arno Press, 1976.
         300p. bibliog.
       The ponderous title is unfortunate, but is an accurate guide
to the contents of this reprinted Ph.D. thesis (Iowa, 1973): thorough,
earnest, heavily reliant on the thesis style manual, hence abandoning
fascination to the dictates of "scholarship." A pity the publisher did
not seek an at least partial re-write, for much of the subject matter
is of considerable interest. Berg's investigation is into the wide

306 / Literature of American Music

variety of reasons for the use of music with the silent film: to neutralize distracting sounds, to enable audiences to adjust to the absence of speech, to provide continuity, to enhance dramatic expression, and to be a special attraction in itself. Chapter 5, which deals with the relationship between music and the events on the screen, is by far the most detailed. Here the antecedents of film music are sought in melodrama, opera, etc., and the methods of realizing a dramatically relevant score are illustrated by examination of the materials for the film musician (cue sheets, handbooks), and by discussion of the guidelines used in choosing appropriate music (for characters, atmosphere, moods). The majority of examples are from the silent film, but there is no index to films, directors or composers (another failure on the part of the publisher).

S.937.   EVANS, Mark. Soundtrack: the music of the movies; drawings of composers by Marc Nadel. New York: Hopkinson and Blake, 1975. 303p. illus.

A useful historical survey of film music that also includes consideration of the functions and esthetics of the genre. The chronological narrative takes the reader from the silent era through the coming of sound, the rise of the symphonic score (Korngold, Steiner), the golden age of the 1940s (Newman, Herrmann, etc.), the outstanding scores of the 1950s (Herrmann again, North, Friedhofer, etc.) up to the emergence of pop music in the scores of Mancini and others. The stylistic features of the music of these composers is described in non-analytical terms and without close references to film sequences from a technical viewpoint. Evans pauses in his narrative after the 1940s to discuss some special perspectives, including concert music and opera in films, and music and animation. The book concludes with an interesting chapter on the functions of the film score (its ability to assist in the pacing of the film, to reflect emotion, etc.) and a final one on "ethics and aesthetics, fables and folklore"--tales of orchestras, conductors, and editors. There are a number of music examples, plus a glossary and an index.

S.938.   HAGEN, Earle. Scoring for Films: a complete text. (New York): Criterion Music Corp., 1971. 253p. illus.

The sole purpose of this technical book, according to the preface, "is to orient the reader to the problems, possibilities, and language of the technique of writing music for Motion Pictures. The technical and psychological methods recommended are the same for Television or Motion Pictures. They are based on the author's experience in writing for films and teaching to professional [composers] the techniques described in this book." Many musical examples are included and segments from actual sound tracks with narration by Hagen are given on two accompanying 7" discs. (Formerly LOAM A255.)

S.939.   LUSTIG, Milton. Music Editing for Motion Pictures. New York: Hastings House, 1980. 182p. illus.

A practical guide to all aspects of music editing. Although aimed at students and teachers involved in the production of motion pictures, its clear exposition of procedures could be illuminating for students and teachers of film music as such. Useful glossary.

S.940. PRENDERGAST, Roy M. A Neglected Art: a critical study of music in film. New York: New York University Press, 1977. 268p. illus., bibliog.
_____. Film music: a neglected art; a critical study of music in films. New York: Norton, 1977. 268p. illus., bibliog.

An attempt to provide a "comprehensive look at the history, aesthetics, and techniques of film music" (p. vii) from a point of view blending musicology and film criticism. By far the longest of the book's three parts is that devoted to history--a useful account of the growth of film music from the silent era to the 1970s. Following his informative discussion of early sound film, the author opts, not for a broad, name-studded survey of the next five decades but for close study of individual film scores, set in their historical context. The most prominently featured composers are Elmer Bernstein, Aaron Copland, Hugo Friedhofer, Jerry Goldsmith, Bernard Herrmann, Leonard Rosenman, Miklos Rozsa, and--especially--David Raksin. A section on animated films looks in particular at the work of Scott Bradley. Throughout this historical part particular sequences are analyzed with music examples, the music related to the action, and its affective role described. (The troublesome question of just how particular phrases, harmonies, rhythms, etc. can express or underline meaning--a vital aspect of film music study--is not discussed; it is taken for granted that one meaning is possible. For a more rigorous approach, using musematic analysis, see Philip Tagg's Kojak--no. S.941.) Part 2, aesthetics, centers on ideas expressed by Copland in 1949, and on problems of form, while Part 3, on techniques, briefly discusses synchronization and dubbing. Index.

S.941. TAGG, Philip. Kojak--50 Seconds of Television Music: toward the analysis of affect in popular music. Gothenburg: Gothenburg University, Dept. of Musicology, 1979. (Studies from Gothenburg University Dept. of Musicology, No. 2.) 301p. illus., bibliog., discog.

Simultaneously a Ph.D. dissertation and a published monograph, this seminal work in the serious study of popular music centers on a minutely detailed, highly original analysis of a particular, short piece of television theme music, but radiates out from there to illuminate the entire, difficult subject of how ideas are communicated in popular music. An intellectual tour de force, it is also humanistically rich, its style a marriage of the rigorous and the "popular," in which the humor of the everyday and the drier abstractions of analysis feed off each other. A wide range of disciplines is drawn upon, but the work is grounded in a musicology which revitalizes and reinterprets older concepts (e.g., hermeneutics),

308 / Literature of American Music

while drawing in more recent ones (e.g., semiology), insisting as it
does so on the need to understand all interpretation as relative, not
universal.

There are two main sections. Part 1, "Background and
Theory," defines the basic terms "popular" and "affect" (the stimu-
lation of feelings), discusses the relevance to the study in hand of
the existing musicological tradition, and the usefulness (and difficulty) of employing concepts drawn from semiology, economics, and
sociology. Affect analysis is then outlined theoretically, with reference to Muzak, and its methodology is described. (The latter
grows out of the perception of three basic units of musical expression: musemes--based on Charles Seeger's concept of the musical
phoneme; paradigmatic musemes--vertical combinations; and syntagmatic musemes--horizontal combinations; in application it seeks to
establish meaning by making use of the techniques of "interobjective
comparison"--between devices, phrases, etc. used in Kojak and elsewhere across the whole range of music, and of "hypothetical substi-
tution," testing whether an idea can correctly be associated with a
particular phrase of music by substituting a different one.)

Part 2, "Analysis of the Kojak Theme," sets the context by
discussing the communication process (transmission, reception) involved, proceeding then to what is perhaps the core of the book,
a musematic affect analysis of the theme itself. Extra-musical dimensions form the subject of the following two chapters--analysis of the
visual sequence accompanying the theme, and of related topics such
as gesture, environment--before the author embarks on analysis of
the syntagmatic level. This, being "congeneric" (as opposed to the
"extrageneric" affect analysis earlier), requires a different approach.
Chapter 9 analyzes each musical phrase syntagmatically, with the
help of a linguistic model based on Chomsky; this leads to an interpretation of the "centrifugal" and "centripetal" processes at work.

The text abounds with music examples (178 in all), with
figures and diagrams (82), and with footnotes (over one thousand).
Equally thorough are the bibliography of books and articles, and
the list of musical references (from Bach to Bacharach) in both score
and recorded form.

S.942. THOMAS, Tony, ed. Film Score: the view from the podium.
South Brunswick, N.J.: Barnes; London: Yoseloff,
1979. 266p. illus., bibliog., discog.

The views of twenty film composers on their art are presented here, in essay form. Several of the pieces originally appeared
in print elsewhere, others see the light of day for the first time,
while a few have been put together by the editor from various
sources. Each is preceded by a biographical introduction. Eighteen
of the featured composers wrote for the American film industry:
Aaron Copland, Miklos Rozsa, David Raksin, Franz Waxman, Hugo
Friedhofer, Max Steiner, Erich Wolfgang Korngold, Dimitri Tiomkin,
Hans J. Salter, Bronislau Kaper, Alfred Newman, Bernard Herrmann,
Elmer Bernstein, Henry Mancini, Fred Steiner, Jerry Fielding, Jerry
Goldsmith, and Leonard Rosenman. The discography, compiled by

Page Cook, includes recordings since 1970 by other composers, in addition to these; the select bibliography, by Win Sharples, lists reference books, monographs, articles and journal titles. No index.

S.943.   ULRICH, Allan. The Art of Film Music: a tribute to California's film composers. Oakland, Calif.: Oakland Museum, 1976. 40p. illus.

This is a catalog that accompanied three days (March 12-14, 1976) of concerts, films, panels, and lectures devoted to five film composers at the Oakland Museum, Oakland, California. The catalog itself contains five sections, each devoted to one of the composers. The sections contain the same seven questions with the questions with the subject's answers, the subject's photograph, a filmography, and a final portion called "Related Activities" and/or the subject's comments about specific film scores composed by him. The five are: Elmer Bernstein, Ernest Gold, Lyn Murray, David Raksin, and Fred Steiner.

S.944.   VAN DE VEN, Luc, ed. Motion Picture Music. Mechelen, Belgium: Soundtrack, 1980. 155p. illus., discogs.

A collection of short pieces on film music composers (mainly American) originally published in the Belgian journal, Soundtrack! (Astridlaan 165, 2800 Mechelen). Besides the editor, the principal authors are W. F. Krasnoborski and John Caps. All the material is in English. There are four articles on Bernard Herrmann, three on John Williams, two on television music, and one each on Jerry Goldsmith, David Shire, Henry Mancini and Bronislau Kaper. There are also filmographies-cum-discographies of Herrmann, Shire, Les Baxter, and Kaper. No index.

h. Individual Composers, Lyricists, and Librettists for Stage and Screen

ABE BURROWS

S.945.   BURROWS, Abe. Honest, Abe: is there really no business like show business? Boston: Little, Brown, 1980. 369p. illus.

"People who write funny, think funny" (p. 106)--and humor on the Broadway musical stage has no better exponent than Abe Burrows (b.1910). His entertaining, anecdotal autobiography is like that humor--crafted, professional, but very human. His account of his experiences as librettist for Guys and Dolls (to which he came "green and frightened" from a successful career in radio and television) extends over seven chapters, and is particularly interesting for the portraits of Frank Loesser, producers Feuer and Martin, members of the cast, and, especially, director George S. Kaufman. Other musicals also prominently featured in his recollections are Can-Can (music by Cole Porter), and How to Succeed in Business Without Really Trying (Frank Loesser). Index.

SAM COSLOW

S.946.   COSLOW, Sam. Cocktails for Two: the many lives of
         giant songwriter Sam Coslow. New Rochelle, N.Y.:
         Arlington House, 1977. 304p. illus., discog.
         High-speed autobiography of an extremely busy, productive
life (1902-1982) as a songwriter (a composer-lyricist with some 500
songs to his credit), and sometime music publisher, bandleader,
vocalist, and film producer. The main part of the book falls into
two halves: Coslow's apprenticeship and early career in Tin Pan
Alley, a ten-year period (1919-1929) which brought him into contact
with virtually all the celebrities of the New York scene, and laid
the foundations for the second part of his career in Hollywood.
Here he wrote songs for a great many films in the 1930s and '40s
(among them "Just One More Chance" for Bing Crosby and "My Old
Flame"), and was at the epicenter of the popular song industry on
the West Coast, until his retirement from the music scene. In the
appendices are a selection of his favorite songs, and a selective
discography of vocal and band versions. A vast index gives some
indication of the size of the cast which Coslow's narrative embraces.

HOWARD DIETZ

S.947.   DIETZ, Howard. Dancing in the Dark; words by Howard
         Dietz. New York: Quadrangle, 1974. 370p. illus.
         _____. _____: an autobiography. New York:
         Bantam Books, 1976. 366p. illus.
         Justly celebrated as a lyricist for shows with music by
Jerome Kern, Vernon Duke, and especially Arthur Schwartz (The
Little Show, The Band Wagon), Howard Dietz (1896-1983) also
created something vastly more famous (if less inspiring, and without
his obvious signature upon it): the trademark and slogan of MGM.
This was one achievement among many during a long, distinguished
career as director of publicity and advertising for the company--a
life in which lyric-writing remained a spare-time activity, a species
of moonlighting for which, like Charles Ives, in another area of music, he will best be remembered. A pivotal figure, therefore, in
the creative and business sides of both stage and screen, Dietz recounts a life story which crossed the path of virtually everybody-
who-was-anybody on Broadway and in Hollywood in the 1920s and
'30s. This is not mere name-dropping, however, but a wise and
witty, detached, and sparely written inside story of show business,
recorded, one can scarcely believe, in the grip of Parkinson's dis-
ease. Regrettably, although many lyrics are quoted, there is relatively little on Dietz's approach to lyric-writing, or on his collaboration with Arthur Schwartz. (Formerly LOAM A251.)

OSCAR HAMMERSTEIN II

See also S.959

S.948.   FORDIN, Hugh. Getting to Know Him: a biography of
         Oscar Hammerstein II. New York: Random House,
         1977. 383p. illus., bibliog.
         Reading this book is a little like watching someone else's
home movies: the atmosphere is relaxed but the content is a little
too intimate for comfort. Eventually the reader starts to feel he/she
is eavesdropping, and there is also a danger of regarding as unim-
portant or even banal events that are meaningful to those involved.
Nevertheless, this is a valuable, blow-by-blow account of Oscar
Hammerstein II's life. He was a meticulous craftsman, occasionally
agonizing over the use of an individual word in a lyric, and this
comes over strongly. The Hammerstein family cooperated fully on
this book; 'there is a minimum of invented dialogue. For some
reason the bibliography omits the publication dates for all titles.
The introduction is by Stephen Sondheim.

LORENZ HART

See also S.960

S.949.   HART, Dorothy, ed. Thou Swell, Thou Witty: the life
         and lyrics of Lorenz Hart; designed by Lydia Link;
         co-ordinated by Elliott Sirkin. New York: Harper &
         Row, 1976. 191p. illus.
         When it comes to words without music, not all lyricists'
work can stand the exposure. That Hart's can readily do so is
confirmed by the display of his stunning talent that forms the backbone for this volume. The editor (Hart's sister-in-law) opts for a
show-by-show arrangement, prefacing her selection of lyrics with
brief details of performance dates, run length, and production
credits, and illustrating the text with a particularly fine array of
black-and-white photographs. Some excerpts from contemporary
reviews are also included. A many-sided portrait of Hart himself
is added by the assorted personal recollecitons of a cross-section
of his friends and colleagues. The editor herself provides a linking
narrative.

MOSS HART

S.950.   HART, Moss. Act One: an autobiography. New York:
         Random House, 1959. 444p.
         _____.   _____. New York: Vintage Books, 1976.
         383p.
         A thespian spirit evidently visited the infant Moss Hart
(1904-1961) in his cradle in the Bronx, and as a result he grew up
with a passion for the theater that took him, eventually, to fame
(and fortune) as a playwright, librettist and director. His

considerable contribution to the musical stage included the sketches for Irving Berlin's As Thousands Cheer (1933), the book for Kurt Weill's Lady in the Dark (1941) and Cole Porter's Jubilee (1935), and the direction of My Fair Lady (1959). Unfortunately for the historiography of the musical theater, if Hart planned Acts Two and Three, he never completed them. His very readable, often amusing autobiography covers only his first 27 years, from his childhood of "unrelieved poverty" through his first ventures in the theater, to his first collaboration with George S. Kaufman (Once in a Lifetime, 1930). Much of the book is devoted to an account of the genesis of this "satire on Hollywood," and is particularly interesting for the affectionate portrait of Kaufman (see also nos. S.952-S.954), and for the lively account of a working collaboration ("Plays aren't written," Kaufman once said, "they're rewritten"). (For a short account of a party held to launch Act One, see Dietz, no. S.947, p. 327ff. Hart's account of his work with Porter appears in The Cole Porter Songbook [New York: Simon & Schuster, 1959].)

BERNARD HERRMANN

S.951. JOHNSON, Edward. Bernard Herrmann, Hollywood's Music-Dramatist: a biographical sketch with a filmography, catalogue of works, discography and bibliography; foreword by Miklós Rózsa. Rickmansworth, Herts.: Triad Press, 1977. (Bibliographical Series, No. 6.) 59p. illus., bibliog., discog.
    Useful handbook by a British critic on the life and work of the composer-conductor whose career spanned film, stage and concert music. The twenty-page biographical sketch outlines his life from birth in New York in 1911 through his career with Columbia Broadcasting System in the 1930s, his tenure of the chief conductor's position with the Columbia Symphony Orchestra, 1940-1955, and his subsequent life in England, up to his death in Hollywood on Christmas Eve, 1975; it also summarizes his main characteristics as a composer, especially of film music. A short article by Herrmann himself, on the music of Elgar, is followed by a list of the feature films for which he composed the scores, from Citizen Kane (1940) to Taxi Driver (1975), a catalogue of his published and unpublished works, and a discography which includes his commercial recordings of his own and other composers' music, his own music on film soundtrack albums and in performances by other conductors, and pirate LPs of his music. The concluding bibliography lists three books and twenty-three articles.

GEORGE S. KAUFMAN

S.952. GOLDSTEIN, Malcolm. George S. Kaufman: his life, his theater. New York: Oxford University Press, 1979. 503p. illus., bibliog. refs.
    Widely acclaimed in his day for the wit and craftsmanship of his plays and libretti, Kaufman (1889-1961) had a long involvement

with the Broadway musical stage (1923-1955), a relationship which
histories of the musical have not adequately assessed (why, for
example, when many of his plays have been successfully revived,
do the musicals he co-authored, despite the music of Gershwin,
Berlin, not seem so durable?). Goldstein's sober official (but not
evasive) biography, telling the story of the illustrious career in
considerable detail, is not concerned with such speculation, nor indeed does it have much to say about Kaufman's view of or contribution to the musical at all (see Teichmann, no. S.954). But the
book's portrait of its odd, diffident, waspish, hypochondriac hero,
as famed for his loves as for his lines, is fascinating, if occasionally
lacking vitality--as are the accounts of his many collaborators (with,
among others, Abe Burrows, Howard Dietz, Edna Ferber, Moss Hart,
Morrie Ryskind). Some attention is paid to each show in sequence,
so we learn some background of Strike Up the Band (1930), Of Thee
I Sing (1931), Let 'Em Eat Cake (1933), Silk Stockings (1955), as
well as of his main success as a director, Guys and Dolls (1950).
The notes indicate extensive research and interviewing on the
author's part. Index.

S.953.   MEREDITH, Scott. George S. Kaufman and His Friends.
         Garden City, N.Y.: Doubleday, 1974. 723p. illus.
         _____. George S. Kaufman and the Algonquin Round
         Table. Abridged ed. London: Allen & Unwin, 1977.
         336p. illus.
         Admiring portrait, placing Kaufman in the context of the
New York literary-cum-social circle (Dorothy Parker et al.), whose
wit and wisdom he generously reflects. (For an incisive review of
the UK edition, see "The Broadway Bit," by John Lahr, Times
Literary Supplement, April 7, 1978.)

S.954.   TEICHMANN, Howard. George S. Kaufman: an intimate
         portrait. New York: Atheneum, 1972. 371p. illus.,
         bibliog.
         Drawing extensively on interviews with some 150 of Kauf-
man's friends and acquaintances, gathered over a ten-year period,
Kaufman's one-time collaborator (on The Solid Gold Cadillac) Teichmann provides a lively, entertaining picture of the many sides of
the enigmatic playwright-author, director, wit, lover, father, friend,
enemy, cardplayer, image-maker (his own).... No apology is given
for resorting, at frequent intervals, to a series of good, quotable
Kaufman anecdotes. Few have musical connections, but in one, perhaps revealing incident, Richard Rodgers stumbled on Kaufman's
"singular distaste for music" (p. 291); Teichmann himself remarks
that "Kaufman's attitude to music was that of a postman towards a
mailbag: odious but necessary" (p. 300). Kaufman's value to Ira
Gershwin, meanwhile, was that "he was one of the most practical
showmen alive" (p. 301). Index.

JEROME KERN

S.955.   BORDMAN, Gerald. Jerome Kern: his life and music.

New York: Oxford University Press, 1980. 438p.
illus.

Meticulously thorough biography of Kern (1885-1945), particularly detailed on his early life and career. Each of Kern's shows,
from the juvenile Uncle Tom's Cabin (1902) to Very Warm for May
(1939) is described in detail, complete with a list of its musical numbers and the names of the characters performing them. The
author's determination to give equal, or almost equal attention to
each show is commendable in many ways, but leads to a feeling that
the book was written to a basic formula (genesis, try-out, premiere,
reception, critical comment) with spaces for personal material at appropriate points. The amount of critical comment is considerable
(especially for musical theater biography), and is especially welcome
for the way it obliges the reader to consider the music, and in
doing so enlightens without recourse to much technical language.
(Alec Wilder's American Popular Song [LOAM 1175] is often quoted.)
Kern himself is affectionately portrayed. While clearly a work of
scholarship, the book unfortunately lacks footnotes and bibliography,
though it has indexes of songs and names. (For consideration of
some of the finer points, see the review by Norman Josephs, Popular
Music 1 (1981), pp. 169-75.)

S.956.   FORDIN, Hugh, ed. Jerome Kern: the man and his music
          in story, picture and song; produced and written by
          Hugh Fordin; book project editor, Joseph Abend; music
          arranged and edited by Dan Fox; art direction, Mel
          Rogers; research and editing, Margaret McGovern.
          Santa Monica, Calif.: T. B. Harms (1975). 192p.
          illus.

This is a collection of 41 of Kern's best-known songs in
simple arrangements for voice and piano. It is included here not so
much for the skimpy three-page biography (with seven photos), but
for the accompanying credits for, and photos from, the shows for
which the songs were written, the text of the eulogy delivered by
Oscar Hammerstein II at Kern's funeral, and the excellent background
notes to each song.

S.957.   FREEDLAND, Michael. Jerome Kern. London: Robson;
          New York: Stein and Day, 1978. 182p. illus.

Freedland's undemanding way with biography, increasingly
smoothly practiced after a series of show business life stories (see
LOAM 1270, 1330, and nos. S.972 and S.1017) to a certain extent
belies the work which goes into them. His life of Kern draws extensively on the recollections of the composer's daughter as well as
on those of numerous show business figures (Guy Bolton, Fred
Astaire...), and embodies research carried out over a two-year
period. The raw material is then transmuted into easy-reading,
pleasant if faintly predictable. Never very strong on background,
Freedland concentrates on character portrayal and major events.
The portrait of Kern is a clear one, tolerant of whims but stopping
well short of devotion; but the gap between the man and his art is

wide. The accounts of Kern's shows include some background on their genesis and production, but are mainly concerned with surface stories, and scarcely ever with analysis or evaluation. A host of Broadway personalities come and go, but few make any impression. Index.

COLE PORTER

S.958. SCHWARTZ, Charles. Cole Porter: a biography. New York: Dial Press, 1977; London: W. H. Allen, 1978. 365p. illus., bibliog., discog.

Schwartz approaches Porter much as he did Gershwin (LOAM 1285)--with a desire to make good the factual failure of previous accounts, particularly in "the key aspects of [his] life that the public know little about, though they add to the full dimensions of the men" (p. 5). He draws on "prime sources wherever possible" (p. x)--personal documents, memorabilia, etc.--and on the results of extensive interviewing to provide a portrait which differs less from Eells (LOAM 1292) in its description of the vain, immaculate socialite than in its revelations of his activities sans culottes. The recitation of details pertaining to Porter's shows, their genesis and reception, is somewhat mechanical, and Schwartz's attention to his music (although he himself is a musician) perfunctory. The realities of one part of Porter's life are no doubt clearer as a result of his investigations, but that, if anything, only makes the creative artist yet more elusive, a situation not helped by the absence of an attempt to locate Porter in the context of the musical theater. The man we meet here is of little significance; his meaning lies elsewhere. The accompanying 74 pages of reference information are useful: a chronological list of shows, with production details and song titles, an alphabetical song list with show titles and date, a selected discography of albums and 78s, and a bibliography of books and articles. There is also an index. For a musicological approach to Porter, see Cole Porter: an analysis of five musical comedies and a thematic catalogue of the complete works, by Lynn Laitman Siebert (Ph.D. dissertation, City University of New York, 1974).

RICHARD RODGERS

S.959. NOLAN, Frederick. The Sound of Their Music: the story of Rodgers & Hammerstein. London: Dent, 1978. illus., bibliog.

A knowledgeable and perceptive account of the celebrated partnership. Beginning with the genesis and reception of Oklahoma! (1943) Nolan turns the spotlight retrospectively, first to the earlier career of Hammerstein, then on to Rodgers' partnership with Hart. Chapters 4-8 describe the course of the Rodgers-Hammerstein collaboration, show-by-show, to The Sound of Music (1959) and Hammerstein's death in 1960. Rodgers' subsequent career, in particular Do I Hear a Waltz? (lyrics by Stephen Sondheim) is briefly told in the final chapter. The many interviews the author conducted (including "several hours" with Rodgers), and the extensive research into contemporary newspapers and journals, give the book an authoritative air, and this is supported by the informative notes and the useful 22-page chronology, 1895-1960. Index.

S.960.   MARX, Samuel, and CLAYTON, Jan. Rodgers & Hart: bewitched, bothered, bedeviled. New York: Putnam's, 1976. 207p. illus.

In a popular style, but with telling use of anecdotes and interviews, and with perceptive characterization, this is an authoritative biography of one of Broadway's most fascinating partnerships. The contrast between Rodgers and Hart, which the authors admit attracted them to the topic, is sharply drawn: Rodgers orderly, self-confident, socially adjusted, adding inspiration to calculation, Hart brilliant but tormented, the victim of his own troubled personality and his age's hang-ups ("his life would have been happier and less guilt-ridden if he were alive today"--p. 10). The course of this 24-year partnership (1919-43) is recorded, not in isolation, but in the richness of the theater world in which it was run. Marx and Clayton are both well-versed in the times and in the characters of their subjects (Marx and Rodgers knew each other from boyhood); Hart, perhaps inevitably, makes a much more interesting subject for the biographer, but Rodgers is not shortchanged. Index.

S.961.   RODGERS, Dorothy. A Personal Book. New York: Harper and Row, 1977. 188p. illus.

Autobiography of the wife of Richard Rodgers; not a book about Rodgers himself, but a portrait of her own upbringing and of the Rodgers' family life. The accounts of their life during Rodgers' early career, with descriptions of their lifestyle in London, New York and Hollywood in the 1930s, form the center of the book. Details become much thinner once the early 1940s have been passed.

HAROLD ROME

S.962.   ROME, Florence. The Scarlett Letters. New York: Random House, 1971. 209p. illus.

Drily witty, entertaining account, by the wife of Harold Rome, of a Japanese project to make a stage musical out of Gone With the Wind, with music by Rome. The book describes the approach to Rome, the initial journey to Japan to prepare the ground, the subsequent stay in Tokyo in 1969 for casting and rehearsals, the ups and downs of the production, and the first night in January, 1970. For much of the time Florence Rome accompanied her husband, so these accounts (in letters to friends at home) are first hand, even though at a "wife's remove," and also provide interesting glimpses of the problems created by cultural differences during such a project. There are illustrations of the production in rehearsal and public performance.

BILLY ROSE

S.963.   ROSE, Billy. Wine, Women and Words; illustrated by Sal-
vador Dali.   New York: Simon and Schuster, 1948;
London: Reinhardt & Evans, 1949.   295p.   illus.
   The lyricist of "Me and My Shadow," "It's Only a Paper
Moon" (etc.), the producer of Carmen Jones, the owner of New York
theaters and night clubs, Rose (1899-1966) enjoyed a formidable
reputation on Broadway.   He was the type who provokes profoundly
differing reactions.   To Helen Morgan he was a "little Napoleon"
(Maxwell, no.S.984, p. 20); to the writer Ben Hecht he was an
authentic New Yorker, whose "true home was the cacaphonic
street....   [His] outside layers ... are made of neon lights and
the best Bessemer steel [but] within exists a man of deep modesty
and astonishing sensitivity" (quoted in Gottlieb, no. S.964, pp. 88-
89).   The chief qualities of Rose's book are the sharpness of wit
(used for entertainment, not harm) and his facility with language.
The book resulted from a column he began writing in 1947, for the
New York Herald Tribune.   Entitled "Pitching Horseshoes." it was
widely syndicated and highly popular, and substantial portions of
it went into the book.   Recollections and opinions of Broadway are
scattered throughout, and numerous celebrities are briefly encountered (Jimmy Durante, Tallulah Bankhead, Danny Kaye).   One particular chapter, "A Funny Thing Happened...," contains some
memories of his earlier life, while his attitude towards survival in
the theater is succinctly put in "Confetti on the Brain."   No index.

S.964.   GOTTLIEB, Polly Rose. The Nine Lives of Billy Rose.
New York: Crown, 1968.   290p.   illus.
   Lively, if slightly disorganized, anecdotal biography by
Rose's sister.   Despite the author's occasionally strange habits with
chronology, the reader gets a vivid picture of Rose's life, his thirst
for success, his rise to the top as writer and producer, the ups and
downs of his career, and of his marriages (to Fanny Brice, Eleanor
Holm, and Joyce Mathews).   The author's position as Rose's "lifetime confidante" provides a sense of accuracy and proximity not always present in show business biographies ("I was the only person
who knew every twist and turn of his life that made Billy tougher
than any tough guy, and I saw money become my brother's muscle"
--p. 25).   Index.

JULE STYNE

S.965.   TAYLOR, Theodore. Jule: the story of composer Jule
Styne.   New York: Random House, 1979.   293p.   illus.
   Enjoyable, if lightweight, show business biography of the
varied career and changing fortunes of the composer of Bells Are
Ringing, Gypsy, etc.   Styne (b.1905) himself assisted Taylor (who
calls him "the main source of this material") and that gives a sense
of authenticity both to the facts (his addiction to gambling is not
glossed over) and to the lively, conversational style.   Best known

for his musicals, Styne's musical life actually began as a child prodigy pianist in Chicago (where his Russian parents settled on emigrating from London, Styne's birthplace, in 1912), but a concert career was closed to him (he was told his hands were too small) and he turned instead, in his teens, to popular music. His knowledge of the Chicago jazz scene in the 1920s, and his early career as pianist, then bandleader, are told in Chapter 2, "The Chicago Story." Chapter 3, "The Hollywood Story," tells of his songwriting career in the movie business, of his partnership with Sammy Cahn, and of the beginnings of his on-off friendship with Frank Sinatra. The Broadway career itself begins only in 1948, with Gentlemen Prefer Blondes. This, and Styne's subsequent successes and failures in musicals, is the subject of the longest chapter, "The New York Story," which brings the narrative up to 1976. Index.

KURT WEILL

S.966.   SANDERS, Ronald. The Days Grow Short: the life and music of Kurt Weill. New York: Holt, Rinehart and Winston, 1980. 469p. illus., bibliog., discog.

This biographical and critical study is the first book to make a serious, substantial attempt to re-examine and re-assess the "American" Weill. Sanders approaches the task from the standpoint of ardent enthusiasm for the works written in the US, and out of a sense that Weill's contribution to American culture has essentially gone unacknowledged. He is not a homiletic writer, however, nor an especially profound critic; his main purpose, admirably achieved, is to set out the course of Weill's American career in detail, and to demonstrate how the composer's adaptability and professionalism permitted him to develop "an American idiom all his own ... frankly rejoicing in its sounds" (p. 359). Half the text is given over to the American years (chapters 16-28). The main focus of attention, within a biographical framework, is on the genesis of each show, the work with collaborators (Maxwell Anderson, Moss Hart, Ira Gershwin, Langston Hughes), and on descriptive accounts of their themes and plots. Commentary on the music and on Weill's relationship to American culture tends also to be descriptive rather than analytical. The 29 pages of sources notes offer valuable guidance, as well as confirming Sanders' own thoroughness in compiling his narrative. There is also a list of Weill's principal compositions, an annotated discography, and an index.

MEREDITH WILLSON

S.967.   WILLSON, Meredith. And There I Stood With My Piccolo. Garden City, N.Y.: Doubleday, 1948. 255p.

Autobiographical reminiscences of a versatile composer-performer (1902-1984), whose apparent aim--to tell as many funny stories as possible--somewhat conceals the varied nature of the first 25 years of its subject's career: as a musician with Sousa's band in the early 1920s, then with the Philharmonic Society of New York under Mengelberg and Furtwangler; as musical director of radio stations in San Francisco and Hollywood; as joint-composer for Charlie Chaplin's Great Dictator; as composer of symphonic works and popular songs. A second volume, Eggs I Have Laid (New York: Holt, 1955) continues in the same vein.

S.968.   WILLSON, Meredith. "But He Doesn't Know the Territory."
         New York: Putnam's, 1959. 190p.
         Willson's hit show The Music Man, based on his own Iowa childhood, opened in New York in December 1957. Here he tells the background story of its genesis in a racy "Iowa-style" that reads as if ad-libbed but is compulsively entertaining. The entertainment does not minimize the evidence of hard work or the grind of the typical Broadway production saga. Willson is particularly informative on his intentions, especially his experiments with "rhythmic speech song." Prominent among the book's cast of characters are Broadway producers Cy Feuer and Ernie Martin (whose quick-fire patter is wonderfully captured), Franklin Lacey, producer Kermit Bloomgarden, director Martin Da Costa, and the show's star, Robert Preston.

P. G. WODEHOUSE

S.969.   WODEHOUSE, P. G., and BOLTON, Guy. Bring On the
         Girls! the improbable story of our life in musical
         comedy, with pictures to prove it. New York: Simon
         and Schuster, 1953. 278p. illus.
         "Writing musical comedies is like eating salted almonds," our two humorists remark, "you can always manage one more" (p. 74). And nothing in this entertaining text by two pioneer lyricists and librettists of the Broadway musical suggests that creation involves any more effort than does consuming gastronomic fancies (life's only punishment is sometimes to make them unavailable). In a class by itself for piquant evocation of a Broadway era, the text relates the story of the Wodehouse-Bolton partnership from Very Good Eddie (1915) to 1927. Their re-created conversations are a theater comedy in themselves. Among the theatrical personalities who appear are A. L. Erlanger, Florenz Ziegfeld, Gertrude Lawrence, the Gershwins, and, of course, Jerome Kern. Index.

S.970.   JASEN, David A. The Theatre of P. G. Wodehouse. Lon-
         don: Batsford, 1979. 120p. illus.
         A chronological catalog of Wodehouse's theatrical work, in London and New York, 1904-1948, including his musicals. Production credits are given, together with cast lists and details of musical numbers. Information on revivals is also included. There is no commentary, but there are a great many illustrations (photographs, sheet music covers, posters, record sleeves), some in color.

i. Stars and Personalities of the Musical Stage and Screen

FRED ASTAIRE

S.971. CROCE, Arlene. The Fred Astaire and Ginger Rogers
Book. New York: Outerbridge and Lazard, 1972.
191p. illus.
From Flying Down To Rio (1933) to The Barkleys of Broadway (1949), Croce proceeds film by film through these ten classics
of the Hollywood musical, paying particular attention to dance routines and with good, interesting (if sometimes effusive) comment on
the movies themselves. For each film there are sections for credits,
general description and assessment, a detailed examination of each
dance number, and production. The scrutiny of the dance routines
produces some revealing insights into the role of music, and into
how music and dance were organically linked in the superb interpretative performances of the two stars.

S.972. FREEDLAND, Michael. Fred Astaire. London: W. H.
Allen, 1976. 277p. illus.
Easy-reading commercial biography, as lean as the man himself but hardly so richly entertaining. Unlike the same UK publisher's biography of Gene Kelly (no. S.976), this is "not an authorized biography" ("although many people who know and admired [As-
taire] co-operated in its preparation"--acknowledgements). It contains more on Astaire's British appearances than in other books, but
it lacks both filmography and discography. Freedland displays little
interest in Astaire's musical contribution, other than occasional perfunctory comments. Index.

FANNY BRICE

S.973. KATKOV, Norman. The Fabulous Fanny: the story of
Fanny Brice. New York: Knopf, 1953. 337p. illus.
Renowned as a unique comedienne (and especially for her
baby impersonations), Fanny Brice (1891-1951) was also an outstanding musical performer in revues, on Broadway, and in Hollywood;
it was her combination of talents that led audiences to prize her so
highly. Katkov's entertaining biography is particularly interesting
on Brice's East Side childhood, and on her early career in burlesque.
For this he uses notes--and witticisms--towards an autobiography
left behind by Brice at her death (for later material he also uses an
unpublished autobiography by Nick Arnstein). Many central figures
in her life were interviewed, among them members of her family,
Eddie Cantor, and Billy Rose. One interview was also conducted
with Brice herself. As the book progresses less attention is paid
to her professional life, and there is little help in assessing the nature of her contribution to the musical stage.

GEORGE M. COHAN

S.974. McCABE, John. George M. Cohan: the man who owned
    Broadway. Garden City, N.Y.: Doubleday, 1973.
    296p. illus.
    Less interested in biographical detail than Morehouse (LOAM
1318), McCabe sets out "to sound Cohan the entertainer from his
lowest note to the top of his compass" (p. xii). This "unforgettable
forgotten man" is seen as a link in the theatrical chain from Harrigan
to Rodgers and Hart, Loesser, etc., and his plays are examined in
the context of his career. Several of his musicals are scrutinized--
Forty-Five Minutes From Broadway (p. 68ff), Hello Broadway (p.
128ff)--without much attention to the music itself. Appendices provide listings of Cohan productions in New York, 1901-1940, and of
his plays, 1895-1941. Index.

DOROTHY DANDRIDGE

S.975. DANDRIDGE, Dorothy, and CONRAD, Earl. Everything
    and Nothing: the Dorothy Dandridge tragedy. New
    York: Abelard-Schuman, 1970. 215p. illus.
    A harrowing personal story of private and public failure,
lightened by occasional success (such as starring in Carmen Jones
and Porgy and Bess, neither of which are dwelt on in any detail).
Dandridge (1924-1965) suffered acutely through the position she occupied between the races--"an experiment in integration." She
worked on this autobiography before her death, although friends
and colleagues discouraged her from doing so.

GENE KELLY

S.976. HIRSCHHORN, Clive. Gene Kelly: a biography. Chicago:
    Regnery; London: W. H. Allen, 1974. 335p. illus.
    _____. _____. (Rev. ed.) London: W. H. Allen,
    1984. 296p.
    An above-average show business biography, but one which,
perhaps because of its success as such, shows up the limitations of
the genre. Hirschhorn effectively incorporates material gained from
a wide circle of family, friends, and associates, and, especially,
from Kelly himself (though his quoted contributions are not always
very revealing), to produce an absorbing narrative of his subject's
life and career from his Pittsburgh childhood (he was born there to
Irish-American parents in 1912) via Broadway to Hollywood. For
each successive show, from Leave It to Me to Pal Joey, and each
movie, from Cover Girl to On the Town, Singin' in the Rain and on,
there are background stories, with special attention to Kelly's
creative role. It is here, however, that the reader may get frus-
trated, for such is clearly the considerable contribution of Kelly to
the stage and screen musical, as dancer, choreographer, singer,
and director, that it requires much more than this descriptive type
of writing, with occasional critical remarks, to begin even to suggest

ways of assessing it adequately. A chronological filmography of
Kelly's 43 movies (1942-1980 in the 1984 edition) provides details
of film company, producer's and director's names, and cast, but
omits all references to music. Index of names and show titles.

S.977.   THOMAS, Tony. The Films of Gene Kelly, Song and Dance
          Man. Foreword by Fred Astaire. Secaucus, N.J.:
          Citadel Press, 1974. 243p. illus.
      Citadel Press's series of illustrated filmographies is familiar
to most movie enthusiasts. Some volumes--like this one and nos.
S.989-S.1010 also have strong musical links, although visual matters
remain the book's chief concern. This is a large lavishly illustrated
book which includes a short biography of Kelly (b.1912) before proceeding to provide details of each film in chronological order--credits,
casts, plot synopses, illustrations. Thomas adds descriptive comments and occasional snippets from contemporary critics.

MARIO LANZA

S.978.   STRAIT, Raymond, and ROBINSON, Terry. Lanza: his
          tragic life. Englewood Cliffs, N.J.: Prentice-Hall,
          1980. illus., discog.
      Idol of many would-be operatic tenors in the 1950s, Mario
Lanza (1921-1959) achieved fame and fortune by making acceptable--
and saleable--in popular culture a figure previously identified with
high culture. He did this in the context of Hollywood musical films
such as The Great Caruso (1951) and The Student Prince (1954).
This biography tells the story of his Philadelphia childhood (he was
born to a modest-to-poor family and was christened Alfredo Cocozza)
and of the course of his career (not overlooking his weight problems,
nervous breakdown, domestic arguments--his wife died soon after
him--and rows with MGM). Though dressed up as a serious biography, the book is in effect an "as told to" account for a more
popular market. The teller is Robinson, a one-time physical thera-
pist and intimate of Lanza, and Stait, author of other Hollywood
biographies (including another "tragic" one) is the professional
writer. Although errors in more sensational accounts of Lanza's life
are corrected, the book is not without its share of melodrama. But
the epithet "tragic" is scarcely deserved; unfortunate--perhaps,
egocentric--undoubtedly.

JEANETTE MacDONALD

S.979.   KNOWLES, Eleanor. The Films of Jeanette MacDonald
          and Nelson Eddy; film credits by John Robert Cocchi;
          music credits and discography by J. Peter Bergman.
          South Brunswick, N.J.: Barnes; London: Tantivy
          Press, 1975. 469p. illus., discog.
      Film-by-film narrative of the Hollywood careers (separately
and together) of the glamorous singing duo. Profusely illustrated
and with full credits and complete song lists for each movie, the

book's chief concern is with the plots; the music interests it only slightly. Biographies of both stars are included, and there is a first-class discography. (For a revealing structuralist insight into the way the MacDonald-Eddy relationship is presented in New Moon, see Rick Altman, ed., Genre: the Musical [London: Routledge & Kegan Paul, 1981], pp. 199-201.) (Formerly LOAM A258.)

S.980.   PARISH, James Robert. The Jeanette MacDonald Story.
        New York: Mason Charter, 1976. 181p. illus.
        It seems unlikely that any biography of the much-loved star of Broadway and Hollywood musicals will ever be able to flesh itself out with the now almost obligatory scandalous tales that decorate most show business biographies. Not that the prim "Iron Butterfly" was a prude. But the life of Jeanette MacDonald (1903-65), despite the stardom, was rather uneventful, as Parish admits. This is nevertheless an enjoyable, quite detailed biography of the singer with the "fragile beauty, dainty manner and magnificent voice" (Chicago Daily Tribune obituary, quoted on p. 179). But no scandals--and no index.

S.981.   STERN, Lee Edward. Jeanette MacDonald. New York:
        Jove Publications, 1979. 159p. illus., bibliog.
        Though containing less biographical detail than Parish (no. S.980), Stern's account has a more passionate commitment to the subject, whom he plainly adores and wishes to see re-assessed. Many portraits and stills illustrate the narrative, which devotes a lot of its time to movie plots and--especially--to Jeanette MacDonald's performance ("the real Jeanette MacDonald was a fascinating performer, literally unique in her combination of innocence and sophistication, earnestness and winning frivolity"--p. 11). Only a modicum of attention is paid to the music. There is a complete filmography of her 29 films.

MARY MARTIN

S.982.   MARTIN, Mary. My Heart Belongs. New York: Morrow,
        1976. 320p. illus.
        The title acknowledges in part the Cole Porter song which made Mary Martin (b.1913) a star in Leave It to Me (1938). Never much at home with innuendo, her voice seemed to Agnes De Mille to resemble "someone calling cows, almost unsexed like a choir boy's, of trumpet clarity" (no. S.920, p. 79). Her autobiography is breathless, endlessly energetic. Besides her early life in Texas, it tells of her rise to fame and her roles in, among others, Annie Get Your Gun, South Pacific, One Touch of Venus, Hello Dolly, and I Do! I Do!

ETHEL MERMAN

S.983.   MERMAN, Ethel. Merman; with George Eells. New York:
        Simon and Schuster, 1978. 320p. illus.

For her second ghosted autobiographical outing (see LOAM 1321 for the first), Ethel Merman retains the same spirited enthusiasm for all that has happened to her. Her confession, "the only things I read are gossip columns" (p. 10), does not hold out the promise of many literary surprises, and so it proves. Retracing, in slightly less detail, the same ground as was covered by the first book, this one continues the story into the late 1950s and the '60s, when the chief events to note are Gypsy (1959), the 1966 revival of Annie Get Your Gun, and Ms. Merman's role as the eighth and final Dolly Levi in Hello Dolly! (1970-1971). The book concludes with a full, chronological listing (credits, cast, musical numbers) of stage shows, a less detailed filmography, and an index.

HELEN MORGAN

S.984.   MAXWELL, Gilbert.   Helen Morgan: her life and legend.
          New York: Hawthorn Books, 1974. 192p. illus., bibliog. refs.
          Popular biography of the torch singer (1900-1941) chosen by Jerome Kern to sing "Bill" in Show Boat (1927), and famous for it ever after. Her other great successes were with the songs especially written for her poignant voice by Kern and Hammerstein for Sweet Adeline (1929), and in Rouben Mamoulian's musical film Applause (1929). Maxwell tells the story--a much-troubled one, despite these successes--with a determination to separate fact from the many fictions about her, and to emphasize that stardom was not painlessly achieved, but was reached "by the endless drudgery route" (p. 178); that her decline was in part by the Hennessey Three Star route he does not deny, though he maintains she was "a self-abusive, sorrowful, tormented artist" (p. 184).

9.   Popular Entertainers

PEARL BAILEY

S.985.   BAILEY, Pearl.   The Raw Pearl.   New York: Harcourt,
          Brace & World, 1968. 206p. illus.
          _____.   _____. New York: Pocket Books, 1969.
          189p. illus.
          Viewing pleasure and pain alike with equanimity, these are somewhat philosophically-inclined memoirs of the singer's life and career, with particular attention to the 1940s and '50s. Though numerous musicians make a brief appearance, there is little about music. Subsequent volumes, Talking to Myself (New York: Harcourt Brace Jovanovich, 1971), and Hurry Up, America and Spit (same publisher, 1976), are increasingly less concerned with performance and more with reflecting on American mores. (The first two books formerly LOAM A268 and A269.)

IRENE CASTLE

S.986.   CASTLE, Irene. Castles in the Air; as told to Bob and
Wanda Duncan. Garden City, N.Y.: Doubleday, 1958.
264p. illus.
_____. _____; new foreword by Ginger Rogers.
New York: Da Capo, 1980. 264p. illus.
The team of Englishman Vernon Castle (1889-1918) and his
American wife Irene (1893-1969), the most popular dancers in the
dance-obsessed 1910s, drew on and in return influenced popular music styles of the era, particularly in their association with bandleader James Reese Europe. A pity that this enjoyable enough autobiography has little of substance to say about the creation of such
dance steps as the foxtrot, or of the relationship between these and
embryo jazz styles, or specifically of the contribution of Europe
(whose drummer Buddy Gilmore was, according to Jean and Marshall
Stearns, "the admitted source of much of their inspiration" [LOAM
1007, p. 97], but not admitted in these pages), or of the musical
shows in which the couple participated. Irene Castle confesses she
was an intuitive dancer (her greatest influence may well have been
in fashion and in changing standards of feminine beauty); Vernon
was the more analytical and inventive of the two, but the affectionate
portrait of him does not plumb any depths. In short, though it may
set the Castles in the air, the book does not put the foundations under them. (Formerly LOAM A271.)

ROSEMARY CLOONEY

S.987.   CLOONEY, Rosemary. This for Remembrance: the autobiography of Rosemary Clooney, an Irish-American singer; with Raymond Strait. New York: Playboy Press,
1977. 250p. illus.
The opening of the book in a Los Angeles psychiatric ward
in 1968 sets the candid, somewhat harrowing tone of the book. The
story of the singer's life and career, from her birth in 1928, her beginnings in the big band era as one of the Clooney Sisters, her experiences on the road, and her big success in the 1950s, tends to
dwell longest on her private life. Foreword by Bing Crosby.

BING CROSBY

S.988.   BARNES, Ken. The Crosby Years. London: Elm Tree
Books; New York: St. Martin's Press, 1980. 216p.
illus., bibliog., discog.
Adulatory mishmash by a British songwriter and record
producer. A biographical outline is followed by reminiscences of
the author's association with Crosby. The most substantial section,
an attempt at a critical assessment of Crosby's vocal innovations,
follows developments in his style over the years, and picks out certain significant records for comment; generally hampered by the
unambitious nature of his approach, the author nevertheless produces

occasional interesting comments. The reference part of the book contains a discography of commercial recordings (chronological, with song title, credits, accompanying orchestra but no record company or label details), a filmography, and a six-item bibliography (sic). The book concludes with the music of the songs particularly associated with Crosby.

S.989.   BOOKBINDER, Robert. The Films of Bing Crosby. Secaucus, N.J.: Citadel Press, 1977. 255p. illus.
Descriptive filmography, from The Big Broadcast (1932) to Stagecoach (1966). Song titles are included in the information given for each film, but no index is provided to facilitate the identification of the film in which a particular song appears. The author's commentary on each film consists of plot summary and brief assessment of the film and of Crosby's performance. Details of film shorts and other miscellaneous appearances are also included.

S.990.   THOMAS, Bob. The One and Only Bing. New York: Grosset & Dunlap, 1977. 158p. illus.
Thomas's text, an affectionate but not entirely adulatory tribute, outlines Crosby's life and career, with the help of a large number of photographs. It is accompanied by an illustrated filmography by Norm Goldstein, and by "Bing's Greatest Hits," in which Mary Campbell outlines Crosby's recording career, with a chronological list of his best records, 1926-1956. No index.

S.991.   THOMPSON, Charles. Bing: the authorised biography London: W. H. Allen, 1975. 249p. illus.
Shallow popular biography; as much insight into Crosby's singular musicianship could probably be gained from a study of his betting slips or his missed birdies. Aficionados of the anecdote, however, can add liberally to their collections. (For the unauthorized view, see the sour Bing Crosby: the hollow man, by Don Shepherd & Robert F. Slatzer [New York: St. Martin's Press, 1981].)

S.992.   ZWISOHN, Laurence J. Bing Crosby: a lifetime of music. Los Angeles: Palm Tree Library, 1978. 147p. illus., discog.
Discography of commercially released studio recordings (i.e., excluding radio and TV shows, soundtracks, bootlegs, etc.). Arrangement is alphabetical by title, with composer and lyricist credits, date of recording, and record company, but no personal listings. The discography is preceded by short biographical chapters on aspects of Crosby's career--his relations with record companies, associations with songwriters, his own songwriting endeavors. Illustrated with black-and-white reproductions of sheet music covers.

DORIS DAY

S.993.   DAY, Doris. Doris Day: her own story; (with) A. E.

Hotchner. New York: Morrow; London: W. H. Allen, 1976. 365p. illus.

_____. _____. London: Star Books, 1977. 357p. illus.

As she is at pains to point out in her opening paragraphs, Doris Day's screen image of "America's wholesome virgin" is neither cinematically accurate, nor anything to do with her personal history (she was, for example, "married at seventeen to a psychopathic sadist"--p. 15, Star Books edn.). Her story, from her Cincinnati childhood through her careers as band singer and movie actress up to the mid-1970s, is indeed rather more riveting than some of her movies (though not than Love Me or Leave Me, in which her own life and her screen role as Ruth Etting were on a par and bore an uncanny resemblance). Although there is information on this and on other musical roles (e.g., in Calamity Jane, Pajama Game), and, at an earlier stage in her career, on her time as a singer with Les Brown and others, these are snippets only, and take second place to the personal side of the story. The narrative is interspersed with recollections of Doris Day by some of her co-stars (James Garner, Rock Hudson) and others. A filmography is included, but no discography or index. (For an analysis of her screen image, see Move Over Misconceptions: Doris Day reappraised, by Jane Clarke and Diana Simmonds [London: British Film Institute, 1980].)

JIMMY DURANTE

S.994.   ADLER, Irene. I Remember Jimmy: the life and times of Jimmy Durante. Westport, Conn.: Arlington House, 1980. 189p. illus.

An affectionate pictorial tribute to the celebrated "schnozz" (photographed, it seems, from all--well, almost all--angles). The accompanying biographical text, is slight; it does include numerous quotations from Durante, Lou Clayton, and Eddie Jackson, but the sources of these are unacknowledged. There is a list of film titles and dates, but no word on recordings. The visual Durante is more highly esteemed than the aural one.

S.995.   CAHN, William. Good Night, Mrs. Calabashz: the secret of Jimmy Durante. New York: Duell, Sloan and Pearce, 1963. 191p. illus., bibliog.

On an unusually early morning excursion, Billy Rose noticed Durante "smacking every tree he passed. 'When I'm awake,' Schnozzola explained, 'no boid sleeps'" (Rose, no. S.963, p. 115). Catching the spirit of such a man is clearly difficult, but Cahn's attempt "to render permanent--through the power of pictures and words--the essence of one of America's great comic spirits" (p. 190) is an eminently readable one. The biographical detail on Durante (1893-1980) is less than in Fowler (no. S.996), but Cahn has more to say about performance style (including Durante's unusual singing), Durante's own music, and the vaudeville and Broadway shows with which he was involved. Numerous reviews are quoted and the bibliography provides a list of sources.

S.996. FOWLER, Gene. Schnozzola: the story of Jimmy Durante.
New York: Viking Press, 1951. 261p. illus.
Enjoyable biography of the "clown laureate of Broadway"
from his Bronx childhood, his apprenticeship in the Coney Island
honkey-tonks (as "Ragtime Jimmy"), his rise to fame via Harlem
nightclubs in the early days of the jazz craze, and his subsequent
career as Hollywood star and radio personality. Durante's humor
and versatility are well reflected; there is little of substance, however, on his contribution to popular music either as songwriter or
performer.

JUDY GARLAND

S.997. DAHL, David, and KEHOE, Barry. Young Judy. New
York: Mason/Charter, 1975. 250p. illus., bibliog.
Garland's early life and her career up to about 1935 (when
she was signed to a seven-year contract by MGM) are examined
forensically by two California social workers. They are particularly
interesting on the family complexities, and point to the sources of
the singer's future problems in these tensions. The bisexuality of
Frank Gumm (Judy's father), which his daughter never knew about,
and the meanness and overbearing manner (according to the authors)
of Ethel Gumm (Judy's mother), which she knew only too well, are
two prominent subjects. But there is also much about the singer's
early love for performance, the stage and, especially, singing. An
appendix lists all her stage appearances into 1935. The text is accompanied by notes, and there is a good bibliography.

S.998. DiORIO, Al. Little Girl Lost. New York: Arlington House,
1973; London: Robson, 1975. 298p. illus., discog.
A devoted Garland fan from a younger generation, DiOrio
began this biography in 1969, shortly before its subject died, and
when he himself was in his freshman year at college. Subsequent
rewriting removed most of the raw edges, but not the enthusiasm.
What makes his account useful is its extensive use of printed
sources, especially reviews, always quoted verbatim, and always
acknowledged. Though this produces a heavy reliance on second-
hand accounts (e.g., in the story of Garland's early days, DiOrio
quotes frequently and at length from her own autobiographical article, "There'll Always Be Another Encore," McCalls Magazine, Jan.-
Feb., 1964), the accumulation of critical reports adds an important
dimension. For some reason, the author--or the publisher?--was
not prepared to complete the task by listing the sources at the back,
but the discography and filmography are extensive. Index. (Formerly LOAM A273. The subtitle "the life and hard times of Judy
Garland" appears on the cover only.)

S.999. EDWARDS, Anne. Judy Garland: a biography. New York:
Simon & Schuster; London: Constable, 1975. 349p.
illus., discog.
Researched with a particular thoroughness, this is a poig-

nant, revealing biography (the author turned down the offer to write an "authorized" life story, preferring the greater liberty of an "unauthorized" account). Although she therefore lacked the access to private papers made available to Gerald Frank (LOAM 1320), the author's extensive interviewing and correspondence, together with her own knowledge of the ways of Hollywood, made a convincing, if profoundly enigmatic portrait. As in most Garland literature (Frank included), one looks in vain for insights into the singer's unique musical talent. A bonus is available, however, in the form of a partial discography (singles and album titles, with catalog numbers). Other supplementary material includes a filmography, lists of television and radio appearances, and an index.

S.1000.   FINCH, Christopher. Rainbow: the stormy life of Judy
          Garland; designed by Will Hopkins. New York:
          Grosset & Dunlap; London: Michael Joseph, 1975.
          255p. illus.
          Though not without biographical hang-ups of his own,
Finch offers a reasonably detached version of the Garland story.
His account of her personal life lacks the detail of some other biographies, but has two distinctive features: the contribution, in interview, by Judy Garland's sister Virginia, and the (perhaps consequential) attempt to rehabilitate the oft-maligned Ethel Gumm, Garland's mother. But Finch's principal interest lies in the films and the Hollywood career, and the book may well interest movie fans most of all. Aside from some observations on the part played by Roger Edens in fashioning the Garland style, those interested in Garland's singing will find little to stimulate them (the most illuminating comments being snippets from Henry Pleasants' The Great American Popular Singers [LOAM 1323]). The most black-and-white photographs are good. Discography and filmography are wanting, but there is an index.

LENA HORNE

S.1001.   HORNE, Lena. In Person, Lena Horne; as told to Helen
          Arstein and Carlton Moss. New York: Greenberg,
          1950. 249p. illus.
          This enduring artist's first autobiography provides insight
into various, linked questions concerning blacks in entertainment.
From her first experiences, touring in Florida in the 1920s with her actress mother, through her work, in turn, at the Cotton Club, on Broadway, with Charlie Barnet's Orchestra, at Café Society, to her coming to Hollywood (Panama Hattie, Cabin in the Sky, Stormy Weather), her account is characterized by a growing, deepening awareness of racial intolerance and injustice. What makes this aspect particularly interesting is the varied ways in which she learns her "lessons in color" from other blacks--negative ones from middle-class Southern blacks and from black society's color codification (her own light skin prevented her getting work at times), positive ones of different kinds from Noble Sissle's "ambassador of good will

theory" of how blacks should behave (which she only partly sub-
scribed to), and Paul Robeson's sympathetic understanding. Another characteristic of the book is its ability to narrate the gradual
find g of a distinctive style, the crucial development in which
comes during her time with Charlie Barnet (p. 155ff). A third
feature is the telling portrait of the conditions under which performers lived and worked; particularly revealing is the description of
the drudgery and exploitation at the Cotton Club.

S.1002.   HORNE, Lena, and SCHICKEL, Richard. Lena. Garden
          City, N.Y.: Doubleday, 1965. 300p. illus.
     The second autobiography repeats the story of Lena
Horne's life and career to the 1940s, recounting many of the same
incidents but generally in less detail; it then continues the account
of an amazingly varied and versatile career, with more emphasis on
the singer as an international star. The same high degree of sensitivity and concern is shown towards racial questions (her life
sometimes appears like one long process of education in the subtleties of racial consciousness), but there is a greater feeling of
toughness and resilience than in the earlier book. Various other
musicians (e.g., Count Basie, Ethel Waters) make noteworthy appearances.

AL JOLSON

S.1003.   ANDERTON, Barrie. Sonny Boy! the world of Al Jolson.
          London: Jupiter Books, 1975. 160p. illus., discog.
     The hyperbole that seems so characteristic of writers
about Jolson hovers around Anderton's preface, but is mercifully
kept in check in the main text, a biographical "tribute" which uses
only a small part of the author's extensive personal archive of Jolson
memorabilia in a brief, factual, well illustrated account of the star's
life and career. The discography is a list of selected song titles
with record label names (no further details: for more information
readers are referred to Dave Jay's Jolsonography [LOAM 1331], the
2nd ed. of which Anderton himself published). A more informative
filmography includes plot synopses. No index. (Formerly LOAM A267.)

S.1004.   OBERFIRST, Robert. Al Jolson: you ain't heard nothin'
          yet. San Diego: Barnes; London: Tantivy Press,
          1980. 341p. illus., discog.
     For those readers who like a biography to read as if it
would rather be a pulp novel, the Jolson shelf is one of the best
places to be. Here's another contribution to the genre (by an
author who is a specialist in short stories); it comes equipped with
all the essential features--predictable rags-to-riches plot, corny
dialogue, the eventual triumph of romance, tearful finale.... One
is driven to suspect that the shallowness of so much Jolson literature cannot be coincidence. Yet his position in American popular
culture is a fascinating one when seen in the wider context of the
role and character of ethnic performers of Jolson's generation, whose

story is essentially one of transition from an authoritarian to a
"liberated" tradition, but who mainly existed in a marginal zone
between cultures--a vantage point which contributed powerfully to
that success of those, like Jolson, willing to exploit it. (See, on
this subject, Ethnicity and Popular Music, by Berndt Ostendorf
[IASPM/UK Working Paper No. 2, Exeter, 1983].) "It is important
that qualities of genius such as Jolson's be analyzed and appreciated," remarks William Morris, Jr. in his foreword. It still is.

LIZA MINNELLI

S.1005.   PARISH, James Robert, and ANO, Jack.   Liza!   an un-
           authorized biography.   New York: Pocket Books,
           1975.   176p.   illus.
           _____. Liza: her Cinderella nightmare.   London:
           W. H. Allen, 1975.   186p.   illus., discog.
           Routine popular biography of Liza Minnelli (b.1946), with
strong supporting roles played by Judy Garland and Vincente Minnelli.   The focus of attention is on the surface of her career and
the course of her relationships; her talent is taken for granted.
The UK edition adds a filmography (with lists of songs), and an LP
discography by T. Allen Taylor--bonuses which scarcely excuse the
bizarre subtitle.

HARRY RICHMAN

S.1006.   RICHMAN, Harry, and GEHMAN, Richard.   A Hell of a
           Life.   New York: Duell, Sloan and Pearce, 1966.
           242p.   illus.
           Ed Sullivan, who knew about such things, called Richman
(1895-1972) "the greatest singer of songs in America."   Al Capone
apparently valued him highly, too.   This autobiography of the
singer, club owner, songwriter and radio personality is chiefly pre-
occupied with his affaires de coeur (et de corps); there is some
information on performance, but not of the musical variety.

FRANK SINATRA

S.1007.   FRANK, Alan.   Sinatra.   London: Hamlyn, 1978.   176p.
           illus., discog.
           Pictorial biography, concentrating on the 1940s and 1950s.
The text steers a generally clear course through hazardous biographical waters, sorting fact from fancy, but allowing some of the legends
a little room.   Frank has little interest in Sinatra the singer, however.   There is a detailed filmography, 1944-1971.   The selected discography lists key albums only.   Index.

S.1008.   HOWLETT, John.   Frank Sinatra.   London: Plexus, 1980.
           170p.   illus., discog.
           A handsome pictorial biography, with a balanced text
which, however, lacks the immediacy of some earlier accounts (e.g.,

Scaduto, no. S.1011, Wilson, no. S.1012). The respective courses
of Sinatra's public and private lives are equally prominent; his
films meanwhile receive some, if slightly scant attention; but his
unique musicianship is, as so often, largely unexamined. A filmography, 1941-1977, gives credits and cast lists; the discography is
a representative selection of album releases, with US catalog numbers. No index.

S.1009.   RIDGWAY, John. The Sinatrafile. Alvechurch, Birming-
           ham: John Ridgway Books, 1977-80. 3v. illus.,
           bibliogs.
        Comprehensive Sinatra reference work. Part 1 contains
details of all complete radio shows, television shows and concerts.
Under each show are given lists of songs performed and names of
other performers. This volume also contains a discography of non-
commercial material. Part 2 is a discography of commercial recordings and V-discs. Ridgway claims he "had access to information
probably previously unobtainable" (p. vii). Part 3 is a filmography
with full cast lists and credits, with information of whether Sinatra
sings in the film and whether a soundtrack album issued has been
released. This volume also includes an update of Parts 1 and 2.
Various indexes.

S.1010.   RINGGOLD, Gene, and McCARTY, Clifford. The Films of
           Frank Sinatra. New York: Citadel Press, 1971. 249p.
           illus.
        Like nos. S.977 and S.989, this is an illustrated filmog-
raphy. Following a broad introduction there is a film-by-film listing
with credits, cast lists, and song titles. Accompanying comments
from contemporary sources are nicely balanced.

S.1011.   SCADUTO, Tony. Frank Sinatra. London: Michael
           Joseph, 1976; London: Sphere Books, 1977. 159p.
           illus.
        Disturbed by a growing realization that Sinatra, his child-
hood idol, whom he has constantly defended against all charges leveled at his behavior, might actually be guilty of them, ex-New York
Post journalist Scaduto sets out to reveal the true man. The results are mostly grim--a distasteful, often sordid tale. Ultimately,
however, the book disappoints in virtually all levels. As an exposé,
it is an anti-climax, despite the evidence; we find Scaduto, in a
bizarre epilogue, quoting G. K. Chesterson on man's secret self and
setting up (and excusing?) Sinatra as "a surrogate for and a symbol
of our own instinctive violent natures" (p. 157). As a biography it
is muddled and muddling, distorting chronology and probably giving
the unfamiliar reader a very confused picture. As a study of the
man, it is--as the author admits--distinctly pop psychology. As for
music ... perhaps the book's greatest irritation is that Scaduto's
random comments on Sinatra's singing suggest a perceptive listener,
who might well have had something to offer.

S.1012.   WILSON, Earl.   Sinatra: an unauthorized biography.
New York: Macmillan; London: W. H. Allen, 1976.
357p.   illus.
_____.   _____.   London: Star Books, 1978.   380p.
illus.
A long, anecdotal biography by a former gossip columnist,
who, after being "for more than a quarter century [Sinatra's] friend,
booster and most consistent defender among the columnists" (preface),
found himself inexplicably out of favor and, for seven years, stopped
writing about him.   Most of this book was written before communica-
tions were restored, but "I have striven to write an honest book,"
Wilson declares; "perhaps I am lucky to have been both out of
Sinatra's favor and in his favor, for I have known both Sinatras.
The book is eminently fair to him, I hope, but in painting the portrait, I have not left out the warts" (p. xiii).   It is a tribute to
Sinatra, of sorts, that what is in effect an extended gossip column
(of the old school) can maintain its interest for so long.   It can't
simply be a question of how many wives one has....   If anything
palls, it is that show biz habit of taking it for granted that this particular world is so important, without producing any genuine reasons
--social, emotional, artistic--why this should be so.   No index.

KATE SMITH

S.1013.   SMITH, Kate.   Living in a Great Big Way.   New York:
Blue Ribbon Books, 1938.   230p.   illus.
This is a chatty memoir of her early years--even several
recipes are included--by the once highly popular singer who was
born in Washington, D.C. in 1907, appeared in stage shows in the
mid-1920, made records, had a regular radio program, and first went
to Hollywood in 1932.   It was especially her radio work in the 1930s
that spread her fame.   Just after this book was written, Smith introduced and recorded Irving Berlin's "God Bless America," the song
most associated with her.   ("In the patriotic schmaltz tradition, so
vital a part of the popular music heritage, the Irving Berlin tune became Kate Smith's, virtually sending to extinction her original theme,
"When the Moon Comes over the Mountain" (Philip K. Eberly, Music
In the Air [New York: Hastings House, 1982], p. 110.   The original
theme was co-written by Smith, with Harry Woods and Harold Johnson.)

BARBRA STREISAND

S.1014.   BRADY, Frank.   Barbra Streisand: an illustrated biography.   New York: Grosset & Dunlap, 1979.   151p.
illus.
A book for fans, but very nicely done.   Skin-deep, but
factual.   Written with a certain flair.   Lots of marvelous photos of
Ms. Streisand--impressive as both a singer and an actress.

S.1015.   JORDAN, René.   The Greatest Star: the Barbra Streisand

story. New York: Putnam, 1975. 253p.
_____. Streisand: an unauthorised biography. London: W. H. Allen, 1976. 253p.

Engaging popular biography of Streisand's life and career from her Brooklyn childhood (she was born there, not in Rangoon, as her earlier self-promotion averred, in 1942) to the movie Funny Lady (1975). Jordan did not enjoy his subject's cooperation, but he conducts extensive interviews with her friends and associates, and a substantial amount of quoted material from these sources appears in the narrative. Among musicians featured in this way are Harold Rome and Jule Styne. Most attention is given to Streisand's stage and movie career, but there are interesting comments on her early nightclub appearances, where her singing offered her a short cut to fame, contrary to her initial expectations ("I'm not a singer, I'm an actress" had been her customary pronouncement). Despite this, Jordan has little to say of any musical interest, though he does dutifully record the appearance of each Streisand album in its chronological place. Collectors of musical theater souvenirs may find most to interest them, in the accounts of the background to shows such as I Can Get It For You Wholesale (1962) (Chapter 6) and Funny Girl (1964) (Chapter 8). No illustrations, and no index.

SOPHIE TUCKER

S.1016.   TUCKER, Sophie. Some of These Days: the autobiography of Sophie Tucker. Garden City, N.Y.: Doubleday, 1945; London: Hammond, 1948. 309p. illus.
_____. Some of These Days: an autobiography. London: Theatre Book Club, 1951. 293p. illus.

According to Michael Freedland (no. S.1017, p. 193), the unnamed co-author of this "highly imaginative, ghosted autobiography" (Dorothy Giles) was an accomplished writer, who "was given the task of assembling Sophie's scribbles on headed hotel notepaper and interviewing people who could best fill the gaps in the Tucker memory." Comparison with Freedland's own book, however, suggests that, while the details of some events and encounters may have been fabricated--Sophie Tucker was a past master at publicity--the story of her life from 1887(?) to World War II as she tells it is essentially correct. Particularly absorbing is her account of her apprenticeship in vaudeville in the early 1900s (in blackface). (There is a similarity in the biographies of many vaudeville entertainers; recognizing the roots of this phenomenon, in a speech made in 1954, Sophie Tucker remarked, "We all sprang from the same source.... We were all swept to the shores of this country as the same tidal wave of immigration, in the same flight from prejudice and persecution. Our life stories are pretty much the same" [quoted in DiMeglio, no. S.889, p. 60). Her own parents came from Russia; she was born "on the road" between Russia and Poland.) Remarkably, she survived the decline of vaudeville in the early '30s, and was able to secure a role in the rapidly changing world of international entertainment. Always generous to worthy causes, she gave all the proceeds of the book to charity. (Formerly LOAM A281.)

S.1017.   FREEDLAND, Michael.   Sophie: the Sophie Tucker story.
          London: Woburn Press, 1978.   221p.   illus.
     The life and career of this most remarkable of all vaude-
ville performers is retold in a readily accessible style.   Freedland
drew heavily on the recollections of Sophie Tucker's long-time ac-
companist, Ted Shapiro, and on her own scrapbooks and memorabilia, preserved at the Lincoln Center, New York.   But the most
successful part of the book is its accounts of her British tours.
From his London base and with the aid of the British press, the
author has a surer grasp of the sense and significance of the "music
hall" and of the spellbinding effect which Sophie Tucker had on it,
which led one critic to remark that she "gives a testimonial to life
every time she opens her mouth" (p. 147).   But a far greater interest in the cultural meaning of ethnic performers is needed--"they
made items of their traditional culture acceptable by Americanizing
them.   Thus they managed to salvage aspects of their traditions by
translating them into popular cultural forms" (Berndt Ostendorf,
Ethnicity, an Popular Music, IASPM/UK Working Paper No. 2,
Exeter, 1983, pp. 18-19).

RUDY VALLEE

S.1018.   VALLEE, Rudy.   Vagabond Dreams Come True.   New
          York: Dutton, 1930.   262p.   illus.
     Scholars of popular culture are always going to have
trouble with a man who could record "Life Is Just a Bowl of Cher-
ries" during the depths of the Depression; but just why this rather
arrogant man with the bland, featureless voice was so immensely
popular in the late 1920s and the 1930s needs to be more closely
examined.   Of Vallee's own books, this first one might be the most
useful, as it discusses informally--and with no false modesty--the
genesis and early career of the Connecticut Yankees, aspects of
playing for dancing, the basics of showmanship, the deliberate decision to adopt a commercially successful style, the development of
orchestration techniques to please a majority taste, and so on.
Other topics covered include song-plugging, songwriting, the inclusion of an element of hokum.   One chapter is devoted to pioneer
saxophonist Rudy Wiedoft and to his influence on Vallee.   (Formerly
LOAM A283.)

S.1019.   VALLEE, Rudy.   My Time Is Your Time: the story of
          Rudy Vallee; with Gil McKean.   New York: Ivan
          Obolensky, 1962.   244p.   illus.
     An informal autobiography of a career lived largely--if
not always contentedly--at the top.   Without any great power to
rivet the reader's attention it describes the course of that career,
from Yale to the commercial music scene of the 1920s, involvement
in George White's Scandals in the 1930s, and subsequent stage and
Hollywood appearances.   Among the cast of characters are Herman
Hupfeld, Rudy Wiedoft, and Irving Berlin.

S.1020.   VALLEE, Rudy. Let the Chips Fall. Harrisburg, Pa.:
          Stackpole Books, 1975. 320p. illus.
          "Since in these forty-seven years in the fascinating yet
sometimes murderous, cruel, shabby, and completely disillusioning
world of 'show business' it has been my fortune to meet everyone
of importance, I have set down some experiences, analyses, and
happy and unhappy results of these associations" (p. 12). In the
event, nobody of any importance stays around on these pages for
long--except the author, and he stays forever. Replete with
long-drawn out episodes of little significance, the book also repeats
much of the autobiographical material of earlier books.

LAWRENCE WELK

S.1021.   WELK, Lawrence. Lawrence Welk's Musical Family Album;
          with Bernice McGeehan. Englewood Cliffs, N.J.:
          Prentice-Hall, 1977. unpaged, illus.
          A slick picture book for fans, light on facts, long on
homeliness. Many of the pictures are in color. Welk himself
manages to be in most of them. (His particular approach to life is
documented in Wunnerful, Wunnerful: the autobiography of Lawrence
Welk. [Englewood Cliffs, N.J.: Prentice-Hall, 1971].)

                       Additional Items

Reference

S.1022.   BARR, Steven C. The (Almost) Complete 78rpm Record
          Dating Guide. Toronto: the author, 1979. 51p.

S.1023.   COMPLETE CATALOGUE of Royalty and Non-Royalty Pro-
          ductions and Grand and Comic Operas, Musical Come-
          dies and Other Musical Productions. New York: Tams-
          Witmark, 1922- . (1922-1929 issues called "Catalogue
          no. 2;" from 1934 called "Catalogue no. 1." Annual
          [?].)

S.1024.   DETHLEFSON, Ronald. Edison Blue Amberol Recordings,
          1912-1914: American popular series, "live" recordings
          and selected recordings, 1915-1928. Brooklyn: APM
          Press, 1980. 206p.

S.1025.   WILMETH, Don. American and English Popular Entertain-
          ment: a guide to information sources. Detroit: Gale,
          1980. 465p.

The Popular Music Life

S.1026.   DURANTE, Jimmy, and KOFOED, Jack. Night Clubs.
          New York: Knopf, 1931. 246p.

S.1027. KENNY, Nick. How to Write and Sell Popular Songs; with advice and special articles by Irving Berlin, Cole Porter (et al.). New York: Hermitage Press, 1946. 255p.

Words and Music

S.1028. CRAWFORD, Richard, ed. The Civil War Songbook: complete original sheet music for 37 songs. New York: Dover Publications, 1976. 157p.

S.1029. EWING, George W., ed. The Well-Tempered Lyre: songs and verse of the Temperance movement. Dallas: Southern Methodist University Press, 1977. 298p.

S.1030. SILBER, Irwin, ed. Songs America Voted By; with words and music that won and lost elections and influenced the democratic process. Harrisburg, Pa.: Stackpole, 1971. 320p.

S.1031. WARNER, James A., ed. Songs That Made America. New York: Grossman, 1972. 151p.

Bands and Their Music

S.1032. BRYANT, Carolyn. And the Band Played On, 1776-1976. Washington, D.C.: Smithsonian Institution, 1975. 54p. (Accompanying a Smithsonian exhibition.)

S.1033. BURFORD, Cary Clive. We're Loyal to You, Illinois: the story of the University of Illinois bands under Albert Austin Harding for 43 years.... Danville, Ill.: The Interstate, 1952. 74p.

S.1034. GILES, Ray. Here Comes the Band! New York: Harper Brothers, 1936. 205p.

S.1035. GRAHAM, Alberta Powell. Great Bands of America. New York: Nelson, 1951. 185p.

S.1036. LINGG, Ann M. John Philip Sousa. New York: Holt, 1954. 250p. (For younger readers.)

S.1037. TAYLOR, George H. The American High School Band. New York: Richard Rosen Press, 1977. 142p.

19th-Century Popular Music

S.1038.   MacGOWAN, R. The Significance of Stephen Collins Fos-
          ter. Indianapolis: privately printed, 1932. 25p.

Popular Music of the Stage

S.1039.   ABBOTT, George. Mr. Abbott. New York: Random
          House, 1963. 279p. (Autobiography of theater director
          and writer--On Your Toes, Damn Yankees, etc.)

S.1040.   CLURMAN, Harold. The Fervent Years: the story of the
          Group Theatre and the thirties. New York: Knopf,
          1945. (Repr. New York: Harcourt Brace Jovanovich,
          1975.) 329p.

S.1041.   CONRAD, Earl. Billy Rose, Manhattan Primitive. Cleve-
          land: World, 1968. 272p.

S.1042.   DUNHAM, Katherine. Journey to Accompong. New York:
          Holt, 1946. 162p.

S.1043.   DUNHAM, Katherine. A Touch of Innocence. New York:
          Harcourt, Brace & World, 1959. 312p.

S.1044.   GILBERT, Louis Wolfe. Without Rhyme or Reason. New
          York: Vantage Press, 1956. 240p.

S.1045.   HIGHAM, Charles. Ziegfeld. Chicago: Regnery; Lon-
          don: W. H. Allen, 1973. 245p.

S.1046.   LACOMBE, Alain. George Gershwin: une chronique de
          Broadway. Paris: Van de Velde, 1980. 204p.

S.1047.   MARX, Henry, ed. Weill-Lenya. New York: Goethe
          House, 1976. 46p. (Published to coincide with an ex-
          hibition at the Lincoln Center, New York, Nov. 1976-
          June 1977.)

S.1048.   NEILSON, Francis. My Life in Two Worlds, 1867-1952.
          Appleton, Wis.: Nelson, 1952-1953. 2v. (Librettist
          for Victor Herbert's Prince Ananias.)

S.1049.   KOTSCHENREUTHER, Helmut. Kurt Weill. Berlin-
          Halensee: Hesse, 1962. 103p.

S.1050.   SCHMIDT-JOOS, Siegfried. Das Musical. Munich: DTV,
          1965. 296p.

S.1051.   STRANG, Lewis C. Celebrated Comedians of Light Opera and Musical Comedy in America. Boston: L. C. Page, 1901. 293p.

S.1052. WHITTON, Joseph. "The Naked Truth!" an inside history of the Black Crook. Philadelphia: H. W. Shaw, 1897. 32p.

Popular Music for the Screen

S.1053. ELLIS, Jack C., et al. The Film Book Bibliography, 1940-1975. Metuchen, N.J.: Scarecrow Press, 1979. 752p. (Includes sections for music and biography.)

S.1054. HENRY MANCINI: an American Film Institute seminar on his work. Glen Rock, N.J.: Microfilming Corp. of America, 1977. 61p. (Microfiche of a text produced by the American Film Institute.)

S.1055. KNOX, Donald. The Magic Factory: how MGM made An American in Paris. New York: Praeger, 1973. 217p.

S.1056. LACOMBE, Alain, and ROCLE, Claude. La musique du film. Paris: Van de Velde, 1979. 516p.

S.1057. MANCINI, Henry. Sounds and Scores: a practical guide to professional orchestration. Northridge, Calif.: Northridge Music, 1975.

S.1058. MEHR, Linda Harris, ed. Motion Pictures, Television and Radio: a union catalog of manuscript and special collections in the Western United States. Boston: G. K. Hall, 1977. 201p. (Includes locations of film scores and manuscripts.)

S.1059. RUSSELL, William. Tumbleweed: best of the singing cowboys. Fairfax, Va.: Western Revue, 1977.

S.1060. SKILES, Martin. Music Scoring for TV and Motion Pictures. Blue Ridge Summit, Pa.: Tab Books, 1976. 261p.

S.1061. STERN, Lee Edward. The Movie Musical. New York: Pyramid, 1974. 159p.

S.1062. TIOMKIN, Dimitri, and BURANELLI, Prosper. Please Don't Hate Me. Garden City, N.Y.: Doubleday, 1961. 261p.

340 / Literature of American Music

Popular Music Personalities

DESI ARNAZ

S.1063.   Arnaz, Desi. A Book. New York: Morrow, 1976. 322p.

FRED ASTAIRE

S.1064.   GREEN, Benny. Fred Astaire. London: Hamlyn, 1979.
          176p.

S.1065.   HARVEY, Stephen. Fred Astaire. New York: Pyramid,
          1975. 158p.

BILL JOE AUSTIN

S.1066.   AUSTIN, Bill Joe. The Beat Goes On and On and On.
          Erwin, N.C.: Carolina Arts and Publishing House,
          1978. 170p.

JOSEPHINE BAKER

S.1067.   BAKER, Josephine, and BOUILLON, Jo. Josephine.
          Paris: Laffont, 1976.
          _____. Josephine; translated from the French by
          Mariana Fitzpatrick. New York: Harper & Row, 1977.
          302p.

S.1068.   KUHN, Dieter. Josephine. Frankfurt: Suhrkamp, 1976.
          159p.

S.1069.   PAPICH, Stephen. Remembering Josephine. Indianapolis:
          Bobbs-Merrill, 1976. 237p.

HARRY BELAFONTE

S.1070.   SHAW, Arnold. Belafonte: an unauthorized biography.
          Philadelphia: Chilton, 1960. 338p.

PAT BOONE

S.1071.   BOONE, Pat. A New Song. Carol Stream, Ill.: Creation
          House, 1970. 192p.

S.1072.   _____. Together: 25 years with the Boone family.
          Nashville, Tenn.: Nelson, 1979. 128p.

BING CROSBY

S.1073.   BAUER, Barbara. Bing Crosby. New York: Pyramid,
          1977. 159p.

S.1074.   SELDES, Gilbert.   The Public Arts.   New York: Simon
          & Schuster, 1956.   303p.   (Includes a chapter on "The
          Incomparable Bing.")

XAVIER CUGAT

S.1075.   CUGAT, Xavier.   Rumba Is My Life.   New York: Didier,
          1948.   210p.

DOROTHY DANDRIDGE

S.1076.   MILLS, Earl.   Dorothy Dandridge: a portrait in black.
          Los Angeles: Holloway House, 1970.   248p.

EDDIE FISHER

S.1077.   GREENE, Myrna.   The Eddie Fisher Story.   Middlebury,
          Vt.:   Eriksson, 1978.   210p.

JUDY GARLAND

S.1078.   BAXTER, Brian.   The Films of Judy Garland.   Bembridge,
          Eng.:   BCW Publishing, 1977.   47p.

S.1079.   MORELLA, Joe, and EPSTEIN, Edward Z.   The Films and
          Career of Judy Garland.   New York: Citadel Press,
          1969.   216p.

DANNY KAYE

S.1080.   SINGER, Kurt.   The Danny Kaye Saga.   London: Robert
          Hale, 1957.   206p.

EARTHA KITT

S.1081.   KITT, Eartha.   Alone With Me: a new autobiography.
          Chicago: Regnery, 1976.   276p.

MARY MARTIN

S.1082.   NEWMAN, Shirlee P.   Mary Martin On Stage.   Philadelphia:
          Westminster Press, 1969.   126p.

EZIO PINZA

S.1083.   PINZA, Ezio.   Ezio Pinza: an autobiography.   New York:
          Rinehart, 1958.   307p.

GINGER ROGERS

S.1084.   DICKENS, H.   The Films of Ginger Rogers.   Secaucus,
          N.J.:   Citadel Press, 1975.   256p.

S.1085.   RICHARDS, Dick. Ginger: salute to a star. Brighton,
          Eng.:   Clifton Books, 1969.   192p.

DINAH SHORE

S.1086.   CASSIDY, Bruce. Dinah! a biography. New York:
          Watts, 1979.   212p.

BOBBY SHORT

S.1087.   SHORT, Bobby. Black and White Baby. New York:
          Dodd, Mead, 1971.   304p.

FRANK SINATRA

S.1088.   GEHMAN, Richard. Sinatra and His Rat Pack. London:
          Mayflower, 1961.   223p.

S.1089.   HARVEY, Jacques. Monsieur Sinatra. Paris: Albin
          Michel, 1976.   229p.

BARBRA STREISAND

S.1090.   ABITAN, Guy. Barbra Streisand: une femme libre.
          (Paris?):   Orban, 1979.   183p.

S.1091.   CASTELL, David. The Films of Barbra Streisand. Bem-
          bridge, Eng.:   BCW Publishing, 1977.   47p.

S.1092.   SPADA, James. Barbra: the first decade; the films and
          career of Barbra Streisand. Secaucus, N.J.:   Citadel
          Press, 1974.   223p.

MEL TORMÉ

S.1093.   TORMÉ, Mel. The Other Side of the Rainbow: with Judy
          Garland on the dawn patrol. New York: Morrow,
          1970; London: W. H. Allen, 1971.   241p.   (UK ed.
          lacks the subtitle.)

LAWRENCE WELK

S.1094.   COAKLEY, Mary Lewis. Mister Music Maker: Lawrence
          Welk. Garden City, N.Y.:   Doubleday, 1958.   280p.

S.1095.   SCHWIENHER, William K. Lawrence Welk: an American
          institution. Chicago: Nelson-Hall, 1980.   288p.

(Note: the literature in book form on rock, rock & roll, and pop
is now very extensive indeed. For further guidance the reader is
referred to the bibliographies by Frank Hoffmann, Rowan Iwaschkin,
and Paul Taylor cited in the Preface.)

1. General Reference Works

(See also S.1139)

S.1096. DALTON, David, and KAYE, Lenny. Rock 100. New
         York: Grosset & Dunlap, 1977. 280p. illus.
     A chronologically-arranged biographical dictionary (or, if
you prefer, a biographically-arranged chronology) of one hundred
major individuals and groups from "the first two (and some) decades
of a lusty, life-or-death music" (introduction); all are performers
who, in the compilers' language, "located the symbolic and vinyl
sites where the real and imaginary feed on each other to create a
star" (ibid.). The biographies, often more critical than factual,
are grouped according to style and period; an index (fortunately)
provides the reference access which the book's arrangement makes
difficult. Some unusual photos.

S.1097. FRAME, Pete. Rock Family Trees. London: Omnibus
         Press, 1980-1983. 2 vols.
     A fascinating and instructive concept: the evolution and
interrelationships of rock bands, mapped out in a series of hand-
drawn genealogical charts ("as in architectural stuff, with drawing
boards and T-squares"--introduction). The "family trees" them-
selves--the lines of descent and inter-marriage--are given in heavier
print, while all the surrounding space, every inch of it, is covered
with snippets of historical, biographical, and often also discographical information. Ten of the 30 charts in Vol. 1 relate to US bands
or groups of bands: Gene Vincent and the Blue Caps; the Byrds;
Jefferson Airplane; Janis Joplin, Big Brother and the Holding Company, Moby Grape; Country Joe McDonald and other San Francisco
groups; Crosby, Stills, Nash and Young; Buffalo Springfield, Flying Burrito Brothers, Eagles, etc.; Frank Zappa and the Mothers of
Invention; Patti Smith, Blondie; New York Dolls, Ramones, etc.
Vol. 2, with a more pronounced British emphasis, includes charts

for Gram Parsons, Flying Burrito Brothers, Emmylou Harris; Little
Feat, Doobie Brothers, Steely Dan. There is also a chronology, in
a different format (square boxes) of the "Rock'n'Roll Era, 1955-
1959." Both volumes have a name index.

S.1098. GIVEN, Dave. The Dave Given Rock'n'Roll Stars Hand-
         book: rhythm and blues artists and groups. Smith-
         town, N.Y.: Exposition Press, 1980. 328p. illus.,
         discog.
         Biographical information and stylistic commentary on some
50 rhythm and blues, rock, and soul performers from the 1950s to
the 1970s.

S.1099. HARDY, Phil, and LAING, Dave, eds. The Encyclopedia
         of Rock. St. Albans: Panther, 1976. 3 vols.
         _____. The Encyclopedia of Rock, 1955-75. London:
         Aquarius, 1977. 287p.
         These volumes represent the best achievement to date in
rock reference (an area which has seen an explosion of works in
the 1980s, many of them of limited value). Now in need of updat-
ing (especially Volume 3), the work as a whole nevertheless maintains, through heavy use by readers of many types, a high reputation for reliability. Each volume covers an approximate span of
time: Vol. 1, "The Age of Rock 'n' Roll," 1955-63; Vol. 2, "From
Liverpool to San Francisco," 1963-68; and Vol. 3, "The Sounds of
the Sixties," 1968-75. The criteria for inclusion are twofold: success, and the editors' judgment on grounds of historical importance
and artistic significance. Coverage is largely restricted to the USA
and Britain. The majority of entries are biographical, but go beyond
performers to include producers, company bosses, session musicians,
and songwriters. Also represented, in a genuine attempt to cover
the entire world of rock, are record companies, places, and genres,
and space is also found to include representatives of blues, country
music, and gospel. The style adopted is a narrative one; this
means that "complete" coverage of hardcore factual data is not attempted, but instead entries offer selected (but generous) information, authoritatively and interestingly conveyed. The list of contributors to each volume is long, but no signs of a stylistic mish-mash
are evident. Each volume contains a name index, with references,
to main entries and to passing mentions. (There is no index in the
one-volume reissue.) No discographical information is given, although the titles of many recordings are referred to in the text.

S.1100. KNEIF, Tibor. Sachlexikon Rockmusik: Instrumente,
         Stile, Techniken, Industrie und Geschichte. Reinbek
         bei Hamburg: Rowohlt, 1978. 252p.
         _____. _____. Rev. ed. Reinbek bei Hamburg:
         Rowohlt, 1980. 194p. bibliogs., discogs.
         The well-established German tradition of subject encyclo-
pedias, with no entries under names of individuals, has never
properly caught on in the English-speaking world, with the result

that reference sources in English often lack the ability to provide information on, or convey a sense of, the many-sidedness of a subject. Rock lends itself to this alternative approach, once the stranglehold of star obsession is broken, and hence Kneif's attempt to redress the balance is very welcome. He provides concise information, with considerable authority, on instruments, styles, genres, musical phenomena, record companies, locations, specialized terminology, etc. There is a well-organized cross-reference system, and very many entries are accompanied by bibliographical and/or discographical information. Access to information on individuals can be obtained via the name index. Any future, serious endeavor to provide a broadly-based reference source for rock (or for popular music as a whole) must take account of Kneif's work, and of the approach he uses. (For the same approach applied to jazz, see Wölfer, no. S.636.)

S.1101.   LOGAN, Nick, and WOFFINDEN, Bob. The Illustrated
          New Musical Express Encyclopedia of Rock. London:
          Hamlyn, 1976; London: Salamander Books, 1977. 255p.
          illus., discogs.
          _____. The Illustrated Encyclopedia of Rock. New
          York: Harmony Books, 1977. 255p. illus., discogs.
          _____. The Illustrated Encyclopedia of Rock. 3rd ed.
          London: Salamander Books, 1982. 288p. illus.,
          discogs.
          Compiled by two writers for London's New Musical Express,
this is a well-designed, large format biographical dictionary, with
occasional subject entries. Coverage is evenly divided between
American and British performers. Arranged in four columns per
page, the 600-plus entries average 250 words each (though major
performers have considerably more, and are given a two-column
spread to distinguish them). They give generally concise career
information in a lively narrative style, with a limited amount of
comment and a general avoidance of hyperbole. Album titles, given
in heavier type, frequently provide the backbone for an entry, so
that biography and recording career are closely linked. Each entry
concludes with a (usually selective) discography giving album titles
and record labels. Index.

S.1102.   MARCHBANK, Pearce, and MILES. The Illustrated Rock
          Almanac. New York & London: Paddington Press,
          1977. 188p. illus.
          Probably of most use to disc jockeys and astrologers, this
is a calendar in which for each day of the year miscellaneous events
from the annals of rock are commemorated ("rock" being liberally
interpreted to include not just some jazz, blues, and country music
occurrences, but a wide, whimsical variety of people and events
with no musical connection whatsoever). Birthdays and death-days
are the most frequent entries, followed by selective recordings and
performances, and filled out by a variety of trivia. Each entry has
a brief descriptive (often biographical) note. Once the initial

fascination of meaningless juxtaposition has worn off, the book's determination to be unsystematic (no indexes, no cross-references from dates of birth to dates of death) becomes frustrating, as all sense of history is subsumed by random coincidence. A genuine chronology, now, that would be worth having....

S.1103. NITE, Norm N. Rock On: the illustrated encyclopedia of rock'n'roll. (Vol. 1). The Solid Gold Years; special introduction by Dick Clark. New York: Crowell, 1974; New York: Popular Library, 1977. 676p. illus., discogs.
_____. _____. Updated ed. New York: Harper & Row, 1982. 722p. illus., discogs.
_____. _____. (Vol. 2). The Modern Years; special introduction by Wolfman Jack. New York: Crowell, 1978. 448p. illus., discogs.
_____. _____. (Vol. 2). The Years of Change, 1964-1978; with Ralph M. Newman. Updated ed. New York: Harper & Row, 1984. 747p. illus., discogs.
_____. _____. Vol. 3. The Video Revolution to the Present; with Charles Crespo. New York: Harper & Row, 1985. 443p. illus., discogs.

A substantial biographical dictionary of performers (and only performers), with over 2,000 entries for individuals and groups in its three volumes. The focus is primarily on rock, but the principal criterion for inclusion (a Top 100 single, or, for Vol. 2, a Top 100 album--no criteria are stated for Vol. 3) ensures the presence also of country, rhythm & blues, and middle-of-the road popular singles. A typical entry provides date of birth (though Vol. 1 is sometimes sketchy on this, and Vol. 3 found many contemporary performers too coy), home town, a short (often very short) biographical sketch, and a list of hit records by date (with label name only). Many entries have accompanying photographs. Apart from the 1974 edition of Vol. 1 each book has a song title index.

S.1104. SCHMIDT-JOOS, Siegfried, and GRAVES, Barry. Rock-Lexikon. Reinbek bei Hamburg: Rowohlt, 1973.
_____. _____. Rev. ed. Reinbek bei Hamburg: Rowohlt, 1975. 445p. bibliog., discog.

Reliable, informative biographical reference work that combines concisely expressed factual data with astute critical summary. Good use is made of quotations, both from the musicians themselves and from critics. The revised edition contains some 600 entries (almost all American and British musicians), each with a short discography. There is a good cross-referencing system, a glossary of subject keywords (see Kneif, no. S.1100, for a fuller treatment of this approach), and a name index.

S.1105. YORK, William. Who's Who in Rock: an A-Z of groups, performers, producers, session men, engineers.... Seattle: Atomic Press, 1978. 260p.

_____ . _____ . London: Omnibus Press, 1979.
237p.

_____ . Who's Who in Rock Music. Rev. ed. New York:
Scribner; London: Barker, 1982. 413p.
The original version of this biographical dictionary contains
over 5,000 entries, based on information "taken almost entirely from
album jackets" (p. 4). A typical entry for a minor figure (of whom
there are many) gives details of instrument(s) played, group(s)
belonged to, and important sessions played for more major musicians;
entries for the latter usually provide a capsule career summary and
a list of major albums with year of release. Entries for groups give
names of participating musicians and major albums. In all three
categories the provision of basic biographical information is very uneven. The 1982 edition expands coverage to over 13,000 entries; it
also corrects erroneous information in the earlier version, and is far
more thorough and accurate in the data provided, without ever wholly convincing the user of its reliability.

S.1106. ZALKIND, Ronald, ed. Contemporary Music Almanac
1980/81. New York: Schirmer; London: Collier Macmillan, 1980. 944p. illus., bibliogs., discogs.
The first, but evidently the only volume in a proposed
series, this is an impressive yearbook-cum-directory of the rock
and popular scene, with a pronounced US slant. The team of 30
writers includes R. Serge Denisoff, Dennis Lambert, Dave Marsh,
John Morthland, and John Swenson. The information is selected
"to focus on what has drawn the most national attention during
1979" (preface), but actually extends well beyond the year itself
to offer retrospective lists (of, for instance, awards). The ten
sections provide: day-by-day chronologies and lists of the top five
1979 albums and singles; feature articles on the music scene past
and present; a who's who, including a list of music professionals;
a chronological list of 1979 albums, with names of producers, engineers, studio, and address lists of record companies, producers,
studios, managers, agents, publishers; guidance on "getting started"
(organizing the business side); contracts; a gazetteer of radio stations, concert halls, publicity firms, attorneys; reference lists of
magazines (with addresses), recent books, and rock films, awards;
puzzles and quizzes.

2. Recordings

(a) Discographies, record lists, charts

(See also S.556-S.558)

S.1107. BERRY, Peter E. "... And the Hits Just Keep on Comin'."
Syracuse, N.Y.: Syracuse University Press, 1977.
278p. illus., bibliog., discog.
During his work as a radio disc jockey and producer,

Berry compiled his own annual list of hit songs, in which he drew
together information obtained from several sources--trade journals
(Billboard, etc.), radio station playlists, and weekly Top 40 charts.
These annual listings, 1955-1976, are the result. Each year's list
is preceded by a highly subjective version of that year's highlights;
the lists themselves are of Top 50 songs for each year, and are followed by lists of Number 1 hits, of Berry's choice of significant
artists, and of Academy Award winners. A discography (pp. 169-
276), arranged by artist, provides a selective listing in chronological
order.

S.1108. BLACKBURN, Richard. Rockabilly: a comprehensive dis-
         cography of reissues. n.p. (England): the author,
         1976. 30p.
         The reissues in question--45s and LPs--are presented in two
groups, anthologies and individual performers; the performer section
is also an index to the 46 anthologies. All were, or had recently been,
available at the time of compilation, and include European labels.
The compiler does not define rockabilly, save to say Elvis Presley's
Sun recordings "constitute the core of true rockabilly music," that
Johnny Cash and Johnny Horton are omitted "due to lack of sufficient black influence and offbeat rhythm," and that Jerry Lee Lewis
and other country boogie pianists are not included, "on the assumption that rockabilly requires a guitar lead" (introduction).

S.1109. BLAIR, John. The Illustrated Discography of Surf Music
         1959-1965. Riverside, Calif.: J. Bee Productions,
         1978. 52p. illus.
         _____. The Illustrated Discography of Surf Music
         1961-1965. 2nd ed., revised. Ann Arbor, Mich.:
         Pierian Press, 1985. 166p. illus., bibliog.
         Much enlarged in its later edition, this fine discography
represents a great deal of patient research. The Southern California sound of the early 1960s, inaugurated mainly by Dick Dale with
the help of Leo Fender's reverb unit, is generally identified with
the Beach Boys, but Blair shows just how many bands were involved
in the scene. He views surf music as unique in being the first musical style to grow up around a sport, and--perhaps more interest-
ingly--as culturally important in being for the most part a "geographically isolated form of pop music" (p. ix). The discography
lists vocals and instrumentals which relate in some specific way to
surfing. It is divided into two sections: singles and albums, each
alphabetically arranged by performer, and chronologically by label
and number. Some biographical information is included. Master
numbers are given for singles when available. Issue numbers are
given for singles and albums, and release dates are added when
known. The LP section generally includes track listings. The text
is profusely illustrated, and is followed by various appendices (including a surfing dictionary) and indexes of names, label and record
numbers, and song and album titles.

S.1110. GOLDSTEIN, Stewart, and JACOBSON, Alan. Oldies But
Goodies: the rock 'n' roll years. New York: Mason/
Charter, 1977; New York: Van Nostrand Reinhold,
1978. 328p. illus.

Based partly on Billboard statistics (according to the dust
jacket, though not stated in the book itself) and partly on the
compilers' preferences, this is a month-by-month listing of "every
oldie that made the Top 40 between 1955 and 1963, the major years
of rock 'n' roll" (foreword). Those records regarded as "non-oldies"
(a category which includes, for example, the Supremes) are omitted
from the main list, and an undertaking in the foreword to include
them in a special chronological section seems to be unfulfilled; instead, there is a two-and-a-half-page alphabetical list with month
and year of arrival in the Top 40 chart. The main chronological sequence is followed by various other lists, bringing together information by different means (artists with number one hits, etc.). Paul
Anka provides a brief introduction.

S.1111. THE MILES Chart Display. Vol. 1. Top 100, 1955-1970,
by Betty T. Miles, Daniel J. Miles, Martin J. Miles.
Boulder, Colo.: Convex Industries, 1973. 1270p.
THE MILES Chart Display of Popular Music. Vol. 2. Top
100, 1971-1975, by Daniel J. Miles, Martin J. Miles.
New York: Arno Press, 1977. 406p.

A unique concept in charting hit records: the rise and
fall of each disc is displayed by means of graphs ("phono/graphs");
one axis shows the week of the Billboard chart, the other the chart
position, thus allowing a more detailed picture of the fortunes of any
one record than is permitted by conventional listing. Details are
provided of artist name(s), record label and number, the date of the
Billboard issue in which the record was first listed, the highest position reached, and the date it left the charts. Vol. 1 contains
over 9,500 graphs, alphabetically by song title. It also includes an
artist index, with record titles and "phono/graph" number; there is
also an index of "corporate" graphs--graphs for songs recorded successfully by more than one performer, and which give a fascinating
insight into struggles for supremacy. Vol. 2 contains an additional
feature: a percentage ranking ("percentile") shows the relative
ranking of a particular record among all records during the period
covered.

S.1112. NUGENT, Stephen, and GILLETT, Charlie, eds. Rock
Almanac: top 20 singles, 1955-73, and top 20 albums,
1964-73. Garden City, N.Y.: Doubleday, 1976. 485p.
discogs.
_____. Rock Almanac: top 20 American and British
singles of the '50s, '60s, and '70s. Garden City, N.Y.:
Anchor Books, 1978. 485p. discogs.

Basically a selection for the US market from the contents
of the British Rock File 1-4 (no. S.1113). The bulk of the book is
devoted to listings ("logs") of "all the singers and musicians,

comedians and narrators, film stars, footballers and animals who ever had a record make the top twenty in America or Britain" (introduction). The lists are in two sections: for singles and albums. Each entry contains details of date of chart entry, highest position reached, and number of weeks in the chart. Of the five essays which precede the lists, the ones relevant to the USA are "Hot One Hundred Singles and Albums," by Gillett and Simon Frith, with Dave Marsh (based on a piece in Rock File 3), and Paul Gambaccini's "American Radio Today" (from Rock File 4).

S.1113.   ROCK FILE; edited by Charlie Gillett. London: Pictorial
           Presentations, 1972. 156p. illus., discog.
           ROCK FILE 2; (edited by Charlie Gillett). St. Albans:
           Panther, 1974. 169p. illus., discogs.
           ROCK FILE 3; edited by Charlie Gillett and Simon Frith.
           St. Albans: Panther, 1975. 224p. illus., discogs.
           ROCK FILE 4; edited by Charlie Gillett and Simon Frith.
           St. Albans: Panther, 1976. 400p. discogs.
           ROCK FILE 5; edited by Charlie Gillett and Simon Frith.
           St. Albans: Panther, 1978. 286p. discogs.
    This British-produced series offers an intriguing mix of reference information (charts, in various forms) and well-informed essays on contemporary developments. The emphasis throughout is on the British scene--and both charts and essays have that bias-- but there is a good deal to interest the Americanist also. Of the various essays, those relevant to the USA include (in Vol. 1) Charlie Gillett's comparative piece on the rock press, (Vol. 2) Pete Wingfield on Philadelphia soul, (Vol. 3) Simon Frith and Charlie Gillett's selection of those 100 rock singles and 100 rock albums which had the most impact, and (Vol. 4) Paul Gambaccini on American radio. The "chartlogs" in the first two volumes contain UK information only. In Vol. 3 the log takes the form of an alphabetical song title list, 1955-1973, with details of composer, publisher, performer, year of chart entry, and comparative UK and US highest positions. In Vol. 4 the log is a performer-arranged list of American/British Top 20 hits, 1955-1974. Under each title the information for the UK and the USA releases--label, date of entry, highest position, number of weeks on chart--is separately listed. The chief architect of these lists is Stephen Nugent. Vol. 5 includes UK information only, but has an unusual feature: an index of producers.

S.1114.   SOLOMON, Clive, et al., eds. Record Hits: the British
           Top 50 charts, 1952-1977, plus U.S. chart positions;
           compiled by Clive Solomon, Howard Pizzey and Martin
           Watson. London: Omnibus Press, 1979. 270p.
    This "log" of the British charts includes useful comparative US chart information, excluding the years 1952-55. The statistics for the USA are drawn mainly from Billboard's Top 100. Arrangement is by artist, and for each title details are given of UK label, date of chart entry, highest position, and number of weeks in the charts. For all records also released in the USA the infor-

mation given takes the same form. Title index. (An earlier 1977 edition does not include the US information.)

S.1115. WHITBURN, Joel. Pop Annual 1955-1977. Menomonee Falls, Wisc.: Record Research, 1978. 623p.

Unlike other Whitburn volumes (LOAM 632, 890, 1340, and nos. S.818, S.819), which are based on artist lists, this one is organized chronologically. Information from Top Pop Records 1955-1970, up-dated and partially expanded, is presented year-by-year. (Top Pop Records 1955-1970 was itself revised and appeared as Top Pop Artists and Singles, 1955-1978 [Menomonee Falls: Record Research, 1979].)

S.1116. WILLIAMS, John R. This Was "Your Hit Parade". Camden, Maine: Courier-Gazette, Inc., 1973. 209p.

"Your Hit Parade," first broadcast in 1935, was a weekly radio program playing the fifteen top songs as determined by nationwide survey. In July 1950 it became a television feature. The last program was broadcast in April 1959. These are the weekly listings, April 1935-July 1958, as used by the program. Song titles only are given. Supplementary lists include first, second and third place songs, arranged by the number of times a song held those positions, and an alphabetical list of all songs with the date each first appeared in the program, the number of times it was played, and its highest ranking.

(b) Record Guides

See also S.810, S.817

S.1117. ANDERSON, Ian. Rock Record Collectors Guide. London: MRP Books, 1977. 178p. illus., bibliog.

This is a British production with record labels and other details geared strictly to a UK audience, but including many American performers. All items, including the books and magazines listed in the "Further reading" section, are informatively annotated, and a star system is used to indicate preferences. "What I have tried to do with this book," the author writes in his introduction, "is to gather together all the most important records of their type within the boundaries of rock music and its influences and roots. Jazz, blues, reggae, folk and ethnic musics, although they are not covered in depth, are therefore included. Perhaps the recommended records ... will lead the reader on to other forms of popular music beyond his or her current taste."

S.1118. COLLIS, John, ed. The Rock Primer. Harmondsworth: Penguin Books, 1980. 335p.

A useful guide through the profusion of recordings, this annotated selection of significant albums combines introductory information with enough perceptive comment to attract the attention of a more knowledgeable audience also. The seven British critics present

their choices in eleven sections, nine of which are relevant to US
music: rock & roll (John Collis), folk and blues (Dave Laing),
rhythm and blues (Ian Hoare & Collis), soul (Hoare), country
(Collis), California sun (Mick Houghton), Dylan and after (Laing),
punk (Ian Birch), and the seventies (Steve Taylor). Each section
is restricted to twenty albums, but more are referred to in the
text, and a short list of outstanding singles follows each list of
albums. Index.

S.1119.   GAMBACCINI, Paul, ed. Rock Critics' Choice: the top
           200 albums; with Susan Ready; with contributions by
           Loraine Alterman. London: Omnibus Press; New York:
           Quick Fox, 1978. 96p. illus.
       The records in question were identified by asking 47 inter-
national rock critics and disc jockeys to name their favorite ten albums. The 200 most frequently nominated albums are listed, by
numerical order of choice, in the first part of the book, with a reproduction of the cover illustration, a photograph of the perform-
er(s), a list of the contents, and details of the label, US and UK
release numbers, producer, and year of release. Each critic's complete selection is listed in the second part, together with a photograph of and a note on each. The definitional lines are broadly
drawn, so the choices include such performers as Simon & Garfunkel
and Miles Davis (neither of whom have albums in the top group).

S.1120.   MARSH, Dave, ed. The Rolling Stone Record Guide: re-
           views and ratings of almost 10,000 currently available
           rock, pop, soul, country, blues, jazz, and gospel al-
           bums; with John Swenson. New York: Random House/
           Rolling Stone Press; London: Virgin Books, 1979.
           631p. bibliog.
           MARSH, Dave, and SWENSON, John, eds. The New Rol-
           ling Stone Record Guide. Revised, updated ed. New
           York: Random House, 1983. 648p.
       An extremely useful, if sometimes distractingly subjective
reference guide through the maze of rock LPs and related music.
The major section, occupying two-thirds of the book, is devoted to
rock, soul, country, and pop. Artist entries in these stylistic
groups are arranged in one alphabetical sequence, coverage for rock
being as comprehensive as possible, with a more selective approach
in other areas. In each entry record albums available in the USA
at the time of publication are listed alphabetically by title (in the
first edn.), without dates, and each is given a rating (from one to
five stars, with an extra symbol to denote "worthless"). The reviews following each list vary from curt two-line dismissals to detached four or five-page assessments, usually constructed on broadly
chronological lines. The other sections of the book deal more
selectively with blues, jazz, and gospel LPs and a final section is
given over to anthologies, soundtracks, and original cast recordings.
Thirty-three contributors assist the editors, who are themselves responsible for a substantial number of the annotations. The revised

edition improves the discographies by adding dates and arranging them chronologically; some non-US releases are also included. A number of the assessments are re-written, though subjectivity is still a basic characteristic of many of them. The glossary of terms and the annotated book bibliography (71 books), both creditable features of the first book, are abandoned in the new version, together with coverage of jazz.

S.1121.   PROPES, Steve. Golden Goodies: a guide to 50's and
          60's popular rock & roll recording collecting. Radnor,
          Penn.: Chilton, 1975. 185p.
          Curiously enough, there seems to be no duplication of information between this book and Propes' other guides (Those Oldies But Goodies (LOAM 888) and Golden Oldies (LOAM 887), but all three books share the same basic format: sections devoted to various individuals and groups with lists of their records, accompanied by label name, record number, and year of release. The lists are preceded by information on the performers and by the average collector prices. A collector himself, the author makes a distinction between "popular" rock & roll of the 1950s and 1960s and other rock & roll of the same period (much of which was popular...). The fine line of the distinction adds little to the debate on what "popular" music is, and seems to have meaning for Propes alone. (Not even his publisher seems to understand: a statement on the dust jacket claims, "Here is the complete guide to record collecting..."--emphasis added.)

3.   Histories

(a) General

S.1122.   MILLER, Jim, ed. The Rolling Stone Illustrated History
          of Rock & Roll; designed by Robert Kingsbury. New
          York: Rolling Stone Press, 1976. 382p. illus., dis-
          cogs.
          _____.   _____. Revised and updated ed. New York:
          Rolling Stone Press, 1980; London: Picador, 1981.
          474p. illus., discogs.
          The views of 29 different writers, spread over 82 short essays (in the revised edition), do not make the history the title claims, even though the broad range of subjects and the generally high standard of criticism are sufficient to produce one of the more consistently interesting and informative rock books. The essays follow a broadly chronological arrangement, but because most of them isolate a subject and follow it through from start to finish (or the late '70s), no overall sense of development or change is conveyed, and there is no interaction between subjects. Each essay becomes in itself a mini-history, whether of a life (around half the pieces are on individuals), a place (New Orleans, Memphis, San Francisco, Philadelphia), a genre (doo-wop, soul, punk, disco), or other aspects

(Top 40, AM shows, payola, festivals, films). As such they are
often excellent brief summaries, and illuminating if used that way,
with no further expectations. All the critics are American (most
have written for Rolling Stone or Village Voice), and include in
their number Lester Bangs, Robert Christgau, Peter Guralnick,
Greil Marcus, Dave Marsh, Robert Palmer, John Rockwell, and Ellen
Willis. About three-quarters of the book is devoted to the US
scene. A useful feature is the discography which follows each essay; bibliographic information, however, is totally absent. Name index.

S.1123.   PASCALL, Jeremy. The Illustrated History of Rock Music.
           London: Hamlyn; New York: Galahad Books, 1978.
           221p. illus., bibliog.
           _____.   _____. New and enlarged ed. London:
           Hamlyn, 1984. 237p. illus., bibliog.
    Pascall exemplifies some of those puzzling contradictions
in rock literature: a fluent writer who has written widely, in books
and in the music press, he believes music should not be written
about (1984 ed., p. 232); not short of ideas himself, he berates
those who set out to approach the music in any kind of intellectual/
analytical way. Setting such hang-ups to one side, his is a
knowledgeable text, above the average for the hack work that customarily accompanies pictorial celebrations. Though reasonably well
balanced in his coverage, Pascall is clearly more at home with
British music than American, with white rather than black; but in
all areas there is a shortage of the kind of detail a true "history"
requires. The illustrations, about two-thirds of them in color, are
well reproduced. The new edition adds a chapter on the 1980s. No
discographical information is given.

S.1124.   YORKE, Ritchie. The History of Rock 'n' Roll; prepared
           in association with CHUM Ltd. Toronto: Methuen;
           New York: Methuen/Two Continents, 1976. 174p.
           illus., discogs.
    Written to accompany a series of radio programs with the
same title, broadcast in Canada by CHUM, this is not a history as
such--there is little explanation or interpretation--but a basic
chronology of rock, 1955-1975. Each year receives its own chapter,
in which the major rock events and trends are summarized, and outstanding individuals and recordings are noted; each chapter ends
with a short list of "other notable records." The illustrations,
mostly in black-and-white, have a standard air (many were supplied
by record companies). (Yorke has the distinction of being ranked
by Dave Marsh as one of the "ten worst rock critics"--see The Book
of Rock Lists, by Dave Marsh and Kevin Stein [New York: Dell,
1981].)

(b) Specific Periods

See also S.1145, S.1195.

S.1125. BURCHILL, Julie, and PARSONS, Tony. "The Boy
Looked at Johnny": the obituary of rock and roll.
London: Pluto Press, 1978. 96p. illus.
This caustic account of punk in the UK by two journalists
on the New Musical Express has several, usually hostile but often
revealing, things to say about punk's American background and
some of the mid-'70s American bands and performers. The opening
chapter, "Germs," is a brief but potent antidote to glassy-eyed accounts of late-'60s rock. Stylistically supercharged itself (it could
be using hypocritical and excessive devices to unveil hypocrisy and
excess, but probably isn't), it attacks the "legacy" of the '60s to
the next generation, in particular the gulf between assertions of
revolutionary sensibility and the lucrative commercial reality. Some
rebellious reputations are dented, among them post-John Sinclair
MC5 ("pure pop pap, sheep-dipped in transparent raiments of youth
and rebellion"--p. 20), Iggy Pop and Lou Reed ("the punky junkie
duo"--p. 24), and the New York Dolls. In later chapters, when
American punk is compared to British, the criticism is somewhat
parochial and less interesting, but the comments on Television, the
Ramones, and Talking Heads are worth noting. No index.

S.1126. OBST, Lynda Rosen, ed. The Sixties: the decade remembered now, by the people who lived it then; designed by Robert Kingsbury. New York: Rolling
Stone Press, 1977. 314p. illus.
Wonderfully illustrated with contemporary black-and-white
photographs, this large format book takes a year-by-year look at
1960s culture and events, through the eyes of over 70 participants,
many of whom were interviewed by the editor for the project. Only
a small proportion of the short pieces are on music, but these include Dick Clark on the Twist, Michael Bloomfield on Dylan going
electric, Lou Adler on the Monterey Festival, Rashied Ali on Coltrane, Myra Friedman on Janis Joplin, Wavy Gravy on Woodstock,
and Greil Marcus on Altamont. Each year is accompanied by a calendar of events.

S.1127. PICHASKE, David. A Generation in Motion: popular music and culture in the sixties. New York: Schirmer,
1979. 248p. illus., discog.
Even the shrewdest critics who came of age in the 1960s
are not immune from a sense that they belong to a generation that
was somehow blessed--a radical, self-aware elite who made music a
uniquely significant cultural force. Pichaske's book rests on--or
sprawls over--this thesis; virtually everything about the '60s rock
generation, even the destructive side, is superior to what went before and what followed. Yet if one can forget this generation obsession (try finding it in a book about black music), Pichaske's text

is frequently perceptive, particularly on the significance of rock lyrics in a counter-cultural situation. Although he declares "motion" to be the hallmark of the decade, counter-culture is the prevailing theme. Its roots in the 1950s are explored, four types of '60s protest are analyzed, alternative life styles, new experiences and experiments are discussed. An interesting chapter on the capacity of Western capitalist society to absorb alternatives and band them to its advantage is marred by righteous indignation, while the "excesses" and "absurdities" of the late '60s, climaxed in the Altamont debacle, are seen as partly to blame for the Nixon era. The absence of musical sound from the author's sphere of investigation is itself significant, for the greater subtlety with which music expresses its cultural changes and continuities would not fit with the argument. Index.

S.1128.　SHAW, Arnold. The Rockin' '50s: the decade that transformed the pop music scene. New York: Hawthorn Books, 1974. 296p. illus., bibliog., discog.

　　A long, fascinating history-memoir of the period when, in Shaw's view, Tin Pan Alley pop was gradually but persistently replaced by rhythm and blues and rock & roll--and when, equally important, the influence of black music became paramount. If some of the performers in the vanguard do not receive quite sufficient space (Little Richard, for example), while others, such as Presley, are singled out for extensive treatment, this may be because much of the book consists of personal recollection--Shaw was very much involved in the music business (publishing) during the decade--and the narrative closely reflects his own experience. As such it provides a valuable perspective, and one whose optimism can be contrasted, tellingly, with the disillusion of a David Dachs (Anything Goes, no. S.825). To fill out his own experience in certain areas Shaw turns to printed sources and to interviews. Among the musicians represented are Bill Haley, Chuck Berry, Fats Domino, Paul Anka, Connie Francis, and Bobby Darin. The discography is limited and the bibliography highly selective. Seven-page index.

(c) Specific Areas

S.1129.　FAWCETT, Anthony. California Rock, California Sound: the music of Los Angeles and Southern California; photographs by Henry Diltz. Los Angeles: Reed Books, 1978. 160p. illus., discog.

　　Diltz's photographs (some in color, some in black-and-white) steal this particular show (see, for example, Joni Mitchell, dressed for Halloween, 1976), a portrait in words and images of ten California-based individuals and groups for whom, the author declares, "the environment and its lifestyle have been a part of [their] daily makeup" (introduction). The ten are: Crosby, Stills & Nash, Neil Young, Joni Mitchell, Jackson Browne, America, Linda

Ronstadt, the Eagles, J. D. Souther, Karla Bonoff, and Warren
Zevon. The discography is a select list of their albums with labels
and release dates.

S.1130. PALMER, Robert. A Tale of Two Cities: Memphis rock
         and New Orleans roll. Brooklyn: Institute for Studies
         in American Music, 1979. (I.S.A.M. Monographs, No.
         12.) 38p. illus., bibliog., discog. refs.
      A concise, informative introduction to the contributions of
two very significant Southern cities to the development of rock &
roll. In his account of New Orleans rhythm and blues performers
such as Dave Bartholomew, Fats Domino, and Professor Longhair,
Palmer points to the continuing stream of tradition in the city, and
the relative self-sufficiency of that tradition. Memphis, by contrast,
Palmer sees as an unpredictable place, given to "sudden bursts of
energy and flashes of intuition" (p. 32). His account of Memphis
concentrates on the catalytic role played by Sam Phillips and the rise
of Elvis Presley.

              4. Collected & Miscellaneous Criticism

S.1131. BENSON, Dennis C. The Rock Generation. Nashville,
         Tenn.: Abingdon, 1976. 80p.
      This curious little book was written by a Presbyterian
minister who hosted a (Nashville?) radio show on which a large number of rock musicians (many of them stars) were interviewed. He
also accompanied Alice Cooper and his entourage on a long mid-West
tour. Each of the twelve chapters ("probes," Benson calls them)
is concerned with a different phase of rock--business, touring,
disc jockeys, etc.; each is also followed by a game based on this
particular aspect, from which it appears that the main audience for
the book is probably Protestant church youth groups. The value
to others lies mainly in the quotes from musicians such as Frank
Zappa, Glen Campbell, and the Osmond Brothers. No index.

S.1132. BIGSBY, C. W. E., ed. Superculture: American popular
         culture and Europe. London: Paul Elek, 1975. 225p.
         illus., bibliog. refs.
      Two essays in this volume explore aspects of the impact
of American music in Europe: Michael Watts, in "The Call and Response of Popular Music," traces the successive waves of transatlantic influence in the field of pop music, and Paul Oliver, in "Jazz
Is Where You Find It," provides a useful overview of "the European
experience of jazz" (a subject later fully explored by Chris Goddard
in Jazz Away from Home, no. S.695).

S.1133. DOWNING, David. Future Rock. St. Albans: Panther,
         1976. 172p. discog.
      Predicting the future of the genre is a risky business;

358 / Literature of American Music

predicting the future of mankind is probably worse, but at least it is more glamorous. Downing's interest in the first is subsumed in his interest in those musicians who have tried their hand at the second. Futurism, whether apocalyptic or fantastical, is explored through the music of, among others, Bob Dylan, Velvet Underground, Jefferson Airplane/Starship. The future may or may not come up to scratch, but for Downing, rock's "moment" is over (p. 9).

S.1134.   EISEN, Jonathan, ed.   Twenty-Minute Fandangos and Forever Changes: a rock bazaar. New York: Random House, 1971. 270p. illus.

"Just like in the old John Cage books," says the preface to this grab-bag, "you can start anywhere"; and just like a Californian at a concert (or a ball game), you can leave anywhere also. Dealing mainly with the West Coast scene in the post-Manson era, the anthology contains rather too many examples of (intentional?) over-writing; the best pieces are the lowest-keyed ones. Among the writers are Robert Abrams, R. Meltzer, Steve Sidorsky, and the editor.

S.1135.   MARCUS, Greil, ed.   Stranded: rock and roll for a desert island. New York: Knopf, 1979. 305p. discog.

Marcus asked twenty writers "an old question and a good one; absurd, but irresistible" (p. ix): which rock & roll record would they take to a desert island, and why? The resulting collection of essays is uneven in quality, with some excessive straining for effect, but extremely wide-ranging both in coverage and style. Though it may well be more interesting for its critical attitudes than for its subject matter, it is appropriate here to list both subjects and authors. Fourteen of the contributions focus on American performers: Ronettes (Jim Miller), Bruce Springsteen (Ariel Swartley), Captain Beefheart (Langdon Winner), Velvet Underground (Ellen Willis), Eagles (Grace Lichtenstein), Little Willie John (Joe McEwen), Ramones (Tom Carson), Jackson Browne (Paul Nelson), New York Dolls (Robert Christgau), Huey "Piano" Smith (Jay Cocks), Thomas A. Dorsey (Tom Smucker), Neil Young (Kit Rachlis), Linda Ronstadt (John Rockwell--easily the longest piece), 5 Royales (Ed Ward). The editor contributes an extensive annotated record guide which endeavors to put personal obsession aside and answer what he calls the "Martian" question--which are the essential records to explain the story of rock & roll?

S.1136.   MITSUI, Toru.   Rock no Bigaku. (The Aesthetics of Rock). Tokyo: Bronza-sha, 1976. 252p. illus.

A selection of 25 articles, in Japanese, by a leading Japanese critic. Originally written for a number of different journals in Japan, they range over a wide area of popular music, from the first, and longest, piece, which gives the book its title, through other aspects of rock, including lyrics, to a series of pieces on blues, featuring Robert Johnson, Charley Patton, Blind Blake, Leroy Carr and Scrapper Blackwell, Elmore James, B. B. King, and Chuck Berry.

5. Rock Lyrics

S.1137.   CHIPMAN, Bruce L., ed. Hardening Rock: an organic anthology of the adolescence of rock 'n roll; with an appreciative essay by X. J. Kennedy. Boston: Little, Brown, 1972. 154p. illus.

This is an illustrated collection of lyrics of early rock & roll songs popular between 1954 and 1963. The lyrics are generously interspersed with photographs of the era (Presley in action, Pat Boone autographing white shoes, teenagers in a convertible, a slumber party, Jimmy Clanton with Frankie Avalon...). The book is intended as a nostalgic reminder of an era in pop music when the rhythms might have been frankly sexual but when all else was comparatively innocent--pre-psychedelia, pre-drugs, pre-political assassination. There is an index of song titles (with the names of their creators included). (Formerly LOAM A284.)

S.1138.   DAMSKER, Matt, ed. Rock Voices: the best lyrics of an era. New York: St. Martin's Press, 1980; London: Barker, 1981. 139p.

A collection of 49 lyrics of the 1960s and 1970s, each with a brief introductory commentary. Bob Dylan, Joni Mitchell, and Bruce Springsteen are each represented by four lyrics, John Prine by three, some others by two (among them Paul Simon, Neil Young), the rest by one. No indexes.

S.1139.   MACKEN, Bob, et al.   The Rock Music Source Book, by Bob Macken, Peter Fornatale and Bill Ayres. Garden City, N.Y.: Anchor Press, 1980. 644p. bibliog., discog.

A subject guide to rock since 1954. Fifty themes are listed "that reflect the deepest personal, social, and political concerns in our world and in the world of rock and roll" (p. 29), among them "America," "Divorce," "Money," "Racism," "Suburbia," "Working"; under each the authors provide a short list of "classics," and longer lists of "definitive songs" and "reference songs." Each category is headed by a definition and by references to related subjects, and most lists also include "thematic albums." Some themes are subdivided. Details of the records themselves include song title, artist, album title and record label, but no further discographical details. Additional information given includes a basic rock library of 50 LPs, lists of "landmark" albums, important live albums, the "best of the greatest hits," and some "sleepers" (good albums which failed commercially); all these provide label name only. Other lists cover a chronology of rock-oriented films, rock movie and TV

soundtracks, a calendar of birth and death dates, a list of record
company addresses, and a brief bibliography with annotations.

S.1140.   SARLIN, Bob.   Turn It Up!   (I Can't Hear the Words):
          the best of the new singer/songwriters.   New York:
          Simon & Schuster, 1974.   222p.   illus.
          Hearing the words probably comes low down the average
listener's order of priority, but this study belongs in that era when
a new style seemed to some enthusiastic ears to have been created,
"the result of the integration of the intellectual and lyrical qualities of folk music and political folk songs with the simplicity and energy of good old rock-and-roll" (p. 17).   The leading protagonists
Sarlin calls "songpoets," and discusses their work in a series of individual chapters: Bob Dylan, Robert Hunter, Van Morrison, Joni
Mitchell, Laura Nyro, Randy Newman, Don McLean.   A group of
"Others," among them Neil Young, James Taylor, Leonard Cohen,
receive shorter treatment.   For one of the book's most interesting
chapters Sarlin interviews critics Ralph Gleason and Greil Marcus.
Other interview material is scattered throughout the book.   No index.

S.1141.   URBAN, Peter.   Rollende Worte - die Poesie des Rock: von
          der Strassenballade zum Pop-Song; eine wissenschaft-
          liche Analyse der Pop-Song-Texte.   Frankfurt: Fischer,
          1979.   317p.   bibliog., discog.
          Well-known in German-speaking countries but virtually ig-
nored elsewhere, this ambitious study probes the content of a broad
cross-section of American and British rock song texts from the 1950s
to the '70s.   Urban's approach is thematic, grouping lyrics around
such topics as love, private and social experience, everyday life, social criticism, etc.   The strengths and weaknesses of applying lit.
crit. to popular song lyrics are well illustrated--many unsuspected
meanings and nuances are revealed, but, in the absence of the
music which is the primary communicator, it is easy to read too
much into texts alone.   The analysis, which occupies 170 pages in
all, is preceded by an outline history of popular music from its folk
roots to the development of "youth-oriented" music after 1955, and
by a discussion and analysis of formal aspects of pop song.   There
are name and song title indexes (the latter containing some 450-500
references).

6.   Social, Cultural & Media Aspects

(a) Rock Life

S/1142.   FARREN, Mick, and SNOW, George.   Rock 'n' Roll Circus:
          the illustrated rock concert.   London: Pierrot Publish-

ing, 1978. 115p.
"Maybe it's time to examine the energy and the people who keep the rock and roll circus on the move" (p. 12); the promised "examination" is gossipy, but in any case mostly visual, with plentiful (often color) photographs taken before, during, and after rock concerts, both onstage and off.

S.1143.   GAMBINO, Thomas. Nyet: an American rock musician encounters the Soviet Union. Englewood Cliffs, N.J.: Prentice-Hall, 1976. 183p.
The only justification for including this odd book here is the hope that Gambino's tale of a winter month spent touring three Russian cities (to provide a rock element for a particular piece in a New York ballet company's repertoire) is, in its insularity, superficiality and cosseted irritability, untypical of mid-'70s professional rock musicians.

S.1144.   GORMAN, Clem. Backstage Rock: behind the scenes with the bands; photographs by Jan Turvey. London: Pan Books, 1978. 205p. illus.
Although concerned very largely with Britain, this informative exploration, by an Australian writer living in London, of how the live gig is created, includes frequent points of comparison between Britain and the USA, and makes numerous general points relating to the presentation of live rock almost anywhere. Part 1 of the book is concerned with "sites and site workers," in particular roadies. Part 2, on planning and business, has interesting accounts of how the design of the live rock show has developed, and of the "reflection" of rock in the market place (shop window, album cover, photograph, etc.). Part 3 describes the world of the hangers-on. Index.

S.1145.   SANDER, Ellen. Trips: rock life in the sixties. New York: Scribner's, 1973. 272p. illus.
An attempt to get close to the spirit of the era, which the author sees as "parenthesized by ambivalence and apathy, yet busting with energy, humor, adventure, a search for the ultimate high..." (p. 10). Using considerable interview material, she gives anecdotal portraits of (among others) Greenwich Village, the Newport and Monterey festivals, the Byrds and the West Coast scene; an appendix offers a "rock taxonomy"--an endeavor to group performers into various categories, with descriptive comments.

S.1146.   SANTELLI, Robert. Aquarius Rising: the rock festival years. New York: Dell, 1980. 291p. illus., bibliog.
From Monterey (1967) to Cal Jam II (Ontario, 1978), via Newport (California), Sky River, Miami, Seattle, Denver, Atlantic City, Woodstock, Altamont, Randall's Island, and Watkin's Glen, this

is a detailed, illuminating history. Most attention is paid to Monterey and Woodstock. Many performers are briefly described, but Janis Joplin, Otis Redding, and Jimi Hendrix stand out. The increasing commercialism, the drug scene, the violence at Altamont are all duly described but without undue sensationalism. A complete chronology c ` festivals is included, together with a bibliography of books and articles, and an index. (Altamont is described in more detail in Jonathan Eisen's book, Altamont: death of innocence in the Wood- stock generation [New York: Avon Books, 1970].)

S.1147. SPITZ, Robert Stephen. Barefoot in Babylon: the crea-
  tion of the Woodstock music festival, 1969. New York:
  Viking Press, 1978. 515p. illus.
  Fascinating, extremely detailed history of the famous Woodstock Festival (actual title: Woodstock Music and Art Fair), which took place on August 15-17, 1969, on Max Yasgur's farm in the White Lake area of upstate New York. The extensive research included interviews, ten years on, with most of the festival's main protagonists, among them its four principal promoters: John Roberts, Joel Rosenman, Michael Lang, and Artie Kornfeld. Aiming to rid the event of the accretions of nostalgia, Spitz declares his object as being to "redefine [the festival] as a vast commercial enter- prise during a time of fascinating, and sometimes ambiguous emo- tions.... I have striven to discover the motivation behind its creation, to gauge the inventiveness of a hippie work force maligned by bigotry and bureaucracy, and to uncover the roots of its mag- netism" (p. viii). Emerging at the other end, not unaided by hav- ing also conceived of his undertaking in terms of an epic novel, Spitz is able to remain positive: "regardless of all the torment and aggravation ... the havoc wrecked (sic) on the citizens ... the economic philandering ... the festival stands as a reminder of how close we came to utopia" (p. 489). The actual musical performances, featured in Part 3 of the book, receive little attention. There is an index. (Roberts and Rosenman told their own version in Young Men With Unlimited Capital [New York: Harcourt Brace Jovanovich, 1974], while Michael Lang joined with Jean Young to write Woodstock Festival Remembered [New York: Ballantine Books, 1979].)

(b) Sociological and political aspects

S.1148. BENNETT, H. Stith. On Becoming a Rock Musician. Amherst: University of Massachusetts Press, 1980. 258p.
  bibliog.
  Based on fieldwork (i.e., in this case, playing in rock groups) done in 1970-72 in Colorado and, less intensively, in other parts of the USA and in France (1972-78?), this is a sober but il- luminating sociological study of the "particular kind of musicianship" (p. vii) appropriate to being a rock musician; being also theoretical- ly based it rises above observation and report to become, in Bennett's

words, "a focussed study of how skills, ideas, and human identities manage to be created and transmitted in the context of industrialized culture" (p. ix). Each of the book's four sections is concerned with one broad aspect of the subject. "Group Dynamics" includes discussion of group formation and recruiting. "Rock Ecology" is concerned with cultural arrangements surrounding instruments, equipment, and gigs. "Mastering the Technological Component," perhaps the most original section, brings together sociology and musicology in studies of the recording process and of practice sessions. "Performance Aesthetics and the Technological Imperative" traces the ways in which the musicians' knowledge and consciousness, built up in the stages of recording, are recapitulated in live performance. An essay guiding the reader through relevant sociological literature precedes the bibliography, and there is a brief index.

S.1149.   FRITH, Simon. The Sociology of Rock. London: Constable, 1978. 255p. bibliog.
_____. Sound Effects: youth, leisure, and the politics of rock 'n' roll. New York: Pantheon Books, 1981; London: Constable, 1983. 294p. bibliog.
Although it concentrates on the British scene, this fine and influential book was intended, according to the introduction to the original version, "to contribute to the understanding of rock as a mass medium which is general to contemporary capitalist culture" (p. 15); in addition, frequent and specific references are made to the USA for both comparative and historical purposes. The part of capitalism which the author emphasizes is youth culture, the relationship of which to rock he sees as crucial to the understanding of both ("the sociology of rock is inseparable from the sociology of youth"--p. 14). Frith's approach is to seek the meaning of rock by analysis, not of the music, but of the twin elements of consumption and production; the former occupies Part 1, with a study of youth groups and their different uses of music, and draws on fieldwork done in Britain, while Part 2 is given over to an excellent account of the processes of commodity production--from A&R men to marketing strategies, and with sections on radio and the music press in Britain and the USA. Part 3 provides an outline of rock ideology, setting out historical relationships to other musics, and seeking to take a fresh look at rock within the mass culture debate (Adorno, et al.). The most fundamental of Frith's conclusions are that traditional manipulationist theories of mass culture are wrong, and that rock can best be understood within the contradictions of an ideology of leisure.
        The academic respectability lent to these discussions by the full use of footnotes and bibliography turns out, with the second version, to be a source of unease. In particular, Frith changes his mind about his earlier, more "academic" assumption--one built into the structure of the first book--that meanings could be deduced from analysis of production and consumption, and that such meanings could be agreed; instead, he suggests that "musical and cultural meanings are continually disputed. It is because of the disputes ...

that rock production and consumption take on their particular forms" (from a conference paper, "The Sociology of Rock: Notes from Britain," in Popular Music Perspectives, ed. D. Horn & P. Tagg [Göteborg & Exeter: IASPM, 1982], pp. 142-154); i.e. discussion of meaning should precede analysis of consumption and production. Hence the biggest change in Sound Effects is in the order: meaning/production/consumption. It has fewer footnotes, but includes a bibliographic guide. Both books have an index.

S.1150.   GROSSMAN, Loyd.   A Social History of Rock Music: from
          the greasers to glitter rock. New York: McKay, 1976.
          150p.
          Any hopes (or fears) aroused by the main title can be quickly dispelled: this is no social history, but a sketchy survey of the main outline of rock's history in the USA and Britain, from the mid-1950s to the mid-'70s; far from springing out of an interest in/analysis of social conditions and their interrelationship to rock, it merely turns an intermittent gaze on certain selected aspects. When he does so (e.g., in sections on business, on technology), Grossman raises interesting points, but the text's basic lack of substance is frustrating, its inability to settle down on any one level of debate irritating. Index.

S.1151.   HARKER, Dave.   One For the Money: politics and popu-
          lar song. London: Hutchinson, 1980. 301p.
          bibliog.
          Harker is a British folk song scholar whose principal interest lies in the struggles connected with the development of working-class consciousness; he also recognizes the importance of 20th-century popular music and accepts the need to understand its politics (though he evidently likes relatively few of its sounds); crucially, however, he cannot accept that the attendant processes --as he sees them--of commercialization, appropriation, and exploitation on the part of the popular music industry can be anything but destructive of genuine, people's music. These subjects--folk song and the British working class; the popular music industry-- form the twin focal points of the book, and this conjuncture, together with its radical, polemical stance, makes it unusual. In his series of argumentatively--often pugilistically--presented case studies, Harker selects for analysis examples drawn almost equally from British and American music. Part 1, "The Industry," is a survey and analysis, in six short chapters, of the connection between various post-war popular music developments and/or artefacts (e.g., electrification, petty bourgeois pre-rock & roll pop songs such as "White Christmas," the advent of rock & roll and its decline) and the music industry. The basic theme--which echoes the work of Chapple and Garofalo (no. S.1153)--is of transformation and innovation expropriated by the industry, which uses the results to control the market. The chapter "Their Music or Ours" sums up Harker's deepest concerns (it also illustrates his aggressive style-- an idiosyncratic mixture of academic analysis, personal prejudice,

sharp insight, and political invective). Though Harker disavows
pessimism, his faith in the creative possibilities of consumption seems
a dim one.

The obverse of this process, at least potentially, forms
the subject of Part 2, "The 'Alternatives.'" Here the main attention
is shared between a discussion of Bob Dylan, especially his early
lyrics, English folk song collectors (Cecil Sharp et al., severely
treated), and north-eastern English pitmen's songs. Part 3, "Approaches," presents two examples of problems encountered when
studying song; one uses Lancashire song as historical evidence, the
other, on commitment, looks at the question of intervention by
singers in class or political movements, with John Lennon and Dylan
texts as examples. In addition to the copious notes, the book's
scholarly apparatus includes a large 38-page bibliography, and an
index.

S.1152. SINCLAIR, John. Guitar Army: street writings/prison
writings; designed by Gary Grimshaw. New York:
Douglas, 1972. 364p. illus., bibliog., discog.

"In the Detroit-Ann Arbor area," writes R. Serge Denisoff, "John Sinclair was both political guru and martyr. He was a
prime catalyst in the Ann Arbor underground scene, one of the
founders of the Detroit-based White Panther party and a self-styled
rock promoter and manager. He served part of a ten-year sentence
in a Michigan penitentiary for the possession of two marijuana ciga-
rettes. In the music world he is best known for his early tutelage
of MC5" (Solid Gold, no. S.1156, p. 326; Denisoff also provides one
of the few serious discussions of Sinclair's ideas). This collection
of Sinclair's writings from 1968 to 1971 centers around the theme of
the connections between rock, drugs, and politics, in particular
the potential of rock to bring about dramatic social change. (There
are more ways than one of making such connections; for a summary,
see "No Satisfaction?" politics and popular music, by John Street
[IASPM/UK Working Paper No. 5, Exeter, 1985].)

(c) Business and Media

See also S.1177

S.1153. CHAPPLE, Steve, and GAROFALO, Reebee. Rock 'n' Roll
Is Here to Pay: the history and politics of the music
industry. Chicago: Nelson-Hall, 1977. 354p. bibliog.

Aiming to be both a source book of historical and economic
data on the industry and a polemic against its politics, Chapple &
Garofalo's "radical analysis" is essential reading on both counts.
While the polemic may be quarreled with, it remains one of the clear-
est statements to date of the deterministic, manipulationist thesis
(Garofalo described it later as a "classical marxist perspective").
Though far from mutually exclusive, the majority of the historical

and similar information comes in the first part of the book, the most important arguments in the second. The first five chapters provide an account of the growth and structure of the industry (records and radio) from its early years (briefly told) to the mid-1970s, with a marked emphasis on post-war developments; a chapter on the contemporary scene includes special profiles of Warner-Reprise and RCA. The amount of detail provided on the industry's various components is impressive. The final four chapters amplify the opening statement that the "development of the music cannot be separated from the politics of the industry" (p. xii) with hard-hitting discussions of the industry's general political character, its relationship with and treatment of black and women performers, and the question of co-optation by the capitalist industrial process. The extensive research included 30 major interviews with industry figures, promoters, managers, broadcasters, journalists, retailers; their names are listed on p. xv. Generous bibliographical notes are provided for each chapter, as well as a bibliography of major books.

In the 1980s, following contact with critics, British and American, of a rather different persuasion on the question of commercialism and the manipulation of consumers (e.g., Simon Frith: rock commercialism "must be the starting point for its celebration as well as its dismissal"--no. S.1149, p. 54), Garofalo shifted his position; while still taking issue with the more optimistic of the "cultural" perspectives, he admitted that he and Chapple were wrong to equate market control with control of the music's form and content (Garofalo, "How Autonomous Is Relative," Popular Music, 6, No. 1, 1987).

S.1154.　CLARK, Dick, and ROBINSON, Richard.　Rock, Roll & Remember.　New York: Crowell, 1976.　276p.　illus. _____.　_____.　New York: Popular Library, 1978. 350p.　illus.

Clark's celebrated American Bandstand, broadcast from Philadelphia's WFIL-TV station, was the first nationally popular television show devoted entirely to rock & roll (it was also the first to exploit the formula of teenagers dancing to mimed records). As host of the program, Clark (b.1929) was in a position to promote a great many performers; to begin with, the majority of these were Philadelphia-based, and this led to national popularity for the Philadelphia "sound." (Not all commentators have seen Clark's influence as benign, or his interests as anything but commercial; see Chapple & Garofalo, no. S.1153, pp. 50-51--"Philadelphia Schlock minimized the impact of whatever good r&b/rock 'n' roll had managed to survive into the treacle period.... The degeneration of the music did not bother Clark in the slightest....") Clark's own story is cast in the familiar style of racy show business autobiographies, complete with precisely recalled conversations. But when that is penetrated there is much interesting inside information on the broadcasting and recording of late 1950s pop music. Not every business detail is given, not surprisingly, but Clark is frank about just how much money his success brought him. Fifty-six pages (pp. 236-292 in the

1978 ed.) are devoted to an account of the 1959 payola hearings. Among a plethora of names, the most frequent appearances are those by Frankie Avalon, Bobby Darin, Duane Eddy, Connie Francis, Elvis Presley, and Bobby Rydell. The story of Chubby Checker and the Twist is briefly told on pp. 137-141 (1978 ed.). Index.

S.1155.   DAVIS, Clive. Clive: inside the record business; with
          James Willwerth. New York: Morrow, 1975. 300p.
          illus.
          _____. _____. New York: Ballantine, 1976. 346p.
          illus.
As Columbia's General Attorney, Davis had the dubious privilege of telling Bob Dylan, in 1963, that "Talking John Birch Society Blues" could not be recorded. As Administrative Vice-President of the company, then President of the Record Division, for eight years, 1965-1973, Davis had a rather more securely based claim to fame, indeed was a central figure in the shift of a major record company away form "MOR" to rock; but some of the ambivalence remained. Nevertheless, his story of these years provides a fascinating insight into the record business. In Davis' mind, the period "spanned a revolution, a massive musical change, a cultural explosion.... Recording personalities became the subject of intense media interest all over the world..." (p. 330, 1976 ed.). His summary dismissal by CBS in 1973, briefly told (pp. 324-330), provided him with the impetus to write the book, not to seek vindication (in any case, he was legally barred from disclosing details of CBS's allegations) but "to see that my first eight years in music will not have been wasted" (p. 330). Some star performers, such as Dylan and Streisand, were already at Columbia when Davis rose in the company's ranks, others joined during his time of office; most prominent among the latter group, in Davis' account, are Janis Joplin, Blood, Sweat and Tears, Simon & Garfunkel, Sly and the Family Stone. Index. (Davis went on to found his own label, Arista.)

S.1156.   DENISOFF, R. Serge. Solid Gold: the popular record
          industry. New Brunswick, N.J.: Transaction Books,
          1975. 504p. illus., bibliog.
One thing which is amply demonstrated by Denisoff's detailed sociological account of the rock record industry is that, while there may be gold, it is rarely solid for long in anyone's grasp (with a few exceptions). The large mound of information, however--economic, statistical, oral-historical, sociological--is itself extremely solid, even if, in the final analysis, the results of this accumulated empiricism leave a lot of questions unanswered. The book opens with an attempt to frame a definition of popular music, on the basis of recognizing the existence and interaction of diverse social, generic and aesthetic groupings. The study of the industry which follows is constructed by following the "life cycle" of a record (no particular record) from artist to audience. Successive chapters consider the performer (motivation and beginnings, dealings with

record companies, promotional tours, performing); the record industry itself (structure, risks and problems, internal workings--
production, promotion, distribution, etc.); the role of radio; rock
journalism, especially reviewing practices; the existence and influence
of political and cultural factors, from marxist left to radical right
(including consideration of John Sinclair and Pete Seeger, festivals,
censorship, and a revealing section on "Christian Crusaders" David
Noebel, Bob Larson and others); and the audience. Risks, vicis-
situdes, confrontations, exploitations, prejudices--all are present,
but Denisoff remains basically an optimist. Though light in tone the
book has all the trappings of scholarship, with extensive notes and
references at the end of each chapter, and a bibliographical essay.
There is also an index.

S.1157.   GAMMOND, Peter, and HORRICKS, Raymond, eds. The
           Music Goes Round and Round: a cool look at the
           record industry. London: Quartet Books, 1980.
           183p. illus.
       These ten essays are mainly concerned with aspects of
the record industry in Britain, but frequently contain points of
cross-reference to the US scene. Three pieces are historical: on
the early history of recording, the coming of the LP, and the "pop
explosion"; others describe functional aspects of the industry--the
producer, the engineer, the publisher, the marketer, the critic.
Though generally popular in tone, most of the pieces are written
with authority.

S.1158.   LAMBERT, Dennis, and ZALKIND, Ronald. Producing Hit
           Records; foreword by Al Coury. New York: Schirmer;
           London: Collier Macmillan, 1980. 196p.
       Record producer (with Brian Potter) and songwriter Lam-
bert's "nuts and bolts" book is an attempt to "provide the reader
with a working knowledge of how to prepare for a session: what to
look for in the studio; how to get a good sound recording [of] the
various instruments, including voice; how to mix and edit multi-
track tapes; how to present the product to a record company; and,
perhaps most crucial, how to cope with the business world outside
the recording studio" (p. 2). The book conveys a mass of information in a well thought-out, clear presentation, with much use of
diagrams, charts, sample track sheets, work sheets, credit sheets,
etc. The lengthy appendixes provide details of building a home
studio, demo recording techniques, a phonograph record labor agreement, the union (AFTRA) national code of practice, a sample independent record contract, and a sample letter on intent. There is
also a useful glossary of terms, and an accompanying 33 1/3 seven-
inch demonstration record, "Diary of a Hit."

S.1159.   MONACO, Bob, and RIORDAN, James. The Platinum Rain-
           bow; (how to succeed in the music business without
           selling your soul. Sherman Oaks, Calif.: Swordsman
           Press, 1980. 239p.

A knowledgeable, entertaining, breezily (sometimes too breezily) written book by two successful members of the music business. According to the preface, "this book is primarily designed for people who want to become successful [rock] recording artists," but there are also sections "devoted to becoming a successful manager, producer, publicist, agent, songwriter, engineer, record label producer, and producer." Headnotes by Frank Zappa and others.

S.1160.   RAPAPORT, Diane Sward. How to Make and Sell Your Own Record: the complete guide to independent recording. New York: Quick Fox, 1979. 167p. Illus., bibliog.
According to the introduction, "this book has been written to help [the independent record maker] benefit from [others'] experience. It is ... especially for you, the musician who has music to share and wants to know the steps involved in making and selling a record before plunging in. It should also be of help to anyone who has become interested in the music of an artist and wishes either to finance their record project or participate in some part of the work." Since users of this bibliography may not be in any of these categories, the book's main interest will lie in the account it gives of the independent record business as such. Information is clearly given, and of a rudimentary character; coverage stretches from recording techniques to legal questions. Strategically placed quotes from independent producers dot the text, and there are eleven sample worksheets. Index.

S.1161.   REDD, Laurence, N. Rock Is Rhythm and Blues: (the impact of mass media). East Lansing: Michigan State University Press, 1974. 167p. bibliog. refs.
The polemical motive for this book ("it is time that every white person learns what every black person immersed in his culture knows--that rock music is really the creation of black people"--p. xiii) has an undeniably solid foundation, though if the book were a study of rock as such it would be, at the least, an unsubtle interpretation. In the event, Redd's central theme is the role of the media--often a duplicitous one--in the advent of rock & roll. Successive chapters in Part 1 are devoted to radio (the growth of black radio stations in the 1940s and '50s, the disc jockey Alan Freed's discovery of r&b, and the subsequent outraged response of the white middle-class audience), to films (from Louis Jordan to Bill Haley), and to television (the discrimination against black music; the impact of Elvis Presley). Part 2, less polemical, is a series of interviews with 'soul poets': B. B. King, Brownie McGhee, songwriter Dave Clark, Arthur Crudup, publisher and songwriter Jerry Butler, and singer-songwriter Jessica Whitaker. The aim is to document the music as its creators see it. No index. (Formerly LOAM A300.)

S.1162.   STOKES, Geoffrey. Star-Making Machinery: inside the

business of rock and roll. Indianapolis: Bobbs-Merrill, 1976; New York: Vintage Books, 1977. 234p. illus.
"The biography of an album" (p. 3--elsewhere it is described as an "odyssey"); not only is this unique, eye-opening book an outstanding account of the business side of rock, it is also, with its acute portrait of the fine intricacies of the record-making process, a powerful antidote to the plague of superficial, hagiographic accounts of star performers. Written by a Village Voice reporter, it tells the story of the making of their fifth album in 1974 by the San Francisco-based group, Commander Cody and His Lost Planet Airmen; the members of the group are only part of a constantly changing cast that includes managers, producers, executives, PR men, critics, all caught up in "the interplay between the giant corporations that invest in and profit from the music that a generation once considered genuinely revolutionary" (ibid.). Index.

(d) The Image of Rock

See also S.1137

S.1163.   HIRSCH, Abby.   The Photography of Rock; designed by George Delmerico. New York: Bobbs-Merrill, 1972; Henley-on-Thames: Aidan Ellis, 1973. 241p. illus.
An impressive anthology of the work of nine American photographers. Location details are provided for each photograph.

S.1164.   JENKINSON, Philip, and WARNER, Alan.   Celluloid Rock: twenty years of movie rock. London: Lorrimer Publishing, 1974. 136p. illus.
Covering a period from the mid-1950s (Blackboard Jungle, 1955, and Rock Around the Clock, 1956) to the early 1970s (Wattstax, 1973), this is a concise, informative chronicle of American and Britain motion pictures centered around rock and pop. If the need to include references to a great many very forgettable movies results in too little space being available for the authors to expand their obviously interesting ideas (e.g., on the relationship between film sound techniques and changes in the sound achieved on rock records), the bonus is a generally reliable reference source. Completely accurate data, the authors discovered, eluded them ("initial research revealed ... a multiplicity of conflicting production and release dates, countless numbers of title changes, incomplete credit lists and changes of ownership"--foreword), and so the filmography at the end, which attempts to provide a full list of film titles, with dates and names of musicians, omits all other credits. There is an index, and there are numerous, mainly black-and-white illustrations.

S.1165.   PEELAERT, Guy, and COHN, Nik.   Rock Dreams. London: Pan Books; New York: Popular Library, 1974. unpaged. illus.
_____.   _____; introduction by Michael Herr. London:

Picador; New York: Rogner & Bernhard, 1982.
unpaged, illus.

In a series of brilliantly conceived paintings Peelaert explores the world of "rock as a secret society, as an enclosed teen fantasy" (Cohn's words). Fantasy it may be, but it is expressed by Peelaert in a succession of images which use photorealist techniques, bold, bright colors, clear outlines, and make much of the sheer physical presence both of the people (mostly star figures) and of the (often popular culture) objects, to produce extraordinarily tactile pictures. At once ironic and sentimental, sympathetic and mocking, fascinated and repelled, they explore a bigger range of conflicting senses and meanings than Cohn's sharp, witty but basically monochromatic captions can suggest with mere words.

Album Covers

S.1166. ERRIGO, Angie, and LEANING, Steve. The Illustrated History of Rock Album Covers. London: Octopus, 1969. 160p. illus.

A well chosen and well reproduced selection of covers, in large format, with a thoughtful accompanying text. The four main sections deal in turn with faces and public images (covers emphasizing a particular persona, etc.), "signs of the times" (sex, gimmicks, jokes), "art for art's sake" (the influence of contemporary art, the work of prominent cover designers, and a series of covers "as a bona-fide art form"--p. 117), and the contemporary scene in the late 1970s. Each section has a preliminary, general text setting and themes, followed by a series of covers, with detailed captions, including information on label, date, designer and photographer. The generous indexes provide access via performer, album title, art studio, art directors and designers, photographers, artists, and illustrators.

S.1167. POLLOCK, Bruce. The Face of Rock & Roll: images of a generation; designed by John Wagman; with a foreword by Pete Fornatale. New York: Holt, Rinehart & Winston; London: New English Library, 1978. 184p. illus.

The "face" in question is the album cover, seen as the visual dimension of the fan's emotional attachment to the music. The point of this selection is not the study of covers as such, but their ability to evoke in "lifelong admirers" (i.e., the authors) "twisted fictions and fantasies" (p. 8). The covers are grouped by broad themes (images of men, of women, fashion, East, West. etc.) and include sections for country and folk, and for jazz and blues. Pollock's accompanying prose (called "impressionistic" and "neither erudite nor definitive" (ibid.)) is organized around the artists portrayed, but is interested, not in connecting text and image, but in attempting to recapture youthful responses to the music. Index.

S.1168. THORGERSON, Storm (Hipgnosis), and DEAN, Roger,

eds. Album Cover Album; introduced by Dominy Hamilton. Limpsfield, Surrey: Dragon's World, 1977. 160p. illus.

An enticingly colorful collection of album cover art, with some--but not too much--pretense at organization. The central section, "Recent Years," is a deliberately subjective, miscellaneous selection of 1970s rock covers, celebrating "good quality" American and British designs without comment. Elsewhere there are sections for jazz, psychedelia, "influence and coincidence" (of design features), portfolios of eight individual designers (including the two British editors), "devices and disguises," and miscellany. Each illustrated cover has an accompanying caption giving details of performer(s), album title, date, record company, and designer. The introduction provides a brief historical perspective. An index of names can be found on pp. 6-7. (A follow-up compilation, Album Cover Album: the second volume, edited by Storm Thorgerson, Roger Dean, and David Howells, was published by the same publisher in 1982.)

7. The Musicians

(a) Collected profiles

See also S.718

S.1169. BUSNAR, Gene. The Superstars of Rock: their lives and their music. New York: Messner, 1980-1984. 2 vols. illus., discogs.

Fannish potted biographies of a selection of 1970s and '80s performers, aimed at a teenage audience. A "Collectors Guide" discography follows each entry.

S.1170. DALLAS, Karl. Singers of an Empty Day: last sacraments for the superstars. London: Kahn & Averill, 1971. 208p. illus.

Somewhat imprecisely located around the themes of decline, communication difficulties, and the problem stars have telling illusion from reality, this is a series of portraits of performers by a British critic and long-time contributor to Melody Maker. The American musicians featured are Frank Sinatra, Elvis Presley, and Bob Dylan (a long chapter), with appearances by Jimi Hendrix and, to a lesser extent, Janis Joplin, in the final chapter, which muses over autodestruction. Index. Illustrated by line drawings.

S.1171. FONG-TORRES, Ben, ed. What's That Sound? the contemporary music scene from the pages of "Rolling Stone." Garden City, N.Y.: Anchor Books, 1976. 426p.

The 28 pieces in this collection appeared in Rolling Stone between 1969 and 1976; they include articles and interviews. Twelve are on American individuals or groups: Dylan (pieces by Nat

Hentoff and the editor), Paul Simon (Jon Landau) Neil Young
(Cameron Crowe), Patti Smith (Dave Marsh), Bruce Springsteen
(John Rockwell), Louis Jordan (Ralph J. Gleason), Ray Charles
(the editor), Sly Stone (Timothy Crouse), Stevie Wonder (the
editor again), the Allman Brothers (Cameron Crowe), and Alice
Cooper (Ed McCormack). There are also essays on jazz-rock by
Bob (Robert) Palmer, and on heavy metal by Jim Miller.

S.1172. LEIGH, Spencer. Stars in My Eyes: personal interviews
         with pop music stars. Liverpool: Raven Books, 1980.
         160p. illus.
         A splendid collection of 23 interviews with a wide range
of performers. Leigh's modus operandi is clearly stated in his introduction: "I've never been too fond of the gossipy style of interviewing where a subject's private life is all-important. I prefer to
concentrate on the music." Outside of specialized sources, it is
rare to come across interviews with some of the Americans featured
here, for instance Burl Ives, Don Williams, Frankie Laine. Among
other Americans included are Tom Paxton, Rod McKuen, Bo Diddley,
and Slim Whitman. A glossary provides the dates of the interviews,
and the credits for the many photographs. No index.

S.1173. PETRIE, Gavin, ed. Rock Life. London: Hamlyn, 1974.
         128p. illus.
         Assorted short profiles from London's Melody Maker, by
Geoff Brown, Steve Lake, Michael Watts, Chris Welch, and others.
Of the sixteen "legends" seven are American: Chuck Berry, Bob
Dylan, Jimi Hendrix, Allman Brothers, Grateful Dead, Jefferson
Airplane, Roger McGuinn. Among six "heroes" there is one Ameri-
can: Steely Dan. In a book by males for males, the only female
performer mentioned is Grace Slick.

S.1174. POLLOCK, Bruce. In Their Own Words. New York:
         Macmillan, 1975. 231p. illus.
         Twenty "lyricists, singer/songwriters, artists and crafts-
men" from the rock world are interviewed by Pollock on their approach to their work and their views on music. The interviews are
grouped in six parts, covering 1955-1974. Among the interviewees
are Hal David, Doc Pomus, Gerry Goffin, Phil Ochs, Buffy Sainte-
Marie, Frank Zappa, Robert Hunter, John Sebastian, Felice and
Houdleaux Bryant, Melvin Van Peebles, Randy Newman, Loudon Wain-
wright, John Prine, Melanie Safka, Harry Chapin, and Linda Creed.
The interviews in each section are prefaced by a brief sketch of the
particular era, centered round a selection of a small number of relevant records. The conversations offer interesting insights, but
could have profited form tighter editing. No index.

S.1175. ROCK GUITARISTS: from the pages of Guitar Player
         Magazine. Saratoga, N.Y.: Guitar Player Magazine,
         1975-1977. 2 vols. illus.
         Like nos. S.95 and S.734, this compendium of pieces from

the reliable Guitar Player Magazine is based on interviews with performers. Some 130 pieces are contained in the two volumes, covering
1967-1976. In addition to the interviews there are articles on aspects of instruments and style. Attention throughout tends to focus
on performance techniques rather than biography.

S.1176.   SAPORITA, Jay. Pourin' It All Out. Secaucus, N.J.:
           Citadel Press, 1980. 204p. illus.
       A miscellany consisting mostly of brief "interviews, pro-
files, anecdotes, and vignettes, all concerned with a single theme--
the world of rock 'n' roll" (introduction). Among those featured are
Billy Joel, Easy (Eddie) Money, Meat Loaf, and Jackson Browne.
Two "chapters" are devoted to Bruce Springsteen. There are also
explanations of the drugs favored in the rock worlds, and of the
meaning of the term "punk." A glossary of rock trade terms is a
useful appendage.

S.1177.   SPITZ, Robert Stephen. The Making of Superstars: ar-
           tists and executives of the rock music business. Gar-
           den City, N.Y.: Doubleday, 1978. 310p.
       An excellent collection of autobiographical interviews with
individuals from various areas of rock and pop, from performers
(such as Janis Ian, Barry Manilow, Neil Sedaka, Grace Slick, Barry
White) to agents, producers (John Hammond, Jerry Wexler), A&R
men, promoters and critics (Dave Marsh, Jon Landau). Spitz himself provides vivid commentary. Index.

S.1178.   TOBLER, John. Guitar Heroes. London: Marshall Caven-
           dish, 1978. 88p. illus., discogs.
       Short biographical portraits of 32 electric guitarists from
the 1940s (Les Paul) to the 1960s. (A similar volume, based on a
BBC radio series, is The Guitar Greats, by John Tobler and Stuart
Grundy [London: BBC, 1983].)

(b) Women performers

S.1179.   ALESSANDRINI, Marjorie. Le rock au féminin. Paris:
           Albin Michel, 1980. 214p. illus., discog.
       This account of the "irresistible rise" of women in rock is
told in a series of lively essays, chronologically arranged with a
common style and/or background. The portraits, mostly quite short,
are all sharply drawn, with a particularly keen eye for a performer's
image. Among the numerous US performers included, the most
prominent are Grace Slick, Janis Joplin, Joni Mitchell, Patti Smith,
and Debbie Harry. Few black performers are featured, nor is the
legacy of black women considered. Index.

S.1180.   GARBUTT, Bob. Rockabilly Queens. (Toronto?): Duck-
           tail Press, 1979. 80p. illus., bibliog., discog.

Biographical sketches of three successful female rock & roll singers: Wanda Jackson, Janis Martin, and Brenda Lee. There are detailed discographies of each.

S.1181.   KATZ, Susan. Superwomen of Rock. New York: Grosset
& Dunlap, 1978. 134p. illus.

The different ways in which female performers have handled the problems posed by a male-dominated medium form the crux of these six fairly generous, if fannish, profiles. The six in question are Debby Boone, Rita Coolidge, Olivia Newton-John, Linda Ronstadt, Stevie Nicks and Carly Simon.

S.1182.   ORLOFF, Katherine. Rock 'n' Roll Woman. Los Angeles:
Nash Publishing, 1974. 199p. illus.

"The purpose of this book is to explore the feelings and the life-styles of some women who make their living in rock and roll, on-stage in front of bands, and on records," writes the author in her excellent introduction. There are a dozen probing interviews: questions as well as answers are printed. Many of the same questions were asked each interviewee, and the variety of answers is fascinating. Accompanying each interview is at least one photograph. Those interviewed are Nicole Barclay, Toni Brown, Rita Coolidge, Terry Garthwaite, Claudia Lennear, Maria Muldaur, Bonnie Raitt, Linda Ronstadt, Carly Simon, Grace Slick, Alice Stuart, and Wendy Waldman.

S.1183.   PAVLETICH, Aida. Rock-a-Bye Baby. Garden City,
N.Y.: Doubleday, 1980. (Repr. as Sirens of Song:
the popular female vocalist in America. New York,
Da Capo, 1980.) 281p. illus.

In the wake of the women's movement the need for a good historical study of women in rock and pop is clear. Pavletich, a Los Angeles-based journalist, does not provide one (to be fair, it is the reprint publisher, not the author, who describes the book as a history--the author herself declares her aim as being to capture a "living, changing scene ... on the wing"--p. 21), but seems torn between a broad survey approach, reeling off names in various contexts, and a more in-depth study of certain individuals and trends. The result is a book which, while offering valuable insights, struggles to find an identity, not altogether helped by a style in which the sentences and the arguments seem afraid of tiring easily, so play safe by stopping short. The focus is on "female vocalists who are primarily recording artists and who perform in concerts and smaller venues" (p. 22). Gospel and jazz are excluded (though Billie Holiday is not). Eight broadly genre-based chapters cover the subject area: the popular singer (from Holiday and Peggy Lee to Dionne Warwick and Barbra Streisand); folk "madonnas" (including Odetta, Joan Baez, Buffy Sainte-Marie, Joan Collins, Maria Muldaur); "teen angels" (e.g., the Shirelles, the Shangri-Las, Lesley Gore, young Carole King); "soul sisters" (especially Gladys Knight and Aretha Franklin); rock (Janis Joplin, Grace Slick, Linda Ronstadt, Bonnie

Bramlett); British and other "birds, thrushes and nightingales" and
the US response (Cher, Cass Elliott, Roberta Flack); country
(Loretta Lynn, Tammy Wynette, Dolly Parton); and singer-songwriters (Joni Mitchell, Dory Previn, Carly Simon, later Carole King).
A concluding chapter relates more contemporary developments broadly
to the changes in the position of women in the 1970s. Interview material is included, and there is an index of names and titles.

(c) Individuals and groups

BEACH BOYS

S.1184.   BARNES, Ken.   The Beach Boys; edited by Greg Shaw.
          New York: Sire Books/Chappell, 1976.   55p.   illus.,
          discog.
     An illustrated biography in nine short chapters, con-
structed around the group's successive recordings, with commentary
on them and on the group's dealings with record companies and
managers.   Full discography, providing chronological lists of singles
and albums, with numbers and labels.

S.1185.   GOLDEN, Bruce.   The Beach Boys: Southern California
          pastoral.   San Bernardino, Calif.:   Borgo Press, 1976.
          59p.   bibliog., discog.
     "This book discusses the Beach Boys' music.   It is not a
biography" (preface).   The study is relatively brief (pp. 7-39) but
good, placing the Beach Boys in the context of early 1960s California, and analyzing their developing style.   Copious notes, a good
bibliography and discography conclude the book.

S.1186.   LEAF, David.   The Beach Boys and the California Myth.
          New York: Grosset & Dunlap, 1978.   192p.   illus.
     This "skimpy version of the 'myth'," scolded critic Greil
Marcus, "is merely an Easterner's conceit" (Rolling Stone, 28 December, 1978, p. 119).   Despite the portentous title, this is more of a
pop-philosophical picture book.   Brian Wilson, in his eccentric way,
occupies the center of attention.   (An in-depth study of the group
is still lacking in 1986, but perhaps, as Marcus suggests [op. cit.],
a study of Californian popular music from Johnny Otis to the late
1970s would be a better idea.)

S.1187.   PREISS, Byron.   The Beach Boys.   New York: Ballan-
          tine Books, 1979.   160p.   illus., discog.
     In an attempt to create what he calls a "visual sound-
track" rather than a straight biography, the author adopts the technique of interspersing his biographical narrative with frequent (very
frequent) conversational extracts derived from interviews with the
group, their families, friends and associates.   These juxtapositions
are designed to let the group and its circle's view of themselves and

their music emerge simultaneously with, but not always as a result of, the main historical sequence of events. At the same time, photographs convey the image they presented to the world, illustrations (most of them in color) provide a decorative response to specific songs, while song lyrics themselves, boxed on the page (and many of them not previously published, Preiss claims), offer a reminder of part of what it's all about. The interesting experiment is only partly successful, chiefly because, as a good correspondence column in a newspaper draws the eye from the news, so here the reader's attention is relentlessly enticed away from the main narrative (which is, admittedly, not very strong) by the interpolated quotations, leaving a disjointed overall impression. The discography provides chronological lists of singles and LPs, with US labels and numbers. There are also lists of major cover versions of Beach Boys' songs, and of unreleased items.

S.1188. TOBLER, John. The Beach Boys; edited by Jeremy Pascall and Pamela Harvey; designed by Bob Burt. London: Phoebus Publishing, 1977; Secaucus, N.J.: Chartwell Books, 1978. 96p. illus.

Principally for the UK market--and not averse to that irony with which the country defends its uncertainties--this is a liberally illustrated biographical outline from the group's beginnings to its rebirth in the mid-1970s. The photographs, often somewhat unimaginative, are mostly in color and have few identifications. The selective discography includes only major releases; US labels are indicated.

BLONDIE

S.1189. BANGS, Lester. Blondie. New York: Simon & Schuster; London: Omnibus Press, 1980. 91p. illus.

In the mid-1980s Lester Bangs is dead (he died in 1982). Blondie is a fading memory. Which matters most? A reading of this book may suggest that here--for once, anyway--the writer has it over those written about, and is the bigger loss. To one critic, Bangs "has been, crucially, the one rock critic whose stance is not rooted in the 1960s" (Simon Frith, Sound Effects, no. S.1149, p. 278). In contrast to the school of criticism which invests rock music with great meaning, Bangs can exclaim of Blondie's LP Parallel Lines, "I still refuse to believe that any of the songs are about anything" (p.64); or, more generally, "Rock'n'roll is not an 'art-form.' Rock'n'roll is a raw wail from the bottom of the guts" (p. 20). This impatience distinguishes Bangs from writers like Dave Marsh, with whom he shares a populist approach ("Rock is for everybody, it should be ... implicitly anti-elitist"--ibid.). Hence the fascination for him of punk, in the context of which this biographical and critical portrait is set. It is a context which gives rise to many doubts, however, for what Bangs sees as Blondie's bland "Post-modernism" (p. 65), their emotional neutrality, seems to contradict his belief that the music should express passion;

another contradiction for Bangs is that between the "pervasive cold-
ness" of the group and the marketing of Debbie Harry as a sexual
image.
These and other arguments say more about Bangs and his
perceptions of rock at this time, in this place, than they do about
Blondie as such, but they are pursued within a broad biographical
structure which takes in the group's (especially Debbie Harry's and
Chris Stein's) beginnings, the New York punk scene (New York
Dolls, Ramones) and the group's late 1970s successes. Bangs'
style is probably flattered by the blurb writer who describes it as
"mutant critical-journalism based on the sound and language of
rock'n'roll," but it is very readable. Mention should also be made
of the large amount of interview material quoted, and of the well-
chosen illustrations, in color and black-and-white, which are themselves aids to understanding the arguments. (For a more dispas-
sionate account of the group, see Fred Schruers, Blondie [London:
Star Books, 1980].)

ALICE COOPER

S.1190.   COOPER, Alice. Me, Alice: the autobiography of Alice
          Cooper; with Steven Gaines. New York: Putnam,
          1976. 254p. illus.
Celebrated for his tastelessness and unashamed to confess
both his total lack of musical talent and his exclusively commercial
motives, the creator of a particularly bizarre form of "theatrical
rock" demonstrates here that ghosted autobiography is not his forte
either. Whatever Cooper (b. Vincent Damon Furnier in 1948) could
achieve on the stage--and it was doubtless memorable--his performance in print is no rival for it. Nor does it reveal much about
Cooper himself, save for his fondness for the bottle, and his ve-
hemently proclaimed heterosexuality.

S.1191.   GREENE, Bob. Billion Dollar Baby. New York: Athe-
          neum, 1974. 364p. illus.
A large, blow-by-blow account of a Christmas 1973 tour
by Alice Cooper and his group. The author, a Chicago-based journalist at the time, traveled and appeared with the group, in order
to write about it as an insider (cf. Shepard, no. S.1202 and Sloman,
no. S.1203); he played the part of a Santa Claus who becomes a
murder victim. At outset, he endorses Cooper's well-established
reputation for being "sick, degenerate, perverted, obscene, and
Nazi-like" (p. 5), but ends by waxing nostalgic about the tour in
general, and by quoting Cooper's avowal of his total innocence
("there are psychotic people who think we're serious"--p. 310).

JOHN DENVER

S.1192.   DACHS, David. John Denver. New York: Pyramid
          Books, 1976. 93p. illus., discog.
Somewhat hollow, press-agent style biography of the (to

quote the cover) "folk composer, concert performer, conservationist and TV personality." Rudimentary discography.

S.1193.   FLEISCHER, Leonore. John Denver. New York: Flash
          Books, 1976. 80p. illus., discog.
     Fan biography, liberally illustrated, and compiled from a range of secondary sources. The discography lists Denver's LPs chronologically, with indication of track titles.

BOB DYLAN

S.1194.   CABLE, Paul. Bob Dylan: his unreleased recordings.
          London: Scorpion, 1978. 192p.
          _____. _____. New York: Schirmer, 1980. 198p.
     Given the mass of Dylan bootlegs, and their importance in any assessment of his work, this is an invaluable reference work. The author's aim is "to provide a comprehensive, chronological cata-logue of that Dylan material ... which has unofficially found its way into circulation, and to appraise that material" (p. 5). Bootleg tapes form the basis of the catalog, but records are noted also. The critical appraisal accompanying the chart of each tape is admit-tedly personal, but shows an extensive knowledge, not just of Dylan's recordings, but of his performances also. Following the catalog there is an "official" discography (in basic outline only), a detailed discography, with evaluations of sound quality, and an in-dex. The 1980 edition includes a "1980 update."

S.1195.   DICKSTEIN, Morris. Gates of Eden: American culture in
          the sixties. New York: Basic Books, 1977. 300p.
          illus., bibliog.
     This series of essays on aspects of 1960s culture includes a chapter, "The Age of Rock Revisited," which is substantially de-voted to a stimulating reconsideration of Bob Dylan. Believing that, in the protean character of Dylan's career, "his shifts reveal those of the age" (p. 188), Dickstein relates Dylan's use of folk and rock to the contrasting and fluctuating cultural sensibilities of the decade. The theme of change is also connected by the author to Dylan's habit of recreating his own songs in successive perform-ances--an aspect often glossed over in Dylan criticism, but one which leads Dickstein, whose main interest, here and elsewhere in the book, is in texts, to assert the paramount importance of Dylan the melodist and performer above Dylan the lyricist.

S.1196.   DYLAN, Bob. Bob Dylan in His Own Words; compiled by
          Miles; edited by Pearce Marchbank; designed by Perry
          Neville. London: Omnibus Press; New York: Quick
          Fox, 1978. 126p. illus.
     The scissors-and-paste format of this type of book is basically unsatisfactory: a compiler assembles snippets of a perform-er's assorted sayings, taken out of context from a variety of sources (in this case, press conferences in 1965 and '66, radio and TV shows

from the same period, interviews from then and from the 1970s--all rather vaguely identified), groups them loosely under general headings ("biographical fragments," "rock 'n' roll lifestyle," etc.), and lets the reader loose to look for nuggets of wit and wisdom. Inevitably, the reader takes things out of context, and reads messages of significance into off-the-cuff remarks; expectations are aroused, and the material is plundered for a means of fulfilling them. The whole concept says more about what we expect of a rock star than anything else.

Yet in Dylan's case at least something different is also on offer, namely ability to respond to noxious prying, and/or ignorant questions with remarkable wit; indeed, his wit is the most serious thing in the book.

S.1197.　GROSS, Michael.　Bob Dylan: an illustrated histeory; produced by Michael Gross, with a text by Robert Alexander.　New York:　Grosset & Dunlap; London: Elm Tree Books, 1978.　149p.　illus.

No very high aims are entertained here: a "scrapbook," Gross calls it.　As such it comes off well.　Alexander's biographical text is a lively account of Dylan's life and career, succinctly condensed from a great many (mostly printed) sources.　Some critical commentary is incorporated.　The many black-and-white photos are excellent, pride of place being taken by those of Jim Marshall. (Gross's name appears on the spine as if he were the author.)

S.1198.　HOGGARD, Stuart, and SHIELDS, Jim.　Bob Dylan: an illustrated discography.　Warborough, Oxon.: Transmedia Express, 1978.　108p.　illus., bibliog.

An excellent annotated discography, in which official albums, bootlegs, singles, interviews, television and film soundtracks are listed in one chronological sequence.　Each item is accompanied by informal background notes, which include some biographical information, but mainly concentrate on the circumstances of each recording.　The 83 bootleg items include masters, demos, concerts, radio and television tapes, and private recordings.　Index of names and titles.

S.1199.　KNOCKIN' ON DYLAN'S DOOR.　New York:　Pocket Books, 1974; London:　Michael Dempsey, 1975.　137p.　illus.

In January and February 1974 Dylan and the Band undertook a national tour, his first for eight years, during which they gave 40 concerts in 21 cities.　These twelve pieces (from Rolling Stone?) follow Dylan around, some giving instant, on-the-spot descriptions and reactions, and others offering more considered responses.　The sense of immediacy is provided by the main contributor, Ben Fong-Torres, who finally succeeds in obtaining his interview with Dylan, which is transcribed in full.　Other views come from Michael McClure, Ralph J. Gleason, and Paul West; "press reviews" are represented by pieces from Nat Hentoff, Lucian K. Truscott, and Ellen Willis.

S.1200.   NASH, Roderick. From These Beginnings...: a bio-
           graphical approach to American History. New York:
           Harper & Row, 1973. 548p. illus., bibliogs.
           _____. _____. 2nd ed. New York: Harper &
           Row, 1978. 2 vols. illus., bibliogs.
           _____. _____. 3rd ed. New York: Harper &
           Row, 1984. 2 vols. illus., bibliogs.
           The thirty-page biographical chapter on Dylan (following
those on Martin Luther King and Richard Nixon) is part of an attempt
to tell "the larger story of the American experience" through a small
series of specially selected lives. History students (for whom the
book is mainly intended) may find the approach refreshing, but the
Dylan who is seen to be speaking for and reflecting the era is a well-
worn topic in rock literature. (Nash's Wilderness and the American
Mind [New Haven: Yale University Press, 1967; new ed. 1982] is,
by contrast, a classic of American cultural history.)

S.1201.   RINZLER, Alan. Bob Dylan: the illustrated record; de-
           signed by Jon Goodchild. New York: Harmony Books,
           1978. 120p. illus., bibliog.
           From Bob Dylan (1962) to Street Legal (1978), this is an
interesting listener's guide to each of Dylan's albums--but, more than
that, it's a triumph for the designer. A large, square page format
permits a kind of simultaneity (or basic polyphony?): essential
events in Dylan's life at the time of each record appear in a column
at the extreme edge of each page, framing the central text; at the
same time separate boxes and panels are given over to short extracts from contemporary critics, or to Dylan's own (often mystifying)
words to interviewers, enabling the reader to obtain some idea, however limited, of the changing attitudes of both parties. These devices absolve Rinzler from having to integrate biographical and critical opinion, but more significantly, together with the numerous illustrations they begin to suggest different levels at which a performer like Dylan should be taken. The main text itself is chiefly
concerned with discussing Dylan's lyrics, and the frequent meta-
morphoses of attitude they contain. Perceptive without ever being
pretentious (unlike some Dylan-ologists), Rinzler nevertheless has
a tendency to overdo a kind of pop journalese; more serious perhaps
is the isolation in which the songs are examined.

S.1202.   SHEPARD, Sam. Rolling Thunder Logbook. New York:
           Viking Press, 1977; Harmondsworth: Penguin, 1978.
           184p. illus.
           Playwright Shepard was invited by Bob Dylan to accompany
the Rolling Thunder revue's New England tour in 1975, to write the
script for a film based on the tour. The role soon became secondary
(the film as originally intended was never made; Renaldo and Clara,
directed by Dylan and Howard Alk, is a fictionalized version of the
tour), and Shepard found himself "a collaborator in a whirlpool of
images and shifting ideas" (p. 1). His "fractured memory" of the
cause of events expresses itself in the fragmentary text which ends

up reading like a cross between a screenplay and a diary. One is never certain, as a consequence, if Joan Baez, Joni Mitchell, Ramblin' Jack Elliot, Allen Ginsberg, and Dylan himself, are seen as actors or as "themselves."

S.1203.   SLOMAN, Larry. On the Road With Bob Dylan: rolling
          with the thunder. New York: Bantam Books, 1978.
          412p. illus.
     Like Shepard (no. S.1202), Sloman traveled with Dylan's Rolling Thunder Revue, and, also like Shepard, experienced similar difficulties and frustrations, especially in "penetrating the circle" (they commiserate on p. 107; Sloman, more reviled than Shepard, is also more ingratiating, and eventually achieves acceptance by the group, albeit as "Ratso," "a sort of spiritual mascot, part fan, part scribe, part pharmacist, part jester"--p. 128). His sprawling, slice-of-life chronicle of the tour attempts to capture as many facets of the enterprise as possible, from Dylan and Baez in performance to obscure hangers-on and miscellaneous unconnected characters encountered in the byways in the small hours. Sloman's talent in depicting this "underside" surpasses his more general descriptive powers or his interview technique (though interviews with Baez, Ronee Blakley, Bob Neuwirth, Joni Mitchell, Hurricane Carter, Allen Ginsberg, and Dylan himself should be dutifully noted); his greatest skill, however, lies in describing his own odyssey, from dejected Rolling Stone vassal to bit-player in Dylan's odd movie, Renaldo and Clara.

S.1204.   THOMSON, Elizabeth M., ed. Conclusions on the Wall:
          new essays on Bob Dylan. Manchester: Thin Man,
          1980. 108p. illus., bibliog.
     These thirteen essays were gathered to commemorate the 1980 "Dylan Revisited" convention; their authors are a cross-section of academics and journalists, both British and American, and their approaches vary from the personal to the studious. No one theme is in control, though several essays grapple with Dylan's recent religious conversion (Robert Shelton, Steve Turner; while Suzanne Macrae reveals the deep vein of religious feeling in a piece written before the conversion). Two deal with music--those by Wilfrid Mellers (also published in a fuller version in Popular Music, 1, 1981), and the editor; one with humor (Patrick Humphries), one with Dylan's influence on popular music (Paul Cable), one with Dylan's Tarantula (Gabrielle Goodchild), one with his influence on 1960s protest (Linda Cantor), one with his "antic disposition" (William T. Lhamon), while a brief contribution from Christopher Ricks discusses Dylan's song endings. More personal reflections come from Mike Porco and Michael Gray.

S.1205.   WILLIAMS, Paul. Dylan--What Happened? South Bend,
          Mich.: And Books; Glen Ellen, Calif.: Entwhistle
          Books, 1979. 125p. illus., bibliog.
     Dylan's conversion to born-again Christianity, rumored in

early 1979, substantiated in the summer with the album <u>Slow Train</u>
<u>Coming</u>, was confirmed in a series of concerts in San Francisco in
November of the same year. Williams attended each of the first
seven, then, in the following days, wrote this "essay" in which,
overwhelmingly impressed by the music and the performance, ambivalent about the sentiments but determined not to be dismissive, he
attempts to think himself through the possible reasons for Dylan's
conversion, and his own conflicting responses. Clues are sought in
close inspection (of an excited, random, not systematic kind) of
Dylan's lyrics, pre- and post-conversion (songs on <u>Blood on the</u>
<u>Tracks</u>, <u>Street Legal</u>, <u>Slow Train</u>, and those subsequently issued on
<u>Saved</u>). Interesting though this is, it is in Williams' own struggle
with his reactions ("even though I'm an outsider I can't help but be
moved"--p. 10) that the book's fascination lies.

GRATEFUL DEAD

S.1206.   HARRISON, Hank. <u>The Dead</u>. Millbrae, Calif.: Celestial
          Arts, 1980. 322p. illus., discog.
Harrison's first account of the Grateful Dead (cited as
LOAM A293) was a somewhat bizarre essay in capturing the spirit of
the 1960s West Coast rock culture. This second book, which "represents Book Two and Book Three of the Dead Trilogy" (opening
sentence) is a little more down-to-earth--as in the retelling of some
major events such as the Altamont Festival--and contains interview
material with members of the group. But the overall purpose is
once again rather obscure: "This book is a presentation of paradigms
and mental models that represent and symbolize the rock and roll
community at the closest level of intimacy, and is not directly concerned with the music or the public legend..." (p. 10). The intimacy in question may refer in part to Harrison's own status as
friend and hanger-on of the band. Interesting photographs, incomplete discography, and five astrological (sic) charts; no index.

JIMI HENDRIX

S.1207.   HENDERSON, David. <u>Jimi Hendrix: voodoo child of the</u>
          <u>Aquarian age</u>. Garden City, N.Y.: Doubleday, 1978.
          514p. illus.
          _____. <u>'Scuse Me While I Kiss the Sky: the life of</u>
          <u>Jimi Hendrix</u>. New York: Bantam, 1981. 384p.
          illus., discog.
          The power of Hendrix's onstage performance contrasted
with his private offstage manner, making a convincing portrait difficult; noting this (p. 380, 1981 ed.), Harlem-born poet and musician Henderson remarks, "it took years, literally, to win the trust
and confidence of ... [his] inner circle of friends." In the event,
he received help from many sources, until a project begun in anger
at Hendrix's death in 1970 ended in a sense of "essence uncovered"
and of enjoyment of Hendrix's life. Less committed readers might
like to reserve judgment, especially about Hendrix's life style, but

Henderson is successful in many aspects of his book: in the integration of biographical data, character portrayal, and musical commentary (the latter often impressionistic but demonstrating great familiarity with the music); in the understanding of Hendrix's roots in black music; and in the clear account of the crucial first period in London, where Hendrix was dropped like a small pebble, but went on to create shock waves. The 1981 edition is a condensed version, with minor revisions, of the 1978 book. The discography is selected, but contains some information on private tapes. No index.

BUDDY HOLLY

S.1208.   GOLDROSEN, John J. Buddy Holly: his life and music.
           Bowling Green, Ohio: Bowling Green University Popular
           Press, 1975. 243p. illus., bibliog., discog.
           _____. _____. London: Charisma Books, 1975.
           256p. illus., bibliog., discog.
           _____. The Buddy Holly Story. New York: Quick Fox,
           1979. 257p. illus., bibliog., discog.
           A thorough, exhaustively researched biography, incorporating the results of "a twenty-thousand mile cross-country drive in search of the people and the places that were part of Buddy Holly's life" (p. 12, Charisma edn.). Goldrosen begins by situating Holly (1936-1959) firmly in his home town of Lubbock, Texas, and attempts successfully in the ensuing narrative to discover the sources and reasons for Holly's particular sound by mapping out his social and musical environment and his personality, by looking in detail at the process of studio recording, and by examining the songs themselves (which he characterizes as "a fusion of surface simplicity and actual complexity"--p. 224). The revised version discusses the film, The Buddy Holly Story, which was loosely based on the 1975 edition, though fictionalized in many respects (p. 221, 1979 edn.). The discography in the 1979 edition ("compiled with the assistance of Bill Griggs") is particularly good.

S.1209.   TOBLER, John. The Buddy Holly Story. London: Plexus;
           New York: Beaufort Books, 1979. 96p. illus., discog.
           A clearly written illustrated biography by a British writer, drawing heavily on material in Goldrosen (no. S.1208). The final chapter is devoted to the movie, The Buddy Holly Story (of whose distortions Tobler quotes Goldrosen as saying, "They could have told the truth and still been commercial"--p. 92). The discography is a thorough listing of singles and albums, 1956-1978.

BILLY JOEL

S.1210.   GAMBACCINI, Peter. Billy Joel: a personal file. New
           York: Quick Fox, 1979. 128p. illus., discog.
           An above-average fan biography, fluidly written and levelheaded. Many direct quotes of Joel's words, taken from various previous magazine interviews, are included.

JANIS JOPLIN

S.1211. DALTON, David. Janis; written and edited by David
          Dalton. New York: Simon & Schuster, (1971). 212p.
          illus.
          _____. _____. London: Calder & Boyars, 1972.
          154p. illus.
          A composite portrait of Janis Joplin (1943-1970) by a con-
tributing editor to Rolling Stone, who followed in the singer's wake
during several of what were to be her last appearances, and who
reflects, often quite tellingly (if in occasionally pretentious terms),
both on her lifestyle and on the true nature of her personality. Besides his own thoughts, Dalton includes a selection of Rolling Stone
articles on Joplin, a large photo section, excerpts from reviews, and
the words and music of fourteen songs by and/or associated with
her. An eight-inch (sic) long-playing record of her singing and
talking is included also with the US edition. (Formerly LOAM A285.)

S.1212. LANDAU, Deborah. Janis Joplin: her life and times. New
          York: Paperback Library, 1971. 160p. illus., discog.
          Published a little over a year after the singer's death (in
October, 1970), this popular biography shows all the signs of a lack
of time to do any serious investigation, or reflection. In part com-
pensation for this, however, the flavor of the contemporary response
to the singer is breathlessly captured. (Formerly LOAM A295.)

CAROLE KING

S.1213. COHEN, Mitchell S. Carole King: a biography in words
          and pictures; edited by Greg Shaw. New York: Sire
          Books/Chappell, 1976. 56p. illus., discog.
          From "Will You Love Me Tomorrow" (1960) for the Shirelles,
via songs for Phil Spector, the Monkees and others, to her own album Tapestry (1971) and on, the career of Carole King (b.1942) deserves closer scrutiny than is on offer here. Cohen's text is rather
more interested in her as singer-songwriter than in the earlier partnership with lyricist and one-time husband Gerry Goffin (Goffin, for
all that this is a pictorial biography, only merits one small illustration). An appendix provides a selected listing of Carole King's
songs, 1958-1970.

AL KOOPER

S.1214. KOOPER, Al. Backstage Passes: rock 'n' roll life in the
          sixties; with Ben Edmonds. New York: Stein & Day,
          1977. 254p. illus., discog.
          An extremely versatile figure in the rock world, Kooper
(b.1944) has been, among other things, a session musician, composer, arranger, and producer; making his name recording with Bob
Dylan (on organ), he later formed--and soon left--Blood, Sweat and
Tears, recorded with Hendrix, and with the Rolling Stones, as well

as making discs under his own name. His account of the rock life, which features all these and others, is intended, he says, "to allow the reader a glimpse of what it is like to build a career in the music business from scratch in New York, circa the dawn of the sixties" ("Introdukshun"). Though a little short on precise factual information, the book offers convincing insights into some of the high, and low, and (perhaps to a lesser extent) the medium points in this particular scene. Other supporting roles are played by Clive Davis, Judy Collins, Paul Simon, Joni Mitchell.

LEIBER & STOLLER

S.1215.   PALMER, Robert. Baby, That Was Rock & Roll: the legendary Leiber & Stoller; introduction by John Lahr. New York: Harcourt Brace Jovanovich, 1978.   131p. illus., discog.
      With songs like "Hound Dog," "Spanish Harlem," "Yakety Yak," Jerry Leiber (b.1933) and Mike Stoller (b.1933) became the song-writing supremos of rock 'n' roll; a study of their partnership, with its profound stamp of black culture, would be most welcome. This celebratory album merely whets the appetite. Palmer's short text has little room to develop its ideas, and is followed by a collage of lyrics and photographs (Presley, the Coasters, etc.). The discography, by Robert Bienstock and Faith Whitehill Koeppel, is arranged by title, and gives artist's name, year, record label and number. There is also a chronological listing of Leiber and Stoller-produced records.

LITTLE RICHARD

S.1216.   GARODKIN, John. Little Richard: king of rock 'n' roll. (Denmark):   Danish Rock 'n' Roll Society, 1975.   71p. illus., discog.
      Until the appearance of Charles White's The Life and Times of Little Richard (New York: Harmony Books, 1984) there was scant material on Little Richard in book form. This little paperback should be noted, though it scarcely filled the gap. It was issued as a special number of the Danish Rock 'n' Roll Society's journal, Keep a Rockin' (replacing, apparently, issues 12-14). Inspired by a Danish tour by the singer, it is a game effort with sections devoted to Little Richard's recordings and to his recording sessions.

BETTE MIDLER

S.1217.   MIDLER, Bette. A View from a Broad; photography by Sean Russell. New York: Simon & Schuster, 1980. 160p. illus.
      Intended apparently as something of a comedy-fantasy, this is a tongue-in-cheek, largely non-literal account of a Midler world tour.

JONI MITCHELL

S.1218.   FLEISCHER, Leonore.   Joni Mitchell.   New York: Flash
          Books, 1976.   79p.   illus.
          More routine fan literature, but the absence of any other
study on this subject makes it necessary to include it here.   There
is a brief consideration of Joni Mitchell's music.

JIM MORRISON

S.1219.   HOPKINS, Jerry and SUGARMAN, Daniel.   No One Here
          Gets Out Alive.   New York: Warner Books; London:
          Plexus, 1980.   387p.   illus., bibliog., discog.
          A best-selling, frequently sensationalist but ultimately te-
dious popular biography of Jim Morrison (1943-1971).   An audacious
performer, Morrison's own self-hype was at least in character; the
authors' apparent belief that their subject was some sort of cata-
clysmic revolutionary (poetic) force is in stark contrast to the story
they actually tell: of one of rock's more pretentious delusions, and
of the great potential of the late 1960s rock environment for nasti-
ness.   Hopkins, whose research for the book took him four years,
wrote two drafts; Sugarman, a Doors aide, produced the final version.   The discography includes singles and albums; the list of
books is limited to Morrison's own poetry.   No index.

PHIL OCHS

S.1220.   ELIOT, Marc.   Death of a Rebel.   Garden City, N.Y.:
          Anchor Press/Doubleday, 1979.   316p.   illus., discog.
          Extremely detailed, unsentimental biography of Phil Ochs
(1940-1976), of whom Melody Maker once wrote, "if Bob Dylan is
the King of protest, Phil Ochs ... is the President."   As Eliot
shows, Ochs' political sensitivity and drive to action far outstripped
Dylan's, but his songs, which so epitomized this period in many
ways, by and large failed to reach a mass audience.   It was, perhaps characteristically of the urban folk rock movement, a politiciza-
tion, as Ochs said, "out of an inner need for expression, not to
change the world" (p. 93).   In his research Eliot, who knew Ochs,
was considerably assisted by the singer's family, and in addition
conducted interviews with "hundreds of people."   The result is an
exceptional portrait of a turbulent, paradoxical, immensely gifted
figure, whose depressive urge finally took its toll as a sense of
failure overwhelmed him.   He was no loner, and his relationships
with social and political movements, with the record industry, with
the establishment, and with friends and fellow musicians, are sharply
drawn.   Refraining totally from moralistic or any other discussions,
Eliot leaves the reader to draw his/her own conclusions from his tale.
The discography lists all the tracks on Ochs's albums, with dates
and label numbers.   Index.

CARL PERKINS

S.1221.   PERKINS, Carl. Discipline In Blue Suede Shoes; with
          Ron Rendleman. Grand Rapids, Mich.: Zondervan,
          1978. 145p. illus.
          Perkins' (b.1932) account of Sam Phillips' Sun Records in
the 1950s forms the most interesting part of this ghosted autobiography. Presley and Cash, as might be expected, make frequent
appearances. Inspirational poems and "born again" interpolations
make the narrative hard to follow at times. Cash provides a brief
foreword.

ELVIS PRESLEY

Note: far more books have been written about Elvis Presley than
any other American rock performer. For further information see
Elvis Presley: a bio-bibliography, by Patsy Guy Hammontree
(Westport, Conn.: Greenwood Press, 1985), Elvis Presley: a
reference guide and discography, by John A. Whisler (Metuchen,
N.J.: Scarecrow Press, 1981), and Robert K. Oermann's review of
38 Presley books in Journal of Country Music, 9/2 (1982), pp. 120-
126. See also the relevant section of Paul Taylor's Popular Music
Since 1955 (London: Mansell, 1985).

S.1222.   CORTEZ, Diego, ed. Private Elvis; with photographs of
          Rudolph Paulini. Stuttgart: Fey, 1978. 199p. illus.
          How West Germany made a young soldier willkommen.
Paulini's photographs are candid shots of Presley with a variety of
consorts from the available nightlife. Cortez contributes an essay
in semiological analysis (in English and German).

S.1223.   ESCOTT, Colin, and HAWKINS, Martin. The Elvis Ses-
          sion File: 20 years of Elvis. Bexhill-on-Sea, Sussex:
          Swift Record Distributors, 1974. 64p.
          _____. Elvis Presley: the illustrated discography.
          London: Omnibus Press, 1981. 96p. illus., bibliog.
          The first version of this discography was designed "as a
guide through the tangled issues of which musicians played on
which sessions and what songs were recorded" (rev. ed., p. 5);
the second, better organized and produced version is a full updat-
ing, incorporating information on the flood of issues that followed
the singer's death in 1977. The main section, a chronological session list, gives details of 81 recording sessions, 1954-77, with some
linking biographical narrative. Titles and personnel are given,
in addition to venue and date. Other supplementary sections are
devoted to albums, singles, EPs, movies and bootlegs. An interesting final section, "Roots," provides a chronological list of all
those songs in Presley's recorded output that were originally recorded by other artists; details are included of performer, record
label and number, and date.

S.1224.   GREGORY, Neal, and GREGORY, Janice. When Elvis
           Died. Washington, D.C.: Communications Press, 1980.
           292p. illus., bibliog.
    The dust jacket adds the subtitle: "a chronicle of national
and international reaction to the passing of an American king." The
world-wide response to the event (Presley's death on August 16,
1977) is meticulously documented, using a wide range of printed and
media sources, backed up by the compilers' own interviews (they
evidently combed the Library of Congress and the British Library,
and watched many hours of old television broadcasts). The depth
and scope of the research are impressive, and the treatment has an
exemplary objectivity. Perhaps the most successful section is the
first, in which, for the first three days after Presley's death, the
media event gradually develops, particularly in and around Memphis
itself. Concluding chapters offer some perspectives concerning the
cultural and other values on display. Three sections devoted to
selected newspaper editorials (reprinted), to sources and notes, and
to a bibliography, contain a wealth of information.

S.1225.   HARBINSON, W. A. Elvis Presley: an illustrated biog-
           raphy; designed by Stephen Ridgeway. London:
           Michael Joseph, 1975; New York: Grosset & Dunlap,
           1976. 160p. illus.
           _____. The Life and Death of Elvis Presley; designed
           by Stephen Ridgeway. Rev. ed. London: Michael
           Joseph, 1977. 160p. illus.
    This well-illustrated volume has a biographical structure
(it opens with a vivid evocation of Presley's background, and concludes, in the revised edition, with his death) but is more noteworthy as an intelligent overall interpretation of Presley as performer and as image, in particular of the inherent contradictions
(remote star/intimate performer, artistic endeavor/cold commerce,
etc.) on display. The two central chapters are devoted to Presley's
films, and to a personal analysis of an amalgam of his Las Vegas
cabaret performances. While he has many harsh words for Hollywood and for the milieu in which Presley lived and worked, the
author has substantial praise for the performer and a sharp sense
of the extent to which Presley was "cornered" by his own celebrity
and mystique.

S.1226.   HOPKINS, Jerry. Elvis: the final years. New York:
           St. Martin's Press; London: W. H. Allen, 1980.
           258p. illus.
    Hopkins' first Presley biography (LOAM 1386), published
in 1971, remains a standard work. Here he picks up the biographical thread in 1970 and continues the narrative, with less enthusiasm
than earlier but equal diligence. A conscientious researcher (he
claims to have interviewed "approximately 75 individuals"--p. v), he
tells the dismal story of Presley's declining years to his death in
1977 without the sensationalism which besets so much writing on the
subject. He is prepared to use some of the material revealed by the

first of the "insider" accounts--and Presley's lifestyle is not dis-
guised--but finds both their motivation and their style distasteful
(for his remarks on West et al., see no. S.1235). If there is a
shapelessness about it all, that is probably inevitable. Presley the
performer takes an increasingly minor role; most of his performances
are mentioned, but there is no attempt to discuss music. No index.

S.1227.   LACKER, Marty, et al. Elvis: portrait of a friend, by
          Marty Lacker, Patsy Lacker, and Leslie S. Smith.
          Memphis, Tenn.: Wimmer Bros., 1979. 317p. illus.
          _____. _____. New York: Bantam, 1979. 369p.
          illus.
     Three contrasting attempts to "tell all" about Elvis and
his lifestyle. Marty Lacker, who worked for the singer and was for
a time a close associate, provides an entertaining, admiring portrait;
his wife Patsy viciously berates the coterie of people by whom Presley was surrounded (especially its female members); and Smith, who
evidently co-ordinated the book, adds his own version of events,
one with particular interest in the drug question.

S.1228.   LICHTER, Paul. The Boy Who Dared to Rock: the def-
          initive Elvis. Garden City, N.Y.: Doubleday, 1978;
          London: Sphere Books, 1980. 304p. illus., discog.
     Lichter's brand of idolatry is not to everyone's taste--Dave
Marsh remarked, in his Elvis (New York: Times Books, 1982),
p. 235, "Lichter's love for Presley is unquestionable--without it he
could never have trivialized him so well"; but at least the factual
data provided is valuable. The book is in four sections: (i) biography (or hagiography: the last chapter in this part, called
"Aloha," begins, "It is with great sorrow that I add this final chapter to a book that was written as a tribute to a Living' Legend!
'That Legend Will Live Forever'"); (ii) a chronological listing of
Presley's live appearances, 1969-1977, with exact dates, venues, etc.,
preceded by descriptions of Elvis the performer ("useful only if
you're contemplating a career as an Elvis impersonator"--Marsh,
ibid.); (iii) a list of all Presley's recording sessions in one chronological sequence, with dates, venues, titles, personnel, matrix nos.;
and (iv) discography and filmography, the former organized by type
of record, including bootlegs and non-American releases, the latter
merely giving studio and year of release. (For a more informative
work on Presley's films, see Lichter's Elvis in Hollywood [London:
Hale, 1977].)

S.1229.   MATTHEW-WALKER, Robert. Elvis Presley: a study in
          music. Tunbridge Wells: Midas Books, 1979. 154p.
          illus., bibliog., discog.
     The subtitle is perhaps misleading: British music critic
Matthew-Walker's book is best thought of as a non-specialist companion to Presley's recordings, rather than as a study of them (we
still await the latter, in its fullest sense). Taking each recording

session in its chronological place, and each of the session's titles alphabetically, he provides general, descriptive comments and guidance (e.g., on the song, on Presley's performance) on each individual item in turn. Musicological language and techniques are both avoided in the interest of reaching the general reader. This item-by-item catalogue approach, for all its merits as an introduction to thinking about Presley's music (an all-too-rare occurrence in Presley literature) is incomplete without an attempt to collate ideas under particular heads (vocal tone, range, rhythm, accompaniment) on a broader level. This concluding summary is insufficient to do. A preliminary biographical chapter is pleasantly free from hype; other bonuses include a good chronological filmography, 1956-1973, with full details of studio, company, credits, and song titles, and a select discography. The bibliography restricts itself to an odd list of eight "especially recommended" books. There are indexes of songs and names.

S.1230.   PANTA, Ilona. Elvis Presley: king of kings. Hicksville,
            N.Y.: Exposition Press, 1979. 247p.
    Ilona Panta is probably not the only Presley fan to have become convinced he was a prophet, even a god, but no other believer can rival her credentials: a clairvoyant from Transylvania, living in Canada, and making public her revelations through the good offices of an aptly-named press in a perhaps even more aptly-named town. This bizarre corner of Presley literature is occupied by a basically autobiographical tale of how--and it's a very odd "how" indeed--visions of Elvis transformed one particular life. Having written him letters setting down her fantasies, the author foresees his demise and heads for Memphis to save him. No matter that she failed; he will be back anyway....

S.1231.   PRESLEY, Dee, et al.   Elvis, We Love You Tender, by
            Dee Presley, Billy, Rick and David Stanley; as told to
            Martin Torgoff. New York: Delacorte Press, 1980.
            395p. illus.
    _____.   _____. London: New English Library,
            1980. 426p. illus.
    Presley's stepmother and her three sons provide their version of the singer's life from the late 1960s. Dee Presley's own life story occupies a somewhat disproportionate amount of space, but, dull as that is, to the reader of "told-to" Presley books there comes a time when almost any diversion is welcome. The picture of Presley himself has many of the familiar ingredients (summarized as his "fall from grace"), without quite the same acerbic quality that marks some other accounts. The authors are keen to emphasize this themselves, and do so by a novel means--lambasting another "told-to" book (West, et al., no. S.1235) for being a "Judas act" (p. 345), a "trivialization and sensationalization" which highlighted "the blackness in Elvis's life ... without allowing him the dignity of understanding or compassion" (p. 351). (What would they have said about the most contemptuous of all Elvis books, Albert Goldmann's and Lamar Fike's Elvis [New York: McGraw-Hill, 1981]?) Index.

S.1232. PRESLEY, Elvis. Elvis in His Own Words; compiled by
              Mick Farren; designed and edited by Pearce Marchbank.
              London: Omnibus Press, 1977. 120p. illus.
              (For general comments on this type of book, see no.
S.1196.) One of the first books to appear after Presley's death was
this miscellany of his own none-too-revealing public utterances. The
book is divided into a great many sections, offering Presley's views
on movies, recording, girls, etc. The comments are taken from various periodical interviews, radio shows, and at least one book (Hopkins' Elvis), but the source of a given comment is not fully identified. Some of the photos are unusual, but the quality is very
grainy.

S.1233. THARPE, Jac L., ed. Elvis: images and fancies. Jack-
              son: University of Mississippi, 1980. 180p. illus.,
              bibliog. refs.
              _____. _____. London: Star Books, 1983. 188p.
              illus., bibliog. refs.
Following in the wake of Greil Marcus' seminal essay,
"Elvis: Presliad" (Mystery Train, LOAM 1369), the majority of the
fourteen pieces in this stimulating collection seek to explore and explain Elvis Presley in the context of the myths, symbols and complexities of American culture. Most pieces are academic, but contrast is provided by several (e.g., Gay McRae's) of an unashamedly
fanatical type. Presley's stylistic roots, his relationship with and
influence on other musical traditions, are explored by Bill C. Malone
(country music) and Charles K. Wolfe (gospel), while Richard
Middleton, in the book's only example of musical analysis, examines
innovations and continuity in his vocal style. The longest and most
wide-ranging piece, by Van K. Brock, is an attempt to unveil the
"forces that shaped and insulated his thinking" (p. 86), a process
replete with (particularly religious) paradox and contradiction. Public reception of Presley is explored by Stephen R. Tucker in a piece
on changing perceptions in magazines such as Time and Newsweek.

S.1234. WERTHEIMER, Alfred. Elvis '56: in the beginning; photo-
              graphs by Alfred Wertheimer; text by Alfred Wertheimer
              and Gregory Martinelli. New York: Collier; London:
              Cassell, 1979. 149p. illus.
              A fascinating photo book featuring Presley on the brink of
celebrity, displaying a mixture of boyish innocence and growing
confidence. Wertheimer, a freelance photographer, was engaged by
RCA to take publicity pictures at the first New York recording session. He also joined the entourage to travel by train to a concert
appearance in Richmond, Virginia, and to the Presley home in Memphis. The accompanying text, in which Wertheimer gives his recollection of events, is of less significance.

S.1235. WEST, Red, et al. Elvis: what happened? by Red West,
              Sonny West, and Dave Hebler; as told to Steve Dun-
              leavy. New York: Ballantine Books, 1977. 332p. illus.

Three Presley bodyguards were dismissed in the summer of 1976, not by the singer himself--which only increased their malevolence--but by his father Vernon ("we're going to have to cut back on expenses"). They told all they knew about Presley's private life, especially his dependence on drugs, to an Australian journalist on (Rupert Murdoch's) World Star; the journalist used the talents which such employment had sharpened to pen the first and most celebrated of the "inside" stories (sometimes known as the "told-to" books). "Not even Howard Hughes seemed so colorful, so eccentric, so sick," commented Jerry Hopkins. "The book was a distortion, a bitter diatribe without perspective or compassion, motivated by a wish to get even and rich.... But there was truth in the book--however narrow its scope--and sometimes the truth hurts" (no. S.1226, pp. 232-3). Presley was indeed hurt, and angered by the book. Red West's protestations that he still loved the "sonofabitch" probably brought him little comfort; he did not live long after its publication to fret, however.

S.1236. ZMIJEWSKY, Steven, and ZMIJEWSKY, Boris. The Films and Career of Elvis Presley. Secaucus, N.J.: Citadel Press, 1976. 223p. illus., discog.

As with most other books in this series detailing the film careers of famous singers (see, for example, nos. S.989 and S.1010), the interest here is more cinematic than musical. The book is basically a discursive filmography of Presley's 31 films and two documentaries. Following a workmanlike biographical account in ten short chapters, the films are taken one by one, with full details of casts, plot, release date, run time, etc., and with general comments. Though fascinated by the films, the authors struggle to find a means of evaluating them (they are reduced to phrases such as "cream-puff musicals"--p. 13). The discography is limited to million-selling singles and albums. Extensively illustrated with film stills.

DORY PREVIN

S.1237. PREVIN, Dory. Bog-Trotter: an autobiography with lyrics; drawings by Joby Baker. Garden City, N.Y.: Doubleday; London: Weidenfeld & Nicolson, 1980. 383p. illus.

Having let her younger self have her say in her first book (see no. S.1238), Dory Previn here recounts something of her adult years, including her songwriting and her marriage to André Previn. There is little interest in documentation, more in a poetic exploration of her inner life. The intense text lacks the impact of the earlier book. Rather more than half of the work (p. 153 on) is devoted to a large collection of the author's song lyrics; other lyrics are interspersed in the narrative itself. (The bog-trotter of the title is a rude word for the Irish; Ms. Previn is herself of Irish extraction.)

S.1238. PREVIN, Dory. Midnight Baby: an autobiography. New

York: Macmillan, 1976; London: Elm Tree Books, 1977. 246p.

_____. _____. London: Corgi, 1978. 140p.

While undergoing therapy in the early 1970s (following the breakup of her marriage to André Previn), Dory Previn had a recurring image of herself as a child. This first volume of auto-biography is an attempt to recapture the life of that child ("I knew I couldn't write any kind of book about my life today, until I let her tell about her life yesterday"--preface). The story is told through the child's eyes and in the child's words--except that "adults haven't the sense to let well enough alone," and she "tried to polish it a bit" (ibid.). The text is rather too self-consciously fragmentary to be truly childlike, but it is certainly vividly evocative of her evidently traumatic New Jersey childhood.

LINDA RONSTADT

S.1239. BERMAN, Connie. Linda Ronstadt: an illustrated biography. Carson City, London: Proteus, 1979. 117p. illus., discog.

Overwritten popular biography, determined to claim for Linda Ronstadt a position "at the zenith of rock" (p. 112), but not really able to say why--and not much interested in any other claimants. More substantial than Vivian Claire's biography (no. S.1240), however.

S.1240. CLAIRE, Vivian. Linda Ronstadt. New York: Flash Books, 1978. 72p. illus., discog.

A brief promotional biography with a concentration on pictorial images of the singer, but with a song-by-song review of her recordings. The discography is of LPs, chronologically arranged, with indication of song titles.

S.1241. KANAHARIS, Richard. Linda Ronstadt: a portrait. Los Angeles: L.A. Pop Publishing, 1972. 79p. discog.

This "portrait" turns out to be a useful source of reference information. Following the sixteen-page biography ("Overview") which occupies Part One, Part Two is devoted to an excellent discography with comments and excerpts from reviews, a sampling of song titles from her concert appearances, an artist list of those Ronstadt has performed with, and more. Part Three is a listing of all songs (with performing personnel) on the Ronstadt albums. (The curious might like to note that the book is dedicated to George McGovern.)

GRACE SLICK

S.1242. ROWES, Barbara. Grace Slick: the biography. Garden City, N.Y.: Doubleday, 1980. 215p. illus.

For this authorized biography the author drew not only on "two years of confidences" (p. 7) with Grace Slick herself, but on the recollections, among others, of another Jefferson Airplane member, Spencer Dryden ("whose mind is a history of rock in San Francisco during the 1960s"--p. 6). The book reports only briefly on the singer's early years (she was born in Chicago in 1939 and moved to San Francisco in 1943), concentrating on her life and career from the time of the band Great Society (1965-66), through her years with Airplane (1966-73) to the formation and early days of Jefferson Starship. Slick's personality, and the particular life-style of the time and the place, come across clearly enough; although there is mention of her songwriting and of her performing style, these are not discussed in any depth.

BRUCE SPRINGSTEEN

S.1243. GAMBACCINI, Peter. Bruce Springsteen. New York: Quick Fox, 1979. 127p. illus., discog.

_____. _____. Rev. ed. New York: Putnam; London: Omnibus Press, 1985. 153p. illus., discog.

Though adequate by the standards of popular pictorial biographies, Gambaccini's book has Marsh for competition (no. S.1244), a rival who shows us what the genre can do, publishers notwithstanding. Like Marsh, Gambaccini has a concern with lyrics, and his chronological account of Springsteen's life and career pauses frequently to focus on these. But there comparisons end. Much of the text consists of excerpts from other printed sources--Springsteen's interviews with magazines such as Newsweek, Playboy, critics' comments from the music press, etc. The revised edition picks up the story at Darkness at the Edge of Town and continues it up to the LP Born in the USA.

S.1244. MARSH, Dave. Born to Run: the Bruce Springsteen Story. Garden City, N.Y.: Doubleday, 1979. 176p. illus.

_____. Springsteen, Born to Run: the story of Bruce Springsteen. London: Omnibus Press, 1981. 191p. illus.

Enthusiasm for one's subject is not unusual in popular music biographies; what distinguishes Marsh's book is that the biographical account takes place in the framework of a clearly stated personal conviction as to what rock & roll is and is not about, and the significance of this particular performer in that context. The argument is laid out in the first pages: 1970s rock "betrayed itself," becoming "just another hierarchical system in which consumers took what was offered without question." Springsteen, by contrast, "made rock and roll a matter of life and death again ... [he] rooted out corruption" (p. 6). In essence, true rock & roll, for Marsh, is street-level music, rawly energetic yet innocent and wholly lacking in cynicism; more than that, it "[reaches] down into homes without culture to tell kids there is another way to live" (ibid.). These unusually forthright views are carried over into the main text in a style which easily avoids the crassly enthusiastic (the "zealot's rant," as he himself calls it), but is still, as he wants it to be, that

of a fan. In keeping with his theme, Marsh draws the portrait of
Springsteen's working-class New Jersey upbringing with care and
affection, and stresses the importance of these roots throughout the
book. In the account of Springsteen's career from his Columbia
audition (for John Hammond) in 1972 to the LP Darkness on the Edge
of Town (1978), Marsh devotes considerable space to commentary on
each recording, with particularly close attention to the lyrics. Another major feature in the narrative is the 1976-1977 lawsuit with
entrepreneur Mike Appel. Interview material with friends and associates is integrated into the text; Springsteen himself was not interviewed (though he read the text before publication), but many,
often lengthy excerpts from his spoken stage introductions prove to
be extremely useful biographical material. There is no discography,
but a list of songs and a chronology of shows, 1972-1979. (For
further evidence of Marsh's fascination with Springsteen, see his
Fortunate Son [New York: Random House, 1985].)

NEIL YOUNG

S.1245. DUFRECHOU, Carole. Neil Young. New York: Quick
         Fox, 1978. 126p. illus., discog.
         An enthusiastic but rather summary account of Young's
life and career, up to his LP Decade. Young's recordings are sub-
jected to general descriptive comment in their chronological place;
more valuable, though not invariably so, are the frequent quotations
from contemporary reviews (from Rolling Stone, Village Voice, etc.),
for which publication details are given in the text. The discography
is divided into solo albums, those with Buffalo Springfield, and those
with Crosby, Stills, Nash and Young; full track listings are given.

FRANK ZAPPA

S.1246. DISTER, Alain. Frank Zappa et les Mothers of Invention;
         en collaboration avec Urban Gwerder. Paris: Albin
         Michel, 1975. (Collection Rock & Folk.) 186p. bib-
         liog., discog.
         Dister spent time with Zappa and the Mothers on more than
one occasion (the first time they transformed the outlook of the
writer's "yeux de Français un peu prude"), and his short biograph-
ical-cum-critical portrait is a perceptive one. It is mainly structured
around the seminal albums of the late '60s and early '70s (Freak Out,
Lumpy Gravy, etc.), and includes (in French) both Zappa's "self-
interview" on 200 Motels, and a "real" interview made in September
1974. Also included is a colorful account of the 1974 European tour
by Urban Gwerder and Kansas J. Canzus. The "gargantuan appendix" contains a chronology of various groups of Mothers, a discography of commercial discs, a filmography, and a bibliography of
writings by and about Zappa.

Additional Items

General Reference Works

S.1247.   DACHS, David. Encyclopedia of Pop/Rock. New York:
          Scholastic Book Service, 1972. 320p.

S.1248.   GREEN, Jonathon. The Book of Rock Quotes. London:
          Omnibus Press, 1977. 128p.

S.1249.   KUHNKE, Klaus, et al. Schriften zur populären Musik:
          eine Auswahl-Bibliographie. Bremen: Archiv für
          Populäre Musik, 1975-1977. 2 vols.

Recordings

S.1250.   ELROD, Bruce C. A History of American Popular Music.
          2nd ed. Columbia, S.C.: Colonial Printing Co., 1982.
          310p. (Cover title: Your Hit Parade; the book is
          chiefly concerned with the radio program of the same
          name.)

S.1251.   HILL, Randall C. The Official Price Guide to Collectible
          Rock Records. Orlando, Fla.: House of Collectibles,
          1979. 391p.

S.1252.   KASEM, Casey. Casey Kasem's American Top 40 Yearbook;
          researched, compiled, and prepared by the staff of
          American Top 40; editor Jay Golsworthy; editor-in-
          chief Don Bustang. New York: Grosset & Dunlap,
          1979. 203p. (Billboard charts.)

S.1253.   MIRON, Charles. Rock Gold: all the hit charts from
          1955 to 1976. New York: Drake, 1977. 160p.

S.1254.   OSBORNE, Jerry, and HAMILTON, Bruce. A Guide to
          Record Collecting; Victoria Erickson, associate editor.
          Phoenix, Ariz.: O'Sullivan Woodside, 1979. 142p.

S.1255.   OSBORNE, Jerry. Record Collector's Price Guide; edited
          by Bruce Hamilton. Phoenix: O'Sullivan Woodside,
          1976. 196p.
          _____. (2nd ed.) Popular and Rock Records 1948-
          1978; edited by Bruce Hamilton. Phoenix: O'Sullivan
          Woodside, 1978. 252p.
          _____. (3rd ed.) Popular and Rock Price Guide for
          45's: the little record with the big hole; associate
          editor Bruce Hamilton. Phoenix: O'Sullivan Woodside,
          1979. 168p.

S.1256.   OSBORNE, Jerry. 33 1/3 & 45 Extended Play Record Al-
          bum Price Guide; Bruce Hamilton, editor; Greg Shaw,
          associate editor for rock and rhythm & blues. Phoenix:
          O'Sullivan Woodside, 1977. 166p.
          _____. (2nd ed.) Record Albums, 1948-1978; Bruce
          Hamilton editor. Phoenix: O'Sullivan Woodside, 1978.
          256p.

S.1257.   VALENTI, Mary Jo, and LARKIN, Linda J., eds. My
          Sisters' Song: discography of woman-made music. Mil-
          waukee, Wis.: Woman's Soul Pub., 1975. 21p.

Histories: General

S.1258.   BOECKMANN, Charles. And the Beat Goes On: a survey
          of pop music in America. Washington, D.C.: Luce,
          1972. 224p.

S.1259.   KUHNKE, Klaus, et al. Geschichte der Pop-Musik; by
          Klaus Kuhnke, Manfred Miller, Peter Schultze. Vol. 1.
          Bremen: Archiv für Populäre Musik, 1977. 472p.

S.1260.   TOBLER, John, and FRAME, Pete. 25 Years of Rock.
          London: Hamlyn, 1980. 252p.

Histories: Specific Periods

S.1261.   MILLER, Douglas T., and NOWAK, Marion. The Fifties:
          the way we really were. Garden City, N.Y.: Double-
          day, 1975. 444p.

Histories: Specific Areas

S.1262.   BURT, Rob, and NORTH, Patsy, eds. West Coast Story.
          London: Hamlyn, 1977. 96p.

S.1263.   SANTOS, Raye, et al. X-Capees: a San Francisco Punk
          Photo Documentary. Berkeley: Last Gasp of San Fran-
          cisco, 1980. 71p.

Collected & Miscellaneous Criticism

S.1264.   WÖLFER, Jürgen. Die Rock- und Popmusik: eine um-
          fassende Darstellung ihrer Geschichte und Funktion.
          Munich: Heyne, 1980. 189p.

Lyrics

S.1265. BRUCHAC, Joseph. The Poetry of Pop. Paradise, Calif.:
         Dustbooks, 1973. 84p.

Social, Cultural & Media Aspects

S.1266. DAVIS, Lorrie. Letting Down My Hair: two years with
         the love rock tribe--from dawning to downing of Aquar-
         ius. New York: Arthur Fields, 1973; London: Elek,
         1974. 279p. illus. (Life with the musical Hair.)

S.1267. KRIEGER, Susan. Hip Capitalism; foreword by James G.
         March. Beverly Hills: Sage Publications, 1979. 304p.
         (San Francisco radio; includes consideration of rock
         broadcasting there.)

S.1268. NOEBEL, David A. The Marxist Minstrels: a handbook on
         Communist subversion of music. Tulsa, Okla.: Ameri-
         can Christian College Press, 1974. 346p.

S.1269. PASSMAN, Arnold. The Dee Jays. New York: Mac-
         millan, 1971. 320p.

S.1270. PINCUS, Lee. The Songwriter's Success Manual. New
         York: Music Press, 1974. 160p.

S.1271. WEIR, William J., and GODDARD, Uno. The Songwriting
         Racket and How to Beat It. N. Palm Springs, Calif.:
         Cherokee Publishing Co., 1977. 187p.

The Image of Rock

S.1272. BENEDICT, Brad, and BARTON, Linda. Phonographics:
         contemporary album cover art and design. New York:
         Collier, 1977. 137p.

S.1273. HASEBE, Koh. Music Life Rock Photo Gallery. New
         York: Sire/Chappell, 1976. 156p.

S.1274. LEIBOVITZ, Annie, ed. Shooting Stars; designed by Tony
         Lane. San Francisco: Straight Arrow Books, 1973.
         152p. (Photos from Rolling Stone.)

S.1275. LEWIS, Laurie. The Concerts; with a foreword by John
         Peel. Limpsfield, Hants.: Paper Tiger; New York:
         A & W Visual Library, 1979. 119p. (Good selection of
         colored photographs of the rock concert.)

S.1276.   SALEH, Dennis, ed.   Rock Art: fifty-two album covers.
          Seaside, Calif.:   Comma Books, 1977.   134p.

Musicians: Collected Profiles

S.1277.   BARSAMIAN, Jacques, and JOUFFA, Francois.   L'âge d'or
          du rock 'n' roll.   Paris: Ramsay, 1980.   255p.

S.1278.   BUSNAR, Gene.   The Superstars of Rock: their lives and
          their music.   New York: Messner, 1980.   223p.

S.1279.   CAREY, Gary.   Lenny, Janis & Jimi.   New York: Pocket
          Books, 1975.   299p.

S.1280.   FOX-SHEINWOLD, Patricia.   Too Young To Die.   Baltimore:
          Ottenheimer, 1979; London: Cathay Books, 1980.
          353p.

S.1281.   McCOLM, Bruce, and PAYNE, Doug.   Where Have They
          Gone?   rock 'n' roll stars.   New York: Grosset &
          Dunlap/Tempo Books, 1979.   254p.

Musicians: Women Performers

S.1282.   SHEVEY, Sandra.   Ladies of Pop-Rock.   New York:
          Scholastic Book Service, 1972.   147p.

Musicians: Individuals & Groups

ALLMAN BROTHERS

S.1283.   NOLAN, Tom.   The Allman Brothers Band.   New York:
          Sire/Chappell, 1976.   55p.

BLONDIE

S.1284.   SCHRUERS, Fred.   Blondie.   New York: Grosset &
          Dunlap/Tempo Books; London: Star Books, 1980.
          134p.

BYRDS

S.1285.   SCOPPA, Bud.   The Byrds.   New York: Quick Fox,
          1971.   136p.

CAPTAIN BEEFHEART

S.1286.   MUIR, John.   The Life and Times of Captain Beefheart.
          Manchester: Babylon Books, 1980.   72p.

ALICE COOPER

S.1287. DEMOREST, Steve. Alice Cooper. New York: Popular
Library, 1974. 159p.

JOHN DENVER

S.1288. DACHS, David. John Denver. New York: Pyramid
Books, 1976. 93p.

S.1289. MARTIN, James. John Denver: Rocky Mountain wonder-
boy. London: Everest, 1977. 148p.

JANIS JOPLIN

S.1290. CASERTA, Peggy. Going Down With Janis; as told to
Dan Knapp. Secaucus, N.J.: Lyle Stuart; London:
Talmy Franklin, 1975; London: Futura, 1976. 267p.

BETTE MIDLER

S.1291. BAKER, Robb. Bette Midler. New York: Popular Libra-
ry, 1975. 190p. illus.
_____. _____. New ed. New York: Fawcett, 1979;
Sevenoaks, Kent: Coronet, 1980. 256p.

NEW YORK DOLLS

S.1292. MORRISSEY, Steven. New York Dolls. Manchester:
Babylon Books, 1980. 52p.

ELVIS PRESLEY

S.1293. ADLER, Bill, ed. Bill Adler's Love Letters to Elvis. New
York: Grosset & Dunlap, 1978. 96p. (Collection of
fan letters.)

S.1294. CANADA, Lena. To Elvis With Love. New York: Everest
House, 1978; New York: Scholastic Book Services,
1979. 126p. (Correspondence between Presley and a
handicapped child.)

S.1295. COCKE, Marian J. I Called Him Babe: Elvis Presley's
Nurse Remembers. Memphis, Tenn.: Memphis University Press, 1979. 160p.

S.1296. HOLZER, Hans. Elvis Presley Speaks. New York: Manor
Books, 1978. 255p. (i.e., posthumously.)

S.1297. JONES, Peter. Elvis. London: Octopus, 1976. 88p.

S.1298.   LEVY, Alan. Operation Elvis. London: Deutsch, 1960;
          London: World, 1962. 151p. (Presley in the army.)

S.1299.   MANN, May. Elvis and the Colonel. New York: Drake,
          1975. 273p.
          _____. The Private Elvis. New York: Pocket Books,
          1977.

S.1300.   PARISH, James Robert. The Elvis Presley Scrapbook.
          New York: Ballantine, 1975.
          _____. _____. Rev. ed. New York: Ballantine,
          1977. 218p.

S.1301.   PARKER, Edmund K. Inside Elvis; sketches by George
          Bartlett. Orange, Calif.: Rampart House, 1978.
          197p. (Memories of Presley's karate instructor.)

S.1302.   REGGERO, John. Elvis in Concert; photographs by John
          Reggero, with an introduction by David Stanley. New
          York: Dell, 1979. 120p.

S.1303.   SHAVER, Sean, and NOLAND, Hal. The Life of Elvis
          Presley. Memphis, Tenn.: Timur, 1979. 299p.

S.1304.   SLAUGHTER, Todd. Elvis Presley. London: Mandabrook,
          1977. 128p.

S.1305.   STATEN, Vince. The Real Elvis: good old boy. Dayton,
          Ohio: Media Ventures, 1978. 150p.

S.1306.   STEARN, Jess, and GELLER, Larry. The Truth About
          Elvis. New York: Jove Books, 1980. 236p. (How
          Presley's hairdresser, Geller, groomed him in mysticism.)

S.1307.   WALLRAF, Rainer. Presley: eine Biographie. Munich:
          Nüchtern, 1977. 151p.

S.1308.   YANCEY, Becky, and LINEDECKER, Cliff. My Life With
          Elvis. New York: St. Martin's Press, 1978. 254p.
          (Recollections of Presley's secretary.)

Elvis Presley--Reference Works

S.1309.   AROS, Andrew A. Elvis: his films and recordings.
          Diamond Bar, Calif.: Applause Productions, 1980.
          64p.

S.1310.   BARRY, Ron. All American Elvis: the Elvis Presley
          American Discography. Phillipsburg, N.J.: Spectator
          Service, Maxigraphics, 1976. 221p.

S.1311.   JORGENSON, Ernest, et al.   Elvis Recording Sessions.
          Stenlose, Denmark: JEE-Productions, 1977.

S.1312.   OSBORNE, Jerry, and HAMILTON, Bruce.   Presleyana:
          the complete Elvis guide.   Phoenix, Ariz.:   O'Sullivan
          Woodside, 1980.   304p.   (Guide to collecting Presley
          records.)

LOU REED

S.1313.   TREVENA, Nigel.   Lou Reed and the Velvets.   Falmouth,
          Cornwall: Bantam, 1973.   36p.

LINDA RONSTADT

S.1314.   MOORE, Mary Ellen.   The Linda Ronstadt Scrapbook.
          New York: Sunridge Press, 1978.   121p.
          _____.   _____.   New York: Grosset & Dunlap/Tempo
          Books, 1978.   154p.

SIMON & GARFUNKEL

S.1315.   COHEN, Mitchell S.   Simon & Garfunkel: a biography in
          words and pictures; edited by Greg Shaw.   New York:
          Sire Books/Chappell, 1977.   55p.

S.1316.   MARSH, Dave.   Paul Simon.   New York: Quick Fox, 1978.
          128p.

PATTI SMITH

S.1317.   ROACH, Dusty.   Patti Smith: rock & roll madonna.
          South Bend, Ind.:   And Books, 1979.   95p.

GENE VINCENT

S.1318.   VINCE, Alan.   I Remember Gene Vincent.   Prescott,
          Lancs.:   Vintage Rock 'n' Roll Appreciation Society,
          1977.

BOBBY VINTON

S.1319.   VINTON, Bobby.   The Polish Prince; with Robert E.
          Burger.   New York: M. Evans, 1978.   189p.

APPENDIX A:

BOOKS PUBLISHED 1981-85:
A PROVISIONAL LIST

Note: All the main sections in this list, A-J, and their principal
numbered subdivisions are basically the same as those in the main
part of the book, with the exception of the shorter sections B and
E, where no subdivisions are used. In Sections A, C, and D-J,
where a numbered subdivision has no relevant titles in this appendix it is omitted, but the numbering remains unaltered. To
facilitate clearer arrangement of this particular collection of material
a few changes have been made at the level of the smaller sub-
sections (those indicated by lower case letters or Roman numerals),
but these, too, remain substantially the same as their equivalents
in the body of the book.

All entries in the indexes with the prefix S/A refer to items
in this supplementary list.

Brief annotations for a considerable percentage of the books
in sections F-J will be found in the "Booklist" in the journal
Popular Music (Cambridge University Press), Vols. 2-5 and 6/3.

A. GENERAL WORKS

A.1. Bibliography and Reference

a. Bibliographies and Discographies

See also S/A.17

S/A.1. DAVIS, Elizabeth A. Index to the New World Recorded

Anthology of American Music: a user's guide to the initial one hundred records. New York: Norton, 1981. 235p.

S/A.2. HEINTZE, James R. American Music Studies: a classified bibliography of master's theses. Detroit: Information Coordinators, 1984. 312p.

S/A.3. HESKES, Irene, ed. Resource Book of Jewish Music: a bibliographical and topical guide to the book and journal literature and programme materials. Westport, CT: Greenwood Press, 1985. 305p.

S/A.4. PERFORMING ARTS BOOKS 1876-1981. New York: Bowker, 1981. 1,656p.

S/A.5. PHIMISTER, William. American Piano Concertos: a bibliography. Detroit: College Music Society, 1985. 323p.

S/A.6. RODGERS & HAMMERSTEIN ARCHIVES OF RECORDED SOUND, New York Public Library. Dictionary Catalog. Boston: G. K. Hall, 1981. 15 vols.

b. Encyclopedias and Biographical Dictionaries

S/A.7. BUTTERWORTH, Neil. A Dictionary of American Composers. New York: Garland, 1983. 523p.

S/A.8. EWEN, David. American Composers: a biographical dictionary. New York: Putnam, 1982; London: Hale, 1983. 793p.

S/A.9. JABLONSKI, Edward. Encyclopedia of American Music. Garden City: Doubleday, 1981. 629p. (includes entries for names, forms, genres & work titles in seven chronological sections)

c. Library Directories
See also S/A.510

S/A.10. BRADLEY, Carol June, ed. Music Collections in American Libraries: a chronology. Detroit: Information Coordinators, 1981. 249p.

S/A.11. KRUMMEL, D. W., et al. Resources of American Music History: a directory of source materials from colonial times to World War II: Urbana: University of Illinois Press, 1981. 463p.

a.2. Histories

S/A.12. HAMM, Charles. Music in the New World. New York:
Norton, 1983. 722p. (designed to be read in conjunction with the New World Recorded Anthology of American Music)

S/A.13. LYNES, Russell. The Lively Audience: a social history
of the visual and performing arts in America, 1890-1950.
New York: Harper & Row, 1985. 489p.

A.3. Miscellaneous Studies

S/A.14. CRAWFORD, Richard. Studying American Music; with a bibliography of the published writings of Richard Crawford.
Brooklyn: I.S.A.M. Special Publications, No. 3, 15p.

S/A.15. HEARTZ, Daniel, and WADE, Bonnie, eds. Report of the
Twelfth Congress (of the International Musicological Society), Berkeley 1977. Kassel: Bärenreiter, 1981.
912p. (includes papers from sessions on African roots,
oral composition (Lester Young), recent research on
American music, and the worldwide transmission of
American popular music)

A.4. Women in Music

See also Sections G.2.C, G.3.b, H.6.b, and J.7.b

S/A.16. CLAGHORN, Gene. Women Composers and Hymnists: a
concise biographical dictionary. Metuchen, NJ: Scarecrow Press, 1984. 288p.

S/A.17. COHEN, Aaron I. International Discography of Women Composers. Westport, CT: Greenwood Press, 1984. 254p.

S/A.18. _____. International Encyclopedia of Women Composers.
New York: Bowker, 1981. 597p.

S/A.19. TICK, Judith. American Women Composers Before 1870.
Ann Arbor: UMI Research Press, 1983. 302p.

S/A.20. ZAIMONT, Judith Lang, and FAMERA, Karen. Contemporary Concert Music by Women: a directory of the
composers and their works. Westport, Conn.: Greenwood Press, 1981. 355p.

A.5. Vocal Music

See also S/A.96

S/A.21. FRIEDBERG, Ruth C. American Art Song and American
Poetry. Metuchen, NJ: Scarecrow Press, 1981-84. 2 vols.

S/A.22. MARCO, Guy A. Opera: a research and information guide.
New York: Garland, 1984. 373p. ("USA": pp. 244-
249)

S/A.23. VIRGA, Patricia H. The American Opera to 1790. Ann
Arbor: UMI Research Press, 1982. 393p.

A.6. Church Music

a. Hymnody

S/A.24. ROGAL, Samuel J. The Children's Jubilee: a bibliographical survey of hymnals for infants, youth, and Sunday
schools published in Britain and America, 1655-1900.
Westport, Conn.: Greenwood Press, 1983. 136p.

S/A.25. ROGAL, Samuel J. Sisters of Sacred Song: a selected
listing of women hymnodists in Great Britain and America.
New York: Garland, 1981. 162p.

b. Gospel Hymn

S/A.26. HEFLEY, James C. How Sweet the Sound. Wheaton, Ill.:
Tyndale House, 1981. 320p.

c. Moravians and German Pietists

S/A.27. ADAMS, Charles B. Our Moravian Hymn Heritage: chronological listing of hymns and tunes of Moravian origin in
the American Moravian hymnal of 1969. Bethlehem, Pa.:
Moravian Church in America, 1984. 144p.

S/A.28. LOEWEN, Alice, et al. Exploring the Mennonite Hymnal: a
handbook. Newton, Kan.: Faith & Life Press, 1983.
358p.

S/A.29. STEELMAN, Robert, ed. Catalog of the Lititz Congregation
Collection. Chapel Hill: University of North Carolina
Press, 1981. 488p.

A.7. Musical Life

a. Regional Studies

S/A.30. ALEXANDER, J. Heywood. It Must Be Heard: a survey
of the musical life of Cleveland, 1836-1918. Cleveland:
Western Reserve Historical Society, 1982. (exhibition
catalogue)

S/A.31. BELFY, Jeanne. The Louisville Orchestra New Music
Project: an American experiment in the patronage of
international contemporary music; selected composers'
letters to the Louisville Orchestra. Louisville: University of Louisville, (1983?). 53p.

S/A.32. BERGENDORFF, Conrad. One Hundred Years of Oratorio
at Augustana: a history of the Handel Oratorio Society,
1881-1980. Rock Island, Ill.: Augustana Historical Society, 1981. 54p.

S/A.33. BRUBAKER, Robert L. Making Music Chicago Style. Chicago: Chicago Historical Society, 1985. 72p.

S/A.34. DICKSON, Harry Ellis. Arthur Fiedler and the Boston
Pops: an irreverent memoir. Boston: Houghton Mifflin,
1981. 174p.

S/A.35. GOODWIN, Francis. An Unfinished History of the Hartford
Symphony from 1934-1976; notes by Jacqueline James
Goodwin. s.l., n.p., 1984. 61p.

S/A.36. HOOGERWERF, Frank, ed. Music in Georgia. New York:
Da Capo, 1984. 343p. (collection of reprinted articles)

S/A.37. KAUFMAN, Charles H. Music in New Jersey, 1655-1860.
Rutherford, N.J.: Fairleigh Dickinson University Press,
1982. 304p.

S/A.38. LAMBERT, Barbara, ed. Music in Colonial Massachusetts
1630-1820. Vol. 2. Music in Homes and in Churches:
a conference held by the Colonial Society of Massachusetts, May 17 and 18, 1973. Boston: Colonial Society
of Massachusetts, 1985. 1194p.

S/A.39. LEDBETTER, Steven. 100 Years of the Boston Pops. Boston: Boston Symphony Orchestra, 1985. 48p.

S/A.40. PIERCE, Frank H. The Washington Saengerbund: a history
of German song and culture in the nation's capital. Washington, D.C.: The Saengerbund, 1981. 203p.

S/A.41. SCHLENKER, Alma H. Music in Bethlehem. Bethlehem, Pa.: Oaks Printing Co., 1984. 64p.

b. Operatic Life

S/A.42. EISLER, Paul E. The Metropolitan Opera: the first twenty-five years, 1883-1908. Croton-on-Hudson: North River Press, 1984. 331p.

S/A.43. HORNE, Marilyn. Marilyn Horne: my life; with James Scovell. New York: Atheneum, 1983. 258p.

S/A.44. JACOBSON, Robert. Magnificence: onstage at the Met; twenty great opera productions. New York: Simon & Schuster/Metropolitan Opera Guild, 1985. 256p.

S/A.45. McKENNA, Harold J., ed. New York City Opera Sings: stories and productions of the New York City Opera, 1944-79, by the New York City Opera Guild Archives Committee. New York: Richards Rosen Press, 1981. 404p.

S/A.46. MARTORELLA, Rosanne. The Sociology of Opera. New York: Praeger, 1982. 228p.

S/A.47. MAYER, Martin. The Met: one hundred years of grand opera. London: Thames & Hudson, 1983. 368p.

S/A.48. NASH, Elizabeth. Always First Class: the career of Geraldine Farrar. Lanham, Md.: University Press of America, 1981. 281p.

S/A.49. SMITH, Patrick J. A Year at the Met. New York: Knopf, 1983. 240p.

S/A.50. SOKOL, Martin L. The New York City Opera: an American adventure. London: Collier Macmillan, 1981. 562p.

d. Musical Instruments

(i) General works

S/A.51. LIBIN, Laurence. American Musical Instruments in the Metropolitan Museum of Art. New York: Metropolitan Museum of Art/Norton, 1985. 224p.

(ii) Organ

S/A.52. ELSWORTH, John Van Varick. The Johnson Organs: the
story of one of our famous American organbuilders;
edited by Donald R. M. Paterson. Harrisville, N.H.:
Boston Organ Club Chapter of the Organ Historical
Society, 1984. 160p.

S/A.53. FESPERMAN, John T. Flentrop in America: an account of
the work and influence of the Dutch organ builder D. A.
Flentrop in the United States, 1939-1977. Raleigh: Sunbury Press, 1981. 114p.

S/A.54. LANDON, John W. Behold the Mighty Wurlitzer: the history of the theatre pipe organ. Westport, Conn.:
Greenwood Press, 1983. 231p.

S/A.55. PAPE, Uwe, ed. Organs in America. Vol. 1. Berlin: the
author, 1982.

(iii) Piano

S/A.56. GILL, Dominic, ed. The Book of the Piano. Oxford:
Phaidon; Ithaca, N.Y.: Cornell University Press, 1981.
288p. (includes chapters on American piano music by
William Brooks, and on jazz and popular piano by Wilfrid
Mellers)

(iv) Guitar

S/A.57. DUCHOSSOIR, Andre. Gibson. Vol. 1. Winona, Minn.:
Leonard, 1981. 191p. (cover title: Gibson Electrics).

S/A.58. KIENZLE, Rich. Great Guitarists. New York: Facts on
File, 1985. 246p.

S/A.59. KOZINN, Allan, et al. The Guitar: the history, the music,
the players. New York: Morrow, 1984. 288p.

S/A.60. SALLIS, James. The Guitar Players: one instrument and
its masters in American music. New York: Morrow,
1982. 288p.

S/A.61. TOBLER, John, and GRUNDY, Stuart. Guitar Greats.
London: BBC, 1982. 191p.

S/A.62. WHEELER, Tom. American Guitars: an illustrated history;
foreword by Les Paul. New York: Harper & Row, 1982.
370p.

(v) Other

S/A.63. ADAMS, Frank. Wurlitzer Jukeboxes and Other Nice Things, 1934-1974. Seattle: AMR Publishing Co., 1983. 200p.

S/A.64. BOTTS, Rick. A Complete Identification Guide to the Wurlitzer Jukebox. Des Moines: Jukebox Collector Newsletter, 1984. 109p.

S/A.65. LYNCH, Vincent, and HENKIN, Bill. Jukeboxes: the golden age; photographs by Kazuhiro Tsurata. Berkeley: Lancaster-Miller; London: Thames & Hudson, 1981. 110p.

f. Education

S/A.66. KEENE, James A. A History of Music Education in the United States. Hanover, N.H.: University of New England, 1982. 396p.

S/A.67. SHETLER, Donald J., ed. In Memoriam Howard Hanson: the future of music education in America; proceedings of the July 1983 conference. Rochester: Eastman School of Music, 1984. 90p.

S/A.68. WENDRICH, Kenneth A. Essays on Music in American Education and Society. Washington, D.C.: University Press of America, 1982. 149p.

g. Phonograph

S/A.69. DEARLING, Robert, and DEARLING, Celia. The Guinness Book of Recorded Sound; with Brian Rust. Enfield, Middlesex: Guinness Books, 1984. 225p.

S/A.70. FROW, George L. The Edison Disc Phonographs and the Diamond Discs: a history with illustrations. Sevenoaks, Kent: the author, 1982. 280p.

B. THE MUSICAL TRADITION TO 1800

See also S/A.23, 38

S/A.71. BANDEL, Betty. Sing the Lord's Song in a Strange Land:

the life of Justin Morgan. Rutherford, N.J.: Fairleigh
Dickinson University Press, 1981. 263p.

S/A.72. BRITT, Judith S. Nothing More Agreeable: music in
George Washington's family. Mount Vernon: Mount Vernon Ladies' Association of the Union, 1984. 120p.

S/A.73. INSERRA, Lorraine, and HITCHCOCK, H. Wiley. The Music of Henry Ainsworth's Psalter (Amsterdam 1612).
Brooklyn: I.S.A.M., 1981. (I.S.A.M. Monographs, No.
15) 126p.

S/A.74. JOHNSON, H. Earle, and HEDGES, Bonnie, eds. Music
in America Before 1825. New York: Da Capo, 1985.
280p.

S/A.75. KELLER, Kate van Winkle. Popular Secular Music in
America Through 1800: a preliminary checklist of manu-
scripts in North American collections. Philadelphia:
Music Library Association, 1981. 140p.

S/A.76. TEMPERLEY, Nicholas, and MANNS, Charles G. Fuging
Tunes in the Eighteenth Century. Detroit: Information
Coordinators, 1983. 493p.

C. THE CULTIVATED TRADITION IN
THE 19TH CENTURY

C.2. Reference Works

S/A.77. GILLESPIE, John, and GILLESPIE, Anna. A Bibliography
of Nineteenth-Century American Piano Music. Westport,
Conn.: Greenwood Press, 1984. 384p.

S/A.78. WILSON, Bernard E., ed. The Newberry Library Catalog
of Early American Printed Sheet Music. Boston: G. K.
Hall, 1982. 3 vols. (covers ca. 1790-1870)

C.3. Individual Composers

WILLIAM WALLACE GILCHRIST

S/A.79. SCHLEIFER, Martha Furman. William Wallace Gilchrist
(1846-1916): a moving force in the musical life of Philadelphia. Metuchen, N.J.: Scarecrow Press, 1985. 209p.

LOUIS MOREAU GOTTSCHALK

S/A.80. DOYLE, John G. Louis Moreau Gottschalk, 1829-1869: a bibliographical study and catalog of works. Detroit: Information Coordinators, 1983. 386p.

S/A.81. KORF, William E. The Orchestral Music of Louis Moreau Gottschalk. Henryville, Pa.: Institute of Mediaeval Music, 1983. 162p.

ANTHONY PHILIP HEINRICH

S/A.82. NOBLITT, Thomas, ed. Music East and West: essays in honor of Walter Kaufman. New York: Pendragon Press, 1981. 403p. (includes "The American Indian in the Orchestral Music of Anthony Philip Heinrich," by Wilbur R. Maust)

JOHN HILL HEWITT

S/A.83. HOOGERWERF, Frank. John Hill Hewitt: sources and bibliography. Atlanta: Emory General Libraries, 1981. 42p.

SIDNEY LANIER

S/A.84. GABIN, Jane S. A Living Minstrelsy: the poetry and music of Sidney Lanier. Macon, Ga.: Mercer University Press, 1985. 192p.

LOWELL MASON

S/A.85. PEMBERTON, Carol A. Lowell Mason: his life and work. Ann Arbor: UMI Research Press, 1985. 264p.

D. THE CULTIVATED TRADITION IN THE 20TH CENTURY

D.1. 20th-Century Music in General

a. Reference Works

S/A.86. BURBANK, Richard. Twentieth Century Music; introduction by Nicolas Slonimsky. New York: Facts on File, 1984. 405p. (chronology, 1900-1979; US events are well represented)

S/A.87. EWEN, David. Composers Since 1900: a biographical and critical guide. First Supplement. New York: Wilson, 1981. 328p.

b. Historical and Critical Works

S/A.88. BATTCOCK, Gregory, ed. Breaking the Sound Barrier: a critical anthology of the new music. New York: Dutton, 1981. 351p.

S/A.89. DeLIO, Thomas. Circumscribing the Open Universe. Lanham, MD: University Press of America, 1984. 105p. (includes pieces on Babbitt and Glass, and essays by Lucier and Wolff)

S/A.90. GRIFFITHS, Paul. Modern Music: the avant garde since 1945. London: Dent, 1981. 331p.

S/A.91. WEISS, Piero, and TARUSKIN, Richard, eds. Music in the Western World: a history in documents. New York: Schirmer, 1984. 556p. (includes 20th-century US sources)

c. Electronic and Computer Music

S/A.92. DODGE, Charles, and JERSE, Thomas A. Computer Music: synthesis, composition, and performance. New York: Schirmer; London: Collier Macmillan, 1985. 381p.

S/A.93. HOLMES, Thomas B. Electronic and Experimental Music. New York: Scribner, 1985. 278p.

S/A.94. MANNING, Peter. Electronic and Computer Music. Oxford: Clarendon Press, 1985. 291p.

S/A.95. ROADS, Curtis, ed. Composers and the Computer. Los Altos: William Kaufman, 1985. 201p.

D.2. 20th-Century American Art Music

a. Reference Works

S/A.96. LUST, Patricia. American Vocal Chamber Music, 1915-1980: an annotated bibliography; foreword by Phyllis Bryn-Julson. Westport, Conn.: Greenwood Press, 1985. 273p.

S/A.97. OJA, Carol J. American Music Recordings: a discography of 20th-century U.S. composers; foreword by William Schuman. Brooklyn: I.S.A.M., 1982. 368p.

S/A.98. SOLOW, Linda, ed. Boston Composers Project: a bibliography of contemporary music. Cambridge, Mass.: MIT Press, 1983. 775p.

S/A.99. WHO'S WHO IN AMERICAN MUSIC: Classical; compiled and edited by Jaques Cattell Press. New York: Bowker, 1984. 1,000p.

b. Critical Works

S/A.100. DeLIO, Thomas, ed. Continuous Lines: issues and ideas in music of the '60s and '70's. Lanham, Md.: University Press of America, 1985. 211p. (includes pieces on Cage, Feldman, Wolff, Ashley and Lucier)

S/A.101. GAGNE, Cole, and CARAS, Tracy. Soundpieces: interviews with American composers; with introductory essays by Nicolas Slonimsky and Gilbert Chase; photographs by Gene Bagnato. Metuchen, N.J.: Scarecrow Press, 1982. 418p.

S/A.102. GARLAND, Peter. Americas: essays on American music and culture, 1973-80. Santa Fe: Soundings Press, 1982. 293p.

S/A.103. KOCH, Frederick. Reflections on Composing: four American composers: Elwell, Shepherd, Rogers, Cowell. Pittsburgh: Carnegie-Mellon University Press, 1983. 89p.

S/A.104. KRAMER, Lawrence. Music and Poetry: the 19th century and after. Berkeley: University of California Press, 1984. 251p. (includes chapters on Ives, Carter and others)

S/A.105. LEVY, Alan Howard. Musical Nationalism: American composers' search for identity. Westport, Conn.: Greenwood Press, 1983. 168p.

S/A.106. MOORE, Macdonald Smith. Yankee Blues: musical culture and American identity. Bloomington: Indiana University Press, 1985. 213p.

S/A.107. ROCKWELL, John. All American Music: composition in the late 20th century. New York: Knopf, 1983. 287p.

c. Individual Composers

GEORGE ANTHEIL

S/A.108. WHITESITT, Linda. The Life and Music of George Antheil,
          1900-1959. Ann Arbor: UMI Research Press, 1983.
          351p.

SAMUEL BARBER

S/A.109. HENNESSEE, Don A. Samuel Barber: a bio-bibliography.
          Westport, CT: Greenwood Press, 1985. 404p.

LEONARD BERNSTEIN

S/A.110. BERNSTEIN, Leonard. Findings. New York: Simon &
          Schuster, 1982. 376p.

S/A.111. GRADENWITZ, Peter. Leonard Bernstein: unendliche
          Vielfalt eines Musikers. Zurich: Atlantis, 1984.
          364p.

S/A.112. ROBINSON, Paul. Bernstein. New York: Vanguard
          Press, 1982. 152p.

JOHN CAGE

S/A.113. GENA, Peter, and BRENT, Jonathan, eds. A John Cage
          Reader; in celebration of his 70th birthday. New York:
          Peters, 1982. 207p.

S/A.114. GRIFFITHS, Paul. Cage. London: Oxford University
          Press, 1981. 50p.

ELLIOTT CARTER

S/A.115. ROSEN, Charles. The Musical Languages of Elliott Carter.
          Washington, D.C.: Library of Congress, Music Division,
          1984. 87p.

S/A.116. SCHIFF, David. The Music of Elliott Carter. London:
          Eulenburg; New York: Da Capo, 1983. 371p.

AARON COPLAND

S/A.117. BUTTERWORTH, Neil. The Music of Aaron Copland; with
          a preface by Andre Previn. London: Toccata Press,
          1985. 262p.

S/A.118. COPLAND, Aaron, and PERLIS, Vivian. Copland: 1900 through 1942. New York: St. Martin's Press; London: Faber & Faber, 1984. 402p.

S/A.119. SKOWRONSKI, JoAnn. Aaron Copland: a bio-bibliography. Westport, Conn.: Greenwood Press, 1985. 273p.

HENRY COWELL

S/A.120. MANION, Martha L. Writings About Henry Cowell: an annotated bibliography. Brooklyn: I.S.A.M., 1982. (I.S.A.M. Monographs, No. 16). 368p.

S/A.121. MEAD, Rita H. Henry Cowell's "New Music." Ann Arbor: UMI Research Press, 1981. 475p.

MORTON FELDMAN

S/A.122. FELDMAN, Morton. Essays; hrsg. von Walter Zimmermann. Kerpen, W. Germany: Beginner Press, 1985. 244p.

ELIZABETH GARRETT

S/A.123. HALL, Ruth K. A Place of Her Own: the story of Elizabeth Garrett. Rev. ed. Santa Fe: Sunstone Press, 1983. 171p.

CHARLES TOMLINSON GRIFFES

S/A.124. ANDERSON, Donna K. The Works of Charles Tomlinson Griffes: a descriptive catalogue. Ann Arbor: UMI Press, 1983. 566p.

ROY HARRIS

S/A.125. STEHMAN, Dan. Roy Harris: an American musical pioneer. Boston: Twayne, 1984. 296p.

CHARLES IVES

S/A.126. BALLANTINE, Christopher. Music and Its Social Meanings. New York: Gordon and Breach, 1984. 202p. (Chapter 4, "Charles Ives and the Meaning of Quotation in Music;" Chapter 5, a consideration of Dylan's Nashville Skyline album)

S/A.127. BURKHOLDER, J. Peter. Charles Ives: the ideas behind the music. New Haven: Yale University Press, 1985. 166p.

S/A.128. PERLIS, Vivian. Charles Ives Papers. New Haven: Yale

University Music Library, 1983. 198p. (catalogue)

S/A.129. REED, Joseph W. Three American Originals: John Ford,
William Faulkner and Charles Ives. Middletown, Conn.:
Wesleyan University Press, 1984. 228p.

EDMUND THORNTON JENKINS

S/A.130. GREEN, Jeffrey P. Edmund Thornton Jenkins: the life
and times of an American composer, 1894-1926. Westport, Conn.: Greenwood Press, 1983. 213p.

GIANCARLO MENOTTI

S/A.131. ARDOIN, John. The Stages of Menotti; photographs edited
by Gerald Fitzgerald; designed by Gregory Downer.
Garden City, N.Y.: Doubleday, 1985. 255p.

PAULINE OLIVEROS

S/A.132. VON GUNDEN, Heidi. The Music of Pauline Oliveros.
Metuchen, N.J.: Scarecrow Press, 1983. 195p.

WALTER PISTON

S/A.133. POLLACK, Howard. Walter Piston. Ann Arbor: UMI Research Press, 1982. 247p.

ROGER REYNOLDS

S/A.134. ROGER REYNOLDS: profile of a composer; with an introduction by Gilbert Chase. New York: Peters, 1982.
48p.

WALLINGFORD RIEGGER

S/A.135. SPACKMAN, Stephen. Wallingford Riegger: two essays
in musical biography. Brooklyn: I.S.A.M., 1982.
(I.S.A.M. Monographs, No. 17) 53p.

GEORGE ROCHBERG

S/A.136. ROCHBERG, George. The Aesthetics of Survival: a
composer's view of twentieth-century music; edited and
with an introduction by William Bolcom. Ann Arbor:
University of Michigan Press, 1984. 244p.

NED ROREM

S/A.137. ROREM, Ned. Setting the Tone: essays and a diary.
New York: Coward, McCann & Geoghegan, 1983.
383p.

ROGER SESSIONS

S/A.138. OLMSTEAD, Andrea. Roger Sessions and His Music. Ann
Arbor: UMI Research Press, 1985. 218p.

WILLIAM GRANT STILL

S/A.139. ARVEY, Verna. In One Lifetime; with an introduction and
notes by B. A. Nugent. Fayetteville: University of
Arkansas Press, 1984. 262p.

VIRGIL THOMSON

S/A.140. RYAN, Betsy Alayne. Gertrude Stein's Theatre of the Absolute. Ann Arbor: UMI Research Press, 1984. 232p.
(includes consideration of Four Saints in Three Acts)

S/A.141. THOMSON, Virgil. A Virgil Thomson Reader; with an introduction by John Rockwell. Boston: Houghton Mifflin,
1981. 582p.

EDGARD VARÈSE

S/A.142. BREDEL, Marc. Edgard Varèse. Paris: Mazarine, 1984.
216p.

d. 20th-Century Musical Life

S/A.143. BECKER, Howard S. Art Worlds. Berkeley: University
of California Press, 1982. 392p.

S/A.144. BOOKSPAN, Martin, and YOCKEY, Ross. Andre Previn:
a biography. Garden City: Doubleday, 1981. 398p.

S/A.145. GUSIKOFF, Lynne. Guide to Musical America. New York:
Facts on File, 1984. 347p.

S/A.146. DANIEL, Oliver. Stokowski: a counterpoint of view.
New York: Dodd, Mead, 1982. 1090p.

S/A.147. KOSTELANETZ, Andre. Echoes: memoirs of Andre Kostelanetz; in collaboration with Gloria Hammond. New
York: Harcourt Brace Jovanovich, 1981. 247p.

S/A.148. LEDERMAN, Minna. The Life and Death of a Small Magazine: (Modern Music, 1924-1946). Brooklyn: I.S.A.M.,
1983. (I.S.A.M. Monographs, No. 18) 211p.

S/A.149. LICHTENWANGER, William, ed. Oscar Sonneck and

American Music; with a foreword by Irving Lowens.
Urbana: University of Illinois Press, 1983. 277p.

S/A.150. McINTOSH, Ruskin. Helen Rice, the Great Lady of Chamber Music. Burlington, Vt.: George Little Press, 1983.
191p.

S/A.151. MARTIN, George. The Damrosch Dynasty: America's
first family of music. Boston: Houghton Mifflin,
1983. 526p.

S/A.152. RUTTENCUTTER, Helen Drees. Previn. New York: St.
Martin's Press; London: Michael Joseph, 1985. 234p.

S/A.153. SILET, Charles L. P. The Writings of Paul Rosenfeld:
an annotated bibliography. New York: Garland, 1981.
214p.

S/A.154. TAWA, Nicholas E. Serenading the Reluctant Eagle:
American musical life 1925-1945. New York: Schirmer;
London: Collier Macmillan, 1984. 261p.

E. THE MUSIC OF THE AMERICAN INDIAN

See also S/A.170

S/A.155. BIERHORST, John. The Sacred Path: spells, prayers
and power songs of the American Indians. New York:
Morrow, 1983. 191p.

S/A.156. BOYD, Maurice. Kiowa Voices: ceremonial dance, ritual
and song. Vol. 1. Fort Worth: Texas Christian University Press, 1981. 164p.

S/A.157. CLEMENTS, William M., and MALPEZZI, Frances M.
Native American Folklore, 1879-1979: an annotated
bibliography. Athens, Ohio: Swallow Press, 1984.
247p.

S/A.158. GILL, Sam D. Sacred Words: a study of Navajo religion
and prayer. Westport, Conn.: Greenwood Press,
1981. 257p.

S/A.159. HETH, Charlotte, ed. Sharing a Heritage: American Indian arts. Los Angeles: American Indian Studies
Center, 1984. 214p. (includes "Update on Indian Music," by Charlotte Heth)

S/A.160. HOWARD, James H. Shawnee! the ceremonialism of a native Indian tribe and its cultural background. Athens: Ohio University Press, 1981. 454p.

S/A.161. LACZKO, Gina. Apache Music and Musical Instruments. Mesa, Ariz.: Mesa Museum, 1981. 26p.

S/A.162. MURIE, James R. Ceremonies of the Pawnee. Washington, D.C.: Smithsonian Institution Press, 1981. 2 vols.

S/A.163. SWANN, Brian, ed. Smoothing the Ground: essays on native American oral literature. Berkeley: University of California Press, 1983. 364p.

S/A.164. VENNUM, Thomas. The Ojibwa Dance Drum: its history and construction. Washington, D.C., 1983. 320p.

F. FOLK MUSIC

F.1. General Works on Folk Music

S/A.165. BERMAN, Leslie, and WOOD, Heather, eds. Grass Roots International Folk Resource Directory. New York: Grass Roots, 1985. 198p.

S/A.166. BRUNNINGS, Florence E. Folk Song Index: a comprehensive guide to the Florence E. Brunnings Collection. New York: Garland, 1981. 357p.

S/A.167. LIFTON, Sarah. The Listener's Guide to Folk Music. New York: Facts on File; Poole, Dorset: Blandford Press, 1983. 140p.

S/A.168. TITON, Jeff Todd, ed. Worlds of Music: an introduction to the music of the world's peoples. New York: Schirmer, 1984. 325p. + cassettes

F.2. Folk Music in the United States

a. Reference

S/A.169. BOGGS, Beverly B., and PATTERSON, Daniel W. An Index of Selected Folk Recordings: a user's guide to a microfiche index of five hundred recordings of traditional music and speech performances from the United States and related countries.... Chapel Hill: University of North Carolina, Curriculum in Folklore, 1984. 75p.

S/A.170. THE FEDERAL CYLINDER PROJECT: a guide to field cylinder collections in federal agencies. Washington, D.C.: Library of Congress, American Folklife Center, 1984- (Vol. 1, ed. Erika Brady et al., 1984; Vol. 2, ed. Judith Gray et al., 1985)

S/A.171. RASAF, Henry. The Folk, Country and Bluegrass Musician's Catalogue. New York: St. Martin's Press, 1982. 192p.

S/A.172. WASSERMAN, Paul, ed. Festivals Sourcebook. 2nd ed. Detroit: Gale Research Co., 1984. 721p.

b. General Studies

S/A.173. FERRIS, William, and HART, Mary L., eds. Folk Music and Modern Sound. University: University of Mississippi Center for the Study of Southern Culture, 1982. 215p.

S/A.174. FORUCCI, Samuel L. A Folk History of America: America through its songs. Englewood Cliffs, N.J.: Prentice-Hall, 1984. 256p.

F.3. Anglo-American Folk Song
Studies and Collections

S/A.175. BURTON, Thomas G. Some Ballad Folks; Annette L. Burton, music editor. Boone, N.C.: Appalachian Consortium Press, 1981. 108p.

S/A.176. DARLING, Charles W. The New American Songster: traditional ballads and songs of North America. Lanham, Md.: University Press of America, 1983. 388p.

S/A.177. PORTER, James, ed. The Ballad Image: essays presented to Bertrand Harris Bronson; with a foreword by Wayland D. Hand. Los Angeles: Center for the Study of Comparative Folklore & Mythology, 1983. 202p.

S/A.178. WARNER, Anne, ed. Traditional American Folk Songs From the Anne & Frank Warner Collection; Jeff Warner, associate editor; Jerome S. Epstein, music editor, foreword by Alan Lomax. Syracuse: Syracuse University Press, 1984. 501p.

F.4. Other Ethnic Groups

a. General

See also Section I.3.6

S/A.179. ETHNIC RECORDINGS IN AMERICA: a neglected heritage. Washington, D.C.: Library of Congress, American Folklife Center, 1982. 269p.

S/A.180. TAWA, Nicholas E. A Sound of Strangers: musical culture, acculturation, an the post-Civil War ethnic American. Metuchen, N.J.: Scarecrow Press, 1982. 304p.

b. Spanish-American

S/A.181. BERGMAN, Billy, et al.. Hot Sauces: Latin and Caribbean Pop. New York: Morrow, 1985. 143p.

_____. Reggae and Latin Pop: hot sauces. Poole, Dorset: Blandford Press, 1985. 143p. (includes salsa and rhythm & blues)

S/A.182. PEÑA, Manuel H. The Texas-Mexican Conjunto: history of a working-class music. Austin: University of Texas Press, 1985. 218p.

c. Other Groups

S/A.183. JANTA, Aleksander. A History of Nineteenth Century American Polish Music. New York: Kosciuszko Foundation, 1982. 186p.

S/A.184. RIDDLE, Ronald. Flying Dragons, Flowing Streams: music in the life of San Francisco's Chinese. Westport, Conn.: Greenwood Press, 1983. 329p.

F.5.   Regional Studies and Collections

ALABAMA

S/A.185. BROWN, Virginia Pounds, and OWENS, Laurella. Toting
the Lead Row: Ruby Pickens Tartt, Alabama folklorist
University: University of Alabama Press, 1981. 180p.

APPALACHIA

S/A.186. BROSI, George, et al., eds. Appalachian Literature and
Music: a comprehensive catalogue. Berea, Ky.:
Appalachian Book & Record Store, 1981. 80p.

S/A.187. WHISNANT, David E. All That Is Native and Fine: the
politics of culture in an American region. Chapel Hill:
University of North Carolina Press, 1983. 340p.

FLORIDA

S/A.188. HARPER, Francis, and PRESLEY, Delma E. Okefinokee
Album. Athens: University of Georgia Press, 1981.
194p.

GEORGIA

S/A.189. ROSENBAUM, Art, and ROSENBAUM, Margo Newark.
Folk Visions and Voices: traditional music and song in
North Georgia. Athens; University of Georgia Press,
1983. 240p.

KANSAS

S/A.190. CHINN, Jennie A., ed. Folk Roots: an exploration of
the folk arts and cultural traditions of Kansas. Manhattan, Kans.: University for Man, 1982. 31p.

KENTUCKY

See also S/A.232

S/A.191. FEINTUCH, Burt. Kentucky Folkmusic: an annotated
bibliography. Lexington: University Press of Kentucky, 1985. 105p.

S/A.192. HIGH, Ellen Clay. Past Titan Rock: journeys into an
Appalachian valley. Lexington: University Press of
Kentucky, 1984. 183p.

NEW ENGLAND

S/A.193. LEMAY, J. A. Leo. "New England's Arrogances": America's first folk song. Cranbury, N.J.: Associated University Presses for the University of Delaware Press, 1985. 163p.

NEW YORK

S/A.194. CAZDEN, Norman. Folk Songs of the Catskills. Albany: State University of New York Press, 1982. 650p.

S/A.195. _____. Notes and Sources for Folk Songs of the Catskills. Albany: State University of New York Press, 1981. 180p.

OZARKS

S/A.196. COCHRAN, Robert. Vance Randolph: an Ozark life. Urbana: University of Illinois Press, 1985. 284p.

SOUTH DAKOTA

S/A.197. KREITZER, Jack, and BRAUNSTEIN, Susan, eds. A Living Tradition: South Dakota Songwriter's Songbook. Vol. 1. Sioux Falls: George B. German Music Archives, 1983. 147p. (contemporary song collection)

TEXAS

S/A.198. ABERNETHY, Francis Edward, ed. Singin' Texas. Dallas: E-Heart Press, 1983. 183p.

S/A.199. BAUMAN, Richard, and ABRAHAMS, Roger D., eds. "And Other Neighborly Names": social process and cultural image in Texas folklore. Austin: University of Texas Press, 1981. 321p. (includes essays on corridos by John Holmes McDonald, on country music in Austin, by Archie Green, and on conjuntos, by Manuel H. Peña)

S/A.200. CASEY, Betty. Dance Across Texas. Austin: University of Texas Press, 1985. 135p.

S/A.201. OWENS, William A. Tell Me a Story, Sing Me a Song: a Texas chronicle. Austin: University of Texas Press, 1983. 328p.

S/A.202. WILLOUGHBY, Larry. Texas Rhythm, Texas Rhyme: a pictorial history of Texas music. Austin: Texas Monthly Press, 1984. 144p.

WEST VIRGINIA

S/A.203. CUTHBERT, John A., ed. West Virginia Folk Music: a
descriptive guide to field recordings in the West Virginia and Regional History Collection. Morgantown:
West Virginia University Press, 1982. 185p.

F.6. Instrumental Folk Music

See also Section A.7.d

S/A.204. ALVEY, R. Gerald. Dulcimer Maker: the craft of Homer
Ledford. Lexington: University Press of Kentucky,
1984. 186p.

S/A.205. BEHAGUE, Gerard, ed. Performance Practice: ethnomu-
sicological perspectives. Westport, Conn.: Greenwood
Press, 1984. 262p. (includes "American Traditional
Fiddling: performance contexts and techniques," by
Linda C. Burman-Hall)

S/A.206. GROCE, Nancy. The Hammered Dulcimer in America.
Washington, D.C.: Smithsonian Institution Press,
1983. 93p.

F.7. The Religious Folk Song Tradition
of White Americans

S/A.207. PATTERSON, Daniel W. Gift Drawing and Gift Song: a
study of two forms of Shaker inspiration. Sabbathday
Lake, Me.: United Society of Shakers, 1983. 112p.

F.8. Occupational Folk Song

a. General

S/A.208. REUSS, Richard A., ed. Songs of American Labor, In-
dustrialization and the Urban Work Experience: a
discography. Ann Arbor: University of Michigan,
Labor Studies Center, 1983. 109p.

S/A.209. SEEGER, Pete, and REISER, Bob. Carry It On: a history in song and pictures of the working men and
women of America. New York: Simon & Schuster,
1985; Poole, Dorset: Blandford Press, 1986. 256p.

b. Cowboys

S/A.210. McCLURE, Dorothy May. The World Famous Cowboy Band, 1923-1973: a history of the first fifty years of the Cowboy Band, Hardin-Simmons University, Abilene, Texas. Abilene: Hardin-Simmons University, 1983. 299p.

S/A.211. TINSLEY, Jim Bob. He Was Singin' This Song: a collection of forty-eight songs of the American cowboy. Gainesville: University Press of Florida, 1982. 255p.

c. Miners

S/A.212. GARLAND, Jim. Welcome the Traveler Home: Jim Garland's story of the Kentucky mountains; edited by Julia S. Ardery. Lexington: University Press of Kentucky, 1983. 231p.

d. Railroads

S/A.213. COHEN, Norm. Long Steel Rail: the railroad in American folksong. Urbana: University of Illinois Press, 1981. 710p.

S/A.214. LYLE, Katie Letcher. Scalded to Death by Steam: authentic stories of railroad disasters and the ballads that were written about them. Chapel Hill: Algonquin Books, 1983. 212p.

F.9. Protest and Social Song Movements

S/A.215. DUNAWAY, David King. How Can I Keep From Singing? Pete Seeger. New York: McGraw-Hill, 1981. 380p.

S/A.216. PHILBIN, Marianne, ed. Give Peace a Chance: music and the struggle for peace. Chicago: Chicago Review Press, 1983. 122p. (exhibition catalogue)

F.11. Country Music

a. General Reference Works and Discography

S/A.217. BUTTERFIELD, Arthur. Encyclopedia of Country Music.

London: Multimedia Publications, 1985. 192p.

S/A.218. KINGSBURY'S WHO'S WHO IN COUNTRY AND WESTERN
MUSIC. Culver City, Calif.: Black Stallion Country
Press, 1981. 304p.

S/A.219. SMYTH, Willie. Country Music Recorded Prior to 1943:
a discography of LP reissues. Los Angeles: John
Edwards Memorial Foundation, 1984. (Special Series,
No. 14) 83p.

b. Miscellaneous Guides and Surveys

S/A.220. HAGAN, Chet. The Great Country Music Book. New
York: Pocket Books, 1983. 189p.

S.A.221. HUME, Martha. You're So Cold I'm Turning Blue: Martha
Hume's guide to the greatest in country music. New
York: Viking; Harmondsworth: Penguin, 1982. 202p.

S/A.222. KASH, Murray. Murray Kash's Book of Country. London:
Star Books, 1981. 509p.

S/A.223. MASON, Michael, ed. The Country Music Book. New
York: Scribner, 1985. 421p.

S/A.224. MORTHLAND, John. The Best of Country Music. Garden
City, N.Y.: Doubleday, 1984. 436p. (Record guide)

S/A.225. OERMANN, Robert K. The Listener's Guide to Country
Music. New York: Facts on File; Poole, Dorset:
Blandford Press, 1983. 137p.

S/A.226. WOOTTON, Richard. The Illustrated Country Almanac.
London: Virgin Books, 1982. 186p.

c. Songs and Songwriting

S/A.227. ETTEMA, James S., and WHITNEY, D. Charles, eds.
Individuals in Mass Media Organizations: creativity
and constraint. Beverly Hills: Sage Publications,
1982. 300p. (includes "The Product Image: the fate
of creativity in country music songwriting," by John
Ryan and Richard A. Peterson)

S/A.228. ROGERS, Jimmie N. The Country Music Message: all
about lovin' and livin'. Englewood Cliffs, N.J.:
Prentice-Hall, 1983. 208p.

d. History and Criticism

    (i) Bluegrass

S/A.229. CANTWELL, Robert. Bluegrass Breakdown: the making
          of the old Southern sound. Urbana: University of
          Illinois Press, 1984. 309p.

S/A.230. KOCHMAN, Marilyn, ed. The Big Book of Bluegrass.
          New York: Morrow, 1984. 277p.

S/A.231. ROSENBERG, Neil V. Bluegrass: a history. Urbana:
          University of Illinois Press, 1985. 447p.

e. Regions and Places

    See also S/A.202

KENTUCKY

S/A.232. WOLFE, Charles K. Kentucky Country: folk and country
          music of Kentucky. Lexington: University Press of
          Kentucky, 1984. 199p.

TENNESSEE

See also S/A.242

S/A.233. BURTON, Thomas G., ed. Tom Ashley, Sam McGee,
          Bukka White: Tennessee traditional singers. Knox-
          ville: University of Tennessee Press, 1981. 240p.

S/A.234. DUFF, Arlie. Y'all Come--Country Music: Jack's
          branch to Nashville. Austin: Eakin Press, 1983.
          194p.

S/A.235. LOMAX, John, III. Nashville: Music City USA. New
          York: Abrams, 1985. 224p.

VIRGINIA

S/A.236. CRUMP, George D. Write It Down: a history of country
          music in Hampton Roads. Norfolk, Va.: Donning,
          1985. 142p.

WEST VIRGINIA

S/A.237. TRIBE, Ivan M. Mountaineer Jamboree: country music
          in West Virginia. Lexington: University Press of
          Kentucky, 1984. 233p.

f. Musicians

   (i) Collected Profiles

S/A.238. BUSNAR, Gene. Superstars of Country Music. New
        York: Messner, 1984. 239p.

S/A.239. BYWORTH, Tony. Giants of Country Music. London:
        Hamlyn, 1984. 224p.

S/A.240. FARAH, Cynthia. Country Music: a look at the men who
        made it. El Paso: C. M. Pub., 1981. 76p.

S/A.241. HAGAN, Chet. Country Music Legends in the Hall of
        Fame. Nashville: Country Music Foundation, 1982.
        256p.

   (ii) Individuals

ROY ACUFF

S/A.242. ACUFF, Roy. Roy Acuff's Nashville: the life and good
        times of country music. New York: Perigree Books,
        1983. 224p.

S/A.243. GREEN, Douglas B., and GRUHN, George. Roy Acuff's
        Musical Collection at Opryland. Nashville: WSM, 1982.
        85p.

ALABAMA

S/A.244. MORRIS, Edward. Alabama. Chicago: Contemporary
        Books, 1985. 109p.

PAT BOONE

S/A.245. BOONE, Pat. A New Song. Nashville: Impact Books,
        1981. 192p.

CARTER FAMILY

S/A.246. CARTER, Janette. Living With Memories. Hilton, Va.:
        Carter Family Memorial Center, 1983. 83p.

JOHNNY CASH

S/A.247. SMITH, John L. The Johnny Cash Discography. West-
        port, Conn.: Greenwood Press, 1985. 205p.

PATSY CLINE

S/A.248. NASSOUR, Ellis. Patsy Cline. New York: Tower Publications, 1981. 410p.

LESTER FLATT

S/A.249. LAMBERT, Jake. "The Good Things in Life Outweigh the
Bad": a biography of Lester Flatt. Rev. ed. Hender-
sonville, Tenn.: Jay-Lyn Publications, 1982. 178p.

LEFTY FRIZZELL

S/A.250. WOLFE, Charles. Lefty Frizzell: his life, his music;
with discography by Richard Weize and Charles Wolfe.
Bremen, W. Germany: Bear Family Records, 1984.
99p.

MERLE HAGGARD

S/A.251. HAGGARD, Merle, and RUSSELL, Peggy. Sing Me Back
Home. New York: Times Books, 1981. 287p.

WAYLON JENNINGS

S/A.252. DENISOFF, R. Serge. Waylon. Knoxville: University of
Tennessee Press, 1983. 368p.

GEORGE JONES

S/A.253. ALLEN, Bob. George Jones: the saga of an American
singer. Garden City, N.Y.: Doubleday, 1984. 291p.

S/A.254. CARLISLE, Dolly. Ragged But Right: the life and times
of George Jones. Chicago: Contemporary Books, 1984.
250p.

GRANDPA JONES

S/A.255. JONES, Louis M. "Grandpa." Everybody's Grandpa:
fifty years behind the mike; with Charles K. Wolfe.
Knoxville: University of Tennessee Press, 1984. 258p.

BASCOM LAMAR LUNSFORD

S/A.256. JONES, Loyal. Minstrel of the Appalachians: the story of
Bascom Lamar Lunsford; music transcribed by John M.
Forbes. Boone, N.C.: Appalachian Consortium Press,
1984. 249p.

HARRY McCLINTOCK

S/A.257. YOUNG, Henry. "Haywire Mac" and the "Big Rock Candy Mountain." s.l.: Stillhouse Hollow Publishers, 1981. 80p. (available from the author, 213 E. Victory Ave., Temple, Texas 76501)

BARBARA MANDRELL

S/A.258. MANDRELL, Louise, and COLLINS, Ace. The Mandrell Family Album. New York: N.A.L., 1983. 250p.

WILLIE NELSON

S/A.259. BANE, Michael. Willie: an unauthorized biography of Willie Nelson. New York: Dell, 1984. 253p.

S/A.260. SCOBEY, Lola. Willie Nelson, Country Outlaw. New York: Kensington, 1982. 414p.

DOLLY PARTON

S/A.261. CARAEFF, Ed. Dolly: close up/up close; photographed by Ed Caraeff; text by Richard Amdur. New York: Delilah; London: Sidgwick & Jackson, 1983. 90p.

S/A.262. WILLADEENE. In the Shadow of a Song: the story of the Parton family. New York: Bantam Books, 1985. 236p.

CHARLIE POOLE

S/A.263. RORRER, Clifford Kinney. Rambling Blues: the life and songs of Charlie Poole. London: Old Time Music, 1982. 104p.

JEANNIE C. RILEY

S/A.264. RILEY, Jeannie C. From Harper Valley to the Mountain Top. Lincoln, Va.: Chosen Books; Eastbourne, Sussex: Kingsway, 1981. 211p.

STANLEY BROTHERS

S/A.265. REID, Gary B. Stanley Brothers: a preliminary discography. Roanoke, Va.: Copper Creek Publications, 1984. unpaged.

S/A.266. WRIGHT, John. Ralph Stanley and the Clinch Mountain Boys: a discography. Evanston, Ill.: the author, 1983. 44p.

MEL TILLIS

S/A.267. TILLIS, Mel. Stutterin' Boy: the autobiography of Mel Tillis, America's beloved star of country music. New York: Rawson, 1984. 270p.

ERNEST TUBB

S/A.268. BARTHEL, Norma. Ernest Tubb, the Original E.T. Roland, Okla.: Country Roads Publications, 1984. 97p.

SLIM WHITMAN

S/A.269. GIBBLE, Kenneth L. Mr. Songman: the Slim Whitman story. Elgin, Ill.: Brethren Press, 1982. 158p.

HANK WILLIAMS

S/A.270. FLIPPO, Chet. Your Cheatin' Heart: a biography of Hank Williams. New York: Simon & Schuster, 1981; London: Eeel Pie, 1982. 251p.

S/A.271. KOON, George William. Hank Williams: a bio-bibliography. Westport, CT: Greenwood Press, 1983. 180p.

BOB WILLS

S/A.272. KINEZLE, Rich. Papa's Jumpin': the MGM years of Bob Wills. Bremen, W. Germany: Bear Family Records, 1985. 31p.

F.12. Cajun Music

S/A.273. ANCELET, Barry Jean. The Makers of Cajun Music/Musiciens cadiens et créoles. Austin: University of Texas Press, 1984. 160p.

S/A.274. BROVEN, John. South to Louisiana: the music of the Cajun bayous. Gretna, La.: Pelican, 1983. 368p.

S/A.275. SAVOY, Ann Allen, ed. Cajun Music: a reflection of a people. Vol. 1. Eunice, La.: Bluebird Press, 1984. 418p.

G. BLACK MUSIC

G.1. Black Music in Works on
Black Culture and Society

a. Reference

S/A.276. ENCYCLOPEDIA OF BLACK AMERICA; W. Augustus Low, editor; Virgil A. Clift, associate editor. New York: McGraw-Hill, 1981. 921p.

S/A.277. KELLNER, Bruce, ed. The Harlem Renaissance: a historical dictionary for the era. Westport, Conn.: Greenwood Press, 1984. 476p.

S/A.278. NEWMAN, Richard, ed. Black Access: a bibliography of Afro-American bibliographies. Westport, Conn.: Greenwood Press, 1984. 294p.

b. Histories, Studies

S/A.279. ANDERSON, Jervis. This Was Harlem: a cultural portrait, 1900-1950. New York: Farrar, Straus & Giroux, 1982. 389p.
_____. Harlem: the great black way, 1900-1950. London: Orbis, 1982. 389p.

S/A.280. BARAKA, Amiri. The Autobiography of Leroi Jones/Amiri Baraka. New York: Freundlich Books, 1984. 329p.

S/A.281. LENZ, Günter H., ed. History and Tradition in Afro-American Culture. Frankfurt: Campus Verlag, 1984. 334p. (subjects include toasts and worksongs, jazz innovation (Shepp), John Coltrane and the poetry of Michael Harper)

S/A.282. LEWIS, David Levering. When Harlem Was in Vogue. New York: Knopf, 1981. 381p.

S/A.283. NEILSON, Kenneth P. The World of Langston Hughes Music. Hollis, N.Y.: All Seasons Art, 1982. 100p. (bibliography and discography of settings of Hughes' writings)

S/A.284. OSTENDORF, Berndt. Black Literature in White America. Brighton: Harvester Press; Totowa, N.J.: Barnes & Noble, 1982. 171p.

G.2.   Black Music--General Works

a.   Reference

S/A.285.   BROWN, Rae Linda.   Music, Printed and Manuscript, in
the James Weldon Johnson Collection of Negro Arts and
Letters: an annotated catalog.   New York: Garland,
1982.   348p.

S/A.286.   CLIFFORD, Mike, et al.   The Illustrated Encyclopedia of
Black Music; consultant Mike Clifford; authors Jan
Futrell (et al.); editor Ray Bonds.   London: Salaman-
der; New York: Harmony Books, 1982.   224p.

S/A.287.   DE LERMA, Dominique-René.   Bibliography of Black Music.
Vols. 1-4.   Westport, CT: Greenwood Press, 1981-84.
(essential work; volumes so far for reference materials,
Afro-American idioms, geographical studies, theory and
education)

S/A.288.   FLOYD, Samuel A., and REISSNER, Marsha J.   Black Music in the United States: an annotated bibliography of
selected references and research materials.   Milwood,
N.Y.:   Kraus, 1983.   234p.

S/A.289.   GRAY, Arlene E.   Listen to the Lambs: a source book of
the R. Nathaniel Dett materials in the Niagara Falls
Public Library, Niagara Falls.   (Niagara Falls, N.Y.:
Niagara Falls Public Library?):   1984.   293p.

S/A.290.   MEADOWS, Eddie S.   Theses and Dissertations on Black
American Music.   Beverly Hills: Theodore Front,
1982.   19p.

S/A.291.   SKOWRONSKI, JoAnn.   Black Music in America: a bibliography.   Metuchen, N.J.:   Scarecrow Press, 1981.
722p.   (14,319 references)

b.   Critical Studies

S/A.292.   BALMIR, Guy-Claude.   Du chant au poème: essai de lit-
térature sur le chant et le poésie populaire des noirs
américains.   Paris: Payot, 1982.   384p.

S/A.293.   BROOKS, Tilford.   America's Black Musical Heritage.
Englewood Cliffs, N.J.:   Prentice-Hall, 1984.   336p.

S/A/294.   HAYDON, Geoffrey, and MARKS, Dennis, eds.

Repercussions: a celebration of Afro-American music. London: Century Publishing, 1985. 192p.

S/A.295. JACKSON, Irene V., ed. More Than Dancing: essays on Afro-American music and musicians. Westport, Conn.: Greenwood Press, 1985. 281p.

S/A.296. KEBEDE, Ashenofi. Roots of Black Music: the vocal, instrumental, and dance heritage of Africa and black America. Englewood Cliffs, N.J.: Prentice-Hall, 1982. 162p.

c. Collected Biography

S/A.297. HANDY, D. Antoinette. Black Women in American Bands and Orchestras. Metuchen, N.J.: Scarecrow Press, 1981. 319p.

S/A.298. SOUTHERN, Eileen. Biographical Dictionary of Afro-American and African Musicians. Westport, Conn.: Greenwood Press, 1981. 478p.

G.3. Black Concert Music Tradition

a. Reference

S/A.299. DE LERMA, Dominique-René. Concert Music and Spirituals: a selective discography. Nashville: Institute for Research in Black American Music, Fisk University, 1981. 44p.

S/A.300. TISCHLER, Alice. Fifteen Black American Composers: a bibliography of their works; with the assistance of Carol Tomasic. Detroit: Information Coordinators, 1981. 328p.

S/A.301. WHITE, Evelyn Davidson. Choral Music by Afro-American Composers: a selected, annotated bibliography. Metuchen, N.J.: Scarecrow Press, 1981. 167p.

b. Studies

S/A.302. GREEN, Mildred Denby. Black Women Composers: a genesis. Boston: Twayne, 1983. 171p.

S/A.303. SAMUELS, William Everett. Union and the Black Musician:

the narrative of William Everett Samuels and Chicago
Local 208; edited by Donald Spivey. Lanham, Md.:
University Press of America, 1984. 150p.

c. Individuals

S/A.304. CAZORT, Jean E., and HOBSON, Constance Tibbs. Born
to Play: the life and career of Hazel Harrison. Westport, Conn.: Greenwood Press, 1983. 245p.

S/A.305. DAVIS, Lenwood G. A Paul Robeson Research Guide: a
selected, annotated bibliography. Westport, Conn.:
Greenwood Press, 1982. 879p.

S/A.306. ROBESON, Susan. The Whole World in His Hands: a pictorial biography of Paul Robeson. Secaucus, N.J.:
Citadel Press, 1985. 254p.

S/A.307. SIMS, Janet L. Marian Anderson: an annotated bibliography and discography. Westport, Conn.: Greenwood
Press, 1981. 243p.

S/A.308. WESTLAKE, Neda M., and ALBRECHT, Otto E. Marian
Anderson: a catalog of the collection at the University
of Pennsylvania Library. Philadelphia: University of
Pennsylvania Press, 1981. 89p.

G.5. Folk Song

S/A.309. WILLIAMS, Brett. John Henry: a bio-bibliography.
Westport, Conn.: Greenwood Press, 1983. 175p.

G.6. Spirituals and Religious Music (except Gospel)

See also S/A.289, 299

G.7. Ragtime

S/A.310. HASSE, John Edward, ed. Ragtime: its history, composers, and music. New York: Schirmer; London:
Macmillan, 1985. 400p.

G.8.   Blues and Race Records (except Gospel)

a.   Reference

S/A.311.   GURALNICK, Peter.   Listener's Guide to the Blues.   New
York: Quarto; Poole, Dorset: Blandford Press, 1982.
138p.

S/A.312.   RUPPLI, Michel.   The Chess Labels.   Westport, Conn.:
Greenwood Press, 1983.   2 vols.   (Discography)

S/A.313.   TAFT, Michael.   Blues Lyric Poetry: a concordance.
New York: Garland, 1984.   3 vols.

b.   Mainly Historical

S/A.314.   BASKERVILLE, Stephen W., and WILLETT, Ralph, eds.
Nothing Else to Fear: new perspectives on America in
the thirties.   Manchester: Manchester University Press,
1985.   294p.   (includes "'Sales Tax On It':   race
records in the New Deal years," by Paul Oliver)

S/A.315.   CHARTERS, Samuel.   The Roots of the Blues: an African
search.   London: Boyars, 1981.   151p.

S/A.316.   KIRBY, Edward "Prince Gabe."   From Africa to Beale
Street.   Memphis: Musical Management, 1983.   176p.

c.   Regional Studies

See also S/A.202, 233

S/A.317.   GOVENAR, Alan.   Living Texas Blues.   Dallas: Dallas
Museum of Art, 1985.   88p.

S/A.318.   GUIDA, Louis, et al.   Blues Music in Arkansas.   Philadelphia: Portfolio Associates, 1983.   26p.

S/A.319.   McKEE, Margaret, and CHISENHALL, Fred.   Beale Black
and Blue: life and music on black America's main street.
Baton Rouge: Louisiana State University Press, 1981.
265p.

d. Individuals

ROBERT JOHNSON

S/A.320. GREENBERG, Alan. Love in Vain: the life and legend
of Robert Johnson. Garden City, N.Y.: Doubleday,
1983. 252p.

MANCE LIPSCOMB

S/A.321. LIPSCOMB, Mance, and MYERS, A. Glenn. I Say Me for
a Parable: the life and music of Mance Lipscomb. El
Rito, N.M.: Possum Heard, 1982. unpaged.

ROBERT NIGHTHAWK

S/A.322. LORENZ, Wolfgang. Robert Nighthawk: complete discography, 1936-1967. Bonn: the author, 1963. 15p.

MA RAINEY

S/A.323. LIEB, Sandra. Mother of the Blues: a study of Ma
Rainey. Amherst: University of Massachusetts Press,
1981. 226p.

BESSIE SMITH

S/A.324. BROOKS, Edward. The Bessie Smith Companion: a crit-
ical and detailed appreciation of the recordings.
Wheathampstead, Herts: Cavendish; New York: Da
Capo, 1983. 229p.

S/A.325. FEINSTEIN, Elaine. Bessie Smith. New York: Viking,
1985. 104p.

JOE WILLIAMS

S/A.326. GOURSE, Leslie. Everyday: the story of Joe Williams.
London: Quartet Books, 1985. 208p.

e. Interpretation

S/A.327. BAKER, Houston A. Blues, Ideology, and Afro-American
Literature: a vernacular theory. Chicago: University of Chicago Press, 1984. 227p.

S/A.328. DAUER, Alfons Michael. Blues aus 100 Jahren: 43
Beispiele zur Typologie der vokalen Bluesform. Frankfurt: Fischer, 1983. 222p.

S/A.329. EVANS, David. Big Road Blues: tradition and creativity
          in the folk blues. Berkeley: University of California
          Press, 1982. 379p.

S/A.330. FEDEREGHI, Luciano. Blues nel mio animo: temi e poesia
          del blues. Milan: Mondadori, 1981. 231p.

S/A.331. HERZHAFT, Gerard. Le blues. Paris: Presses Universi-
          taires Françaises, 1981. 128p.

S/A.332. OLIVER, Paul. Blues Off the Record: thirty years of
          blues commentary. Tunbridge Wells: Baton Press;
          New York: Hippocrene Books, 1984; Exeter, etc.:
          IASPM, 1986. 297p.

S/A.333. OLIVER, Paul. Songsters and Saints: vocal traditions on
          race records. Cambridge: Cambridge University Press,
          1984. 339p.

S/A.334. PALMER, Robert. Deep Blues. New York: Viking, 1981.
          310p.

S/A.335. PEARSON, Barry Lee. "Sounds So Good to Me": the
          bluesman's story. Philadelphia: University of Pennsyl-
          vania Press, 1984. 175p.

S/A.336. SPRINGER, Robert. Le blues authentique: son histoire
          et ses thèmes. Paris: Filipacchi, 1985. 239p.

S/A.337. VENTURINI, Fabrizio. Sulle strade del blues. Milan:
          Gammalibri, 1984. 466p.

S/A.338. YOURCENAR, Marguerite. Blues & gospels. Paris:
          Gallimard, 1984. 192p.

f. Collections of Music and Texts

S/A.339. OLIVER, Paul, ed. Early Blues Songbook. London:
          Wise, 1982. 192p.

S/A.340. TAFT, Michael. Blues Lyric Poetry: an anthology. New
          York: Garland, 1983. 378p.

S/A.341. TITON, Jeff Todd, ed. Downhome Blues Lyrics: an an-
          thology from the post-War II era. Boston: Twayne,
          1981. 214p.

G.9. Rhythm & Blues, Soul, Gospel

a. Rhythm & Blues

(i) History and Reference

S/A.342. ALSMANN, Götz. Nichts als Krach: die unabhängigen
Schallplattenfirmen und die Entwicklung der ameri-
kanischen populären Musik, 1943-1963. Drensteinfurt:
Huba, 1985. 160p.

S/A.343. HANNUSCH, Jeff. I Hear You Knockin': the sound of
New Orleans rhythm and blues. Ville Platte, La.:
Swallow Publications, 1985. 374p.

S/A.344. McGOWAN, James A. Hear Today! Hear to Stay! a personal history of rhythm & blues. St. Petersburg, Fla.:
Sixth House Press, 1983. 194p.

S/A.345. PAVLOW, Big Al. The R & B Book: a disc-history of
rhythm & blues. Providence, R.I.: Music House,
Publishing, 1984. 111p.

S/A.346. RUPPLI, Michel. The King Labels: a discography.
Westport, Conn.: Greenwood Press, 1985. 2 vols.

(ii) Individuals

CHUCK BERRY

S/A.347. DeWitt, Howard A. Chuck Berry: rock 'n' roll music.
Fremont, Calif.: Horizon Books, 1981. 228p.
_____. _____. 2nd ed. Ann Arbor: Pierian Press,
1985. 291p.

S/A.348. REESE, Krista. Chuck Berry: Mr. Rock 'n' Roll. London: Proteus, 1984. 128p.

PROFESSOR LONGHAIR

S/A.349. CROSBY, John. Professor Longhair: a biodiscography.
London: the author, 1983. 11p.

b. Soul and Motown

(i) History and Reference

S/A.350. FULLER, Graham, and MACK, Lorrie, eds. The Motown
Story. London: Orbis, 1983. 96p.

S/A.351. HIRSHEY, Geri. Nowhere To Run: the story of soul music. New York: Times Books, 1984. 384p.

S/A.352. RYAN, Jack. Recollections: the Detroit years; the Motown sound by the people who made it. [Michigan?]:
the author, 1982. 132p.

S/A.353. WALLER, Don. The Motown Story. New York: Scribner,
1985. 256p.

(ii) Individuals

MARVIN GAYE

S/A.354. RITZ, David. Divided Soul: the life of Marvin Gaye.
New York: McGraw-Hill; London: Joseph, 1985.
367p.

DIANA ROSS

S/A.355. BROWN, Geoff. Diana Ross. London: Sidgwick &
Jackson, 1981. 144p.

STEVIE WONDER

S/A.356. DUFAYET, Jean-Jacques. Stevie Wonder. Paris: Plasma,
1982. 192p.

c. Gospel Music

See also S/A.333, 338

S/A.357. BROUGHTON, Viv. Black Gospel: an illustrated history
of the gospel sound. Poole, Dorset: Blandford Press,
1985. 160p.

S/A.358. CARD, Caroline, et al., eds. Discourse in Ethnomusicology, 2: a tribute to Alan P. Merriam. Bloomington:
Indiana University Ethnomusicology Publications Group,
1981. 216p. (includes essay by Joyce M. Jackson on
parallels between black American chanted sermons and
the West African tradition)

S/A.359. DAVIS, Gerald L. I Got the Word in Me and I Can Sing
It, You Know: a study of the performed Afro-American
sermon. Philadelphia: University of Pennsylvania
Press, 1985. 185p.

G.10. Rap

S/A.360. GRANDMASTER BLAST. All You Need to Know About
Rappin'. Chicago: Contemporary Books, 1984. 63p.

S/A.361. HAGER, Steven. Hip Hop: the illustrated history of
break dancing, rap music, and graffiti. New York:
St. Martin's Press, 1984. 112p.

S/A.362. TOOP, David. The Rap Attack: African jive to New York
hip hop. London: Pluto Press; Boston South End
Press, 1984. 168p.

H. JAZZ

H.1. Reference Works

S/A.363. ALLEN, Daniel. Bibliography of Discographies. Vol. 2.
Jazz. New York: Bowker, 1981. 239p.

S/A.364. HEFELE, Bernhard. Jazz-Bibliographie. Munich: K. G.
Saur, 1981. 368p.

S/A.365. MEADOWS, Eddie S. Jazz Reference and Research Materials: a bibliography. New York: Garland, 1981.
300p.

S/A.366. STRATEMANN, Klaus. Negro Bands on Film. Lübbecke:
Uhle & Kleimann, 1981. 124p.

H.2. Discographies

a. General

S/A.367. BRUYNINCX, Walter. Jazz Discography. Mechelen: the
author, 1984- . (series of volumes, based on LOAM
932, 2nd ed.; titles include Modern Jazz, Progressive
Jazz, Modern Big Band Jazz)

S/A.368. TULANE UNIVERSITY. William Ransom Hogan Jazz Archive. Catalog of the William Ransom Hogan Jazz Archive: the collection of 78 rpm phonograph recordings.
Boston: G. K. Hall, 1984. 2 vols.

b. Special

S/A.369. BELL, Malcolm F. Theme Songs of the Dance Band Era.
Memphis: KWD Corp., 1981. 52p.

S/A.370. LAING, Ralph, and SHERIDAN, Chris. Jazz Records:
the specialist labels. Copenhagen: Jazzmedia, 1981.
2 vols.

c. Individuals and Bands
(Note: the number of discographies published shows no sign of
declining; the following is a selective list of some of the more
major publications)

LOUIS ARMSTRONG

S/A.371. SCHAAP, Phil. Louis Armstrong Festival Discography.
New York: WKCR, 1982. 183p.

S/A.372. WESTERBERG, Hans. Boy from New Orleans: Louis
'Satchmo' Armstrong on records, films, radio and television. Copenhagen: Jazzmedia, 1981. 226p.

ART ENSEMBLE OF CHICAGO

S/A.373. JANSSENS, Eddy, and CRAEN, Hugo de. Art Ensemble
of Chicago Discography. Brussels: New Think Publications, 1984. 114p.

S/A.374. HAMES, Mike. Albert Ayler, Sunny Murray, Cecil Taylor,
Byard Lancaster & Kenneth Terroade: on disc & tape.
Ferndown, Dorset: the author, 1983. 63p.

WARDELL GRAY

S/A.375. SCHLOUCH, Claude. In Memory of Wardell Gray: a
discography. Marseille: the author, 1983. 32p.

COLEMAN HAWKINS

S/A.376. VILLETARD, Jean-François. Coleman Hawkins. Amsterdam:
Micrography, 1984- . (Vols. 1-2 published so far;
to 1957)

DUKE JORDAN

S/A.377. SJØGREN, Thorbjørn. The Discography of Duke Jordan.
Copenhagen: the author, 1982. 52p.

LEE KONITZ

S/A.378. FROHNE, Michael. Subconscious Lee: 35 years of records
and tapes; the Lee Konitz discography. Freiburg: Jazz
Realities, 1983. 132p.

CHARLES MINGUS

S/A.379. LINDENMAIER, H. Lukas, and SALEWSKI, Horst J. The
Man Who Never Sleeps: the Charles Mingus discography
1945-1978. Freiburg: Jazz Realities, 1983. 103p.

S/A.380. RUPPLI, Michel. Charles Mingus Discography. Frankfurt:
Ruecker, 1982. 47p.

THELONIOUS MONK

S/A.381. BIJL, Leon, and CANTÉ, Fred. Monk on Records: a
discography of Thelonious Monk. Amsterdam: Fred
Canté, 1982. 88p.
_____. _____. 2nd ed. 1985. 180p.

MAX ROACH

S/A.382. GOLDBERG, Bill. Max Roach Discography. New York:
WKCR, 1983. 76p.

SHORTY ROGERS

S/A.383. HOFMANN, Coen, and BAKKER, Erik. Shorty Rogers: a
discography. Amsterdam: Micrography, 1983. 148p.

SONNY ROLLINS

S/A.384. SJØGREN, Thorbjørn. The Sonny Rollins Discography.
Copenhagen: the author, 1982. 50p.

ARCHIE SHEPP

S/A.385. CERUTTI, Gustave, and MAERTENS, Guido. Discographie
Archie Shepp 1960-1980. Sierre, Switzerland: Jazz
360 Degree, 1981. 24p.

ART TATUM

S/A.386. LAUBICH, Arnold, and SPENCER, Ray. Art Tatum: a
guide to his recorded music. Metuchen, N.J.: Scarecrow Press, 1982. 330p.

d. Annotated Record Guides

S/A.387. HARRISON, Max, et al.. The Essential Jazz Records.
Vol. 1. London: Mansell; Westport, Conn.: Greenwood Press, 1984. 545p.

S/A.388. SWENSON, John, ed. The Rolling Stone Jazz Record
Guide. New York: Random House/Rolling Stone Press,
1985. 219p.

H.3. General Books on Jazz

a. General Guides and Handbooks

S/A.389. LEVY, Joseph. The Jazz Experience: a guide to appreciation. Englewood Cliffs, N.J.: Prentice-Hall, 1983.
158p.

S/A.390. McCALLA, James. Jazz: a listener's guide. Englewood
Cliffs, N.J.: Prentice-Hall, 1982. 152p.

b. The Jazz Life

(i) General

S/A.391. DANZI, Michael. American Musician in Germany 1924-
1939: memoirs of the jazz, entertainment, and movie
worlds of Berlin during the Weimar Republic and the
Nazi era. Frankfurt: Ruecker, 1985. 292p.

S/A.392. JOST, Ekkehard. Jazzmusiker: Materialien zur Soziologie
der afroamerikanischen Musik. Berlin: Ullstein, 1981.
311p.

S/A.393. JOST, Ekkehard. Sozialgeschichte des Jazz in den USA.
Frankfurt: Fischer, 1982. 265p.

S/A.394. WHITE, Andrew N. Hey Kid! Wanna Buy a Record? a
treatise on self-production in the music business.
Washington, D.C.: Andrew's Music, 1982. 58p.

(ii) Photographic and Other Visual Studies

S/A.395. DRIGGS, Franklin, and LEWINE, Harris. Black Beauty,
White Heat: a pictorial history of classic jazz, 1920-
1950. New York: Morrow, 1982. 360p.

S/A.396. FRIEDMAN, Carol. A Moment's Notice: portraits of American jazz musicians; text by Gary Giddins. New York: Schirmer, 1983. 144p.

S/A.397. GOLDBLATT, Burt. Jazz Gallery 1. (New York?): Newbold, 1982. 201p.

S/A.398. KLAASE, Piet. Jam Session: portraits of jazz and blues musicians drawn on the scene; Mark Gardner, J. Bernlef, text. Newton Abbot: David & Charles, 1985. 192p.

c. Practical Guides to Arranging, Composing, and Improvising/Jazz in Education

S/A.399. DURANT, J. B. A Student's Guide to American Jazz and Popular Music: outlines, recordings, and historical commentary. Scottsdale, Ariz.: the author, 1984. 748p.

S/A.400. FRICH, Elizabeth. The Matt Mattox Book of Jazz Dance. New York: Sterling, 1983. 128p.

S/A.401. GRIDLEY, Mark. How to Teach Jazz History. Manhattan, Kans.: National Association of Jazz Educators, 1984. 193p.

S/A.402. HENRY, Robert E. The Jazz Ensemble: a guide to technique. Englewood Cliffs, N.J.: Prentice-Hall, 1981. 117p.

S/A.403. JAFFE, Andrew. Jazz Theory. Dubuque, Iowa: Brown, 1983. 198p.

S/A.404. SPENCER, Ray. Piano Player's Jazz Handbook. Metuchen, N.J.: Scarecrow Press, 1985. 99p.

S/A.405. STANTON, Kenneth. Jazz Theory: a creative approach. New York: Taplinger, 1982. 221p.

d. General Analytical and Critical Works

S/A.406. HOFSTEIN, Francis. Au miroir du jazz. Paris: Pierre, 1985. 150p.

S/A.407. MALSON, Lucien. Des musiques de jazz. Paris: Editions Parenthèses, 1983. 216p.

S/A.408. POLILLO, Arrigo. Jazz: la vicenda e i protagonisti della musica afro-americana. Milan: Mondadori, 1983. 789p.

S/A.409. REDA, Jacques. Anthologies des musiciens de jazz. Paris: Stock, 1981.

S/A.410. REDA, Jacques. L'improviste: une lecture du jazz. Paris: Gallimard, 1981. 208p.

S/A.411. REDA, Jacques. Jouer le jeu: l'improviste 2. Paris: Gallimard, 1985. 214p.

S/A.412. RIEFLER, Wolfgang. Jazz: eine improvisierte Musik; dargestellt an vergleichenden Analysen des "St. Louis Blues." Menden, W. Germany: Der Jazzfreund, 1984. 45p. (compares Armstrong and Goodman versions)

S/A.413. SALES, Grover. Jazz: America's classical music. Englewood Cliffs, N.J.: Prentice-Hall, 1984. 246p.

S/A.414. SCHENKEL, Steven. The Tools of Jazz. Englewood Cliffs, N.J.: Prentice-Hall, 1983. 119p.

S/A.415. VULLIAMY, Graham. Jazz and Blues. London: Routledge & Kegan Paul, 1982. 158p. (introduction aimed at schools)

e. General Histories

See also S/A.395

S/A.416. GODBOLT, Jim. A History of Jazz in Britain, 1919-1950. London: Quartet, 1984. 306p.

S/A.417. MEGILL, Donald D., and DEMORY, Richard. Introduction to Jazz History. Englewood Cliffs, N.J.: Prentice-Hall, 1984. 259p.

S/A.418. MONGAN, Norman. A History of the Guitar in Jazz. New York: Oak, 1983. 274p.

S/A.419. SANDNER, Wolfgang. Jazz: zur Geschichte und stilistischen Entwicklung afroamerikanischer Musik. Laabe: Läber–Verlag, 1982. 152p.

S/A.420. STARR, S. Frederick. Red and Hot: the fate of jazz in the Soviet Union, 1917-1980. New York: Oxford University Press, 1983. 321p.

S/A.421. TAYLOR, Billy. Jazz Piano: a jazz history. Dubuque, Iowa: Brown, 1983. 264p.

S/A.422. WERNER, Otto. The Origin and Development of Jazz. Dubuque, Iowa: Kendall/Hunt, 1984. 163p.

f. Collected Criticism and Appreciation

S/A.423. BALLIETT, Whitney. Jelly Roll, Jabbo, and Fats: 19 portraits in jazz. New York: Oxford University Press, 1983. 197p.

S/A.424. _____. Night Creature: a journal of jazz, 1975-80. New York: Oxford University Press, 1981. 285p.

S/A.425. BROWN, Charles T., ed. Proceedings of NAJE Research. Manhattan, Kans.: National Association of Jazz Educators, 1981- . (ongoing series of conference papers; cover title, Jazz Research Papers)

S/A.426. FERGUSON, Otis. The Otis Ferguson Reader; edited by Dorothy Chamberlain and Robert Wilson. Highland Park, Ill.: December Press, 1982. 305p.

S/A.427. GIDDINS, Gary. Rhythm-a-ning: the jazz tradition and innovation in the '80s. New York: Oxford University Press, 1985. 291p.

S/A.428. _____. Riding on a Blue Note: jazz and American pop. New York: Oxford University Press, 1981. 313p.

S/A.429. LARKIN, Philip. Required Writing: miscellaneous pieces, 1955-1982. London: Faber & Faber, 1983. 315p. (includes some further material not included in All That Jazz, no. S.705)

S/A.430. VIAN, Boris. Autres écrits sur le jazz. Paris: Bourgois, 1981-82. 2 vols.

S/A.431. WILLIAMS, Martin. Jazz Heritage. New York: Oxford University Press, 1985. 253p.

S/A.432. YOUNG, Al. Bodies and Soul: musical memoirs. Berkeley: Creative Arts, 1981. 129p.

S/A.433. ZWERIN, Mike. Close Enough for Jazz. London: Quartet Books, 1983. 246p.

S/A.434. _____. Broken Up and Down. Paris: Handshake Editions, 1982. 126p.

H.4. History and Criticism of Specific Periods

a. Origins to 1930

S/A.435. DAUER, Alfons Michael. Tradition afrikanischer Blasor-
chester und Entstehung des Jazz. Graz: Akademische
Druck- und Verlagsanstalt, 1985. 2 vols.

b. The Swing Era

S/A.436. GAMMOND, Peter, and HORRICKS, Raymond, eds. The
Big Bands. Cambridge: Stephens, 1981. 183p.

S/A.437. LYTTELTON, Humphrey. The Best of Jazz. Vol. 2.
Enter the Giants. London: Robson, 1981. 239p.

c. Bebop and After

S/A.438. CANE, Giampiero. Canto nero: il free jazz degli anni
sessanta. Bologna: Cooperative Libraria, 1982. 296p.

S/A.439. HELLHUND, Hubert. Cool Jazz: Grundzüge seiner Entstehung und Entwicklung. Mainz: Schott, 1985. 302p.

S/A.440. LITWEILER, John. The Freedom Principle: jazz after
1958. New York: Morrow, 1984. 324p.

H.5. Regions

CHICAGO

S/A.441. TRAVIS, Dempsey. An Autobiography of Black Jazz.
Chicago: Urban Research Institute, 1983. 543p.

DETROIT

S/A.442. BOYD, Herb. Detroit Jazz Who's Who. Detroit: Jazz
Research Institute, 1983. 96p.

NEW ORLEANS

S/A.443. CRAWFORD, Ralston. Music in the Street: photographs
of New Orleans. New Orleans: Historic New Orleans
Collection, William Ransom Hogan Archive, 1983. 36p.

S/A.444. SPEDALE, Rhodes. A Guide to Jazz in New Orleans. New
          Orleans: Hope Publications, 1984. 276p.

S/A.445. TURNER, Frederick. Remembering Song: encounters with
          the New Orleans jazz tradition. New York: Viking,
          1982. 123p.

SAN FRANCISCO

S/A.446. STODDARD, Tom. Jazz on the Barbary Coast. Chigwell,
          Essex: Storyville, 1982. 192p.

H.6. Jazz Musicians

a. Collected Profiles

S/A.447. BRITT, Stan. The Jazz Guitarists. Poole, Dorset:
          Blandford Press, 1984. 128p.

S/A.448. GOURSE, Leslie. Louis' Children: American jazz singers.
          New York: Quill, 1984. 366p.

S/A.449. GRIME, Kitty. Jazz Voices. London: Quartet Books,
          1983. 184p.

S/A.450. LYONS, Les. The Great Jazz Pianists. New York: Mor-
          row, 1983. 322p.

S/A.451. RUSCH, Robert D. Jazztalk: the 'Cadence' interviews.
          Secaucus, N.J.: Lyle Stuart, 1984. 190p.

b. Women Jazz Musicians

S/A.452. DAHL, Linda. Stormy Weather: the music and lives of
          a century of jazz women. New York: Pantheon, 1984.
          371p.

S/A.453. PLACKSIN, Sally. American Women in Jazz, 1900 to the
          Present: their words, lives and music. New York:
          Seaview Books, 1982. 532p.

S/A.454. UNTERBRINK, Mary. Jazz Women at the Keyboard. Jef-
          ferson, N.C.: McFarland, 1983. 184p.

c. Individuals

LOUIS ARMSTRONG

S/A.455. COLLIER, James Lincoln. Louis Armstrong. New York:
Oxford University Press, 1983. 303p.

CHARLIE BARNET

S/A.456. BARNET, Charlie. Those Swinging Years: the autobiography of Charlie Barnet; with Stanley Dance. Baton
Rouge: Louisiana State University Press, 1984. 225p.

COUNT BASIE

S/A.457. BASIE, Count. Good Morning Blues: the autobiography
of Count Basie; as told to Albert Murray. New York:
Random House, 1985; London: Heinemann, 1986. 399p.

S/A.458. MORGAN, Alun. Count Basie. Tunbridge Wells: Spellmount; New York: Hippocrene Books, 1984. 96p.

BARNEY BIGARD

S/A.459. BIGARD, Barney. With Louis and the Duke: the autobiography of a jazz clarinetist; edited by Barry Martyn.
New York: Oxford University Press; London: Macmillan, 1985. 152p.

WALLACE BISHOP

S/A.460. KLEINHOUT, Henk, and EYLE, Wim van. The Wallace
Bishop Story. Alphen aan de Rijn: Micrography,
1981. 72p.

MARION BROWN

S/A.461. BROWN, Marion. Recollections: essays, drawings, miscellaneous. Frankfurt: Juergen A. Schmitt, 1984. 285p.

RED CALLENDER

S/A.462. CALLENDER, Red, and COHEN, Elaine. Unfinished Dreams
the musical world of Red Callender. London: Quartet,
1985. 239p.

BENNY CARTER

S/A.463. BERGER, Morroe, et al. Benny Carter: a life in American music. Metuchen, N.J.: Scarecrow Press, 1982.
2 vols.

JOHN COLTRANE

S/A.464. FILTGEN, Gerd, and AUSSERBACHER, Michael. John
Coltrane: sein Leben, seine Musik, seine Schallplatten.
Gauting-Buchendorf: Oreos, 1983. 220p.

S/A.465. GERBER, Alain. Le cas Coltrane; préface de Francis Mar-
mande. Marseille: Editions Parenthèses, 1985. 155p.

S/A.466. WHITE, Andrew. Trane 'n Me: (a semi-autobiography);
a treatise on the music of John Coltrane. Washington,
D.C.: Andrew's Music, 1981. 64p.

BOB CROSBY

S/A.467. CHILTON, John. Stomp Off, Let's Go! the story of Bob
Crosby's Bob Cats and Big Band. London: Jazz Book
Service, 1983. 284p.

CHARLIE DAVIS

S/A.468. DAVIS, Charlie. That Band From Indiana. Oswego,
N.Y.: Mathom, 1982. 157p.

MILES DAVIS

S/A.469. CARR, Ian. Miles Davis: a critical biography. London:
Quartet; New York: Morrow, 1982. 310p.

S/A.470. CHAMBERS, Jack. The Music and Times of Miles Davis.
Toronto: University of Toronto Press, 1983-85. 2
vols.

S/A.471. NISENSON, Eric. 'Round About Midnight: a portrait of
Miles Davis. New York: Dial Press, 1982. 244p.

S/A.472. STEINER, Wendy, ed. The Sign in Music and Literature.
Austin: University of Texas Press, 1981. 237p.
(includes "Miles Davis Meets Noam Chomsky," by Alan
M. Perlman & Daniel Greenblatt)

S/A.473. WIESSMUELLER, Peter. Miles Davis: sein Leben, seine
Musik, seine Schallplatten. Gauting-Buchendorf:
Oreos, 1984. 194p.

DUKE ELLINGTON

S/A.474. GEORGE, Don. Sweet Man: the real Duke Ellington.
New York: Putnam, 1981. 272p.
_____. The Real Duke Ellington. London: Robson,
1982. 272p.

S/A.475. RULAND, Hans. Duke Ellington: sein Leben, seine Mu-
          sik, seine Schallplatten. Gauting-Buchendorf: Oreos,
          1983. 189p.

GIL EVANS

S/A.476. HORRICKS, Raymond. Svengali; or, The Orchestra Called
          Gill (sic) Evans. Tunbridge Wells: Spellmount; New
          York: Hippocrene Books, 1984. 95p.

HELEN FORREST

S/A.477. FORREST, Helen. I Had the Craziest Dream: Helen For-
          rest and the big band era. New York: Coward, McCann
          & Geoghegan, 1982. 305p.

ERROLL GARNER

S/A.478. DORAN, James M. Erroll Garner: the most happy piano.
          Metuchen, N.J.: Scarecrow Press, 1985. 481p.

DIZZY GILLESPIE

S/A.479. HORRICKS, Raymond. Dizzy Gillespie and the Be-bop
          Revolution. Tunbridge Wells: Spellmount; New York:
          Hippocrene Books, 1984. 95p.

BENNY GOODMAN

S/A.480. CONNOR, Donald Russell. The Record of a Legend:
          Benny Goodman. New York: Let's Dance Corp.,
          1984. 382p.

COLEMAN HAWKINS

S/A.481. JAMES, Burnett. Coleman Hawkins. Tunbridge Wells:
          Spellmount; New York: Hippocrene Books, 1984. 93p.

BILLIE HOLIDAY

S/A.482. JAMES, Burnett. Billie Holiday. Tunbridge Wells:
          Spellmount; New York: Hippocrene Books, 1984. 95p.

INTERNATIONAL SWEETHEARTS OF RHYTHM

S/A.483. HANDY, D. Antoinette. The International Sweethearts of
          Rhythm. Metuchen, N.J.: Scarecrow Press, 1983.
          258p.

JAMES P. JOHNSON

S/A.484. TROLLE, Frank H. James P. Johnson, Father of Stride

Piano. Alphen aan de Rijn: Micrography, 1981. 2
vols. (48p., 48p.)

KING SISTERS

S/A.485. REY, Luise King. Those Swinging Years. Salt Lake
City, Utah: Olympus, 1983. 154p.

CHARLES MINGUS

S/A.486. LUZZI, Mario. Charles Mingus. Rome: Lato Side, 1983.
208p.

S/A.487. PRIESTLEY, Brian. Mingus: a critical biography. London: Quartet, 1982. 300p.

S/A.488. WEBER, Horst. Charles Mingus: sein Leben, seine Musik, seine Schallplatten. Gauting-Buchendorf: Oreos,
1984. 178p.

WES MONTGOMERY

S/A.489. INGRAM, Adrian. Wes Montgomery: biography/discography. Gateshead: Ashley Mark, 1985. 150p.

JELLY ROLL MORTON

S/A.490. CHARTERS, Samuel Barclay. Jelly Roll Morton's Last
Night At the Jungle Inn: an imaginary memoir. London: Boyars, 1984. 168p.

S/A.491. MORTON, Jelly Roll. The Collected Piano Music; (edited
by) James Dapogny. Washington, D.C.: Smithsonian
Institution Press; New York: Schirmer, 1982. 513p.
(includes substantial textual matter)

TURK MURPHY

S/A.492. GOGGIN, Jim. Turk Murphy - Just For the Record. San
Francisco: Traditional Jazz Foundation, 1983. 356p.

ANITA O'DAY

S/A.493. O'DAY, Anita. High Times, Hard Times; with George
Eells. New York: Putnam, 1981. 349p.

CHARLIE PARKER

S/A.494. PARKER, Chan. To Bird with Love; Francis Paudras, conception.... Poitiers: Editions Wizlov, 1981. 409p.
(mainly illustrations)

S/A.495. PRIESTLEY, Brian. Charlie Parker. Tunbridge Wells:
Spellmount; New York: Hippocrene Books, 1984. 96p.

OSCAR PETERSON

S/A.496. PALMER, Richard. Oscar Peterson. Tunbridge Wells:
Spellmount; New York: Hippocrene Books, 1984. 93p.

BUDDY RICH

S/A.497. MERIWETHER, Doug. We Don't Play Requests: a musical
biography/discography of Buddy Rich. Chicago:
K.A.R. Publications, 1984. 234p.

S/A.498. NESBITT, Jim. Inside Buddy Rich; with Buddy Rich.
Delevan, N.Y.: Kendor, 1984.

SONNY ROLLINS

S/A.499. BLANCQ, Charles. Sonny Rollins: the journey of a jazzman. Boston: Twayne, 1983. 142p.

WILLIE RUFF

S/A.500. ZINSSER, William. Willie and Dwike: an American profile. New York: Harper & Row, 1984. 170p. (Willie
Ruff & Dwike Mitchell on tour)

FATS WALLER

S/A.501. MACHLIN, Paul. Stride: the music of Fats Waller.
Boston: G. K. Hall; London: Macmillan, 1985. 167p.

PAUL WHITEMAN

S/A.502. DeLONG, Thomas A. Pops: Paul Whiteman, king of jazz.
Piscataway, N.J.: New Century, 1983. 360p.

LESTER YOUNG

S/A.503. GELLY, Dave. Lester Young. Tunbridge Wells: Spellmount; New York: Hippocrene Books, 1984. 94p.

S/A.504. PORTER, Lewis. Lester Young. Boston: G. K. Hall;
London: Macmillan, 1985. 190p.

I. POPULAR CURRENTS

I.1. General Reference Works

a. Bibliography and Reference

S/A.505. BOOTH, Mark W. American Popular Music: a reference guide. Westport, Conn.: Greenwood Press, 1983. 212p. (very useful series of bibliographical essays)

S/A.506. COOPER, B. Lee. The Popular Music Handbook: a resource guide for teachers, librarians, and media specialists. Littleton, Colo.: Libraries Unlimited, 1984. 415p.

S/A.507. GRAY, Michael H. Bibliography of Discographies. Vol. 3. Popular Music. New York: Bowker, 1983. 205p.

S/A.508. INGE, M. Thomas, ed. Handbook of American Popular Culture. Vol. 3. Westport, Conn.: Greenwood Press, 1981. 558p.

S/A.509. LANDRUM, Larry N., ed. American Popular Culture: a guide to information sources. Detroit: Gale Research, 1982. 435p.

S/A.510. SCHROEDER, Fred E. H., ed. Twentieth-century Popular Culture in Museums and Libraries. Bowling Green: Bowling Green University Popular Press, 1981. 268p.

S/A.511. WICKE, Peter, and ZIEGENRÜCKER, Wieland. Handbuch der populären musik: Rock, Pop, Jazz, Folk. Berlin, E. Germany: Deutscher Verlag für Musik, 1985. 583p.

S/A.512. WILMETH, Don S. The Language of American Popular Entertainment: a glossary of argot, slang and terminology. Westport, Conn.: Greenwood Press, 1981. 305p.

b. Song Indexes

See also S/A.655

S/A.513. LAX, Roger, and SMITH, Frederick. The Great Song Thesaurus. New York: Oxford University Press, 1984. 665p.

c. Discographies and Guides to Recordings

S/A.514. CLEE, Ken. The Directory of American 45 rpm Records. Philadelphia: the author, 1981-85. 4 vols.

S/A.515. DANIELS, William F. The American 45 and 78 rpm Record Dating Guide, 1940-1959. Westport, Conn.: Greenwood Press, 1985. 157p.

S/A.516. FAGAN, Ted, and MORAN, William R. The Encyclopedic Discography of Victor Recordings ... 12 January 1900 to 23 April 1903. Westport, Conn.: Greenwood Press, 1983. 442p.

S/A.517. TUDOR, Dean. Popular Music: an annotated guide to recordings. Littleton, Colo.: Libraries Unlimited, 1983. 674p.

c. Collected Biography

S/A.518. WHITE, Mark. "You Must Remember This": popular songwriters 1900-1980. London: Warne, 1983; New York: Scribner, 1985. 304p.

I.2. The Popular Music Life

a. General Works

S/A.519. CAMPBELL, Patricia J. Passing the Hat: street performers in America. New York: Delacorte Press, 1981. 260p.

S/A.520. DASILVA, Fabio, et al. The Sociology of Music. Notre Dame, Ind.: Notre Dame University Press, 1984. 186p. (includes a number of case studies of popular music)

S/A.521. WEISSMAN, Dick. Music Making in America. New York: Ungar, 1982. 147p.

b. Business and Media Studies

S/A.522. EBERLY, Philip K. Music in the Air: changing tastes in popular music, 1920-80. New York: Hastings House, 1982. 406p. (on radio)

S/A.523. RACHLIN, Harvey. Encyclopedia of the Music Business. New York: Harper & Row, 1981. 524p.

S/A.524. RYAN, John. The Production of Culture in the Music Industry: the ASCAP-BMI controversy. Lanham, Md.: University Press of America, 1985. 159p.

S/A.525. SANJEK, Russell. From Print to Plastic: publishing and promoting America's popular music. Brooklyn: I.S.A.M., 1983. (I.S.A.M. Monographs, No. 20). 71p.

S/A.526. WALLIS, Roger, and MALM, Krister. Big Sounds From Small Peoples: the music industry in small countries. London: Constable; New York: Pendragon, 1984. 419p. (on the impact of the US/multi-national record industry on the local situation in various parts of the world)

c. Clubs, etc.

S/A.527. ERENBERG, Lewis A. Steppin' Out: New York nightlife and the transformation of American culture, 1890-1930. Westport, Conn.: Greenwood Press, 1981; Chicago: University of Chicago Press, 1984. 291p.

I.3. Historical and Critical Studies

a. General Works, Including Popular Music of the USA

S/A.528. ATTALI, Jacques. Noise: the political economy of music; translated by Brian Massumi; foreword by Frederic Jameson; afterword by Susan McClary. Minneapolis: University of Minnesota Press; Manchester: University of Manchester Press, 1985. 179p.

S/A.529. BOOTH, Mark W. The Experience of Songs. New Haven, Conn.: Yale University Press, 1981. 226p.

S/A.530. HORN, David, and TAGG, Philip, eds. Popular Music Perspectives: papers from the First International Conference on Popular Music Research, Amsterdam, June 1981. Göteborg, Exeter: IASPM, 1982. 250p.

S/A.531. HORN, David, ed. Popular Music Perspectives 2: papers from the Second International Conference on Popular Music Studies, Reggio Emilia, September 19-24, 1983. Göteborg, Exeter, etc.: IASPM, 1985. 517p.

S/A.532. MARRE, Jeremy, and CHARLTON, Hannah. Beats of the Heart: popular music of the world. London: Pluto Press, 1985. 254p.

S/A.533. NORMAN, Philip, ed. The Road Goes On Forever. London: Elm Tree Books; New York: Simon & Schuster, 1982. 206p. (collection of pieces from London Times & Sunday Times)

S/A.534. OPEN UNIVERSITY. Popular Culture. (Block 4, Units 16 & 17). Form and Meaning, 2. Milton Keynes: Open University Press, 1982. 75p. (includes "Reading Popular Music," by Richard Middleton)

S/A.535. OPEN UNIVERSITY. Popular Culture. (Block 5, Units 18 & 19/20). Politics, Ideology and Popular Culture, 1. Milton Keynes: Open University Press, 1981. 92p. (includes teaching material on sub- and countercultures)

S/A.536. SHEPHERD, John. Tin Pan Alley. London: Routledge & Kegan Paul, 1982. 154p. (introduction aimed at schools)

S/A.537. TAYLOR, Rogan. The Death and Resurrection Show: from shaman to superstar. London: Blond & Briggs, 1984. 24p.

b. USA

See also Section F.4

S/A.538. COOPER, B. Lee. Images of American Society in Popular Music: a guide to reflective teaching. Chicago: Nelson-Hall, 1982. 282p.

S/A.539. DENNISON, Sam. Scandalize My Name: black imagery in American popular song. New York: Garland, 1982. 594p.

S/A.540. KANTER, Kenneth Aaron. The Jews in Tin Pan Alley: the Jewish contribution to American popular music, 1830-1940. New York: KTAV Publishing House, 1982. 226p.

S/A.541. OSTENDORF, Berndt. Ethnicity and Popular Music. Exeter, etc.: IASPM/UK, 1984. (IASPM/UK Working Papers, No. 2) 22p.

S/A.542. RIMLER, Walter. Not Fade Away: a comparison of jazz age with rock era pop song composers. Ann Arbor: Pierian Press, 1984. 221p.

S/A.543. SAVAGE, William W. Singing Cowboys and All That Jazz: a short history of popular music in Oklahoma. Norman: University of Oklahoma Press, 1983. 185p.

S/A.544. SLOBIN, Mark. Tenement Songs: the popular music of the Jewish immigrant. Urbana: University of Illinois Press, 1982. 213p.

S/A.545. TAWA, Nicholas. Music for the Millions: antebellum democratic attitudes and the birth of American popular music. New York: Pendragon, 1984. 211p.

S/A.546. TOLL, Robert C. The Entertainment Machine: American show business in the twentieth century. New York: Oxford University Press, 1982. 284p.

I.4. Words and Music

a. Sheet Music

S/A.547. HOOGERWERF, Frank W. Confederate Sheet-Music Imprints. Brooklyn: I.S.A.M., 1984. (I.S.A.M. Monographs, No. 21) 158p.

b. General Guides and Studies

See also Section J.6.c

S/A.548. CAHN, Sammy. The Songwriter's Rhyming Dictionary. New York: Facts on File, 1983. 224p.

S/A.549. DAVIS, Sheila. The Craft of Lyric Writing. Cincinnati: Writer's Digest, 1985. 350p.

I.5. Bands and Their Music

S/A.550. BIERLEY, Paul E. Hallelujah Trombone. Columbus, Ohio: Integrity Press, 1982. 156p. (on Henry Fillmore)

S/A.551. _____. The Music of Henry Fillmore and Will Huff. Columbus, Ohio: Integrity Press, 1982. 61p.

S/A.552. BODDIE, David L. We've Come a Long Way Together: the story of a drum corps. New Rochelle, N.Y.: C. W. Dickerson, 1981. 135p.

S/A.553. DELAPLAINE, Edward S. John Philip Sousa and the National Anthem. Frederick, Md.: Great Southern Press, 1983. 113p.

S/A.554. NEWSOM, Jon, ed. Perspectives on John Philip Sousa. Washington, D.C.: Library of Congress, 1983. 144p.

S/A.555. OLSEN, Kenneth E. Music and Musket: bands and bandsmen of the American Civil War. Westport, Conn.: Greenwood Press, 1981. 299p.

I.8. Popular Music of the Stage and Screen

a. General Historical Works

S/A.556. HOFFMANN, Gerhard, ed. Das amerikanische Drama. Berne: Francke, 1984. 324p. (includes "Vorformen und Nachbarformen des amerikanischen Theaters: Minstrel Show, Vaudeville, Burlesque, Musical, 1800–1932," by Berndt Ostendorf)

S/A.557. MATES, Julian. America's Musical Stage: two hundred years of musical theatre. Westport, Conn.: Greenwood Press, 1985. 252p.

S/A.558. TRAUBNER, Richard. Operetta: a theatrical history. London: Gollancz, 1984. 461p.

b. Blacks on Stage and Screen

S/A.559. FOX, Ted. Showtime at the Apollo. New York: Holt, 1983. 221p.

S/A.560. SCHIFFMAN, Jack. Harlem Heyday: a pictorial history of modern black show business and the Apollo Theatre. Buffalo: Prometheus Books, 1984. 280p.

S/A.561. WOLL, Allen. Dictionary of Black Theatre: Broadway, off-Broadway, and selected Harlem theatre. Westport, Conn.: Greenwood Press, 1983. (includes information on black musicals)

c. Minstrelsy, Medicine and Tent Shows

S/A.562. ASHBY, Clifford, and MAY, Suzanne DePauw. Trouping

Through Texas: Harley Sadler and his tent show.
Bowling Green: Bowling Green University Popular
Press, 1982.   188p.

d. Burlesque, Vaudeville, Revue, etc.

S/A.563. BORDMAN, Gerald. American Musical Revue: from The
Passing Show to Sugar Babies. New York: Oxford
University Press, 1985. 184p.

S/A.564. LAHR, John. Automatic Vaudeville: essays on star
turns. New York: Knopf; London: Heinemann,
1984. 241p.

S/A.565. ROOT, Deane L. American Popular Stage Music, 1860-
1880. Ann Arbor: UMI Research Press, 1981. 284p.

S/A.566. SLIDE, Anthony. The Vaudevillians: a dictionary of
vaudeville performers. Westport, Conn.:   Arlington
House, 1981. 172p.

S/A.567. STEIN, Charles W., ed. American Vaudeville As Seen By
Its Contemporaries. New York: Knopf, 1984. 392p.

e. Broadway Musical Comedy

(i) Reference Works

S/A.568. APPELBAUM, Stanley, and CAMNER, James, eds. Stars
of the American Musical Theater in Historic Photographs:
361 portraits from the 1860s to 1950. New York: Dover
Publications, 1981. 168p.

S/A.569. BLOOM, Ken. American Song: the complete musical theatre companion. New York: Facts on File, 1985.
2 vols.

S/A.570. LEONARD, William Torbert. Broadway Bound: a guide to
the shows that died aborning. Metuchen, N.J.:   Scarecrow Press, 1983. 618p.

S/A.571. RAYMOND, Jack. Show Music on Record: from the 1890's
to the 1980's; a comprehensive list of original cast and
studio cast performances issued as commercial phonograph records, covering the American stage, screen and
television; with composer performances and other selected collateral recordings. New York: Ungar, 1982.
253p.

(ii) Histories and Studies

S/A.572. BORDMAN, Gerald. American Musical Comedy: from
Adonis to Dreamgirls. New York: Oxford University
Press, 1982. 224p.

S/A.573. BORDMAN, Gerald. American Operetta: from HMS Pina-
fore to Sweeney Todd. New York: Oxford University
Press, 1981. 240p.

S/A.574. BRAHMS, Caryl, and SHERRIN, Ned. Song by Song:
the lives and work of 14 great lyric writers. Bolton,
Lancs.: Anderson, 1984. 281p.

S/A.575. LONEY, Glenn, ed. Musical Theatre in America: papers
and proceedings of the Conference on the Musical
Theatre in America. Westport, Conn.: Greenwood
Press, 1984. 441p.

S/A.576. MASSON, Alain. Comédie musicale. Paris: Stock, 1981.
417p.

S/A.577. MORDDEN, Ethan. Broadway Babies: the people who
made the American musical. New York: Oxford University Press, 1983. 244p.

S/A.578. THOMAS, Tony. That's Dancing. New York: Abrams;
Harmondsworth: Penguin, 1985. 272p.

(iii) Practical Aspects

S/A.579. LYNCH, Richard Chigley. Musicals! a directory of musical properties available for production. Chicago:
American Library Association, 1984. 197p.

(iv) Individual Shows

S/A.580. KING, Larry L. The Whorehouse Papers. New York:
Viking, 1982. 283p. (on The Best Little Whorehouse
in Texas)

f. Film Musicals

S/A.581. ALTMAN, Rick, ed. Genre: the musical; a reader.
London: Routledge & Kegan Paul, 1981. 228p.

S/A.582. AYLESWORTH, Thomas G. A History of Movie Musicals.
Greenwich, Conn.: Bison Books; London: Hamlyn,
1984. 256p.

S/A.583. BABINGTON, Bruce, and EVANS, Peter William. Blue
Skies and Silver Linings: aspects of the Hollywood
Musical. Manchester: Manchester University Press,
1985. 238p.

S/A.584. BERGAN, Ronald. Glamorous Musicals: fifty years of
Hollywood's ultimate fantasy. London: Octopus Books,
1984. 160p.

S/A.585. DELAMATER, Jerome. Dance in the Hollywood Musical.
Ann Arbor: UMI Research Press, 1981. 313p.

S/A.586. FEUER, Jane. The Hollywood Musical. Bloomington:
Indiana University Press; London: Macmillan, 1982.
192p.

S/A.587. GREEN, Stanley. Encyclopedia of the Musical Film. New
York: Oxford University Press, 1981. 344p.

S/A.588. HIRSCHHORN, Clive. The Hollywood Musical. London:
Octopus Books, 1981. 456p.

S/A.589. MORDDEN, Ethan. The Hollywood Musical. New York:
St. Martin's Press; Newton Abbot: David & Charles,
1982. 261p.

S/A.590. SENNETT, Ted. Hollywood Musicals. New York: Abrams,
1981. 384p.

S/A.591. WARNER, Alan. Who Sang What (On the Screen). London: Angus & Robertson, 1984. 167p.

S/A.592. WOLL, Allen L. The Hollywood Musical Goes to War.
Chicago: Nelson-Hall, 1982. 186p.

g. Music for Films and Television

S/A.593. ATKINS, Irene Kahn. Source Music in the Dramatic Motion Picture. Rutherford, N.J.: Fairleigh Dickinson
University Press, 1983. 190p.

S/A.594. LIMBACHER, James L. Keeping Score: film music 1972-
1979. Metuchen, N.J.: Scarecrow Press, 1981. 510p.
(Supplements LOAM 1309)

S/A.595. REHRAUER, George. The Macmillan Film Bibliography.
New York: Macmillan, 1982. 2 vols.

S/A.596. THIEL, Wolfgang. Filmmusik in Geschichte und Gegenwart. Berlin: Henschel, 1981. 447p.

S/A.597. WESCOTT, Steven D. A Comprehensive Bibliography of Music for Film and Television. Detroit: Information Coordinators, 1985. 432p.

h. Individual Composers, Lyricists and Librettists for Stage and Screen

AL DUBIN

S/A.598. McGUIRE, Patricia. Lullaby of Broadway: a biography of Al Dubin. Secaucus, N.J.: Citadel Press, 1983. 204p.

GEORGE GERSHWIN

S/A.599. JEAMBAR, Denis. George Gershwin. Paris: Mazarine, 1982. 256p.

S/A.600. LIPMANN, Eric. L'Amérique de George Gershwin. Paris: Messine, 1981. 224p.

BERNARD HERRMANN

S/A.601. BRUCE, Graham. Bernard Herrmann: film music and narrative. Ann Arbor: UMI Research Press, 1985. 248p.

OSCAR HAMMERSTEIN II

S/A.602. HAMMERSTEIN, Oscar. Lyrics. Milwaukee: Hal Leonard Books, 1985. 270p.

JEROME KERN

S/A.603. LAMB, Andrew. Jerome Kern in Edwardian London. Littlehampton, Sussex: the author, 1981. 32p.
_____. _____. Rev. and enl. ed. Brooklyn: I.S.A.M., 1985. (I.S.A.M. Monographs, No. 22) 85p.

ERICH WOLFGANG KORNGOLD

S/A.604. CARROLL, Brendan G. Erich Wolfgang Korngold, 1897-1957: his life and works. Paisley, Scotland: Wilfion Books, 1984. 42p.

JOHNNY MERCER

S/A.605. MERCER, Johnny. Our Huckleberry Friend: the life, times and lyrics of Johnny Mercer; collected and edited by Bob Bach and Ginger Mercer. Secaucus, N.J.: Lyle Stuart, 1982. 252p.

MIKLÓS RÓZSA

S/A.606. RÓZSA, Miklós. Double Life: the autobiography of Miklós Rózsa; foreword by Antal Dorati. Tunbridge Wells: Midas Books; New York: Hippocrene Books, 1982. 224p.

DIMITRI TIOMKIN

S/A.607. PALMER, Christopher. Dimitri Tiomkin: a portrait. London: T. E. Books, 1984. 144p.

KURT WEILL

S/A.608. JARMAN, Douglas. Kurt Weill: an illustrated biography. Bloomington: Indiana University Press; London: Orbis, 1982. 160p.

S/A.609. SCHEBERA, Jürgen. Kurt Weill: Leben und Werk; mit Texten und Materialien von und über Kurt Weill. Königstein: Athenäum, 1984. 350p.

VINCENT YOUMANS

S/A.610. BORDMAN, Gerald. Days to Be Happy, Years to Be Sad: the life and music of Vincent Youmans. New York: Oxford University Press, 1982. 256p.

i. Stars and Personalities of the Musical Stage and Screen

S/A.611. GOTTFRIED, Martin. In Person: the great entertainers. New York: Abrams, 1985. 263p.

FRED ASTAIRE

S/A.612. CARRICK, Peter. A Tribute to Fred Astaire. London: Hale, 1984; Bridgeport, Conn.: Merrimack Publishing Corp., 1985. 188p.

S/A.613. CEBE, Gilles. Fred Astaire. Paris: Veyrier, 1981. 272p.

S/A.614. MUELLER, John. Astaire Dancing: the musical films. New York: Knopf, 1985; London: Hamish Hamilton, 1986. 440p.

S/A.615. THOMAS, Bob. Astaire, the Man, the Dancer. New York: St. Martin's Press, 1984; London: Weidenfeld & Nicolson, 1985. 340p.

JUDY HOLLIDAY

S/A.616. CAREY, Gary. Judy Holliday: an intimate life story. New York: Seaview Books, 1982. 271p.

S/A.617. HOLTZMAN, Will. Judy Holliday: only child. New York: Putnam, 1982. 304p.

LIBBY HOLMAN

S/A.618. BRADSHAW, Jon. Dreams That Money Can Buy: the tragic life of Libby Holman. New York: Morrow, 1985. 431p.

S/A.619. PERRY, Hamilton Derby. Libby Holman: body and soul. Boston: Little, Brown, 1983. 300p.

ETHEL MERMAN

S/A.620. THOMAS, Bob. I Got Rhythm! the Ethel Merman Story. New York: Putnam, 1985. 239p.

I.9. Popular Entertainers

TONY BENNETT

S/A.621. JASPER, Tony. Tony Bennett. London: W. H. Allen, 1984. 192p.

NAT KING COLE

S/A.622. HASKINS, James. Nat King Cole. New York: Stein & Day, 1984. 204p.

BING CROSBY

S/A.623. CROSBY, Gary, and FIRESTONE, Ross. Going My Way. Garden City, N.Y.: Doubleday, 1985. 304p.

S/A.624. CROSBY, Kathryn. My Life With Bing. Wheeling, Ill.: Collage, 1983. 351p.

S/A.625. SHEPHERD, Don, and SLATZER, Robert F. Bing Crosby: the hollow man. New York: St. Martin's Press; London: W. H. Allen, 1981. 320p.

JUDY GARLAND

S/A.626. GLICKMANN, Serge. Judy Garland. Paris: La Pensée Universelle, 1981. 192p.

S/A.627. MEYER, John. Heartbreaker. Garden City, N.Y.: Doubleday, 1983. 322p.

S/A.628. SPADA, James. Judy and Liza; with Karen Swenson. Garden City, N.Y.: Doubleday, 1983. 216p.

LENA HORNE

S/A.629. HASKINS, James. Lena: a personal and professional biography of Lena Horne; with Kathleen Benson. New York: Stein & Day, 1984. 226p.

S/A.630. HOWARD, Brett. Lena. Los Angeles: Holloway House, 1981. 218p.

AL JOLSON

S/A.631. KINER, Larry F. The Al Jolson Discography. Westport, Conn.: Greenwood Press, 1983. 194p.

SPIKE JONES

S/A.632. YOUNG, Jordan R. Spike Jones and His City Slickers: an illustrated biography. Beverly Hills: Disharmony Books, 1984. 191p.

FRANK SINATRA

S/A.633. GOLDSTEIN, Norm. Frank Sinatra: ol' blue eyes. New York: Holt, 1983. 160p.

S/A.634. JEWELL, Derek. Frank Sinatra: a celebration. London: Pavilion Books, 1985. 192p.

S/A.635. LONSTEIN, Albert I. Sinatra. New York: Musicprint Corp., 1983. 176p.

S/A.636. PETERS, Richard. The Frank Sinatra Scrapbook: his life and times in words and pictures. New York: St. Martin's Press; London: Souvenir Press, 1983. 157p.

S/A.637. ROCKWELL, John. Sinatra: an American classic. New York: Random House/Rolling Stone Press, 1983. 157p.

S/A.638. SHAW, Arnold. Sinatra the Entertainer. New York:
          Delilah, 1982. 156p.

S/A.639. TURNER, John Frayn. Frank Sinatra: a personal por-
          trait. Tunbridge Wells: Midas Books; New York:
          Hippocrene Books, 1984. 168p.

S/A.640. SINATRA, Frank. Sinatra in His Own Words; compiled
          by Guy Yarwood. New York: Delilah, 1983. 126p.
          _____. Sinatra on Sinatra; compiled by Guy Yarwood.
          London: W. H. Allen, 1982. 126p.

BARBRA STREISAND

S/A.641. CONSIDINE, Shaun. Barbra Streisand: the woman, the
          myth, the music. New York: Delacorte Press, 1985.
          335p.

S/A.642. MOLINE, Karen. Streisand Through the Lens; photo-
          edited by Frank Teti. New York: Delilah; London:
          Sidgwick & Jackson, 1982. 137p.

S/A.643. SPADA, James. Streisand: the woman and the legend.
          Garden City, N.Y.: Doubleday; London: W. H. Allen,
          1982. 249p.

S/A.644. ZEC, Donald, and FOWLES, Anthony. Barbra: a biog-
          raphy of Barbra Streisand. London: New English Li-
          brary; New York: St. Martin's Press, 1982. 384p.

RUDY VALLEE

S/A.645. KINER, Larry F. The Rudy Vallee Discography. West-
          port, Conn.: Greenwood Press, 1985. 190p.

J. ROCK, ROCK & ROLL, POP

J.1. General Reference Works

a. Bibliographies

S/A.646. HANEL, Ed. The Essential Guide to Rock Books. Lon-
          don: Omnibus Press, 1983. 95p.

S/A.647. HOFFMANN, Frank W. The Literature of Rock, 1954-1978.
          Metuchen, N.J.: Scarecrow Press, 1981. 337p.

S/A.648. TAYLOR, Paul. Popular Music Since 1955: a critical guide to the literature. London: Mansell; Boston: G. K. Hall, 1985. 533p.

b. Dictionaries, Encyclopedias, Biographical Dictionaries

See also S/A.511

S/A.649. BANE, Michael. Who's Who in Rock; researcher, Kenny Kertok. New York: Everest House, 1981. 259p.

S/A.650. BIANCO, David, ed. Who's New Wave in Music: an illustrated encyclopedia, 1976-1982 (the first wave). Ann Arbor: Pierian Press, 1985. 430p.

S/A.651. CLIFFORD, Mike, et al. The Illustrated Rock Handbook; consultant, Mike Clifford; authors, Pete Frame ... (et al.) London: Salamander, 1983. 272p.

S/A.652. COUPE, Stuart, and BAKER, Glenn A. The New Rock 'n' Roll. London: Omnibus Press, 1983. 192p. (New Wave)

S/A.653. DELLAR, Fred. NME Guide to Rock Cinema. London: Hamlyn, 1981. 192p.

S/A.654. FORMENTO, Don. Rock Chronicle: today in rock history. London: Sidgwick & Jackson, 1983. 372p.

S/A.655. GARGAN, William, and SHARMA, Sue. Find That Tune: an index to rock, folk-rock, disco and soul in collections. New York: Neal-Schuman, 1984. 303p.

S/A.656. HEBEY, Jean-Bernard. Encyclopédie illustrée du rock. Paris: R.T.L. Editions, 1981. 256p.

S/A.657. HELANDER, Brock. The Rock Who's Who: a biographical dictionary and critical discography.... New York: Schirmer; London: Collier Macmillan, 1982. 684p.

S/A.658. HENDLER, Herb. Year by Year in the Rock Era. Westport, Conn.: Greenwood Press, 1983. 656p.

S/A.659. HIBBERT, Tom. The Dictionary of Rock Terms. London: Omnibus Press, 1982. 96p.

S/A.660. JASPER, Tony, et al. The International Encyclopedia of Hard Rock and Heavy Metal. London: Sidgwick & Jackson; New York: Facts on File, 1983 (i.e., 1985). 400p.

S/A.661. KNEIF, Tibor. Rock Music: ein Handbuch zum kritischen Verständnis. Reinbek: Rowohlt, 1982. 394p.

S/A.662. LEDUC, Jean-Marie, and OGOUZ, Jean-Noël. Le rock de A à Z: dictionnaire illustré. Paris: Michel, 1984. 511p.

S/A.663. MARSH, Dave, and STEIN, Kevin. The Book of Rock Lists. New York: Dell; London: Sidgwick & Jackson, 1981. 644p.

S/A.664. PARELES, John, and ROMANOWSKI, Patricia, eds. The Rolling Stone Encyclopedia of Rock & Roll. New York: Rolling Stone Press/Summit Books, 1983. 617p.

S/A.665. ROLLING STONE ROCK ALMANAC: the chronicles of rock and roll. New York: Macmillan; London: Collier Macmillan, 1983. 371p.

S/A.666. SHAW, Arnold. Dictionary of American Pop/Rock. New York: Schirmer; London: Collier Macmillan, 1982. 440p.

J.2. Recordings

a. Discographies, Record Lists, Charts

S/A.667. ALBERT, George, and HOFFMANN, Frank. The Cash Box Country Singles Charts, 1958-1982. Metuchen, N.J.: Scarecrow Press, 1984. 596p.

S/A.668. THE BOOTLEG BIBLE. Manchester: Babylon Books, 1981. 272p.

S/A.669. BROOKS, Elston. I've Heard Those Songs Before: the weekly top tunes from the past fifty years. New York: Morrow, 1981. 444p.

S/A.670. BRONSON, Fred. The Billboard Book of Number One Hits. New York: Billboard, 1985. 616p.

S/A.671. DELLAR, Fred, and LAZELL, Barry. The Omnibus Rock Discography. London: Omnibus Press, 1982. 192p.

S/A.672. DUXBURY, Janell R. Rockin' the Classics and Classicizin' the rock: a selectively annotated discography. Westport, CT: Greenwood, 1985. 188p.

S/A.673. GEORGE, B., and DEFOE, Martha. Volume: international

discography of the New Wave. New York: One Ten
Records, 1980.
_____. The International New Wave Discography.
Vol. 2. With Henry Beck, Nancy Breslaw and Jim
Linderman. London: Omnibus Press; New York: One
Records, 1982. 736p.

S/A.674. GEORGE, Nelson. Top of the Charts: the most complete
listing ever. Piscataway: New Century, 1983. 470p.

S/A.675. HIBBERT, Tom. Rare Records: wax trash and vinyl
treasures. London: Proteus, 1982. 128p. (Mainly
UK releases)

S/A.676. HOFFMANN, Frank, and ALBERT, George. The Cash Box
Singles Charts, 1950-1981; with the assistance of Lee
Ann Hoffmann. Metuchen, N.J.: Scarecrow Press,
1983. 860p.

S/A.677. HOUNSOME, Terry, and CHAMBRE, Tim. New Rock
Record: a collector's directory of rock albums and
musicians. Poole, Dorset: Blandford Press, 1981.
526p.
_____. _____. Revised ed. Poole: Blandford
Press, 1983. 719p. (two private editions were published by the authors in 1978-79)

S/A.678. QUIRIN, Jim, and COHEN, Barry. Chartmasters' Rock
100: an authentic ranking of the 100 most popular
songs for each year, 1950 through 1981. 3rd ed.
Covington, La.: Chartmasters, 1982. 84p.

S/A.679. THEROUX, Gary, and GILBERT, Bob. The Top Ten,
1956-Present. New York: Simon & Schuster, 1982.
302p.

S/A.680. WHITBURN, Joel. The Billboard Book of Top 40 Hits,
1955 to Present. New York: Billboard; London:
Guinness, 1983. 509p.

S/A.681. WHITBURN, Joel. Bubbling Under the Hot 100, 1959-
1981. Menomonee Falls, Wisc.: Record Research, 1982.
234p. (records which failed to make the Billboard
charts)

b. Record Guides

S/A.682. CHRISTGAU, Robert. Christgau's Record Guide: rock
albums of the seventies. New Haven, Conn.: Ticknor
& Fields, 1981. 480p.

S/A.683. COLLECTABLE EPs. January 1950-December 1975. London: Vintage Record Centre, 1982-85. 3 vols.

S/A.684. COLLECTABLE 45s: price reference guide to singles, January 1950-December 1964. London: Vintage Record Centre, 1981. 2 vols.

S/A.685. DICKERSON, P. J., and GORDON, M. A., eds. Collectable 45s of the Swinging Sixties. London: Vintage Centre, 1984-85. 2 vols.

S/A.686. JAKUBOWSKI, Maxim. The Rock Album: a good rock guide. London: Muller, 1983. 224p.
_____. _____. Vol. 2. London: Zomba Books, 1984. 194p.

S/A.687. KIRSCH, Don R. Rock'n'Roll Obscurities. 2nd ed. Tacoma, Wash.: the author, 1981. 99p.

S/A.688. REES, Tony. Rare Rock: collectors' guide. Poole, Dorset: Blandford Press, 1985. 352p.

S/A.689. SANTELLI, Robert. Sixties Rock: a listener's guide. Chicago: Contemporary Books, 1985. 304p.

S/A.690. THE TROUSER PRESS GUIDE TO NEW WAVE RECORDS. New York: Scribner, 1983. 416p.

J.3. Histories and Surveys

a. General

S/A.691. BROWN, Charles T. The Art of Rock'n'Roll. Englewood Cliffs, N.J.: Prentice-Hall, 1983. 202p. (for schools & colleges)

S/A.692. CHAMBERS, Iain. Urban Rhythms: pop music and popular culture. London: Macmillan; New York: St. Martin's Press, 1985. 272p. (historical-cultural study of pop music in Britain, with particular attention to transatlantic influences)

S/A.693. THE HISTORY OF ROCK. London: Orbis, 1982-84. (121 weekly parts, heavily illustrated, cumulating in 10 vols.)

S/A.694. JERRENTRUP, Ansgar. Entwicklung der Rockmusik von den Anfängen bis zum Beat. Regensburg: Bosse, 1981. 378p.

S/A.695. KENT, Jeff. The Rise and Fall of Rock. Stoke-on-Trent: Witan Books, 1983. 484p.

S/A.696. ROGERS, Dave. Rock'n'Roll. London: Routledge & Kegan Paul, 1982. 148p. (introduction for schools)

b. Specific Periods

S/A.697. BAKER, Glenn A., and COUPE, Stuart. The New Music. London: Ring Publications, 1980; New York: Harmony Books, 1981. 128p.

S/A.698. BARSAMIAN, Jacques, and JOUFFA, François. L'âge d'or de la pop music. Paris: Ramsay, 1982. 244p.

S/A.699. PALMER, Myles. New Wave Explosion: how punk became New Wave in the 80's. London: Proteus, 1981. 128p.

S/A.700. POLLOCK, Bruce. When the Music Mattered: rock in the 1960s. New York: Holt, Rinehart & Winston, 1984. 243p.

S/A.701. POLLOCK, Bruce. When Rock Was Young: a nostalgic review of the Top 40 era. New York: Holt, Rinehart & Winston, 1981. 214p.

S/A.702. RUSSELL, Ethan A. Dear Mr. Fantasy: diary of a decade; our time and rock and roll. Boston: Houghton Mifflin, 1985. 253p.

S/A.703. SCULATTI, Gene, ed. The Catalog of Cool. New York: Warner Books; London: Vermilion, 1983. 216p.

c. Specific Areas

S/A.704. BELSITO, Peter, and DAVIS, Bob. Hardcore California: a history of punk and New Wave. Berkeley: Last Gasp of San Francisco. 1983. 128p.

S/A.705. BELSITO, Peter, et al., eds. Streetart: the punk poster in San Francisco. Berkeley: Last Gasp of San Francisco, 1981. 128p.

S/A.706a. McDONOUGH, Jack. San Francisco Rock: the illustrated History of San Francisco Rock Music. San Francisco: Chronicle Books, 1985. 224p.

S/A.706b. PERRY, Charles. The Haight-Ashbury: a history. New York: Random House, 1984. 306p.

476 / Literature of American Music

S/A.707. SCULATTI, Gene, and SEAY, Davin. San Francisco
Nights: the psychedelic music trip. New York: St.
Martin's Press, 1985. 191p.

S/A.708. TOURVILLE, Tom W. Minnesota Rocked!! the 1960's; a
discography and guide to the music and the people of
Minnesota from the 1960's. Spirit Lake, Iowa: the
author, 1983. 72p.

S/A.709. WOODS, Brenda, and WOODS, Bill. Louisville's Own: an
illustrated encyclopedia of Louisville area recorded pop
music from 1953 to 1983. [Louisville?]; De Forest,
1983. 173p.

J.4. Collected and Miscellaneous Criticism

S/A.710. ARANZA, Jacob. Backward Masking Unmasked: backward
satanic messages of rock and roll exposed. Shreveport,
La.: Huntington House, 1983. 115p.

S/A.711. BAKER, Paul. Contemporary Christian Music: where it
came from, what it is, where it's going. Rev. ed.
Westchester, Ill.: Crossway Books, 1985. 279p.

S/A.712. BANE, Michael. White Boy Singing the Blues. New York:
Penguin, 1982. 269p.

S/A.713. DUNCAN, Robert. The Noise: notes from a rock'n'roll
era. New York: Ticknor & Fields, 1984. 293p.

S/A.714. KERSHAW, Alan Roy, and HOHENSEE, Michael. The Rock
Reader. Vol. 1. 1953-1978. Leura, New South Wales:
Afloat Press, 1982. 227p.

S/A.715. KRAMARZ, Volkmar. Harmonieanalyse der Rockmusik:
von Folk und Blues zu Rock und New Wave. Mainz:
Schott, 1983. 212p.

S/A.716. LAWHEAD, Steve. Rock Reconsidered: a Christian looks
at contemporary music. Downers Grove, Ill.: Inter-
varsity Press, 1981. 156p.

S/A.717. McGREGOR, Craig. Pop Goes the Culture. London: Pluto
Press, 1984. 156p.

S/A.718. McGREGOR, Craig. Soundtrack For the Eighties: pop
culture, Australia, politics, suburbia, art and other essays. Sydney: Hodder & Stoughton, 1983. 203p.

S/A.719. MARSH, Dave, et al. The First Rock & Roll Confidential Report: inside the real world of rock & roll, by Dave Marsh and the editors of Rock & Roll Confidential. New York: Pantheon, 1985. 306p.

S/A.720. MARSH, Dave. Fortunate Son: essays and criticism by America's best-known rock writer. New York: Random House, 1985. 337p.

S/A.721. WILLIS, Ellen. Beginning to See the Light: pieces of a decade. New York: Knopf, 1981. (Repr. New York: Wideview Books, 1982) 320p.

J.5. Rock Lyrics

S/A.722. PICHASKE, David R. The Poetry of Rock: the golden years. Peoria, Ill.: Ellis Press, 1981. 173p.

J.6. Social, Cultural and Media Aspects

a. Rock Life

S/A.723. FULLER, John G. Are the Kids All Right? the rock generation and its hidden death wish. New York: Times Books, 1981. 262p.

S/A.724. HERMAN, Gary. Rock'n'Roll Babylon. London: Plexus, 1982. 192p.

S/A.725. LANDY, Elliott. Woodstock Vision. Reinbek: Rowohlt, 1984. 128p.

S/A.726. STALLINGS, Penny. Rock & Roll Confidential. Boston: Little, Brown, 1984. 256p.

S/A.727. WHITCOMB, Ian. Rock Odyssey. Garden City, N.Y.: Doubleday, 1983; London: Hutchinson, 1984. 360p.

b. Sociological and Political Studies

S/A.728. DURANT, Alan. Conditions of Music. London: Macmillan, 1984. 256p.

S/A.729. FLETCHER, Peter. Roll Over Rock. London: Stainer & Bell, 1981. 175p.

S/A.730. HIBBARD, Don, and KALEIALOHA, Carol. The Role of
Rock. Englewood Cliffs, N.J.: Prentice-Hall, 1983.
216p.

S/A.731. LIPSITZ, George. Class and Culture in Cold War America:
"a rainbow at midnight." South Hadley, Mass.: Bergin
& Garvey, 1982. 254p. (Chapter 13, "Class Origins
of Rock & Roll")

S/A.732. LONDON, Herbert I. Closing the Circle: a cultural history of rock. Chicago: Nelson-Hall, 1984. 198p.

S/A.733. MARSH, Dave. Sun City, by Artists United Against Apart-
heid: the struggle for freedom in South Africa; the
making of the record. New York: Penguin, 1985. unpaged.

S/A.734. MARTIN, Bernice. A Sociology of Contemporary Cultural
Change. Oxford: Blackwell, 1981. 288p.

S/A.735. ORMAN, John M. The Politics of Rock Music. Chicago:
Nelson-Hall, 1984. 209p.

S/A.736. STREET, John. "No Satisfaction?": politics and popular
music. Exeter, etc.: IASPM/UK, 1985. (IASPM/UK
Working Papers, No. 5) 24p.

c. Business and Media

S/A.737. BENNETT, Roy C. The Songwriter's Guide to Writing and
Selling Hit Songs. Englewood Cliffs, N.J.: Prentice-
Hall, 1983. 161p.

S/A.738. CONNELLY, Will. The Musician's Guide to Independent
Record Production. Chicago: Contemporary Books,
1981. 208p.

S/A.739. DENISOFF, R. Serge. Tarnished Gold: the record industry revisited. New Brunswick, N.J.: Transaction
Books, 1985. 350p.

S/A.740. HURST, Walter E. The Music Industry Book: protect
yourself before you lose your rights and royalties.
Hollywood: Seven Arts, 1981. 92p.

S/A.741. OPEN UNIVERSITY. Popular Culture. (Block 6, Units
24-25). Science, Technology and Popular Culture, 1.
Milton Keynes: Open University Press, 1982. 86p.
(includes "The Rock Music Industry," by Dave Elliott)

S/A.742. RAMSEY, Dan. How To Be a Disc Jockey. Blue Ridge
Summit, Pa.: Tab Books, 1981. 226p.

S/A.743. SHORE, Michael. The History of American Bandstand;
with Dick Clark. New York: Ballantine, 1985. 235p.

S/A.744. SIEGEL, Alan H. Breakin' In the Music Business. Port
Chester, N.Y.: Cherry Lane Books, 1983. 275p.

S/A.745. SKLAR, Rick. Rocking America: how the all-hit radio
stations took over: an insider's view. New York:
St. Martin's Press, 1984. 220p.

S/A.746. USLAN, Michael, and SOLOMON, Bruce. Dick Clark's The
First 25 Years of Rock and Roll. New York: Dell,
1981; New York: Greenwich House, 1983. 465p.

S/A.747. WILLIAMS, George. The Songwriter's Demo Manual and
Success Guide. Riverside, Calif.: Music Business
Books, 1984. 193p.

J.7. The Image of Rock

S/A.748. BURT, Rob. 25 Years of Teen-Screen Idols. Poole, Dorset: Blandford Press; New York: Delilah, 1983.
208p.

S/A.749. EHRENSTEIN, David, and REED, Bill. Rock on Film. New
York: Delilah, 1982. 275p.

S/A.750. ELLIS, Robert. The Pictorial Album of Rock. London:
Salamander Books, 1981. 224p.

S/A.751. FITZGERALD, f-stop. Weird Angle. Berkeley: Last Gasp
of San Francisco, 1982. 64p.

S/A.752. OCHS, Michael. Rock Archives: a photographic journey
through the first two decades of rock & roll; introduction by Peter Guralnick; designer by Vincent Winter.
Garden City, N.Y.: Doubleday; Poole, Dorset: Blandford Press, 1984. 401p.

S/A.753. ROWLANDS, John. Spotlight Heroes. New York: McGraw-
Hill, 1981. 146p.

S/A.754. SHORE, Michael. The Rolling Stone Book of Rock Video.
New York: Quill, 1984. 319p.

S/A.755. STEWART, Tony, ed. Cool Cats: 25 years of rock'n'roll
style. London: Eel Pie, 1981. 160p.

a. Collected Profiles

S/A.756. COLMAN, Stuart. They Kept On Rockin': the giants of rock 'n' roll. Poole, Dorset: Blandford Press, 1982. 160p.

S/A.757. GAMBACCINI, Paul. Masters of Rock. London: BBC, 1982. 223p.

S/A.758. HERBST, Peter, ed. The Rolling Stone Interviews, 1967-1980: talking with the legends of rock & roll; introduction by Ben Fong-Torres. New York: St. Martin's Press; London: Barker, 1981. 426p.

S/A.759. SCHMIDT-JOOS, Siegfried, ed. Idole. Frankfurt: Ullstein, 1984. 3 vols.

S/A.760. TOSCHES, Nick. Unsing Heroes of Rock & Roll. New York: Scribner, 1984. 245p.

S/A.761. WEINBERG, Max, and SANTELLI, Robert. The Big Beat: conversations with rock's great drummers. Chicago: Contemporary Books, 1984. 197p.

S/A.762. WHITE, Timothy. Rock Stars. New York: Stewart, Tabori & Chang; Bromley, Kent: Columbus Books, 1984. 287p.

b. Women Performers

S/A.763. BETROCK, Alan. Girl Groups: the story of a sound. New York: Delilah, 1982. 176p.

S/A.764. JUGE, Pascale, et al. Rockeuses: les héroïnes de jukebox. Paris: Grancher, 1982. 135p.

S/A.765. STEWARD, Sue, and GARRATT, Cheryl. Signed, Sealed and Delivered: true life stories of women in pop. London: Pluto Press; Boston: South End Press, 1984. 168p.

S/A.766. THOMSON, Liz, ed. New Women in Rock. London: Omnibus Press; New York: Delilah, 1982. 96p.

c. Individuals

PETER ALLEN

S/A.767. SMITH, David, and PETERS, Neal. Peter Allen: 'Between the Moon and New York City.' New York: Delilah, 1983. 149p.

BEACH BOYS

S/A.768. ELLIOTT, Brad. Surf's Up: the Beach Boys On Record 1961-1981. Ann Arbor: Pierian Press, 1982. 494p.

S/A.769. MILWARD, John. The Beach Boys Silver Anniversary. Garden City, N.Y.: Doubleday, 1985. 240p.

BLONDIE

S/A.770. HARRY, Debbie, et al. Making Tracks: the rise of Blondie, by Debbie Harry, Chris Stein and Victor Bockris, New York: Dell; London: Elm Tree Books, 1982. 192p.

MICHAEL BLOOMFIELD

S/A.771. WARD, Ed. Michael Bloomfield: the rise and fall of an American guitar hero. Port Chester, N.Y.: Cherry Lane Books, 1983. 135p.

JACKSON BROWNE

S/A.772. MANZANO, Alberto. Jackson Browne. Madrid: Júcar, 1982. 218p.

S/A.773. WISEMAN, Rich. Jackson Browne: the story of a hold out. Garden City, N.Y.: Doubleday, 1982. 177p.

THE BYRDS

S/A.774. ROGAN, John. Timeless Flight: the definitive biography of the Byrds. London: Scorpion, 1981. 192p.

CROSBY, STILLS & NASH

S/A.775. ZIMMER, Dave, and DILTZ, Henry. Crosby, Stills & Nash: the authorized biography. New York: St. Martin's Press; London: Omnibus Press, 1984. 268p.

BOBBY DARIN

S/A.776. DiORIO, Al. Borrowed Time: the 37 years of Bobby
Darin. Philadelphia: Running Press, 1981. 256p.

DEAD KENNEDYS

S/A.777. KESTER, Marian. Dead Kennedys: the unauthorized version. Berkeley: Last Gasp of San Francisco, 1983.
64p.

THE DOORS

S/A.778. LISCIANDO, Frank. An Hour For Magic: a photojournal
of Jim Morrison and the Doors. New York: Delilah;
London: Eel Pie, 1982. 152p.

S/A.779. SUGARMAN, Daniel, ed. The Doors: the illustrated history. New York: Morrow; London: Vermilion, 1983.
203p.

BOB DYLAN

S/A.780. ANDERSON, Dennis. The Hollow Horn: Bob Dylan's reception in the United States and Germany. Munich:
Hobo Press, 1981. 280p.

S/A.781. BAULDIE, John. Bob Dylan and "Desire." Bury, Lancs.:
Wanted Man, 1984. 58p.

S/A.782. BOWDEN, Betsy. Performed Literature: words and music
by Bob Dylan. Bloomington: Indiana University Press,
1982. 239p.

S/A.783. COTT, Jonathan. Bob Dylan. New York: Rolling Stone
Press; London: Vermilion, 1984. 246p.

S/A.784. DORMAN, James E. Recorded Dylan: a critical review and
discography. Pinedale, Calif.: Soma Press, 1982.
124p.

S/A.785. DOWLEY, Tim, and DUNNAGE, Barry. Bob Dylan: from
a Hard Rain to a Slow Train. Tunbridge Wells: Midas
Books; New York: Hippocrene Books, 1983. 177p.

S/A.786. GANS, Terry Alexander. What's New and What Is Not:
Bob Dylan through 1964; the myth of protest. Munich:
Hobo Press, 1983. 160p.

S/A.787. HERDMAN, John. Voice Without Restraint: a study of
Dylan's lyrics and their background. Edinburgh: Paul
Harris; New York: Delilah, 1982. 164p.

S/A.788. HEYLIN, Clinton. Rain Unravelled Tales: (the nightingale's code examined); a rumourography. Juarez (i.e.,
Sale, Cheshire): Ashes & Sand, 1982. 135p.

S/A.789. KROGSGAARD, Michael. Twenty Years of Recording: the
Bob Dylan reference book. [Copenhagen]: Scandinavian Institute for Rock Research, 1981. 608p.

S/A.790. MELLERS, Wilfrid. A Darker Shade of Pale: a backdrop
to Bob Dylan. London: Faber & Faber, 1984. 255p.

S/A.791. ROWLEY, Chris. Blood on the Tracks: the story of Bob
Dylan. London: Proteus, 1984. 157p.

S/A.792. SCHMIDT, Mathias R. Bob Dylan's "Message Songs" der
sechziger jahre und die anglo-amerikanische Tradition
des sozialkritischen Liedes. Berne: Lang, 1982.
233p.
_____. Bob Dylan und die sechziger Jahre: Aufbruch
und Abkehr. Frankfurt: Fischer, 1983. 191p.

THE EAGLES

S/A.793. SWENSON, John. The Eagles. New York: Ace, 1981.
192p.

EVERLY BROTHERS

S/A.794. WHITE, Roger. Walk Right Back: the story of the Everly
Brothers. London: Plexus, 1984. 158p.

CONNIE FRANCIS

S/A.795. FRANCIS, Connie. Who's Sorry Now? New York: St.
Martin's Press; London: W. H. Allen, 1984. 332p.

GRATEFUL DEAD

S/A.796. GANS, David, and SIMON, Peter. Playing the Band: an
oral and visual portrait of the Grateful Dead. New
York: St. Martin's Press, 1985. 191p.

S/A.797. GRUSHKIN, Paul, ed. Grateful Dead: the official book
of the Dead Heads. New York: Morrow, 1983. 209p.

S/A.798. JACKSON, Blair. Grateful Dead. New York: Delilah,
1983. 256p.

BILL HALEY

S/A.799. SWENSON, John. Bill Haley: the daddy of rock and roll.

London: W. H. Allen; New York: Stein & Day, 1982; London: Star Books, 1903. 174p.

DARYL HALL & JOHN OATES

S/A.800. TOSCHES, Nick. Daryl Hall/John Oates: dangerous dances; the authorized biography. New York: St. Martin's Press, 1984. 136p.

JIMI HENDRIX

S/A.801. HOPKINS, Jerry. Hit and Run: the Jimi Hendrix Story. New York: Putnam, 1982. 320p.

S/A.802. PURPLE HAZE ARCHIVES. Jimi Hendrix: a discography; compiled by the Purple Haze Archives and Dave Armstrong. Tucson, Ariz.: Purple Haze Archives, 1981. 46p.

BUDDY HOLLY

S/A.803. GRIGGS, Bill, and BLACK, Jim. Buddy Holly: a collector's guide. Sheboygan, Wisc.: Red Wax Publishing Co., 1983. 92p.

MICHAEL JACKSON

S/A.804. BROWN, Geoff. Michael Jackson: body and soul; an illustrated biography. London: Virgin Books, 1984. 127p.

S/A.805. GEORGE, Nelson. The Michael Jackson Story. New York: Dell; London: New English Library, 1984. 191p.

JANIS JOPLIN

S/A.806. ABERNETHY, Francis Edward, ed. Legendary Ladies of Texas. Dallas: E-Heart Press, 1981. (Publications of the Texas Folklore Society, No. 43) 224p. (includes "Janis (Joplin) and the Austin Scene," by Stanley G. Alexander)

JERRY LEE LEWIS

S/A.807. BOER, Wim de. Breathless: the Jerry Lee Lewis long play album guide. Best, Holland: DeWitte, 1983.

S/A.808. CAIN, Robert. Whole Lotta Shakin' Goin' on: Jerry Lee Lewis, the rock years, the country years, the triumphs and the tragedies. New York: Dial Press, 1981. 143p.

S/A.809. LEWIS, Myra. Great Balls of Fire: the uncensored story of Jerry Lee Lewis. New York: Morrow, 1982. 291p.

S/A.810. PALMER, Robert. Jerry Lee Lewis Rocks! New York: Delilah; London: Omnibus Press, 1982. 128p.

S/A.811. TOSCHES, Nick. Hellfire: the Jerry Lee Lewis story. New York: Dell, 1982. 276p.

LITTLE RICHARD

S/A.812. WHITE, Charles. The Life and Times of Little Richard, the Quasar of Rock. New York: Harmony Books; London: Pan, 1985. 256p.

BARRY MANILOW

S/A.813. PETERS, Richard. The Barry Manilow Scrapbook: his magical world in words and pictures. London: Pop Universal, 1982. 95p.
_____. Barry Manilow: an illustrated biography. New York: Delilah, 1983. 95p.

BETTE MIDLER

S/A.814. SPADA, James. The Divine Bette Midler. New York: Collier; London: Collier Macmillan, 1984. 214p.

GRAM PARSONS

S/A.815. GRIFFIN, Sid. Gram Parsons: a music biography. Pasadena: Sierre Records & Books, 1985. 189p.

IGGY POP

S/A.816. POP, Iggy. I Need More: the Stooges and other stories; with Anne Wehrer. Princeton: Karz-Cohl, 1982. 128p.

ELVIS PRESLEY

(i) Reference

S/A.817. COTTEN, Lee, and DeWITT, Howard A. Jailhouse Rock: the bootleg records of Elvis Presley, 1970-1983. Ann Arbor: Pierian Press, 1983. 367p.

S/A.818. CRANOR, Rosalind. Elvis Collectibles. Paducah, Ky.: Collection Books, 1983. 366p.

S/A.819. HAMMONTREE, Patsy Guy. Elvis Presley: a bio-bibliography. Westport, Conn.: Greenwood Press; London: Aldwych, 1985. 301p.

S/A.820. SAUERS, Wendy. Elvis Presley: a complete reference; biography, chronology, concerts list, filmography, discography, vital documents, bibliography, index. Jefferson, N.C.: McFarland, 1984. 194p.

S/A.821. WHISLER, John A. Elvis Presley: reference guide and discography. Metuchen, N.J.: Scarecrow Press, 1981. 258p.

(ii) Other Works

S/A.822. BURK, Bill E. Elvis: a 30-year chronicle. Temple, Ariz.: Osborne Enterprises, 1985. 351p.

S/A.823. CABAJ, Janice. The Elvis Image. Smithtown, N.Y.: Exposition Press, 1982. 184p.

S/A.824. CARR, Roy, and FARREN, Mick. Elvis: the complete illustrated record. London: Eel Pie, 1982. 191p.

S/A.825. COTTEN, Lee. All Shook Up: Elvis day-by-day, 1954-1977. Ann Arbor: Pierian Press, 1985. 580p.

S/A.826. CRUMBAKER, Marge, and TUCKER, Gabe. Up and Down with Elvis Presley. New York: Putnam, 1981. 256p.

S/A.827. DUNDY, Elaine. Elvis and Gladys: the genesis of a king. New York: Macmillan; London: Weidenfeld & Nicolson, 1985. 350p.

S/A.828. GOLDMAN, Albert. Elvis. New York: McGraw-Hill; London: Allen Lane, 1981. 598p.
_____. _____. Harmondsworth: Penguin, 1982. 727p.

S/A.829. MARSH, Dave. Elvis. New York: Rolling Stone Press; London: Elm Tree Books, 1982, 246p.

S/A.830. PETERS, Richard. Elvis: the golden anniversary tribute. London: Pop Universal/Souvenir Press, 1984. 128p.

S/A.831. RIJFF, Ger. Elvis: long lonely highway. Amsterdam: Tutti Frutti Productions, 1985. 184p.

S/A.832. SHAVER, Sean. Elvis' Portrait Portfolio. s.l.: Timur, 1983. 304p.

S/A.833. TOBLER, John, and WOOTTON, Richard. Elvis: the legend and the music. London: Optimum Books, 1983. 192p.

S/A.834. TORGOFF, Martin, ed. The Complete Elvis; art direction
by Ed Caraeff. New York: Delilah; London: Virgin
Books, 1982. 256p.

S/A.835. WORTH, Fred, and TAMERIUS, Steve D. All About Elvis.
New York: Bantam, 1981. 414p.

PRINCE

S/A.836. FELDMAN, Jim. Prince. New York: Ballantine Books,
1985. 146p.

LOU REED

S/A.837. CLAPTON, Diana. Lou Reed and the Velvet Underground.
London: Proteus, 1982. 127p.

LIONEL RICHIE

S/A.838. PLUTZIK, Roberta. Lionel Richie. New York: Dell,
1985. 185p.

NEIL SEDAKA

S/A.839. SEDAKA, Neil. Laughter in the Rain: my own story.
New York: Putnam, 1982. 200p.

SIMON & GARFUNKEL

S/A.840. MATTHEW-WALKER, Robert. Simon & Garfunkel. Tunbridge Wells: Baton Press; New York: Hippocrene
Books, 1984. 165p.

S/A.841. SWENSON, John. Simon & Garfunkel. London: W. H.
Allen, 1984. 222p.

BRUCE SPRINGSTEEN

S/A.842. GAMBACCINI, Peter. Bruce Springsteen. New York:
Perigree, 1985. 159p.

S/A.843. HUMPHRIES, Patrick, and HUNT, Chris. Blinded by the
Light: Bruce Springsteen. London: Plexus, 1985.
250p.

S/A.844. YOPP, Chuck, and FENTON, Donna. Greetings from
Asbury Park, N.J.: a look at the local scene; the
Bruce Springsteen photo discovery. Asbury Park,
N.J.: Greetings Publications, 1983. 299p.

DONNA SUMMER

S/A.845. HASKINS, Jim, and STIFLE, J. M. Donna Summer: an unauthorized biography. Boston: Little, Brown, 1983. 136p.

TALKING HEADS

S/A.846. GANS, David. Talking Heads. New York: Avon Books, 1985. 168p.

TINA TURNER

S/A.847. MILLS, Bart. Tina. New York: Warner; Sevenoaks, Kent: New English Library, 1985. 127p.

S/A.848. WYNN, Ron. Tina: the Tina Turner Story. London: Sidgwick & Jackson, 1985. 158p.

CONWAY TWITTY

S/A.849. ESCOTT, Colin. The Conway Twitty Rock'n'Roll Years; with Richard Weize. Bremen, W. Germany: Bear Family Records, 1985. 80p.

VELVET UNDERGROUND

S/A.850. BOCKRIS, Victor, and MALANGA, Gerald. Uptight: the Velvet Underground Story. London: Omnibus Press, 1983. 128p.

GENE VINCENT

S/A.851. HAGARTY, Britt. The Day the World Turned Blue: a biography of Gene Vincent. Vancouver: Talon, 1983; Poole, Dorset: Blandford Press, 1984. 262p.

NEIL YOUNG

S/A.852. ROGAN, Johnny. Neil Young: the definitive story of the musical career. London: Proteus, 1982. 170p.

FRANK ZAPPA

S/A.853. OBERMANNS, Norbert. Zappalog: the first step of Zappology. Grevenbroich, W. Germany: the author, 1981; Los Angeles: Rhino Books, 1982. 127p.

APPENDIX B:

Revised Editions

This appendix provides details of some important revised editions of books listed in The Literature of American Music (1977). They are given here in the order of their original LOAM numbers.

178. GELATT, Roland. The Fabulous Phonograph, 1877-1977. 2nd revised ed. New York: Macmillan, 1977. 349p.

291. REIS, Claire R. Composers in America: biographical sketches of contemporary composers with a record of their works; with a new introduction by William Schuman. Revised and enlarged ed. New York: Da Capo, 1977. 399p.

447. NETTL, Bruno. Folk Music in the United States: an introduction. 3rd ed., revised and expanded by Helen Myers. Detroit: Wayne State University Press, 1976. 187p.

466. COFFIN, Tristram Potter. The British Traditional Ballad in North America. Revised ed., with a supplement by Roger deV. Renwick. Austin: University of Texas Press, 1977. 297p.

479. RANDOLPH, Vance. Ozark Folksongs. Revised ed.; introduction by W. K. McNeil. Columbia: University of Missouri Press, 1980. 4 vols.
_____. _____; edited and abridged by Norm Cohen. Urbana: University of Illinois Press, 1982. 590p.

525. DAVISSON, Ananias. Kentucky Harmony...; facsimile edition with an introduction by Irving Lowens. Minneapolis: Augsburg, 1976. 140p.

606. MALONE, Bill C. Country Music USA. Revised ed. Austin: University of Texas Press, 1985. 562p.

610. STAMBLER, Irwin, and LANDON, Grelun. The Encyclopedia of Folk, Country and Western Music. 2nd ed. New York: St. Martin's Press, 1983. 902p.

489

645. WILLIAMS, Roger M. Sing a Sad Song: the life of Hank
Williams. 2nd ed., with a discography by Bob Pinson.
Urbana: University of Illinois Press, 1981. 318p.

694. ROACH, Hildred. Black American Music, Past and Present.
Revised ed. Boston: Crescendo, 1976. 199p.

697. SOUTHERN, Eileen. The Music of Black Americans: a history. 2nd ed. New York: Norton, 1984. 602p.

806. DIXON, Robert M. W., and GODRICH, John. Blues and Gospel Records 1902-1943. 3rd ed. Chigwell, Essex: Storyville, 1982. 898p.

901. CHILTON, John. Who's Who of Jazz: Storyville to Swing
Street. 4th ed. London: Macmillan; New York: Da Capo,
1985. 375p.

914. KENNINGTON, Donald, and READ, Danny L. The Literature
of Jazz: a critical guide. 2nd ed., revised. London:
Library Association, 1980. 236p.

915. MECKLENBURG, Carl Gregor, Herzog zu, and RUECKER,
Norbert. International Bibliography of Jazz Books. Vol.
1. 1921-1949. Baden-Baden: Koerner, 1983. 107p.

921. MEEKER, David. Jazz in the Movies: a guide to jazz musicians 1917-1977. (Revised ed.) London: Talisman
Books, 1977. unpaged. (amendments to the book appeared
in Jazz Journal International, July 1978)

930. RUST, Brian. Jazz Records 1897-1942. 4th ed., revised and
enlarged. New Rochelle: Arlington House, 1978. 2 vols.

932. BRUYNINCKX, Walter. 60 Years of Recorded Jazz, 1917-
1977. Mechelen, Belgium: the author, 1977-1983(?).
(looseleaf discography)

1045. SIMON, George T. The Big Bands. 4th ed. New York:
Schirmer, 1981. 614p.

1080. WILLIAMS, Martin. The Jazz Tradition. 2nd ed. New York:
Oxford University Press, 1983. 256p.

1146. AMERICAN SOCIETY OF COMPOSERS, AUTHORS AND PUB-
LISHERS. ASCAP Biographical Dictionary. 4th ed.,
compiled by Jaques Cattell Press. New York: Bowker,
1981. 589p.

1161. SHAPIRO, Nat, and POLLOCK, Bruce, eds. Popular Music,
1920-1979: an annotated index of over 18,000 American
popular songs.... Detroit: Gale Research, 1985. 4 vols.

1205. BIERLEY, Paul E. The Works of John Philip Sousa. Columbus, Ohio: Integrity Press, 1984. 234p.

1228. SMITH, Cecil, and LITTON, Glenn. Musical Comedy in America: from The Black Crook to South Pacific, by Cecil Smith; from The King and I to Sweeney Todd, by Glenn Litton. New York: Theatre Arts Books, 1981. 367p.

1239. PASKMAN, Dailey. "Gentlemen, Be Seated!" a parade of the American minstrels. Revised ed. New York: Potter, 1976. 253p.

1259. LEWINE, Richard, and SIMON, Alfred. Songs of the Theater: a definitive index to the songs of the musical stage. New York: Wilson, 1984. 916p.

1260. SALEM, James M. A Guide to Critical Reviews. Part 2. The Musical 1901-1974. 2nd ed. Metuchen, N.J.: Scarecrow Press, 1976. 619p.

1298. RODGERS AND HAMMERSTEIN FACT BOOK. New ed., edited by Stanley Green. New York: Drama Book Specialists, 1980.

1338. ROXON, Lilian. Rock Encyclopedia; compiled by Ed Naha. New York: Grosset & Dunlap, 1978; London: Angus & Robertson, 1979. 565p.

1342. ESCOTT, Colin, and HAWKINS, Martin. Sun Records: the brief history of the legendary record label. New York: Omnibus Press, 1980. 184p.

1350. GILLETT, Charlie. The Sound of the City. Revised ed. London: Souvenir Press, 1983. 515p.

1369. MARCUS, Greil. Mystery Train: images of America in rock 'n'roll music. New ed., revised and expanded. New York: Dutton, 1982. 320p.

1373. DYLAN, Bob. Lyrics, 1962-1985. New York: Knopf, 1985. 524p.

1374. GRAY, Michael. The Art of Bob Dylan: song and dance man. New ed. London: Hamlyn, 1981. 236p.

1388. WALLEY, David. No Commercial Potential: the saga of Frank Zappa then and now. 2nd ed. New York: Dutton, 1980. 184p.

INDEXES

<u>Notes for the Reader</u>

1) The prefix "S," which appears before all items in the text of the bibliography, is omitted in the index entries.

2) Entries for individuals (as authors or subjects), companies, institutions, and organizations will be found in the INDEX OF NAMES. To find entries for names of individual buildings (e.g., Apollo Theatre), see the INDEX OF SUBJECTS.

3) The INDEX OF TITLES contains entries for each book listed in the bibliography. Entries for titles of films, stage shows, radio and television programs, journals and magazines, and individual songs referred to in the annotations will be found in the SUPPLEMENT TO THE INDEX OF TITLES.

Europe, James Reese 213, 533, 695, 881, 986
Evans, Bill 664
Evans, Charles 135
Evans, David A329
Evans, Edward G. 58
Evans, Gil 704, A476
Evans, Herschel 640, 726
Evans, Mark 617, 937
Evans, Mary Anne 94
Evans, Mary Garrettson 26
Evans, Peter William A583
Evans, Tom 94
Evensmo, Jan 640, 646
Everly Brothers A794
Ewen, David 157, 834, A8, A87
Ewing, George W. 1029
Eyle, Wim van A460

Faber, Charles F. 359
Fagin, Ted A516
Fallwell, Marshall 363
Famera, Karen McNerney 163, A20
Fancourt, Leslie 548
Farah, Cynthia A240
Fark, Reinhard 779
Farrar, Geraldine A48
Farren, Mick 1142, 1232, A824
Farrar, Claire R. 248
Farwell, Arthur 12, 66, 199
Faulkner, William A129
Fawcett, Anthony 1129
Fay, Amy 20
Feather, Charlie 389
Feather, Leonard 630, 678, 691, 702-704, 719, 734, 839
Federeghi, Luciano A330
Fedor, Ferenz 864
Fehl, Fred 907
Feinstein, Elaine A325
Feintuch, Burt A191
Feist, Leonard 829
Feldman, Jim A836
Feldman, Morton 155, A100, A122
Fellers, Frederick P. 57
Felton, Harold W. 337
Fender, Leo 89, 1109
Fennell, Frederick 45, 222
Fenton, Donna A844
Ferber, Edna 922, 925, 952
Ferguson, John Allen 130
Ferguson, Otis A426
Ferlingere, Robert D. 556
Ferretta, David 275
Ferris, Sharon Paugh 7
Ferris, William 269, 544, A173

Fesperman, John T. A53
Feuer, Cy 945, 968
Feuer, Jane A586
Ficcio, Catherine 241
Fichter, George S. 237
Field, Marshall 87
Fielding, Jerry 942
Fields, Dorothy 915
Fields, Lew 880, 890, 893
Fife, Austin E. 340
Fifth Dimension 568
Fike, Lamar 1231
Fillmore, Henry A550, A551
Filtgen, Gerd A464
Finch, Christopher 1000
Fine, Vivian 22
Finnell, Judith Greenberg 163, 193, 210
Finney, Ross Lee 167
Firestone, Ross A623
Fisher, Eddie 1077
Fisher, Fred 821
Fisher, John 822
Fisher, William Arms 602
Fishwick, Marshall 354
Fisk University 608
Fiske, Isaac 97
Fitzgerald, Ella 836
Fitzgerald, f-stop A751
Fitzgerald, Gerald 74, A131
5 Royales 1135
Flack, Roberta 1183
Flanagan, Cathleen C. 272
Flanagan, John T. 272
Flanagan, Tommy 735
Flanagan Brothers 298
Fleischer, Leonore 1193, 1218
Flemming, Herb 747
Flentrop, D. A. A53
Fletcher, Curley 340
Fletcher, Peter A729
Flippo, Chet A270
Florida West Coast Symphony Orchestra 120
Floyd, Carlisle 217
Floyd, Samuel A. A288
Flying Burrito Brothers 1097
Fong-Torres, Ben 1171, 1199, A758
Foote, Alan 190
Foote, Arthur 144
Forbes, John M. 405, A256
Ford, John A129
Ford, Larry R. 833
Ford, Les 94
Ford, Tennessee Ernie 400, 413
Fordin, Hugh 948, 956
Formento, Don A654

Gordy, Berry 565, 574
Gore, Lesley 1183
Goreau, Laurraine 577
Gorman, Clem 1144
Gottfried, Martin 908, 913, A611
Gottlieb, Jack 175
Gottlieb, Polly Rose 964
Gottschalk, Louis Moreau 13, 61, 69, 824, 840, A80, A81
Gottwald, Clytus 156, 180
Gourse, Leslie A326, A448
Govenar, Alan A317
Grabs, Manfred 209
Gradenwitz, Peter A111
Graham, Alberta Powell 1135
Grainger, Percy 66
Grame, Theodore C. 290, 446
Grandmaster Blast A360
Grant, Mikki 500
Grappelli, Stéphane 698
Grashey, Don 408
Grateful Dead 1173, 1206, A796-A798
Gratovich, Eugene 190
Graue, Jerold C. 14
Graves, Barry 1104
Graves, Milford 724, 725
Graves, Morris 177
Gray, Andy 388
Gray, Arlene E. A289
Gray, Henry 543
Gray, Judith A170
Gray, Michael 1204
Gray, Michael H. 5, 6, A507
Gray, Ronald Palmer 342
Gray, Wardell 752, A375
Green, Adolph 675, 915
Green, Al 569
Green, Archie 405, A199
Green, Benny 513, 1064
Green, Carol Hurd 23
Green, Douglas B. 358, 367, 368, A243
Green, Jeffrey P. A130
Green, Johnny 803
Green, Jonathon 762, 1248
Green, Mildred Denby A302
Green, Myrna 1077
Green, Stanley 900, A587
Greenberg, Alan A320
Greenblatt, Daniel A472
Greene, Bob 1191
Greenfield, Elizabeth Taylor 507
Greer, Sonny 831a
Gregg, Maxine 735
Gregorio, Juan 245
Gregory, Janice 1224

Gregory, Neal 1224
Gridley, Mark C. 664, A401
Griffes, Charles Tomlinson 13, 185, A124
Griffin, Johnny 676
Griffin, Sid A815
Griffiths, Paul 171, A90, A114
Griggs, Bill 1209, A803
Grime, Kitty 676, A449
Grimshaw, Gary 1152
Grissim, John 377
Gritzner, Charles F. 833
Groce, Nancy A206
Gronow, Pekka 298, 299
Gross, Michael 1197
Grossman, F. Karl 58
Grossman, Loyd 1150
Grubbs, John W. 15
Gruen, John 195
Gruhn, George A243
Grundy, Stuart A61
Grushkin, Paul A797
Guckin, John P. 710
Guida, Louis A318
Guntharp, Matthew G. 326
Guralnick, Peter 389, 1122, A311, A752
Gusikoff, Lynne A145
Guthrie, Marjorie 348, 349
Guthrie, Mary 349
Guthrie, Woody 345-349, 351, 675, 833
Gutman, Bill 792
Gwerder, Urban 1246

Hackett, Karleton 129
Hackley, E. Azalia 496
Haden, Charlie 722, 724
Haden, Walter D. 402
Hadley, Henry 53
Hadlock, Richard 678
Haefer, J. Richard 250
Haeussler, Armin 30
Hagan, Chet A220
Hagarty, Britt A851
Hagen, Earle 938
Hager, Steven A361
Haggard, Merle 377, 389, 390, A251
Hague, Douglas 708
Hague, Eleanor 435
Haines, Connie 751
Hakim, Taleb Rasul 505
Hale, Monte 932
Haley, Bill 1128, 1161, A799
Haley, J. Evetts 321(6)

INDEX OF TITLES

Note: Subtitles are normally included only when necessary to distinguish between identical main titles. Where books have identical titles and no subtitles, authors' names are given in parentheses.

546 / Literature of American Music

Modern Jazz 720
Modern Music A 90
Modern Music, Published By the
League of Composers 1924-1946
166
Molly O'Day, Lynn Davis, and the
Cumberland Mountain Folk 410
A Moment's Notice A396
Monsieur Sinatra 1089
Moravian Music For the Bicentennial
108
More Than Dancing A295
The Mormon Tabernacle Choir 64
Mother of the Blues A323
Mother Wit From the Laughing Bar-
rel 520
Motion Picture Music 944
Motion Pictures, TV and Radio 1058
The Motown Story (Fuller) A350
The Motown Story (Waller) A353
Mountain Ballads For Social Singing
430
Mountain Songs of North Carolina
315
Mountaineer Jamboree A237
Move Over Misconceptions 993
The Movie Musical 1061
Movin' On Down de Line 750
Murray Kash's Book of Country
A222
Music and Dance in Northwest
Coast Indian Life 249
Music and Dance Research of South-
western United States Indians
238
Music and Edgar Allan Poe 26
Music and Its Social Meanings A126
Music and Musket A555
Music and Poetry A104
Music and Politics 722
The Music and Times of Miles Davis
A470
Music and Theater in Minnesota
History 123
Music Collections in American Li-
braries A10
Music East and West A82
Music Editing For Motion Pictures
939
Music For Patriots, Politicians, and
Presidents 860
Music For the Millions: antebellum
democratic attitudes and the birth
of American popular music A545
Music For the Millions: the Kimball
Piano and Organ Story 87
The Music Goes Round 132

The Music Goes Round and Round
1157
The Music Hunter 267
Music in America and American Music
16
Music in America Before 1825 A74
Music in American Education 102
Music in American Society, 1776-
1976 17
Music in Bethlehem A41
Music in Colonial Massachusetts 1630-
1820 49
Music in Colonial Massachusetts 1830-
1920 A38
Music in Georgia A36
Music in New Jersey 1655-1860 A37
Music in Lexington Before 1840 56
Music in the Air A522
Music in the New World A12
Music in the Street A443
Music in the Western World A91
Music in Willa Cather's Fiction 510
The Music Industry Book A740
Music Is My Faith 213
Music Life Rock Photo Gallery 1273
Music Machines--American Style 99
Music Making in America A521
Music Master of the Middle West 118
The Music of Aaron Copland A117
The Music of Corktown 450
The Music of Elliott Carter A116
The Music of Henry Ainsworth's
Psalter A73
The Music of Henry Fillmore and Will
Huff A551
Music of Many Cultures 243
Music of Our Time 160
The Music of Pauline Oliveros A132
Music of the Bailes of New Mexico
436
Music of the Maidu Indians of Cali-
fornia 247
Music of the Spanish Folk Plays of
New Mexico 437
Music of the Twentieth Century 159
Music of Three Seasons 217
Music Periodical Literature 8
Music, Printed and Manuscript, in
the James Weldon Johnson Collec-
tion of Negro Arts and Letters
A285
Music Scoring For TV & Motion
Pictures 1060
Music Since the First World War
162
Music Under the Moon 54
Das Musical 1050

SUPPLEMENT TO INDEX OF TITLES

For a note on the contents of this supplement, see the information given at the beginning of the Indexes (p. 493). An asterisk (*) indicates a journal.